# Every Monument Will Fall

ALSO BY DAN HICKS

*The Brutish Museums: The Benin Bronzes,
Colonial Violence and Cultural Restitution*

DAN HICKS

Every Monument Will Fall
*A Story of Remembering and Forgetting*

HUTCHINSON
HEINEMANN

HUTCHINSON HEINEMANN

UK | USA | Canada | Ireland | Australia
India | New Zealand | South Africa

Hutchinson Heinemann is part of the Penguin Random House group of companies whose addresses can be found at global.penguinrandomhouse.com

Penguin Random House UK,
One Embassy Gardens, 8 Viaduct Gardens, London SW11 7BW

penguin.co.uk

First published 2025

001

Copyright © Dan Hicks, 2025

The moral right of the author has been asserted

Penguin Random House values and supports copyright. Copyright fuels creativity, encourages diverse voices, promotes freedom of expression and supports a vibrant culture. Thank you for purchasing an authorised edition of this book and for respecting intellectual property laws by not reproducing, scanning or distributing any part of it by any means without permission. You are supporting authors and enabling Penguin Random House to continue to publish books for everyone. No part of this book may be used or reproduced in any manner for the purpose of training artificial intelligence technologies or systems. In accordance with Article 4(3) of the DSM Directive 2019/790, Penguin Random House expressly reserves this work from the text and data mining exception.

Typeset in 10.5/14pt Sabon LT Std by Jouve (UK), Milton Keynes
Printed and bound in Great Britain by Clays Ltd, Elcograf S.p.A.

The authorised representative in the EEA is Penguin Random House Ireland, Morrison Chambers, 32 Nassau Street, Dublin D02 YH68

A CIP catalogue record for this book is available from the British Library

ISBN: 978–1–529–15274–6 (hardback)
ISBN: 978–1–529–15275–3 (trade paperback)

Penguin Random House is committed to a sustainable future for our business, our readers and our planet. This book is made from Forest Stewardship Council® certified paper.

*For the memory of Professor Mary C. Beaudry (1950–2020)
archaeologist, anthropologist, storyteller*

# Contents

Prologue: Legacy Monumentality … 1

## I *The Rule of Names* … 39

*fall*, noun. i) (of a structure) a collapse;
by extension (of currency or a commodity),
a steep reduction in value

1. LAND ACKNOWLEDGEMENT … 47
2. HOW MYTHS DIE … 54
3. ABOLISH THE MUSEUM … 61
4. MILITARIST REALISM … 72
5. INVISIBLE STATUES … 82

## II *The Fold* … 91

*fall*, noun. ii) (of a body of water) the fact
of subsiding, ebbing, or receding; a fast-flowing
or turbulent section of a river where it flows over
a precipice or ledge (hence, waterfall)

6. DEREALISATION … 95
7. RELIC TABLE … 103
8. THE MASTER'S TOOLS … 113
9. A TIME CAPSULE … 122
10. CRASH … 133

## CONTENTS

### III *The Unseen Hand*     142

*fall*, noun. iii) the descent of
an estate or inheritance (obsolete)

11. COUNTER-TRIANGULATION     150
12. A DEAD WHITE MAN     158
13. NECROSTRATIGRAPHY     166
14. THE KILLER STORY     175
15. CULTURE AND ANARCHY     181

### IV *No Humans Involved*     189

*fall*, noun. iv) the cadence with which words
or melodies conclude. See also (wrestling)
a throw which keeps an opponent on
the ground for a specified period

16. THE MORANT BAY RACE MASSACRE     200
17. THE CANNIBAL CLUB     207
18. REVOLVER     218
19. PIANO WIRE     227
20. FUTURE PROGRESSIVE EXONERATIVE     235

### V *Panic Attack*     248

*fall*, noun. v) (of a person or animal) the action
of falling as a consequence of stumbling,
losing balance or becoming dizzy or weak

21. A KIND OF WARNING     250
22. TECHNOVIOLENCE     255
23. DRILLED BODIES     261
24. ARGO     266
25. WAR OF POSITION     275

## VI *Choc en Retour*  286

*fall*, noun. vi) (military) the surrender of an army
or capture of a fortress. see also (military)
to 'fall in': to form and move in a line

26. GRAND TOUR  290
27. SOME GREAT WAR  304
28. AUTOMATIC ACTION  316
29. THE ARROW AND THE BOOMERANG  327
30. WHEN THE WORLD SCREAMED  336

## VII *Culture War*  350

*fall*, noun. vii) the decline or closing part of a day, year,
or someone's life. By extension, autumn,
the season in which leaves fall from trees

31. THE MUSEUM  354
32. THE MONUMENT  367
33. THE SUBJECT  383
34. SPITTING ON BRITAIN  393
35. FLATLINE  406

*Acknowledgements*  415
*Notes*  421
*Bibliography*  495
*Index*  545

# Prologue: Legacy Monumentality

I

Ever felt you've been lied to? Not by a politician or a salesman or an ex, but by a museum, or a statue, or by words in black and white on the page or the screen that you hold in your hand. Lied to by an object that is, something that seemed to be given, in the two primary senses of that word: both self-evident and authorative, and also offered freely, free from subjectivity or obligation. Lied to *through* an object that is, you said, I remember. So some old lie can come to seem like an eternal truth, something hammering itself into your mind, your body, absorbed through your skin, brought even into your sense of the past, without you even noticing, as if someone else's memory had come to be your own. A lie driven so deep into your consciousness that when someone calls attention to it, it seems as solid as the granite plinth that holds up the bronze major-general sitting on his horse. As certain as the bright white letters that spell out a name in all-caps on the glazed blue surface of a round ceramic plaque, fixed by unseen brass screws sunk deep into the mortar joints of a red brick wall. As real as the rough texture of the grey cotton binding of the book spines on every shelf of the library stack. Lies where the liar is long dead, that is, but where the lie lives on nonetheless, hardens into concrete fictions, a manufactured reality that endures but also evolves, mutates, decomposes and recomposes, soaks into the fabric of a place, you continued. Falls on its rooftops and runs up from its drains like blood from a vein. A lie that gathers like archival dust, like a storm gathers, then in some future moment might be seen as it drops as fallout.

Or lied to by something very much less tangible, I replied. I see from my diary entry it was mid-November 2016, and we were walking back to my office against a vile wind in the dusk with the news of the election result still ringing in our ears. Lied to by a mental framing, or a set of attitudes and prejudices; by what the theorists used to call an ideology or a discourse. Lied to by a claim to neutrality, a strategy of unending counterargument and the imposition of a balanced view. An old and familiar lie that thunders like the echo of machine-gun fire from colonial battlefields into the present, repeating its false claim: that a balance sheet could be drawn up to justify every atrocity and horror from Omdurman to Gaza, as if the sociocultural debris piled up from every democide and industrialised mass slaughter ever witnessed by humankind were always a curate's egg – 'good in parts' as the saying goes. Lies chiselled from thin air by a chorus of mouths, vocal tracts and tongues like sculptures in a gaseous state, pulmonic utterances that can hang in the atmosphere, words that are not just heard but also swallowed, internalised and parroted – transmitted like a language is transmitted across generations. Words in an intangible and yet physical form that can harden into assumptions and so come to seem like facts – through cultural habits, learned behaviour, institutional rites or ritual, repetition and preservation, memorialisation and commemoration. Tradition, culture and sometimes prejudice, I said, I remember: perpetuated through remembrance and inheritance to tell stories of heritage, progress or destiny. How much changed in the decade or so since then.

Lied to even by a silence, you continued. By what seems at first to be just a pause or hesitation, an inadvertent omission or oversight, but then the absence comes to feel like part of a pattern. The silence grows into a sonic void so prolonged and so deafening that at some point you have to think of that silence as a speech act in its own right. You might think that someone would call out the fiction, but the lie is a silence that no one dares break. A chilling effect develops, as if a dead hush had blown from the library as a vapour into the seminar room, condensed in public discourse – crystallising to frame what can and can't be said, then falling thickly across the voices of the past. Lied to by how an academic discipline might train you to look the other way, you said. Silence, that is, in its verbal sense, active and transitive, as if the writing of history had become, as the Haitian anthropologist Michel-Rolph Trouillot once put it, a 'practice of silencing' – silencing the past like a silencer silences a gun.[1] Lied to like an archive might lie to you where facts may not just be voiceless but destroyed – colonial documents redacted or dumped at sea, museum artefacts censored by being simply buried in some inaccessible warehouse, family papers burned, names erased, houses bulldozed, graveyards desecrated, as if the skulls, bones, teeth, hair and skin of the dead were smashed up then made to live on in death, preserved like specimens locked inside a museum, each human fragment forced noiselessly to repeat the lie.

You're talking about White supremacy? I interrupted you as we arrived back at the museum. The heavy door closed against a swirl of the cold dark air. Like the lies that Stephen Jay Gould excavated and catalogued in his book *The Mismeasure of Man* back in 1981. Gould debunked the fake 'race science' in nineteenth- and twentieth-century anthropology, exposing the misrepresentations built into the racist craniometry, phrenology, polygenism, eugenics and hereditarian theories that sought to correlate intelligence with physical features, from the legacies of Louis Agassiz at Harvard and Samuel Morton at Penn to the enduring forms of biological determinism that ran from the American Civil War through the Jim Crow era and long into the twentieth century.[2] That's one part of it, you replied. But this isn't just about natural history and ideas of biological determinism; it's also about cultural history and ideas of cultural determinism. Ideas of Whiteness to some extent, yes – but *cultural* Whiteness. Ethnosupremacism, legacy militarist ideologies of barbarism and 'primitiveness' as distinct from a solely fake-scientific racial supremacism. It's about patriarchal infrastructures interdigitating not just with science and laboratories but with ideas of heritage, museums, the arts, the humanities, inherited through statues, galleries, libraries, lecture rooms – monuments of all kinds. Structures through which militarism, racism and colonialism can get inbuilt so they seem like historical norms, natural and eternal, inevitable, right and true, and yet somehow strangely vulnerable. Like something that needs to be defended.

Outside my office window snow had started to fall, lit up in the dusk, and the sky was the colour of a television tuned in to white noise. Recalling that conversation today, I thought of that foundational line of cyberpunk fiction: 'To call up a demon you must know its name.'[3] To address these cultural histories demands something other than just scientifically correcting the evidence, you assured me. Fact and fiction are always already blurred here, as that chilling effect kicks in. If I were pushed to classify this phenomenon in art historical terms, I said, I'd have to say it is some variety of Neo-Gothic. There must be a better name, you told me, for this deafening apparatus of silence, seen and unseen, material and immaterial. You should try to write something about it, these forms of militarism, inherited structures of supremacism, of cultural Whiteness, racism and colonialism. A legacy monumentality in all its shifting forms. Surely this fake culture war has a history? A prehistory, even?

## II

'The most terrible thing about war, I am convinced, is its monuments,' W. E. B. Du Bois wrote in 1931.[4] He was talking about the warping of truth through the Confederate monuments which had been built in their hundreds in public spaces across the American South in the previous half-century. If you were to plot the places and dates of their erection on gridded paper as a seriation graph, it would take the form of a battleship curve – an armoured grey mass that probably reaches its maximum width sometime around 1910. And that's not to mention the naming of public squares and parks. Practices of commemoration were brought from the military cemeteries into the streets and transformed in the process, in the name of the Confederacy as a living tradition. 'The war memorial as we know it today took form here,' the historian Kurt Savage has argued – memory was inscribed into physical space in this new manner 'decades before such monuments were built in Europe'.[5] I want to think that argument through, and consider what it means for the modern transatlantic histories of racism, violence and memory culture, and debates about preservation, heritage and monumentality.

Confederate monuments were erected in public parks or on the main street in front of the county courthouse, building quotidian statements about justice, freedom, incarceration and the rule of law into the townscape, and also becoming the focus of various annual days of remembrance, with marching, bands and speeches. Some were abstract forms, like obelisks, monoliths or fountains, but most were figurative statues of rank-and-file soldiers or famous generals – holding a flag or a bugle, or carrying a rifle, or simply sitting on a horse.[6] They served alongside the circulation of battle flags, the rebuilding of war cemeteries, the publication of pamphlets and the distribution of medals, not just as symbols but as myths.[7] These Robert Lees and Jefferson Davises will always be depicted as tall and handsome, Du Bois observed, but the lies don't stop there, as if a monument to those who 'fought a bloody war for the perpetuation of slavery' could bear the text 'Died Fighting for Liberty'.[8]

Like, for example, the one in Oxford, North Carolina (population 8,628). For 111 years the seven-foot-tall bronze figure of a gunman, wearing a slouch hat and holding his rifle in the ready position, looked down on this town, perched atop a thirty-four-foot column of Warren County granite. Two crossed Confederate flags were carved into the stone, alongside the words 'To Our Confederate Dead' and the initials CSA and UDC – Confederate States of America and United Daughters of the Confederacy. The local chapter of the UDC was the sponsor for the public subscription of $3,000, and they published a pamphlet that recorded the speeches made when this monument to the 'citizen soldiery' of Granville County was installed outside the courthouse in 1909.[9]

Speaking in the courthouse in the same year, the state governor railed against ideas of racial equality, celebrated how 'the invisible empire sprung up, and Ku Klux came as a method necessary' and paid tribute to what he called the 'onward march' of the 'white race'.[10] The local press reported that the leader of the Klan in Granville County 'commended the fervid eloquence' of the speech.[11] The governor had form for racial incitement, even while serving as a member of the House of Representatives. Eleven years earlier, and 150 miles to the south of Oxford, he'd been among the ringleaders of the Wilmington Race Massacre.[12] Just as the United States was entering a new phase in naval-militarist colonialism in Cuba, Puerto Rico and the Philippines, the American South was witnessing new forms of extremism. On 10 November 1898, 2,000 soldiers and vigilantes armed with Winchester rifles and a Gatling machine gun overthrew the municipal government of the port city of Wilmington. An editorial in the *Wilmington Messenger* described what was at stake as 'race, not politics' and 'the furtherance of White Supremacy', since 'the Anglo Saxon race MUST and WILL rule'.[13] Martial law was declared as a pretext for a planned coup d'état, days after local elections. A White mob looted and burned scores of Black-run businesses, slaughtering and wounding perhaps as many as 300 African-American citizens, and displacing thousands who fled the violence.[14] A month before this episode of insurrection and mass murder the governor had declared, 'Before we allow the negroes to control the State as they do now we will kill enough of them that there will not be enough left to bury them.'[15]

Now in 1909 in Oxford, NC the cornerstone of the monument was being laid by the grand master of the Lodge of Masons. A crowd of thousands cheered as soldiers and cadets marched with 150 veterans, by now in their seventies and eighties, 'Southern immortals' they called them, as if each were a kind of animated statue worn by time and war, periodically emitting that ghoulish falsetto *yee-haw* scream, the Rebel Yell. The pamphlet claimed the statue was a monument to the living as well as the dead: 'an everlasting sentinel to keep eternal vigils, by night and by day', it said, through which 'the busy man of affairs may in after years be here reminded of the glories of his race'. Far more than just war memorials, such Confederate monuments, whether canonised Confederate heroes or those figures of rank and file citizen soldiery, were icons of the pseudo-historical ideology of the so-called 'Lost Cause' – that cultish nostalgia which twisted the facts of the Civil War to portray it as a glorious military sacrifice of a generation of grandfathers and great-grandfathers born in the 1830s and 1840s who defended agrarianism against industrialism, rather than a racist struggle to retain the institution of slavery. Such images sought to engender a genealogical, intimately ethnopolitical form of patriotism among the descendants of Confederacy soldiers. A demand for 'loyalty to monuments' that would 'perpetuate the truth ... and immortalize its facts and traditions' came hand in hand with other forms of indoctrination, including banning books in schools. White children could represent 'living monuments', the Daughters claimed, defending the supposedly sacred principles for which their ancestors had died.[16] In effect, the event horizon of this revisionist, negationist, ethnonationalist monument, and hundreds more like it, came to slip forward in time, becoming tacit glorifications of Jim Crow-era ideas of racial supremacy and segregation and ongoing paramilitary vigilante campaigns of terror and lynching. The monument was built to make the war last, even after it was lost; indeed to deny the war had been lost in the first place.

Much of this had been foreseen by Frederick Douglass, decades earlier. In December 1870, a few weeks after the death of Robert E. Lee, he had reflected on reports of a planned monument to the general. Douglass predicted that such monuments would perpetuate the warped memory of the Lost Cause, and thus 'reawaken the conflict, by cultivating hatred'.[17] The hatred certainly endured, just as the statues did. And a century after Douglass was writing, when an African-American military veteran named Henry D. Marrow was gunned down and killed by White supremacists during civil rights demonstrations in 1970, the connections between that hatred and the legacy monumentality came back into view. The first community-led attempts to have Oxford's monument to slavery and gun violence removed came about, and it was moved around the corner. There it stood for another fifty years, outside Granville County Public Library on Main Street.

The new phase of the civil rights movement that was catalysed by racist murders of Eric Garner and Michael Brown at the hands of police officers, in July and August 2014, brought Civil War monuments into focus in a new way. The Black Lives Matter movement brought longstanding attempts to remove the cultural icons of the Confederacy, some dating back over half a century, to a tipping point. One watershed moment came in August 2017. In Charlottesville, Virginia the city council resolved to remove the statue of Robert E. Lee and rename Lee Park, in which it stood, Emancipation Park. A fascist rally was convened to try to 'defend' the statue and the name from these developments. Under the banner of Unite the Right there was an attempt to bring together White supremacist groups across the alt-right, from Klansmen to far-right militias, neo-Confederates and neo-Nazis. Counter-protests were organised, and during the rally, a White supremacist drove his Dodge Challenger car into the crowd of anti-fascist protestors, injuring thirty-five people and murdering 32-year-old Heather D. Heyer.[18]

Across the American South, White supremacist monuments hidden in plain sight for a century or more were now coming into view.[19] The slogan that emerged in summer 2017 was bold and clear – 'All Monuments Must Fall'.[20] The question was parallel to the issues that Angela Y. Davis raised when she posed her famous question in 2003: 'Are prisons obsolete?' Davis asked whether prisons could be reformed, or whether as part of a wider carceral-industrial complex that has deep historical connections to enslavement, the issue should be abolition rather than reform.[21] And just as mass incarceration has a longstanding historical connection with the unfinished work of abolition and emancipation, since freedom is still a racialised entity, so too it is with memory culture, the latent, post-slavery regimes of White supremacism that run in parallel with legacy monumentality.

Back in Oxford, it had seemed since the 1970s that there was 'seemingly little threat' of the statue being removed.[22] But in the wake of further campaigning against police brutality and anti-Black violence, including protests after the massacre of nine people in the Charleston church shooting in 2015, the removal came. When on 22 June 2020 the monument was finally removed from public view, the efforts to achieve this had lasted for more than half a century. That summer, as another Confederate statue in another southern town fell every day after another long campaign, questions hung in the air. What war was this exactly, which produced these monuments? Was it the Civil War itself? Or some other war, another kind of war, one with a long history? A war about culture, memory and freedom. A war that isn't over.

### III

There's a parallel story from Oxford, England (population 163,257). A story with a twist. An unfinished story. We can pick it up earlier that day in 2016. I'd met you from your train and we walked straight there: past the Business School, along Park End Street, then dodging the buses as we continued straight on Queen Street. When we got to Cornmarket I told you about how in May 1936 a trade unionist rally had convened to protest a speech by Oswald Mosley of the British Union of Fascists at the Carfax Assembly Rooms. On May Day 1933,

PROLOGUE

Mosley had addressed the inaugural meeting of the Oxford University Fascist Association in the same building. In November 1935, the *Sunday Times* reported how, when addressing their annual dinner, he 'predicted that Fascism would triumph in this country in 1938', and 'exhorted his Oxonian Blackshirts to take courage'.[23] Mosley had been ramping up his attempts to lodge fascist ideas in the heart of the British establishment, and even set up a private dining club in Mayfair to which he invited key military officers and aristocrats. But in Oxford a grassroots anti-fascist sentiment was growing.[24] So when Mosley ordered his Defence Force of twenty uniformed paramilitary thugs, armed with black rubber truncheons, to eject hecklers that evening in May 1936, they were outnumbered by a loose coalition of students, bus-drivers and car workers, who fought back. Mosley continued with his speech later on, but the damage was done. The bloody scrum that ensued in the hall and on the street, which became known as the Battle of Carfax, had exposed the violence of his movement in the sedate environment of this medieval university town.[25]

We were still talking about the history of anti-fascism as we weaved along the pavement on the delicate Hawksmoor curve of High Street. Arriving at the University Church, we leaned our backs against the church door, our view framed by the Baroque twists of the seventeenth-century barley-sugar columns of the south porch, and craned our necks up to meet the gaze of the diminutive figure of the man built into on the north wall of Oriel College.[26] The demolition work began in 1909, I told you, and the new building took two years to complete. At the ceremony in 1911 there were cheers as the façade was unveiled, punctuated by seven statues in white Portland stone. The man being commemorated had dreamed of a new unity of English-speaking people across the British Empire; a new kind of ethnolinguistic pan-nationalist supremacism that might, he said, require abolishing the monarchy.[27] It was a vision of another kind of sovereignty. No wonder then that the figure was installed in an alcove on the uppermost storey, one floor above the twin statues of King Edward VII (who died in 1910) and King George V (who succeeded him), a tier above not one monarch but two, both the living and the dead. Standing thirty feet in the air under a faux-shell canopy, the statue looks down from the tower on the city. It wears the three-piece suit of a businessman, but holds the slouch hat of the Imperial Yeomanry in its right hand. That hat might as well be a Lee-Enfield rifle, given the chilling message of the iconography. 'It feels not so much like a memorial as like a threat,' I remember you saying.

Long before his image became a weapon pointed at the city and the university, this man had been a student at Oriel. He matriculated in 1873 but studied only intermittently. His main concern in those years was developing his mining activities in southern Africa. During his visits to Oxford he played polo; joined student private members' clubs like the Bullingdon Club, famous for its dinners, and Vincent's; became a Freemason (Oxford University Apollo Chapter of the Masonic Order); and served as master of the Oxford University drag hunt.[28] There are stories about a pushy, attention-seeking young man who would strut around town with uncut diamonds in a matchbox in his waistcoat pocket, which he'd show off at any opportunity. Eventually in 1881 he had accumulated the nine terms 'in residence' required to graduate, and, aged twenty-eight, received a passman degree in Classics.[29] This man lived for only another two decades, but such was the accelerationism of his life-course that he became wealthy on an almost unimaginable scale.

The biography has been told and retold so many times. There are four intertwined strands. First there is the story of the brutal multi-millionaire diamond- and gold-mining tycoon whose operations ran across what is today South Africa, Zimbabwe and Zambia, with a royal charter for his company and sidelines in railways and telegraph networks. Second, the story of the land-grabber in the so-called 'scramble for Africa', a war criminal and mass murderer responsible for tens of thousands of deaths, through military slaughter, scorched earth policies and starvation as a tactic of war, and implicated in the history of the Second Boer War, where the British interned civilians in concentration camps. Third comes the story of the politician and privy counsellor to the British government who was the architect of legal structures that laid the authoritarian foundations for Apartheid, and argued that Black Africans should be treated as 'a subject race', and as 'fellow tribesmen of the Druids' who were conquered by the Roman Empire in Britain.[30] The man who tried to overthrow an elected government with a force of 500 mounted policemen, artillery and Maxim machine guns, in a putsch known as the Jameson Raid. Last but not least, there's the story of how this man is the most significant benefactor in Oxford's 1,000-year history. And yet the strange truth is that, technically speaking, he never donated a penny to the university.

The Oriel statue is like a night watchman, Amit Chaudhuri has observed, a gatekeeper standing guard on a door below him which is never opened.[31] Looking up, his name can be read in the inverse spaces of six hand-scrieved letters running along the stone ledge on which the statue stands:

## RHODES

But this isn't about the man who died on 26 March 1902. It's about the statue that was erected there nine years after his death, and still stands. I mean, it's about a culture of memorialisation. About how his image evolved through constant repetition and copying. It started during his lifetime, most famously when *Punch* published a cartoon in 1892 which used a silly pun on the man's name and redrew him as a modern Colossus – as if the massive figure of the Greek sun god Helios that was one of the Seven Wonders of the Ancient World, erected at Rhodes harbour in the third century BCE had been reincarnated. His arms outstretched, his head in the clouds, a pith helmet in his right hand, a rifle slung over his shoulder, one vast boot on Cape Town and the other on Cairo, the giant holds a telegraph wire that runs the entire length of the continent, a line of imperial red rendered in black and white print.[32]

In part it was self-fashioning.[33] The entry for this modern colossus in the *Oxford Dictionary of National Biography* records that he was 'strongly impelled to bestow his likeness upon posterity'.[34] That was no understatement. One biographer describes how he was not only an avid commissioner of images of himself, but was also known to slash or stamp on portraits of himself which he disliked. 'I find I am human,' he wrote in 1891, 'and should like to be living after my death.' He desired, as he put it, to 'leave a monument to posterity which shall convince mankind that I had really lived'.[35] He fantasised that he would be remembered for 4,000 years.[36] And in 1893, a postscript to one of the many rewrites of his will presented a loose translation of one of the *Odes* of Horace, a poem called *non omnis moriar* ['I shall not wholly die']:

> I have erected a monument more enduring than bronze and higher than the royal pyramids, which neither the corroding rain nor the wild North Wind could destroy, nor a countless series of years, nor the passage of time. I shall not wholly die; a large part of me will elude the Goddess of Funerals and I will continue to grow, renewed through posthumous praise.[37]

This taste for auto-memorialisation and fantasies of immortality was outdone tenfold by the vigour with which this iconography was taken up and reproduced by others after his death. The Oriel statue was just the most prominent of a multiplying battalion of simulacra of the colossus from the 1890s and long after his death: score upon score of public memorials, like a cultural counterpart to a police force or a militia, and the circulation of his image or name in every conceivable medium: busts, medals, portraits, prints, photographs, named buildings, professorships, banknotes, postage stamps, parks, roads, memorial dinners, and so on. One visitor to Cape Town in 1909 observed that Rhodes was still somehow present and ubiquitous, as 'a haunting sense of some dominating personality present but unseen everywhere'.[38] The monumentality spread across his sphere of influence in southern Africa as well, from the equestrian statue of him erected at Kimberley in 1907 to his gravesite on the summit of the hill known as Malindidzimu ('Hill of Ancestral Spirits') twenty miles south of Bulawayo in Matobo National Park – a park itself originally named after him.[39] At a mock ancient Greek temple with a portico and Doric columns and a bronze bust built as his memorial at Devil's Peak in Cape Town, an inscription composed by Kipling reads:

> The immense and brooding spirit still shall quicken and control
> Living he was the land and dead his soul shall be her soul.

Things named after him ranged from a steam ship on Lake Tanganyika to a school in Winnipeg, Canada, a university in the Eastern Cape of South Africa, a future chief inspector of the City of London Police, a

1930s block of flats in Camden, and even an archaic human species from the Middle Pleistocene.[40] There was even an improbable and unsuccessful approach to Auguste Rodin to make a sculpture of him. At times it could feel like a 'cult', as historian Paul Maylam once suggested; but mostly it was just that the name and the image sank into a tacit ubiquity.[41] The man's name was even applied to a nation state, adopted by the British South Africa Company from 1895 and formally recognised by the British government in 1898. In Oxford, there was a plaque attached to the wall of his former undergraduate lodgings in 1906, a portrait hung in the college, and a memorial tablet installed in the Examination Schools, just along High Street.[42] The proliferating images of the man entered public collections in increasing numbers, from the Bodleian Libraries, to Tate, the Royal Collections and Oriel College itself.[43] In the National Portrait Gallery alone there are no fewer than twenty-eight drawings, paintings, prints, photographs and sculptural busts, plus a plaster cast of his death mask. Portraits were hung in the Constitutional Club in London, the Kimberley Club in South Africa, the Bulawayo Club in what is today Zimbabwe, and even the North Foreland Golf Club near Broadstairs in Kent. And the month after Prime Minister Margaret Thatcher came to power in 1979, the Government Art College purchased a lithograph of this man at a Sotheby's auction – an image that was hung in the Department for International Trade by Liam Fox MP in 2017.[44]

There was also an instance of destruction as a kind of memorialisation. In 1935, Southern Rhodesia took over the offices of the British Medical Association (BMA) on the Strand to house its high commission. A series of eighteen Portland stone sculptures by Jacob Epstein called *The Ages of Man* ran around the building's façade. The artist's first major public commission, these realistic naked images depicting the different life stages of the human body had been installed by the BMA in 1908. At a high commission dinner at the Trocadero in 1935, a toast to the memory of the man, 'our founder', celebrated the 'kind of mystical presence' that he still had, welcomed the move to the new building, and announced that the Epstein sculptures would be replaced with statues of former governors.[45] From the mid-1930s the high commissioner was also pushing for a twelve-foot bronze statue of the colossus to be put up either somewhere on the Strand, or perhaps at some other site in London such as outside the Imperial Institute in the Albertopolis.[46]

The high commissioner proceeded to try to have the Epstein statues removed and sold off.[47] Their lack of 'austerity' was 'not in keeping with the building,' he told the press, and after all 'everyone is entitled to their own views on art'.[48] The Royal Fine Art Commission intervened to stop them being removed, but two years later on 20 July 1937, the day after the opening of the Nazi Degenerate Art exhibition in Munich, the high commissioner issued a statement saying there would be 'no reprieve' for the sculptures, which represented 'a public danger'.[49] 'Epstein Statues Must Go', read the headlines. A report commissioned by the embassy suggested the statues might be loose, cracked, decaying, insecure and unsafe. The Jewish artist denounced it as 'vandalism' – 'just a whitewashing affair to destroy the statues'. Expressing the hope that casts of the figures might be placed in a museum, in the following weeks the high commissioner oversaw the mutilation, with limbs and faces hacked off with chisels, 'amputated' as the *Daily Mail* put it.[50] The mutilated figures still stand today on what is now Zimbabwe House as a lasting memorial to a Rhodesian model of monumentality. As for the statue of the colossus, the war intervened, and the prospect of a new figure of the man after the defeat of Nazi Germany was no longer an idea of the times, if it ever had been.

The story of *Physical Energy*, George Frederic Watts' fantasy seven-ton bronze equestrian statue, shows how this 'cult' evolved and shifted. Adapted from elements of the Parthenon marbles and commissioned from Watts as a grave monument for Rhodes, it was displayed in the courtyard of the Royal Academy in 1904–5, shipped to South Africa in 1906, and eventually installed at the Rhodes Memorial in Cape Town. After Watts' death a cast of the memorial was commissioned by the British government and installed in September 1907 in London's Kensington Gardens, close to where in his later years this man would ride every morning while in London. In 1960, the year in which seventeen African nations gained independence, the British South Africa Company doubled down on the serial commemoration of their founder, and a third cast commissioned by them was installed outside the high court building in Lusaka, and unveiled by the Queen Mother.[51] The story was that Lord Malvern, resident director of the company, described the meaning of the sculpture: the rider was the European and the horse the African.⁵² Then in November 2017 the Royal Academy installed a fourth cast of *Physical Energy* in the courtyard, 112 years since it was last there. It stood for four months outside the main entrance to the museum in this courtyard space shared with five learned societies at Burlington House, including the Society of Antiquaries of London.

With each cast, the name and meaning shifted. Nowadays people will even claim the Kensington Gardens cast isn't a copy of the Rhodes memorial. A constellation of signifiers was detaching from what they signified and coming to stand for something else. For what, exactly?

The timing of Rhodes' death is significant here. It came the year after the nation had mourned Queen Victoria, whose own cult of monumentality led to a proliferation of statues, portraits and many other forms of memorialisation. It was also two months before the end of the Second Boer War (1899–1902), for which a quarter of a million soldiers were mobilised from Britain, more than double the numbers sent to the Crimean War half a century earlier, the largest military deployment since the Napoleonic Wars.⁵³ In a conflict that brought British war crimes and mass slaughter, including the killing of tens of thousands of civilians as well as the deaths of African, British colonial and Boer troops, more than 22,000 British soldiers were killed. It was a similar number to the British losses in Crimea, and more than 2,500 memorials to the dead were erected to mark a loss that reached to every city, town and parish – in churches, cathedrals, schools, police stations, public parks and on the streets of towns and cities. Some are brass or marble plaques with lists of names; others are metal statues of men pointing rifles. In the first years of the new century, as the monumentality of Confederate statues was shifting gear on the other side of the Atlantic, the remembrance of the colossus came to be mixed up with the wider memorialisation of national loss. The genre of the war memorial was evolving into something else, as if remembrance of the fallen could be twisted into images that would never fall. And like the figure of a Confederate general, this man's image came to merge in public consciousness with losses of ordinary soldiers, as a supremacist memory culture, a monumentality of cultural Whiteness, a transatlantic culture war, entered a new phase.

We ran our eyes along the lower storey of the college's statuary.

Below this man, flanking the two British monarchs, stand four figures representing former provosts of the college. The man who was provost in 1911 remarked upon how the Rhodes statue seemed to break with some of Oxford's traditional visual regimes of remembrance, I told you. It had been common practice for centuries to exhibit portraits of former fellows and heads of house in the dining hall or the Senior Common Room. But a contrast could be drawn between that conservative traditionalism and this new mode of more ostentatious and populist monumentality. 'Our great benefactors of the fifteenth century are commemorated in our chapel shrines and by the shields over the doorways in the Old Quad,' the provost said in his speech at the unveiling ceremony, while 'this building will stand as the visible monument of the generosity and loyalty' of this man.[54]

This monument to a benefactor had few precedents. There's the statue erected for the slave-owner Christopher Codrington across the road at All Souls College in 1734. This freestanding white marble statue of a seventeenth-century benefactor and Caribbean plantation-owner still stands on a high pedestal at the centre of the long library, above the heads of readers, dressed for war in a Roman *sagum* (cloak) and cuirass (body armour), a military baton in his right hand.[55] But that's inside the college library, very much not in a public space. And there's the Pitt Rivers Museum, a brisk ten-minute walk from Oriel, named for its donor (1827–1900) in 1884. What is this connection between empire, public art and benefaction then? you said as we started out on that walk to my office in the museum. Look at the list of other All Souls donors, and it's Lascelleses, Dawkinses and Beckfords, profits that ran from Caribbean plantations to the English landscape.[56] It's more than just artwashing imperial fortunes, surely? It's about changing how and what is remembered. A model of benefaction with genealogical links to Atlantic militarist-colonialism. Memory culture isn't just stories like history or biography; it's about physically intervening. Shaping the future, of course, but doing so by changing the past.

## IV

Follow the money, as they say. Under the terms of his will, two sums of money came into play. On the one hand there was £22,500 for

Oriel College, one of the self-governing colleges of the collegiate university, for the construction of new buildings on High Street. A decade after his death there was the northern façade, with the statue atop it, which now a century later we were leaving behind us as we walked north past the Radcliffe Camera and the Bodleian Library. That bequest came with a further £77,500 to increase the income of the fellows of the college, pay for the maintenance and repair of college buildings – and enhance what the will called 'the dignity and comfort' of the college's High Table.[57]

On the other hand, there was a vastly larger fortune, more than £3 million, from his residuary estate, which endowed a trust which later adopted his name. Again, this was not a donation to the university. The Rhodes Trust was set up to be in Oxford but not of Oxford, so to speak: wholly independent from the university and the colleges, but giving bursaries to students to study at them. With a chunk of that money they bought a parcel of land next to the Pitt Rivers Museum from Wadham College, and built a walled and gate-kept presence in the city, and thus another monument to this man, Rhodes House.[58] Stylistically, the building is an Arts and Crafts country house wrought in the Cotswoldian yellow of its rough Bladon stone with some elements of Cape Dutch grafted on. A sustained mood of the Neo-Gothic runs from the lead-lined dormer windows to the sheer creepiness of the vast dark rotunda vestibule that forms its main entrance like the internal cavity of a skull, forming a shrine to the eponymous benefactor. 'The Gothic is conducive to pious irreason', 'pseudo morality' and a 'crazed decor of fear', the visionary architectural writer Jonathan Meades once observed.[59] Never was that 'quasi-religious architectural psychosis' more vivid than here, where a portrait bust of the man is entombed and gobbets of Latin and Greek are engraved on the walls, including the title of that ode by Horace above the internal lintel – *non omnis moriar*. On the roof stands an outsized copy of a carved soapstone bird from the archaeological site of Great Zimbabwe, where the colossus commissioned an archaeological expedition in 1891 after the British South Africa Company had invaded Mashonaland – a memorial to how this man used archaeology falsely to claim that all African monuments had been built by Phoenicians under European influence, a geographical lie that echoed his transcontinental ambitions.[60]

To look at these memorials on the one hand, and at the work of the trust on the other, is to see what Hannah Arendt pointed out in her 1951 book *The Origins of Totalitarianism* as the two contrasting sides of this man's expansionism. On the one hand there is the 'monstrous innate vanity', she observed; on the other there is a secrecy and silence that bordered sometimes on mysticism.[61]

Rhodes' fantasy was to use his vast wealth to establish a 'secret society' that would promote his White supremacist beliefs – beliefs first outlined in a document known as his 'Confession of Faith' written while still an undergraduate in 1877:

> I contend that we are the first race in the world, and that the more of the world we inhabit, the better it is for the human race. I contend that every acre added to our territory provides for the birth of more of the English race who otherwise would not be brought into existence ... The absorption of the greater portion of the world under our rule simply means the end of all wars ... The furtherance of the British Empire, for the bringing of the whole uncivilised world under British rule, for the recovery of the United States, for the making the Anglo-Saxon race but one Empire [sic]. What a dream! but yet it is probable. It is possible.[62]

These ideas were picked up and reinforced in the atmosphere of the Oxford of the 1870s. Later in life he recalled the 'deep impression' that John Ruskin's lectures had on him then, with one particular text making, he said, 'a forceful entry into my mind'.[63] It was the first of Ruskin's inaugural *Lectures on Art*, in which he delivered the infamous lines about the future of the British nation:

> This is what she must either do, or perish: she must found colonies as fast and as far as she is able, formed of her most energetic and worthiest men; – seizing every piece of fruitful waste ground she can set her foot on.[64]

Ruskin's view was uncompromising:

> There is a destiny now possible to us – the highest ever set before a nation to be accepted or refused. We are still undegenerate in race; a race mingled of the best northern blood.[65]

In 1891, the idea of a 'United English', 'Pan-Britannic or 'Pananglian' Festival was proposed in a letter to *The Times*. It would take place every four years or so, with athletic competitions, industrial exhibitions, and also a 'cultural section' with 'national scholarships'.[66] Seven years later, this man took this idea of cultural scholarships as a blueprint. It was a vision that came to him in 1898 while at Madeira en route back to London – came to him, he said, 'from the sea'.[67] The author of that letter was the editor of a periodical called *Greater Britain*, and 'the expansion and consolidation of Greater Britain' came, as one of his closest supporters put it, to be 'his one dominant idea'.[68] As Oswald Mosley would do in 1932 when he published a book called *The Greater Britain*, so in 1898 Cecil Rhodes was expanding a Victorian idea about how a shared language and culture could represent bonds akin to the concept of 'race' in colonial-militarist expansion. Where Mosley repurposed this concept in his fascist rhetoric about how to 'preserve and elevate European culture' in 'a tradition of civilisation and progress', the colossus operationalised an anglophone psychogeography at a global scale in the idea of an Anglo-Saxon unity not just across the British Empire in Canada, the Caribbean, southern Africa, Australia, and India, but to the United States and Germany as well.[69]

The history of precisely which organisations and projects this man's vast eponymous posthumous trust funded over the years has not been written, although given his talk of a secret society there is no shortage of conspiracy theories.[70] What is certain is that much of its activity involved a programme for young men to study at Oxford. His vision was that a programme of scholarships would build an imperialist fraternity, training a new battalion of settlers with each new year of entry. Scholars were drawn from across what he saw as the Anglo-Saxon world – from Germany as well as from America and across the British Empire.[71] The intention was for an elite transatlantic club of colonists, selected for their demonstrable 'instincts to lead' rather than just academic 'book worm' merit.[72] Candidates should demonstrate four qualities, the man said: 'smugness' (scholarly attainment), 'brutality' (success in outdoor sports), 'tact and leadership' (moral force of character) and 'unctuous rectitude'. It was the vision of someone, as one supporter put it, 'whose Imperialism was that of Race and not that of

Empire' – and who wanted Oxford to be 'the educational centre of the English-speaking race'.⁷³ The destiny of British imperialism would require 'the best souls of the next two hundred years', he believed. An annual dinner named for the man to celebrate the scholarships was inaugurated, with a toast to his memory – a toast that included, to take the example of the 1914 dinner, held at the Randolph Hotel, a celebration of his three aims – the consolidation of the British Empire, the unification of the Anglo-Saxon race, and the peace of the world.⁷⁴

The monumentalisations were resisted all along. In 1898 when he received the honorary degree of doctor of civil law (DCL) at the university's annual Encaenia ceremony, a letter of objection was signed by ninety-four dons, including the Bodley's librarian, the principal of Pusey House, master of Balliol College, and both the junior and senior proctors.⁷⁵ After his death a proposal to erect a statue in his hometown of Bishop's Stortford was unsuccessful, and the idea of erecting a drill hall in his honour was opposed by the town council.⁷⁶ A proposed statue to him in Westminster Abbey was the subject of public debate, and a powerful committee was formed with the purpose of constructing a national memorial to the man.⁷⁷ No such national memorial was ever built – although Oxford's statue (and arguably London's *Physical Energy*) came *de facto* to fill that role, and in 1953 a small memorial plaque was finally installed in the Lady Margaret Chapel of Westminster Abbey.⁷⁸ Meanwhile, although in their conception the scholarships were 'a sort of glorified Ku Klux Klan', one biographer reflected in 1933, there was little evidence that the students really developed 'a raging thirst for universal Nordic domination'.⁷⁹

As the history of post-war decolonisation unfolded across the continent of Africa, the regime of monumentality began to be dismantled. He described the nation that bore his name as part of his 'indelible' memory, Lady Randolph Churchill recalled in her memoirs – but the names Zambia and Zimbabwe were adopted in 1964 and 1980 respectively.⁸⁰ Just as the first Colossus had stood for only half a century, collapsing in the earthquake of 226 BCE and never rebuilt, so in this slow collapse the name had stuck for just sixty-six and eighty-two years respectively. With independence, statues commemorating the man began to be removed. In Lusaka in 1964, the *Physical Energy* sculpture installed just four years earlier was removed by crane.⁸¹ In

August 1980, a statue of him was removed from Main Street, Bulawayo in the newly independent nation of Zimbabwe, and placed in a museum, and in the same month another from Jameson Avenue (itself renamed Samora Machel Avenue in the early 1980s) in the capital Salisbury (renamed Harare in 1982).[82]

In March 2015 at the University of Cape Town, the Rhodes Must Fall protest movement formed to remove yet another statue of the man, one erected in 1934 at the centre of the campus. On 7 March an activist named Chumani Maxwele threw human faeces onto the sculpture, and following a month of demonstrations, the figure was removed on 9 April. The argument was simple. Twenty-one years after the end of Apartheid, students at the university still experienced racism, in all its forms. The persistence of an image of Rhodes was not just a metaphor for this persistence – it was part of the apparatus through which a culture endures. The ability for a community to remove an image, because it wishes to remember different people, and to build a different future, is a basic test of freedom and democracy. Art and culture matters more than some people might claim. At the memorial in Cape Town, the nose of the bronze bust was removed in 2015 but later repaired and the head was removed entirely in 2020, but then again replaced.[83]

In Oxford, as a new academic year was getting underway in October 2015, a parallel grassroots campaign group called Rhodes Must Fall Oxford formed and called for the removal of Oxford's own statue of Rhodes. Like in Cape Town, as Natalya Din-Kariuki has pointed out, the campaign was about much more than the statue.[84] It was, the group's founding statement said, also 'more importantly the culture that inculcated his imperialism in the first place':

> In Oxford, the spirit of imperialism is not simply kept alive by buildings but also by what is inside them. The habits of mind and ways of relating that stoked colonialism continue to hang in Oxford's halls and infuse its institutional cultures. Oxford continues to colonise the minds of future leaders through its visual iconographies, the concepts and histories on its curricula, the networks of power, the cultural capital, and the 'civilised' culture of 'taste' in which students are steeped.[85]

One way of looking at this history is to walk east from Oriel, across Magdalen Bridge, to the roundabout at the bottom of the Iffley and Cowley Roads, known as The Plain. Stand next to the fountain installed for Queen Victoria's diamond jubilee, then turn and look back west towards town. It was the site of the former churchyard of St Clement's Church. Here, on 19 September 1903, the Bishop of Oxford unveiled a block of Portland stone that stood nine feet tall, a memorial to the men of the Oxfordshire Light Infantry who had died in the Second Boer War. On the sides were brass tablets that listed the battle honours, the names of those killed or who died of disease, and an image of a bugler playing the Last Post. The manufacture of the statue planned to stand on top was delayed for a couple of years, but in the meantime the memorial served its purpose perfectly well. Eventually when it was installed in 1906, it came as a shocking contrast. A life-size statue of a soldier in a pith helmet and wearing South African War campaign dress was holding his rifle raised in the ready position, and pointing it straight down High Street.[86] Oxford's South African War Memorial stood there for almost half a century. After the Second World War, like many industrial British cities, Oxford welcomed a new generation of migrants from the British Commonwealth, and many found accommodation in east Oxford. In 1950, when the new roundabout was created as part of traffic management works, the city council took the opportunity quietly to remove the statue. It was relocated first to the Cowley Barracks in east Oxford, then later to the nearby Territorial Army Centre at the Slade Park Barracks, and then when that site was demolished and sold by the city council in 2008, the statue moved to the Edward Brooks Barracks in Abingdon. It's no longer pointing a gun down the High Street.[87] One of Oxford's monuments to Rhodes' legacy, a prime example of how the memorialisation of the Boer War brought the Confederacy style of statues of gun-toting soldiers to the built environment of urban England, was calmly and straightforwardly taken down and relocated. There was no outcry at the time, and there are no campaigns to have this violent image reinstated.

But what was simple in 1950 proved more complicated in the twenty-first century. Pressure was immediately put on the college by powerful voices to resist the campaign. 'It's not the job of the present to tick off the past,' the Cambridge University classicist Mary Beard wrote in her *Times Literary Supplement* blog in December 2015. 'I mean you can't whitewash Rhodes out of history, but go on using his cash,' she continued, referring to the cash spent on the monuments a hundred years ago, and what remains in the trust and the college rather than the university itself.[88] 'Where does it stop?' asked Stephen Pollard, editor of the *Jewish Chronicle*, a few days later, accusing the campaign of the 'censorship' of 'free speech'.[89] Tony Abbott, former Australian prime minister and former beneficiary of a Rhodes scholarship, wrote that the university's task was 'not to reflect fashion but to seek truth and that means striving to understand before rushing to judge' someone who was 'a man of his times'.[90] And then in January 2016 Lord Patten, the then chancellor of Oxford University, added his voice. Although Oriel is a self-governing college, and the trust is not a department of the university, at the inauguration of Louise Richardson as the university's new vice-chancellor he claimed that 'Oxford will not bow' to the campaign, arguing: 'History is not a blank page on which we can write our own version of what it should have been according to our contemporary views and prejudices.'[91] All were perhaps unfamiliar with the advice given by Evelyn Waugh, printed in a souvenir programme for the New Theatre, Oxford on 28 February 1930 under the title:

RECOMMENDATION
to those who wish to preserve Oxford

Waugh's text suggested adopting 'a policy less of Preservation than of judicious destruction', observing that 'a very small expenditure on dynamite should be enough to rid us forever of ... the High Street front of Oriel', and that if Magdalen Bridge were partially demolished then 'the Boer War memorial could lapse into repose'.[92]

From here on, the story gets a little strange. By 2017 it felt to many like the Rhodes Must Fall in Oxford had failed as a movement. All those arguments that mixed up the statue with the man seemed to have hit home, as if a chunk of carved stone had a right to free speech, as if what was needed was to listen to all sides, and in so doing kick the can forever down the street. But in 2020 the movement was further catalysed by the second wave of Black Lives Matter protests during the Covid lockdowns. In Bristol on Sunday 7 June, following a longstanding campaign over more than two decades, a statue of a seventeenth-century slave trader named Edward Colston, which had been erected in 1895, was toppled and thrown into the harbour water.[93] Speaking to the press later that week, Oxford's vice-chancellor doubled down, claiming that the question facing Oriel was 'how to evaluate historical figures morally', and that 'hiding your history is not the route to enlightenment'.[94] On the same day the Birthplace Trust named after this man announced they would be renamed the Bishop's Stortford Museum.[95] Ten days after Colston fell, Oriel's governing body voted to relocate its statue.[96] It was three days before the removal of the Confederate monument from Oxford, North Carolina. A college commission was established, and after it reported in April 2021 the college reaffirmed its position on removal the following month. An application for listed building consent was expected, both for the statue and for the small plaque on King Edward Street put up in 1906.[97] Then, very slowly, nothing happened.

In London in September 2021, a 1930s block of flats in King's Cross that bore the man's name was renamed Park View House by Camden Borough Council.[98] The campaign for that name change stretched back even longer than the Colston campaign, having been put forward in 1984 in an anti-racism initiative by the Greater London Council.[99] But in October 2021 a sign which the college described as 'a temporary contextualisation' was erected which read: 'In June 2020 Oriel College declared its wish to remove the statue but is not doing so following legal and regulatory advice.' What exactly that advice was, or from whom it came, was left unspecified.

An obfuscatory commentary posted on the college website explained that its commission had advised that relocating the statue would be a protracted and time-consuming process, 'highly costly to take through to completion', and that there was 'a very strong likelihood that the process would fail in the end'.[100] A series of actions to address equality and diversity in the college would therefore be taken instead, including staff training in 'race awareness'.[101] The position of the secretary of state for housing, communities and local government, Robert Jenrick, on the idea of 'retaining and explaining contested heritage' was mentioned. The timing of this shift in Oriel's position coincided with Jenrick's replacement in that role by Michael Gove, future editor of *The Spectator*, on 15 September 2021.[102] Through a combination of denial, anxiety, obviation, paralysis, weakness, whataboutism, wherewillitendism, excuses, bullying, threats, lies, and above all meek deference to unseen and possibly nonexistent authorities, the statue remained, undemocratically, unfallen.

Oxford is 'a place of dead languages and undying prejudices'. That was the verdict of the Radical MP John Bright in 1880, and it is a line that took on new resonance in 2021.[103] It's not that the prejudice seems to be undying, because it doesn't feel that way. The prejudice is dying, albeit slowly. It's that the legacy monumentality is itself a kind of dead language. But if it's possible to remove a White supremacist statue erected in 1911 in Oxford, North Carolina, or in Bristol in 1895, why would it be impossible to remove a White supremacist statue of the same genre and a similar date from Oxford, England? The thing's gaze says everything it needs to: it believes it will outlive us all. Like he always said he would. 'It's a very Oxford solution, I guess,' someone who had sat in those meetings told me recently, 'to decide we want to do something and also that we won't do it.' As if that were the end of the matter. But no one can be sure how this ends. In fact, we're still very much at the beginning of the story I want to tell you.

In those examples I mentioned it took decades before the eventual removal. Widen the frame and they were part of a long history of 'fallism', the loose movement of grassroots anti-colonial, anti-racist, anti-militarist movements that began with efforts to remove White supremacist statues in the 1960s and 1970s, from Mozambique and Algeria as well as Zambia, Zimbabwe and the American South, and has expanded to encompass other kinds of monument.[104] As a transatlantic phenomenon the history of fallism is far from over. It's a history of what counts as a monument, and what counts as a fall.

The journalist and academic Gary Younge has questioned the national obsession with statues, suggesting that the best response would be to take every last one down, so as not to 'burden future generations with the weight of our faulty memory and the lies of our partial mythology', or to 'petrify historical discourse, lather it in cement, hoist it high and insist on it as a permanent statement of fact, culture, truth and tradition that can never be questioned, touched, removed or recast'.[105] This book takes an alternative approach. It traces a history of slippage in order to cut a sondage into the memory culture of White supremacy and corporate-militarist colonialism. The unfallen status of the Cecil Rhodes statue in Oxford makes the writing of this book possible. I've come to think of it as a form of sustained speculation. Because it has in some real sense already started to fall. Through documenting the history of the fall, as these opening pages have, it may be possible to flip it as it is still unfolding, and begin to trace out its obverse: the 150-year history of Oxford's legacy monumentality in all its forms, the transatlantic geography of the nameless cultural and artistic movement that can be glimpsed as it falls, and the deeper prehistory of this so-called 'culture war'.

## V

As we walked away from Oriel through the cold dusk air the streetlights were coming on in Radcliffe Square, making the rain sparkle like cumulus clouds of dust as it fell. It's about how what was unnoticed and tacit can become visible, I was saying, about an institutional culture that's failed to keep up with the reality outside. And when you replied you offered an image that has become my talisman for thinking about this question. In 1865, you told me, when the Confederate troops had started to surrender, and the American Civil War began gradually to come to an end, Emily Dickinson wrote a poem in which she imagined a new law of physics. It wasn't a law of gravitation, of motion or of thermodynamics; not a law of the movement of bodies in space, but their fragmentation over time. 'Crashe's Law', Dickinson wrote, you continued, concerns 'slipping'. Falling, dilapidation, decay, ruin and failure will never, this law states, happen in an instant – but will always unfold over time, 'consecutive and slow'. The poem bore the title 'Crumbling is not an instant's Act'.[106]

This is a book about that Dickinsonian sense of slippage. About how a monument can remain standing, unfallen and yet already be in the process of falling. A fall, any fall, will always be just the most visible moment in the unfolding of some wider, deeper, more long-standing process of descent or failure. Naturally it is this moment that will command attention, not least because of the dominant, sublime, iconoclastic power that the sight of falling masonry, whether from real or metaphorical structures, will always bring. The crash appears to have come from nowhere, but it has not come from nowhere, any more than a financial crash or a train crash would just appear out of thin air. Don't mistake the moment of toppling for the longer process of the fall, you told me. The process of slippage means that there is, to revive some old Marxist jargon, no longer just a structure, but *a conjuncture*.

Any scientific law, even the kind imagined by a poet, will be concerned with observable phenomena, and with causality. As if it were Newton's autumnal apple or the splash of Archimedean bathwater, when the thing bursts into view, as a monument does when it topples, the first question people ask will often be: 'What is the reason for the fall?' But the archaeologist's questions will include another kind of causality, which requires a different kind of inference from that of the physicist, because the work of culture is about more than just the force of gravity or the calculation of volume. To ask *Why did it fall?* is essential; but to answer that fully there must be a prior question: *How was it made to endure for so long?*

If you know the feeling I'm describing, that feeling that you've been lied to, then you might guess what I want to say next. The work that's needed to keep a lie going can be as minimal as a collective participation in the idea that the lie must be preserved. And participation is more often a case of holding your nose or simply looking the other way, rather than fighting for lies to be preserved. *Interpellation*, that's what the Althusserians used to call it, this process of participation, the way that people take a structure on board as part of their subjectivity. People can come to normalise and internalise a self-contradictory, supremacist account, like race-awareness training in an institution with a monument to Apartheid for example. Such structures only persist because the community maintains them. But, crucially, people start to take it personally, as they spend time, acquire knowledge, learn the codes. That's how participation works. People come to identify with a tradition, to embody socially transmitted behaviour which anthropologists call 'culture'. It's as if they have been duped into confusing someone else's ideology with their own thoughts, someone else's lies about the past with their own memories, even when those memories are just memories of being part of the tradition. And when that ideology or those lies are about cultural Whiteness, it becomes a kind of identity politics. You become part of the lie. Multiply that and that's how the lie endures.

I'm talking about myself, of course, when I talk about those people, those cultural dupes, I told you when we were back in my office. No kidding, you said, with a wide gesture of the arm, a gesture that seemed to encompass the melancholic vitrines of the museum galleries fifty feet from us in the building, and the university administrators who would seek to defend that cursed monument on High Street and its legacy model of benefaction, but also the books on my shelves, and thus the disciplines in which we were both trained. Anybody who spends time in any part of this nexus of disciplines, the 'four As' – anthropology, archaeology, art, architecture – will understand the thrilling sense they give you of being part of something centuries or millennia old, and transcontinental in scope, an entity that goes under a variety of names like the human past, world culture or universal history – or, in an older language, civilisation, expansion and destiny.[107] These cultural disciplines were among what historian Peter Mitchell has described as late Victorian Oxford's 'spiritual reclamation of imperial subjects'.[108] They created new public spaces – museums, galleries, public art, libraries, lecture theatres, and so on – that can hold a halo effect, seeming sacred, unquestionable, eternal.

So there is always this bourgeois, establishment dimension to how the lies persisted. The currency is distinction and taste, esoteric knowledge mixed with pleasantries, cultural capital and civic values. It is possible then to find oneself, without even noticing it, part of a Defence Force for culture, drilled through structures of participation. Just as a statue can serve to mix up the person depicted with their transubstantiated likeness carved in stone or wrought in bronze, so it's possible to mistake your own life story and values for those of a tacit inherited subculture hard-wired into the arts, culture, heritage and education sectors since the mid-nineteenth century; since the Crimean War or the American Civil War if you like. These fields are unlikely battlefields; their regimes of display improbable weapons for a war about dead prejudices and attitudes, their public spaces surprising sites in which to find extreme views seeping into the mainstream and sticking there, like time-bombs with long-delay timers, operating at the pace of toxic pollution or radioactive waste, years after anybody held them. But the improbability was always the point. How could these things, the arts, culture, heritage, a statue in the streets, be seen as anything other than forces for good, after all? They are built to seem like something that demands our protection, that must be preserved. Something you'd fight to defend.

## VI

'Why is it so difficult to study monuments?' the prehistorian Richard Bradley has asked. 'Is it because they cut across our everyday experience of time?'[109] These are questions to ask of White supremacist statues as well as of ancient sites like Stonehenge. Part of the answer is the variety of ways in which they 'cut across' the present, as Bradley puts it. Because as every archaeologist knows, monumentality is neither an eternal nor a constant dimension of social life. Writing in 1950, Gordon Childe defined the presence of monuments as one of his ten criteria that distinguish a city from a village. A decade later the American anthropologist Elman Service suggested monument-building was a signature of a phase of social evolution that he called 'chiefdoms'.[110] The role of monuments in urban life and hierarchical power is still a topic worthy of consideration today. But since the 1960s archaeologists have come to understand that monumentality is not the prerogative of city-dwelling or indeed agricultural societies alone. Monumentality, and the diverse practices of genealogy and commemorating the ancestral past that can accompany it, can take many different forms, forms which are as diverse as their potential meanings. There are public buildings, temples, pyramids and statues, and there are earthen barrows, shell mounds and stone tombs. A monument may contain the skulls, bones or cremated remains of the dead, or it may be concerned with remembrance without physically containing or burying human bodies.[111] Sometimes even natural places like mountains, caves, rivers or springs can be a kind of monument – because of the human practices or ritual activities that take place there.[112] The same might be said of ancient monuments which a nation designates for restoration and preservation. It's the process that is key. Monuments emerge through physical actions concerned with duration and memory.

Just like their meanings and their possible forms, the physical substance of monuments is always unstable too. The intention may be a particular statement, inscribing space for the remembrance of the dead or simply conspicuous consumption as a statement of authority and wealth.[113] But just as a fall is only one moment in the slippage, so the expression of such a statement or design should not be mistaken for the longer processes of building and unbuilding. As the archaeologist Lesley McFadyen has argued, a monument is a 'lively' form of architecture which may give the appearance of finality but is in fact always in a continually unstable stability. People will participate and improvise in prolonged practices of building and bricolage that carry on even when it appears to be completed, and which will always include deconstruction as well as construction.[114] Indeed, building and unbuilding can take many forms. They can even happen at the same time as each other.

That was the argument that the artist Robert Smithson advanced in his lecture on Hotel Palenque, read in 1972 to the architectural faculty at the University of Utah. Smithson described a ramshackle Mexican hotel that was undergoing a process of renovation which simultaneously involved the dismantling of some of its wings alongside the construction of others. He saw a simultaneous process of renovation and decay in the ancient Mayan ruins in the landscape as well as in the dilapidated modern building. Smithson's image of landscape monumentality was one of a process of continual building and unbuilding. Something similar can be seen in museums, he suggested in another essay. In a museum, 'the "cave-man" and the "space-man" may be seen under one roof', in juxtapositions of extreme pasts and futures that have the quality of provisionally fossilised 'pseudo-events'. This form of monumentality is akin, he wrote in the mid-1960s, to how an artificial intelligence would 'fabricate "memories" that are neither dead nor alive' as 'coded information feigns the possibility of immortality' – a 'tombic communication'.[115]

The forms, meanings and even the substance of a monument are therefore never stable. A monument may be made of stone or metal, or may be in some tacit, unseen or wholly immaterial form. But its medium is constant. It may appear to represent a fixed moment in time, but that is part of the illusion produced by monuments as a technology. The medium of monumentality is always duration. Preservation is just one mode of monumentality, a kind of construction that uses the found materials of the past to rewire cultural memory.

These observations are helpful when it comes to understanding the culture-warrior postions of the former chancellor and vice-chancellor of Oxford, of Mary Beard and Tony Abbott and the mob of culture warriors who followed them in their defence of Oxford's public monument to colonial-militarist violence. Some may imagine monuments to be epiphenomenal: a by-product, a superstructure that should not distract from the 'real' functioning of political and social life, or indeed the 'real' work of anti-racism or historical enquiry. As if social relations and political formations were more real than stone, or bronze, or silence. It's just the past, anyway. And the past, we were taught, was not just a very long time ago, it was a foreign country. They did things differently there, the heritage theorists used to insist in the 1980s. It's the way things are. You can change most things in this world, but you can't change the past. Four attack lines emerge:

*Stop rewriting history*, they say – as if historians should never question the accepted version of events, but remain stuck in the imperialist positivism of late Victorian historians who claimed their task was the accumulation of the facts, following that old, faux-naïve, impossible Rankean ideal of writing history *wie es eigentlich gewesen* ['as it really was']; as if every history book were a mere encyclopaedia, every chunk of propaganda an eternal truth.[116]

*Retain and explain*, we are told – as if the historic built environment should never change, as if everything must always be preserved, as if there were not complex longstanding formal processes to manage such change and preservation, through which more than 20,000 applications for listed building consent, and hundreds of demolitions of listed buildings, are approved each year in England alone.

*Don't try to cancel Cecil Rhodes or General Robert E. Lee or Christopher Columbus, etc, etc*, you will hear – as if the claim that these were simply 'men of their times' could confuse the listener into mistaking the statue for the man; as if a society cannot choose whom it commemorates, as if any random statue must demand the respect that we pay to a gravestone, or the bones of the ancestors.[117]

*Don't judge the past by the standards of the present*, they insist – when in reality the past is simply now catching up with legacy monumentality.[118]

Part of what is in play here, as Paul Gilroy once argued, is melancholy. Melancholy, Gilroy showed, is a common reaction to 'the loss of a fantasy of omnipotence'. He made this observation in his Wellek Library Lectures, delivered at the University of California Irvine in 2002, and published in 2004 under the title *Postcolonial Melancholia*. The third lecture took its cue from Alexander and Margarete Mitscherlich's 1967 book *The Inability to Mourn* – a psycho-historical study of West Germany's relationship with its recent past in the aftermath of the defeat of fascism. Gilroy brought this pathology of denial, guilt, trauma, silence and intergenerational conflict into dialogue with the theme of his talk. He was speaking about how British people might come to terms with the ideologies of 'race' and supremacy that formed the master narratives of European colonialism. Before British people 'can adjust to the horrors of their own modern history and start to build a new national identity from the debris of their broken narcissism', Gilroy argued, 'they will have to learn to appreciate the brutalities of colonial rule enacted in their name and to their benefit'. Time to stop avoiding the subject.[119]

It's like the stages of grief; a grief for legacy monumentality as it slowly fails across its three main fields: public memory in the streets, the displays and collections of world culture museums, and the humanities and social sciences disciplines in universities. First comes denial, then anger, then depression. Another view is possible, and it's nothing to do with passing judgement on people from the past. Instead it's about transparency, choice, consent and the democratic ownership of the means of public memory. About the insistence that monumentality is about memory rather than history, and that new forms of public memory and monumentality are always possible. About how much art, culture, heritage and our knowledge of the past matter. About human dignity. And ultimately about reconciliation – the potential for new modes of inheritance to emerge where old toxicities fall away;

for a new abolitionism in arts and culture that is willing to excise racist legacies where that is what a community decides. The second half of the 2020s is unquestionably a time of genuine hope in the fields of art, culture and heritage. More than a decade into this new phase of the Black Lives Matter movement, these sectors are starting to follow the guidance that Stuart Hall, the scholar who recreated the field of cultural studies in the 1970s, 1980s and 1990s, offered about his own discipline. 'Turn your face violently towards things as they exist now,' Gramsci said, Hall wrote.[120] 'Not as you'd like them to be,' he continued, 'not as you think they were ten years ago, not as they're written about in the sacred texts, but as they really are: the contradictory, stony ground of the present conjuncture.'[121]

## VII

The aim of an anthropology of lying, Carole McGranahan has argued, cannot be to correct the lies; it is to ask how we might understand them as claims to truth.[122] Sometimes it's not a direct lie but a culture: those tacit practices of framing and classification or ordering that go unchallenged, unnoticed, passing, changing, shifting from one generation to another. The proper names become generalised, the pronouns identified with and thus words become a form of kin terminology, in that we come to feel part of something intergenerational. Passed down like inherited privilege, unremarked on; or passed down like vicarious trauma, repressed. Don't dare to challenge it, betray it, any of it, is the inculcated attitude, an unspoken threat. Lies sublimated to such an extent that they come to feel like personal knowledge and metahistory at the same time. Don't be a traitor.

If I told you that I was thinking of writing a book about this legacy monumentality and its transatlantic prehistory, about museums and academic disciplines as types of monument too, then I know that you'd tell me to start by finding the right language to describe that body of tacit propaganda, this kind of informal, corporate colonialism that occupied art and culture as if it were empty territory to be settled, a militarist, Gothic, supremacist mode of monumentality to which art historians have not yet given a name. Fight magic with magic then, you'd tell me; name the reality so as to provincialise its fictions. Meet unreality on its own terms. Thirty years ago the Jamaican writer and critic Sylvia Wynter talked of a need for the 'mutation of knowledge' in our universities as the right framing to deal with the systemic prejudice that we collectively inherit.[123] This could be part of the pact we make with each other, as reader and writer, in this zone where non-fiction encounters fictions: the promise not to lie to one another. You once told me about a 'rag tree' you visited, which struck me as a different form of monument. Here, the folklorists record, each knotted strip of fabric is made as a wish or an oath on the site of an ancient holy spring. Maybe I can try to write each paragraph as if tying another coloured ribbon to a hawthorn branch, and then as you turn the leaves of the book you could make each note in the margin, each underlined or highlighted word, the first line of a new spell, an improvised charm that protects against some ancestral evil eye. As if reading and writing could be ways of attending to slippage in a mode of monumentality.[124] Of bringing that slippage about, even, through a form of speculation.

Break the spell. As a lie this legacy monumentality is just an incantation that tries to make a fiction eternal. The magic works quite simply: it makes a gamble that this lie will become self-fulfilling. There are so many ways and places in which the same lie has been told. It can feel like a bewitchment that could never be shattered. An inevitability. But since a monument requires collective participation, it is important to insist that to keep something standing is always a choice. There are other kinds of monumentality, of protection, of salvage. Other stories. This is not just about the idea that people continually reinterpret their past. Let's be clear: all human societies constantly *change* their past, its physicality and its tacit structures as well as its meaning. Look outside the window. The landscape you see is full of citations and omissions just like the words on the page, each actively made and remade. Human societies constantly build new structures, keep old ones standing, or let them fall. That goes for words and ideas just as for bricks and mortar, marble or bronze. Any society, any community bears the responsibility for how it remembers, which monuments and what forms of monumentality it chooses to value, protect, preserve, maintain and thus inherit and pass on to the next generation.

This monumentality may take linguistic forms. It can make a particular use of voice. For example, in a book, a newspaper article, a 'contextual plaque' on some colonial monument, or the printed label for a looted object in a museum display, colonial-militarist violence might be described in the 'past exonerative'. It's that familiar euphemistic passive verbal construction in which agency is concealed and the nature of actions seem to be transformed. Thefts become acquisitions. Killings become deaths. The horrors of the transatlantic slave trade might be presented as a triumphant and virtuous story that begins and ends with abolition and emancipation. Or the monumentality might make particular use of proper nouns. Names that evoke certain victories and foundations and benefactions and dead White men that should be remembered, so as to forget others, to unname them, even. The kind of voice where every mention of a name is a tool for silencing someone else. Even retelling the history can become a kind of monumentalism, repeating their name again and again, and so centring them still further. If you're going to write this book you'll need to think about whose name gets mentioned, you'd tell me. Sometimes you could just say he or him.

I want to pay attention to the pronouns too. An innocent 'we' conjures the image of a community into which some are invited, and some are not. That 'we' may become an 'us', the framing may expand to a 'them', and before you know it we are mapping our present onto old segregations, the division that asserts 'the West' above 'the Rest' for example, or of civilisation above barbarism, or of different degrees of humanity between human groups, or other such persistent old lies. And the possessive corollary of that we, 'our', can index possession and dispossession, ownership and custodianship, so for example in 'our' self-proclaimed 'universal' museums, stolen objects are presented as salvaged for the world. Our heritage, our past, our culture, our borders, our country. There was once even a Twitter account called Save Our Statues, I don't know if the bloke is still running it or not. Save them all, defend them, we hear. They are under attack, we are told. Whether made of stone or made of thin air, they are vulnerable, we read. Before you know it you're being interpellated again. Participating, so you can feel you're part of something bigger than yourself, something you owe allegiance to, loyalty even, or else you'll be shut out. It's us and them, those lies will claim.*

An older academic language might have described this legacy monumentality as the naturalisation of inequality, or 'the invention of tradition'. That was the name offered in 1985 by Eric Hobsbawm and Terry Ranger in their book of that title for a phenomenon of collective memory and the forging of the national past that they saw as unfolding between the years 1870 and 1914. Their timeframe isn't far off the story I want to tell here, although the phenomenon at the heart of this story lasted a little longer, into the 1920s and 1930s, and it's about ethnosupremacism rather than nationalism. I would have to find a name for this phenomenon, as it unfolds over time – a structure of myths and a hardening of those lies into something I still need to find the words to describe.

As we said our farewells that evening ten years ago you made a comment about the voice that would be needed to write a book that took slippage in Emily Dickinson's terms as its theme. What is needed to grasp this history is an archaeology that doesn't try to piece the past back together, you told me. One that refuses to limit its work to filling gaps and reconstructing the past in the way that one might cross-mend some broken potsherds. There are other ways of seeing the past, forms of memory, strategies for digging into the present. Sometimes allowing an image to fall and shatter can be a way to

---

* And that's part of the reason why the 'you' in this text will constantly shift its referent. In most of the text the second person reflects a wide range of conversations with colleagues, friends and loved ones with whom I have discussed the ideas in this book and made some field trips, in other cases exchanges with my editors, and many other people too: the students with whom I have discussed and read some of the material presented here, and with many international audiences for lectures and conversations. Through this provisional community of arguments and agreements, the preparation of this book has become a form of co-authorship. I am thankful to all, for their integrity and honesty, as we have brought legacies, silences and untruths into dialogue with each other. At some points the second person refers more specifically to a dialogue with my dear late colleague, collaborator, co-editor and friend Professor Mary C. Beaudry (1950–2020) of Boston University. I still miss our conversations, Mary, and the very long emails you always sent afterwards. Those messages still flash up on the screen sometimes when I search my inbox, as if I could still send you a reply. This book is in part an attempt to send you that reply, even though you're no longer there to read it.

expand understanding and memory. Resist all that wishful thinking about holding onto the past as it is, as if every fracture could be undone, or pasted over. Stay with the fragments, you said, but don't trust them to be your framework. Sometimes, there's a breakage, a shattering, and that's the history. Sometimes even the gap can be the monument.

As I wrote this book, that came to be one of its two mottos. Now, in the contradictory, stony ground of the present conjuncture, as Stuart Hall would have it, a decade on from the beginning of the Rhodes Must Fall campaign, there is another story to be told, about another slippage. One about a different Oxford college, and another violent, Neo-Gothic, proto-fascist form of cultural supremacism. About a further dimension of this legacy monumentality. Another unfinished story. Whose story is it? Whose heritage?

# I
# The Rule of Names

*fall*, noun. i) (of a structure) a collapse; by extension (of currency or a commodity), a steep reduction in value

It's unsettling to come face-to-face with a myth. It is mid-autumn in Oxford, and in the streets the wind is blowing orange leaves in great handfuls from the trees. The college archivist is placing a medium-sized, acid-free cardboard archival box in front of me on the wooden desk in her office. It is white. The afternoon sunlight streams in through the sash window and breaks in folds across the floorboards. I untie the two white cotton twill bows that hold the square box closed, lifting off the lid, and as I reach inside a line from a book written by H. G. Wells resurfaces, across more than a hundred years, in my head:

> And as I stood there, stupid and perplexed with this dumbfounding relic in my hand, something very soft and light and chill touched my hand for a moment and ceased to be, and then a thing, a little white speck drifted athwart a shadow. It was a tiny snowflake, the first snowflake, the herald of the night.[1]

'Calvaria' is the name given to the uppermost part of the human neurocranium. The Latin word is the source of the more familiar name Calvary, a translation of the Aramaic and Greek term *Gogulpha* or *Golgotha*, the name given to the place where Christ was crucified – the Place of Skulls. This calvaria has been sawn with a metal blade from the roof of somebody's skull, then ground, polished, and lacquered or waxed. A silver rim and stand have been added to turn the calvaria into some sick variety of tableware. A name is engraved on the rim, but it is not the name of the nameless, un-named, de-named person whose thoughts, knowledge, understanding, perceptions and memories once pulsed inside this skull. Any memory of the person's name has been erased. Instead the name of a dead man who once owned this drinking vessel runs around the circumference, alongside the name of this college, his college, Worcester College, Oxford. That name in fact indexes two men, two generations of owners. There's the man who gave it to the college in 1946. And there is his grandfather, the man with whom he shared a name and from whom he inherited this artefact, the man whose long shadow seemed, as I sat down just now, to rise from the floor of this room and tilt across from the window-blind to the surface of this desk before vanishing. The light readjusts, falls in a different way. Ten letters and a hyphen spell it out:

PITT-RIVERS

Ask around in the seminar rooms of Oxford and Cambridge, or the antiquarian clubs of London, or the public houses of rural Wiltshire, or down the line for coffee between sessions at anthropological meetings in the USA or Canada, as I have done over the years. You'll hear many different, overlapping, layered, disparate descriptions of that grandfather. In no particular order, let me bring some of them to mind. And no, we don't need endlessly to repeat the name. First, an aristocrat who inherited perhaps the single largest private fortune of the Victorian age. (The name came with the inheritance.) Second, Britain's first inspector of Ancient Monuments. (He played a key role in shaping modern ideas of heritage protection and preservation.) Third, the founder of archaeology as a scientific field. (As every undergraduate in the discipline he forged must learn, he pioneered new, militarily precise field methods of excavation and post-excavation analysis.) Fourth, the collector of vast arrays of archaeological and anthropological objects brought back from the frontlines of the British Empire, and dug out from every layer of the human past. (At the Oxford Museum which bears the inherited name, with no hyphen, you find yourself immersed in his ideas about museum displays as powerful tools for education and instruction.)

When I pick the skull-cup up, the hollow mass is lighter than

I expect; delicate even. Putting on curatorial white cotton gloves would be pointless; this skull already bears tiny smudges of countless tens of thousands of fingerprints all over it, the traces of the thousands of hands through which it passed. Because the story of this skull is that, until just a few years ago, well into the twenty-first century – I mean, like, 2011 or 2015 – it remained in periodic use in the Senior Common Room (SCR) during dessert after formal High Table dinners, guest nights and 'schools dinner' graduation celebrations. We don't know how many hundreds or thousands of graduating students and college dons and honorary fellows and their guests drank claret or Sauternes, blood-red or deep yellow, from the skull-cup over the years, just as we don't know the name or identity of the person whose skull this once was, but the crude modern repair to the stand suggests heavy use. On the face of it, the trail goes cold right here. Nobody seems to know when the practice started, or how it morphed and hardened into a tradition. And it seems not just like a practice of unclear depth, but also a memorial with uncertain intent.

That list of fractured personas runs on, as if the descriptions were the roll call for a body of soldiers, rather than fragments of the biography of one dead white man. Fifth, a major-general of the Grenadier Guards who distinguished himself testing and adopting the Enfield rifle as the new service weapon for the British Army. (He devised drills and training for soldiers in musketry in the run-up to the Crimean War, where the improved weapon represented a decisive military technological factor in the Allied victory.) Sixth, a soldier who played a key role in how we think about three civic institutions that were transformed in the late Victorian age, redefined and reloaded in ways with which we still live today. (The museum, the monument, the university.) Seventh, the brusque administrator of learned societies, editor of their proceedings and journals, a deliverer of lectures and the chairman of scientific meetings, a serial convenor and secretary of special subcommittees of enquiry. (A man whose approach to life, death, inheritance, posterity and even administration looks something like an arms race.) Eighth, a foundational figure in the study of material culture. (He wove together a model for the comparative study of art, architecture, anthropology and archaeology across millennia and around the globe, and played a key role in the creation of anthropology as an academic discipline.) The Grandfather-General claims ancestry in every one of these fault lines of descent and more. And yet nobody reads him any more. Seven heavy oversized volumes bound in blue calf leather glare at me from the bottom shelf in my office as I type this, those ten letters and the hyphen in a neat gold font on every spine. I look up the entries that cite his work in the Oxford English Dictionary, and the list of words is revealing of the esoteric nature of his technical work on material culture: 'ward-plate' (*n.* the ridges inside a lock), 'collery stick' (*n.* a throwing weapon from southern India), 'screw' (*n.* the rotation of a boomerang), 'wing-wader' (*n.* Australian wading bird), 'spring' (*n.* the elasticity of wood suitable for use for a bow), 'tussore' (*n.* a kind of silk). And then there are three more: 'crouched' (*adj.* of a burial), 'Stone Age' (*adj.* a stage of human development, which he claimed 'the Fijians were in at the time of their discovery') and 'unfinish' (*n.* an unfinished state).

It wasn't even his real name, you pointed out to me when I said all that in an email. And anyway, there's the open question of the Grandson, who gained such fame and notoriety for trying to merge anthropology with fascism. Like ice shelves calve off from a glacier, you said. That was 2015. For the first time the weather forecasters started to issue names to the storms of the coming winter in the British Isles. I looked up the roll call of anticipated storms, from Abigail and Barney to Vernon and Wendy. Over the winter months some storm-names came in as amber or red, while others never came at all.

Over time, I'm told, the skull began to leak. And when this brought its function as a communal wine goblet to an end – so the stark, sharp truth of the real-life body-horror mythoreality as it was told to me runs – the ritual transformed. Placed night after night on the table at dessert to hold the chocolates. One emeritus fellow took particular glee in passing the skull to a new fellow or a guest, I learned from one eyewitness, to elicit a sudden horror in the candlelight as that person recognised what they were holding in their hands.

Was this even legal? the bursar of another college had asked, I heard, at third or fourth hand. It kept me away from then on, another person told me, scared me off. I just didn't understand how it was possible, someone else said. That was back in 2004 or 2005. In those years, on the days on which it was not in use the vessel was kept with the rest of the silverware in the SCR, illuminated by candlelight on special occasions. Gradually, more and more fellows and staff expressed disquiet. It was like the gradual removal of a monument, but less visible, I guess. There were retirements and departures. Eventually, in the year 2015, it was removed to the SCR safe, and then in 2019 relocated to the archival box which is now open on the desk before me, and placed in a closed safe.

I asked you questions you can't answer. How does such a practice come into being? Through what energy or force is it passed down? As what kind of invented or inherited tradition might we classify it? Was the skull sliced out with a spade from a robbed grave, or sheared off a cadaver on the slab in the name of science, or picked up as some kind of conflicted memento from a battlefield, geographically if not temporally distant? Would it be possible to attribute motivation or intentionality at any point in this unending desecration? Is it an anomaly, an aberration – or just the tip of an iceberg? A moment where the mask slips, to reveal – well, what exactly? Something surely must be done to address this legacy, but what? Something must be undone, but how? How could it be possible to find the words and actions to begin to address the existence of this skull, once lit up in the display case by candles, and periodically placed, with measured detachment, on the polished oak surface in the Senior Common Room at that point in the meal when everyone has already been given too much to drink; and now in this white box, in the archives, in limbo?

It's not a metaphor, you replied. This denigrated, fragmented skull is a monument, in every possible meaning of the word. The dictionary offers at least six intersecting senses that might hold currency here, you wrote:

> *monument*, noun. i) a structure erected to commemorate a notable person or event, or more generally in memory of the dead; ii) a site of historic or archaeological significance or interest; iii) something that through its survival comes to memorialise some enduring aspect of a person, group, period, way of life, etc; iv) a significant text or a written record; v) (in US law and surveying) a fixed object in the landscape used to map property boundaries; vi) (obsolete) a portent; a thing that gives a warning.

So to say that the story of the skull-cup is a story of a monument would be to say it is a structure; a site; a survival; a text; a forewarning. A kind of landmark that could be used to triangulate between enduring forms of supremacism or militarist colonialism encountered in the disorienting form of dinner-table schlock-horror. When you're dealing with a monument in all these senses at once, then its peculiar form of monumentality produces, it seems, a special kind of artefact – one that is built to interfere with the passage of time, to transform and warp the past, to shape the weft of the future. More than a structure, as a monument the skull-cup is a conjuncture when it comes into view. Try to write about it and it's like when your fingers used sometimes to hit two typewriter keys at once and arrest the staccato of writing as the typebars jammed hard together before they could click against the ribbon. The skull-cup is an erasure. Its presence indexes an absence, it's as if the engraved silver band emits silence, like white noise broadcast by some defunct technology that's somehow still operating, a transformation of substance. Say nothing. Nobody says that directly, but everyone around the table heard the injunction, deafening and muting at the same time. But in this case the silence was a violence. What I was holding in my hands was the erasure, redaction, dehumanisation, un-naming, degradation, an unfinished silencing, an unfinished violence. The effect is something like what the poet Robert Frost expressed when he described 'a time made simple by the loss / Of detail, burned, dissolved, and broken off'.[2] Tell the part of the story that is in your hands, you always told me. Stay with the fragments but don't trust them as your framework.

On the surface there's some Gothic fantasy of the necromancer and the ghost. Look closer and there are the omissions, silences, redactions, untruths that take the form of collective traditions. The dehumanisation of a human skull reduced to a dead, empty vessel; it's strange, I told you, how this abjection feels familiar, as if it's a genre I can't quite put my finger on. It's something different from a piece of evidence that might be used for piecing together the past, something closer to how the text on the silver rim is incised, spelled out letter by letter through the removal of the metal. We talked about the leak, the claret dripping red on the white napkins, saturating the fabric and running onto the floor as if the table were drenched in ancestral blood, you suggested. And we talk about the crude repair. Sometimes addressing the past requires more than filling in the gaps, you repeated to me. When I began to try to write about it, I told you, it was with an image from Marcel Proust's *Time Regained* in mind. An image of a book that is like a vast graveyard, where most of the stones are effaced so you can no longer read the names.[3] Sometimes memory has to be the remembrance of loss. Sometimes the monument is the gap.

I run my finger along the ten-letter name shared by the Collector-Grandfather-Soldier-Theorist and the Grandson, a fascist incarcerated during the war, and I try to picture a speculative approach of writing that would start from the silver dust that was removed by the burin to engrave the letters. To write a history where so much has been destroyed would require a method that could picture, consolidate, multiply and reuse that silver dust; to write the fragments, I mean, rather than trying to reassemble what has been broken. The name stands there in relief. To write about it would require a form of prosopography, not writing against the grain exactly but something more like trying to write the inverse of a name repeatedly incised and set down to obscure other names, like a document on which the same name has been written and rewritten so many times that everything becomes illegible, the paper begins to tear, nothing but an inky palimpsest remains. What you see before you is the redaction, like how the initials of that name came to be handwritten on every one of the 300,000 objects that are in the museum today, printed on 300,000 printed labels, reproduced on the database and the website, and the full name carved in bold Gothic lettering above the entranceway into the cavernous void of the Victorian galleries. This will have to be about very much more than one man, or one museum, or one name, because it's a story about how a claim was made to a single, privileged, universal, unified, jeweller's-eye, synoptic view of humanity, past and present.

The risk would be to write about this history as if erecting a monument. We all know those books. I mean, it's the biggest section of the bookshop. Biographies of men where every turn of the page offers another hagiographic turn of phrase. Histories of world wars, of big ideas, of Enlightenment or commerce or discovery or 'civilisation'. Books where the reader is invited to reinforce their worldview, or identify with a particular hero or ideal, books where each full stop is a steel screw sunk flush to fix a commemorative plaque, books that don't so much silence the past as speak over its voices, writing over alternative memories. And then there's the risk of reproducing this framing by writing as if pulling a monument down and offering nothing in its place. There are other forms of memory, you reminded me, other modes of monumentality, not just the monolithic stories of that original identity politics, the cultural heritage of militarist Whiteness.

It's already clear that it's going to be necessary to mix metaphors, to collide them against one another to the extent that any possible symbolism in this story breaks down. The men who set the story in play have mixed themselves into a slipstream of objecthood and subjecthood to such an extent that an ancestor like the Grandfather-General exists more as an inheritance and a memory than a human figure. I mean the name has come somehow to be detached from the person, applied to an institution and yet detached from the place, and in the same gesture somehow generalised into the fields where he is seen as a 'founding father' (archaeology and anthropology, two disciplines that take as their area of enquiry the whole of the human past and the entirety of human cultures in the present; the museum and the monument, the two institutions that preserve and display those pasts and cultures in the present). The name has become deterritorialised. In these respects this is a story about how personhood can be distributed, and thus quietly weaponised. This isn't the kind of past that you simply receive across the decades, or even the kind that rips into the present, with the velocity, cadence and spin of a brass bullet fired from a rifled barrel. It's more like the corrosive fallout from a bomb detonated in another millennium being borne back down now to the surface of the earth in rain, hail or snow, blown like dust, gathering like loess. This is the unfinished history of a gap. As if a statue had been carved from negative matter, as if a museum were filled with the absences its collecting histories left behind in every part of the world, as if a tradition were constructed from nothing but prejudice and violence, and now these pasts are catching up with the present.

So a biography, whether hagiography or character assassination, a hero myth or a hit-job on the archetype, is the last thing that's needed. There's no point in making this into an allegory, or a cautionary tale. This is a history to be mourned. Something closer to a necrography then; maybe, by which I mean a history of loss, of death, of dispossession. You could write a book as if putting up a statue of a man pointing a gun, literal or metaphorical, and you could write a book as if pulling such a statue down. But this is a history of the decimation of some human figures, and the hyperrealisation of others. A history of one form of monumentality, one that might, I believe, be written by letting it fall. Every monument will fall. Unless, that is, a choice is made to keep it standing.

A container leaking in the candlelight. Grandfathers and grandsons. Illegible gravestones. Potential storms so strong that they require names to describe them. It's not a fragmented history that you could assemble, you told me, it's a history of fragments that are an inheritance, and what to do with them. And the manner in which you inherit is always about how you choose to remember the ancestors.

## 1. LAND ACKNOWLEDGEMENT

This book was not written on stolen land. Then again, European empires never exactly confined themselves to the land that they stole and colonised. Settler colonialism was only ever one strand in a wider bundle of colonial practices, practices which involved much more than colonisation or occupation. Occupied territory was only ever one part of the imperial map.

In the wake of a hundred flags planted on a hundred supposedly newly discovered lands, from sea to shining sea, the creation of Crown colonies and sovereign dominions, there emerged over the course of the nineteenth century a wide spectrum of new, informal imperialisms. There were protectorates, mandates and trust territories; suzerainties and condominiums; 'dependencies' and 'spheres of influence'; forms of indirect rule that ran from joint stock companies to 'gentlemanly capitalism'.[4] In recent years scholars have begun to offer some alternative names for this tacit arsenal of deterritorialised, corporate, more violent, less visible, constantly shifting forms of conquest and structures of control: extractivism, carcerality, militarism, plantocratism, missionarism, racial capitalism, disaster capitalism, ecocide, necropolitics. In these proliferating forms, for some of which names have not yet been found, colonialism took the entire globe as its theatre of operation, Europe included.

These histories are closer than you might think. They're not even histories. I mean, this is about the here and now. And yet you still sometimes hear people talking about 'postcolonialism', as if colonialism, in these many different forms, were simply over. Just open a newspaper or doomscroll your social media, from Russian imperialism in Ukraine, to Israel's mass slaughter of Palestinians in Gaza, to a newly confident far right in Germany, Britain and the United States. The question of whether the idea of postcolonialism was ahistorical, de-politicising or simply overly optimistic was discussed quite a lot in the Nineties. Scholars like Anne McClintock questioned how it seemed to involve an 'entranced suspension of history', suggesting that in reality 'colonialism returns at the moment of its disappearance'. Arif Dirlik argued the term was even 'celebratory of the so-called end of colonialism' – since it implied that the project of 'decolonisation' in the post-war period was genuine rather than spurious or partial.[5] Today the idea of 'postcolonialism' is best classed alongside that other fin-de-siècle narrative, the right-wing claim of 'the end of history', which was the counterpart of the story of the fall of the Berlin Wall as a last victory for capitalism as if it brought wars to an end. Call it late colonialism if you like, whether in war, securitisation and policing, in cultural policy or culture war, but call it colonialism. A nostalgia for that theoretical prefix 'post' is now obstructing understanding and explanation of this ongoing militarism. And in any case, the unilinear model of time that it's mortgaged to was always going to fail to describe a multifaceted phenomenon that seeks, in every single one of its many different forms, to dissemble, collapse, destroy, annihilate time. Perhaps then it is possible to proceed by agreeing, with apologies to Fredric Jameson, that postcolonialism was simply part of the cultural logic of late capitalism: the 'unforeseeable return of narrative as the narrative of the end of narratives'.[6]

When something survives from the past, the archaeologist will ask not just why, but also how? That goes for ideas and practices, just as it does for prehistoric artefacts buried in the ground or ancient monuments in the landscape. (Even Stonehenge was rebuilt in the 1950s and 1960s, the lintels lifted onto the trilithons by crane, the sarsen stone upright bases set in concrete, underground toilets installed in a light brutalist architectural style, and a car park and ticket machine put in place.) It is possible to imagine a field of enquiry called *militarist taphonomy* – the study of how the violence of White supremacy comes, eight decades after the defeat of the fascists in the Second World War, to be not over. It requires work for something to endure, so in this case certain places, institutions, practices, discourses, have been built, rebuilt or co-opted over the past century and a half. Still are. Such a study would, I believe, turn out to be a history of the mythologies, framings and justifications that were built alongside the forms of informal empire set out above. A history of a certain kind of realism.

Not on stolen land. You hear that statement quite a lot in European universities and museums these days, this acknowledgement of nonpositionality. I mean, you hear it without anyone actually moving their lips. Nobody types it out and sticks it at the bottom of their email signature, or says it out loud in the welcoming comments before a lecture or a conference. It's expressed unambiguously nonetheless, by inaction. The kind of questions being asked in North American, or South American, or Australian, or African, or Indian, or Caribbean universities and museums, they are different here, we are told, silently, implicitly but clearly, tacitly but loudly: things are different here, as if there were no history of enclosure in Europe, as if there were nothing for these legacy colonial institutions to 'acknowledge'. As if stolen art were a totally different question from stolen land, stolen lives, stolen freedom, stolen culture, stolen knowledge. Sometimes even the bodies of dead were stolen, and put into museums. And if you want to see how all this dispossession is still ongoing in the present, think about the stolen climate. All these thefts remain unceded. And yet it is as if restitution were nothing to do with reparations, or remembrance, or reconciliation. In the face of all that theft and violence, what good is an acknowledgement anyway?[7] That's my question as well as theirs. In the museums, demands to return stolen art to their rightful owners are gradually being acceded to. Restitution is an urgent and necessary but also insufficient first step, surely. It's the thin end of the wedge, they will tell you without actually telling you, with that familiar blend of whataboutism and wherewillitendism. No. The question is about understanding the unfinished history of late nineteenth-century and early twentieth-century colonialism in all its forms. This has to be about more than just returning the Benin Bronzes. But what restitution shows is that the work is always about what happens next.

Not on stolen land. With the theft of tens of billions of acres of land, the killing of untold millions of Indigenous people, and the enslavement of uncounted millions of African people in the 400-year history of transatlantic slavery, came new evolving forms of extraction. From the stolen land there were furs ripped from slaughtered animals, timber harvested from felled trees, gold and diamonds dug from the ground, art and culture looted. Through the unfree labour forced to work the land of the Americas and the Caribbean, enslaved human bodies were, as Ta-Nehisi Coates has put it, 'transfigured' into cotton, indigo, tobacco, coffee and sugar.[8] The Marxists used to call this process, this generation of capital, 'primitive accumulation'. 'Cleverer than the alchemists,' Marx wrote, capitalism seemed to generate gold out of nothing: 'The treasures captured outside Europe by undisguised looting, enslavement, and murder floated back to the mother-country and were there turned into capital.' Capital, Marx continued, is 'dead labour that, vampire-like, only lives by sucking living labour, and live the more, the more labour it sucks'.[9] Not for nothing was Marx's favourite place to write the reading room of the British Museum (seat G7).

Not on stolen land. Then again, stand in Oxford's Radcliffe Square and ask who paid for this architecture, the built environment of this university, the libraries, offices, museums, the silverware in the mahogany-panelled rooms of those ancient colleges? The infrastructure in play involves, among other things, layer upon layer of benefactions where the wealth may be said to derive from corporate-militarist colonialism, an army of alumni who were colonisers, imperial administrators, merchants, bankers, soldiers, missionaries, especially in the later nineteenth and early twentieth centuries. The money matters, of course. The debate about 'decolonisation' should not operate, Kojo Koram persuasively argues in his book *Uncommon Wealth*, 'as if the legacy of empire is almost entirely carried within the symbolic and cultural register'.[10] But symbols and culture can be infrastructure too, not just a distraction from the real work of dealing with what Koram calls 'the aftermath of empire', but the way in which that aftermath is still being produced. Like when what was given came in the form of material objects, solid statues and stone architecture, rather than hard cash. Capital does not just take many forms, Marx taught us, its forms constantly change, to the extent that it can even appear to be its own origin or cause, as it comes to appear to produce and infinitely reproduce itself.

Following the money only gets you so far. 'The problem with capital,' the artist Isaac Julien has observed, 'is that it is abstract.' How can you depict something that can't be seen or even pictured? In a performance-talk in 2012, Julien asked the geographer David Harvey why capital is so hard to depict, and in his answer Harvey used a Newtonian analogy:

> In the same way you can only intuit gravity exists by its effects, you can really only intuit capital by its effects. The apple falls from the tree and you say, 'Oh, it must be gravity.' The factory closes down and you say, 'Ah, it must be capital.'

Julien has described how since the 1980s his filmmaking has attended not to the 'fact-based approach' of a documentary, but has blended the work of the curator and the artist, and thus the realms of fact and fiction. His visual and sonic installation-experiments have tested the power of the imagination to intervene with the past, in works that Julien has said are 'simultaneously fiction and documentary'. So, for example, Julien has sought to evoke capital through the 'unstoppable movement' that it drives.[11] In the story I want to tell, a further dimension of the problem with depicting capital will come into focus – how it constantly changes shape and form. Documentation or even interpretation must be the wrong tools when the object of study has always been a misrepresentation. Julien reveals the potential and need for a mode of analysis that tries to visualise the unseen forces in play, whether in the fall of an apple, or some wider socio-cultural process.

'You can't change the past.' That's one of the things you hear quite a lot round Oxford without anyone actually saying it; as if the monument or the museum were already something other than a transformation of the past. Like those other lines I mentioned before:

'These contested pasts are entangled'; 'Don't judge the past by the values of the present'; 'Stop trying to rewrite history'; 'Stop asking us to apologise on behalf of the dead.' The desire is to shift this question to a kind of cliometrics of past ethics, as if a balance sheet could be used to retrofit the work of contemporary ethical donation reviews back onto imperial capital, with those familiar shaky calculations about what any particular historic sum would be worth in modern money. The only aim is to distract, to exhaust. On social media they call it 'shitposting'; deliberate attempts to derail conversations, provocatively distract, make it seem the whole dialogue is two extreme sides between which a middle course has to be found. It's often a one-two: their wing-men and women will fill the middle ground and repeat the same old militarist-colonial lines to keep it all the same. The strategy is to create a chilling effect. That is the nature of the attacks that some claim constitutes a 'culture war', but which in reality tries simply to portray change as a threat. In any case, to be constrained by this framing would be to misunderstand what colonial capital is, how it operates. Because just as capital is transforming, so too the forms in which debt can be repaid are mutable too, across time and space. Fifty years ago the anthropologist Jack Goody pointed out that in any society the modes of land ownership and mechanisms of inheritance between generations will always shape one another, so there is always a two-way process between forms of production and reproduction.[12] In the same way today, when deterritorialised forms of colonial militarism are transmitted into the present as an intergenerational legacy, whether in a museum or a monument or a university, they will create their own distinctive conditions of inheritance and indebtedness.

In settler colonies, acknowledgements of land or country should not be 'vapid proclamations', Michael Lambert, Elisa Sobo and Valerie Lambert have written, but rather 'a truth-telling, a demand for accountability, and a call to action'. Such an acknowledgement should, they argue, seek to 'disrupt'.[13] Otherwise they are just speech acts that don't deliver what they seem to promise, simply allowing a state of affairs to continue, or worse helping it to persist, by restating an inequality that comes to seem eternal and unchanging. Acknowledge and move on, the implication can be. Such acknowledgements can be prime examples of what Sara Ahmed calls 'non-performativity' – the process through which institutions expend a lot of time and effort, produce much noise and heat, on questions of diversity and inclusion for example, and yet fail, as she puts it, to 'bring into effect what they name'.[14] Denialism can take the form of the blank inaction when it comes to those forms of colonialism that stretched all the way to the metropole, to institutions in Oxford, for example, that came to be used as structures of cultural descent.

Try to name it, to call it out, and the traditional position round here has always been a kind of lowering of the gaze, or a simple looking away. If someone, anyone, a curator or a visitor or a student, asks a difficult question then the response is to change the subject, and then when pressed to challenge their tone, or question their motivation. How gauche to ask such a question, how naïve. It's complicated. Entangled, don't you see? Stop attacking culture, they say, without even having to say it. That chilling effect on open dialogue, on scholarship, would have to be a central concept if the field of *White taphonomy* were ever to get going. It's part, I suppose, of the structures that emerge through the lies, a generation or two onwards, as the narrative gets so ingrained, the facts so solidly flattened out, so that the story comes to seem like reality, like the only possible state of affairs, to the extent where someone can't even ask a question without the culture warriors calling them a culture warrior. That's the predicament, so what should you call it?

There's more than one way to break a silence, you always assured me. I thought of that when I was rereading how Stephen Jay Gould concluded his book *The Mismeasure of Man* with a chapter that he called 'Debunking as Positive Science'. The story of the cultural formations at stake here picks up where that sorry history of the misuse of science left off. These stories are hard-wired not into the natural sciences but into the fields of art, culture, heritage, education, civic institutions; racisms that didn't lay claim to science, but to culture, in all its senses, and still do. *The Mismeasure of Man* paid attention to how 'systems of classification direct our thinking and order our behaviours'.[15] But words and actions can construct reality as well as thought and behaviour, and lies and redactions are words that can destroy reality. Sylvia Wynter once advised that the question might be posed like this: 'Where did this system of classification come from?'[16]

Perhaps that is the difference between acknowledgement and disruption. If what's at stake is how a lie gets repeated, hardens first into a story, and then into some kind of reality, then how is it possible to undermine the structure that is inherited? Perhaps it's possible to switch registers, from what lies may have been said and heard to what lies might be visible and invisible. Treat this as a question of visual anthropology, by which I mean that this may have to be a story about not what has been, but *what appears to have been.*

## 2. HOW MYTHS DIE

Can you find another way to start this? you ask me. Sure, here goes. I first heard the story of the skull twenty years or more ago. I assumed at first it was just that, a story – one of those myths that gets told and retold in places like this ancient university, the facts shifting and eroding with the duration of time like the gradual decomposition of the limestone that softly shears and crumbles from the walls of Oxford's colleges, chapels and libraries, dusting new shapes onto the streets before the rain washes them away overnight.

Once or twice a year one colleague or another would approach me and ask again in a hushed tone: 'Have you heard about the Worcester skull?' Recalling those exchanges now, I think of that childhood game where you whisper a word around the table from one ear to the next, and the meaning slips and transforms as it's passed down the line. (The Americans call it 'Telephone'; in my youth in the English West Midlands we used to call it 'Chinese Whispers'.) At the dénouement we see and hear how the message has changed in form and therefore meaning. Was the story of the skull-cup a myth, or a reality, or a distorted mix of the two? A silent monument so small that you could fit it into your palm like a hand grenade caught in mid-air, the pin already pulled from the cast-iron pineapple casing of the weapon that is built to kill through its own violent fragmentation. That was my feeling before I'd held it in my hands. And before I learned of the connection to him – the Grandfather-General, the man who bought this human skull-cup at auction and set another story in motion. This story.

If it were possible to write a book about this story, it would have to be about the person whose body this was, rather than the dead White men whose names were attached to someone else's unfinished death; and therefore a book about chains of transmission and how to break them, and about the lossiness and transformativity and the thickening and attenuation and hardening and brittleness in the stories people tell each other and tell themselves: in institutions, in their working lives and in public culture. I mean, stories that are at once about ourselves and about each other: who we think we are and where we think we came from; what we have received from those who stood here before us and what we might choose to pass on to the next generation. It's that question of pronouns again: these are stories about what exactly that 'we' denotes or demarcates. More potential gaps, or omissions, or silencings. I place the skull back in the box and light and shadow moves again across the wall.

The history at stake here concerns how ideas, stories and practices can coalesce around objects, artworks and institutions, and how certain modes of monumentality might confuse these human lives, memories and places. With a theoretical training in anthropology, archaeology, art or architecture you might, if you weren't careful, find yourself employing the jargon of 'material agency', or 'entanglement' or 'the social life of things', and so on, to try to describe how the worlds of people and things interdigitate. But in this case to press such theories upon this delicate shrapnel of silver and human bone would be a revealing violence. I have become familiar with some of the history of where those ideas come from by working in these disciplines and in this university town. I'll get to that later but for now let me say that this is a history where the violence lay precisely in an attempt to confuse and blur the categories of humanity and materiality, to degrade, and to have others join in with the degradation. It's in such wilful category errors that a sense of eternal verity can be engendered, as if this hybrid figure of an object-subject were a normal state of affairs. This intellectual inheritance, I have come to believe, is what is falling. I will work through some of the different senses of that word in the chapters that follow, but for now let me start with the sense of where 'fall' meets failing: a collapse, or a sudden reduction in value.

I want to try to begin to unpick what on the one hand falls to us through inheritance, and what on the other is simply falling apart, I told you. Sounds like the Neo-Gothic when you put it like that, you said. Yeah, I replied, and then there's this structuralist part.

In an essay written in 1971, the French anthropologist Claude Lévi-Strauss asked: *How do myths die?* In any given society, myths, he wrote, are far from stable. They are always transforming: being retold and elaborated upon; reformulated over generations. Myths wax and wane. And as well as being passed down over time, they also spread out across space, are overheard or copied, reduplicating and crossing thresholds from one group of people to another – and here the transformations are especially intense. The framework and the code of the myth may change, and the meaning or message may even completely invert. Myths start to die when they no longer function as myths, but become just eroded stories, curiosities, relics or legendary traditions. There exists, Lévi-Strauss argued, a universal phenomenon which he called 'a kind of principle of conservation of mythic matter'. According to this principle, as they degenerate and die myths become unmoored. Belief fades away and, with nobody to believe in them, myths take on a new cultural or literary form, like an echo of some final deathbed murmur. On the surface it can take on the outline of a self-evident and virtually unexaminable truth, a kind of informal received wisdom. In other words, something of the integrity of the myth's structure survives, even when the storytellers are long dead. What does this undead structure look like? It is like a kind of recycling: a special kind of inheritance, one in which the recipients do not exactly see themselves as heirs. Lévi-Strauss describes this as the '*carrure*' of a melody – a French word which in 1974 the English translator rendered as 'lilt', but which in fact more accurately denotes the rhythmic structure of music, and also suggests the word's primary meaning of 'stature' and 'build', both physically and figuratively, whether the physical breadth of the shoulders or the influence of a body of imagery. With nothing more to say, and nobody alive to speak it, the dead, mute hulk of an implicit myth lives on in form alone as a cultural infrastructure, or an ideology, or a tool of legitimation through which contemporary ideas might be made to seem timeless. The dead or dying myth, Lévi-Strauss concludes, comes to operate as part of 'what must be called politics'.[17]

Take an imaginary jemmy in your hand, you said, and picture us creeping across formal gardens at dusk and breaking into some ancient, abandoned museum together. Forcing the window, in the first gallery our counter-expedition finds dinosaur fossils that have been slowly decomposed by condensation, heat, light and algal blooms in their locked cases, bathed in slatted beams of illuminated, scattered dust that shine with a feeble light as if the cracked roof were an openwork screen. Like the intermittent passage of air and torchlight through the space, the names of the collectors and excavators, themselves now long since extinct, are partially legible, stuttering down the decades, inked on blotted cards or punched into the limestone walls like letters carved into a gravestone. This gang of men imagined themselves to be preserving specimens for posterity. But having lain unchanging for countless millions of years in the ground, their extraction – the interventions of digging up and collecting and putting on display – has after all simply restarted processes of decay that had been halted an eternity ago. The fossils' formation began with the burial of a creature soon after death by sand, silt or clay – conditions that allow the form to be preserved as the organic tissue is gradually replaced by minerals, to be hardened as rock, you told me.

In a second ruinous gallery we find the damp, decaying remains of pinned butterflies brought from every corner of the globe. They have bled a pool of dulled colour in tones of brown onto the bottom of a tall, cracked, glass-fronted case; around a corner, we see the barrelled-out carcasses of stuffed lions and antelope that were shot on safari, their dried and painted hides long since rotted away to leave just the wire mannequin framework, cotton wads and the tangled threads of the taxidermist standing on a powdery mound of decayed moths. Fragments of plaster casts of wings, jaws, teeth and claws. A smeared bell jar holding the blurred remains of an animal foetus of now indistinguishable taxonomy leaching out into pale saffron-coloured liquid. Under a cuticle of smeared ash, one bleak alcove houses a glass jar holding the smashed, disarticulated remains of what was once the skeleton of a dodo, its skull dissected, the faded label tells us, by the museum authorities in 1848. A hundred years after its extinction in the seventeenth century, the dodo was thought by many to be just a myth. By the time this became 200 years and the cranium was sawn up, it had become an allegory for extinction.

Picture the men busy with their rifles and oversized nets and the wooden crates in which they shipped these trophies home, you continued, dissecting the surface of this planet ligament by ligament. Listen for the echoes of the gunshots with each step you take, you said, I remember. Think of the toolbox from which the anatomist-professors chose the right bone-saw to open up the crania of dead birds. They disarticulated and decomposed the world they inherited down to the sinews of landscapes conquered. Flayed, and studied, animal bodies were suspended in impossible liquid shades of deep ochre and light blue. A small platoon of nineteen statues of great men of science once metaphorically clicked their heels around the court perimeter: Aristotle, Linnaeus, Galileo, Newton, Darwin. Now that silent, impossible chorus of boots clicking is a kind of echo. Each figure lies cracked and crushed amid scores of fallen columns of polished decorative rock. Those rocks were brought from every corner of the British Isles – British marbles from Cornwall, Cork, Aberdeen, Mull, Leicestershire. The broken gold lettering that once labelled their provenance and the names of the stones now lies like Scrabble tiles, like a destroyed map of the United Kingdom, a strange Victorian stratum of drift geology, each with some story to tell about the lord who lays claim to the geology from which it was mined: mottled red granite, carboniferous limestone, pink syenite, gypsum, 'trap rock', quartz porphyry, calcareous breccia, black serpentine.

The frozen circus of desolation before us was already contained in the gesture of collecting, which was the gesture of the butcher. Along one cracked, rust-stained wall, in the disfigured light unidentifiable forms hang from exhibition mounts like carcasses from meat-hooks. Silent for a moment, we shine our phone torches onto a mildewed sign above the entranceway to a third gallery in the destroyed museum. It reads 'Anthropology and Archaeology'. But we hesitate and cannot bring ourselves to take our living, breathing bodies beyond the threshold to witness the sheer scale of the entropic horrors of loot, skin, hair and human bones that might remain warehoused in this place where the dead and the killed were treated as if they were fossils rather than ancestors. As scrappy, empty vessels. But to be filled up with what: what fictions or what facts? With memory? is my best attempt at an answer at this point. Or simply raw consciousness. This Gothic tone isn't my kind of thing, I said when you first read me those passages. But the horror and gore is already there, you replied, and not so far below the surface; so how would you suggest trying to write about it, if not speculatively?

Your image of the monument-museum in ruins is hardly new, I told you. At least three further images lie behind it, it seems to me. I sent you the list by email, once I'd got my references straight. First there is chapter ten of H. G. Wells' 1895 classic of speculative fiction *The Time Machine*. Weena and the Time Traveller are somewhere south-west of what was once Battersea when they approach the ruined pinnacles of the Palace of Green Porcelain silhouetted against the pale yellow banners of the sky, only ragged vestiges of glass remaining in its windows. This colossal abandoned museum is now an 'ancient monument of an intellectual age' containing fossils for which 'the inevitable process of decay that had been warded off for a time' was now 'with extreme sureness, if with extreme slowness, at work again'. Among the derelict mineralogy displays, the Time Traveller describes how the sight of a block of sulphur sets his mind running on gunpowder, and then further in he enters a gallery of decaying stands of the arms of all ages, including rusty guns, pistols and rifles whose cartridges and powder have rotted into dust. Time has disarmed the museum. The Time Traveller breaks off an iron rod as an improvised weapon.

Second, there's a passage with which the French philosopher Michel Serres opens his 1987 book, *Statues*. It describes a live globally televised event that unfolded at 11.39 a.m. on 28 January 1986. The Space Shuttle *Challenger* blasts off from Cape Canaveral in Florida and disintegrates 74 seconds later, enveloped in flaming liquid propellant, incinerating and fragmenting the bodies of the seven crew members, and hurling all that remains of the crew compartment at terminal velocity against the surface of the ocean. Footage of the explosion and the burning debris falling from the sky is replayed again and again on TV news so that people come repeatedly to witness it and remember it, a phenomenon that Serres compares with the worship of a vast figure of the god Baal in Carthage in the sixth century BCE. He describes how crowds of people come to witness the spectacle. A massive fire of laurel, cedar and oil is lit, and human sacrifices are burned in the white heat of the metallic shell. It's as if the figurative statue and the military rocket share a common genealogy, a destructive power. There is an anthropology of these technologies, he writes, and 'the humanities teach this anthropology without knowing it: when they speak of statues they shed light on those of our museums or cemeteries, but also and above all on torpedoes and missiles'.[18] In drawing this comparison, Serres calls into question any imagined line between civilised and 'barbaric' societies. In the philosopher's hands the burning rocket is a burning statue full of living bodies, blazing tombs in a militaristic rite of sacrifice. An anthropologist might add a further entry to this line of descent. The space shuttle was named after HMS *Challenger*, a Royal Navy copper-bottomed screw-driven corvette that was the flagship of the Australia Station and undertook a punitive expedition in 1868, shelling villages and burning houses supposedly in retribution for the killing of a Methodist missionary the previous year.[19] The ship was converted into a kind of maritime laboratory for a Royal Society-sponsored expedition that set out from Portsmouth in 1872. Fifteen of its seventeen guns were removed to make space for scientific laboratories, as if the dissection knives and jars of ethanol were themselves a kind of weapon for another kind of expedition. The *Challenger* expedition travelled around the globe and brought back tens of thousands of specimens from its four-year mission, which were deposited in more than a dozen museums, and included human crania from South Africa, Patagonia, Tierra del Fuego, Australia, New Zealand, the Admiralty Islands and the Hawaiian Islands.[20]

Third, skip back to 1968 and there's the ending of that movie when Taylor and Nova are riding on horseback along the beach in the Forbidden Zone and encounter the Statue of Liberty buried in the sand long after an ancient nuclear war. I look the scene up on YouTube and we play back Charlton Heston's lines, delivered on his knees in the surf: *You finally did it. You maniacs! You blew it up! Oh, damn you! God damn you all to hell!*

Fallen museums. Liberty buried in the fallout. Blazing metallic tombs. The missile as a prototype for the monument. The monument operates by standing for something else, and projecting itself into our present. What then of the skull-cup? Let the metaphors fall against each other, you told me. That way you might see which ones are more than just metaphors. And before the smoke clears, before the dust has settled, what will be certain is that, in Lévi-Strauss' terms, this story of the skull is a dead myth. Which is of course to say, it has become an artefact of politics. I spelled out each character punched into the silver rim, and those carved into the skull itself, and you asked me: Why has nobody told this story before? Now there's a question.

## 3. ABOLISH THE MUSEUM

It's late in the evening. This afternoon I took the ten-minute walk back from Worcester College, down Beaumont Street, across St Giles, along Lamb and Flag Passage, onto Museum Road then skirting the museum lawn as the sun emerged and sliced it with amber light. My thoughts kept returning to that image of the ruins of a museum and I walked up the steps and into the phantasmagoric space of the University Museum. Now known as Oxford University Museum of Natural History, it was built to John Ruskin's ornamentalist, semi-Venetian Neo-Gothic, cast-iron style. It is glass-roofed like a vast greenhouse today just as it was when it opened in 1860. You have to walk through this museum to get to the second museum, the one where I work, at the back, built as an extension to the first museum a quarter of a century later, building out from nature into culture. This second museum, a museum of cultural history within a museum of natural history, was created by another dead man, not Ruskin. The Soldier-Grandfather had it built for his collection to be displayed; founded in his name seventeen years before he died. The first museum of two he created. I've been one of the curators here for eighteen years now, more than half my working life. There have been changes over its century and a half of existence, of course, mostly to keep the place the same. I recall towards the end of my second year in post, after a new shop had been installed at the entrance, reading a report in the *Daily Telegraph* that claimed, quite accurately in fact, that 'after a ten-month overhaul', my workplace was now 'even more Victorian'.[21] A world within a world, a museum placed behind another museum, as if it were a lens placed against another lens, like at the opticians. (Clearer now? Or now? And how about now?) In a collective, psychological, institutional sense, where memory, artifice, annihilation, science fiction and latent supremacism interdigitate.[22]

When we sit together in my office in the museum sometimes I tell my students about what the American ethnographer Roy Wagner once said about the discipline of anthropology. Like all academic traditions, he wrote, it lives with 'the persistence of theoretical fossils', but the hope lies in the fact that anthropology tends to remain disparate and eclectic as a field, the disciplinary instinct being somehow not 'to institutionalize this persistence, or indeed, to institutionalize a consensus at all'.[23] There is a humanity to the subject, the subjectivity that the humanities can bring. Hold onto that humanity, I can hear you saying. Listen to the building's creaking silence and you might imagine you hear the fossilisation, the stratification of eclectic accretions, taking place, one specimen at a time. That's an image it's been built to project, from the beginning and over the years. The institution appears at first glance to be some Victorian vision preserved in aspic for posterity and for eternity, a museum of museums, an endpoint or a cul-de-sac. And yet, to those who come to know it well it has come to seem, as one former director of the museum expressed it, like 'the least moored, stable, or pre-constituted entity imaginable'.[24] It's that relative lack of fixity and coherence that means it always feels like it will always somehow have the last word on any matter, and yet perhaps it's there that one might find hope. Perhaps it's not just unstable or untethered, I remember you once suggested, not just some ongoing exercise in steampunk fanfiction refracting the Gothic Revival style of its architecture, but a place preserved by the curators while holding out for its own obsolescence. An overwound clock that no longer keeps time. After all, when any structure approaches the end of its life questions will inevitably arise about which parts might need to be dismantled, and what will need to be built in their place, unless the whole structure, in which there surely might be some future value, is to fall.

Thirty yards from where we sit and talk, my students or visitors and me, the museum galleries are now in darkness, locked and alarmed. A dozen narrow red diodes blink at each other within the light Gothic architectural form of exposed brick walls and steel girders, two mezzanine floors above a dizzying main hall. Part warehouse where objects are stored, part barracks or gymnasium where bodies are drilled, part Victorian railway station where ideas are freighted, part bank vault, part penitentiary, part cargo hold, part gun barrel or time-bomb, part monument, part mortuary. It is as if each of these dimensions were an integral component of an explosive device strapped to the body of a self-consciously medieval university, where the timer still counts out each second with an unerring noiseless metronomic tick. Outside the window the rain has eased off. I stand up from my desk, turn the key in my office door, set the security system, and walk out into the cool night air and the wet streets.

In the year 1880, at the age of fifty-two, the Grandfather-General came into a vast fortune. He used this opportunity, among other things, to found Oxford University's Museum of Anthropology and World Archaeology, donating the nucleus that was the personal collection he had been amassing for thirty years or so. With the inherited land and fortune came an inherited name. The museum still bears it, the new name that this man adopted for the final two decades of his life. The Grandfather-Theorist became interiorised, fossilised, embodied in a named museum in the oldest university in the English-speaking world. It's like an occlusion in a tree, you tell me. Potentially invisible from the outside, it can play havoc come timber time, when you try to build something with it. Through the initial act of donation the collection came to possess a kind of soft, expansive solidity, like driftwood swollen with salt water. The name is even written into the traffic signs that direct the tourist coaches around the university town with a clearly inscribed vector or one-way arrow: *Pitt Rivers*.

For thirty years, and slowly to start with, the Grandfather-General assembled a collection of 30,000 'ethnological' and archaeological objects. He displayed them privately at first in the London townhouses where he lived, and then to the public: at an outstation of the South Kensington Museum at Bethnal Green in the East End, and later at what is now the Victoria and Albert Museum in South Kensington, before donating them to Oxford. There was no endowment. The university officials were presumably expecting a sum to be left in his will when they agreed to take the collection on, so as was customary for donors they awarded him an honorary doctorate of civil law (DCL). His invitation letter to the university's Encaenia, the annual ceremony that commemorates past benefactors to the university by inviting prospective ones, came from the provost of Oriel College, and he attended to receive the award in June 1886. Thirteen years later in 1899 at the same annual ceremony Cecil Rhodes received his DCL alongside Field Marshal Kitchener – who was fresh from his bloody military campaign in Sudan.[25] Benefaction. That's one word for it.

The Grandfather's relationships with the men who most closely oversaw the museum's installation and development – Edward Burnett Tylor, Oxford's first reader in anthropology (and, from 1895, the world's first professor in the subject), and Henry Balfour, a much younger man, who worked as an assistant at the museum straight after graduating from Trinity College, Oxford (animal morphology, 1885), and was the principal custodian and curator of the collection from 1891 right up to his death half a century later in 1939 – grew increasingly fractious. Indeed, it was perhaps because of a permanent falling out with these two men, the professor and the curator,[26] that when he died in 1900 there was no financial bequest for Oxford in the will. Instead, two Pitt Rivers Museums were formed. The Grandfather-Collector had created a second, rival museum (closed and dispersed after the Grandson died in 1966) eighty miles to the south-west on the vast estate that he inherited on the Wiltshire–Dorset borders, to which he also gave the name Pitt-Rivers Museum (hyphenated). Any provisional sense of the Oxford museum's coherence started to dissemble and scatter like ash.

Over the century and a half since its foundation, the Oxford collection has grown to more than ten times its original size, more than 300,000 artefacts. Objects from the collections of Christ Church, including items taken from the Pacific islands during the first two voyages of Captain Cook, objects from other Oxford colleges, from the university's Indian Institute Museum, and from the university's Ashmolean and Natural History Museums were assimilated year by year. Layers of global extractivist asset-stripping sedimented in the medieval university. Like hundreds of psycho-killer hoards, someone once said to me when I was showing them round. New lines of inheritance and descent coursed through this amorphous, shifting, chaotic, pressure-cooker mass of collections upon collections, each running like quicksilver through a barometer, the poisoned liquid metal waxing and waning with each change in the atmosphere. The atmosphere is definitely changing today. And if the glass cracks, spilt mercury is hard to get rid of, its toxic beads are near impossible to gather up. And I thought again of the silver dust from the rim. Did I tell you there are Greek letters incised into the skull itself as well?

Most of the museum's subsequent growth came from taking in accessions from more than 5,000 new donors. Some were twentieth-century alumni who became colonial soldiers, administrators, missionaries and travellers; others were anthropologists whose bequests emptied their sealed chests and cupboards after they died, and drew the things together. Their names were dutifully recorded in the vast expanding prison-space of the accession registers. More than a quarter of a million further items brought home were piled up as secondary layers in this place, a tangle of locked drawers that monumentalise loss. The legacy of this accelerating growth emits a kind of necromantic magic that sinks into the ground and crushes the visitor's sense of where precisely they might be standing: Oxford, or New Guinea, or Virginia, or the Torres Islands, or Lagos, or Lahore. Walk in the galleries and this place somehow blurs the line between the dead and your living, breathing body, like a statue would blur that line. In the 1890s, the curator would tell people that was the point; he had a line I remember reading that ran something like: 'in this museum, we show you the living to show you the dead'.[27]

I got an early hint of the necromantic stories of this place within the first months of taking up my job. I looked up the archaeological report that had been written when an extension was being built onto the south side of the museum in 2005, the building in which my office is located, and where I'm writing this now. It had occurred to me that the excavation might have revealed something the ground into which the foundations of the museum were cut, this unsettled para-colonial space that I was finding it so hard to describe. In two test trenches a horizon of red-brown silty sand dappled with pockets of tree-root disturbance was recorded, I read. Five and a half inches thick, this layer was sandwiched between the deep natural undisturbed river gravels below and the soft brown sandy parkland loams above. Not a single artefact was recovered from this red-brown deposit. But its strange blurring of the natural geology and the historic disturbance above led the excavator to conclude that underneath the museum there runs a thin interface, which he described as 'a supernatural subsoil'.[28] Sounds like that short story by H. P. Lovecraft, you told me. A writer famous for blending his racism with his command of the powerful language of Gothic terror. It was called 'The Horror in the Museum'. At a waxworks museum in Southwark, a ramp leads down from the vaulted chamber of displays to an incarcerated, diabolical presence so ferocious and dangerous that the curator finds himself torn apart, killed and preserved as an exhibit. What is there about this nineteenth-century institution that can still evoke Lovecraft's twentieth-century fear of other cultures to the extent that the twenty-first-century archaeologist wanted to hint at supernatural presences in the ground on which it is built?

Imagine you come to the museum and ask for me at Front of House. This place is about far more than one man's lone, eccentric acquisition of cultural curios and specimens from a network of dealers and auction houses and looters returning from military, administrative, corporate or missionary colonial service. Or his purchases fire-sold from defunct contemporary museums like that of the Anthropological Institute in London, or the Blackmore Museum in Salisbury, to build his collection: building a narrative by putting one thing after another. No, this is a question of how the dead are made to live on.

We walk upstairs and start in the upper gallery. Every morning before the museum opens, the bank of Bakelite switches is flicked and the yellowed, subterranean glare of electric light blinks three or four times, then illuminates what's here on the second floor. We walk around the mezzanine and become gradually aware of the acoustics, how our voices bounce off the tongue-and-groove ceiling and into the void of the two further levels of the museum below. Behind glass against red-brick walls under lock and key scores of tall display cases built like upended glass coffins hold clubs, spears and spear-throwers, swords, knives and daggers, slings, blowpipes, boomerangs, axes, staffs, polearms, bows, crossbows, firearms of every variety. Even the shields, breastplates and helmets are classed as weapons in this place. The air is restless with silences and mentions: the unnamed people slaughtered while fighting with these weapons, and those collectors, many alumni of the university, whose names are meticulously documented on gallery texts as having 'acquired', to use the familiar euphemism, weapons taken from the battlefields of empire, or taken as trophies and mementoes from corpses and captured bodies.

The original plate glass roof always leaked. In November 1928 a storm ripped a great section of it away, exposing the artefacts and cases to the wind and rain.[29] During the Blitz the replacement glass roof was painted over to avoid breaking the blackout. Then in the 1970s the roof and single window were finally boarded up, like screwing down the lid of a tea chest, or shovelling spoil to backfill a trench. The longer you spend here, as your eyes become accustomed to the conditions, your pupils growing in the dark and then tightening in the spotlights, the more you come to wonder whether it is really a museum at all, or rather a weapon, a kind of incendiary device lobbed into the future by the Grandfather-Grenadier. As if each glass case were a retina that retains the flashing bleached outline of the bright light of an explosion, shots fired in that man's culture war. How could anyone ever disarm an institution so overloaded with weapons of every conceivable kind, or exorcise a space crammed with so many forms of the undead? Start with reconfiguring the memory culture perhaps, as Walter Benjamin put it in those famous lines: 'taking hold of a memory as it flashes up in a moment of danger'.[30]

The handwriting on the labels runs in strips like a barbed-wire fence, each repeating his name in initials: P. R. Coll. These thousands of miniature manuscript panels read like a roll call of Victorian colonial massacres. There is a sword and a dagger taken during the Indian Rebellion at Lucknow in November 1857.[31] A longbow and four arrows taken during the bombardment of Shimonoseki in Japan, when British, French, Dutch and United States forces sacked the Tokugawa/Edo domain of Chōshū in September 1864.[32] An axe seized in an attack on an Aboriginal camp at Mackenzie River, Queensland in September 1865.[33] A tomahawk collected by one of General Custer's soldiers from the site of the Washita River Massacre in Texas in November 1868.[34] An Ethiopian iron spear taken by troops at Magdala during the Abyssinian Expedition in April 1868.[35] A Mahdi spear, five bronze and textile cavalry helmets, two bronze arm guards, a padded *jibbeh* fighting coat, a coat of chain mail, a hide shield and two swords taken from corpses at the battlefield at

Omdurman in Sudan in September 1898. In the aftermath, Kitchener ordered the Mahdi's body to be dug up and thrown in the River Nile and his tomb to be exploded with lyddite shells, but not before his head was taken as a trophy and carried to Queen Victoria in a kerosene can.[36] One account describes how Kitchener had planned to have the skull made into an inkstand or a drinking cup, or else have it 'forwarded as a curiosity to the Royal College of Surgeons'.[37]

Further along, a carved wooden Herero club purchased by the museum the year after the Herero-Nama genocide was carried out in German South West Africa, now Namibia, in 1904. There is a wooden composite bow captured at the Dongtse Monastery during the British punitive mission to Tibet in 1905.[38] Half a dozen spears and swords from the Sulu Archipelago in the Philippines which arrived in the museum a few months after the massacre of Moro people by the United States Army at Bud Dajo in 1906.[39] I remember how in 2010 my colleagues juxtaposed two improvised Mau Mau rifles with these trophies, their roughly cut wooden stocks attached to lengths of metal tube, taken by a British Army captain in May 1955.[40] In every case the names of the colonial officers are remembered; in none the names of those who resisted colonial violence. The silent insinuation is deafening: that those unnamed fighters, bodies slain and possessions looted, died because they held a less destructive weapon, and that was because theirs was a technologically inferior culture. Interspersed among the militaria looted from the scenes of massacres and battles are the weapons that were pointed in the opposite direction. A rifled Lefaucheux pin-fire revolver used against Jamaican people in the Morant Bay rebellion of 1865.[41] An example of the 1870s Colt 45, 'frontier model', from the United States, known as 'the Peacemaker'. A mid-1930s aluminium Italian Breda Model 35 hand grenade. A 1980s Israeli Defence Forces Uzi 9mm submachine gun, handed in to an English police station during the 1988 National Firearms Amnesty and displayed in the museum since 2010.[42]

The catalogue of this monument to militarism at the heart of the university goes on. Periodic reviews by explosives experts declare the bullets and powder flasks safe. Regular inspections by Thames Valley Police deem the gun cases adequately secured. But if you shone your phone's torch into this thick necromass of tomb-like cases I could show you slug-holes in the hide shields and the leather armour. Turn a corner and these weapons are juxtaposed with archaeological displays: excavated prehistoric stone arrowheads, hand-axes, Bronze Age swords, Roman helmets, presented as if the violence of 200 years of colonial war were merely the latest chapter in an eternal and inevitable process, rather than an unprecedented apocalypse. Press your phone against the glass and you'll find out how hard this jumbled arsenal of Palaeolithic stone axes, barbed and tanged arrows, and knuckle-dusters is even to photograph, never mind comprehend.

We walk back down one level. In the lower two galleries you encounter the stuff that is also displayed as if it were weaponry, even if it's not formally classed as such. If the upper gallery consists of the 'open carry' cabinets of guns and knives, down here there is a kind of concealed quality to the display of hundreds of different classes of material culture, tools and technologies as if they were offensive weapons of some kind. Navigation devices, fire-lighting devices, locks and keys, horse furniture, house furniture, musical instruments, voice-disguisers, devices of writing and measurement, tools of bodily transformation, for piercing and tattooing, smoking pipes, children's toys, lamps, clothing, medical instruments, fishing kit, animal-traps and man-traps, pots and bags and baskets, decorative art and sculpture representing the human form, and the paraphernalia of magic and religion and the treatment of the dead. All presented as if every wooden cane held a hidden sword-stick and every ivory handle contained a flick-blade, as if every braided string were a strangling cord, every basket a thorn-lined trap.[43]

Some of the exhibits are recorded as picked up on some far-flung battlefield. There's the triple display cabinet of Benin Bronzes of course, but also many other examples of such violent mementoes and loot. An eagle's claw necklace, for example, which, if you read the tiny manuscript label carefully, you will learn was worn by a Zulu chief at the Battle of Ulundi in 1879, and taken from his body by a 21-year-old soldier who had joined the 91st Highlanders in the February of that year, a young man who brought it home to give to his father, the museum's founder.[44] There is an Imperial Flag of China taken from a tower during the First Opium War in 1840.[45] An Aboriginal Australian grass basket with geometric chevron designs in black, white and red taken in 1861 from a village attacked in reprisals for the Cullin-la-ringo massacre in Queensland, Australia.[46] An Afridi woman's loom taken on the Tirah Expedition of 1898 in what is today Pakistan.[47] There's even a leather-bound Qur'an looted from the King's Palace at Kano in northern Nigeria in a punitive mission in 1902.[48] The Collector-General called these displays 'the arts of life', but the lens he offered for the understanding of them began with weapons seen in colonial conflict and slaughter – the art of war and the technologies of death applied not just to human bodies but to human culture.

Imagine ourselves suddenly set down at the bottom of the stairwell, on ground level. The elevator has always broken down periodically. As we walk past its metal doors, cordoned off because it's out of order again, we talk about what constitutes the next layer down, whatever dumped clay or rubble or other deposit into which the elevator shaft of this basementless institution is sunk. The horizon below the asphalt of the parking spaces that lies in turn above eroded fragments of Victorian gravel, and the layer below that. The sand below the cobblestones, as they used to say in Paris. Or that layer the excavator called the museum's 'supernatural subsoil'. Walking forward into the compound-like Court of the museum, it is rammed with cabinets, rectangular forms gathered like a flotilla of steam launches. Each is fully loaded, except one, recently disarmed.

We stop at the empty case that until recently housed an infamous and particularly grisly display installed by the curator in 1903, three years after the Grandfather-General's death. It bore the title *The Treatment of Dead Enemies*. The case stands close to the entrance, operating for more than a century as a kind of introductory case for the museum as a whole. The 'Dead Enemies' cabinet displayed an global, allochronic jumble of human skulls, skin, hair and teeth from Canada, the United States, Brazil, Borneo, Nigeria, Malaysia, India, Fiji, Vanuatu, Papua New Guinea and the Solomon Islands, alongside ten examples of 'shrunken heads' (*tsantsas*) from Ecuador and Peru made from human, sloth and monkey heads. There was even a bamboo knife from Melanesia with a label that claimed it was 'used for cutting off heads during head-hunting raids', two notches supposedly representing two victims.

By the 2000s the Dead Enemies cabinet had become for many visitors a kind of star exhibit of the museum, a favourite destination for Home Counties grandparents wishing to terrify their confused grandchildren in the half-term holidays. Like the hipster dads who now lurked between the cases, pairing flat caps and country tweed with a baby-carrier, it was part of the wider phenomenon of a non-ironic ironic take on Victoriana or Edwardian heritage that mapped itself onto legacies of cultural Whiteness. As Matthew Sweet has shown, the 'invention' of the idea of the Victorians has a long history, reaching back to the 1920s. But this was a new phase in what Elizabeth Ho described as the memory of empire in 'neo-Victorianism', something akin to the 'the retro-Victorian novel', from A. S. Byatt to Graham Swift, but seen now in marketing strategies that were monetising culture and rebranding heritage and museums. In part it was a knock-on effect of the Blairite vision of Cool Britannia in the late nineties, mixed up with the shock waves of the gentrification of the East End of London.[49] This Oxford museum fell, quite by accident, into step with that retro-cultural filmic imaginary of the noughties: *Sherlock* box sets on the iPlayer, Ripper 'whodunems' in the bookshop windows, *Sweeney Todd* at the local renovated arthouse cinema, the bleak Gothic-horror nostalgia of the Mark Gatiss–Tim Burton 'steampunk' aesthetic that leached out from the laptop screens into everyday material culture, marketing, fashion. A taste for this new canonisation of Victoriana as a British resource to be extracted and marketed. The non-authentic authenticity of vintage connoisseurship included exposed brickwork in coffee shops, barbers and fashion retailers; single-speed bicycles; bushy beards not seen since the 1890s, waxed moustaches and hand-made leather shoes. And a day trip to see the traditional White supremacist display in the university museum.

In reality, the cabinet was from the start dedicated to promoting the myth of cannibalistic 'headhunter' cultures as a meaningful sociological class or type for comparative anthropology. This was an idea that had been introduced by Tylor in his 1884 textbook *Anthropology*, where he claimed that 'low tribes keep up the fierce hatred and pride of battle by trophies of the enemy – his head dried and hung as an ornament of the hut, or his skull fashioned into a drinking-cup'.[50] At the same time, the installation was a kind of in-joke by the Edwardian curator, suggesting that the main rationale of this colonial-militarist museum was to display objects and heads raided from the supposedly 'barbarous' and 'primitive' 'dead enemies' of the British Empire. Perhaps the inclusion of objects collected by the founder in this new case meant it was even a kind of commentary on the recent death of the man who had made an enemy of the curator. The display was dismantled in 2020, and the wood-glass case interior stood empty.

What kind of monument was the Dead Enemies case: a memorial, some kind of attempt to exorcise the ghost of the founder, or a statement of intent? As he caught his own eye in the reflection of the glass of this dark case, did Balfour ever, as I have, get the sudden uncanny sense that he was encountering the Grandfather-General himself, whom he mistook at first for a another hipster dad with waxed hair and a herringbone shooting jacket, but with not a leather satchel slung over his shoulder but an Enfield rifle, returning my gaze with eyes that seem to pierce through the decades? Did he ever catch that distinctive aroma that rises as a warm, fine, musty dust through the interlaced mesh of the circles and latticework of the wrought iron grilles of the exhibition hall's antiquated heating system, and imagine the smell to be something like damp tweed and waxed cotton mixed with spent gunpowder? Next time you're there look down at that locked grid of Anglo-Celtic knotwork, which runs like the Gothic grates of a prison cell window under your feet when you walk the tile-floored galleries of the museum.

Later that evening you send me a message. What exactly, you ask, is being contained here? I try to take it as a rhetorical question, although I know that we still need to find an adequate reply. It's a question of reform, you might think. But then I look at the subject line of your email. It reads: Abolish the Museum.

## 4. MILITARIST REALISM

What's being contained? You could flip the question, I reply. Begin by describing the acts of containment in the vitrines not just of this 'world culture' museum but the hundreds of others like it across Europe and North America. We start to make a list.

First, there's the warehousing of material culture in hollow frames, each display case and storage box like the hold of a ship or a cattle truck, practices of freighting things as if they were commodities, crowding this cargo together. Through this abject hyperconcentration, cultures are objectified, presented as alien or dead, reduced to status of the spoils of war, even when they weren't actually taken from a battlefield; a war that took many forms, had many military tactics, among which were confiscation and imprisonment. There were 'scavengers of all sorts' in this history, Michel-Rolph Trouillot reminds us – 'colonists, diplomats, warriors, and archaeologists'.[51]

Second, there's the policing of collective memory, a redacted, expurgated archive of the human past with a tiny proportion of what's been brought together on display. Artefacts ripped from their contexts and jumbled together, anonymised human body parts scattered across storage facilities. Inside these places, histories of theft, extraction and erasure are called preservation, heritage and tradition. They could become places to write those histories, if it weren't for the secrecy. These nineteenth-century classificatory museums are blueprints for a shift in the meaning of the term 'classified' information over the course of a hundred years – evolving from the High Victorian ideal of meticulous ordering and categorisation into that familiar, more modern sense: being filed as top-secret, confined, accessible only to certain authorised people, or perhaps not even to anyone if the basic cataloguing has never been done. And of course possibly binned, dumped at sea or incinerated. These are 'images of ash and fragments', as Caroline Elkins has put it: archives can 'conceal as much as they reveal', as the resulting gaps become an 'imperial legacy' in their own right.[52]

Third, there's the locking-in of a distinctive sensibility, an aesthetic which nobody has bothered to try to name. Neo-Gothic for sure, with all its horror and fear, fear of the unknown foremost among the fear-mongering; a conjuring of the kind of sudden, generalised terror elicited by the architecture of a semi-lit gallery, or by vacuity, darkness, solitude and silence, or by the sound of distant gunfire, elements that contributed to the terror that Edmund Burke described as aroused by what he called 'the artificial infinite', a form of the sublime, as if every privation visible in the presence of an artefact, and every typescript word on every museum label, threatens to lodge in your skull and return in a nightmare. But also with elements that are proto-Expressionist, semi-mystical, esoteric, militarist, coldly emotional, hipster, retro, coded as culturally White.[53]

Above all there is a sort of looseness, a sense of an intricate metaphor that has lost its tenor, a figure without a ground, a place antithetical to the present. From a gradual, tacit fusion of militarism and monumentality something more abstract and intangible has emerged. Through insouciance, or through arrogance, or through mere neglect and lack of vision, it has been made to survive, and to grow. It could be that, put plainly, at this point in these museums' histories, the institutions don't have the stomach to look at what they have become; neither the stomach nor the guts. And so the blurring of representation and misrepresentation continues. Study the labels and the interpretation boards, or look at the websites of any world culture, legacy colonial or self-styled 'universal' museum. Reservation is the word that comes to mind, in at least two senses: scepticism and enclosure. The texts read like they have been hollowed out of any clear emplotment, of causality, of motivation, of any rationale or justification for their existence today. That's precisely how they have survived. What can be said about the artefacts is held back, contained by this sustained vagueness, just as the artefacts are contained, like an enemy would be contained by an army so it can't break out and operate elsewhere.

As for the Grandfather-General's museum, in the 1980s the children's author Penelope Lively described this place as 'the attic of the human mind'. Around the same time, the poet James Fenton called it 'a boxroom of the forgotten or hardly possible laid with the snares of privacy and fiction'.[54] Four decades on it still operates like a vast novel, a suggestive raft of legacy fictions about cultural alterity and technological supremacy. But in these fictions it reveals a reality that is much harder to discern in the real world outside. In and among these places of amazement and wonder the great sadness is that you will see things that are hard even to see in a statue of General Lee or Cecil Rhodes – violence, extraction, militarism, brute force, hatred, White supremacy. Amazing to think that for some people it would be impossible, or even controversial, to think about changing that, I said to you. Don't mistake the museums for churches, for sacred spaces, no matter how much Neo-Gothic they threw into the architecture.

In her book *Carceral Capitalism*, American poet-scholar Jackie

Wang shows how practices of captivity have constantly slipped between registers over the past two centuries. She interlaces the histories of imprisonment, of slavery, of policing, of looting, of debt, of gratuitous violence and execution. The unfinished work of abolition emerges as an urgent thread running through these shifting forms of mechanised death continuing by other means across different locations and periods. The history runs across many sites, from the plantation, through the long history of the military-industrial complex, to the prison-industrial complex of our contemporary world.[55] There is a kind of compound interest at work: looting valuables, enslaving human bodies, laying claim to land, extracting resources, and then ultimately extending the idea of 'reservation' from the sepulchral nature of the settler landscape to the human imagination, bastioned against the escape of the boldest thoughts. Any resulting debts or obligations surely then take multiple forms as well.

An acknowledgement, an apology, the return of a few objects or ancestral bones, those surely necessary but insufficient first steps. Museum abolitionism – which would include allowing the failed narratives of a museum, the fictions it still presents as facts, its co-option for the purposes of White supremacy, to fall away – would be a process akin to allowing a monument to fall when a community wants to remove a hurtful or racist image, because the ideology has failed, has no place in our contemporary world. 'Colonialism works to de-civilise the coloniser,' Aimé Césaire wrote, 'to numb him in the true sense of the word, to degrade him, to awaken in him buried instincts, lust, violence, racial hatred and moral relativism.'[56] When the damage that can be done in the name of culture can be seen, when the unspoken, ongoing nature of cultural brutalisations becomes visible, then we must allow the museum or the monument to fall. Not to destroy the idea of a museum, or to stop sculpture as an artistic practice or a form of collective memorialisation, but to allow the world of art and culture to keep in step with our times. To release the trap, unlock the door, exit the proverbial vampire castle.

To think of a museum or a monument or an academic discipline like archaeology and anthropology as carceral spaces would be to see them as latent weapons, collectively half forgotten, only half visible, but still holding a violence. Like a trap. In his ethnographic studies of entrapment as a technology, Spanish anthropologist Alberto Corsín Jiménez has analysed how snares, bait or poison laid in advance transform the hunter's spear-throw or the archer's arrow-flight, or the direct mêlée of the chase, into an anticipatory artefact of captivation. Such strategies of predation and attack defer action through mediating devices like the dragnet, or the pitfall disguised with leaves and branches, or even those practices of mimicry and disguise which turn the body of the hunter itself into a kind of latent weapon.[57] Corsín Jiménez looks back to a paradoxical example given by Claude Lévi-Strauss about eagle-hunting among the Hidatsa people of what is today North Dakota. Carrion is placed above a pit into which the hunter has climbed and is hidden. When the eagle swoops down and perches to take the bait, the hunter reaches up suddenly to grab its legs with his bare hands. 'The man is the trap,' wrote Lévi-Strauss. Which is to say, he adopts the position of the hunted animal and the hunter at the same time, while in fact he is simply waiting in the subterranean position of a trapped animal in order to kill the bird, who in turn is tricked by the mediation of a dead creature.[58]

As a spike-lined pit transforms the operation of the edged weapon, or as the booby-trap transforms the work of the grenadier's bomb hurled into the void, so it may be with the legacy supremacist museum, monument or discipline. And how might this switching of position play into the carceral history of the museum or the skull-cup or the monument? Think back to the boarding-up of the museum's glass roof; that post-hoc lidding-over of this state of affairs, as if the whole collection could be slid into an archival box, as if the disciplines of anthropology and archaeology, the art, technology and architecture of the human past and the Victorian present, were destined for nothing but some vast future haunted mausoleum. Perhaps this whole story will turn out to be about the foxhole from which the gunner kills – delivering their execution by assuming the position of the dead in their graves.

I try to picture the dugout cut through a fine-grained stratigraphy of layers made from colonial-militarist accumulation by dispossession: inherited wealth made through slavery; that wealth used to buy objects accumulated through colonial warfare and punitive expeditions; a future of endurance through sublimation. With these images of negative space and deferred action in hand, it may yet be possible to piece together the after-history of dehumanisation. To see legacy colonial museums and monuments as proxy horrorscapes that stretch across the Atlantic from the ship's hold to the plantation, ersatz landscapes of internment camps, border walls, checkpoints and those gun emplacements in the upper gallery. Necroscapes that reach from the killing fields of colonial war, the new phenomenon of the machine gun and the mass graves it brought into existence, to the vicarious regimes of the snuff-displays of battlefield trophies. Just like the border regimes of the nation state don't exist solely at the physical border. What you find at national borders today is something closer to what Nicholas De Genova has called 'border spectacle' – a term he introduces to describe how certain border locations and infrastructures of enforcement can become key images or icons that enact and perform borderwork across the media as if they were 'the symbolic and ideological production of a brightly lit scene of "exclusion" that is always in reality inseparable from an obscene fact of subordinate (illegalised) inclusion that transpires in its shadows'.[59]

In his book *Capitalist Realism* the philosopher Mark Fisher, better known at the time under his blogging handle k-punk, discussed that famous slogan 'It's easier to imagine the end of the world than it is to imagine the end of capitalism'. The 'realism' here, Fisher wrote, 'is analogous to the deflationary perspective of a depressive who believes that any positive state, any hope, is a dangerous illusion'.[60] It's an idea that Ursula Le Guin picked up in an acceptance speech at an awards ceremony in November 2014, you tell me. 'We live in capitalism,' she said. 'Its power seems inescapable. But then, so did the divine right of kings. Any human power can be resisted and changed by human beings. Resistance and change often begin in art. Very often in our art, the art of words.'[61]

In George's Orwell's *Nineteen Eighty-Four*, Big Brother's regimes of surveillance and control were limited to watching you awake and asleep, indoors or outdoors, with no escape except, Orwell wrote, for 'the few cubic centimetres inside your skull'.[62] In this history, in contrast, thought itself was always already contained, reserved, as if any new idea would be already framed before it is even formed. Close your eyes and try to formulate the right questions, ones that won't simply make things worse, another futile scratch on the wall, marking time in a place where the prisoners and warders are long dead and yet the carceral regime somehow still persists, harsher than ever. In these inner spaces, time and geography collapse into one another, just as capital appears to short-circuit the hours, days and months that the movement of commodities takes, to tear down every obstacle for the sake of its own self-valorisation, to conquer the whole world and thus, in the famous expression, to 'annihilate space by means of time'.[63] The upshot is that hatred and theft long stripped of any possible past scientific validity or antiquarian justification, ideas long since dead and buried, are still here in form and structure, implicit and implicated, taking place in the present. An inherited body of habitual gestures of thoughts and action that are not so much naturalising as desensitising. The subjective comes to appear objective, as a partial reflection in the cabinet places a hand on your shoulder, and then comes a push through the looking glass. Strange to think that the Collector-General's great-grandson was briefly married to George Orwell's widow, I remember you once observing; and how his great-grand-niece Diana Mitford married Oswald Mosley. That book I imagined I might write one day, it would have a lot to say about those lines of descent and alliance, I replied.

We can pick up Mark Fisher's account in the halls of the British Museum, founded in 1753, in the same decade as Burke published his treatise on the sublime. The sheer scale of superintended archives, online databases and raw data handwritten on abandoned card-index systems, operating like the unexploded land mines from some long-forgotten war, brings about a technical complexity that produces a kind of halo effect: a vast, chaotic, chilling sublime that can dumbfound the onlooker and curator alike. Here, Mark Fisher wrote, 'you see objects torn from their lifeworlds and assembled as if on the deck of some Predator spacecraft'.[64] As a cultural technique, as a genre, as an aesthetic, extractivist containment became unconscious, habitual, internalised to the point that 'all that is left is the consumer-spectator, trudging through the ruins and the relics'.[65] The consumer-spectator is, in other words, still going in this ancient device built to create the images of a divided humanity, and pass them on: the living and the dead, the 'fit' and the dying, the civilised and the barbaric, 'the West and the rest', even after he has destroyed so much. In what follows, we're going to have to find a name for this movement, art-historical but part of intellectual history too, a bundle of inherited attitudes and prejudice that takes the form of sculpture in the streets and objects in exhibition cases as well as words on the page and frameworks in the mind. A movement that normalised dehumanisation, mainstreamed debasement, but by using not the fake science but culture and art, which ran from the 1870s to the 1920s through the museums, the monuments and the lecture rooms, and hardened across subsequent generations, sometimes brittle and sometimes resilient, a phenomenon of phantasm, spectacle and silencing that endures to the present day. It's characterised by a certain resemblance to the real, the appearance of fidelity in representation, but a sense of fidelity that emerges purely from duration, from a myth told slowly so as to try to outlast reality. You could call it Gothic brutalism, you tell me, or magical futurism, White constructivism or accelerationist materialism; speculative monumentalism perhaps, or nihilist nostalgism. All of those could work, I reply; but how about we name it simply *militarist realism*?[66]

The Inspector-Grandfather had another term in mind. 'Primitive Warfare' was the title he gave to a series of three annual lectures in the late 1860s, delivered to the Royal United Service Institution in their lecture room located just off Whitehall at Middle Scotland Yard between Whitehall and the Thames Embankment. This framing bore an echo of an address given by John Ruskin nine miles to the east across London, south of the river, to a group of graduating cadets at the Royal Military Academy at Woolwich in December 1865. War is the foundation stone of all art, Ruskin told the assembled teenagers, boys of the generation that would become the officers in countless battles in the name of Queen and Country and Empire in the closing years of the nineteenth century. 'You must have war to produce art,' he continued. No great art ever yet rose on earth, he claimed, but among a nation of soldiers.[67]

In the Grandfather-General's lectures, the lines of argument started to interlock, as if heavy steel levers were shifting in a railway signal box. As all introductory textbooks read by first-year archaeology students recount, his was a general theory of the continual development of all aspects of human material culture, based on the gradual improvement of weapons technology. In terms of intellectual history, this was a crude blend of ideas. Somewhere in the mix was Thomas Hobbes' mid-seventeenth-century theory that the original condition of society was that of war – *bellum omnium contra omnes* (the war of all against all). So too was Thomas Malthus' late eighteenth-century idea of society as a 'struggle for existence'.[68] These were expanded through two new, current ideas – Charles Darwin's account of 'natural selection, or the preservation of favoured races in the struggle for life', and Herbert Spencer's development of this as the 'survival of the fittest' and their 'multiplication'.[69] But its ambition was more twentieth-century in character, more complex than a soldier's crass evocation of what Thomas Huxley, the man known as 'Darwin's Bulldog' because of his promotion of evolutionary ideas in ethnological thinking, later called the 'gladiatorial theory of existence'.[70]

The Royal United Service Institution had a museum of weapons, a collection that is today long defunct and dispersed, from which the General purchased many of his first museum objects. The 'Primitive Warfare I–III' lectures offered an account of the gradual evolution of weaponry inspired by his own involvement in the perfection and adoption of the improved Enfield rifle as the service weapon of the British Army, and from his military service in Crimea, Malta, North America and most recently Ireland. From this perspective, the weapons expert delivered what was on the face of it a standard Victorian improvement narrative, based on the idea of applying evolutionary thinking to the world of human material culture, giving the history and prehistory of weapons technology a primacy as the catalyst and ur-metaphor for technological change. It was a theory of the primacy of violence, and of primeval violence dwelling close to the surface of English society because of persistences from the past. In this theory of primitive warfare, objects were imagined to develop as if the museum in which they could be studied were a barracks, as if the disciplines of archaeology and anthropology should be properly located within war studies, as if an idea could be a weapon and its use drilled into the population as if the lecture room were a parade ground.

The lectures attempted to impose, very lightly and yet in thickly descriptive and empirical layers, a narrative line of 'the West and the rest' onto the present and the past, encompassing the whole of human history and prehistory, and the entire diversity of human technology, inventions and improvisations. From tools to textiles to objects used for magic or in the treatment of the dead, a picture of incremental improvements inherited was presented, alongside periodic episodes of 'degeneration', when knowledge and skill were lost. The Grandfather-General's 'Primitive Warfare' lectures relied on the 'three-age system' of prehistory, in which periods of time could be defined by the materials used for the technologies of weapons and tools, and he encouraged his audience to consult the recently published book *Prehistoric Times* to see the 'evidence upon which the succession of the stone, bronze and iron ages has been determined'.[71] His interest was in how these periods of time, as they ran from the prehistoric to the present day, overlapped, as some parts of the world saw changes in material culture, thus gaining military superiority from technological improvement, and others did not. In one typical assertion, for example, he suggested that 'the Fijians, at the time of their discovery, were still in the Stone Age'.[72] One of his colleagues offered the metaphor of the refraction of light, writing that 'like the three principal colours of the rainbow, these three stages of civilization overlap, intermingle, and shade off the one into the other', proportions of the spectrum varying in different countries.[73] Strikingly, in that account the Iron Age was one in which Victorian society still found itself.[74] There was a sense of a pinnacle in the evolution of material culture coming as the Iron Age peaked in a world of steel, as if the percussion of the Stone Age technology of the knapped flint against the steel frizzen of a gun were a metaphor for the military supremacy, now itself superseded by the percussion lock of a modern rifle. Steel, and the sheer shift in scale in industrial production that it brought, ran through the proliferating nineteenth-century forms and locations of colonialism. The rifles and machine guns of the battlefield, battleships and steam packets, the new industrial landscapes of the steel works, the structural steel of the buildings and bridges of the metropolis, the steel wheels of rolling stock running along steel railway lines from one steel-girdered station to the next, the steel wire of electricity and the telegraph, the steel-edged ruler of the archaeological surveyor or draughtsman, steel engravings and the steel shell of a camera, steel pocket knives, an Age of Steel that fought using steam, electricity, telegraphic communication. From the steel bars of the prison to the steel-girdered museum.

The anonymised skull and the hyperaccumulation of artefacts. A supremacist sublime and the impossibility of imagining the world otherwise. The carceral, the trap and the soldier's foxhole. Ruskin's image of war as the origin of all art and Trouillot's scavengers. The military Grandfather-Theorist blasted, galvanised and sharpened like a bayonet in an Age of Steel. His arms-race theory of history, how it sought to make a worldview stick. That vision of permanent war as human instinct and human fate seems to prefigure a line often misascribed to Hermann Göring, but in fact spoken by a jaded and angry German First World War veteran, brutalised by trench warfare and spoiling for the next conflict, given a voice by the minor inter-war dramatist Hanns Johst in an infamous 1933 Nazi propaganda biographical drama *Schlageter*, which memorialised a Freikorps soldier executed by the French during the occupation of the Ruhr and celebrated as a martyred national hero under the Nazi regime: 'When I hear the word culture, I slide the safety-catch off my Browning.'[75] When I was looking up that line you told me about how as well as the play, scores of streets in German towns and cities were named after Albert Leo Schlageter (1894–1923) in the so-called 'Schlageter cult' from 1923 to 1939, and a hundred or so physical monuments to the man were erected. There were even two monuments built at Dachau concentration camp. Most have been removed, you said. Some of them still survive today.[76]

## 5. INVISIBLE STATUES

Let us leave behind us for now the playwright's image of the National Socialist holding his American light machine gun to the hip for marching fire, at war with culture. It must be possible find something more to say about how the silver rim bent onto this violated, anonymised skull is inscribed with that name, Pitt-Rivers. Consider a parallel story from Berkeley, California. In Ursula K. Le Guin's 1960s fantasy series *The Earthsea Trilogy*, to know someone's name is to hold power over them. 'To speak the name is to control the thing,' she wrote in her 1964 short story 'The Rule of Names', the text where she first introduced this aspect of Earthsea cosmology and magic. As an eleven-year-old boy I was struck by Le Guin's description of how, in the fictional world she wove, at puberty, people give up their given name, the 'child name' assigned to them at birth, and take on a 'true name' – a new identity which must be kept secret.

Perhaps Le Guin got this idea about the magic of names from an episode in her own family history. It concerned her anthropologist father, Alfred Kroeber (1876–1960). Kroeber was, the textbooks and obituaries record, a man who through 'pioneering toil, sacrifice and imagination' won the 'secure niche' that anthropology enjoys today. He specialised in the American West and used linguistic analysis to identify Native American 'culture areas'.[77] His education began as a home-schooled boy in a German Protestant family living in New York City in a five-storey brownstone on the corner of 78th and Madison Avenue;[78] a boy who collected specimens of rocks, plants and beetles from Central Park and built models of the siege of Troy on the beach during summer vacations on Long Island. You could see the Metropolitan Museum from the top-floor bedroom windows.[79]

In 1898, Alfred Kroeber took a course in physical anthropology at the American Museum of Natural History, making anthropometric measurements of skulls and skeletons.[80] He went on to study for a doctorate at Columbia. Later, when he became professor at Berkeley, Kroeber oversaw the removal of the bodies of Native American ancestors from grave sites for the museum collections. In his monumental *Handbook of the Indians of California* (1925), he wrote that the native Muwekma Ohlone people were 'extinct so far as all practical purposes are concerned'. This verdict of cultural death contributed to their removal two years later from the Office of Indian Affairs' National Register of Native Peoples, an administrative act which, by removing recognition, directly led to the Ohlone tribe being dispossessed of land and political power.[81]

Kroeber took custody of a Native American man and kept him as his ward at the museum at Berkeley. Or you could say that he captured and imprisoned him, and put him to work for his theoretical programme.[82] 'Ishi', as he was named by Theodora Kroeber, Alfred's wife, Ursula's mother, worked as a museum janitor and as a 'living specimen' – on display to visitors and informing anthropological research. As the anthropologist James Clifford has put it, when it comes to any possibility of telling 'Ishi's story' there are only 'suggestive fragments and enormous gaps: a silence that calls forth more versions, images, endings', told and retold.[83] He was a member of the Yahi Nation, a Native American group that were subjected to extermination by White settler militia during the Gold Rush in their tribal lands, in what is today northern California. Bounties were issued: fifty cents for a Yahi's scalp, five dollars for a Yahi's head. Attacks by the settlers were recorded in the press: blowing out their brains and splitting open their skulls, the heads of little children and babies smashed apart, those who managed to run being hunted down and shot.[84] Part of one of just a few groups of his people who managed to survive these genocidal impulses, on 13–14 August 1865 when 'Ishi' was around four years old, the settlement he lived in was attacked in the Three Knolls Massacre. He and his family went on the run in the hills.[85] His uncle, mother and younger sister died after their camp was found by a group of land surveyors in 1908. Surviving for three more years alone in the wilderness, after forest fires in August 1911, so the story goes, he was discovered early one morning, starving and exhausted, leaning against a fence-line in the corral of a slaughterhouse at Oroville, California, the dogs' barking awaking the butchers. Handcuffed, the man was handed first to the sheriff and imprisoned at Oroville Jail, and then to the university, where he became the subject of continual research and public exhibition, which might be read, as Clifford has put it, as an inexorable path towards 'the future' – 'white civilisation and death in the anthropology museum' – or as something very different from 'walking into civilisation' or giving himself up.[86] He died of tuberculosis four and a half years later.

His home in the museum, from 1911 to 1916, was next to the storage facility for thousands of human skulls and bones. Within hours of his death, and against his express will, his corpse was dissected by the Berkeley medics, an object of enquiry in death as he had been a subject for research in life. The body was cremated but not before his brain was removed and preserved, then placed by Kroeber in a deerskin-wrapped Pueblo Indian pottery jar and sent by rail across America to the laboratory of eugenicist and 'race' scientist Aleš Hrdlička at the Smithsonian Institution in 1917 – as if the museum were a kind of reservation for the Indigenous dead.⁸⁷ There, as anthropologist Orin Starn recorded in his book *Ishi's Brain*, the brain was held until, after years of protest about its continued incarceration, it was, in the words of the museum, 'rediscovered' in 1999. In August 2000, it was eventually restituted to representatives of the tribes who trace their bloodlines to the Yahi Nation, and laid to rest in a secret location.⁸⁸ Kroeber recorded 148 wax cylinder recordings, fifty hours of this man's language, stories and songs, which were eventually deposited in the Library of Congress's National Registry in 2010.⁸⁹

Kroeber Hall was the name given in his honour to the building that houses the University of California Berkeley's anthropology department and its museum. The museum became a monument to a foundational figure in modern anthropology. But on 27 January 2021, in light of the enduring legacy of his anthropological practice, through which he became a 'public symbol of discrimination against and disdain for Native American people', Kroeber Hall was un-named by the university chancellor.⁹⁰ On YouTube you can watch a workman chiselling off the metal type of his name from the outer wall of the building letter by letter.

Le Guin's 'Rule of Names' was published four years after her father's death, and three years after her mother Theodora Kroeber had published her own best-selling book, *Ishi in Two Worlds*. Theodora's book bore the subtitle *A Biography of the Last Wild Indian in North America*. 'Ishi startled the modern world,' the author claimed, 'by accidentally walking into it from the Stone Age.'⁹¹ He never revealed his Yahi name. The name Theodore Kroeber chose to call him, 'Ishi', is simply the word for 'man' in the Yana language.⁹²

Concepts and practices got passed down from one generation to another in this twentieth-century White settler family in post-war California. There was the double 'discovery' of 'Ishi': the first time as a living man in the corral, and the second as a forgotten brain soaked in formaldehyde on the other side of the United States. And then there was Le Guin's manner of transposing the Indigenous worlds studied by her father into her science fiction and fantasy writing, in a process that has been criticised as complicit in cultural extractivism and 'poaching'.⁹³ Looking back on his life's work, Kroeber suggested that the anthropology he practised was a kind of cult, which was concerned with 'laying bare the skeletal structures of culture'.⁹⁴ In the mid-1990s, Le Guin wrote her own ambivalent note of reflection, published with the title 'Which Side Am I On, Anyway?', in which she described her anthropologist father as 'a postfrontiersman' whose fieldwork 'among the wrecks of cultures, the ruin of languages, the shards of an infinite diversity swept aside by a monoculture' was both 'an act of imperialism' and 'an act of human solidarity'.⁹⁵ Alternative readings are possible, as always when tropes of balance and both-sidesism are deployed. Settler-miner extractivist societies can try to take cosmologies as well as human lives, landscapes, minerals and property. Creative co-option can go hand in hand with killing and destruction, or can follow in its wake; in the hands of the pioneering anthropologist, or of the writer of fiction.

In her book *Argonauts*, Maggie Nelson writes: 'Once we name something, you said, we can never see it the same way again. All that is unnameable falls away, gets lost, is murdered.'⁹⁶ Call it what it is, then. I mean, the un-naming, the naming, the de-naming – the choices of memory. A debate between past and present, between racism and anti-racism, is the last thing that anyone needs. (Except that vocal one per cent who, due to their personal sensitivities, claim, improbably, that they simply want to keep everything exactly the same as it is, whereas in fact they just refuse to face up to the different forms of legacy colonialism in the academy or the museums or the realm of public art and memorialisation.) There is the question of who is named in the memory culture of museums and statues and academic disciplines, and the question of whose names are erased. And listen out for the third question: who is it that we wish to remember?

It might be possible to break with that pernicious, endless both-sidesism through triangulation. Right now, for example, sitting in the Common Ground café on Little Clarendon Street, I can locate myself in relation to three Oxford monuments, none very far away – the skull-cup at Worcester College, the museum named for the Grandfather-General, and that hateful image memorial to the origins of Apartheid at Oriel College with that man in the business suit holding a slouch hat in his right hand.

Triangulation is a strategy of self-location; the kind of mapping that they used to do with a plane table, where you measure out in three or more directions from a single vantage point in the landscape, and end up finding out where you are standing. Think about it for a moment, how this cartographic technique with a history that connects settler colonialism or military surveying with archaeology might be repurposed in the present. I mean, how far are you right now from an unnamed skull in an acid-free archival box? From a statue erected for the purposes of militarist realism? And a museum of 'world culture' with displays built to normalise dispossession and dehumanisation? See if you can draw the map, sketch it out or Google it, situate yourself. I could imagine it as a kind of salvage project, you tell me. To understand your positionality, foreground your situatedness, not just to acknowledge it but as a kind of survey of what is going to need to change, document these colonial legacies so people recall and understand what they were, and to point to the ways in which they are still taking place. That would be a method of positionality for these times in which communities are addressing these legacies, transforming these places for the better, one after another.

In the seminar rooms, the scholarly journals and the academic conferences, the Rule of Names inflects citation practices. Who is on the curriculum, which names appear in the reading lists or bibliography, who is centred? But also, who teaches, researches and works in the academy; who's around the table in the first place? In the wake of the toppling of the Cecil Rhodes statue in South Africa in 2015, a project called Dismantling the Master's House based at University College London posed these two parallel questions directly. First: 'Why is my curriculum White?' At stake here, Neda Tehrani argued, was not just institutional complicity in cultural forms of White supremacy, but also its 'contribution to its very foundations through the legitimisation of racist ideologies'. And second: 'Why is my professor not Black?' 'Now, that is a loaded question,' wrote Yewande Okuleye, a UCL alumnus and doctoral researcher. 'What do you know – the Elephant in the room is coming into focus.'[97] From citation and inclusion to redaction and exclusion – the Rule of Names is about pronouns: I, you, we, they – who exactly is indexed by these words?

Those ten letters and their hyphen are still above the door, but like I said, hardly anyone actually reads the Grandfather-Theorist any more. It would be unusual for anyone even to consider assigning his writings to their students. And yet every student of archaeology, anthropology, the museum, the monument, learns his name in passing, internalises it, through the names of those who claim intellectual descent, or whose forefathers and foremothers did and now they have forgotten. His theories are third-hand refractions echoing in that internal space that shapes the mainstream expert conceptions of the human past and human cultures in the present. His misrepresentations, prejudice, desire for posterity. In my office, I find myself idly staring at the layered spines of the heavy volumes of his excavation memoirs, now piled one on top of another under my laptop for Zoom calls like stacked strata of some artificial archaeological site. I think again of what Proust wrote about a book as a series of forgotten names: 'sometimes on the contrary you remember the name very well, but without knowing whether something of the person who bore it survives in these pages'.[98]

The name of the Grandfather-General is a dead myth, through which some form of tacit knowing, hardly knowledge, something more like an attitude or a prejudice, lives on. Tell me, whose deaths are we talking about in this myth? From South Africa to California to Israel to Australia, the labels on the guns in the museum cases do not give the names of those they slaughtered, or how many. The skull-cup remains anonymised, and yet now bearing the name inherited by the Grandfather and the Grandson on the rim. As if these two dead men can live on in this university town, despite everything. Imagine the triangle between those three monuments: from the corner of Beaumont Street and Walton Street to the corner of Parks Road and South Parks Road, and on to High Street. Draw the line in your head or look it up on Google maps. Find a spot in the space that this triangle maps out, whether on foot in real life or on street view online, and take stock. Sit in the reading rooms of the Bodleian's Old Library if you've got a ticket or in the café of Blackwell's bookshop, on a bench on St Giles or High Street or at a table on the Ashmolean Museum's roof terrace. Join the dots, now multiply the triangulation.

Behind the Oriel façade stand countless statues of colonists and soldiers guarding the public squares and city parks across the United Kingdom and its former empire. A brigade of the patriarchy in bronze and stone. (Women didn't go to sea in the Royal Navy until the Gulf

War of 1990, you remind me, and couldn't undertake combat roles in the British Army until 2016.) Behind the museum stand a thousand other museums of 'world culture', mixing anthropology with archaeology, from Birmingham to Berlin, from Boston to Berkeley. Behind the skull at Worcester College stand untold millions of other human beings whose skulls and bones are stacked, de-named, in collections and archives around the world, classified alongside photographs of people's faces, heads and bodies taken for the purposes of 'racial science' or cultural supremacism. And all three corners of this triangle established in such a relatively short space of time – a monumentality mania from, let's say, the 1870s to the 1930s. If you bring the art history into view, then you also bring the lives and deaths and ideologies into focus, like the first crack in the silverware that starts to leak during the dessert would come suddenly into view. No wonder there's been such sustained silence.

I think again of those names given to warn of a storm that may or may not come, pre-emptively, and I think of my own position in all this. Not exactly complicit in the silence, but hardly passive. Certainly, in Michael Rothberg's term, 'implicated' in some sense – a word which, he tells us, means 'folded in'. Folded in, that is, in the sense of being a participant: inhabiting, inheriting and benefiting from, contributing to as well, a group that 'occupy the histories and structures of racial privilege and white supremacy'.[99] Lines from Christina Sharpe's book *Ordinary Notes* offer clarification:

> The architecture of the memorial stages encounter
> A memory that is not mine returns to me
> Every memorial and museum to atrocity already contains its own failure
> The answer to these obscene questions? Return the bones. Return the photographs. Repatriate the statues. Empty the museums.[100]

The buses pile east down High Street as I sit on the bench. The museum is half a mile north, the skull-cup half a mile to the west, the statue is right here. A triangulation can throw your location into relief, but this particular map will be one of suppressed, contained, unspoken collective grief. Remember, you say at the end of our last call. This kind of countermapping brings stuff to the surface, into view, throws it into relief. That silver rim into which the text is punched runs along a saw-line in the bone, you remind me. You send me a poem by Denise Riley, where she writes about how grief can 'arrest time': not stopping the flow of time, but placing you outside of it with a prolonged cessation, so that time can even start to run in the wrong direction. 'This arrested time,' Riley writes, 'is also a question about what is describable; about the linguistic limits of what can be conveyed.'[101]

Naming can be part of remembrance, of course, and sometimes not. In some societies or situations there may be a prohibition on speaking the names of the dead, as Lévi-Strauss once observed. And when this is the case it might be understood as an effect of particular systems of naming.[102] Lévi-Strauss' discussion of naming practices among the Penan of Borneo was presented in his 1962 book *La pensée sauvage* (a book title traditionally rendered in English as *The Savage Mind*, but that might just as well be translated as *Wild Thinking*). Here, he introduces the idea of a death name. Alongside personal names (the 'autonym') and terms that refer to someone's offspring (the 'teknonym') there exists among the Penan what he says might be called the 'necronym'. This term refers to a person in terms of their 'ascendants' rather than descendants, which is to say that it expresses the kin relationship of a person to a deceased relative: that their father is dead, or their niece is dead, and so on.

The necronym contains no proper name, indeed it is the reverse, Lévi-Strauss tells us, of a proper name: it is simply the statement of a kin relationship, a definition of the self by a deceased relative. A name, in other ways, can come to represent a structural position. Individuality or personhood can become an effect of classification. In what follows, let us try to flip the logic of Ursula Le Guin's speculative universe; not to de-name the museum but to call the Grandfather-Collector, the army general who founded the quasi-eponymous museum in Oxford and acquired the skull-cup, by the name he had from birth; to start to tell a story of the dead and how they live on and so begin this necrography without the necronym. Cut the network. Lean closer and let me whisper his name in your ear:

FOX.

# 11

# The Fold

*fall*, noun. ii) (of a body of water) the fact of subsiding, ebbing, or receding; a fast-flowing or turbulent section of a river where it flows over a precipice or ledge (hence, waterfall)

The cranial sutures under the translucent varnish run along the sides as if they were some kind of applied decoration. Their tightly wound serpentine grooves fold from peak to trough and back again like radio waves. As my fingertip traces them I make an involuntary exhalation, beginning so deep in my lungs that it comes out first as a sigh and then as a groan, meeting the still breath of an empty space then breaking into the silent triangle between the archivist and me and the skull-cup before us. The sound falls hollowly, and there is the strange sensation that the void of the calvaria holds a kind of gravitational pull. I stand up. Motes scatter and blaze through the sunbeam that streams through the window, as if you were seeing stars. The dust is impossible to discern until for just a moment in a certain light it finds itself an illuminated, luminous cloud, a visible mass, as if particles were dispersed so lightly and densely that a spontaneous combustion could take place any moment.

A vast constellation of literature, running from the Baroque into Romanticism and the Gothic Revival, makes up the history of the macabre contemplation of the human skull as a body-object. In such reflections, human remains are made to stand for something other than themselves. In the 1920s in his study of German tragic drama of the eighteenth century, Walter Benjamin described part of this metaphorical gesture. A distinctive cult of the relic or the ruin came about, Benjamin wrote, in which 'allegories are in the realm of thoughts as ruins are in the realm of things'. So too, he continued, in a manner quite unlike the living body, the dead body and its broken-up parts could operate as 'emblems' of something else: an idea, or a sensibility, or a history.[1]

There is a fragmentary autobiographical text that Rainer Maria Rilke wrote in Switzerland in 1919, just after the war had ended – a part-modern, part-Romantic, Neo-Gothic, retro-mystical, sub-Byronic text, meditative to the point of self-indulgence. It was Kroeber's daughter Ursula who introduced him to Rilke.[2] In this partial essay, Rilke recounts how two memories came to be folded together, intertwined to such an extent that they took the form of a recurrent thought. The first concerns how, as a young cadet at the lower military academy in Sankt Pölten in Lower Austria in the late 1880s, his science master had the class conduct an experiment with the new technology of sound recording.[3] They made an improvised phonogram using what materials they had to hand: a roll of cardboard, a sheet of greaseproof paper, candlewax, glue, a small wooden cylinder fitted with a hand-crank, the bristles from a clothes brush, and clear varnish to fix the wax after the recording had been made. When the cadets listened back they were shocked to hear the words which, so to speak, had been theirs but no longer were. The wavering, trembling quality of the voices replayed seemed, Rilke wrote, to confront them from a totally new position in reality. This new technological medium, assembled with their own hands, seemed to the schoolboys simultaneously more advanced than them and yet somehow more immature, 'enduringly delicate' as Rilke puts it. But the deep impression that stayed across the years was not that of the sound of the recorded voice, but of the marks etched in the wax.

The second memory that Rilke describes comes from two decades later, in Paris sometime around 1905. The poet was in his late twenties. Attending anatomy lectures at the École des Beaux-Arts, he found himself contemplating the dry bones of the human skeleton displayed during the lecture, and especially the skull. The function of the skull, it seemed to him, he writes, was paradoxical in the sense that it protects the organ of the body that is most boundless in scope by confining and containing it in solid bone, an interiorised world. Soon afterwards Rilke purchased a skull and lived with it around his apartment. He recalls how whenever he caught a quick, sideways glance of it by candlelight at night, the cranial sutures seemed particularly visible.

Now in 1919, in his mid-forties, in the aftermath of those years of bloody industrialised slaughter, Rilke describes how these two old memories came to fold into a single idea or image: that the cranial sutures might be played by running a phonogram needle along them like the spiral grooves of a wax cylinder. What kind of sound, or sequence of sounds, or music, or white noise would result? What feelings would that raw, unnameable, imaginary 'ur-sound' elicit: disbelief, awe, fear, reverence? And what line or contour, in any part of life or landscape, could you not try to run a needle along so it can make itself felt, transformed into another field of the senses or another time, as if being read out loud?[4]

This account of the imagination contained and kept within a skull, written by the poet who conflates inner and outer worlds to such effect, echoes the description of the function of a phonograph offered by its inventor Thomas Edison in 1878: 'the gathering-up and captivity of sound-waves heretofore designated as fugitive, and their permanent retention'.[5] In the wake of four dehumanising years of anonymised, mechanised mass death, memories of the nameless skull and the extrasomatic retention of words in the wax cylinder fused. The memory-trails of those two past moments in two different educational institutions, a science lesson and an art lecture, twist together. Folds of time. I think again of the etymology: complicated, complicit, implicated, implicit: folded together, folded in, folded out.

Something in the Rilke text reads like a prefiguration of Alfred Kroeber's lines about how anthropology should lay bare the skeleton of culture. Its ur-mystical, para-phenomenological, uncanny allegory feels like a warning in how it collapses humanity into materiality into memory in purely contemplative terms. How the human body can be rendered as an object and a fantasy. How the settings of education can fuse with the brutalisations of industrial war, the lecture theatre or anatomical laboratory becoming one with the military barracks or frontline trench. How a kind of contemplative, distanced attitude to human bodies, bones and skulls might appear, or reappear, first as an aesthetics and then as a theoretics. It is a kind of intellectualism that I recognise from my own disciplinary training, one that blurs the line between people and things. A self-reflection that contemplates the boundaries between humanness and materiality and, in that distanced contemplation, in that reflexivity, can, paradoxically, dehumanise.

Sitting down again, I set my elbows on the table, press my palms into my forehead and hairline. My hands are cupping the brow of my own skull. I put my hands back down, look up, fold and unfold my arms, and think of that word again: calvaria. If we were in that other Place of Skulls, I mean the museum with the ten hyphenated letters above the door, then the database entry would numbly classify this item as 'modified human remains'. It would be just one of the many composite objects in the collections made using materials from a dead human body: skin, hair, teeth, fingernails, or in this case the white bone of the calvaria.

With the torchlight from my phone I transcribe the inscription that is incised in an uneven hand directly into the bone, a horizontal band of Ancient Greek that enfolds and circumscribes. Later I found the text carved into the bone was a quote, and tracked it down. It's a line from a sepulchral epigram from the sixth century CE, written by Julianus the Egyptian. The Egyptian? you ask me, checking you've heard it right. Yes, or Prefect of Egypt, take your pick. I type out the Greek text:

ΠΙΝΕΤΕ ΠΡΙΝ ΤΑΥΤΗΝ ΑΜΦΙΒΑΛΗΣΘΕ ΚΟΝΙΝ

which means something like:

Drink, before you are clothed in this dust.[6]

## 6. DEREALISATION

Sitting in the upper reading room of the library, I decide to look up that line I half remember from the Pitt Rivers Museum curator Henry Balfour. The one about the living and the dead. Turns out it's from a lecture Balfour gave at the Royal Society of Arts in London on 10 April 1894 in the Great Hall, the lecture room of their Adelphi premises, specially built for the society in the 1770s. That room is enfolded by James Barry's vast imperialist-allegorical frieze titled *The Progress of Human Culture*. Installed in 1784, as an all-encompassing encircling band, this cycle of six epic oil paintings stands almost twelve feet high and runs to more than a hundred feet in length. The narrative concerns cultural improvement.

First there is the mythical figure of Orpheus, the poet who accompanied the Argonauts on their quest. He is depicted in 'a wild and savage country, surrounded by people as savage as their soil'. Orpheus offers instruction from the gods with his lyre. At the other end, the final section shows Elysium crowded with a crouched army of figures gathered impossibly from across ancient and modern times: Homer, Plato, Brutus, Columbus, Shakespeare, Hogarth.[7] But it's the fourth section in the sequence that detains the eye. Titled *Commerce, or the Triumph of the Thames*, it depicts the colossal white figure of Father Thames enthroned in his sea-car, a compass in his left hand, the tiller in his right, steering downstream. Waist-high in the water around him the mariner-colonists Francis Drake, Walter Raleigh, Sebastian Cabot and James Cook, shown as Tritons, pushing the boat forward, surrounded by a ring of nereids carrying items of industrial manufacture from Manchester and Birmingham. 'Good God,' exclaimed the artist in a letter to the society in 1793, 'how much do we want a manly history of our islands!'[8] Ahead, figures personifying the different continents lay goods at the river-god's feet: Asia with silk and cotton, Europe offering grapes and wine in an ancient vase, America with a basket of furs, and Africa in manacles, his weeping eyes uplifted to the sky, himself the commodity to be traded. Australia is simply not depicted. In the distance are the chalk cliffs of the southern coast of England. Mercury flies above, blowing a bronze salpinx, the military horn of antiquity used to summon troops to war. In 1843, one visitor described this series as a vision that 'looks over the field of human history as a superior being might be supposed to look over it'.[9]

It was against this backdrop that Balfour's lecture set out his vision of the relationship between anthropology and archaeology. Under the title 'Evolution in Decorative Art', it folded this epic vision of improvement back upon art itself. I try to picture how the seated bodies of the assembled audience joined the hundred-year-old figures on the murals. The coughs and the clearing of the throats as proceedings were about to start, Sir George Birdwood in the chair calling the room to order. The bodies that had been freighted in damp woollen jackets, leather boots, felt hats on that rainy Tuesday night by hansom cab and by underground rail. Bodies that had carried themselves on foot from different directions, past Nelson's Column and along the Strand, or across Waterloo Bridge along the Embankment past Cleopatra's Needle, or emerging from the District line at Charing Cross,[10] that sharp sulphurous underground smell still in their nostrils. Three minutes into the talk, the words now lit up in the pdf on my screen were read aloud. Balfour said: 'The present is offered in explanation of the past, the living as representative of the dead.'[11]

A generation earlier, in pamphlets penned and lectures delivered in other parts of London during the mid-1870s, Fox (not yet the Grandfather-General and not yet bearing the necronym) had introduced this analogical transposition of the living and the dead, and folded it into a method. This analytic procedure was, he claimed, foundational to both archaeology and anthropology, those emerging academic disciplines he was helping to create, whether in the excavated trench or the museum galleries or landing on some remote beach as an explorer, colonial officer or army general. The method began with a transposition of the dead onto the unknown, and the living onto the known. The 'descriptive ethnology' of travellers' accounts, Fox argued, represents a lens through which to understand the past through its 'relics', as if the world were inhabited by two broad categories of people: living men and half-dead survivals from the past.[12] It was a vison and a division that came in part from a distinction that had been made in German ethnology between 'Naturvölker' ('nature people') and 'Kulturvölker' ('culture people'), which in the 1840s Gustav Klemm had distinguished as 'active' races in a condition of civilisation and freedom and 'passive' races in a condition of savagery.[13] A central idea that ran through Fox's writing was, *The Athenaeum* recalled in his obituary in 1900, the idea that 'the modern savage' might 'represent primeval man'.[14]

The twist came like a Möbius strip: these inductive disciplines, he stated, and by extension any cataloguer of museums or monuments, must always act 'upon the orthodox scientific principle of reasoning from the known to the unknown' – indeed anthropology is 'entitled to a standing in the ranks of science' precisely because of its method of 'interpreting the past by the present, the unknown by the known'.[15] The past approaches the present from the unknown, Fox argued, with an 'unbroken continuity'. And as it does so, in its continual repetition of cultural forms, reality warps, curves, transforms, evolves, decays.

It was in another lecture, delivered to the Royal Institution in 1875 with the title 'The Evolution of Culture', that Fox set out this argument as his programme. He compared the way in which we inherit knowledge from the past with how a concept when expressed through speech 'is liable to change as it passes from mouth to ear'. Another forty years would pass before Ferdinand de Saussure's *General Linguistics* formalised the distinction between the sound-image (signifier) and the concept (signified), but in Fox's hands the transformation of meaning was traced like the arc of a grenadier's bomb.

When it comes to ideas expressed through art, he continued, these have more stability than a spoken word, before the invention of writing at least, because a physical image can be inherited across time whereas spoken words cannot. Studying the weapons of 'savages', Fox continued, therefore teaches us about the earliest phases of human life far more than the study of language ever could. The names for things may change with every passing generation, Fox said, but the physical things themselves are passed down 'from father to son, faithful records of the condition of the people by whom they were fabricated'.[16]

In a folder of Fox ephemera in the archives in Salisbury, a card handwritten by Fox in a bold military or railway-sign-like sans-serif font sets out the rules for a parlour game that was instructive on this point:

INSTRUCTIONS GIVEN TO DRAUGHTSMEN IN COPYING.

YOU ARE REQUESTED TO COPY THESE DRAWINGS AS FAITHFULLY AS POSSIBLE. FIRST EXAMINE THE DRAWINGS CAREFULLY AND ENDEAVOUR TO TAKE IN THE EXACT MEANING OF THE FIGURES. IF YOU NOTICE ANYTHING IN THEM WHICH YOU CONSIDER TO BE AN IMPERFECTION OF DETAIL ACCORDING TO YOUR IDEAS OF THE ORIGINAL DESIGN YOU MAY CORRECT IT. BUT DO NOT INTRODUCE ANY ORIGINAL VARIATIONS.

NO DRAUGHTSMAN WAS ALLOWED TO SEE ANY BUT THE COPY IMMEDIATELY PRECEDING HIS OWN AND FROM WHICH HIS OWN COPY WAS TAKEN.[17]

This was 1883, a century before my schoolfriends and I were playing the game we called, with that Cold War inflection, Chinese Whispers. In Fox's day, from say the late 1860s, it was known, with a parallel anti-eastern framing, as 'Russian Scandal'.[18] Russian Scandal worked not with a single word but a short story a few sentences in length. The story was repeated out loud by the final person in the circle, and the variation was compared with the original words. Fox changed the rules. To draw a line between language and art, Fox argued, was 'a subjective delusion'.[19] 'It occurred to me that the same thing might be done to show the successive copies of drawings,' he recalled in a lecture delivered at the Blackmore Museum in Salisbury in 1890.[20] Like the verbal version, this was a game that worked with transmission and change. But in place of spoken word passed around the table Fox's game worked with a sequence of drawn images.[21]

Fox used this analogy to discuss what he called 'the development of ornament' over time, arranging objects into sequences. One of his examples was a series of imitations of a gold 'stater' coin of Philip II of Macedon, which was copied many times by late pre-Roman Iron Age metalsmiths in Britain. In a drawing presenting the coins in succession, over time the figures on the coins could be seen to change gradually, becoming simpler or shifting in form. Thus, the head of the ruler gradually disappears from the obverse, leaving just his wreath as a band across the coin, which is replaced in turn by a cross. On the reverse a chariot with horses becomes just a single horse and wheels, the chariot vanishing. In one later copy, the body of the horse disappears to leave only four lines as echoes of the animal's legs, and in another only the head survives but now it has, Fox said, grown a pair of wings.[22]

In 1872, Fox had offered another example of the same process, this time from human figures depicted on wooden paddles and clubs from New Ireland in Papua New Guinea – a group of islands, he noted as he set the scene, 'adjoining the one in which Bishop Patterson was lately murdered'.[23] He arranged the objects, through pure conjecture in this case, so as to show a realistic representation of a human figure in his first example changing during successive copies, first to a more stylised face, then to the figure represented from the side thus 'lopping off an arm and a leg on one side', then to the disappearance of the legs, next to the whole body disappearing leaving only the head, and then to nothing but the nose, and then to a shape something like a moustache, and finally to the abstract shape of a crescent moon.[24]

Fox called the phenomenon that he identified on the prehistoric coins and the Melanesian paddles 'realistic degeneration'. It is the result, he wrote, not of the physical decay of artworks, but of 'the decomposition of the mental ideas which produced them'. He claimed to have identified the same process in myths. The history of myth, he argued, is one of the ongoing decay. In archaeology, in anthropology, in museums, the task is to study the 'manifestations of the mind' to trace this continual degeneration of the real. These principles of continuity, Fox argued, applied also to his own new ideas. To get them accepted would be 'a work of development', he wrote, that 'will require time and the labours of many individuals to establish it as the truth, if truth it be'.[25]

In the Society of the Arts, Balfour was taking on Fox's ideas and evolving them as if the drawing had been passed from one player to the next. He talked about survivals. Look at the form of an Austrian air rifle for example, he said. With air rifles there is no need for an external lock and lock-plate, but there is an engraving on the breach end, where these would have been. A functional part of a previous technology survives in the form of decoration. And he talked about 'unconscious variations' brought about by successive copying, giving the example of a famous watercolour made in the 1580s by John White. The image depicts a group of Algonquian people dancing at a circle of timber posts, holding gourds, rattles and corn or tobacco leaves. Examining the detail of reproductions of this image from 1634, 1724 and 1875, Balfour shows how the artwork is variously reversed, simplified and elaborated upon, for example a rattle evaporating into a shadow, and in the latest image the wooden posts becoming a stone circle, as if this Native American dancing circle at Secotan in what is today North Carolina were being transformed into a monument of the British Neolithic. Balfour also described his own experiments with the parlour game, in which over nine successive copies, an image of a snail on a twig appears to 'evolve' into the image of a bird.[26] When I looked up the original John White watercolour on the British Museum online catalogue, the curator's notes describe the confusing effect of how the image is offset and has also been folded in half, another leaf in a history that's not so much layered as origamied, pleated, turned in upon itself for self-preservation.

Looking back along the sequence of Fox's theory of the decomposition of reality, you come to a lecture delivered at the Dorchester School of Art in Dorset in February 1884. Here he described experiments he had undertaken over the previous few years with people whom he described as 'untaught aborigines of different savage countries who have come to England', and 'untaught country children and adults of our own race'. The method was to provide pen and paper, to take them one by one into a room, and to ask them to draw his own portrait. (Fox gives no record of his state of dress, or undress, in these incidents.) One of the subjects was a Zulu woman called 'Adsumvola', Fox continued. Her first drawing depicted the General's head, arms and legs as disarticulated, as if pulled away and detached from each other. Taking the paper away and giving her another, Fox said, he instructed her to draw his body again. And again she drew Fox's body as a disarticulated figure, only this time switching the positions of the legs and the arms, so his feet were where his hands should be. Fox talks about these drawings as experiments in understanding the development of realistic drawing, but there is surely another reading of this story, another method. A method I mean in the sense in which 'Adsumvola' herself (if that was even her name) resisted the experiment, and thus conducted her own exercise, or at least brought it onto her own terms. She disarticulated his form, detaching his head, arms and legs from the trunk, making an image that decomposed and distributed the man, plucked him limb from limb.

I think back to the eagle's claw necklace that Fox's son brought back among his trophies of war from Ulundi, the final battle of the Anglo-Zulu War in July 1879, in which the Zulu Kingdom was defeated and the royal kraal of oNdini was sacked and burned, just months before the inheritance and the necronym passed on. And I use the museum database to look up the other trophies of war that he brought home to his father: metal armlets and anklets made of brass and coiled copper and iron wire, a neck ornament of beads, hair ornaments of bone, and ear ornaments made of horn and sea urchin shells – taken from the bodies of men and women, disarticulated, distributed, enshrined in the display cabinets to keep the violence going.[27]

And I remember that you once told me about Field Marshall Lord Grenfell, who recorded in his memoirs how he had returned to the old battlefield at Ulundi two years later in June 1881. Finding the spot at which he had witnessed a Zulu Induna shot in the head by one of the Gatling machine guns, he paced out the terrain and dug up the man's skull, which still lay where the Zulu commander had fallen. 'A splendid skeleton, his bones perfectly white, his flesh eaten off by the white ants,' Grenfell wrote, 'I felt I could not part with him.' An amateur antiquarian and collector of Egyptian artefacts, Grenfell took the skull back to his manor house, where he displayed it alongside other 'curiosities'.[28] Such treatment of the bodies of ancestors was not without parallel, you tell me, and perhaps not even uncommon. The scale of the slaughter at Ulundi meant that skulls were taken by the 'sackful' and given to museums including the Hunterian collection at the Royal College of Surgeons in London, or simply kept as trophies.[29]

There's also the case of Major-General Sir Frederick Carrington, the great friend and ally of Cecil Rhodes, who displayed a skull on the mantelpiece of his Gloucestershire country house dining room, which he said was a Xhosa chief named Sandile, or 'Sandilli, Chief of the Gaika Nation'.[30] The anthropologist Simon Harrison, in his studies of how the British treated the dead in modern warfare, has shown how these transgressive, dehumanising behaviours were connected to ideas of 'savagery' on the part of the colonial enemy. The taking of body parts in some cases included ears, teeth and hair as well as bone. What is clear, Harrison argues, is that these practices did not take place in the Napoleonic or Crimean Wars, and were not applied to Dutch settlers in the Boer Wars. The dehumanisation had a racial dimension. They became techniques for keeping the enemy dead.[31]

I couldn't believe it, you tell me, when I realised it's the same Grenfell. I mean, the one that Grenfell Tower was named after, the block of flats in Kensington, three miles west of Hyde Park, just off the Westway, where 72 people died in 2017 when the cladding caught fire. I didn't know what to think, what to say, you add.

The library is closing. I shut the pdf document, close my laptop, pull on my coat and hat, swing my bag on my shoulder. The stars still bore the names ascribed to them by Ptolemy right the way into modern times, I once read, so that legends were still written in them, like the constellation Argo Navis, the ship of Jason's Argonauts, persisting hundreds of light years away, billions of years old, two millennia on, the keel, deck and sails punctuating the southern sky like a spray of bright holes in the dark, each one a floating signifier. That's the term Lévi-Strauss used to describe a concept that belongs not to the order of the real, but to the order of thinking, so it signifies an idea rather than a fact.[32] 'Race', Stuart Hall later argued, is an example of a floating signifier that operates at the same time as a prism.[33] This prism, Paul Gilroy wrote in a commentary on Hall, is 'located at the epicentre of our volatile environment bounded by nationalism and civilisationism'.[34] Lean in, shine a torch through the prism, follow the fold. Because the non-study of an idea can enable an idea to endure as a floating signifier. Like the non-study of legacy-proto-fascism, for example. Or the non-study of these enfolding remnants of Victorian classificatory schemes that were in the first place assembled to prop up a worldview of dehumanisation and militarism and cultural supremacy.

Take a look at Sayak Valencia's book *Gore Capitalism*, you suggest.[35] Valencia writes about corporeal politics, in which capital accumulation gets redirected, to the extent that the destruction of bodies has become a kind of product or commodity. The 'B-side' of globalisation is the body count, death as profit, capital transforming into new ultraviolent forms of killing, extraction and 'necroempowerment'. The screen media of 'snuff capitalism' filter and spectralise this violence, so that 'derealisation' becomes a tactic of war, derealised bodies seeming distanced, alien and illegitimate, facilitating a normalisation of violence, abuse or transgression. Has the college, or the museum, or the monument operated as a similar kind of borderline medium, to process and refract a similar kind of patriarchal violence in the past as Valencia identifies as surfacing in the present – murder, dismemberment, terror, horror?[36]

After all, in building a self-image of what they called 'the civilised', anthropology, archaeology, the monument and the museum each in different ways tried to fit the vast majority of people on the planet, along with almost all of the human past, into what Michel-Rolph Trouillot called 'the savage slot'.[37]

How then to keep pulling at those limbs by applying pen to paper, to learn from and extend the gesture of analytic counterwork begun by the woman whom Fox called Adsumvola? I read you some lines from that famous scene in Lewis Carroll's *Alice's Adventures in Wonderland*, published ten years before Fox described how reality decays, in which the Cheshire Cat 'vanished quite slowly, beginning with the end of the tail, and ending with the grin, which remained some time after the rest of it had gone'.[38] As I look away from the night sky and keep walking through the unreality of this university city, it's as if that single, persisting smile were the northern hemispheric arc marked out by the gait of Cecil Rhodes turned by ninety degrees, a transatlantic axis from Berlin and Leipzig to New York City or Berkeley, California. One jackboot on Oxford, England, the other on Oxford, North Carolina.

## 7. RELIC TABLE

The practice of writing on archaeological artefacts is one example of what Fox described as making words last. It was a nascent museological practice that Fox took to a new level, beyond the etching of statements of ownership by those who looted the past, and beyond the numbering systems of the museum curator. The requirements of the future, he argued in 1888, 'demand that everything should be recorded and tabulated in such a way as to be of easy access hereafter'.[39] In the chair as the President of Section H (Anthropology) at the annual meeting of the British Association for the Advancement of Science at Bath, Fox was describing to the assembled audience how he had established a system of 'relic tables' on his excavation campaigns, which was designed to allow every detail, 'however small and apparently trivial', to be inserted without confusing the text. He had first introduced the system when he dug at Mount Caburn, an Iron Age hillfort overlooking the English Channel in East Sussex which he repeatedly sondaged in 1877–78, and then he used it when publishing his fieldwork from the site of 'Caesar's Camp' (Castle Hill) in Folkestone in Kent – a Norman ringwork that he initially believed might have been Romano-British in origin, before his excavations showed it to be a medieval castle. He used the tables again in his extensive fieldwork in the 1880s on his inherited estate on Cranborne Chase. Widely thought of ever since as a key innovation for the practice of archaeology, the tables listed every object alongside line-drawn illustrations to the scale of each one. These long and exhaustive lists of artefacts gave exact locations and measured depths for each find, along with descriptions, quantification of the number of sherds and fragments, the date of discovery, and the number and dimensions of the feature or deposit in which each was found – a pit, a ditch, a foundation trench, the surface of the site, and so forth. The facts were copied from cardboard tickets tied or glued to each artefact by the excavators, turning the 'relics' into documents of some kind, folding objects into texts, running the ink-blue lines of their pens from things to words.

With the very model of the precision of a Victorian quartermaster overseeing ammunition supplies for a military expedition, among these 'relics' special attention was given to the many human skulls he exhumed. Detailed measurements and calculations were provided for each: Fox believed intelligence could be measured by reading them against 'cephalic indices', the key metric of the racial 'science'. This fake science was evolving: from the racist mid-nineteenth-century pseudoscience of craniology promoted by Paul Broca in Paris, Gustav Klemm in Leipzig and Samuel Morton in Philadelphia into the descendant, also-fake science of eugenics, as it emerged as a new form of supremacist discourse after Sir Francis Galton's 1869 book

*Hereditary Genius*. Galton, heir to a family fortune made in gun-making and banking, was Erasmus Darwin's grandson and Charles Darwin's cousin. That racist episode in the history of science formed part of what Stephen Jay Gould called *The Mismeasure of Man*.[40]

Broca made colour charts for eye and skin tone. Morton had African American skulls dug up from nearby graveyards. And Klemm built a museum of weapons: artefacts of the body. Fox learned from each of them. His craniometric measurements were calculated according to the method of Paul Topinard in his *Anthropologie générale*, by dividing the maximum width or 'biparietal diameter' by the maximum length or 'occipitofrontal diameter'. He used this method to distinguish so-called long-headed or 'dolichocephalic' human specimens from the so-called round-headed or 'brachycephalic' people. He saw this anatomical distinction as evidence of different periods of British prehistory, reading off from the bone of the head to the artefact in the hand, claiming that 'long skulls are generally associated with stone implements, and bronze implements with short skulls'.[41] There was even a suggestion that the transition in burial monuments, from long barrows to round barrows, evidenced the shape of the head reflected in the landscape. Fox had two craniometers specially made to his own design, which he introduced at the meeting of the British Association for the Advancement of Science in Oxford in August 1894, for the measurement of both 'skulls and living heads'; and he devised his own charts of colour standards for skin, hair and eyes.[42] But Fox's relic tables were more than just an exercise in anatomical measurement of what had been dissected from the earth; they were an extension of its logic. He came to see his work, he wrote in his 1875 lecture titled 'On the Evolution of Culture', as 'classifying and arranging in evolutionary order', as in comparative anatomy, 'the manifestations of mind, as seen in the development of the arts, institutions, and languages of mankind'.[43]

The lists and drawings of artefacts, bones, bone fragments and skulls thus crowded together at the end of his excavation reports in appendices; 'recapitulations' of the things discovered that formed a kind of paper exhibition, a form of display that contained facts in the columns and rows of a grid like relics in the crypt, or living bodies in prison cells, or books on the shelves of a reading room. Typeset in small print and arranged between horizontal and vertical lines, part landscape and part portrait, they did not, he told a meeting of the Royal Archaeological Institute at Dorchester in 1897, 'trespass upon the text'. Everything was recorded in this way, he continued, no matter how tedious this might seem, down to the minutest fragment of pottery.[44]

The statistical table had from the later eighteenth century developed into a key technology of imperialist imagination, colonial-militarist governance and bureaucratic domination.[45] As a mode of representation and an instrument that created norms and deviations, through quantification and listing its arithmetical sleight of hand was to transform human lives into 'populations' and guns or bullets into the ordered matériel of war. The characteristics, demographies and sheer quantities of each could be classified and controlled as numbers, letters and words across two axes, ordered as part of the metrical toolbox of statecraft in what Ian Hacking once called 'an avalanche of printed numbers'.[46] Ruled lines in account books were translated onto the printed pages of reports and journals. Alongside censuses and the imposition of patronyms and national language, the surveying of cadastral maps, and the auditing of taxation, military infrastructure and conscription, tables played a central role in nineteenth-century bureaucracy. As James Scott observed in his book *Seeing Like a State*, tabulated knowledge laid the foundations for the high modernist forms of administrative governance of the twentieth century. As classificatory grids came to reach into every part of life, Scott wrote, a new kind of 'legibility' based on 'the hieroglyphics of measurement' gained momentum: documented, static, aggregate, standardised facts, where detailed examples, often just a tiny fraction, were made to stand for the whole phenomenon or 'type'.[47] From 'data' flowed generalised norms, behaviours and averages, statistical reasoning, generalisation by extension, and thus, of course, the naturalisation of patterns as 'laws' and images of outliers as 'deviancy'. Practices of legibility, Scott argued, 'transformed the reality they presumed to observe'.[48] And so it was with the meticulous recording of every last fragment in Fox's relic tables, through which he applied those bureaucratic methods of numerology to create and control the data of the past. Methods that were refracted through the measurement of human skulls and bones, and the quantification of broken pottery and abraded flintwork. The resulting archive, even more than most archives, was a fiction. How then to read it?

In Fox's hands, the classificatory grid was a technology of artificial memory. The legibility of tabular knowledge became mnemonic. As memory devices, Fox's relic tables folded fragments into an image of the human past. He understood, not least through his military training, how the grid could not only misrepresent reality but also intervene, inscribing and in the same gesture redacting the undocumented, broken or incommensurable. As Lévi-Strauss put it in his discussion of masks, so it was with Fox's relic tables, the question is 'not primarily what it represents but what it transforms, that is to say, what it chooses not to represent'.[49] Fox was no bean-counting empiricist. He interpreted the past by the present, created precise methods for misremembering through minutiae, for making a restricted field of vision appear universal, comprehensive, all-encompassing, of importance disproportionate to the facts, everything blandly listed, mummified. He conjured the past as if divining the future, the table's rows like strata below the surface, its columns like siege works, modes of showing and telling; a way of seeing like inscriptions bathed in light on a museum case label. He ensured that the arguments he put in his texts operated at a second order from his tables, never 'trespassed' over by the numbers but folded onto them like a dog-ear marks a page, as if they were just as much part of the art of memory as the objects contained within them, drawn up on large cards for display in the ritualised environment of lectures for learned society. An anthropologist might describe it as a system of belief.

The archaeologist's sondage is surely always dwarfed by the vast landscape in which it lies, but Fox presented his datasets as one abridged, synoptic, microcosmic, universal map of the past. All were forms of speculation, I mean in the way that a calculation of how to shoot a bullet to hit its target is speculative, or the investment in an emerging market is speculative. The grids were also containments, not unrelated to that phrase coined by Max Weber in 1905 to evoke bureaucratic confinements which was rendered in the first English translation in 1930 by the sociologist Talcott Parsons as 'iron cage', a phrase that has stuck as it has been learned and repeated down the generations, but read in the original German *stahlhartes Gehäuse*, which translates more accurately as 'steel-hard casing': a machinic, industrial, rust-proof metaphor, more like the casing of a shell, or a steel-plated gunboat, or the metal body of a train carriage.[50]

Archaeology, anthropology, the museum, the monument. In Fox's belief system, all face from present to past, from surface to depth, the known to the unknown. They are probabilistic tools, in other words, weapons of inference, a means for sounding belief as a shared memory. Speculative frames, if you like, since the rationale for classification is after all never just a desire for order or regulation; as the anthropologist Rodney Needham once pointed out it's always already 'an urge to speculate in metaphysical terms'.[51] As the soil piles up around the baulks of the trench, the story takes shape from the purely conjectural to something you can hold in your hands, a conjecture enacted, fragments that can be marked, bagged and listed. Like a strange premonition of the image of the Angelus Novus in a famous passage written by Walter Benjamin on 'the concept of history' in 1940, in Fox's account the curator and the excavator hold their backs to the future, facing the past as wreckage after wreckage is hurled at their feet, desperate to awaken the dead or to make whole what is smashed. But the fragmented spoils of excavation and the sifted spoil-heaps of earth dug out and arranged by Fox to illustrate his ideas of progress are not a product of the flapping of the wings of the Angel of History but the debris of the excavator's own spadework like the spoil that lodges in the folds of the digger's skin.[52] Just as the zoology museum curator might be taught how not to mention in the gallery text the processes of hunting and killing through which the carcasses were brought here, so the student of anthropology may not learn the history of their theories of material culture and methods of bricolage, of those dead fragments gathered by the Soldier-Archaeologist.

If you take something to pieces, whether a pocket watch or a Gatling gun, then that's your best chance of understanding how it works, of revealing the structure. Is it then possible to turn Fox's method upon him, as 'Adsumvola' pulled him limb from limb? To excavate him, start in the present, look backwards, dig down, fold the past against itself, disarticulate it, decompose this constructed reality? Is it possible to bring Fox's methods to bear upon his own endurances, and to find words with which to speak about the skull-cup? A basis for comparison through description, taxonomy, the anatomy of a list? The risk is clear. On TikTok they call it Main Character Syndrome. In anthropology they sometimes call it reflexivity. How then not to centre Fox as hero, or indeed the descendant-curator as protagonist, and nonetheless to use that name, Pitt-Rivers, the name of the man christened Augustus Henry Lane Fox, who lived between 1827 and 1900, was known to his comrades as Gus, this man who sometimes signed his name with the acronym ALF, and later in life took the necronym Pitt-Rivers and the fortune that came with it. How to use that name to guide our understanding, as some fragment of further truth for the de-named person, whose fate has for almost two centuries been reduced to a necrography, a death strung out to the clink of cutlery and the chit-chat of High Table conversation. (The first rule of Oxbridge dinners is: don't talk about politics, I once advised you. Or offer your views too freely on questions of transubstantiation, you later replied.)

Here then is a provisional list of the fragments that lie on the surface of this man's afterlife; part landscape and part portrait, a relic table of the raw facts of his life drawn into a single diagram, folded one page against another, verso to recto.

FOX, Augustus Henry Lane (PITT-RIVERS), Lieutenant-General, DCL, FRS, JP[53]

OTHER POST-NOMINALS: FSA, FLS, FASL, etc.

High Sheriff of Dorsetshire; President of the Anthropological Institute of Great Britain and Ireland; President of the Royal Archaeological Institute; Vice-President of the Society of Antiquaries of London.

BORN: A. H. L. Fox 14 April 1827 Hope Hall, Yorkshire. Only surviving son of Captain William Augustus Lane-Fox (1795–1832) of the Grenadier Guards, Cornet in the Yorkshire Hussar Yeomanry Cavalry,[54] and Lady Caroline Lane-Fox (née Douglas, 1797–1873) granddaughter of Edward Lascelles, 1st Earl of Harewood.

ARISTOCRAT: great-grandson of George Pitt, 1st Baron Rivers. Under the will of his great-uncle George Pitt, 2nd Baron Rivers, after the death of his cousin once removed Horace, 6th Baron Rivers inherited the Pitt-Rivers estate and assumed the additional names of Pitt-Rivers by royal licence 25 May 1880.

MARRIED: 1853, Alice Margaret Stanley (1828–1910), daughter of Edward John Stanley, 2nd Baron Stanley of Alderley (Postmaster-General and President of the Board of Trade) and Henrietta Maria Stanley (née Dillon-Lee), Baroness Stanley of Alderley (d. 1895); six sons, three daughters.

EDUCATION: Royal Military Academy Sandhurst, Cadet 1841.

CAREER: British Army Staff Officer, commissioned directly by purchase as Lieutenant into the Grenadier Guards 16 May 1845, aged eighteen.[55] Made a collection of weapons and then other objects from 1852. Conducted rifle experiments at Woolwich and Enfield, 1850–53. First Instructor of Musketry at Hythe, Kent 1853; served in the Eastern campaign of 1854 as Deputy Assistant Adjutant-General/Quartermaster-General, including Battle of Alma (mentioned in dispatches, Crimean Medal with two clasps, 5th Class of the Medjidie, Turkish Medal); Instructor of Musketry at Malta 1854–58; Special Service in North America 1862; Assistant Adjutant-General/Assistant Quartermaster-General at Cork, Ireland 1862–67; commanded depot at Guildford 1873–76.

Exhibited collection in Bethnal Green from 1874 then South Kensington 1878; Lieutenant-General 1 October 1882; first Government Inspector of Ancient Monuments from 1 January 1883; founded two museums both named the Pitt Rivers Museum, one at Oxford University (1884) and a second in Wiltshire (1884, now dispersed).

MILITARY RANKS AND PROMOTIONS: Ensign and Second Lieutenant, 16 May 1845;[56] Lieutenant and Captain, 2 August 1850;[57] Brevet Major, 12 December 1854;[58] Captain and Lieutenant-Colonel, 15 May 1857;[59] Colonel, 22 January 1867[60] (half pay from 6 July 1867 to 1 April 1873); Brigadier, 1 April 1873; Major-General, 2 October 1877;[61] Lieutenant-General, 1 October 1882;[62] remained on the active list until 1896.

1st or Grenadier Regiment of Foot Guards (Grenadier Guards); West Surrey Brigade Depot; Colonel of Prince of Wales Volunteers (South Lancashire Regiment) 1893–96.[63]

FAMILY: nephew of George Hamilton-Gordon, 4th Earl of Aberdeen (Prime Minister 1852–55)[64]; nephew of Lord John Russell (Prime Minister 1846–52 and 1865–66); nephew of the 17th Earl of Morton; nephew of the 18th Earl of Morton; nephew of Lord Haddo; son-in-law of the Lord Eddisbury, 2nd Baron Stanley of Alderley; brother-in-law of the 9th Earl of Carlisle; brother-in-law of the Countess of Airlee; brother-in-law of Lord Ogilvy, the 10th Earl of Airlie; father-in-law of John Lubbock MP, 1st Baron Avebury; great-great-uncle of Princess Alexandra of Kent.

FAMILY (CONT.): uncle of philosopher Bertrand Russell, 3rd Earl Russell; uncle of Algernon Bertram Freeman-Mitford, 1st Baron Redesdale; great-uncle of Sir Winston Churchill (Conservative Prime Minister 1940–45 and 1951–55);[65] grandfather of the Mosleyite fascist Captain George Pitt-Rivers; great-great-uncle of the Mitford sisters; great-great-uncle of Lieutenant Sir Oswald Mosley MP (6th Baronet, founder and leader of the British Union of Fascists 1932–40).

CHILDREN (SELECTED): Alexander ('Alex') Edward Lane Fox-Pitt-Rivers (landowner, Sheriff of Dorset, adopted the name Pitt-Rivers in 1900, aged forty-four); Captain William Augustus Lane-Fox-Pitt (served in the 91st Highlanders in the Zulu War of 1879, Medal with clasp, and in the Sudan Campaign of 1885, Khedive's Star and Medal with clasp); Douglas Henry Fox-Pitt (painter, part of the Camden Town Group); Agnes Geraldine Fox-Pitt (Lady Grove, essayist, suffragist and anti-vaccination campaigner); St George William Lane Fox-Pitt (inventor of the iridescent light bulb and the 'bayonet' bulb mount, and paranormal researcher).[66]

RECREATIONS: Hunting; shooting; excavation.

POLITICAL MEMBERSHIPS: Liberty and Property Defence League; Primrose League.

PUBLICATIONS: *Treatise on Musketry*, 1854; *Lectures on Anthropology, Archaeology, Warfare and the Arts*; *Records of Excavations*.

ADDRESS: Rushmore, Salisbury; 4 Grosvenor Gardens, London SW.

MEMBERSHIPS: Royal Society; Royal Institution of Great Britain; Society of Antiquaries of London (Vice-President, 1871); Royal Archaeological Institute (President of the Salisbury and Dorchester Meetings, 1887 and 1897); Royal Asiatic Society; Royal Society of Arts; Royal Society of Antiquaries of Ireland; Royal Geographical Society; Royal Horticultural Society.

MEMBERSHIPS (CONT.): Anthropological Society of London; Ethnological Society of London; Anthropological Institute (twice President, 1875–77 and 1881–83); British Association for the Advancement of Science; Folklore Society; Geological Society; International Congress of Prehistoric Archaeology; National Association for the Advancement of Art and its Application to Industry; Zoological Society.

MEMBERSHIPS (CONT.): Cambridge Antiquarian Society; Dorset Field Club; Hampshire Field Club; Lancashire and Cheshire Antiquarian Society; London and Middlesex Archaeological Society; Society of Antiquaries of Newcastle upon Tyne; Somersetshire Archaeological and Natural History Society; Wiltshire Archaeological and Natural History Society (President 1890–93); Society of Antiquaries of Scotland; Cork Royal Institution; Cork Antiquarian Society; Kilkenny Archaeological Society; Société des Antiquaires de France; United Service Institution (museum committee).

HON. MEMBERSHIPS: Anthropological Society of Washington; Cuvierian Society of Cork; Royal Irish Academy; Société d'Anthropologie de Paris; Società Italiana di Antropologia e di Etnologia.

CLUBS: United Service, Athenaeum.

DIED: 4 May 1900 aged seventy-three, after a long illness including dropsy and diabetes.[67]

WEALTH AT DEATH: £414,586 7s. 6d. Owned more than 27,000 acres, property in London that included 19–20 Penywern Road and 4 Grosvenor Gardens, and several million pounds' worth of art and material culture.[68]

Some of the facts of Fox's life are laid out in black and white on these pages before us, like sherds ploughed to the edge of a field and washed out after rainfall. You could almost imagine that the art of what archaeologists call 'cross-mending' might now begin – piecing together whatever fragments survive, looking for where the fracture lines match up so as to estimate the form in which his life might now find expression. Or you could stay with the fragments. Fox's afterlife takes the form of a body of writing and a body of artefacts and a body of theory and practice, and surely the bodies of living people who work in the tradition or shadow of his work, including my own body to some extent as well; bodies, metaphorical and real, that have been intercut, redeposited, jumbled around, left behind, burned to ash and yet somehow remain resilient and flourishing like the proverbial green bay tree. There's iconoclasm and iconodulism, sure; but then again sculptors and archaeologists can collapse those twin impulses, use a hammer or a trowel to chip away stone or clay, melt wax from a mould or wash earth from sherds – each a partial outline of endurance and remembrance.

## 8. THE MASTER'S TOOLS

It's just not working, you tell me. In the face of this loss, incalculable and irreparable, what use could such a line-by-line listing, part curriculum vitae, part obituary, part parody of Debrett's, really be? We don't need his *Who's Who* or *Who Was Who* entry. When he died in 1900, *The Athenaeum* described him as 'without any exaggeration one of the first men of the century as an anthropologist and exact antiquary'.[69] So what does this table add, other than more Great-Man history like that? If you're in some sense sentimental for the genre why not email the editor of the *Oxford Dictionary of National Biography*, and see if they'll let you update his entry? Another dead White mediocre man with letters after his name, an inherited fortune, some made-up landed gentry title, come on. That book you were talking about writing couldn't be a biography, you say. I mean, how could a biographical study dismantle militarist-colonial legacies? The master's tools will never dismantle the master's house.

The phrase is one we both know well, the title of a talk given by Audre Lorde. On 29 September 1979 at the New York Institute for the Humanities, Lorde delivered what became her best-known speech, a commentary that bore this warning as its title delivered in a panel themed on 'The Personal and the Political' at a conference that marked the thirtieth anniversary of Simone de Beauvoir's book *The Second Sex*. Those tools 'may allow us temporarily to beat him at his own game', she said, 'but they will never enable us to bring about genuine change'. Lorde's argument dug into structural disregard and exclusion of Black women in the feminist movement, and thus into who does the urgent work of subverting systems of oppression. 'This is an old and primary tool of all oppressors to keep the oppressed occupied with the master's concerns,' she wrote – 'a diversion of energies and a tragic repetition of racist patriarchal thought.'[70]

Subsequent discussions of the implications of Lorde's crucial intervention in feminist discourse have sometimes suffered from failing to read further than the title itself. As Micah M. White has observed, her words have sometimes found themselves employed as 'the ultimate meme of cynical inaction', presented as a logic that must lead to mere resignation, inaction, silence, an acceptance of the status quo, and a scepticism towards the potential ever to flip or misuse vehicles of dispossession and oppression. Writing in the wake of the Occupy Wall Street movement, White described how Lorde's text was an early critique of an exclusionary tendency in straight White feminism, in which the intersectional project of overcoming patriarchal structures can serve to reinscribe inequalities and silences based on 'race', sexuality or class. But surely any tool of domination, he argued, was once at some earlier point appropriated from someone else by racial, patriarchal, ultraviolent capitalist-colonialism. The case for working from within systems to deconstruct them, rather than giving in to a 'reactionary shutdown mode', is therefore far from lost.[71] But it is complicated. That etymology again: folded together. In her book *Abolition Geography*, Ruth Wilson Gilmore shows how Lorde's caveat was concerned quite precisely with 'who controls the conditions and the ends to which any tools are wielded'. There are, Gilmore writes, two essential elements in motion here. On the one hand, the image of the master's house 'guides our attention toward institutions and luxury' that must be dismantled and recycled for new ends. On the other, her image of tools reminds us that 'if the master loses control of the means of production, he is no longer the master'.[72] I am a partial descendant to Fox's ideas and methods and objects and disciplinary and institutional structures. Part of my role must surely, I reply to you, be to accelerate that process of relinquishing control, and of dismantling structures that have outlived their time. But finding the right method is trickier than expressing the goal. Reading and writing, of the kind in which I am trained, is in part Fox's own disciplinary training. What then of using the master's methods?

Take a metaphor. In a lecture called 'The Principles of Classification', Fox said, 'Progress is like a game of dominoes; like fits on to like.' We never know in advance how these 'adhesions' will unfold, Fox continued: all we know is that 'the fundamental rule of the game is sequence'.[73] Against this image of layering and piecing together I think of how in my childhood we used dominoes to play that other game: not fitting one numbered block against another flat on the table with numbers matched end to end, but instead balancing the rectangular tiles on their narrow ends, spaced to make a line across the floor or table. One gentle flick of the finger would set the whole run falling with the sound of serial clicks like ticker tape and down it went, leaving a fallen line in black and white in a sudden chain reaction. That might be another kind of progress. All I have here are the master's tools. How then to misuse them? Not to represent Fox like a portrait, but to abstract him as he did with the past and the present; to produce not a likeness but a kind of resemblance. This, after all, is the French philosopher Gilles Deleuze's approach to his inheritance from Gottfried Leibniz, in a book that he called *The Fold*.[74] Meanwhile Leibniz's most famous axiom – that nature never acts by leaps – was central to the thinking both of Fox and in Tylor's 1871 account of what he called 'the science of culture'. Both used it to turn an argument about how material culture 'evolved' into an argument for conservatism and against revolution.[75]

With that in mind, let me bring what Deleuze suggested about the body into the mix. Deleuze suggests, 'The body is analogous to Theseus's ship, which the Athenians were constantly repairing.'[76] This sense of the periodicity of renewal, I mean the way in which new parts are added over time not all at once, may take us a step closer to understanding how, as a monument, a dead man, or a past body of thought, or an old lie, some unspoken, tacit, inherited method, framing or discipline can seem like it could never fall. It's not a question of ghosts or haunting; it's that question again about what appears to be real. The archaeologist who dug up the dead is himself long dead. We know that. Mostly dead, at least, since he's still here in name if not in bodily form. If I am to fold him against himself, from each end of his life, then it must be something closer to the domino run than to the relic table of his life. So let me try to repurpose his own tools, and return to his death.

A Monday morning, 28 March 2022. Basingstoke, Whitchurch, Andover. The neat market-town commuter-belt railway stations scroll by. I'm on my way to consult Fox's archive at Salisbury and South Wiltshire Museum. I try to imagine the final round-trip made by his body after death. The household servants followed the lord of the manor's instructions to the letter, it appears. The *Western Gazette* reported that Fox's remains were 'conveyed in a plain elm coffin, being entrained at Tisbury'.[77] The news desk of the *Bristol Mercury* reported that Fox 'was well known as an ardent archaeologist; he will be cremated at Woking'.[78] Looking out of the train window I wonder whether the pun on the word 'ardent' was intentional. And think about how the steam locomotives that ploughed the Salisbury and Yeovil branch line between Tisbury Station and the furnace at Woking Cemetery freighted the corpse in the elm box in one direction, and the ash and burnt fragments of bone encased in a specially made metal casket in the other, a dark copper alloy, some kind of gunmetal. I picture a shell fired into the void like a firework, falling back from a burst of light as ash, burnt fragments and shrapnel. A body destroyed, or a body scattered, distributed. Fox died on 4 May 1900, a Friday, the feast day of St Florian, patron saint of firefighters. The internet is sketchy as the thin steel shell of this train moves across the Hampshire Downs, but I manage to google the date range on my phone. Cremation was not formally legalised in Britain until 1902, but in 1884 a practising Druid had been tried for attempting to cremate his infant son, and following his acquittal the first quasi-legal modern cremation had taken place at Woking in March 1885, under the auspices of the Cremation Society of England.[79] Out of the window the steep eroding grassy embankments of the narrow railway cutting turn from gravel and loam into the chunky white soil that means we're now moving across the chalk downlands west of the army town of Andover. I listen as the wheels turn on steel lines with the metre and dactyls of a John Betjeman poem, listen to the hum of the electric light and imagine a pull of the cord on the steam train whistle, the fire flaring up in the engine of the railway, and the Woking furnace.

The train cuts like a gramophone needle through the gentle folds of the southern English landscape. I open the library book I've brought with me and start to read. It bears the title *The Art of Bookbinding*, and was published in 1880 by a London-based bookbinder named Joseph Zaehnsdorf. The book introduces the practical skills of his profession, presenting a chapter-by-chapter treatise for the aspiring unskilled and amateur maker of books. Towards the beginning the reader learns how to beat the paper fifty or sixty sheets at a time with a wide-ended, bell-shaped stone hammer on an iron slab to make the pages thinner and more solid when they are passed between thumb and forefinger. This is an early stage in what bookbinders call 'forwarding' a book with a sewn binding: to prepare it structurally, and make it ready to be decorated and finished. Zaehnsdorf moves on to how to collate the sheets, to cut them with a tenon saw and sew them with a needle and cotton thread. Later comes the trimming, sticking, backing, covering and finishing using paste, glue, paper, cord, cotton wool, sponges, calf skin, ink, solid brass type, sharp iron blades, gold leaf for the cover font, and so on. To marble the endpapers, I read, requires a zinc trough, small stone jars of colour each with their own brush, a slab of marble with a stone muller to crush up the pigment, burnishers and palette knives, ox gall and turpentine, beeswax and soap, combs made of brass wire set into wood, and gum suspended in water and strained through a muslin or linen sheet as the colours are thrown and floated, hues with names like King's Yellow, Vermillion and Rose, Flake White, Lamp Black, Prussian Blue.

The work of the bookbinder encloses the book, the author explains. It is a phase of production after the work of the writer, the papermill and the printing press is complete. Words are contained, and through this containment they can be arranged, ordered and categorised on the shelf. Zaehnsdorf suggests certain standard colours that might be selected for the cover based on a book's content, to create a pleasing sense of order in a personal library: military matters in bright red, naval matters in blue, poetry in orange or light green, archaeology in dull red, law in white.[80]

I turn back to the first chapter. It is concerned with the subject of folding. Folding, Zaehnsdorf explains, is the first task when forwarding a book, that is, when giving it a structure. As a method, in folding the bookbinder turns one body of words against another, repeatedly, reversing and turning so opposite sides fall one against another. And in bookbinding it must be performed carefully if the margins are to be uniform and the bleed sufficient so that when the book is cut there's no risk of chopping into the text. I have none of the tools or materials that Zaehnsdorf describes to hand. But flick back a couple of pages further and in his preface Zaehnsdorf offers a remarkable double image of how he will write: 'I have endeavoured in the following chapters, step by step, to forward and finish an imaginary book.'[81] And I think about the preparation of this book, the one I'm thinking of writing. It occurs to me that it might be necessary to sew and bind these paragraphs and chapters loosely, to rearrange the positions of things and people to bring them in or out of focus, so as to tell a story that remains unfinished.

I've been reading about the history of bookbinding because of a donation that was made to the archival collections of the Pitt Rivers Museum in 1918. Only scant details of the circumstances under which the photograph of the dead body was delivered eighteen years after the death of its subject are recorded. But what is certain is that the donor was a fifty-year-old man named Alfred Henry Maltby. Before the war, Alfred had taken over the family business on Oxford's St Michael's Street from his father, Alfred senior – bookbinder to the Bodleian Library. Since the 1830s, Maltby's had been binding books and theses for Oxford's students, dons, libraries and publishers. They remained in operation at the same premises until 2015 when they moved out of town to an industrial estate. The building became a bike shop/café. I find a few biographical details for Alfred Maltby: he was a church warden, a Liberal, and a member of several fraternities: a Freemason, a Druid, and an Odd Fellow.[82] Maltby's name is recorded in the museum accession book as the donor.

The photograph is taken from the right-hand side of the corpse. It is a breathless cadaver with a spade-shaped beard. The heat is draining away from the body which lies face up on a brass bedstead under a crisp white sheet. We see two small vases of late springtime flowers, a water jug and wide bowl on a dresser, an empty chair, white towels hung on a wooden rail, an empty wooden side-table, no bible. The ironed creases of the sheet fall to the floor in the foreground and are themselves creased in turn left to right down the middle of the photograph where it has been folded, like a horizon or a line of ectoplasm hovering from feet to head above the body, as if the spirit were departing in that very instant between the camera shutter closing and opening. Above all, it is a photograph of the head in profile: the hair combed back, eyelids closed, a facial expression like a stopped clock, the contour of a high forehead, the shape of the nose and cheekbones, skin powdered white, a grey-white untrimmed moustache, and the blade-like beard. The photograph bears a two-line caption, inked in all-caps at the bottom. It reads:

> General Pitt-Rivers
> Two Hours After Death.

A later hand, with a fatter fountain pen line, slightly blotted as if it were written in bold, the ink sucked into the paper, has added another word at the start of the first line:

> Taken Two Hours After Death.

The practice of post-mortem deathbed photography among men of Fox's class was far from uncommon at the time. There's a wide literature on how it became part of a late-Victorian-elite sensibility around death; modern visual relics, not so much mummifying that frozen moment of loss before the grief kicks in as making the death last longer. I spend time with the image. Look at the stillness around the form of the head and imagine it might hint at the stillness in the air between forgotten heaves of late springtime rainfall from a century and a quarter ago. I try to picture where in Rushmore, his vast country house on the Wiltshire–Dorset border, the photograph was taken. And I resolve to follow the bookbinder's method as I try to tell this story. I mean, to reflect on that part of writing the past that is both making and telling, hammering and sewing, folding back the binding to break the spine as you annotate the text. Part of reading this kind of past is not simply about receiving the narrative, but something more like taking a paper-knife in your hand to cut the pages open, one after another. It's always possible to improvise for any task, of course, including the task of continuing an unfinished story. To cut the unread pages of a book with a steel ruler for example, or a library card; or to choose to skip some pages, leaving them uncut, folded upon themselves until a later reader opens them up.

Getting off at Salisbury, there's a chill in the air. I imagine how the cremated remains in the metal box, a residue of solid bone fragments sunk into grey-brown dust, continued their return journey west, to the gas-lit platform of Tisbury railway station and thence six miles by carriage to the village of Tollard Royal, part of the Rushmore estate, a stone's throw from the estate house. The roar of the train's engine and the rattle of the baggage carriage and scream of the whistle echoed, I imagine, the thunder of artillery fire, the firing of rifles and the shrill, demented wail of shells. Something catches in my throat, as if some sluggish trace of the crematorium smoke that blew into the slow dusk of the Surrey sky all those years ago were still present in the Wiltshire air this morning. On its return, the casket was placed on a small handbier, covered with a pall, in the centre of the entrance hall to St John's House, opposite the church, surrounded by wreaths placed by four grandchildren. The hallway was decorated with flowers and foliage from the estate gardens, ready for the funeral the next morning. The next day, six days after the death, in a ceremony that commenced at 3 p.m., the last rites were performed. As the funeral bell tolled, a procession brought the casket, borne by four of Fox's servants, like a saintly relic or like an unexploded fallen bomb, across to the thirteenth-century flint and limestone parish church of St Peter ad Vincula (capacity 150).

'The gloomy, threatening state of the weather possibly stopped many from attending who otherwise would have been present,' the *Western Gazette* reported. When the rector delivered a sermon about Fox at the following Sunday's communion service, he remembered him as 'a brave soldier, a dear friend, an honourable neighbour, a staunch supporter of our schools and church, a liberal benefactor not only towards the poor in our midst' (the words rang out in the medieval space) 'but to mankind in general'. This death 'deprives science of one of its ablest exponents, especially in the direction of anthropology', the priest continued. 'He is no longer a warrior but a triumphant conqueror in the Heavenly Kingdom.'[83]

This time two years ago, in the second week of January, we stood in that Gothic church and listened for an echo of the eulogy. We stayed the night in the nearby Museum Inn pub, opened by Fox in the 1880s, for visitors to his second collection to stay in. We went for a run along the darkening lanes under a threatening sky, up towards the old museum and back again, but already earlier that day, when we were in the car somewhere along the serpentine drive out of Rushmore, unsure whether we'd trespassed by driving in past the gateposts and up this narrow line of macadam, this chunk of Wiltshire–Dorset borderland had taken on the quality of one vast unreal illusion. 'You wore the wrong colour shoes, then.' Back at the pub, after we had showered and changed, the landlady was gesturing at my white trainers. We ate a meal, drank two wines, smoked three cigarettes on the porch. So do you reckon everyone in this pub works for the estate? you asked me in a hushed voice, and we looked around the bar and wondered who was the gamekeeper, who the poacher. When I closed my eyes to sleep that night, I saw the damp, frosted, ploughed fields, the chalk and flint stretching out in furrows, acre after acre of hedgerows, deaneries and tithes. I dreamed of a symbol cast in gunmetal on the wall in the church; and awoke wondering again how any of this might help in understanding a dehumanised, de-named skull, or even the silver rim that bears that necronym: Pitt-Rivers.

## 9. A TIME CAPSULE

'It is an impossible writing which attempts to say that which resists being said (since dead girls are unable to speak). It is a history of an unrecoverable past; it is a narrative of what might have been or could have been.'

It was fifteen years ago, winter, some part of the East Coast, when you read me that line. We were meeting at a diner for breakfast – eggs, coffee and grits – before walking in for the third day of one of those vast annual American academic conferences, laid out like a trade fair, in a Hyatt hotel, taxis freighting grad students and professors to and from the airport, 5,000 people weaving from roundtable luncheon to panel discussion to plenary lecture to award banquet between the publishers and poster displays in the exhibit hall, the queues for the coffee and the groups at the bars.

Away from all that, catching up with one other, you were excited, energised, telling me about a paper you'd just read by Saidiya Hartman, a writer and scholar I'd never heard of at the time. The paper was called 'Venus in Two Acts'. Her account of 'critical fabulation' could challenge and expand the body of work on 'storytelling' in feminist historical archaeology, including your own vision of 'documentary archaeology' or 'ethnography in retrospect', you told me.[84] In the context of the history of enslavement, Hartman offers a kind of literary method for 'remaking the document, for assembling and composing alternative narratives of Black existence'.[85] Michel-Rolph Trouillot got us to attend to how through such mentions and silencings events become codified: first as sources, then as archives, then as narratives, and then as history.[86] But Hartman goes so much further to show that where there are gaps and erasures in the archival record, the imagination might be put to work in a narrative strategy to tell a new story. Speculative narrative might even jeopardise the status and solidity of historical events, she says, you told me, and rearrange the basic elements of the story in a kind of double gesture: one that strains against the limits of the archive that narrates the past, without ever fully representing it.

Storytelling can bridge the gaps, you continued. To address a lie on its own terms you need to erode the distinction between fact and fiction, archive and redaction, words and silences; blend genres. And you know excavation, you said, of course, is always speculative. You can never know what you will dig up; but you know it will be assemblages and fragments, not wholes. When it comes to the knowledge of the past that archaeology creates, this is a method that works with residuality; things that survive. To use the imagination to change the narrative could even be a method for changing the course of history.[87]

In the month after you died, Mary, I read a reflection by Hartman on her method, where she described critical fabulation as encompassing 'speculative history', 'close narration', 'documentary poetics', 'radical narrative', 'intimate history', 'remaking the document', 'errantry', a series of responses to 'the limits, the lies, the omissions, the fabrications' of the archive.[88] The purpose is not to give a voice to the silenced, but instead to imagine what can't be verified. It's an 'impossible' form of writing, Hartman says; one that seeks 'to exceed the limits of the sayable dictated by the archive'.[89] To go beyond what can be represented. And I read Marlene NourbeSe Philip's line that 'perhaps, the fragment allows for the imagination to complete its missing aspects – we can talk, therefore, of the poetics of fragmentation'.[90] And I realised that part of what was now missing was you; how the other side of our dialogue continues after your death. I return to Hartman, without you this time. Hartman's method opens up a potential to refuse those old distinctions between objective science and subjective interpretation, between past and present. And I read what she says about grief, both personal grief and the collective grief of the enduring, 'extant' time of slavery, the 'horizon of loss'. 'We are coeval with the dead,' she writes.[91]

Mary, you taught me so much about the relationships between words and things; about how anthropology must always attend to language as well as to objects, bodies and human relationships. Your studies of written lists of objects in colonial-period America especially, excavating the probate inventories made when somebody died to try to understand the everyday living environment of households, to reconstruct vernacular classifications. In your hands this was the study of 'modifiers' – those adjectives or descriptive labels that can change the meaning of a word, set a thing apart. There are words for vessels, for example: beaker, bottle, bowl, cup, dish, flagon, jar, pipkin, porringer, posnet, roundlet, skillet, tumbler. And there are modifier words for age, composition, size, capacity, function, colour, shape, weight, contents, condition, and so on. Pewter, brass, copper, iron (composition). Large, small, great, little (size). Teapot, drinking-pot, wine-pot, sugar-pot, mustard-pot, cream-pot, batter-pot, flower-pot, glue-pot, piss-pot (function). Empty, full (contents). Broken, cracked, repaired (condition). These 'variables', as you described them, sit on the page alongside 'unmarked' words.[92] There is privilege in the ambiguity that comes with the unmarked position, you told me, in its neutrality, its zero-degree style, opposition or confrontation or binarism replaced by slight or subtle difference. Reframing. The most obvious examples would be masculinity, or Whiteness, but you flipped this to try to resist classification. And there must be hope in the act of modification, I learned from you; how one word on the page can transform the next. As if that could be the basis of a particular kind of speculative writing, where fiction and non-fiction transform one another.

Last time I saw you, as things turned out, we talked about the history of the word 'fabulation', how Michel Foucault talked about 'scientific fabulation'.[93] I was suggesting that what 'militarist realism' – although I didn't have that vocabulary then – perpetuated was more than just a worldview, but a tissue of lies and fictions. Sometimes the reality only exists because of the story, we told each other. The text isn't descriptive of something separate from it; words are already part of the enactment of human lives.

In the little history of ideas of fabulation in our conversation, we started back in the 1930s. There was Henri Bergson, whose account of 'the fabulation function' was about its outdated, conservative role; the idea that an image, if vivid enough, may 'masquerade as perception and in that way prevent or modify action ... enjoining compliance with the status quo through images of powerful beings overseeing human affairs and demanding obedience'.[94] In feminist science and technology studies, Donna Haraway had recently been publishing on her concept of 'speculative fabulation', with no reference to Saidiya Hartman (although she'd clearly been reading her, you assured me), but instead claiming inspiration from Ursula Le Guin for what she called 'a mode of attention, a theory of history and a practice of worlding'.[95] In anthropology, Anna Tsing's writing at the time chimed with this, evoking what she called stories that might be 'simultaneously true and fabulous'.[96] And somewhere in the mix there was Gilles Deleuze, who called for a new kind of legend-making or 'fabulous memory', arguing in 1990 that 'we ought to take up Bergson's notion of fabulation and give it a political meaning'.[97] The terms on which such politics would develop were expanded the following year, when, with Félix Guattari, he defined the monument as a form of auto-embodiment, a self-sustaining fabulation:

> The monument here is not something that commemorates a past, it is a block of contemporary sensations that owe their preservation to nothing but themselves, and that give the event [*événement*] the composition that celebrates it. The act of the monument is not memory, but fabulation.[98]

There was an echo of Friedrich Nietzsche here, his line that 'monumental history deceives by analogies: with seductive similarities it inspires the courageous to foolhardiness and the inspired to fanaticism'.[99] What if I were to tell you I was trying to find a method for comparing stories, as a way of trying to excavate how Fox collapsed the statue and the antiquarian into one another, I mean how he tried to turn the past itself into a monument? The result might look something like what the cultural anthropologist Stuart McLean calls 'fabulatory comparativism' at 'the edges of the human'.[100] Start with one story and look to the analogies. That might be the method to trace the outline of militarist realism.

There's one story that I keep hearing, perhaps factitious, perhaps not. It's the story that Fox left instructions for his head to be removed before he was cremated, boiled down to leave just the skull. The plan was to donate it to a London museum for posterity. At first, I'm not sure of the source of this story. Perhaps it was a mix-up with Fox's sometime disciple or follower, the archaeologist Flinders Petrie. In 1942 Petrie certainly donated his head to the Royal College of Surgeons of England, as what he described as 'a specimen of a typical British skull', a bequest described by one anthropologist as 'the final act of a life-long adherent to the cause of racial "science" [to] allow his personal whiteness to legitimize these very methods and theories'.[101]

Such ideas certainly circulated also among Fox's relatives. For example, in the years running up to her death in 1895, Fox's mother-in-law said that she wished to leave her brain to the Royal College of Surgeons in London. The philosopher Bertrand Russell, her grandson and adoptive son, recalled in 1937 how she would often exclaim, 'It will be so interesting for them to have a clever woman's brain to cut up!'[102] So was Fox's head cremated with the body, or did it continue the journey from Woking to Waterloo, ending up in some acid-free archival box for future anthropologists to study – as if a part of his own body were a projectile carried into the future?

Talking of bones being used as weapons, I remember an argument we once had about Ursula Le Guin. We'd just rewatched that movie, the one where the monolith appears in some imaginary prehistoric landscape three million years ago, and the actors are in monkey-suits playing Australopithecines, and Richard Strauss' *Thus Spoke Zarathustra* is the soundtrack. One of the hominins picks up an antelope thighbone and begins to smash up the skeleton of the dead animal. Then when his troop confronts a rival group at the waterhole, several of them now have thighbones in their hands, and they beat one of their monkey enemies to death. As the parable draws to a close, the ape protagonist throws the bone-weapon into the air in triumph. This opening sequence of the movie bears the title 'The Dawn of Man'. It culminates in that iconic match cut, one of the most famous moments in modern cinema, from the spinning bone in flight to a satellite in space.

You know what Le Guin wrote about *2001: a Space Odyssey*, right, you asked me? It's this 1968 movie opening that she sets up, in an essay from 1986, as the opposite of what she calls 'The Carrier Bag Theory of Fiction'. The image is of two opposite kinds of storytelling. The first is concerned with hunting and killing; in fact Le Guin suggests that hunting and killing was a prehistoric beginning of this kind of storytelling. What was brought back from the mammoth hunt, Le Guin writes, was 'a load of meat, a lot of ivory, and a story'. And not just any kind of story, but one with action, and a hero. Le Guin offers us an alternative mode of storytelling, which begins from an alternative image, not hunting but gathering. Practices of collecting nuts and berries are less remarkable or eventful as stories, unfolding slowly as one wild-oat seed after another is removed from its husk, but they involve a distinctive kind of cultural technology, Le Guin argues. Rather than tools for doling out violence, 'that wonderful big, long, hard thing, a bone', as she puts it, the murder weapon that becomes a spaceship 'thrusting its way into the cosmos', the first cultural devices in human prehistory may have been 'recipient technologies': 'a leaf a gourd a shell a net a bag a sling a sack a bottle a pot a box a container. A holder. A recipient.'[103]

The distinction here is between the weapon and the container as the origin of culture, and thus between linear, progressive, 'ascent' narratives – stuff that counts as news made by sticks, spears, swords, 'long, hard objects for sticking, bashing, and killing' – and stories made through bricolage, assemblage, re-collection.[104] Perhaps statues and monuments and the shaft of the archaeological trench and the model of the anthropologist going straight into ethnographic immersion like a paratrooper, perhaps all these, I asked you, are genres of narrative, or forms of memory, or patterns of knowledge, that are gendered in this way, patriarchal, an example of what Le Guin calls 'the killer story'? Stories that have a beginning and an end like the incremental improvement of any weapon, from the musket to the machine gun, from the hand grenade to the atom bomb.

Sure, you said, but look again at the 'carrier bag' device Le Guin offers in its place. Her countermodel, if you held too closely to its metaphor, would involve a storytelling based on containment. It begins with an image of putting 'something you want, because it's useful, or edible, or beautiful, into a bag' and taking it home, and then quickly the language slips into talking about storing things in 'a solider container' or putting them in 'the museum, the holy place'. And she says that doing so, day after day, is human – not 'unaggressive' or 'uncombative', simply not 'Techno-Heroic'. A book, she says, you said, contains words. Words hold things. You quote Le Guin: 'The natural, proper, fitting shape of the novel might be that of a sack, a bag.'[105] This narrative model may not be a 'weapon of domination' like the bone raised in anger as a club, but its hero-free containment narrative is a carcerality full of people, and could surely in some sense be a form of domination too? When you read 'The Carrier Bag Theory', you told me, you pictured Le Guin's father in his museum, and the man he called Ishi, held in the museum as if it were a sling, or a ceramic jar, or one vast vitrine. In any case, we all know how bad carrier bags are for the environment. And then there's the question of Donna Haraway's citation practices, the wider history of fabulation as a central issue for the question in hand. Which I see now, you continued, is a question not so much of modes of writing as of modes of inheritance. I argued with you so much. We disagreed as often as we agreed. On the carrier bag I think I now see that you were right. In thinking about writing this book, I've learned something about containment, and the shapeshifting forms the idea of the monument can take.

Fox once expressed the desire for his own skeleton to be preserved. The wish turns up in an 881-word fragment of a manuscript text written in 1875, the same year as he gave his lecture on 'The Evolution of Culture', two years after his mother's death left him without either parent. Surviving in the Pitt-Rivers family papers, the text reads like the beginning of an abandoned autobiography, in which he reflects on questions of heredity and inheritance. In its feel, it reminds me for some reason of that fragmentary text from Rilke, I told you. We were still in Dorset, that night that we stayed in the Museum Inn, when I read some of the lines from the text back to you:

> Now that I am in my forty-*ninth* year and begin to feel that I am no longer young, it occurs to me to write a brief account of such events of my life as I can remember. Our growing knowledge of the laws of heredity gives an interest to all that relates to the physical and mental constitution and culture of our ancestors which must increase rather than diminish as years roll on [...] Hence an autobiography, if truthfully written, may be of some scientific value to a man's offspring even *tho* it may in no sense be a record of stirring events or contain anything of which the family may have especial reason to be proud. I have myself found the want of such a record. My mother had a fancy for burning every scrap of paper which had writing on it, even my father's letters to his father written from the Peninsular, where he served with the Grenadier Guards, which I remember reading with much interest.

I found after her death that she had burnt them with everything else that belonged to her in the way of papers. I wish to pursue a different course in my own case. I do not indeed propose to make a clean bosom of all my innermost thoughts but I desire to write with as little bias as can reasonably be expected of a man when speaking of himself. I have kept no journal, not being a man of methodical habits and must rely on memory for the past years of my life [...] I would wish that if it could be done without inconvenience and without jarring on the feelings of those that I leave behind a post mortem examination should be made of my body and the particulars of my physical constitution recorded by a competent anatomist for the information of my descendants, more particularly the form and peculiarities of the cerebral convolutions, and I should even think it reasonable if it were practicable to preserve the skeleton for comparison with those of any of my progeny who might be similarly minded to have it done.[106]

It would be simple to suggest that Fox simply failed to finish this autobiography. But an alternative reading would be to consider how he took what Le Guin calls the 'killer story' to another level, writing his life into something much bigger than some volume of memoirs of an army officer, a genre of publishing of which there was surely no shortage in the later Victorian era. Perhaps Fox's killer story was the carrier-bag-museum and a bone-gun-rocket type of narrative at the same time. I mean a desire to achieve a particular state of monumentality whether through the destruction of the body in the furnace or through the curation of two museums and the preservation of the skull or skeleton, superintended in the archive forever. What kind of cyborg monumentality was this: his ideas, his writing, his body, his ashes? I remember that you told me once about what Klaus Theweleit wrote about the genre of autobiography in 1920s Germany. The first-person voice of the diary became an important mode of writing for former First World War soldiers who'd fought for the Kaiserreich – a mode in which bound pages and rows of letters became vehicles for what he called 'the preservation of the self in body armour'.[107] In Fox's case, half a century earlier, that armour was wilfully fragmented and partial, anonymising and at the same time identifying, like a mask or a monument, like the necronym.

One thing is certain. I don't know the fate of his skull. But this isn't the gravedigger scene in *Hamlet*, that quintessential literary moment of some contemplative male holding someone else's skull in his hand. Flick back from Act 5 to Act 3, where Hamlet has a line that's far more relevant:

> There's hope a great-man's memory may outlive his life half a year
> But by our Lady he must build churches then.[108]

What secular churches were built in Fox's ambition for posterity and afterlife, not for his body but for his thinking, his prejudice, his fictions, his self-delusions, his violence, his lies? It will be evident by now that this text will not be an exercise in history or biography, whether hagiography or hit-job. Instead of thinking myself back into some past life and working forward in time, I want to try to rewire that latent archaeological sense of writing in the present with the remains of the past. Archaeology is the science of human duration. It can be the inverse of history, in that the discipline works with what survives. It remakes the past in the present. Rewrites the past, but changes it. Destroys it even, sometimes, since excavation is always an unrepeatable experiment; it deconstructs what it studies, and transforms what had survived there into knowledge of the past. In that sense archaeology could prove to be an unlikely but important part of the toolkit for addressing enduring structures of White supremacy.

From the early modern period into the Victorian age, antiquarianism was always in part a secular reflection on death and the body. Fox was for example undoubtedly familiar with Thomas Browne's 1658 antiquarian text *Hydriotaphia, Urn Buriall, or, A Discourse of the Sepulchrall Urnes Lately Found in Norfolk*, published half a century after *Hamlet* was first performed. Browne discussed the early medieval cremation cemetery at Walsingham in Norfolk, and reflected on the desperate hope inherent in the idea of cremation that, as carbonised fragments, the substance of a person might outlast the corpses of others, outlast even the bones of those yet unborn, a futile attempt to defeat the passage of time. Browne reflected on the vanity of the living who try to control their remains in death when he wrote: 'But who knows the fate of his bones, or how often he is to be buried? Who hath the Oracle of his ashes, or whether they are to be scattered?'[109]

Last year when we were making plans to visit his monument in the church together, you sent me an article by the anthropologist Michael Taussig called 'History as Sorcery'. Taussig describes the study of 'what makes the real real and what makes the normal normal'.[110] And we talked about how science sometimes created myths, rather than dispelling them. About the trope of explorers who make up stories, from early modern fabulous geographies of fantastic, impossible worlds to the later fictional folds in this genre, from Professor Challenger in Conan Doyle's *The Lost World* and George MacDonald Fraser's reimagination of Harry Flashman to the 2006 movie *The Lost City of Z* and the Indiana Jones franchise. The historian of finance Marc Flandreau has even suggested that the beginnings of anthropology as a discipline lie in the fabricated knowledge of distant places that was used for the so-called 'puffing' of joint-stock ventures, a quick profit through scientific intelligence borne by unreliable narrators. What then of distant, future times, like our own? Fictions laid down for that future. I go back to Fox's writing; read and reread his words; underline and strike through; annotate his ideas on the page, scattered particles of thought that imagined some future reader. You asked me again: Is it possible to turn Fox's dehumanising tools upon him, to disarticulate him? I didn't know then what I would later dig up in the archives in Yorkshire, and what might or might not be in the museum in London. But I shouldn't get ahead of myself.

We found Fox's urn, as we had read online that we would, at Tollard Royal, in St Peter ad Vincula, the Gothic church named for Peter, the saint whose name means 'stone'. The shape of the marble sarcophagus is like a fireplace surrounding a semi-circular recess that houses the urn, cut into the medieval chancel wall. There is a strange picture on the gunmetal casket, like an oversized coin or medal. Sometime around his change of name, Fox commissioned a quasi-heraldic emblem, designed by a fellow archaeologist – a numismatist, Quaker, expert classifier of stone and bronze axes, heir to a paper-mill fortune, and author of that metaphor about the colours of the rainbow.[111] The symbol is a kind of personal logo. It is made up of a distinctive assemblage of six components: a human skull, a Bronze Age ceramic collared urn used to hold funerary ashes, an early Bronze Age battle-axe, the archaeologist's pickaxe and survey level on its tripod, and a bronze dagger buried in the ground below. Fox had the emblem reproduced on brass discs or planchets, which he called 'medalets', and which he deposited at the bottom of every trench his archaeological teams excavated before backfilling, each punched with the year of excavation in order, he wrote, 'to show future explorers that I have been there'.[112] In 1983, a group of archaeologists uncovered one from a site known as South Lodge, on the centenary of its deposition, a time-capsule message for the future, the initials of that name again: 'PR 1883'. It was as if a strange precursor of the Pioneer plaque, which was famously blasted into space in 1972, had fallen back to earth, so fast it had been driven into the ground, and was now disinterred, a communication from one generation of archaeologists to another.[113] Before us in the church the same image stood, much larger than on the medalets, in relief on the outside of Fox's metal funerary casket. I framed it up on my iPhone screen, took a few photos, and tried to start to think through what kind of posthumous self-presentation this represented, as if the endurance in play were not his body reduced to fragments of ash, but a page repeatedly folded onto itself until it could be folded no further, a message for the future. And the image of the powdered silver removed from the cup came back to me again. Don't ask what it means, ask what it does, you said.

'How are you getting on?' asks the Cheshire Cat as it slowly reappears, the words coming 'as soon as there was mouth enough for it to speak with'. Isn't there a later scene in which the King of Hearts claims that even a disembodied head can be beheaded? you ask.[114] I think back over what still moves in the idle shadows of Fox's past and future. The sallow-faced death photo of the corpse in the bed. The train rolling across the wide-open chalk downlands as if along a fold in a map. That laundry list of the bare facts of Fox's life set out like a table of what he called relics from one of his own excavations. The contrast between the scattering of his collections and the containment of his cremated ashes behind that symbol of the skull with the archaeologist's pickaxe and the prehistoric battle-axe. That haunting autobiographic fragment with its lines about memory, heredity and donating his skeleton to science for comparison with his descendants. The white marble portrait bust and his head and limbs chopped off and drawn on the page by the Zulu woman that he called Adsumvola, a paper bodyscape. I think of the skull-cup. How after death – how long after death? – it was hollowed out, sawed down, polished and varnished. And I think of Fox's desire posthumously to control the fate of his own body and its partibility.

## 10. CRASH

The conditions that make archaeology possible will always begin with some kind of fold, a collapse of distance across time and space. A kind of jump-cut, if you like. In the case of Fox he tried to fold himself into the future. The work of the biographer is to trace a life course, but the work of the archaeologist is evaluative in character, and works in the opposite direction, digging down, tracing horizons where they lead, studying how the past and the present can be juxtaposed through the physicality of layers and cuts, and thus confronting the different ways in which life and death are folded together. Let me try to give an example, from when I was first thinking about how it might be possible to write about these themes. There were two fragments from the scattered records of Fox's life that came into view together during an archival trip for this book. Encountering these two different layers reminded me of something that all archaeologists must learn: when it comes to backfilling a trench very rarely will you fit all the spoil back into the hole you dug. And it forced me to consider what would be left behind if the Grandfather and Grandson were excavated themselves. What would happen when the fragments won't all fit back neatly where they had been, like silver dust, or chalky loam, or human bones? The aim of this book I'm thinking of writing, I told you then, is to confront precisely this. At the heart of the thing would be an aim to have, by the end, more at hand on the surface than could be packed back down into the hole that was dug.

Layer one is a derailment. It was Bradford, May 2022, when I read about it, but the event took place a long way to the south. I'd spent the afternoon in the special collections archive. Turning the page of the nineteenth-century newspaper I came upon the correspondent's report. The 8.45 a.m. express train from Brighton to London

Bridge was halfway through its journey on Monday 4 January 1847, it read. Just to the south of Croydon, shortly after it had passed a place known as Stoat's Nest, the axle of the first carriage broke away. A jolting was felt in first class, adjoining the luggage-box behind the locomotive and the coal, then there was an alarming sinking of the floor as sherds of the steel undercarriage began to shear off and fall away. Alarm grew in second and third class as the juddering gave way to the wheels actually breaking upwards through the floor. Fragments of broken axle-trees from the front carriage were seen flying over the 25-foot-high embankment, and the train was dragged off the line as the engine-driver applied the brakes, the first carriage falling onto its right-hand side, the second and third derailing to the left. Among the list of passengers named in the press was 'Col Lane Fox'. This could or could not be a reference to the nineteen-year-old Fox.[115] Let me put it this way, having looked at the evidence, and assessed the other possible relatives with that name, I believe it was him. Whether or not I can place him there with 100 per cent certainty is immaterial at this stage. The point is simple. The jack-knife was a prefiguration.

You and I read up together about how the trauma that resulted from train crashes came, in the 1860s, to be referred to by Victorian doctors as 'railway spine'; about how a series of lectures on this condition was given in 1866 by Sir John Erichsen (who went on to be surgeon-extraordinary to Queen Victoria and the president of the Royal College of Surgeons of England). You ordered up copies of those talks and we spent a day reading them together. Erichsen introduces the term 'railway spine' to refer to 'injuries of the nervous system' related to railway accidents: emotional or psychological effects that emerged in the absence of any visible physical injury, as if some form of neurasthenia could result from an inflammation or concussion of the spinal column.[116] A medical debate about early neuroscience played out in the subsequent years. At stake was the relationship between the body and the brain, whether nervous conditions could be purely psychological or had a somatic dimension, and the effects on the human body of rail travel more generally, spurred on by compensation claims made by those who had been in train accidents and reported symptoms.

The affected patient, Erichsen recorded, presents with a range of symptoms, some immediate and some slow-progressing: pain, tension, giddiness, confusion, an aversion to bright light. He hears loud, incessant noises – roaring, singing, sawing or thundering; he bursts into tears, has feelings of revulsion, becomes unusually talkative; his memory is defective; his sleep is disturbed, full of dreams and punctuated by distressing nightmares that wake him in a sudden alarm; he is irritable or otherwise changed in character, looks pale, wears an anxious expression, even sometimes 'looking much older than before the accident', the doctor recorded. 'He is not the man he was,' Erichsen concluded, and he offered a metaphor: it's like when a horseshoe magnet is struck with a heavy hammer-blow, and the iron loses its magnetism.[117]

In 1889, a Philadelphia neurologist described how a railway accident involves 'a combination of the most terrible circumstances which it is possible for the mind to conceive':

> The vastness of the destructive forces, the magnitude of the results, the imminent danger to the lives of numbers of human beings, and the hopelessness of escape from the danger gives rise to emotions which in themselves are quite sufficient to produce shock or even death itself.[118]

I reread the newspaper reports. When the wreckage was examined, the wheels were entirely gone from the first-class carriage, but it was still attached to the other carriages by the coupling chain in a twisted series. The afterimage is one of everyday technology suddenly transformed into an imminent danger, of the machinery of modern life suddenly revealed. The steel wheels freighting passenger bodies at sixty miles per hour suddenly pushed up like circular saws through the floor under their feet, smashing the car to the ground, the reports recorded, in a violent wreckage of human and machine.[119] For those who got out unscathed from the derailed railway carriages, just like so many more who experienced industrial accidents in factories and coal mines in those years, you said, perhaps it now felt as if any part of life could break apart at any given instant, as if your social world were a steel container that broke off from its linear track and burst like a shell, smashed like a bottle, ripped like a leaf, folded like a bag, fractured like the bodies fractured. What stories do people start to tell each other to make sense of such injury, death, collapse, loss, such sublime horror? Then start to tell themselves? And then start to set down for future generations to hear?

Layer two is a drawing. I was in Swaledale the following morning. The air was cooler up here, and it was a relief to be out of the archive in Bradford, going for a bright morning run in the fields in a part of the West Riding of Yorkshire I had never been to, before my appointment at the house later. I was still processing something I'd learned in the archives the day before, which I promise I'm going to try to explain later. But for now I want to recall how the wind came in small blusters, slowly lifting the mist in which the landscape had been draped overnight. And how that mist now rose like radiant gauze from rough pasture, from fence-lines and stiles, and from stone walls. The landscape came into view, the sun shone and I felt its heat on my skin with the joy that comes after a long winter is over and the days are getting longer. In the warm morning air, I felt then like there might be hope for how this story could end. Pathetic fallacy, you told me.

An hour later I was driving my car south across Wharfedale, almost as far as the north-east outskirts of Leeds, to the west of the village of Bramham cum Oglethorpe. I was paying a visit to the place where Fox was born and spent the first years of his life. It was his uncle's estate back then. I hadn't grasped how near Bramham is to the modern trunk road of the A1, a route that retraces the line of the old Great North Road. The highway has its origins in the Roman Ermine Street and connects the north of England with London, running up to Scotch Corner and as far as Edinburgh. This section skirts the eastern boundary of the Bramham estate. Fox was born at the height of the era of turnpike roads and stagecoaches, before the railways came and changed so much about the time-geography of the nation. There were stagecoach services several times a day from Tadcaster in all directions: east to York, west to Leeds, north and south on the Great North Road. For twenty shillings and at an average speed of eight or nine miles per hour pulled by four horses, you could travel with the London Service mail coach through Ferrybridge, Doncaster, Newark, Grantham, Stamford and Stilton in two long days of travel to the capital, broken at a coaching house, and reach the end of your journey, 185 miles away at the George and Blue Boar on Holborn.[120]

The estate landscape ran to more than 15,000 acres in extent in the nineteenth century. Today it is punctuated by ruins and rebuildings. Three houses come into view: Bramham Park (the manor) and the smaller properties of Hope Hall to the east and Bramham Biggin to the south, on the road up to the manor.[121] One of the many descendants and cousins in the complex Fox dynasty now lives in the renovated manor house, and it is here that the drawing hangs on the wall. He also bears the name Fox. He accommodates my visit and is interested and generous with his time. When Fox's uncle lived there, he tells me, you could see York Minster to the east from the bedroom of the manor, and in the opposite direction the skyline of the smoking chimneys of the Leeds factories in the distance.[122]

I am shown the marks of a massive fire that survive in the hallway, where the heat permanently blackened the fine white limestone ashlar. A big chunk of the house burned down on the night of 29 July 1828, he explains, when Fox was a one-year-old baby, and it remained in ruins until the early twentieth century, becoming a kind of monument to intergenerational loss and destruction.[123] The fire took hold at one in the morning on the very night that the lord of the manor, Fox's uncle, a Member of Parliament, had been attending the funeral of his father, the 2nd Baron Rivers. The death of that man, Fox's great-uncle, was a significant development in the unfolding of Fox's inheritance, as will be seen later in this story. For now the image is of a vast blaze which the firemen called from Tadcaster and Parlington did not manage totally to extinguish until about 6 p.m. the next evening. Two statues – one of William Pitt, 1st Earl of Chatham, and another of William Pitt the Younger – were destroyed. So too was a portrait beloved by the uncle, depicting a horse named Old Jack which the great-uncle had ridden the twenty-six miles from the Doncaster Races back to Bramham in just eighty minutes, a feat during which he'd whipped the horse so hard that he would never let him mount him again.[124] I read that a marble bust of Napoleon was also lost to the flames, but a portrait of the 2nd Baron was among the artworks that were salvaged.[125]

Today, my host explains, the main business of the estate involves an annual international horse trials each June, and the Leeds Festival in August. Fox was born at Hope Hall, near enough for us to reach in a fifteen-minute run if you were up for it. It was also abandoned for a long time, between serving as the kennels of the Bramham Moor

Hunt, although it's since been sold and they're now doing it up. Look it up online and you'll find posts from 2008 on urban exploration sites, standard noughties 'dereliction tourism' fare; the 'ruin porn' aesthetic of peeling paintwork, ivy pulling at the walls, smashed bricks where a period fireplace has been removed with a hammer and chisel, abandoned chairs, tables and mattresses from the most recent inhabitants, and the stopped mechanism of an early twentieth-century Gillett and Johnston clock in the tower.[126] When Fox was two years old, the young family moved half a mile into Bramham Park to the larger property at Bramham Biggin. Fox lived here until his father died, aged thirty-six, in 1832. His mother then moved with her two sons, shortly before Fox's fifth birthday, to live in central London.[127] We walk around the building at Bramham Biggin which is currently encircled by steel security fencing. The ground-floor windows are boarded up. Some of the interior scenes for the Gary Oldman movie *Darkest Hour* were filmed here, I am told, that 2017 movie about Winston Churchill. Fox's great-nephew, I am reminded.

Back at Bramham Park, at my request we lift the framed drawing down from the wall and I photograph it with my phone on the pile of a massive Persian rug on the hall floor. The drawing is rectangular, about four feet in width by three in height, and in the bottom right-hand corner there is a title that reads: 'Plan of Black Fen. Augustus Lane Fox, Grenadier Guards. May 1847'. This paper landscape has ridged and bubbled over the years with changes in temperature and humidity, and the ink is fading through exposure to light, but it's all still legible. When he'd just turned twenty, this was Fox's first chronicle of a collection, depicting the planting of a small arboretum of thirty trees around a network of criss-crossing avenues measured, triangulated and drawn at a scale of 120 feet to one inch. A constellation of numbers is indexed by a key, which lists each tree, many of which still survive in the gardens outside today: fir, pine, sycamore, maple, willow, horse chestnut, cedar, larch, walnut, berberis, oak. I tried to picture the geography of the species represented as I read the list of thirty entries out loud to you:

1. Black Italian Poplar and Balm of Gilead Fir; 2. Turkey Oak; 3. Huntington Willow; 4. Beech and Spruce Fir; 5. Scarlet Horse-Chestnut;

6. Variegated Sycamore and American Arborvitae; 7. Purple Beech and Weymouth Pine; 8. Evergreen Oak and Pink Horse-Chestnut; 9. Common Horse-Chestnut; 10. Lime Tree and Black Spruce Fir; 11. Sugar Maple; 12. Red Cedar; 13. Lombardy Poplar; 14. Ulmus Fastigiata and Pinus Cembra; 15. Fraxinus Ornus; 16. Douglas Fir and Lucombe Oak; 17. Pinus insignis and Gleditsia triacanthos; 18. Cedar of Lebanon and Tulip Tree; 19. Cedrus deodara and ailanthus glandulosa; 20. Abies smithiana, or Himalayan fir; 21. Variegated Sycamore; 22. Cedar of Lebanon; 23. Platanus Occidentalis and Abies cephalonica; 24. Common beech and Pinus austriaca; 25. Larch, Pine, and Bastard Acacia or Locust Tree; 26. Spanish Chestnut and Pinus excelsa; 27. Walnut tree and Pinus excelsa; 28. Double blossomed Whin and Berberis Aquifolium; 29. Abies smithiana and Berberis Aquifolium; 30. Araucaria imbricata.[128]

The first edition Ordnance Survey map of this area had been published in 1840, and it plotted the Fox estate's drives, ditches, parkland, lakes, plantations, a gravel pit named Nova Scotia; thatched houses; and the avenues, temples and follies of the seventeenth-century formal gardens of the estate; a network of minor Roman roads and the town of Tadcaster, known in the Roman period as Calcaria, a few miles to the east. This is high ground amid undulating moorland, riding country. The geology is a pale, solid dolomite, part of an outcrop era that runs under the motorway from Nottingham through Yorkshire towards Durham, laid down over 250 million years ago in the Late Permian, and from which the stone buildings in the village of Bramham are constructed. Bramham is a ten-minute drive from the British Library's Document Supply Centre on the Thorp Arch Industrial Estate at Boston Spa. You might imagine the British Library to be located in Kings Cross. But in reality perhaps a hundred million items, including the newspaper collection from which the rail crash was digitised as grainy pdfs, are preserved here under controlled conditions, waiting to be called up. Every library has its stack just as every museum has its storerooms filled with the stuff that's never on display, and in this case the library storage facility was opened in 1961 on the former site of ROF Thorp Arch, a Second World War Royal Ordnance Factory that produced ammunition and land mines for the army and bombs for the Royal Air Force, manufacturing hundreds of millions of items of matériel. The ordnance factory closed in 1958. Today the library shares the former factory site with a prison, HMP Wealstun.

In the eighteenth century Boston Spa became famous for the sulphur springs that percolate through the limestone. People would visit to take the waters. Close to where Watling Street crossed the Wharfe, on the north bank of the river, one of those springs is the site of a well and a former chapel dedicated to St Helen. By Fox's day it had become a sacred site and there was a rag tree on the spot, where knots of coloured fabric were tied for luck and healing: people would tear a strip off from clothing, dip it in the water, and knot it with a wish. These tattered strips hung in a variety of faded colours on barb and thorn. In 1869, Fox collected three specimens of these rags, which are still on display in the museum in Oxford: Case 78: 'Idols and objects connected with religion'.[129] What species of hopes and wishes are these strips of cloth, what mode of monumentality? Reviewing the evidence in 1939, in a paper titled 'Documents of British Superstition in Oxford', the folklorist Ellen Ettlinger noted that according to one tradition the waters could heal damaged sight, and the rags were thus an example of 'Contagious Magic'.[130] I don't know what Fox believed or understood of such a vision of healing or magic or providence when he untied them from the elm tree in 1869, and folded them into his jacket pocket for preservation in his collection. But the tree-planting, listing and drawing from two decades earlier holds some sense of a soldier recuperating on leave from duty in London, and a glimpse of what was to come.

Sometimes the killer story needs to be retold, undone, subjected to a counter-memory. When 'the fiction is already there', as the novelist J. G. Ballard once wrote, 'the writer's task is to invent the reality'.[131] Here were two prefigurations among so many that fold back onto each other. There is the train carriage reduced in a moment to the screech and roar of hot metal, split wood, knocked skulls, cracked spines. And there is a list of trees, each carefully numbered and named in a paper landscape, like torn strips knotted to a branch for luck, for protection, or to mark a moment in time for the future. Stay with the fragments — that would have to be the motto for this book you say you want to write, you told me. The story will have to move a step beyond that method now, and face up to a process of fragmentation: the enduring nature of the destruction and abuse of human bodies and human life through enslavement. Pay a visit with me to St Helen's spring next summer, I wrote to you. Walk down from the trading estate towards the bank of the River Wharfe and there's little trace of the chapel or the sacred well. But people still knot the coloured rags or 'clooties' to the branches, as the spiritual tradition endures. We could tie two rags together there for luck: a blue one as a wish for healing in the future, and a white one to recall the passing of the dead.

# III
# The Unseen Hand

*fall*, noun. iii) the descent of an estate or inheritance (obsolete)

There's a recurrent story that the skull was that of an enslaved woman, that the skull-cup was made from some racist trophy brought back from the Caribbean or from the American South. This would be virtually impossible to prove. I can't even remember where I first heard it. But then again that's how this history seems to operate. I mean, it's a strange kind of history when the facts can't be proved with archival sources because the history was one of the active erasure of the evidence and its replacement with some generic narrative of extinction. As their body was abused after death this person's story was untold, told and retold in different measures and phases, so that today the history remains unfinished. Someone told me that the unfinished state of the story may be the whole point, a detemporalisation just like the destruction of the name was dehumanisation. It's an idea that's worth thinking through. If this were a relic of slavery, this body part turned into a vessel, then it might be precisely how the knowledge would come down the generations – through family whispers that transform into a purchase at auction, institutional rumours and silencings rendered endurant through tradition, open secrets and innuendo, and in the middle of this sequence part of the unburied, uncremated body of this person; not an afterlife but an unfinished death. When it comes to enslavement, Saidiya Hartman has argued, it is important to attend to 'diffuse terror and the divisions it created between life and not life', through what she calls 'scenes of subjection . . . not those of spectacular violence' but instead a 'habitual violence'.[1]

The dead don't bury themselves. That's the main lesson of the subfield of social anthropology that's dedicated to the study of death. The foundational text was published by Robert Hertz in 1905, where he described those aspects of death that involve collective representation of one kind or another. We are accustomed to thinking of death as being quick or slow, deriving from an accident or violence on the one hand, or a long illness on the other. And yet there are ways of describing the pace of death after the moment that life is extinguished. There's always the possibility of holding a supernatural belief in the afterlife, of course. But Hertz's faith lay not in a hope for eternal life or a belief in ghosts, but in comparative sociology. Bringing together what he learned from months of research in the reading room of the British Museum, Hertz traced how across different cultures the aftermath of death is a question of ideas and practices among the mourners and survivors, across three dimensions: the body, the soul and the living. In his 1960 introduction to the English translation of this work, the Oxford anthropologist E. E. Evans-Pritchard observed that the changing condition of the body after death, from rigor mortis to 'the onset of dissolution . . . signifies changing mental states in the survivors'. Death 'destroys the social being grafted upon the physical individual', Hertz wrote, and those who survive the dead person will use rites to render the invisible, transforming the person into an ancestor.[2]

Three different silver parts have been attached to the skull at different points in time, each serving to further transform a human skull into an item of tableware. The earliest of the three is clearly the rim around which the Latin runs in worn lettering, and on which there are four legible hallmarks. From right to left these marks show the following symbols:

> An uncrowned leopard's head, meaning the item was authenticated by the London Assay Office after 1821.
> The letter C, indicating a date of manufacture of 1838–39.
> A lion passant, meaning the sterling silver is at least 92.5 per cent pure.
> The sovereign's head: Victoria 1838, meaning 'duty paid'.

To the right, a punched recess is probably a maker's mark, an 'S' I think, but I can't make it out to be sure of the silversmith's name. Peering through a magnifying glass a few months later in the Ashmolean

Museum's lab, the conservator tells me there are tiny, layered traces of silver polish on the bone where the liquid was smeared and rubbed over the edge of the rim each time the butler performed the termly ritual of polishing the college silverware. Nobody really knows exactly what's in silver polish, she explains to me: it can be a mix of kaolin, soda ash, propylene glycol, and who knows what else; chemicals to dissolve the tarnish, substances that leave their own residue.

At the British Library I called up the sale catalogue for Wednesday 14 May 1884 from the archive of Sotheby's London auction rooms. The bound volume of catalogues was heavy. The list is headed: 'Furniture of War, offensive and defensive' and the subheading is 'European Daggers and Swords'. I found the entry at the bottom of the page, a line below a lot consisting of a sixteenth-century German pike bundled with 'a Chinese beheading sword', and transcribed it:

> 211. A DRINKING BOWL FORMED OF A HUMAN CRANIUM, with a SILVER RIM, resting on a stem and carved wood foot, bound with silver, underneath is inlaid a shilling of Victoria, round the border is a Greek inscription.[3]

The shilling is now gone, and the wooden foot has been broken off and replaced by the silver stem and base. The form persists even as the parts are replaced and the material is changed. The Greek text is still there incised into the bone, a graffito worn down with a patina formed by decade after decade of physical handling, use and misuse. Stripped of skin, flesh, hair, sawn off from the top of the skull to fragment the body. The body horror possesses a kind of flatness or blankness, but there must be the possibility of saying or writing something, you tell me. Look at the contours of the item as you would see the veins that run through a block of marble, hinting at some future statue that might be sculpted, the ancient stone remade into something new.

The necronym that the Grandson who donated the cup shared with the Grandfather who purchased it is etched into the silver rim just as it is carved above the museum entrance. In the British Library the same name is also there in front of me, recorded there in the faded auctioneer's ink hand along with the price paid, the sale of a human body part and its purchase as chattel by the highest bidder:

Five pounds and five shillings; Pitt-Rivers.

It's the record of a purchase of the skull of a dead human being, sawn down, drilled and polished, sold off among weapons – fifty-five of which Fox purchased for a total sum of £119 and nine shillings. The British Museum bought weapons too: a *khond* axe from India, a dagger from Sumatra, a brass Asante sword from what is today Ghana, an iron dagger from what is today Zimbabwe, a Mende dagger from what is today Sierra Leone.[4] There are politics at stake here, as with any dying myth. Any idea of the skull as a protective containment, that image that Rilke would later evoke, is sliced through and evacuated. The character of this brutalisation means you must attend not just to motivations, but to actions and consequences. So that we might recognise how and where the same violence endures, passed down the generations, unseen, like uncut pages in some Victorian library book.

The silver mark indicates that the calvaria was made into a tableware vessel in 1838 in the City of London. The Greek inscription appears to date from the same time. This was the year of Queen Victoria's coronation, and also the year of the emancipation of enslaved people in British colonies; a kind of Ground Zero for this story; a moment of crisis and evolution for an ideology of supremacy that had undergirded one transatlantic dimension of British imperialism for two centuries, which unfolded two centuries ago, and is still not over.

At some point after 1838, the skull-cup came into the possession of a man, known as 'The Armourer', who lived at 3 Eaton Place, Belgravia.[5] After this man died, his widow sold parts of his collection through Sotheby's, and that was when Fox bought the skull. Born on Manchester Street in Marylebone in 1818, the Armourer read law at Oriel College, Oxford in the late 1830s, and was called to the bar at London's Middle Temple in 1842. The earlier histories are circumstantial, speculative. His father was a commander in the Royal Navy at the time of the abolition of the slave trade in the British Empire, and lived until 1844.[6] Perhaps the skull was a relic from the father's naval service. Maybe when the rim was fitted in 1838 it was a gift from father to son, who would have been nineteen or twenty years of age then, a matriculated student at Oxford. There are a few scattered sources that document the father's career: midshipman, lieutenant from 1808, commander from 1812. Later in life, a director of the British Channel Harbours Railway, a scheme to connect up the Hampshire, Sussex and Kent coasts from Portsmouth to Ramsgate by rail.[7] One story tells how in April 1805 he commanded the twelve-gun HMS *Gracieuse*, a tender-boat to HMS *Hercule* which was based at the Jamaica Station, and oversaw the destruction and capture of a Spanish schooner named *Don Carlos* and an unnamed French vessel sailing out of Santo Domingo. In 1829, the *London Gazette* reported that what was called 'head money' would be retrospectively distributed to the former crew of the *Gracieuse*, a bonus or prize for the capture of prisoners from the French schooner, calculated by the head to the value of £149, 15 shillings and 3¾ pence for a 'first-class' share.[8]

It's possible to assemble a few more scrappy genealogical fragments for this man, in stark and shocking contrast again with the person whose redacted life and abused body is at the centre of this story. The Sherlock Holmes approach is not the only way of documenting a crime scene, as a mere prelude to the deductive leap and the dénouement, you told me. Stay with the fragments and see what emerges. On his father's side, the family history involved trading in the English Factory at Kronstadt in the eighteenth century. On his mother's side (she was born in Sylhet, which is today in Bangladesh, in 1790) it was the East India Company.[9] The Armourer's grandfather was born in St Petersburg, was a lieutenant in the 12th Regiment of Foot, and when he died in 1791 one of the executors was a man who, eight years later, became the commander-in-chief of the Windward and Leeward Islands Station.[10] His father-in-law had studied at the Queen's College, Oxford in 1832, lived with Goethe in Weimar as a young man, and translated Goethe's *Reynard the Fox* into English.[11] The Armourer's son was the author of the authoritative text *Poisonous Plants of All Countries*, which set out and classified the range of natural substances that act on the brain (narcotics, deliriants and inebriants), that act on the spinal column (depressants, asthenics), and that act as 'irritant poisons' (purgatives, irritants with nerve symptoms, simple irritants) and 'specific irritants' comprising fungi and bacteria. In essence this was a catalogue of potential recreational narcotics, crystallising two or more generations of knowledge born from drug-dealing freighted through military and corporate-colonial travel. This became crystal clear in 1923 when, in an expanded, semi-confessional, second edition, the Armourer's son, now entering old age, combined his interests in medicine and literature by cross-referencing each entry in his comprehensive discussion of uppers, downers and hallucinogens with their appearances in poetry – from Horace to Shakespeare, Keats, Shelley, Coleridge, Robert Browning, and even Housman, etc.[12] Whether procured at the London club or prescribed by the private doctor, when it comes to the late Victorian ruling class the historian's questions must always include: who was on what?

Back in the real world, there's no trace. No document, scrap or a clue to tell the story of the nameless, unnamed, de-named person whose skull this was. The story is the erasure. The gap is the monument, passed down like a habit or an addiction. Orlando Patterson applied Hertz's sociological sense of how the slowness of dying may extend after life is extinguished to the condition of slavery. Patterson defined slavery as 'social death'. He traced how the violence of enslavement involved dislocation, a severing of social relationships, and a destruction of ancestral relations for those born into slavery.[13] With Patterson's idea of social death in hand, Saidiya Hartman's text *Venus in Two Acts* extended this analysis. Hartman writes of enslavement as 'a realm of experience that is situated between two zones of death – social and corporeal death'. She asks how it might be possible 'to reckon with the precarious lives which are visible only in the moment of their disappearance'.[14]

Writing his PhD in economic history in Oxford in the 1930s, and working in the Rhodes House library, the Trinidadian historian and politician Eric Williams developed his famous thesis.[15] Revised and published in 1944 under the title *Capitalism and Slavery*, when the author had moved to a professorship at Howard University, the 'Williams Thesis' showed the centrality of the profits from the transatlantic slave trade to Britain's industrial revolution. It also documented how economic self-interest lay at the heart of the abolitionist movement, overturning the accepted narrative of the dominant concern being humanitarian in character, a history of moral progress.[16] In this analysis, Williams drew on C. L. R. James' demonstration, in his 1938 book *The Black Jacobins*, that the resistance and revolution of enslaved people from the Haitian Revolution of 1791–1804 also formed an important element of support for the abolition of the slave trade, alongside economic self-interest and rivalry with French Caribbean colonies. Later scholarship has shown how ongoing rebellions, especially in Jamaica in 1831, were a principal factor that drove the subsequent legislation for the emancipation of enslaved people introduced by the British government in 1833.[17]

Williams demonstrated the importance of the so-called 'triangular trade' to British industrial history: manufactured goods like brassware, textiles and guns exported to West Africa, sold for enslaved people who were transported to the Caribbean and America, from where plantation staples like sugar and cotton were imported back to Bristol, Glasgow, Liverpool and London. The profits of bankers, insurance companies, shipbuilders, arms dealers, sugar traders and textile factory owners formed a central part of the history, as did shifting ideologies of White supremacism. Because although it was framed as a study in economic history, the Williams Thesis included a crucial argument about the cultural history of White supremacy. Anti-Black racism was a product of the Atlantic slave trade, not its cause, Williams wrote: 'Slavery was not born of racism; rather, racism was the consequence of slavery.'[18] Colonialism brought more than just its profits home, then. It is after all in the nature of capital to continually transform. So today this can't just be about following the money. There were other alchemical types of capital. But how to follow the alchemy?

When I read Hartman's text with you last week, the image of the Atlantic as a triangle re-emerged in the story we are trying to tell between us. One version of the history at stake here is that the skull of an enslaved African, African-Caribbean or African-American person is brought back by the naval officer who received those bonuses for head money. It is a story of a body possessed and abused, then forced in death to make a further journey across the ocean, to Britain this time, as a kind of trophy. The triangle's three sides are redrawn in this necro-cartography, as if there were a diasporic wave of death that returned across the ocean after abolition and emancipation, at a time when some historians will tell you that every Royal Navy officer was an anti-racist abolitionist fighting the slave trade. There's a glimpse here of how White supremacy was transforming in post-slavery circumatlantic societies, you told me; an evolution of carcerality from the Caribbean plantation into new forms, whether the museum vitrines or the metropolitan dining table. This was a triangulation in both senses of the word: the marking out of a three-sided geographical space in colonial seascapes, and also the surveying of distances and measurements of angles to locate the surveyor, to map difference, to assert power and possession.

Despite the economic realities highlighted by Williams, a crisis for the logics of White supremacy emerged in the face of the ascendance of the new popular model of liberal humanism in the name of which it was claimed that enslaved people were freed. With the idea of a common humanity shared by all the people of the world, how would any rationale for colonial subjugation be retained? This was the problem to which Fox and the theorists of violence and colonialism he associated with came to devote their thinking and writing. This was a logical problem that represented an existential risk for lasting structures of supremacy: militarist realism, anthropology, cultural supremacy, the myths of civilisation above barbarism, these became the improvised responses. Reactions from another time and place, but reactions that we inherit today as framings, prejudices and structures.

Drive a stake solidly through the heart of his memory then, you tell me, and bury it at the crossroads at Grosvenor Place. If only it were that simple. His ideas and his personhood are, like his body burned at Woking, distributed like ash in the wind. His concern was with inheritance and warfare, and how the first might justify the second, you see. His expertise lay in the making and remaking of things from the remains of the past: technology, tradition, heritage, culture and the arts. It lay in the relationships between the living and the dead, and how these might be redrawn across a new image of the living dead and dying in the present. Extinction and the 'unseen hand'.

## 11. COUNTER-TRIANGULATION

I describe it as naval blue, but you correct me. We're standing in Belgravia and looking up on a bright early autumn afternoon at the façade of number 4 Grosvenor Gardens, which was Fox's city residence from 1880 for the final two decades of his life, after he inherited the money and that necronym Pitt-Rivers. The steel boot-scraper is still here although the dirt from the archaeologist's boots has long since washed away. I don't mean the blue of the sky, that electric blue that still freights some vestige of the quality of late summer light above us. We're talking about the blue of the circular ceramic commemorative plaque screwed to the wall. As we stand there and argue about colour perception you tell me about a line from a book by Maggie Nelson: '"We love to contemplate blue, not because it advances to us, but because it draws us after it," wrote Goethe, and perhaps he is right.'[19] Just don't call it wine dark. It's the colour not of the sea but it has that energy, and the energy of the colour of inkwells and regret and melancholy, torn raincoat blue, spilt ink blue. It's *true* blue, you offer. You're right again, of course.

We read the short text that has been pulsing in front of us in letters as white as bone against this blue in the sunlight:

> Greater London Council
> Lieutenant General
> AUGUSTUS HENRY LANE FOX PITT-RIVERS
> 1827–1900
> Archaeologist and Anthropologist
> lived here

The experience of looking up at this tall, narrow house is oddly vertiginous, dizzying, phantasmagoric. Two cable-tied estate-agent signs declare that it's empty for now, a hollowed-out architectural shell, and offer a telephone number. When the GLC fixed the blue plaque to this wall in 1983, the building was the home of the English Tourist Board, I believe.[20] It was the height of Margaret Thatcher's first term in government, and this plaque was a prime example of the Janus-faced zeitgeist of those years which was captured so well by Patrick

Wright in his book *On Living in an Old Country*, years when the national past was being reshaped across cities and landscapes for an immediate, impatient future, narrated as 'precious and imperilled traces, a closely held iconography of what it is to be English', as he put it.[21] Those layers never just existed as physical strata or swatches of colour on some image of the past, but also as behaviours, bodily comportments, attitudes driven by a desire to keep some kind of record, to draw you towards them, as if the past were a lifestyle you could buy into. It was another legacy-colonial layer in the history of cultural Whiteness as the original identity politics.[22]

This is such a weird part of London, sandwiched between the traffic piling north from the Vauxhall Bridge Road no matter what time of day it is, the sedate headquarters of the National Trust, near-neighbours at number 20, and the tall red-brick wall of Buckingham Palace that runs along the other side of the road. Look up and you'll see that this 'heritage asset' is topped with tight lines of weapons-grade barbed wire. The last suicide to be traditionally buried at the cross-roads, here where Grosvenor Place meets Lower Grosvenor Place, was in 1823. Today it's supposedly the most expensive postcode in Britain. The neighbours include Andrew Lloyd Webber and David Beckham, someone told me. Lord Lucan lived a stone's throw away. And you'll never guess which are the closest blue plaques to Fox's one, I said. Chester Square has two, one to Matthew Arnold and one to Mary Shelley, and then the next nearest are a plaque to Fox's son-in-law on Eaton Place, and one to his uncle on Chesham Place.[23] Go a little further, from Belgravia to Victoria, and there's Joseph Conrad. There's definitely a theme emerging, you replied. In 1941, Fox's great-great-niece Diana Mitford leased a house round the corner at Eaton Square from the Duke of Westminster, and used it to distribute fascist publications. From autumn 1936 the German ambassador rented a house from Neville Chamberlain on Eaton Square, too. And Enoch Powell used to live on South Eaton Place. But there's no blue plaque to Mitford, Mosley, Herr von Ribbentrop or Powell, not yet at least.[24]

We take the fifteen-minute walk up the road to Hyde Park from the south-east. I want to show you some more places where a nineteenth-century afterglow shines into the contemporary landscape like office lights left switched on overnight storey after storey in the London skyline. We stop for a moment on the pavement, still crowded with people at this time of the evening, as you light a cigarette, and we look up to the left just before the bus stop. The marble, alabaster, Portland stone and carved lion heads of 10 Grosvenor Place are still here, now a hair-loss clinic but once the home of William Horace Beckford (known by his middle name Horace), born in 1777, died in 1831. That was the 3rd Baron Rivers. He'd inherited the house with the title; it was where the second lord had died three years earlier, Fox's great-uncle, after whose funeral the house at Bramham had burned. The third lord's mother was Fox's great-aunt Louisa Pitt, which made them first cousins once removed. I want to hold onto that minor genealogical detail because the rest of our walk is going to be retracing that man's last steps. We don't need to know the whole ancestry-dot-com family tree, you tell me. Especially if you want to get to the park before they lock the gates.

It's a hassle to navigate the traffic and the scaffolded pedestrian walkways that seem always to run along the frontages of these houses, as if the eastern boundary of the Grosvenor estate were a kind of eternal building site. The city's flow of vehicles and bodies is funnelled along this borderwork into the bottleneck created by the obstruction that the palace wall presents. But five minutes later we come to the second site on our route – the Wellington Arch. Built in 1830, in 1846 a vast public sculpture was placed atop the arch at the edge of the palace grounds. The bronze equestrian statue of the 'Iron Duke' Arthur Wellesley, the 1st Duke of Wellington, was wrought from melted-down French cannon taken from the battlefield at Waterloo. Six decades before *Physical Energy* was installed in Kensington Gardens, it was at the time the largest equestrian statue in Britain.[25] The transformation of the spoils of the battlefield into public art came to be a longstanding theme of the built environment of nineteenth-century London. The lamp posts on John Rennie's New London Bridge (1831) were also cast from French cannon captured in the Peninsular War. Then later in 1861 came John Bell's Guards Memorial, which stands in Waterloo Place at the junction of Pall Mall and Regent Street, in a triumphal, monumental landscape gradually remodelled for soldiers to march through. It was cast from Russian cannon captured at the siege of Sevastopol, commemorating the more than 20,000 British lives lost in the Crimean War. I read the other day that Wellington was given an estate house from the Pitt-Rivers dynasty as a reward for his victory, fifteen years before Fox was born. It was Stratfield Saye in Hampshire, bought for the nation from the 2nd Baron Rivers in 1814, and gifted to the duke, another shape-shifting monument, another one of these financial transactions where the landed gentry get bonuses for their violence from the nation state. Like the soldiers that we don't see marching and riding through the streets so often these days, but who are nonetheless always ready and close by in one barracks or another: Finsbury, Wellington, Regent's Park, Hyde Park.

Five of the horses from the Household Cavalry unseated their riders and broke away last week, first thing on a Wednesday morning, I told you in an email. They'd been preparing for the coronation. There were videos on social media as they smashed into a taxi outside the Clermont Hotel, near Buckingham Palace, then ran bleeding up Lower Belgrave Road, and then out across London, two of them along the Strand and Fleet Street, one getting as far as Limehouse. Later they were brought back to their stables at Hyde Park Barracks. They didn't know why the horses bolted; perhaps it was after hearing a loud noise from a building site, the newspapers said. It was right next to Fox's house on Grosvenor Gardens where the soldiers were thrown. And then the horses ran past where the Armourer lived, on Eaton Place. For a moment the hypermilitarised, securitised nature of this part of the city chaotically flashed up, and then it was gone.

We look up again at the Wellington Arch. The caped figure of the duke on his charger was removed in 1882, when the arch was shifted a few yards to its current location. The statue was later re-erected thirty-five miles away in Aldershot, Hampshire – a town celebrated as 'the home of the British Army' since the first permanent training camp was established there during the Crimean War. Then in 1912 a replacement figure was installed on the arch: Nike, Goddess of Victory, riding the four-horse chariot known as the *Quadriga*. Supposedly the largest bronze sculpture in western Europe this time, its form referenced Berlin's Brandenburg Gate, thus reaching back to index the ancient Greek Mausoleum at Halicarnassus.

The arch, it turns out, is hollow inside. In 1999, the 'arms-length' quango English Heritage took over the management of the monument, and in 2013 they staged an exhibition in this unlikely venue between the streams of taxis and buses at Hyde Park Corner. I get my phone out of my back pocket and google it to remind myself how the show was described. An English Heritage webpage is one of the few remnants of the exhibition, and its title lights up my iPhone screen in all-caps:

A MONUMENTAL ACT: HOW BRITAIN SAVED ITS HERITAGE

'Visitors are taken back to the first half of the twentieth century,' reads the breathless copy, 'to see how a new law and a small band of determined people saved Britain's most historic buildings from decay and destruction, in the process creating a national outdoor museum.' This small exhibition marked the centenary of the Ancient Monuments Consolidation and Amendment Act of 1913, which strengthened the powers of the Office of Works 'to collect, or take into guardianship, monuments of outstanding importance'. Celebrating the work of 'Men from the Ministry' in rescuing the past from vandalism or ruin, it presented a series of images and text panels, alongside an eight-volume series of reports comprising *A History of the National Heritage Collection*.[26] The first volume reproduces a pen-and-ink drawing of Fox standing next to the fragmentary surviving stones of the Neolithic long barrow known as Kit's Coty House in Kent. Fox had taken up his final public appointment in 1883, becoming the first inspector of Ancient Monuments for England, Wales and Scotland.[27] The exhibition text describes how Fox arranged for the commissioners of works to construct a spiked iron fence to his own design around the site, four foot six inches in height, sixteen foot square. Lying close to a main road to the seaside, the monument was being visited by passing 'excursionists', Fox noted. The fence needs to be installed, he said, I read to you, to 'keep the people off and at the same time enable them to see the stones over it'. It was an act that, together with a label-like notice on a board that detailed the penalties for damage to the monument, turned this fragmented long barrow into a kind of outsized outdoor museum artefact, unfolding the layered nature of the English landscape through an act of enclosure. Fox wrote to the chief constable of Kent, instructing him to ask the police to 'give attention to the monument as far as practicable, and prevent people climbing up or otherwise injuring it'.[28] Protecting heritage involved policing, borderwork, the erection of boundaries, invisible as well as visible, but always with sharp edges. Fox combined his inspectorate travels to document and preserve monuments with undertaking ethnographic surveys of different populations across the nation, measuring bodies, the shape of noses, and recording hair, eye and skin colour from Orkney to Cornwall. This was no longer simply salvage; it was preservation as a kind of national defence.[29]

During his seventeen-year stewardship (he died in post), no monument in the General's care was destroyed, the English Heritage report tells us, and a large number of additional sites were preserved. Through his efforts, 'the foundations of a government system for heritage protection were established'. The doggedly bloodless, bureaucratic prose of the heritage professionals is undoubtedly right when it claims that Fox's efforts to preserve monuments were foundational to how the British think about the past.[30] The main thing you learn from this is about another centenary: how in 1983, the year that the screws were being sunk in to fix Fox's blue plaque, the Tory administration created something called 'English Heritage' from its predecessor government body the Ministry of Works – and how this change marked a century since 1 January 1883, when the Ancient Monuments Protection Act 1882 was adopted by Parliament.

But 'heritage' was not a word that Fox ever used in print. What do we even mean by it? The dictionary suggests four principal meanings:

> *heritage*, noun. 1) inherited property, especially land; 2) a condition or state that comes from circumstances of birth or is transmitted from ancestors; 3) sites or features of historical, cultural or scenic interest that are preserved or exploited, e.g. for tourism; 4) a chosen people (e.g. the Church of God)

I want to keep these four meanings in play when thinking about Fox and his legacy. He wrote about 'protection', certainly, of 'ancient monuments', and about surveying archaeological sites and collecting 'relics', and about 'survivals' and 'salvage' in human cultures. But he didn't use that word 'heritage', with its oddly postmodern ring. Most common among the themes that Fox addressed on these issues was what he described as 'inheritance'. In lectures he spoke about 'the transmission of inherited forms' in art, and of 'hereditary capacity' in terms of intellectual and practical ability. He discussed the mechanisms of such inheritance, which today would be called epigenetics, in a manner that mixed natural or biological and cultural propensities and processes, informed by the eugenics and 'racial science' of his milieu and especially Francis Galton's 1869 eugenicist text *Hereditary Genius*.[31] Fox extended the Lamarckian idea that the experiences and learned skills acquired by ancestors may pass down to descendants, as if White supremacy could be justified through some inherited habits that came with the creation of civilisation.[32] Past, present, future; here, there, everywhere: this was how Fox triangulated himself and also 'anthropology', the subject which he helped to create, in time and space to make them seem universal. Through his personal inheritance down the Pitt-Rivers line he took possession of a vast landscape filled with unexcavated archaeological sites. So how was the history of the idea of protecting ancient monuments bound up with the idea of inheritance for this new Victorian class of landed elite, this new feudalism, you ask me? And with the sources of their wealth across the previous couple of generations? Ideas of the subject, modes of subjection, methods of subjectification were all shifting.

I want to think of this walk as a kind of counter-triangulation, I say, as we leave the hollow arch at Hyde Park Corner behind us, weave through the cyclists and joggers, and proceed into the park for the third and final stop. I mean, if triangulation is a strategy of self-location, then its inverse might be a kind of return, an unfolding of folded time, retracing lines of flight in the city landscape like contrails whose opacity grows in the fading light as the sun sets, or paths drawn in Photoshop that could be undone point by point, anchor by anchor.

As we approach the eastern edge of the Serpentine, it's colder than before, but with an hour of daylight in hand and the rain holding off I buy us both a coffee from the kiosk. We circumambulate the goose crap and find an empty bench looking out at the darkening, still water of the lake. Sitting down, I start to try to pull at some of the threads, to unravel this idea of 'heritage'. A bud of ash at the end of your cigarette burns orange and drops to the grey concrete slab beneath our feet, and I want to hold onto that sense of the instability of things, their pace. It's possible to love someone else's work so hard, Roland

Barthes wrote, as his translator Kate Briggs once noted, that 'it is altered in the process':

> The work – or, as is more often the case, a small part of the work, a paragraph or a line – is distorted by the force of your feeling for it. A bit of the work has acted upon you. But it would appear that you have already, also, acted upon it. It addresses you, because it reads as if it had always been written *for you*.[33]

You wonder aloud whether every act of reading involves something like this. Even the stuff you don't love, far from it. Would it be possible not to misrepresent what's there in black and white, but nonetheless in some sense to change it? You think you have a good example, you say: a second-hand ex-library copy of the English translation of Roland Barthes' *Mythologies* bought on AbeBooks a few years ago. And ten or eleven of the forty or so short essays that make up the book were thickly layered with smudgy biro underlining, double underlining, circles, asterisks and strikethroughs; with bright yellow and luminous green highlighting that'd soaked into the paper, breaking the surface, roughening it; and with the occasional word written in the margins or scrawled in the endpapers. The effect was of course, you continue, to bring certain pages, lines or words to the attention as fragments from the predecessor reader or readers, students who are in some sense also now co-authors. Words get connected on the page in jumps between what's annotated and what isn't. Some lines are rendered almost illegible by the way the ink has blotched and run in the intervening years. I've still got it somewhere, you add, and the next day you WhatsApped me some photos to show what you meant:

> page 43: 'those archaeologists who go and gather <u>old stones</u> all over the excavation site and with their cement, <u>modern as it is</u>, erect a delicate wayside altar'

> page 68: 'Einstein's brain is a mythical <u>object</u>, a true museum <u>exhibit</u>'

> page 76: 'To select only monuments suppresses the <u>reality</u> of the land and its people, accounts for nothing of the present, the monuments become undecipherable therefore <u>senseless</u>, constantly in the process of <u>vanishing</u>'

Then there's the question of how people read a landscape, or an object, or the past. Can that happen in the same interventionist way as the student with a biro and a highlighter? you ask. For a moment I try to imagine my relationship with Fox as like the connection you have with the former annotator of a library book, when you try to read past their interminable underlining. Just because you're doing a close reading it doesn't mean you're in love with the words or the author or the time and place in question. Other emotions could change the words on the page too. Like grief, for example.

That book about monumentality, the one I told you I was thinking of trying to write, would have to blur the conventional line between reading and writing, documentation and speculation, if it were properly to navigate how fiction and fact are blended as they're passed down over time, how they can transform from myth to realism. All history is rewriting history, of course; but can archaeology actually change history, intervening and retracing rather than describing or interpreting? Invert the triangle, you say, as if marking out a magic spell, or turning an arrow back on itself, a counterflow. We came from the inherited house at Grosvenor Gardens to the war memorial with the absent Duke of Wellington at Hyde Park Corner, but let me now tell you a story about the fence-lines in front of us. I want to try to begin to close a counter-triangle by picturing what happened here in the fog in the early hours of a Monday morning, 24 January 1831, when Fox was not yet four years old, living 200 miles away from the flat water of the Serpentine, up on the Yorkshire estate. If we must, you reply, with a white cigarette filter between your lips, reaching into your pocket for another folded paper.

## 12. A DEAD WHITE MAN

There were no signs of violence. His clothes weren't torn and his pale skin was unbruised. There was not ice of sufficient thickness on the Serpentine, in this mild January of 1831, to support even the weight of a child, and anyway this man was not wearing ice-skates. The Royal Humane Society had dragged the entire length of the water and were close to giving up, but then at the head of the river, near the waterfall, at three in the afternoon, directly in front of where we are sitting right now in Hyde Park, 'an obstruction was met with, which proved to be occasioned by the body of His Lordship'.

The dragnet couldn't bring it ashore. The body lay beyond the mesh grating, nine yards out from the pathway. So two servants of the Humane Society were sent to fetch ropes, life-girdles and poles from the society's Receiving House, close by on the north riverbank, so a hand-drag could be performed. Established for the preservation of life in cases of near-drowning, the society saved swimmers in the summer and skaters in the winter, but this body had lain submerged in the cold shallow water for more than seventy-two hours. There was not the most remote sign of life when he was found, the *Sunday Times* reported.[34] In his waistcoat, jacket and trouser pockets they found: a sovereign, 3s 6d in silver, a gold repeating watch with appendages, a pocket-book, a number of calling-card cases, a pencil and six unopened letters.

A hearse was called and Constable Jones, No. 50, with the assistance of two constables of T Division, took the cadaver to the Fox and Bull public house, a few streets away in Knightsbridge, and heaved it up the stairs, setting it down on two tables pushed together as a makeshift bier. The spot at which the lord drowned was a ten-minute walk from his townhouse at 10 Grosvenor Place. Think back to that upmarket hair-loss clinic, two centuries on, holding back the effect of the passage of time on living human pates, for a while at least. When we walked past the thirteen Regency windows of its front elevation earlier on, they were staring out unblinking across Buckingham Palace Gardens this evening just as they did that night two centuries ago – when the richest man in England drowned himself in the Serpentine.

They held the inquest on Thursday 27 January in the upstairs room of the pub and when the coroner's jury inspected the body they were, according to one contemporary report, 'much struck with the fine handsome appearance of the corpse'.[35] John Baker, the lord's long-serving footman, was the last person to see him that Sunday night. He had dined at home with his family. 'It was usual for him to go out in the evening,' Baker told the jury, 'usually rather late.'[36] That evening, he had left at quarter to nine. The alarm was raised when he had not returned home by nine the following morning, and that afternoon an application was made at the A Division of Police Station House in Gardner's Lane, Parliament Street for assistance to drag the canal in St James' Park and the Serpentine. By the time they fished him out of the water, it was shortly after three in the afternoon on the following Wednesday. It was ascertained that his lordship was last seen in Hyde Park between nine and ten o'clock on Sunday evening, and so it was supposed he must have drowned himself.[37]

There was no desire to admit this as an act of suicide. The dead man was a 53-year-old called Horace Beckford, known as Pitt-Rivers for the final three years of his life, having inherited from the estate of his late uncle and adopted that necronym to become the 3rd Baron Rivers.[38] The name reflected a vast fortune, much derived from sugar and slavery: a combination of some of the largest Caribbean fortunes conjoined through marriage across country estates in Essex, Gloucestershire, Wiltshire, Dorset, Yorkshire, and beyond. On his Hanover and Westmoreland estates in Jamaica, more than a thousand enslaved people worked the land for sugar cane. 'Lord Rivers, we believe, held no appointment of any description at his death,' one report stated, 'but was an influential member of the West India proprietors.'[39]

Quickly a counter-narrative emerged. Surely the lord must have slipped from the footpath in an accident? Witnesses from the household explained to the inquest that his lordship was very near-sighted. He could only distinguish between persons or objects by aid of a glass, and yet felt a disinclination to wearing spectacles, explained one retainer. One of the jurors offered that he had recently written to the commissioners of woods and forests to point out the dangers of this particular area of the parkland riverside. He had brought a fair copy of the letter with him, and passed it to the coroner. A representative of the Royal Humane Society testified that the pathway was most shockingly dangerous, claiming that any person passing on a dark night, especially if near-sighted, might easily fall into the water. There was neither rail nor fence, and on foggy nights the Society stationed men there with gaslights. His lordship might have been giddy, said the coroner in his summing up. Or the accident may have been due to the darkness or shortsightedness. Accordingly, the coroner's jury returned the verdict:

FOUND DROWNED NEAR THE PUBLIC PATH AT THE HEAD OF THE SERPENTINE RIVER CONSIDERED VERY DANGEROUS FOR WANT OF A RAIL OR FENCE WHERE MANY PERSONS HAVE LATELY FALLEN IN.[40]

It was a tragedy, so the story went. A Tory peer of the realm had died for want of a proper railing on a dangerous causeway at the head of the river. Something must be done to improve safety on this, the main thoroughfare across the park from Knightsbridge barracks to Cumberland Gate. But rumours continued to circulate. Lord Rivers left no suicide note, but circumstantial evidence raised suspicions about the official narrative. There was a report that when the body was taken out of the water, his hat was secured with a handkerchief tied under the chin, 'with the evident intention of preventing its floating to the surface'.[41] And then there was the matter of his lordship's umbrella. The landlord of the pub interrupted proceedings, saying a woman had brought this item to the police, which she had discovered early on Monday morning set down a short distance from the spot where he drowned – a find that had triggered the search of the water in the first place. If it was an accident, why had the umbrella not fallen in with him?

The *Preston Chronicle* reported the widespread strong suspicion that he had drowned himself.[42] The *Bury and Norwich Post*, reporting the coroner's verdict, added that it was rumoured that this catastrophe was not an accident.[43] 'The death of Lord Rivers is now supposed not to have been accidental,' chimed *The Spectator*.[44] And as far away as North Carolina, the *Fayetteville Observer* reported bluntly that Lord Rivers, a husband and a father, drowned himself in the Serpentine River in Hyde Park – owing, as was supposed, to losses at play.[45] A few weeks later the *Sunday Times* reported on a woman who took her life near the same spot.[46] And some recalled the case of Harriet Westbrook, the 21-year-old pregnant wife of the poet Percy Bysshe Shelley, who had drowned herself there fifteen years earlier.

Questions began to be asked about Lord Rivers' gambling habit. His uncle had restricted his financial access to £4,000 per year, retaining ten times that amount under the control of trustees, because of concerns over his nephew's gaming. According to a letter to the editor of *The Age*, from a correspondent who called themselves Amicus and described themselves as 'the intimate friend' of his lordship, the coroner's verdict may lead readers to 'a false conclusion'. On the Saturday night and Sunday morning Lord Rivers had reportedly been gambling until the small hours at Graham's Club, St James' Street, and had lost thousands of pounds playing *écarté* with a skilled player.[47] Six years later, it was being freely reported by the *Sunday Times* that Lord Rivers drowned himself in the Serpentine after massive gambling losses at Graham's.[48]

Horace Beckford might appear to be a relatively distant relative to the three-year-old Fox, but the odd cocktail of feudalism and capitalism, cousinhood and cash, meant that events set in train at this moment led, through a complex sequence of further deaths, to Fox's eventual inheritance of this vast intergenerational fortune in the year 1880. The money and land finally came to Fox through this 'feudal capitalism' when he was about the same age as Horace was when he died. And when it finally did come, he used it to commission his own works of sculpture, to build his own monuments – and even to conjure them from the prehistoric past. Meanwhile, shortly after the coroner's verdict, the ranger of Hyde Park and St James' Park oversaw the erection of a new fence. He ordered it to be installed, *Bell's Life in London* reported on 6 February, 'on the spot where the late Lord Rivers threw himself into the water'.[49]

The railings were swiftly manufactured and delivered by the ironfounders Messrs Bramah of Pimlico. Running 200 yards along the public footpath at the head of the Serpentine, newspaper reports questioned whether they would really help prevent accidents on dark nights or in foggy weather.[50] What was actually being protected was a reputation; what was being enclosed was a story about the dead. The railings were a monument to one version of a death: the pretence that this was not suicide. There's no obvious trace of the fence-line now. Sometimes the enclosure, not what is enclosed, is the lie. And as in this case, sometimes the lie itself is now missing from the landscape, erased or recycled. Although the railings still stand around that Neolithic monument in Kent, I tell you, the one Fox designed with the sharp uprights shaped like spears pointing skyward. Do you know when they lock up here? With this question, you get up and walk over to consult a park map. When you come back you recite the names of the park gates you just read like a royalist-imperialist-militarist fantasy zombie roll call: Achilles, Albert, Alexandra, Apsley, Clarendon, Cumberland, Curzon, Grosvenor, Rutland, Victoria.

These time-warps are unreal, you continue. The future Queen was eleven years old at the time of the lord's drowning, living just across the park to the west in Kensington Palace. There's a statue of her there, a seated figure of Victoria in her coronation robes cut from milk-white marble on a ghost-white Portland stone base, white on white, depicted at age nineteen, a melancholic figure like a stuck clock hand, like the fictional Miss Havisham, sculpted it was said by her daughter Princess Louise, or more probably by Sir Joseph Boehm, to celebrate her Golden Jubilee in 1887, but only finished and erected six years later, unveiled by the Queen herself, aged seventy-four. Its nose was replaced after shrapnel from a Nazi bomb damaged it in 1945, and when I saw it the other year it was still missing the sceptre. I read that someone took a lump hammer to it, prised it away and walked off with it in broad daylight.[51]

The question of suicide is something I talk about in my lectures every year, because it was the topic of one of the foundational texts of modern sociology. In 1897, Émile Durkheim's *Le suicide* outlined what he saw as different types of suicide, and tried to account for their causes, from egotism to altruism, fatalism and *anomie* (confusion). Analysing patterns in suicide from the 1860s to the 1890s, Durkheim took what appears on the face of it to be the most individuated imaginable of acts and to explain it in terms of wider social factors. This last category, *anomie*, was, Durkheim suggested, a common effect of big changes in someone's circumstances, including cases of what he calls 'fortunate crises' such as 'an abrupt growth of power and wealth' as well as the more obvious example of total financial ruin. In both instances there is a dangerous period of readjustment in which 'time is required for the public conscience to reclassify men and things', he suggested.[52]

The case of Beckford, the 3rd Baron Rivers, is clearly one of someone who had suffered enormous financial losses. But in the subsequent years, the largest financial windfall in British history took place, a phenomenon that affected the intergenerational passage of the Pitt-Rivers fortune as well as hundreds of the other largest and richest landed estates. This vast windfall – 'the single largest financial operation undertaken by the British state' in its history is how one historian has described it – took the form of payments made under the 1833 Slavery Abolition Act, under which enslaved people in the British Caribbean, Mauritius and the Cape of Good Hope gained freedom between 1838 and 1840, after a period of 'apprenticeship'.

His Majesty's Government called the payments 'compensation'.[53] The scale of the debt was brought into sharp focus almost two centuries later, when on 9 February 2018, HM Treasury @hmtreasury tweeted to its hundreds of thousands of followers:

> Here's today's surprising #FridayFact.
> Millions of you helped end the slave trade through your taxes.

The tweet included a picture which bore the further text:

> Did you know? In 1833 Britain used £20 million, 40% of its national budget, to buy freedom for all slaves in the Empire. The amount of money borrowed for the Slavery Abolition Act was so large that it wasn't paid off until 2015. Which means that living British citizens helped pay to end the slave trade.

Tone deaf. In payments made to around 20,000 individuals during the second half of the 1830s, the Slave Compensation Commission compensated former 'owners' for the supposed financial loss when more than 800,000 enslaved people were given their freedom, treated as chattel property forfeited through emancipation. No payments were made to the people who had been enslaved. At least half of the claimants were based in Britain, and these large metropolitan payouts went to many MPs, clergy, and military officers. The Barbadian historian Hilary Beckles has called this episode 'Britain's Black debt' – 'the slave-owners' reparations' that rewarded the 250-year-long national crime of Black enslavement and Indigenous genocide. A government response to a freedom of information request stated that the total cost of redemption for this loan was £218,338,715.22.[54] For 180 years the British taxpayer paid back the money as part of national debt. 'How long do racial contracts of credit and debt continue?' Kris Manjapra has asked of this episode.[55]

David Olusoga has pointed out that this meant that up to 2015 millions of Britons, including British descendants of enslaved people, had been paying back a loan made to pay the former Caribbean plantocracy.[56] In the longer run, this immense governmental largesse created a new super-wealthy British ethnoclass, reshaping British society in a manner that still lives on today through a landed elite expanding in untold numbers with each generation, inheriting not just the profits of that phase of racial capitalism, but this windfall with compound interest.

Follow the money, you tell me. What about Fox's connections to slavery, the past profits and compensation he inherited and spent on archaeology and two museums? I'm no economic historian, I reply. Outlining the pattern and process of descent is definitely important, and let me give that a try in what follows. But seeing Fox's story as part of the violent effects and opportunistic responses that came about after this sudden injection of immense wealth for the former plantocracy and absentee estate-owners is what I'm better placed to try to do. I mean, holding onto Durkheim's sense of what a windfall might destabilise.

In the context of the United States, Christina Sharpe's account of the unfinished nature of the undead legacies of enslavement, in a book she called *In the Wake*, might be a touchstone for the parallel British story. In her hands, this word, 'wake', expands to evoke the track left on the water's surface by a ship; the disturbance caused by a body moving in water; a state of wakefulness or consciousness; the air currents behind a body in flight; a region of disturbed flow; the recoil of a gun. Reflecting on how racism affected her own family's ambitions and desires when she was growing up, she writes how 'racism, the engine that drives the ship of the state's national and imperial projects, cuts through all of our lives and deaths inside and outside the nation, in the wake of its purposeful flow'.[57]

So writing from Oxford or on field trips to Dorset or Yorkshire, or mapping Fox's travels to New York and Washington, DC, to Canada, to Malta, to Germany and Italy, to Crimea, to Ireland, to Egypt, or simply sitting with you right now in Hyde Park amid this army of monuments in the dying light, sure, I'll follow the money as best I can, but also try to follow the alchemy, the evolving, transmuting forms of racial capitalism down the generations. Read the militarist realism like a fiction that could be rewritten, not by piecing together the facts but by staying with the fragments. Inheritance across generations. The treatment of the dead. Enslavement and debt. Gaslights. The themes are going to recur in this story.

## 13. NECROSTRATIGRAPHY

How to audit the sources, scale and timeline of Fox's inheritance? I want to think of it like the lake that's in front of us, I say. The water used to come from the Westbourne, a tributary of the Thames that ran in a brick-lined culvert from Hampstead through Paddington to the Chelsea Embankment. Today it's pumped up into the park from bore-holes that run deep into the white chalk bedrock, into the water table perhaps forty yards under our feet. Nobody saw any change on the flat, silent surface of the Serpentine, but now below the pleats of reflected light there are small noiseless eruptions like unseen waves. When the waters enveloped the body of the suicidal lord, it was as if some intangible bore tide, a reverse passage moving upriver from the ocean into the city, had been contained, for now, to give the artificial impression of a static body of water. These hydraulics are more than metaphorical. When I look at this lake, with what I have learned, there is a sense of death, suffering and profit born of enslaved human labour that is still freighted against the current, as if it could at any moment rise up from the very geology under Hyde Park itself, an eruption of salt water into the park, the substance of the ocean and of tears. Water always finds its own level, you tell me, finds the points of ingress.

Fox was six years old when the 1833 Act was passed, setting emancipation gradually in motion twenty-six years after the Slave Trade Act of 1807 had abolished the slave trade in the British Empire. At the moment of the suicide two years earlier, the Pitt-Rivers estate already rolled together three main sources of capital, three Caribbean waves that hit the Dorset shores, hard, and ran all the way inland to Cranborne Chase. First was what the 3rd Baron Rivers inherited with the Pitt-Rivers title from his uncle. This was a vast tangle of property in Hampshire, Dorset, Gloucestershire, London and the Caribbean, which had fallen to him through heirs and dowagers, cousins and second cousins, lords and MPs.⁵⁸ Second, to this the suicidal lord had brought an inheritance from his father Sir Peter Beckford MP, who died in 1811. In 1764, Beckford had inherited 662 enslaved people from his father, along with the Hanover estate in Jamaica.⁵⁹ Married to Louisa Pitt and inheriting from her on her early death in her mid-twenties in 1791, this man, Fox's great-uncle, was a central figure in the Beckford Caribbean sugar dynasty: an absentee owner of plantations in Jamaica and other Caribbean islands, and the owner of an estate in Dorset and at least one commercial wharf on the Thames in London. Third, Horace's marriage in 1808 to the heiress Frances Hale Rigby brought another vast fortune into the estate. This had been built up since the seventeenth century over four generations of the Rigby family through Caribbean sugar and coffee plantations, slave trading and shipping operations from their manor at Mistley, a village on the Stour estuary near Harwich, where the family built quays, dockyards and warehouses for their mercantile activities. Their large portfolio of estates in Jamaica, Antigua and Grenada had been sold up by Frances' father in the early 1800s, cashing in before the abolition of the slave trade.⁶⁰ Rivers, Beckford, Rigby, pretty clear how that fortune of his was made then, you say to me.

But quite apart from the evolving Pitt-Rivers inheritance that would come to him, other sources of slavery fortunes percolated down the female lines of a series of wealthy Yorkshire families towards Fox. His paternal grandmother was Marcia Lucy Fox-Lane (née Pitt, 1756–1822), the daughter of George Pitt, 1st Baron Rivers, and his maternal grandmother was Frances Douglas (née Lascelles, 1762–1817), daughter of Edward Lascelles, 1st Earl of Harewood (1740–1820). In 1795, that man, Fox's great-grandfather, had inherited a vast portfolio of Caribbean plantations and enslaved people, established through his family's longstanding involvement in the slave trade, plantations and the East India Company.⁶¹ The earl's inheritance made him one of the richest men in Britain.⁶² Harewood House has been described as 'one of the greatest monuments to British slavery'.⁶³ In the same year, 1795, at Bramham Park, an eight-mile horse-ride east of Harewood, Fox's father William was born, and two years later Fox's mother Caroline Douglas was born at Goldsborough on the Harewood estate, granddaughter to the earl. In Oxfordshire, meanwhile, Fox's wife Alice Margaret Stanley had been born at Ditchley Park, the estate of her uncle, the 14th Viscount Dillon of Ditchley, who had large landholdings in Ireland, was a trustee of slave-holdings in Montserrat, received compensation payments from plantations on Jamaica, and was married to the granddaughter of Sir Francis Baring, the founder of Barings Bank and a director of the East India Company.[64] And on Fox's side of the family, in 1833 his uncle married a wealthy heiress who inherited significant Jamaican plantations from her father, along with a large estate on Anglesey in North Wales, near the coastline along which ships from the Caribbean came into Liverpool, and slave vessels loaded with guns and textiles departed for West Africa.[65]

Today, Goldsborough, where Fox's mother was born, is a five-star hotel that styles itself as 'the former home of Princess Mary, in landscaped grounds with unspoilt views over tranquil gardens'. I considered staying there during my research trip to Bradford and Bramham, I explain to you, but it turned out to be like £500 a night. Last time I looked, the hotel's website still opened with a video showing a Union Jack mown into the lawn, with the strapline: 'a stately home which you can visit, dine, stay and explore' [sic] as if there were strata of privilege that undergird the gardens from the turf into the loam to the sedimentary rock below.[66] Those strata clearly include the family trusts, of which little documentation survives but which were a central factor in the inherited wealth of women like Fox's grandmothers and his mother; more silences.

It would be hard to trace the detail of how many of these accumulating layers of family wealth found their way to Fox personally. You could imagine a table that set out in sequence the deaths that cut into his life course, described like the excavated features in an archaeological report. Nine horizons of death punch out the successive moments through which Fox's fortune came towards him like an express train accelerating through a series of cuttings in the landscape to the metropole. Then there was his donation of the collection to Oxford with the deed of gift signed on 20 May 1884, and, just under sixteen years later, at the start of a new century, his own death on 4 May 1900. It would look something like this, a sequence that might best be read from bottom to top:

| Date | Death | Fox's age | Details |
|---|---|---|---|
| 1900 | Death of Augustus Henry Lane Fox Pitt-Rivers | 73 | Augustus Henry Lane Fox Pitt-Rivers died on 4 May 1900. |
| 1880 | Death of Horace, the 6th Baron Rivers | 52 | Horace Pitt-Rivers, the 6th Baron Rivers since 1867, and the cousin of Fox's father, died childless aged sixty-five, on 3 March 1880 at 23 Wilton Crescent, London. After Horace's first (estranged) wife died in September 1872, in June 1873 he married for a second time to Emmeline Laura Bastard (1848–1918), but there were no children from that marriage. The Beckford male line, and thus the barony, was now extinct, and the Pitt-Rivers estate and name passed to Fox.[67] |
| 1873 | Death of Caroline, Fox's mother | 46 | Caroline Lane Fox died on 7 November 1873. She never remarried after her husband died, and at her death left around £30,000 to Fox as her only surviving son. |
| 1867 | Death of Henry, the 5th Baron Rivers | 39 | After less than a year as the 5th Baron Rivers, Henry Peter Pitt-Rivers died from 'congestion of the lungs' on 15 March 1867, a few weeks before his eighteenth birthday.[68] 'Thus has culminated in the extinction of the direct male line the overwhelming flood of sorrow and death with which the Rivers family was visited in the past year, and which excited the sympathy of the whole country,' the *Western Gazette* reported.[69] The Pitt-Rivers estate passed to Horace, the 6th Baron, former lieutenant-colonel of the Royal Horse Guards, who was thirteen years Fox's senior. Fox was now presumptive to the Rivers fortune. |

| 1866 | Death of George, the 4th Baron Rivers | 39 | George Pitt-Rivers, the 4th Baron Rivers, died on 28 April 1866, and his wife, Lady Susan, died forty-eight hours later. Three of their four sons had died of tuberculosis, and the barony passed to their final son Henry, then seventeen years old, also chronically unwell. |
|---|---|---|---|
| 1852 | Death of William, Fox's elder brother | 25 | Fox's elder brother William Edward Lane Fox died, aged thirty-four, on 13 June 1852, making Fox presumptive to his mother's inherited fortune through the Douglas and Lascelles sides of her family.[70] |
| 1832 | Death of William, Fox's father | 4 | Fox's father, William Augustus Lane Fox, cousin of the 3rd Baron Rivers, died on 11 February 1832, aged 36.[71] |
| 1831 | Death of Horace, the 3rd Baron Rivers | 3 | Horace Pitt-Rivers (William Horace Beckford) died on 23 January 1831. He was Fox's great-uncle. His eldest son George Beckford, then twenty years old, inherited and took the title of the 4th Baron Rivers.[72] |
| 1828 | Death of George, the 2nd Baron Rivers | 1 | George Pitt, the 2nd Baron Rivers, died on 20 July 1828 at 10 Grosvenor Place. On his death the Rivers estate and name passed to his nephew William Horace Beckford (son of Peter Beckford and Louisa Pitt) as the 3rd Baron Rivers, becoming known as W. Horace Pitt-Rivers.[73] |
| 1818–1822 | Death of Fox's grandparents, James, Marcia, John and Frances | 0 | All four of Fox's grandparents died before he was born, concentrating the intergenerational wealth in Fox's parents. In 1766, one of his great-grandfathers, the 14th Earl of Morton, had sold off his estates on Orkney and Shetland to a man who had made his fortune from sugar and slavery in the Caribbean.[74] |

One watershed clearly came in the penultimate layer on 3 March 1880 when the sixth lord died and, with his four uncles along with his father, mother and only sibling all dead, Fox survived to come into the Rivers fortune.[75] On 25 May 1880, he received formal permission from the Queen to assume the arms and authority to adopt the necronym of Pitt-Rivers.[76] That process began in January 1831 when Fox was three, with the umbrella on the Hyde Park grass and the handkerchief knotted under the chin of the bloated white floating corpse in the Serpentine, and with his father's death a year later. But it's clear that in every direction on his family tree, the sources of Fox's wealth had connections of one kind or another with plantation slavery and the slave trade: from the Pitts, the Beckfords, the Lascelles, the Rigbys, the Douglases, the Pennants, the Dillons, the Foxes, the names of generals, ladies and lords of the manor, enslavers. In his 1944 book *Capitalism and Slavery*, Eric Williams observed that 'there are few, if any, noble houses in England ... without a West Indian strain' – showing how through their profits such dynasties represented a newly ascendant ethnoclass of gentry, just as they had been the masters of plantation estates in the Caribbean. A new 'feudal capitalism' moving colonial profit as capital through British and Irish landscapes. No wonder they were so concerned with the past; and with preservation, as we will see later in this story.

For now, let's be clear that to draw up a balance sheet, to drill into the numbers, the wills and the trusts, and try to come up with precise sums of enrichment through enslavement, might be possible, who knows, but this economic history approach might miss the constant transformation of capital. Such transformations run from the sale of shipyards and plantations divesting themselves so as to cash in before abolition in 1807 to the investment of the 4th Baron Rivers, like so many other beneficiaries of emancipation payments, in the railways in the 1860s, in his case as chairman of the Somerset and Dorset Railway Company. Or indeed the pro-slavery lobbying such as the 4th Baron Rivers' attendance at the General Meeting of Proprietors, Merchants, Bankers, Ship Owners, Manufacturers, Traders and Others Interested in the Preservation of the West India Colonies on 5 April 1832, with Fox's great-uncle, the 2nd Earl of Harewood, in the chair.[77] There are surely other ways to read these layers of wealth and extraction. The kind of economic history practised by Eric Williams, in other words, extending into the cultural world as Stuart Hall always showed was possible, and as Christina Sharpe does in a different way today. Funny how archaeologists use that English word 'relations', a kinship terminology employed to describe siblings or cousins or parents or offspring, to put physical deposits from the ground into sequence, you once said to me. And you reminded me of the line from Saidiya Hartman: 'Slavery is the ghost in the machine of kinship', and we talked about how relations can be destroyed, denied, killed off.[78]

Like an archaeological site, we might think of family inheritance or a human life as formed of successive strata layered one on top of the other, each different in texture, composition, tone and duration, each containing different fragmented traces of events and memories. But no monument was ever formed simply by one stone being placed upon another. As every archaeologist must learn, there are layers, yes, but also cuts and fills: pits, or post-holes, or ditches, or graves. There are bricks and mortar, but also acts of underpinning, punching a window through a wall, capping off the ruin, robbing the foundations of a building for stones, and so on. Today, working in a tradition of thinking about site formation begun by Fox himself, we talk as archaeologists in particular technical terms about different relations between features as they develop over time. Some interfaces are positive, horizontal – one layer placed on top of another, or material filling a pit – but there are also always negative interfaces, vertical interfaces if you like: some kind of scission into earlier material as when a ditch or a pit or a trench is dug. And the archaeologist's pick or trowel will always be the most recent cut among many. A cut has no physical substance – it is simply a relationship, an event, a removal or redeposition. The archaeologist records the material that constitutes deposits, layers and fills: the compaction of the soil, its colour, inclusions of gravel or stones, thickness; and they also trace the form of cuts made into earlier horizons: their shape in plan, dimensions and depth, break of slope, base, orientation, and any later truncation. What kind of relation is a truncation, then? The cut is always an extraction.

The apparent solidity of horizons in this table of inheritance across Fox's life course, each marking a death and a passing-on of land and wealth, is intercut by moments that trespass laterally across the horizontal lines of the table. The inheritances from the slave trade, from plantations that used enslaved labour, and from emancipation payments, are jumbled like redeposited earth. Let me say they are intercut. And what intercuts them, what a purely economic history will never reveal, is perception. Perceptions of the past, of course, but also those future-oriented perceptions that Charles Dickens, in the novel about a boy named Pip to which Fox once referred in one of his lectures, called 'expectations'. Fox's expectations rose up through this necro-stratigraphy like the water table would rise in the London gravels after heavy storms.

This mixed metaphor might offer a lens for interpreting the matrix of Fox's inheritance as cuts made by expectation. Back in the day, Horace Beckford's expectations, half a century before 1880, of becoming the 3rd Baron Rivers, were quite clear. As one biographer observed, part of the context for Horace's spending and gambling habit in his thirties and forties must have been his 'feeling that he was going some day to inherit the title and estate of his uncle, and was led into living far beyond his means'.[79] At some point along the first seven strata, the idea that Fox might inherit the title and estate from his great-uncle, quite straightforwardly as the second son of a second son, must have gained a solidity, just as 'expectations' had done for Horace.[80] But that's not how Fox's biographers have told it. The 1880 inheritance has been consistently described as an unexpected, life-changing event that came out of the blue, suddenly thrust upon him through a complex series of wholly unpredictable and fortuitous deaths.[81] That image of unimaginable wealth appearing unanticipated, out of the blue through chance and providence has dominated his posthumous image. For example, an obituary published within days of his death recalled how Fox had visited the Dorset estate of his great-uncle in the 1850s, he had 'noticed the signs of abundant prehistoric remains' and 'the thought flitted through his mind how desirable such an estate would be to an antiquary of his tastes'. But he had dismissed the thought as impossible – only then for 'a strange series of accidents and incidents' to bring the land into his hands as 'a most happy hunting-ground for a prehistoric archaeologist'.[82] In 1977 one biography of Fox wrote of his 'slight expectations, of which he must have been very conscious in early life' but added that he was not 'living in expectation of great wealth'.[83] Four years later, another biographer described how Fox was 'suddenly, and apparently unexpectedly, the beneficiary of a major inheritance'.[84] And in 1991, the most recent biography of Fox claimed that he 'had no expectation of becoming a major landowner himself' when he was 'thrust into the possession of the Rivers estates'.[85] Like a hundred-year whispered game of Telephone or Russian Scandal, the source of this narrative, evolving into a kind of exonerative voice in which the inheritance was a total surprise, comes in how Fox talked, in what can only be described as mystical terms, about how he came to own a vast pristine archaeological landscape where he could dig into the prehistory of England. In the preface to the first volume of *Excavations on Cranborne Chase* (1887), Fox told the story his way. He connected what he saw as the somehow fated nature of his inheritance with the opportunity and resources he then had to begin a programme of excavation at a scale never seen before:

> I had an ample harvest before me, and with the particular tastes that I had cultivated, it almost seemed to me as if some unseen hand had trained me up to be the possessor of such a property, which, up to within a short time of my inheriting it, I had but little reason to expect.[86]

The biographers' language of surprise and chance is hard to square with the facts, then. After all, in 1852, when his elder brother died of malaria at the British Mission at Cava de' Tirreni near Naples, where he had been assistant to the British envoy to the Kingdom of the Two Sicilies, Fox's marriage to Alice Stanley was finally agreed to by her parents after a long period of courtship because of what they perceived as his improved prospects. Quite possibly this was due purely to the expected inheritance of a fortune from his mother, but the will of Fox's late father's uncle, the second lord, was surely also in the mix.[87] By the time that George, the fourth lord, died aged fifty-five on 28 April 1866, things were more certain. Leaving a combined estate of the Pitt-Rivers, Beckford and Rigby fortunes, George had had thirteen children, of whom four were male, but by 1866 three of the four sons had already died of chronic lung disease.[88] The seriousness of this family illness had become increasingly clear over the previous decade or two. For example, in a visit to the Rushmore estate in November 1858, Fox's father-in-law, the Lord Eddisbury, had written to his wife, with a clear sense of the likelihood of the inheritance, describing the sickness of the brothers.[89]

In March 1867, the last remaining sickly son of the fourth lord died within a year of assuming the title of the 5th Baron Rivers. Fox was thirty-nine and the cards were on the table. The childless sixth lord was the last of his male line. The 'short time' of Fox's expectations, his strong sense of the imminent extinction of the barony and the likelihood of his own inheritance, began in that month, April 1867, and ran for thirteen years up to 1880. Fox did not spend his anticipated inheritance on gambling and London clubs as Horace had done; instead, he took half-pay leave from the army as if it were an academic sabbatical, and began to collect, to excavate, to give lectures, to make public exhibitions and to write. For now, however, let me underline that the biographers' story of surprise, and Fox's claim that he had little reason to expect the fortune, misses the reality of the situation from the mid-1860s, when he returned from Ireland, took half-pay and, from around the age of forty years old, began his antiquarian and anthropological work as a major occupation. His expression about the 'unseen hand' could be read as concerned not with an unexpected nature of his inheritance as with weaving a story in which his past is a foreshadowing, and his future is destiny – a story that came in time to apply to his conceptions of 'race' and of 'culture'.

But for now we can be clear of one thing at this point. Like the tributaries that run into the Thames, the Evenlode, Kennet, Windrush, Lea and so on, before it flows out to sea, so it was with this inheritance. When Fox bought the skull-cup for five pounds and five shillings on the afternoon of Tuesday 13 May 1884, four years after he came into the Rivers fortune and took the necronym, he did so using a fortune made through slavery. With this purchase of a fragment of a dead human body, capital generated through the trade in living human bodies was shifting form across the generations.

## 14. THE KILLER STORY

If it's not going to be a biography, that book you're thinking of writing, you say as we sit here, then tell me about the narrative arc of the necrography or whatever you please to call it. The water of the Serpentine is silently reflecting the twilight. The stars behind a bank of cloud above us, uplit by the city's glow, are invisible constellations behind the skyglow. The light is scattered. Let me start with Fox's boyhood then, I reply. But then again the risk is immediately clear: what Marx described as the counter-revolutionary tactic of 'Bonapartism', or what Antonio Gramsci diagnosed as 'Caesarism', an authoritarian cult of an imagined heroic past based around a charismatic present-day figure of destiny, of which fascism is simply the most famous popular form. The charismatic, heroic figure of the archaeologist holds perhaps a special place in the cult of biographies of the great and the good, the worship of one semi-divine apical ancestor or another. How then could this part of the story be told without reinforcing all those patriarchal, colonial, militarist tropes of a pioneer, a trailblazer, a discoverer, a founding father, a figurehead? Without, in other words, falling back into the frame that Ursula Le Guin was calling the 'killer story'?

Fox's father had been a captain in the Peninsular War and when he died, a year after the suicide of his cousin, shortly before Fox's fifth birthday, a hurried move from Bramham to number 3, St James' Square in Mayfair followed.[90] It's just under a mile to the east of where we're sitting now, I tell you, along Piccadilly past Buckingham Palace and then turn to the right as if you were going to Pall Mall, or Downing Street. Fox grew up in that London townhouse, a brisk twenty-minute walk to the British Museum in one direction, a similar distance in the other to where we're sitting now. The house had been remodelled by John Soane in 1819, and today its next-door neighbours are the London headquarters of BP on one side, and the Army and Navy Club on the other. Elsewhere on the square are the East India Club and the London Library.[91]

We've all met kids like Fox: a list-maker, a scrapbooker, a modelmaker, anxious, empirical, fond of order, a collector, shy, prone to introspection, an impatient reader. Perhaps you were quite like him yourself at that age, you interject. Right. To answer your question, I want to use that as a method for forging the narrative, I mean to identify with the figure of Fox, not the man or his ghost but his image or his memory. Just as you might identify with a line of prose on the page, to the extent, like in that idea from Roland Barthes, that you can rewrite it without having to love it. Unwrite it by becoming its co-author in some sense.

In Fox's surviving notebooks, which bear the title 'Notes made from daily readings' in his adolescent hand, there are lists of the great battles of ancient, medieval and modern history, and sections documenting the history of gunpowder, different types of fortification from crusader castles onwards, 'a Condensed View of Egypt', 'a Condensed View of Rome', 'a Short History of Belgium', 'the Russian Army', the relative range of different artillery weapons, the heroes of Waterloo, the sieges of the Peninsular War, the names of the Roman gods. His military training included mathematics, both theoretical and practical – geometry, trigonometry, mechanics, fortification, engineering and surveying, the movement of ordnance through the air.[92] I try to recall some of the fragmented facts I read in these juvenilia manuscript notes on science, manhood and discovery:

> Attraction of Cohesion: the force by which the particles of bodies are held together.
>
> Balloons were first invented by Montgolfier in 1782. Pilatre de Rozier the first who ascended in one 1783.
>
> Scipio Africanus was the first man who conferred his name on a nation vanquished by him.
>
> Of all the Spanish possessions in America, Cuba is the only one remaining 1843 February.

Oh, and I remember now there was also a hand-drawn teenage diagram, a drawing of the parts of the human skull.[93]

People still talk of Fox as 'the great pioneering archaeologist'.[94] For example in the title of the 2017 pamphlet produced by the Salisbury and South Wiltshire Museum: 'General Pitt-Rivers: founding father of modern archaeology'.[95] The irony of this posthumous figure of Fox is that he mistrusted the genre so much himself. In a letter to

*The Spectator* in 1878 Fox explicitly denied the theory of the utility of 'great-man history', using the ideas of Herbert Spencer in his argument:

> That men of transcendent ability have done great things cannot be denied, but my own study of the subject in relation to the Arts leads me to infer that we are inclined to overrate rather than underrate the influence of individual men [...] As in organic nature, it is the loss of connecting links which give colour to the idea of a special fiat of creation, so in superorganic nature it is the difficulty of tracing the succession of ideas in the minds of men which supports the 'great-man theory of progress', a theory which the most ingenious of modern philosophers, Mr Herbert Spencer, has taken pains to refute.[96]

Quite apart from Marx or Gramsci then, the most famous rebuttal of such a biographical approach came in 1873 in Herbert Spencer's attack on what he called 'the great-man-theory of History'. In contrast with, to give one influential example, Thomas Carlyle's 1841 book *On Heroes, Hero-Worship and the Heroic in History*, Spencer's 1873 *Study of Sociology* called for an alternative approach grounded in 'social science', and in his 1898 *Principles of Sociology* he went further, criticising the genre of biography itself. 'If we go back to a group of savages sitting round a camp fire,' he wrote, 'we find that there is nothing to talk about but their own doings and the doings of others in war and the chase.' Such storytelling focuses naturally, Spencer continued, on:

> the victories of the courageous man, the feats of the strong man, the manoeuvres of the cunning man. Thus in the first stages, merely from lack of other exciting matter, there goes, after the narratives of individual successes in the day's hunt or the day's fight, a frequent return to the always-interesting account of the great chief's exploits, his ordinary doings, his strong sayings.[97]

This passage in Spencer must of course be the source of the account of the 'killer story' in Ursula Le Guin's (unfootnoted) 'Carrier Bag Theory of Fiction'. But Spencer was not exactly offering a critique of the inbuilt patriarchal and elitist politics of the genre. His account of this 'incipient biography' claims that it is a kind of narrative that requires 'the smallest intellectual power' and 'the lowest intelligence'. Fox used Spencer's term 'superorganic' to describe how a theory of the evolution of culture would 'lead us as far as possible from great-man worship'. In Fox's worldview, credit should not be given to those responsible for the 'last finishing stroke' of some new technical or artistic invention or other. Instead, the focus of the social scientist should be on how 'the final result has been built up in the minds of a succession of workers'. The Fox–Spencer view thus was not a critique of cultural supremacy, but a different version of such supremacy based on culture and society rather than individuals and heroes. Culture, society – and 'race', in fact. In his 1873 book, Spencer stated his case against 'great-man-theory' by questioning whether 'two European parents may produce a Negro child, or that from woolly-haired prognathous Papuans may come a fair, straight-haired infant of the Caucasian type', or whether 'a Newton might be born in a Hottentot family, that a Milton might spring up among the Andamanese, that a Howard or a Clarkson might have Fiji parents'. Rather, Spencer continued, 'biological science' shows that 'by no possibility will an Aristotle come from a father and mother with facial angles of fifty degrees', and that 'out of a tribe of cannibals, whose chorus in preparation for a feast of human flesh is a kind of rhythmical roaring, there is not the remotest chance of a Beethoven arising', since 'the genesis of the great-man depends on the long series of complex influences which has produced the race in which he appears, and the social state into which that race has slowly grown ... All of those changes of which he is the proximate initiator have their chief causes in the generations he descended from.'[98]

The critique of Great-Man history as a killer story begins, then, not with Le Guin's alternative image of the carrier bag, but with the Fox–Spencer version of cultural supremacy driven not by individuals but by certain groups with inherited stock, both biological ('organic') and cultural ('superorganic'), an army of people, a 'race'. This was an image, as Fox put it in his *Spectator* letter, of a division among humans between passive drones and active workers, in which the workers should be increased 'at the expense of the drones', albeit not too quickly, since a kite, he wrote, should never be 'without a tail'.[99] We begin here to get a sense of what Fox's idea of the unseen hand, the superorganic inheritance, the hybrid of eugenicism and nascent epigenetics, the supremacist group identity based on colonialism technological supremacism and cultural Whiteness, involved.

That ethnoclass of absentee planters, lords of the manor, generals and bankers, as it emerged from the late eighteenth century, had developed its own killer stories. Starting with blood sports. Peter Beckford, the enslaver, Dorset landowner, MP for Morpeth in Northumberland, and Fox's great-uncle on his father's side is credited with the invention of modern hunting when he published his 1781 book *Thoughts on Hunting*. It represented the first account of fox-hunting as a sport, accused at the time of promoting 'barbarity' and 'wanton abuse and torture' in the name of 'fictitious victory'.[100] Meanwhile another of Fox's great-uncles (this time on his mother's side), Henry Lascelles, the 2nd Earl of Harewood, a Tory peer, enslaver and slave trader, Lord Lieutenant of the West Riding of Yorkshire, took his love of the killer stories of blood sports to a fatal degree. He died in late November 1841 from protracted exposure to the cold when a fox had gone to ground. He sat on horseback, refusing to withdraw before witnessing the kill. 'He would always dig for a fox if he thought his hounds deserved him,' a historian of the Bramham Moor Hunt wrote, 'and under these circumstances he stayed to the end.'[101]

Hunting was not it seems one of Fox's own regular pursuits, although after he inherited the estate in Dorset he did install a statue titled *The Hunter of the Early Days*, depicting an ancient British hunter on horseback with a spear in his hand, at the Larmer Tree Pleasure Gardens that he laid out for the public on his estate.[102] Fox's blood sport of preference was shooting, although he commended flint-hunting as a field sport alongside deerstalking and pigeon-shooting: 'whilst the sportsman pushes forward to be in at the death,' he wrote, so 'the goal of the flint hunter is to be in at the birth of a fresh discovery'. I tell you about Paul Rocher's book examining the introduction of so-called 'non-lethal' weapons in France in the 2010s: tear gas, water cannon or rubber bullets as a 'softer' law enforcement but in reality inflicting irreversible injuries, hurting, mutilating, leaving scars, blinding, sometimes killing. In Fox's hands the killer story evolved in a similar way, from the kill to the chase, from the individual to the group, from the hero to the 'race', a story that was about the carrier bag, containment, the museum as well as the bullet or the arrow. And as the story evolved, so it became a narrative method for mixing up the living and the dead, the present and the past.[103]

The water is dotted with the reflected light like a vast brass rubbing of white crayon on black sugar paper. The horizon to our south is broken by the huge rectangle of the barracks of the Household Cavalry Mounted Regiment. It's where they keep the poor animals that panicked, bolted and ran across London the other week, and where they took them back to. The bloodied black and white horses in the videos were like a dream, or an omen, or some strange flash of memory from the past. When the Brutalist tower block, designed by Basil Spence, was built in 1970 (a building never reclad to appease the park-goers of the twenty-first century), it replaced the earlier Knightsbridge barracks where Fox was stationed in the 1850s and 1860s. The gates don't get locked until midnight, the sign said. We've got time for one more story then before we leave.

## 15. CULTURE AND ANARCHY

You're lighting one more cigarette as the wind picks up. We see only hints of the fence-line in the dark from where we're sitting; a line of arrow-tipped paling. It's not the original railing installed in 1831, pointing into the sky to dispel the shadow of suicide. So much ironwork was ripped out from this country's parks and gardens in the Second World War, requisitioned and removed for use in munitions factories under Regulation 50 of the Defence (General) Regulations of 1939, emergency powers that saw parts of the historic built environment melted down and turned into ammunition.[104] And then along the south-eastern line of the park there's the void still left by the Great Exhibition, 2,000 feet long, 400 feet wide, where you can download an app from a QR code and walk with your phone in front of you as if the structure is still there. To understand Hyde Park as a monumental and a military landscape you need to get your eye in to what's been moved, removed, replaced or restored; what's been weaponised. Each unmarked gap in the railings may be a small monument to anti-fascism, shot at the enemy. Or it may be a monument to an event that happened in 1866, when the railings were weaponised in a different manner.

On 23 July 1866, at the Reform Movement demonstration for male suffrage in Hyde Park, an incident that became known as the 'Hyde Park Railings Affair' took place. Called in the wake of the recent defeat of the Reform Bill, the protest was banned by the new Conservative government under Disraeli, which had been in power for less than a month. The Reform League questioned whether this ban was legal, but at 5 p.m. on the 23rd, under direct instructions from the home secretary, the gates and perimeter of the park were closed and policemen and soldiers on horseback were posted on guard. The protestors sought to claim their right to protest in a public space, and a sustained clash ensued.[105] The force employed in attempting to prevent the crowds entering Hyde Park was interpreted as an act of wanton provocation, encouraged by those around Walpole who were fervent supporters of martial law and heavy-handed restraint.[106] When the mounted police charged to break up groups, using their truncheons freely and briskly, stones and brickbats hailed down on them. Branches were torn from trees and rubble collected and improvised as weapons and missiles.

Fox, recently returned from service in Ireland, his expectations rising by the day, was on duty that night. As junior acting major of the 2nd Battalion of the Grenadier Guards, stationed at Buckingham Palace, he was in command of the detachment of Foot Guards sent in to keep order.[107] Fox and his men took up position at the gate at Hyde Park Corner, the gate we walked in through earlier as we left the Waterloo Arch behind us. Fixing their bayonets, the soldiers were there to defend the fence-line and the monuments.[108] Some reports suggested that 200,000 people broke into the park that day; perhaps it was half that number, but it was a big crowd nonetheless.[109] 'Irritated and outnumbered', as *The Spectator* put it, the guards were derided by the protestors as 'butchers' because of how they brandished their weapons when trying to break up the crowd. As the crowds breached the park's fences *en masse* from all sides, an occupation in protest at the closure of the space for public protest, railings were broken off and transformed into weapons in the mêlée. Flowerbeds were trampled underfoot, the press later reported. But the lasting image was of the soldiers who stood solemnly guarding the prostrate iron rails and stones, rather than going on the attack.[110]

Under Fox's command, the guards were still futilely defending the gate and the monuments despite the fence being breached around them across much of the eastern and northern boundaries of the park. Crowds gathered where gas-pipes, broken off when the fence was pulled down, were now aflame around the edge of the park, and it was in that strange blue flickering light that the guards finally marched back to the barracks at midnight, to mocking howls. Yard after yard of palisading had been dismantled, so not a piece was left standing along Park Lane from Marble Arch to the gate near Apsley House, an extent of about half a mile in length. Tens of thousands of workers thronged the park over the next two days, and tensions were only dissipated on the 25th when an agreement between the League and the Home Office led to troops and police being stood down.

As workmen started to replace the fencing and the gardeners began to put the shrubbery back in order, Victorian society took stock of what this incident meant. The newspapers reported the affair as 'the insurrection of the manhood of the metropolis against what was believed to be police-made law, military terrorism, and governmental repression of the French type'.[111] Karl Marx imagined that if the crowd had fought more actively with the railings, and if, say, policemen had been killed, then the military would have had to step in instead of merely standing there with guns cocked and swords drawn.[112] The political outcome was the Second Reform Act of 1867, which brought enfranchisement to sections of the urban male working class the very next year, effectively doubling the number of people who were able to vote in British elections though still excluding women. 'It is scarcely too much to say that the fall of the Park railings did for England in July 1866 what the fall of the Bastille did for France in July 1789,' suggested the critic John Dover Wilson in 1932.[113]

The following May, 1867, Matthew Arnold took the Hyde Park riot as his theme in his final lecture as Oxford's professor of poetry, under the title 'Culture and its Enemies'. 'We in Oxford,' he wrote, 'brought up amidst beauty and sweetness', understand the importance of these qualities. It is culture, he argued, that stands as a sentiment against the 'hideousness and rawness' of machinery and hatred, grounded in 'a passion for sweetness and light,' but above that, a desire to create 'the perfect man'.[114]

Arnold published this lecture two years later in 1869 in his book *Culture and Anarchy*. He offered the Hyde Park Railings Affair as a prime example of the fragility of societal norms of law and order, and the constant risk of their breakdown if individual freedom were placed above the supposed good of civic society. He took a hard-line view. The working class displayed a precocious readiness 'to take upon them all the functions of government'. But why had the militia, policemen and soldiers allowed them to run riot? For fear of a bigger riot, or fear of their rifles being taken from them and used against them? Arnold contrasted his belief in culture as 'the best that has been thought and known', with what he caricatured variously as the barbarian, philistine and Jacobin-like idea of 'the Englishman's right to do what he likes': 'his right to march where he likes, meet where he likes, enter where he likes, hoot as he likes, threaten as he likes, smash as he likes. All this, I say, tends to anarchy.'[115]

Alfred Kroeber, in his overview of ideas of culture published in 1952 with Clyde Kluckhohn, described Arnold's book as giving the word culture 'an ultra-humanistic sharpening'.[116] But rereading it today, Arnold's instrumental, Hobbesian image of culture as preventing a descent into chaos and a breakdown of law and order verged on moral panic. In this origin myth of 'barbarism' there was also a kind of totemism, in that violence was imagined to lie in a state of nature. As Raymond Williams showed in his book *Culture and Society*, Stuart Hall once argued, Matthew Arnold was hiding 'partisanship ... behind the invocation to a fixed set of standards nominated as Culture with a capital C'.[117] Culture in these terms was a canon to be defended from commerce, industry and wealth (what he glossed as the 'mechanical' dimensions of modern civilisation), and from populism. Why had the authorities not dared to defend against disorder and damage to property even if it had to be 'at the cost of bloodshed'? Arnold asked. Why not deal with the mob with force?[118] Sitting on his horse at Hyde Park Corner, Fox was looking up from inside his helmet at the outsized bronze statue of the Duke of Wellington sitting on his bronze horse, and trying to count how many melted-down cannon made up its mass. As he listened to the shouts and breaking glass around him, he was formulating his own answer to the same question.

Fox also wrote a lecture in the aftermath of the Hyde Park riot, and he delivered it in London on 28 June 1867, one month after Arnold's in Oxford. It was the first of his three annual lectures on 'Primitive Warfare' delivered under this title in the Junes of 1867, 1868 and 1869 at the Royal United Service Institution. Fox's lecture sought to naturalise a particular cultural worldview just as Arnold's did. But here the rhetoric drew from and reshaped Charles Darwin's account of 'modification through natural selection' in *On the Origin of Species*, which had been published eight years previously. Darwin had evoked an image of how 'savage races of man', surviving in marginal parts of the world, 'serve as a record of the former inhabitants'.[119] Fox expanded this account by detailing three instincts that he claimed are shared among the 'higher animals' for survival: 'alimentiveness' for the sustenance of life, 'amativeness' for the propagation of the species, and 'combativeness' for the protection of the species. Fox gave combat a special place above food and sex in his account, since it represented, he claimed, not just an instinct for 'the protection of the species', but also the means through which the natural selection of 'the most energetic breeds' is propagated.[120]

Just as the club and the sword and the gun and the prehistoric stone axe could be understood as prosthetics for the hand raised in anger, so a theory of design in all aspects of human innovation could be found in warfare. There was always the risk of 'halts and relapses', but 'the march of the human intellect has been always onward', Fox continued:

> Civilisation appears always to have been confined to particular races, whose function it has been by means of war and conquest, to spread the arts among surrounding nations, or to exterminate those whose low state of mental culture rendered them incapable of receiving it.[121]

Imagine the 'primitive' societies with which the British Army fought as children, he argued. Or even as animals, in early stages of development. Understood as a struggle against 'primitive warfare', colonial conflict should be seen as akin to a conflict with subhuman beasts. In this evolutionary rhetoric, Fox suggested that the weapons of the prehistoric past were equivalent to those used against colonial officers in imperial wars, and assembled and displayed in museums. They evolved like prosthetics from the body parts of animals like claws or teeth. So, for example, Fox suggested that the development of edged weapons involved a prehistory of successive gradual rudimentary imitations of the function of human or animal incisors, or the long-pointed bill of the swordfish, or the sharp, grasping, raptorial forelegs of the praying mantis. Piercing weapons were invented, Fox theorised, through millennia of improvisations by weapon-makers learned from the action of the spiked horn of an antelope or the elongated ivory canines of the walrus, or the single massive tusk of the narwhal, or the beak of a bird. With the same logic, he suggested that arrows borrow their form from the sting of a bee. The club extends the logic of a tiger that strikes out with its paw, or a swan or eagle with its wing, or the kick of a horse's hoof. Long before the hammer or the grinder, missiles find their origin in a nut hurled by a chimpanzee against a rock to crack it open. Body armour copies the hides of mammals and the scales of the pangolin and the armadillo, sometimes even using these very materials taken from the cadaver of a beast slain in the hunt. The shield held in the African or Indigenous warrior's hand who faced the British soldier on the battlefield recalls the shell of the mollusc or the turtle.[122] And even the idea of hafting an axe began by observing and utilising the natural phenomenon of roots growing around stones.

These just-so stories still draw the reader in. Imperial war presented as part of the state of nature, a necessary conflict between the 'primitive' and the civilised. In the context of the unfolding of British colonial war at a new geographical scale and a new intensity of violence – from the Second Ashanti War of 1863–64 to the Duar War against Bhutan in 1864–65 and the Tauranga campaign against Māori people in 1864, and anticipating the punitive expedition against Abyssinia launched in December 1867 – it invoked the teleological to make the imperial violence of the present appear necessary, somehow timeless and inevitable at the same time, a fixed eternal verity. Indeed, warfare represented the invisible driver for culture, Fox argued: tools evolving from weapons, clothing from armour, shelter from shields, advanced machines from the first defences, one 'race' replacing another, in a struggle for survival that, far from having taken place untold millennia ago, was still happening and indeed reaching its apex in the colonial-militarist present, the dénouement of a process of extinction the invisible motor of which was the subject matter of anthropology, archaeology, the collections of a museum of culture. And just as 'man' in his supposedly 'primitive' state might 'receive instruction from the beasts' in the making of weapons, so, Fox claimed, in a proto-anthropological argument that recalled Alexander Pope's famous suggestion that 'the proper study of mankind is man', Victorian society might receive instruction from warfare in understanding culture. The central lesson of this, he concluded, would be 'the law which consigns to destruction all savage races when brought into contact with a civilisation much higher than their own, now operating with unrelenting fury in every part of the world' as the 'uncivilised' fall 'like wheat before the sickle'.[123]

So why not deal with the mob with force? It's a minute or two before we rouse ourselves from this thought. You zip up your coat, and as we walk out of the royal park, we pass the fence-line and monuments that Fox defended, and come out into the bright lights and late-night traffic of Hyde Park Corner. The thing is, I suggest, that in Fox's account, offensive actions like striking out or firing missiles represent only one of three types of weapons common to animals and 'savages'. Other types of weapons are 'defensive' (hides, scales, solid and jointed plates) and 'stratagems' (concealment, tactics, war cries, columns, artificial defences). The strategy of defending the statues and monuments, therefore, was still a deployment of force, and a tactical one where the guards were outnumbered by a crowd counter-evolving the fence-lines into iron spears.

But a second rationale was in play as well. As weapons of defence, the monuments were like the museums and the sciences of antiquity and ethnology, which, combined with physiology and geology, Fox argued, were 'destined to throw a flood of light' on the question of the evolution of 'mankind'. All depended, in his view, on an image of racial destiny. An image that was very close to how both the abortive 1866 Reform Bill and the successful Conservative government's Reform Act of 1867 defined and rewarded 'respectable' working men and artisans, and excluded the categories of unskilled men, the criminal poor, and, of course, women.[124] And one thing about a royal park, or a museum or indeed a lecture room, is that they could operate as border controls for such social categories.

It's worth repeating, the fact that on 13 May 1884 when Fox bought this skull-cup at Sotheby's for five pounds and five shillings he did so with an inherited fortune made largely from slavery. The enduring violence of slavery, Marlene NourbeSe Philip writes, reflecting on her poem about the massacre of 130 enslaved people on the Liverpool ship *Zong*, revolved around an ideology of non-being – as if humans could be 'without a history, name, or culture': 'in life but without life; without life in life; with a story that cannot but must be told'.[125] Through what it has destroyed and erased and 'broken by history' – the name of the person, their life, their identity – the violence reshapes any potential for how the history can be told, she shows, in that to mutilate or fragment the text might mirror the fragmentation and mutilation that slavery perpetrated, and thus reveal it. Understood in the context of the crisis for the idea of Whiteness after emancipation, Colonel Fox's first 'Primitive Warfare' lecture was not a bullet shot into an occupying crowd but a gun salute fired upwards, into the void, marking a new front in an ongoing war, a war about culture, about how to differentiate subjects, a different kind of race war, one that was about the past as well as the present, that tried to use the past to justify the present. About theories of origins and destiny, and that 'unseen hand' that might play between the two. Above all it was a war that was waged not only in the lecture rooms of London and Oxford, but also in the growing colonial violence of the British Empire. A culture war. An ongoing war. A war about who counts as human.

# IV

# No Humans Involved

*fall*, noun. iv) the cadence with which words or melodies conclude. See also (wrestling) a throw which keeps an opponent on the ground for a specified period

That small silent silver disc that was at some point used to replace the shilling that bore the head of Victoria stares up blankly from the centre of the cavity. Perhaps it was Fox who took the Queen's head out after he bought it; perhaps it was his Grandson. What's certain is that eleven years after the Sotheby's sale, when the skull-cup was put on public display in a special exhibition between 2 and 9 September 1895 at the Larmer Tree Pleasure Gardens, which Fox had created on his private estate, the catalogue entry didn't mention the coin. The skull-cup was simply listed between entry number 242 ('pewter flagon, dated 1727') and 244 ('skull of Flathead Indian from Marmaduke Island, artificially compressed'):

> 243. Cup constructed out of a Human Skull, with inscription in Greek; 'Drink ere you take on this dust.' Exhibited by General Pitt-Rivers.[1]

The fixing of an image of Victoria's head inside the cavity of a skull was one thing. But its removal must have transformed the character of the act of toasting, of passing the drink around the table in the direction dictated by tradition and etiquette. Another kind of sovereignty was being celebrated. Something less, you know, Westphalian, I said to you; I mean less subject to territorial borders, less bound to one particular nation state or another. I want to understand what were they toasting then, you ask me, if it was no longer the Queen? And you tell me about something the Caribbean novelist Merle Hodge once wrote about making sure that 'you can recognise a military invasion when you see one'. There are techniques, she said, of trying to negate a world by offering someone else's world in its place. And one of the main weapons of such subjugation, such claims to sovereignty, she continued, is fiction – because fiction 'gives substance to reality', even when it takes the ambiguous form of culture. And yet it might be possible to use the ability of fiction to 'recreate reality' against itself, to resist the fake realisms.[2]

In this case the stories are told lightly, suggestively, with a practised ambiguity, a learned noncommittalness; it was the oddly abstract, deterritorialised quality to the dehumanisation, the desecration, which means that somehow, impossibly, it can come to be tolerated. A dinner ritual in which everyone is participating but nobody is sure who sets the rules. And through that lowering of levels of toleration, keeping quiet and looking the other way, an implication in this blank violence, this debased sovereignty, collective and individual, begins to grow. At that point the shutters come down. Nobody will say anything. The cultural-supremacist myths have hardened into militarist realism. Don't even ask the question, nobody says, because nobody has to. Don't make things worse. Don't attack the institution, the culture of silence.

There's no doubt that Fox thought of the skull-cup as a weapon of some kind. As we have seen, the man from whom he bought it was a barrister, known to his friends, the obituary in *The Times* recorded, as 'the Armourer', owner of a large private collection of 'swords and weapons of war and of the chase and armour'.[3] The relics that passed through his hands involved a range of different forms of attack, defence and torture. In 1879 he donated a backplate with a bullet-hole in it to the Royal United Service Institution Museum, reputedly worn by the French General Pierre Dupont de l'Étang when he was shot and injured at the Battle of Bailén, surrendered to the Spanish, and was later court-martialled and stripped of rank and title.[4] This trophy of the armour of a disgraced enemy officer was a kind of inversion of the triumphant statues that were increasingly lining the London streets outside. And in the 1856 edition of *Archaeological Journal* he published a drawing and description of an iron head-piece in the collection of Ludlow Museum, which took the form of an instrument of torture used to crush the forehead and 'to keep the head steady during the infliction of branding'.[5] His donations to the Royal College of Surgeons include a 'cattle whip' from the Caribbean.[6] The more I read about the collections of the Armourer, the more it's clear that he wasn't just collecting weapons, but mainly items related to humiliation, shaming, torture and, above all, punishment.

I start to read up on some of the history of exhibiting the criminal body at Tyburn (where Marble Arch is now) and at Temple Bar (close to the Armourer's office). As the archaeologist Sarah Tarlow has traced, the Anatomy Act of 1832 shifted these display regimes, made them evolve.[7] The anthropologist Simon Harrison has observed that two new institutions – the anatomical and ethnological museum, and the personal cabinet of the military officer – quickly replaced Temple Bar as a site for 'the exemplary display of body parts of enemies of the state'.[8] And when I think of the Royal College of Surgeons at Lincoln's Inn Fields, which still stands in that part of London sandwiched between Somerset House, the legal chambers of Temple and the Bank of England, I think of how it has already recurred in this story. Fox's mother-in-law saying she wanted to donate her head to that museum, Fox's fellow archaeologist Flinders Petrie actually doing so, General Kitchener writing about donating the skull of the Mahdi he dug up there too, or else having it made into a drinking cup. And how Fox himself fantasised about his corpse being handled by 'a competent anatomist' and his bones preserved for posterity.

And then there's the combination of human bone and silver. When I was a student, one of my tutors for the archaeology of later prehistoric Europe once suggested in a tutorial that there's a longstanding connection between silver, slavery and ships: what he called a 'package' of metal, bodies and maritime movements that ran across these three Ss, a kind of nexus of portability and substances of transformation. It's seen, he said, in the Iron Age Mediterranean and then re-emerges, in a transmuted form, in the early modern Atlantic. I don't know about that, but who knows what capital was transformed into the many donations of apparently innocuous silver plate to Oxbridge colleges from alumni who forged careers in slave trading, sugar-planting or colonial warfare? You point me towards an auction record at Sotheby's: an ornate silver ewer that was in 1841 the gift of the West India Committee of Absentee Slave Owners and West India Merchants to the Slave Compensation commissioners, to thank them for their service.[9] There's something about that technology of the transformation of substance, of capital, of bodies living and dead in play here maybe. Transformations that are there somehow in the idea of turning a dead skull into a container, which seems to write the killer story onto the containment of the carrier bag to keep the violence going.

The risk of reinscribing the violence, the dehumanisation and the desecration which is still unfinished, is real. But so too is the hope that the claims about humanity and nonhumanity and cultural sovereignty that were in play here, the question about who gets named and who get de-named, can be overturned, like that line in a poem by Aimé Césaire: 'my very worn face on a coin suddenly rediscovered in your excavations'.[10]

Like Fox, the Armourer was a regular attendee of the London meetings of the Archaeological Institute from the early 1850s. By 1881, Fox was living at 4 Grosvenor Gardens, the house in Belgravia where we began that park walk last night, a minute's walk from his neighbour the Armourer at 3 Eaton Place.[11] The man with the skull-cup on his dining table was nine years Fox's senior. It's hard to believe that Fox didn't know of this object before he bought it at the auction after the Armourer's death, easy in fact to imagine him joining in its use and abuse over dinner or drinks at his neighbour's house.

The origin of the skull prior to 1838, before that missing coin was added and the silver was marked with those stamps, is unclear, that much is sure. A comparative, cross-cultural history of the practice of turning calvarias into drinking vessels would certainly be possible. In fact, the Pitt Rivers Museum curator once wrote such a history, of sorts, in 1897. He'd doubtless had dinner at Fox's place sometime after 1884. The curator gave his paper a long title. It read: 'Life History of an Aghori Fakir; with Exhibition of the Human Skull Used by Him as a Drinking Vessel, and Notes on the Similar Use of Skulls by Other Races.'[12] It opened by explaining the curator's most recent curatorial accession from 'Rajputana' (which is today Rajasthan):

> BEING anxious to obtain for the Pitt Rivers Museum a specimen of the human calvaria used as a drinking vessel by Aghori Fakirs in India, I wrote to Surgeon Captain H. E. Drake Brockman IMS asking him to try and obtain one for me. This he not only succeeded in doing, having obtained the specimen which I am exhibiting, but he also very kindly obtained all the information which he could.[13]

The anxiety concerned expanding Oxford's collection of skulls that had been used to venerate the ancestors in certain Buddhist, Hindu and Indigenous Australian sacred contexts, and to use them to tell a different story. Such objects were periodically collected by antiquarians and accessioned into museums during the second half of the nineteenth century. For example, here in Oxford among the collection that Fox donated in 1884, there was one of two such modified skulls, from South Australia, that he exhibited at a meeting of the Ethnological Society of London on 11 January 1870.[14] On the museum database it is catalogued alongside comparable examples from Tibet, India, Australia and China in the museum collections today.[15] In 1890, the curator purchased a copper-lined calvaria for the expanding collections of the museum Fox had given to the university. It was recorded as having been originally mounted in gold and set with diamonds since removed, stolen by the 19th Lancers from a Lama temple during the East India Company's looting of the Beijing Summer Palace in 1860. It had been exhibited in the Chinese Court at the London International Exhibition of 1862, and back then newspaper reports described it as either the head of Confucius, or perhaps the head of an enemy presented to the Emperor like John the Baptist's head was served to Herodius on a platter – although a commentator in 1864 stated that it was more probably 'a sacred relic' of a Buddhist priest.[16]

A further example had been donated to the Oxford University Museum in 1862, two years after it was founded, and ownership was transferred to the growing anthropology collections in the 1880s. This skull-cup had been looted by a British army officer during the Second Opium War from a temple within the precincts of what was described as 'a great Lama Monastery at Peking'.[17] The letter that accompanied the donation described it as an example of how Buddhist priests, so the looter imagined in a moment of intense colonial-militarist projection, 'drink confusion to their enemies'.[18] You could try to write that comparative history by pointing out that from Herodotus' *Histories* to Strabo's *Geographica* we have stories of the Scythians killing their enemies and making their skulls into drinking cups. Colonialism is surely, after all, as old as the Bronze Age, they say. Slavery as old as the Romans, at least. There are archaeologists and classicists out there who have devoted whole books to proving there's nothing new under the sun. But that was, after all, always part of the self-justification of the abuses, horrors and killings of imperialism. That everybody does it. There was something new under the sun in Victorian Britain: that emerging fiction, the fact-warping impulse that I'm calling militarist realism, and the 'compensation' payments that bankrolled it. To start to get to grips with this aesthetic you could borrow another line from J. G. Ballard: 'Freud's classic distinction between the latent and manifest content of the dream, between the apparent and the real, now needs to be applied to the external world of so-called reality.'[19]

The thing is, reading the curator's survey today, it's clear that in any possible account of such objects, we are forced to begin with the brutal layer of their death-histories, their necrographies, which witnessed an attempt to overwrite any sacred or ritual context of such items in the veneration of ancestors with an image that implied barbarity, or cannibalism, or savagery. In July 1897, the same year as he wrote this paper, the Museums Association held their annual meeting in Oxford. In his comments to the conference, the curator reflected that 'the day of the "curiosity shop"' may be over in museums', but: 'He himself did not share in the prejudice against sensational or even gruesome exhibitions; he believed that they did good by arresting the attention of casual visitors.'[20]

True to his curatorial word, five years later, two years after Fox's death, with this para-Byronic passion for melodrama and shock, this Penny-Dreadful freeness with the exhibitions of violence and body horror, the curator installed that case to which he gave the name 'The Treatment of Dead Enemies'. Across the generation after Fox, a certain part of the genre of the anthropological vision was growing, as sacred objects looted from shrines as spoils of war in the 1860s were presented as the heads of slain enemies, rather than the venerated sacred remains of ancestors used in religious observance. It was a militarist vision of anthropology that sought to fill the gap left by the failing 'racial' sciences with a kind of cultural phrenology, a measuring-out of an image of the cannibal head-hunter in the closing years of the nineteenth century; one that chimed with John Ruskin's view of the degenerate character of what he called 'the arts of savage races' which evidenced, he argued in his Oxford lectures of 1870, how 'the animal energy of such races necessarily flames into ghastly conditions of evil, and the grotesque or frightful forms assumed by their art are precisely indicative of their distorted moral nature'.[21]

But let me suggest that the Worcester College skull-cup, with its date-stamp of 1838, comes from a rather different, earlier layer in this history of horror. Before sacred, venerated skull-cups were being looted in the name of ethnology, there was a primary layer of the creation of skull-cups from the dead bodies of enemies.

To have a skull specially adapted for use as a vessel for drinking would not have been without parallel in early nineteenth-century Britain. It was an idea familiar from antiquarian writers, including Thomas Browne's observation of the humiliation of the dead enemy: 'to be knaved out of the ground, to have our skulls made drinking bowls, and our bones turned into pipes to delight and sport our enemies, are tragical abominations'.[22]

From the 1820s, there were reports of African leaders undertaking such acts, most famously in the story about the conversion of the skull of the British governor's skull into a drinking vessel for the Asante king (Asantehene) Osei Bonsu in the First Ashanti War of 1824. Officers of the Royal Navy were returning with their Russian Scandal chains of fact and myth. As Simon Harrison has observed, there is no evidence of British soldiers in Africa 'souveniring' skulls at any significant scale before the 1820s.[23] These stories gradually came to be deployed as justifications for what Harrison has called 'out-savaging the savages'. They reached back to longstanding traditions of retaining trophies from hunting.[24] And they reached forward to horror stories of trophy-hunting from the American Civil war, like those of Confederate soldiers using fence-railings to extract the corpses of Union soldiers from their graves in the aftermath of the First Battle of Bull Run (1861) to make finger rings from long bones and drinking cups from the tops of the skulls, (one such item even being displayed at the Metropolitan Fair in New York in April 1864). A century later the practice re-emerged in Vietnam in 1968 as an air cavalry troop initiation ritual for female cadets involving 'beer and dinner leftovers' imbibed from a skull cap vessel made from the sawn-up head of a Viet Cong casualty.[25] These stories today evoke the body horror of lynching souvenirs, where White supremacists would pose for photographs with the tortured corpse, keeping lengths of the lynch rope and even body parts as mementoes. We butt up against another history of museums and cultures of display here. Back in Britain – alongside that story about the Mahdi's head being sent to Victoria – there are stories of a later governor-general of Sudan, a man known by his nom de guerre 'Wingate of the Sudan', drinking champagne from the Khalifa's skull on the anniversary of the Battle of Omdurman as a supposed revenge for the death of Gordon. I read somewhere that the contemporary outcry over the treatment of the Mahdi's remains meant that his skull was buried by the British consul-general to Cairo at Wādī Ḥalfā in Sudan. And I read a story about a captain of the *Schutztruppe* in German East Africa, who took the head of the Hehe tribal leader Chief Mkwawa who had killed himself when cornered in 1898, boiled it to remove the flesh, and kept it as a 'family trophy' before donating it to a German museum, retaining one of the teeth set in a gold necklace.[26] It makes me think not so much of the Royal Navy and Jolly Roger, you tell me after I said all this, as of some extremist Totenkopf badge that proclaims 'loyalty to death', or to the symbol of Marvel Comics' brutal Vietnam-veteran character 'the Punisher' that's appeared in recent years on police cars and uniforms as part of the so-called Blue Lives Matter movement.

Sometimes the violence is the story being told. The storyteller after all, counterintuitively, as Merle Hodge writes, holds out a vision that's somehow more coherent than our experience of the world – 'more readable'.[27] The skull-cup is still here on the desk. I turn it upside down. It's suddenly much clearer: this is the top of somebody's head.

There's another precedent. In form, someone tells me, the silverwork bears similarities to a vessel with a silver rim but no wooden or metal stand that sold in 2017 at Charterhouse Auctioneers and Valuers in Sherborne, Dorset. The sale room is just twenty-five miles from the estate Pitt-Rivers inherited at Rushmore. I have no idea who bought it, but here it is on the webpage, with the words etched into metalwork that reads:

SKULL DRINKING CUP USED BY LORD BYRON AT NEWSTEAD ABBEY.[28]

That cup was made, according to some accounts, from the skull of a nameless monk found by the gardener while digging on the poet's ancestral estate at Newstead Abbey in Nottinghamshire, a former Augustinian priory, and was seized upon by Byron as 'of large dimensions and peculiar whiteness'. Press stories in 1816 described how Byron oversaw a Bacchanalian group called The Golgothans, or The Charnel Club, whose 'sepulchral banquets' would involve the use of a human skull as a drinking cup 'lined with silver with elaborate ingenuity' and 'mounted on a human thigh bone ... in imitation of the tyrannic vengeance of husbands over adulteresses, related in some old romantic tales'.[29]

According to other accounts, it was the skull of a former mistress defiled in an act by a man whose Gothic sensibilities made him akin to 'a sort of vampire'.[30] The transformation of the skull was performed by a silversmith in Nottingham, and it was filled with burgundy or claret after dinners, passed around.[31] When Byron sold Newstead Abbey to a captain of the 2nd West India Regiment in 1818, the skull-cup passed with it. The captain, who curated it alongside other 'Byron relics', presumably continued to use the cup when hosting visitors for dinners in the Grand Saloon, with its paintings of hunting scenes, portraits of royalty, weapons and a series of cuirasses supposedly 'taken from the fallen dead on the plains of Waterloo' hung on the walls. The cup was kept in a special gilt cabinet inlaid with tortoiseshell and silver.[32] The inside of the skull, one visitor noted in 1827, 'is darkly imbued with the juice of the grape'.[33] A report from the June 1860 meeting of the Leicestershire Architectural and Archaeological Society at the Town Hall reported that at Newstead 'the skull-cup is exhibited' and 'the courteous housekeeper still produces it, with its silver rim and engraved pedestal, as the choicest gem of the mansion'.[34]

The purchase of the abbey was made with profits from a vast

Jamaican plantation that Thomas Wildman and his cousin James Beckford Wildman had received as a gift from, or swindled out of, depending on which account you're reading, William Beckford of Fonthill. The dots are important to join here: this William Beckford, author of the gothic novel *Vathek*, was the cousin of Fox's great-uncle Peter Beckford – and the lover of his wife, Fox's great-aunt Louisa Pitt, daughter of the 1st Lord Rivers (and so potentially Fox's biological great-uncle).[35]

This the sawn-off human skull with its inscribed silver rim inspired Byron's 1808 poem 'Lines Inscribed Upon a Cup Formed from a Skull':

> I lived, I loved, I quaff'd, like thee:
> I died: let earth my bones resign;
> Fill up – thou canst not injure me;
> The worm hath fouler lips than thine.
>
> Quaff while thou canst – another race,
> When thou and thine like me are sped,
> May rescue thee from earth's embrace,
> And rhyme and revel with the dead.

The tone of these lines of verse certainly fits with Pitt-Rivers' chosen translation of the Greek text: 'Drink, ere you take on this dust.' Given the captain's family links to the legal profession, to the army, to the Beckfords and to Caribbean fortunes, it's not impossible that when the Byron skull-cup entered their milieu it became a prototype for this skull-cup, an idea and a set of practices transformed from the Byronic into the emerging ethnoclass of British enslavers and compensation recipients. This phase of the Gothic Revival mutated towards something not unlike Rilke's unsettling, uncanny treatment of that other skull, to somewhere between an appreciation of ruins, of stone mullions, finials and hood moulds, and an appreciation of terror and the sublime. It's a necro-aesthetic seen in brick-built museums, railway stations and Neo-Gothic townhouses, crenellations, domes, Frankenstein towers, laboratories and cabinets – an aesthetic like the style of metropolitan cemeteries but more cathedral-like, like Salisbury Cathedral but more college-like, like St Pancras or Brighton railway stations, I mean, like Manchester Town Hall or the Manchester Museum. The Gothic of *Wuthering Heights* crossed with the violence in *Jane Eyre*, of how the glass and iron of the Crystal Palace was combined with limestone pillars and lead windows in Oxford's Museum of Natural History. The architectural aesthetic of the Pitt Rivers Museum too. A style already containing its own ruination.[36] This Gothic aesthetic that John Ruskin embraced above the Classical for Oxford's museum is one which surely stands in some relationship to what he said in his inaugural lecture for the Slade Lectureship at Oxford in 1870, that statement of a new form of settler colonialism which moved from telling his audience that 'we are still undegenerate in race; a race mingled of the best northern blood', to arguing that that unless England is to 'perish', the nation 'must found colonies as fast and as far as she is able, formed of her most energetic and worthiest men; – seizing every piece of fruitful waste ground she can set her foot on'.[37]

Far from Byron's Newstead Abbey, on the other side of the world, one more fold in the story of the skull-cup was being made. It's a fold that perhaps represents the first shot above the parapet in what I'm calling this cultural phrenology: the use of the skulls of the deceased to dehumanise. It wasn't mentioned by the curator in his survey, but it's one of the earliest examples of a skull-cup being recorded by a European. In fact it's the earliest illustration of such an object that I have managed to find. It comes from a book called *Journals of Expeditions of Discovery*, published in 1845. The illustration is included in a plate that bears the title 'Native Implements'. It shows a skull with the jaws removed, and a caption that reads: 'Drinking cup, being the scull [sic] of a native with the sutures closed with wax or gum.'[38]

The text describes the treatment of the dead among Aboriginal people at Encounter Bay, at the mouth of the Murray River in South Australia, a place that is today sixty-two miles from Adelaide, on the traditional land of Ngarrindjeri people. The body is placed in a tree for excarnation. A fire is lit underneath during an initial period of mourning, until the flesh is gone. The skull is then 'taken by the nearest relative for a drinking cup'.[39]

And then as I'm typing out the footnote, I look up the author of this explorer-ethnologist who drew that skull-cup in Australia and realise who he was, who he became. The last thing we need is the inscription of yet another name of yet another dead White man, you tell me. So let's not give this chapter of the story his name. Call him the future governor if you like. This part of the story is an excavation that digs into the foundations of contemporary White supremacist ideologies; a prehistory of the idea of NHI: No Humans Involved.

## 16. THE MORANT BAY RACE MASSACRE

One thing about White supremacist violence, you say, is that it just sits there waiting for a pretext, to make reprisals that are always out of all proportion to the initial incident. The violence is a timeline, it's always present, even if just as a threat, or as a memory, or as fear, or as silence. And then when the violence breaks cover, it's described as an isolated incident, a necessary response, and becomes attached to individuals. It's the original 'bad apple' strategy, the #NotAllMen response. In the museums it sometimes takes the form of that line 'it's not all looted'. It's the hero narrative transformed into a villain story, as if the violence has to be contained, the story contained, so as to keep the wider implications, the structural violence, out of sight. The killer story flips into the containment narrative, that carrier bag theory again.

The violence in question, the massacre that followed a rebellion, was a campaign of terror undertaken in the name of British colonialism that I definitely wasn't taught about at school. It happened in Jamaica in October 1865, more than three decades after the Slavery Abolition Act 1833 had been passed and those 'compensation' payments had been triggered. Towards the centre of the violence stood the figure of the fifty-year-old governor, a careerist militarist-bureaucrat who held positions of increasing power across the British Empire in the mid-nineteenth century. Born in 1815, a curate's son, a grammar-school boy in South Yorkshire and Lincolnshire, with interests in fishing, climbing and shooting above books and learning, the Bildungsroman of his masculine endeavour and bravery was set down in the pages of the *British Army and Navy Review* for 1866.

His 'time-honoured' and 'ancient' English family history shows, it claimed, the governor came from 'a brave, energetic, determined race of men'. He took the boat to South Australia aged seventeen with £200 in his pocket 'to seek his fortune in a new world', we read.[40] He received the gold medal of the Royal Geographical Society after making an expedition from New South Wales to South Australia, etc, etc. That kind of thing. The man has managed to stay at the centre of the story ever since.[41] But this can't be a question of one man's biography. It's about the history of the idea of 'man' itself. About freedom, and equality, and how you define 'humanity'.

Sometimes you have to tell the killer story, you tell me, if you want to break the containment. In this case what needs to be broken is the sheer hubris of the patriarchal centring – which was how he wanted to tell it, like he was both the hero and the victim. To tell the story otherwise would be to trace the growing hatred and militarist-colonial brutality as it hardened when the man's career – the governor – moved from one part of the British Empire to another:

> 1842 magistrate and 'Black Protector' on the Murray River, South Australia; 1847 Lieutenant-Governor of the South Island of New Zealand; 1854 Lieutenant-General of St Vincent; 1859 interim Governor of the Leeward Islands at Antigua; 1862 interim Governor of Jamaica; 1864 Governor of Jamaica.[42]

This bureaucratic trajectory collided with the dangerous atmosphere of post-emancipation White settler society in Jamaica. The Confederate defeat in the American Civil War grew closer, and then emancipation finally came to enslaved people of the United States on 19 June 1865. Political tensions were running high, and there were growing protests and civil unrest over ongoing efforts by the colonial authorities to limit political representation and democratic participation by Black Jamaicans. This was now developing into plans for a full-blown rebellion, especially through the activism of George Gordon and Paul Bogle in the parish of St Thomas in the far east of Jamaica and its main town, Morant Bay.[43] In 1854, the power of the Executive had been raised above the Assembly, and in 1859 a new poll tax had been introduced which meant that the vast majority of the 430,000 Black Jamaicans were unable to vote, unlike the 14,000 or so Whites. This disenfranchisement combined with an increasing White fear of 'black ascendency', a sense of crisis for White cultural supremacism that ran from Kingston to London.[44] From the start, the governor's regime in Jamaica was authoritarian and violent. Now it entered a new phase with the Morant Bay Race Massacre.

On Saturday 7 October 1865, a group protesting a wrongful arrest and imprisonment broke into the Morant Bay courthouse and freed the prisoner, a man named James Geoghegan.[45] On the following Monday, the authorities issued a warrant for the arrest of twenty-eight people at the nearby town of Stony Gut, and when a contingent of eight police arrived, an aggressive stand-off ensued with a crowd of 300 people armed with sticks, spikes and cane-field cutlasses.[46] In response, on the Tuesday the 'custos' of the parish, a German aristocrat named Baron Maximilian von Ketelhodt, wrote to the governor at Kingston asking for reinforcements.[47] A hundred soldiers arrived from Port Royal. The following day, Wednesday 11 October, Baptist deacon Paul Bogle led a protest march of several hundred people into Morant Bay, and the group raided the police station for guns. At the courthouse, a volunteer militia of thirty or more men, consisting mainly of plantation overseers and bookkeepers, confronted them.[48] Stones were thrown as the custos tried to read the riot act, and then the amateur soldiers opened fire, killing seven protestors. In the ensuing hours of violence, eighteen of the local militia were killed, the courthouse was set on fire, and prisoners were released from the jailhouse. On the Thursday, the governor ordered further troops to be sent on the gunboat *Onyx*. He declared martial law and convened the Assembly and Privy Council for a Council of War, to prevent what he claimed was a risk of a wider rebellion. 'No white people were assaulted subsequent to the fearful outrage on the 11th,' the Admiralty reported.[49] The fighting was contained by the 12th, but now the coming violence had its pretext. With the military and naval forces in full control, a sustained period of brutal reprisals began. As John Stuart Mill put it at the time, a 'disturbance in Jamaica, provoked in the first instance by injustice' came to be 'exaggerated by rage and panic', and thus became:

the motive or excuse for taking hundreds of innocent lives by military violence, or by sentence of what were called courts-marshall, continuing for weeks after the brief disturbance had been put down; with many added atrocities of destruction of property, flogging women as well as men, and a general display of the brutal recklessness when fire and sword are let loose. The perpetrators of those deeds were defended and applauded by the same kind of people who had so long upheld slavery.[50]

An immense military force of army, marines, bluejackets, police and special constables, militia and volunteer reserves, and mercenary troops was marshalled together, and deployed against the unarmed civilian population of Black Jamaicans. There were soldiers from the 1st and 2nd West India regiment, the Royal Artillery, the 2nd battalion of the 6th Royal Regiment, the 3rd Buffs (Royal East Kent Regiment), the 17th (Leicestershire Regiment of Foot), the Rural Constabulary and the Police Force of Jamaica – a specially formed auxiliary detachment of 150 Maroon mercenaries – and the St Catherine's and Kingston Militias. Military operations on the land were supported by a fleet of Royal Navy men-of-war and gunboats: the screw corvette HMS *Wolverine*, the troopship HMS *Urgent*, the screw sloops HMS *Rosario* and HMS *Fawn*, the racer-class sloop HMS *Cordelia*, the gunboats HMS *Steady*, HMS *Lily*, HMS *Nettle* and HMS *Onyx*. These were joined by further warships: the twenty-six-gun screw frigate HMS *Galatea* and the ninety-gun HMS *Aboukir*. Naval steamers brought reinforcements: a battalion of 250 men came on the steamer *Plantagenet* from Nassau, 537 men and officers from Barbados and later the 17th Regiment from Nova Scotia on HMS *Duncan* and HMS *Sphinx*.[51] There are records of the military supplies carried by HMS *Urgent* when it shipped the troops from Barbados: 197 shells for two nine-pounder field guns, 108,100 cartridges, 360,110 percussion caps, 260 muskets, 19 rockets and more besides.[52] On the night of Friday 13 October, one eyewitness recalled that the governor 'read martial law to the sailors and marines – about 100 of them – telling them afterwards that he hoped they would do their duty'.

For mile after mile, the British military mobs burned and destroyed more than a thousand houses of the Black residents of the parish, both makeshift shacks and affluent houses with cedar and mahogany furniture, Baptist chapels, gardens and livestock, everything reduced to splinters, ash and sherds.[53] Where there was resistance, it was with muskets and agricultural cutlasses. Displaced people ran into the fields to escape the militia without clothing or food, hiding wherever they could in the torrential storms of the autumn rainy season.[54] An expeditionary force was sent out into the Blue Mountain Valley to pursue the refugees fleeing the violence.[55] Meanwhile Royal Navy steamers brought troops, weapons and ammunition from Port Royal and Kingston, and returned carrying White women and children from what the governor had turned into a war zone.

Following summary trials under martial law for conspiracy, Paul Bogle was hanged on the gibbet outside the Morant Bay courthouse, and George Gordon, Assembly member for the parish of St Thomas, was brought from Kingston and hanged from the yardarm of the Wolverine.[56] The government inquiry named more than 260 further men and women who were hanged in the next few weeks, including at least one pregnant woman, and a similar number are recorded as being shot, most unarmed, many while running away.[57] Official reports recorded that almost 500 people were killed. Hundreds more were 'barbarously' beaten, flogged, tortured, or hurriedly sentenced to imprisonment with hard labour, penal servitude and up to 100 lashes, it was documented. Thirty years ago, in his assessment of the available evidence, historian Gad Heuman suggested that over 1,000 Black Jamaicans were killed in this chaotic free-for-all of extra-juridical executions.[58] It was described by those on the ground as a 'bush hunt after rebel negroes', and at the time some suggested that, given the numbers shot in the fields, a death toll of 1,500 'would perhaps be a moderate computation'.[59] Official bounties had been placed on the heads of the rebels, and indiscriminate murder proceeded.[60] In one instance, a man named Arthur Wellington was tied to a tree and a firing squad of ten men discharged their rifles at 400 yards to kill; 'I do not feel there was any waste of ammunition', their commanding officer wrote.[61] The troops, the historian Bernard Semmel wrote in 1962, 'thought themselves to be fighting a racial war'.[62] 'They seem to have regarded the whole negro race as their deadly enemies', one contemporary report put it, 'and to have revelled in the opportunity of wreaking vengeance upon them.'⁶³ The fact that even the bare numbers of the killed and injured men, women and children are not known is the point; that's how this dehumanising violence works.

In London, a group calling itself the Jamaica Committee, chaired by John Stuart Mill and with Charles Darwin and Herbert Spencer among its supporters, petitioned the prime minister (Fox's uncle), and began a series of legal attempts to prosecute the governor for the murder of British subjects, which continued for the next two and a half years.⁶⁴

A counter-organisation called the Eyre Defence and Aid Fund was formed, led by Thomas Carlyle, and it celebrated the governor (Edward John Eyre, the same man whose *Journals of Expeditions of Discovery* had described the skull-cup in Australia in 1845) as an English hero.⁶⁵ Its subscribers included Charles Dickens, John Ruskin, John Tyndall, the poet laureate Alfred Lord Tennyson and Matthew Arnold – as well as 71 peers, 6 bishops, 20 MPs, 40 generals, 26 admirals, 400 clergymen and 30,000 others.⁶⁶ They sought to justify the extended period of martial law, presenting the Morant Bay Race Massacre as the suppression of a revolt or insurrection, which would have led to the overthrow of the colonial assembly or the mass extermination of the White population.⁶⁷ There were rumours of a plot for a mass slaughter of all the White people in Jamaica to be carried out on Christmas Day.⁶⁸ The racist character of the debates was captured by the leader comment of *The Times* on 18 November 1865, which compared freed Black Jamaicans with that newspaper's favoured stock image for any anti-Black storyline: the 'treacherous' King of Dahomey 'ready for hideous deeds of blood' to 'slay thousands to fill a trench with human gore'.⁶⁹ Analogies were made with the Indian Rebellion of eight years earlier, or with the growing Fenian movement in Ireland. And closer to home for the post-emancipation Jamaican planter ethnoclass was the example of the Haitian Revolution, which had begun with an uprising three quarters of a century earlier, and led in 1801 to the defeat of the French and the formation of the Caribbean's first independent republic – just 120 miles across the water from the east Jamaican coastline. 'Most naturally,' one defender of the governor wrote, 'our soldiers must act as the ministers of wholesale execution in retaliation for wholesale murder, or even contemplated murder.'[70]

The comparisons foremost in the mind of the governor probably came from other parts of the empire. The New Zealand Wars had, in the five years since he had left for the Caribbean, entered a new phase of intense British military violence.[71] And this was true of British colonialism wherever their sea power could reach, a World War Zero starting to unfold from West Africa to Asia and the Pacific Ocean. The Morant Bay Race Massacre bore all the hallmarks of the racist, ultraviolent logic that came to underpin British militarist colonialism in the final third of the nineteenth century – the 'punitive expedition'. Some of the naval commanders were even veterans of the most infamous incidents of mass-killing, destruction and looting in colonial warfare in South and West Africa, India and China.[72]

Comparisons were drawn with the policing at Hyde Park eight months earlier, and here the figure of Fox re-emerges. John Tyndall downplayed the significance of the killing of Gordon, asking, 'Who dreams of making Jamaica a precedent for England?':

> We do not hold an Englishman and a Jamaica negro to be convertible terms . . . I decline accepting the Negro as the equal of the Englishman, nor will I commit myself to a position that a negro insurrection and an English insurrection ought to be treated in the same way.[73]

As an extension of suffrage to more British male citizens was debated and gradually yielded to by the aristocracy through Parliament in 1867, the definition of freedom and humanity in the years after emancipation in the British Caribbean came into focus, dividing metropolitan opinion in the 1860s. It was a divide that formed an important context for Matthew Arnold's intervention in *Culture and Anarchy*. As Edward Said pointed out in *Culture and Imperialism*, most modern readers of Arnold's celebration of culture have no idea that he connected the 'administrative massacre' ordered by the governor with 'tough British policies toward colonial Eire and strongly approved both', so that Arnold's case for culture was directly linked to a desire to deter 'rampant disorder' – 'colonial, Irish, domestic'.[74]

The opposing political outlooks that divided opinion in London revealed differences in how the limits of emancipation were conceptualised – geographical, cultural and ethnopolitical limits; limits that were about degrees of humanity and freedom. The divide mapped directly onto the positions of two rival anthropological learned societies: the Ethnological Society of London (established 1843) and the Anthropological Society of London (established 1863). Characteristically, Fox was a member of both. I look again at the future governor's 1845 drawing of the Australian skull-cup, and it feels like a statement of intent, a warning of a coming war of cultural supremacy, one that reaches forwards to our definition of 'the humanities' today, and that even sought to marshal 'science' towards its goals. Because the key point was that unlike those 'small wars' on the edges of empire, which were in reality massive military operations of growing scale and ferocity, the victims of the Morant Bay Massacre were subjects of the British Crown. Why then should they be treated differently from British citizens demonstrating in London?

The rationale for Fox's decision not to go on the attack is surely clear. This was about a differentiation between British and foreign people, not in terms of 'race' alone, but on something closer to Matthew Arnold's account of culture. Whiteness and Blackness were certainly in play, but imagined in cultural forms, as civilisation and inheritance; culture itself was being weaponised. The Railings Affair was about new forms of borderwork.

## 17. THE CANNIBAL CLUB

In 1863, at the height of the American Civil War, a group of members of the Ethnological Society of London, then twenty years old, formed the breakaway Anthropological Society of London. Within a few months, the splinter group had grown to the size of a significant learned society, electing over 200 fellows.[75] Its founders Richard Burton (explorer and former captain in the army of the East India Company) and James Hunt (a speech therapist) saw the group as a kind of sister society to the Société d'anthropologie de Paris, but with an explicit political agenda.⁷⁶ The aim was to provide a venue for the discussion of ideas of 'polygenism'. In contrast with the 'monogenetic' position set out by Charles Darwin in *On the Origin of Species* (1859), this was a belief not in a single human origin but multiple origins for different human 'races'.⁷⁷ The society hoped to catalyse the study of 'Man and Mankind' in what they claimed was 'a strictly scientific manner', from physical anthropology and phrenology to 'the mental and moral characteristics of mankind'.⁷⁸ 'Our object of study being MAN in all his relations, physical, moral, psychical and social,' Burton declared in a lecture to the new group, they would require 'a liberty of thought and a freedom of speech' which will offend 'the *mauvaise honte*, the false delicacy and ingrained prejudices of our age'. What Burton was referring to was the virulent racism that ran through everything that the society published. He began his talk with a Latin phrase: '*Hic Niger est, hunc tu, gens angla caveto!*' ('Here is the negro: beware of him, English race!').⁷⁹ The Anthropological Society hosted talks on 'The Negro Question, the Irish Question, the Aryan Question', one member recalled in 1917. Its members founded their own private museum containing hundreds of skulls, housed in rented apartments on St Martin's Street that it shared with the Ethnological Society, now the site of the National Portrait Gallery.⁸⁰ In the window, the agenda of the group was made vivid by the display of a large stuffed gorilla alongside a human skeleton.⁸¹

There was an inner circle of the society, a Byronian dining club that styled itself 'the Cannibal Club'. The sense that this select group was where the power lay in this new society led to the Anthropological Society or 'Anthropologicals' coming to be known colloquially as the Cannibals or the Anthropophagi ('the man-eaters').⁸² The Cannibal Club called their meetings to order with a ceremonial mace which they called 'Ecce Homo'.⁸³ This ivory gavel had a piece of ebony attached at one end, carved in the form of an African man's head eating into the long white handle in the shape of a thighbone.⁸⁴ Between 1865 and 1869, between the afternoon meetings of the council of the society and the evening lectures, this group met at Bertolini's near Leicester Square.⁸⁵ With the president in the chair, their dining commenced with a reading of their member Algernon Charles Swinburne's poem 'The Cannibal Catechism', written specially for this purpose in 1865.⁸⁶ Part mock grace, part club anthem, part parodic hymn, it opened with the invocation:

> Preserve us from our Enemies
> Thou who art Lord of sun and skies
> Whose meat and drink is flesh in pies
> And blood in bowls!
> Of thy sweet mercy, damn their eyes
> And damn their souls!'⁸⁷

Over ten stanzas the poem continued to celebrate how the 'chosen nation' was on its way to glory, while their enemies would be damned, crammed in pits of burning sulphur, chained up, their gin, whiskey and rum cursed, ground into small, gritty pieces, and roasted until their faces turned brown, or black faces turned 'even blacker':

> Scourge him with anger as a whip
> O Mumbo-Jumbo!⁸⁸

The Cannibal Club, especially through the influence of Richard Burton, operated as an exclusive male pseudoscientific debauched space for the comparative discussion of sex, sexuality, sexual organs and related bodily practices, and also, according to some accounts, for sadomasochism and the exchange of colonialist pornography.⁸⁹ In a particular constellation of bodies, sex and militarist-colonial violence, the Gothic horror of the image of the cannibal merged with the dining rituals, and ideas of 'savagery' were attached to uncontrolled sexual desire and to bodily abuse and violence. It was an early instance of a long-lasting Neo-Gothic trope of British colonialism, a reversal in which the insatiable appetite for violent extraction and consumption at a global scale coded the colonised as the debauched, transgressive violator.⁹⁰ In one case in 1863, Burton promised a friend to procure human skin flayed from the thighs of *une négresse vivante* to bind one of his erotic books.⁹¹ Sick bastards, you replied. White men in their thirties, mostly, you added, who wore tweed jackets, hand-made shoes and wax in their hair. Fox joined the Anthropological Society in 1865, and was elected to its council in 1867, shortly before his first 'Primitive Warfare' lecture. The society inaugurated their own symbol or 'logo', formed of a double triangle. I googled it, you told me. In the outer triangle, the Masonic design of three dots was echoed or referenced by a skull, a brain and an eye; within the inner, inverted triangle was a Stone Age hand-axe. The image was later echoed in the design Fox used for his excavation medalets and funerary urn.[92] It's unclear whether Fox was formally a member of the Cannibal Club, but certainly as a council member and close friend of Richard Burton he was familiar with their dining rituals.[93]

Bastards, you say again. You're scrolling through Jstor looking at the tables of contents of the papers read at the meetings and the articles published by the society's journals. There's a clear sense of how the racist rhetoric of this fake science of Black inferiority, centred on brains, skulls and fantasies about 'race', gained momentum as the 1860s moved on. Read it out to me then, I say, taking my AirPods out, if you must.

'Wild Men and Beast-Children'[94]
'On the Difference Between Man and Brutes'[95]
'The Influence of Race on Art'[96]
'Notes on the Capabilities of the Negro for Civilisation'[97]
'Pictet on the Aryan Race'[98]
'The Extinction of Races'[99]
'The Negro in Relation to Civilised Society'[100]
'On the Supposed Increasing Prevalence of Dark Hair in England'[101]
'Notes on Scalping'[102]
'An Inquiry into Consanguineous Marriages and Pure Races'[103]
'Miscegenation'[104]
'Anthropotomy'[105]
'Slavery'[106]
'Observations on the Skeleton of a Hottentot'[107]
'Race and History'[108]
'Race in Religion'[109]
'On the Value of Phrenology in Anthropological Investigations'[110]
'Knox on the Celtic Race'[111]
'What is a Teuton?'[112]
'On the Alleged Sterility of the Union of Women of Savage Races with Native Males, After Having Had Children by a White Man, with a Few Remarks on the Mpongwe Tribe of Negroes'[113]

'Comments on the Essential Differences Observable between the Larynx of the Negro and That of the White Man'[114]
'The Brain of a Negro of Guinea'[115]
'On the Headforms of the West of England'[116]
'On the Headform of the Danes'[117]
'On the Weight of the Brain of a Negro'[118]
'The Negro as a Soldier'[119]

This was how anthropology began? you ask me. I open one of these papers and start to read, to listen to the framing, to try to understand the narrative structure, the words written and delivered as lectures not just to describe the world but to change the facts. Told lightly, like you said before, with a practised ambiguity and innuendo.

The title page reads *Journal of the Anthropological Society of London, 1864, Vol. 2* and I try to picture Fox pulling it from the shelf in the library after dinner, lighting a cigar, sipping a brandy in an armchair, the leather glowing like mahogany in the gaslight, opening at the first page of a paper delivered on 19 January 1864 with the title 'The Extinction of Races', and starting to read. Reviewing mass deaths in Tasmania and New Zealand, the author acknowledges that 'the most relentless butcheries were at one time practised in that colony, for many years past': 'so great was the slaughter practised by the early settlers', he argues, that the number of Aboriginal people of Van Diemen's Land was reduced from 5,000 to 340. Ninety-three per cent mortality, Fox would doubtless have done the long division. If you believe the 5,000 figure, that is. But more recently, when 'the Aborigines have been under the immediate protection of the government', deaths have continued apace. More mysterious processes, the paper continues, must be 'in operation to produce an extinction of certain races', processes that 'at present cannot be clearly defined'; indeed such 'disappearances' might be taken as a 'type' of what might happen at a future period of the world's history. I imagine Fox's manuscript annotation, the fat blue military-issue pencil, underlining the word: TYPE. A word that connotes both a foreshadowing and a kind of diagnostic example. A word that definitely stuck in Fox's mind.

The rest of the paper presents one White supremacist fantasy after another, in which the relentless process of killing and extermination is presented as a process of inevitable extinction in which some undefined, higher hand of providence or destiny is implicated for a new future. 'Glancing over the surface of the globe', it states, it is clear that:

> a new era will be inaugurated ... Europe is now the centre from which this flood of civilised life is overspreading the globe, and our own Anglo-Saxon race constitutes one of the chief elements which are sweeping before them every vestige of earlier inhabitants ... Europe, now pre-eminent in all the attainments of man – the home and the cradle of the noblest arts and profoundest sciences, may have for her destiny to repopulate the globe.[120]

The governor was a member of the Anthropological Society too, and here his changing perspectives as a colonial administrator can be set into a metropolitan context. In 1845, in the preface to his book on his travel in South Australia, the governor-to-be had described what he saw as 'a people who are fast fading away before the progress of a civilisation'.[121] Twenty years later the *British Army and Navy Review* reported that this man 'stands accused of being the exterminator of the black race', 'a cold-blooded, cowardly murderer', by those who want to see 'the domineering whites reduced to their proper position', who say 'we' (that pronoun again) should 'bend the knee to Hindoos, Musselmans, New Zealanders, and negro slaves'.[122] The continuity here was in his anthropological sensitivity, which in the atmosphere of the 1860s meant that he was concerned not so much with 'race' as with what he called 'barbarism', 'habits' and 'character': sociocultural dimensions of inferiority, as it were.[123]

From the massacre at Morant Bay to the debauchery at Bertolini's, questions of slavery, civil war and extermination were foremost in the minds of the Cannibals. On 3 January 1866, in the immediate aftermath of the massacre, the president's address to the society took the form of a eulogy to the governor. He quoted a prediction from Robert Knox's 1850 book *The Races of Man*, which he claimed had now been proved true: 'From Santo Domingo, the Negro drove out the Celt; from Jamaica he will expel the Saxon.'[124] Such revolutions, he concluded, will occur wherever 'the Negro is placed in unnatural relations with Europeans'.

Since their split from the Ethnological Society in 1863, the Cannibals had represented one entrenched side of that divide in opinion about the limits of freedom. A generation after emancipation in the British colonies, it was a divide that was loosely aligned with the two sides of the American Civil War. Lincoln's Emancipation Proclamation of 1 January 1863 had widened this gap in Europe, especially among the sons and daughters who profited from the slave-holding of their parents and grandparents, Fox included.[125] A commercial agent, a protagonist for the South who has been described as 'the most important Confederate strategist in Europe', was the key connection between the Confederacy and the Cannibals.[126] In 1856 he had published an English translation of Joseph Arthur de Gobineau's *Essai sur l'inégalité des races humaines* (1853), a foundational text for the fake 'racial science' that introduced the idea of an 'Aryan race' and the supremacy of its 'Nordic strain', under the title *The Moral and Intellectual Diversity of Races*.[127] Now the 'Anthropologicals' wrote to him to say that the Confederacy 'should and must take a strong interest in our objects, for in us is your only hope that the negro's place in nature will ever be scientifically ascertained and fearlessly explained'.[128]

Some of the funding to establish the Anthropological Society came through this propagandist, originating from American anti-abolitionist interests.[129] The president made his anti-Darwinian, polygenist position clear, stating in 1863 that the new 'Science of Man' promoted by the society would involve 'classifying the Negro as a distinct species'.[130] Addressing a crowded room in the Ethnological Section of the British Association for the Advancement of Science in Newcastle on the evening of 26 August 1863, his paper 'The Mental and Physical Characters of the Negro' offered a list of racist assertions. 'There is far greater difference between the Negro and Anglo-Saxon than between the gorilla and the chimpanzee,' the president argued.[131]

A man stood up in the audience to object. William Craft was an African-American delegate at the conference, a fugitive from enslavement in the American South, who was delivering a paper in the same section.[132] A Black abolitionist who was born into slavery in Macon, Georgia, in 1848, he had escaped with his wife Ellen to the North, and thence to London. In 1860, Ellen and William had jointly published an account of their journey, titled *Running a Thousand Miles for Freedom; or, The Escape of William and Ellen Craft from Slavery*. It described how light-skinned Ellen had bandaged her face and dressed in men's clothing to pass in disguise as a crippled White man travelling with William. In his response to the president's paper, Craft pointed out that there is just as much difference between individual Africans as between individual Englishmen and, in a famous phrase, observed that 'not all Englishmen are Shakespeares'. And then he told a story:

> A lion and a man were walking together along the road, and disputing as to which of the two could claim to belong to the superior race. By and by they came to a public house, the sign of which was a lion violently held down by a man. The man triumphantly pointed to this in confirmation of his superiority; but the lion sagely inquired who painted the picture.[133]

As if the man in William Craft's story were repainting such a picture, the president went on to read a revised version of his paper before the society on 17 November 1863 under the title 'On the Negro's Place in Nature', a play on the title of a recently published book by the man known as Darwin's Bulldog, titled *Man's Place in Nature*. The president repeated the kind of racist views about emancipation for which the Bulldog became well known: 'the Negro is more humanised when in his natural subordination to the European, than under any other circumstances' and 'the Negro can only be humanised and civilised by Europeans'.[134] When the text was published in the *Journal of the Anthropological Society of London* it was simultaneously distributed in the United States in a White supremacist pamphlet series called 'Anti-Abolition Tracts', selling for fifteen cents.[135] But this was far more than just the anti-abolitionist Confederate case in the American Civil War being played out in the pages of English scientific journals.[136] The main agenda of the Anthropophagi lay in the interests of justifying British colonial-militarist violence. On 1 February 1866 the society heard a paper titled 'The Negro and Jamaica'. Interest was so high that they moved the venue from the society's rooms at St Martin's Place to the much larger St James' Hall. The talk ranged from Egyptian mummies to the juvenilia of Virgil and to travellers' accounts of African civilisations in a vitriolic attempt to 'fix the position of the negro at the earliest period in the world's history'.[137] The argument was clear:

> Let us take the negro as we find him, as God designed him, not a white man, nor the equal of a white man. That he can exist in a community of Anglo-Saxons on terms of political and social equality, is both physically and morally impossible.[138]

In the discussion, audience members claimed that abolitionism in America had been an anthropological theory for which 'some of their best blood' had been spilled in the war, and which was now revealed as 'rotten at the core'. 'In some places a white face is now as rarely seen as a black in London,' one man complained, while another advocated 'killing savages as a philanthropic principle', since there may be 'mercy in a massacre'.[139]

This was far more than just a marginal group of adherents to the fake 'racial science' of mid-nineteenth-century physical anthropology breaking away from a more humanistic, even humanitarian, Ethnological Society (the original foundation of which had been as an offshoot of the Aborigines' Protection Society in 1843). Rather, from this nexus of concern – bodies, skulls, violence and White supremacism – a new anthropological voice developed: a new way of expressing ideas of fate or destiny in which ideas of 'culture' and its intergenerational transmission were central. The propaganda was not simply racial; this was about cultural supremacy too. About civilisation.

The hand of the Protagonist (that Confederate agent who sat on the Anthropological council) is detectable in the publication by the society during its first year of an expanded translated edition of Theodor Waitz's 1859 book *Anthropologie der Naturvölker* under the title *Introduction to Anthropology*. Written in the atmosphere of the aftermath of the pan-European revolutions of 1848, the German title had used the term *Naturvölker* ('nature people') which as seen above in the nascent ethnology of Gustav Klemm in Leipzig and of Adolf Wuttke in Breslau had come, with its corollary term *Kulturvölker* ('culture people'), to be used to present a simple, universal binary distinction between 'active' and 'passive' human 'races'.[140]

The Protagonist's adherence to an emerging transatlantic

anthropological ideology that connected culture with 'race', contrasting 'activeness' with extinction, could be seen in a letter he had written to the Comte de Gobineau in July 1856, where he described the United States as 'a country in which the footstep of the red man is scarcely yet erased and where there is not a white man's homestead that dates half a century back'.[141] Waitz's argument added a layer of complexity to this position. Writing from the Hessisch university town of Marburg, he critiqued what he called the 'American School': the simplistic idea that 'the higher races are destined to displace the lower'. He criticised the view that 'all wars of extermination, whenever the lower species are in the way of the white man, are then not only excusable, but fully justifiable ... in order to afford space to higher organisms'.[142] According to that American 'doctrine', he wrote:

> This extinction of the lower races is predestined by nature, and it would thus appear that we must not merely acknowledge the right of the white American to destroy the red man, but perhaps praise him that he has constituted himself the instrument of Providence in carrying out and promoting this law of destruction. The pious manslayer thus enjoys the consolation that he acts according to the laws of nature which govern the rise and extinction of races.[143]

Waitz was setting out a different kind of supremacism, a vision of destiny and extermination based on the idea that differences between human groups were determined by culture, not just nature or biology. Isolated traditional cultures across the globe would inevitably become connected because of ever-developing technology, 'drawn into the vortex', as he put it. Civilisation was 'the universal destination of mankind', he argued, 'the development which nature designs for man, in which all human beings participate, though the parts which they take in it may greatly differ'.[144] Rather than justifiable killings, the extermination of Indigenous people was simply a cultural inevitability, a kind of *force majeure*. Certain sections of the world were simply fated to die out, while others would bear culture, civilisation and freedom forward into the future. When you put it that way, these German arguments sound more 1930s than 1860s in character. But in truth the goose-step was being led from a militarising, proto-fascist London, in dialogue with German, French and American theorists. 'Black races' were, as one typical paper read to the society in March 1866 argued, doomed to 'rapid, entire, and inevitable extinction', and this was somehow part of 'the highest destinies of mankind': 'Far from being influenced by civilisation, they disappear from before the face of it as surely and perceptibly as the snow recedes before the advancing line of sunbeams.'[145] Racist excuses for mass slaughter in a new phase of corporate-militarist colonialism were shifting frame, evolving, in a translation from nature to culture, like another round of Russian Scandal. Alongside natural history, the idea of culture was now a second barrel of the anthropological shotgun.

In 1881 in Berlin, Adolf Bastian set out one of the clearest iterations of this particular form of supremacy, in which, through a use of what could be called the 'present exonerative', or perhaps more accurately the *future progressive exonerative*, colonial slaughter could be denied, presented as an inevitable process, fated, destined:

> The existence of Naturvölker is ephemeral for us, in terms of our knowledge of them, in terms of our relationships with them, and indeed insofar as they exist for us at all. At the very instant that we get to know them they are doomed. The Angel of Death seizes them.

Extinction, Bastian continued, may or may not involve physical demise; but it is always 'without exception, a psychic demise' at the moment of contact with 'civilisation'.[146]

Taken together, what was emerging between Waitz and Bastian was quite different from the fake 'racial science', and a kind of prototype for an enduring, exonerative, supremacist evolutionist model of culture: an equally spurious and hateful cultural science but one somehow better adapted for the long twentieth century.

Waitz's version of this focused on heredity. The unified study of humans as a species would remain incomplete, he argued, until all long-term, slow-changing, external, intergenerational processes were taken into account. This was a theory that contrasted the slow pace of cultural inheritance over the centuries with the fast pace of technological change in the present. It may be that adaptations to 'civilisation' simply cannot happen at a fast enough pace to keep up with change, it was suggested. The idea of progress, in the line of that more commonly associated with missionaries or socialists, thus came to be expressed with a kind of fake humanitarianism, as an inevitability or even a mercy, and was thus turned into an indirect weapon, an idea that made the killing inevitable, the extinction a law of science, a fact of life. A form of cultural anthropology slowly began to fashion itself into a sub-Romantic exercise in the study of loss – as a form of salvage. Anthropology was evolving. More than just 'race', it now had the theme of 'culture' in its arsenal, and thus a new means for naturalising inequality, and killing, and death. A new means of denial, that is. And it now started to speak in that new tense, the future progressive exonerative. The discipline was being forged as a weapon, in a fight about destiny, providence, and who gets to be defined as 'human'. When the Protagonist wrote in July 1863 in his publication *The Index* (described as 'a weekly journal devoted to the exposition of the mutual interests, political and commercial, of Great Britain and the Confederate States of America') that 'the most dangerous dogma of modern times is the dogma of the equality of man', he was expanding this argument to include more than just the measurement of skulls.[147]

## 18. REVOLVER

There's a handgun from Morant Bay in the Pitt-Rivers museum in Oxford. You wouldn't notice it if I didn't point it out. It's the one I mentioned when we saw it on display when we visited the museum before, in a desk case on the upper gallery: the Lefaucheux pin-fire revolver. I look up the accession register and read it to you:

> Rifled pin-fire revolver with integral cartridge extractor, and case. Stamped on the barrel: 'E. LEFAUCHEUX INV BREVETE'. Also stamped with numbers '907' and 'F P 439'. MRS C. HAUGHTON, West Worthing, Sussex. Collected in the 1920s by her husband, Colonial Service. FRANCE. .45 Pin-fire revolver patented by Eugene G. Lefaucheux in 1845. Said by donor to have been used in the Jamaican Rebellion in 1865. In wooden box fitted with slots for cartridges. Length: 29.2 cm. Box: 29.6 x 18.3 x 6.6 cm.[148]

The current display case label was written in 2010, or rather rewritten, transposing certain words and making certain editorial-curatorial changes to the text:

> Lefaucheux pin-fire revolver, France, c. 1845. Casimir Lefaucheux invented pin-fire in the 1830s. His son Eugene developed this open-frame, double-action, 12mm pin-fire revolver, which was popular in Scandinavia, Mexico, America, southern Europe and Egypt in the 1850s and 1860s. Lefaucheux revolvers had a bored-through cylinder to permit rapid loading. The cartridges themselves were waterproof and could be re-used after extraction using the ejector rod beneath the barrel. According to the donor, this gun was used during the Jamaican Rebellion of 1865. Collected by Mr. Haughton c. 1920 and donated by his wife in 1966.

The database offers further details. The gunmaker's mark reads 'AF' surmounted with a crown, and indicates it is from the factory of Auguste Francotte of Liège, Belgium. The self-contained cartridge consists of a paper casing holding the bullet and powder and a metal base with an integral primer pellet and a small metal pin, which protruded through the cylinder to be struck by the hammer and forced into the primer pellet. Then at the bottom of the screen, in a serif red font: 'This gun was safety- and condition-checked by the National Army Museum Conservation department 29 October 2008. Found Not Loaded.'

There are so many potential questions about this memento or relic of the Morant Bay Race Massacre, about the transatlantic arms trade during the American Civil War or the folk memories among Jamaican Whites or Colonial Service administrators in the 1920s, or the motivations and framings of the donor who offered the object or the curators who accepted the gift in 1966. But museum labels are obdurate, silent, passive-aggressive, like this text in a desk-case in the upper gallery. The president would have approved of the dehumanisation, you suggest. And Fox would have appreciated the stratigraphy of what is recorded, that institutional Russian Scandal effect again.

The display label and the original accession book entry read: 'Said to have been used in the Jamaican rebellion of 1865'. But in the archives there's the first display label, which dates to the late 1960s or early 1970s, and it reads: 'Said to have been *carried* in the Jamaican rebellion of 1865'. As the story is whispered down the line, the killings at Morant Bay come in and out of focus: carried, or being fired or being used to kill. But don't worry, the gun isn't loaded now, the database tells us, as if it could therefore do no further harm.

The oddest thing is the sheer inadequacy of the vocabulary of our discipline, of curators and anthropologists and archaeologists, historians of art or technology or conflict or ideas alike, to describe this kind of process, to keep in step with our times, I say. We get talking about Waitz's attempt, in the aftermath of the German Revolutions of 1848–49, to overcome the distinction between 'the ideal and the material'; his attempt to begin an anthropology of culture that got passed on to become a new supremacist tool. It was a new weapon in its own right, one still with us, morphed in expression but unchanged in form over the generations as it has transmuted into theories of 'material culture', like that proverbial wooden ship that persisted in form despite there being so many episodes of repair that not a single plank of the original vessel was left.

What are we holding onto, you ask me, when we address our students with the latest jargon, new mystifications of inherited ideas (very often unreferenced)? The codes seem to be just gatekeeping exercises, keeping things the same. They're monuments in their own right, those theories of objects and subjects, and often not very accomplished ones, these critical materialities, entanglement studies, posthuman futurities, symmetrical archaeographies, nonhuman geographies, multiversal ontologies, material semiologies, you name it.

Each latest brand of thought or theory seems to promise new insights through a framing of 'human–nonhuman relations' that feels to me like it's straight out of the 1860s, some inherited tradition of setting up a distinction between people and things, or ideas and objects, and then claiming to overcome that very distinction by saying they're related, or entangled, or whatever. What's missing is that the category error of mixing up people and things, objects and subjects, has a past. It's part of the prehistory of the war on culture, one of the intellectual and practical dimensions of militarist realism.

Pre-eminent in this genre of para-anthropological discourse today is the strange evangelical growth of a body of thought known as actor–network theory, or ANT for short, and the language of agency, nonhumans, factishes, inscription, symmetry and so on, that it has brought into the social sciences and humanities over the past three decades. As a kind of relational, universal, easily digestible theory of the social and natural worlds, ANT has been adopted so widely that it's now by far the most dominant approach to talking about material culture without ever, it seems to me, adding anything to our understanding. I mean, you have often asked me, what do you learn from saying that an object 'has agency'? And on the other side, what assumptions are you making, what attitudes are you reproducing? All you do is apply a particular account of society, in which agency is a problem to be solved. Then you say you can resolve your particular framing of this problem by extending this thing called agency to everything in the world, and in doing so you distract from the agency that some people might have, and diminish suggestions that other people might have a right to agency that they are denied. I always found ANT pretty reactionary, you tell me. Theories of material culture lifted from late Victorian anthropology and sold back to the anthropologists a century later without any sense of their provenance. Is that really what passes for theory in the social sciences and humanities these days?

There's a small moment in which this museum became tangled up in the gradual takeover of material culture studies by ANT, I offer in reply. In 1993, an object acquired for the collection in 1920 ended up on the cover of one of its foundational texts. That's how these institutions work, I guess, that latency, that time-warping. The book in question is the English translation of Bruno Latour's *We Have Never Been Modern*. The photo shows a German *Pickelhaube* (military helmet) that was taken as a trophy of war from the trenches of the Western Front in 1917–18 by an unnamed Chang man serving for the British Expeditionary Force in the Naga Labour Corps. Back in India, it was made into a traditional dance hat through the addition of the large horns and hair of a sacrificed mithun (wild ox), and then eventually brought back to the museum by a prominent Oxford-trained ethnographer and Indian Civil Service official around 1920.[149] The traditional treatment of an enemy's head, the addition of horns and tassels to the skull, is applied to the helmet. The helmet stands in for the skull, in an act that one anthropologist has described as 'a symbolic substitute of a captured enemy head and proof of valour in battle'.[150] This skeuomorphic object transforms a modern relic of industrialised slaughter with traditional modes of commemorating warfare and the taking of heads. It's a memento of the violence of the British Expeditionary Force, as so many other items of 'trench art' made by soldiers with the detritus of modern warfare, and a symbol of the defeat of the German armies. But it's also an index of another history, in which accusations of 'head-hunting' were used as a pretext for the British punitive expeditions that burned Naga villages in the name of putting down such practices.[151] Latour saw the helmet when it was on loan to Cambridge University's Museum of Archaeology and Anthropology in 1990 in an exhibition titled *The Nagas*, and when Harvard University Press published the translation, he chose it as the cover for his book.[152] It had been loaned from the Oxford display where it had been since the 1920s the central item in the 'Treatment of Dead Enemies' case.

Latour didn't write about the object; it just sits there in the photograph on the cover. He does provide one line that might refer to it, where he talks about Nietzsche, and argues that 'the moderns ... want to keep everything, date everything, because they think they have definitively broken with their past':

> The more they accumulate revolutions, the more they save; the more they capitalize, the more they put on display in museums. Maniacal destruction is counterbalanced by an equally maniacal conservation.[153]

'If I explain that revolutions attempt to abolish the past but cannot do so, I again run the risk of being taken for a reactionary,' Latour writes.[154] The context of the *Wende*, the fall of the Berlin Wall, is very close to the surface here, of course, in this book the title of which asserted *We Have Never Been Modern*, and was published in the original French the year before Francis Fukuyama's reactionary declaration that in 1989 heralded *The End of History*.[155] Also close to the surface is that macabre, gravitational pull of the cephalic relic of a killing, the one we encountered in Rilke and in the Cannibals. The intellectual move had something in common with the anthropologist who presented the Naga–German helmet to a museum that, a generation earlier, had been founded with a host of other weapons and armour taken from the battlefield, including the Russian helmets brought back by Fox himself from the trenches of the Alma. While making an argument about the enduring presence of the past, ANT was itself reintroducing the image of the 'non-human' into accounts of social life – an image that had begun in Victorian museums like this one.[156] The language of humans and nonhumans, and the idea that 'nonhumans', whether animal, vegetable or mineral, could be actors in social life, was recycled from Edwardian anthropology and merged with science studies, a kind of recycling and transformation at the same time. The idea of the nonhuman had surfaced in this museum and places like it around anthropological theories of 'totemism' and 'animism'. For example, in 1909, as the demolition work for the Rhodes building was getting underway, the Oxford anthropologist R. R. Marett published his classic discussion of the power of magical objects, describing how they can come to be 'medicine men' in their own right:

> We may see why the medicine man is so ready to press into his service that miscellaneous mass of 'plant', dead men's bones, skins of strange animals, and what not; and why these objects in their turn come to be able to work miracles for themselves, and in fact develop into non-human medicine men.[157]

J. H. Hutton, deputy commissioner of the Naga Hills and director of ethnography in Assam for the Indian Civil Service, wrote in his book about the Naga people from whom the helmet was collected – writing indeed in the very year, 1921, that his junior colleague and co-researcher brought it back to Europe – about the power of 'inanimate or non-human'.[158] And in what is probably still the most famous anthropology book of all time, *Argonauts of the Western Pacific*, in 1922 Bronislaw Malinowski even wrote about what he called 'non-human agency'.[159] Old wine in new skins, then, okay. But what else did these old ideas, rebranded with the jargon of networks, *actants*, cosmopolitics, factishes and so on, bring with them, what kind of attitudes to humanity? Sometimes the things displayed as objects in museums have ancestral, spiritual or other significant subjecthoods and powers. They may even constitute ancestors rather than simply representing them. But to widen, abstract and flatten out that observation into a general theory of 'material agency' will always continue the legacy violence of the decontextualisations of military realism.

You suggest we take another look at one influential text which Latour wrote about guns. It's a classic of this kind of Nineties theory as it travelled across the humanities and social sciences, from science studies to literary studies to management studies to art history, under various brands and submovements in the neoliberal economy of academic theory. The chapter was from a 1999 book that bore the name *Pandora's Hope*. The argument starts with a discussion of the motto of the National Rifle Association which adorns bumper-stickers across the American South: *Guns don't kill people. People kill people.* Forged in the management schools of Copenhagen and Oxford and in the École des Mines in Paris, Latour's theory was quite simple. He called it a 'symmetrical anthropology', but looking back it wasn't really so far from the 'science of culture' that we saw back among the Anthropologicals. 'Humans and nonhumans', he argued, form a kind of collective made up of ongoing mediations in which the 'actors' identified in traditional accounts of social life include things as well as people. I always snag on that language, you confess. Me too, I concur.

We might think of stuff as passive or neutral, he wrote, but in fact material objects are 'are fully fledged actors in our collective'. So in the case of the gunshot, who is the actor? The gun? That would be a technological determinism, seeing the weapon just as a tool or an intermediary. The citizen holding the gun, then? That would be a pure sociology, that fails to examine the difference between a shooting and a punch-up. 'Who is responsible for the act of killing?' asks Latour. Who is the actor? Surely the gun is different when held in the hand rather than lying unused in the armoury? And the human actor is different in turn when holding a gun. The twin mistake of the materialists and the sociologists is to start with purified essences, those of subjects or those of objects, Latour continued. Social life is far more entangled, he claimed. We should understand the figure of the gunman as a combination of two agents, the gun and the human: 'Agent 1 enlists the gun or is enlisted by it – it does not matter which – and a third agent emerges from a fusion of the other two.'[160]

In other words, to study the 'technical mediation' of social relations through an 'actor–network' approach might reveal that there are not just guns and citizens, but a third entity: 'a citizen-with-a-gun', both someone and something else, where the hyphens are just as important as the words. Latour applies this argument to the question of the 'symmetrical' responsibility for action, arguing: 'It is neither people nor guns that kill. Responsibility for action must be shared among the various actants. We must learn to attribute – redistribute – actions to many more agents.'[161]

Latour's discussion of the gun lobby slogan was framed as an attack by an imaginary figure that he called 'the science warrior'. That figure of the science warrior represented, he argued, a 'critical modernist' who with all the 'rage and violence and power' of the iconoclast seeks to fight between the opposite poles of relativism and realism, who tries to smash up idols or 'fetishes' but always misses and just shadow-boxes with their own projections.[162] Claiming to chart a middle course, he launched a critique of a famous essay called 'The Question Concerning Technology' written by Martin Heidegger in 1954, which paints a picture of the dominating control that technology can exert over the modern human subject. 'Heidegger is mistaken,' Latour argued, because there is no mastery of nonhumans over humans, or vice versa.[163] To say that 'we have been made by our tools' is the kind of *Homo faber* myth that you might read in Karl Marx, or Henri Bergson, he said.[164] 'I am folded into nonhumans', declared Latour.[165] It's time (yes, you guessed it) to bypass 'the old subject–object dichotomy', he said.[166] Latour substituted the category of human–nonhuman for what he called the 'subject–object fairy tale'. He claimed he wanted to conceptualise 'a different political regime from the war forced upon us by the distinction between the subject and object'.[167] What then is this new political regime? A politics freed from science. A politics of peacetime, since the nonhuman is, Latour wrote, 'what an object can be called in peacetime'. The argument was to free objects from their objectivity, and to free subjects from subjectification.

Some may accuse this approach of being 'reactionary', Latour wrote in the 1999 chapter, repeating the point he made back in 1993.[168] But for millions of years, he continued, humans have extended their social relations to other material actors, with which they have swapped properties and formed collectives.[169] The story begins with a bow and arrow, a javelin, a hammer or a net. Here, we see an image of the 'prehuman' using tools and skilled techniques, he wrote, channelling (presumably unknowingly) Fox's 'Primitive Warfare' lectures from 130 years earlier.[170] Humanity becomes less pure as the world of nonhumans gets more complex, he argued, from stone tools to nuclear power stations.[171] What is this idea of purity, you ask me – rhetorically, because it's clear you have a view. Is this what he means when he criticises the binary contrast between people and stuff, claiming that 'we are sociotechnical animals'?[172]

That pronoun, 'we', again. And that wilful confusion of objects and subjects, that pretends that actions are the product of circumstances, apparatuses, networks, of *force majeure*, rather than of human beings.[173] We do not live in societies, he claimed, but in entangled 'imbroglios', 'collectives of humans and nonhumans'.[174]

Sounds like Margaret Thatcher when she said she didn't believe in society, you tell me. Above all it's striking that in *Pandora's Hope*, a postmodernist study that relied so much on that neologism 'nonhuman', and which provided a nine-page glossary defining sixty-three keywords it uses, from 'actor' to 'translation' to 'society' and of course to 'nonhuman', the word 'human' was never defined. I think I understand now the politics of what he means when he says 'we are not at war', you continue. As if the war that was militarist-colonialism was finally over in the final year of the last millennium, and the fragments of colonialist thought can now be picked back up and reused, rehabilitated without so much as a nod to the history. *There's a history of men holding guns, and it's not unrelated to the parallel history of men theorising about men holding guns.*

The point is that Latour is just one particularly prominent example of a whole generation who have played this human–material game, and in doing so have resurrected the old latent model of the human and have thus tacitly rehabilitated the old universal, flattening, colonial, curatorial category of the 'nonhuman'. It's a theoretical position that you simply can't dissociate from the legacy of mixing up these categories by reducing humans to objects.

Others have discussed the 'militaristic and imperialistic language' that characterises Latour's writing, and the oddly depoliticised way in which on those rare occasions when he discusses European colonialism, he tries to depict it as a kind of laboratory experiment, just at a larger scale.[175] 'I have nothing against a good fight,' Latour wrote, 'but I would like to be able to choose my terrain, my witnesses, and my weapons – I want, above all, to decide for myself what my war aims are.'[176] (But the strange thing here is how, like revenants, the concerns of nineteenth-century anthropology resurface one by one in actor–network theory, and the legacy colonial museum re-emerges in plain sight; both on the book cover and when Latour states, 'I believe in a universalist anthropology.'[177]

So against the theorists' complaints about distinguishing subjects from objects, people from things, entangling one disciplinary subject with another in the name of 'agency' and 'materiality' – all those arguments that owe so much to just repeating that mid-nineteenth-century proto-anthropological propaganda, and its preferred denialist voice of the future progressive exonerative – please let's talk some more, you tell me, about humanity, humanness, subjects in all their complexity. The beginning of anthropology in a collection of trophies of war gives way, more than a century later, to another battlefield relic on the cover of the book. So tell me, you ask me, whose finger is really on the trigger here? And in answering that, let's keep in mind an observation that Christina Sharpe once made: 'All modern subjects are post-slavery subjects.'[178]

## 19. PIANO WIRE

Skip back from those 1990s actor–network theorists to the lecture room of the Royal United Service Institution – on the page, that is ... The date was Friday 5 June 1868, and Fox was on his feet this time to deliver his lecture titled 'Primitive Warfare Section II: On the Resemblance of the Weapons of Early Races, their Variations, Continuity, and Development of Form', much of which was about the weapons of insurrection. In the beginning, Fox argued, you tell me, in a semibiblical construction, 'All men were warriors.' And before the division of labour brought by civilisation between the arts of peace and the arts of war into specialisation, he continued, the same implement will be used by the 'primeval savage' as both a tool and a weapon. The weapon-tool combination is also found in more recent times, Fox continued, and 'especially amongst those semi-civilised and savage races of our own times, whom we regard as the representatives of antiquity'. The implements of husbandry were always used by 'subject people' fighting for their freedom, he argued, and he read out a passage from the First Book of Samuel (the King James version, of course):

> Now there was no smith found throughout all the land of Israel: for the Philistines said, Lest the Hebrews make them swords or spears. But all the Israelites went down to the Philistines, to sharpen every man his share, and his coulter, and his axe, and his mattock. Yet they had a file for the mattocks, and for the coulters, and for the forks, and for the axes, and to sharpen the goads. So it came to pass in the day of battle, that there was neither sword nor spear found in the hand of any of the people that were with Saul and Jonathan.[179]

These shares were the blades of the ploughshare, Fox explained to his audience. A coulter a kind of knife, and the mattock a kind of agricultural pickaxe (also used by archaeological excavators). And just like the Israelites in biblical times, in the first revolts of the German peasantry in the fifteenth and sixteenth centuries, we read, Fox continued, you say, the insurgents armed themselves with threshing flails and the blades of scythes. So too in Poland in the Kościuszko Uprising of 1794 and the November Uprising of 1830–31, and in the Hungarian Revolution of 1848. Then comes the case of Jamaica, Fox continued. Again, there were the 'weapons of husbandry'. In his proclamation, Fox reported, you tell me, Paul Bogle said, 'Every one of you must leave your house, take your guns; who don't have guns, take cutlasses' – meaning, Fox explained, the sharp, steel, curved machete-like tools used to cut sugar cane.[180] If the uprising hadn't been put down, Fox noted – you read the exact words here: *'ably and powerfully put down'* – it would have led to 'the destruction of the whole white population'.[181]

Fox's image of the transformation of tools into arms pushed at the boundaries of what might be classed as a weapon. In some cases, the repurposing of agricultural implements had brought innovation in weapons technology, he argued, and without such adaptation, weapons like the military flail, the bill (a kind of pole-arm), and the yataghan (a variety of short sword) would never have been invented. The image he wanted to convey was one of everyday objects used for violence, a modern parable that was a direct inversion of that verse in Isaiah, where the prophet speaks of a time when nations will 'beat their swords into ploughshares, and their spears into pruning hooks'.

It's a part of the mindset of the punitive expedition, you tell me, part of the trick of turning the tables, of White projection: of the killer presenting as victim as a pretext, the aggressor self-presenting as protector, to imagine that tools in the hands of other people are always already weapons, and thus to present acts of violence as acts of disarmament, opportunistic acts of mass slaughter as self-defence. Have you tried getting into the British Museum recently? you ask me. A generation ago, when Norman Foster installed the museum's famous glass canopy, the idea had been to open up a pedestrian link from north to south. The architect imagined it as part of a 'new heritage route' from Kings Cross to the South Bank. There are lines of concrete blocks and metal crash barriers at both entrances today.

To get into the galleries now begins with an airport security-style examination of objects, and what I find interesting, you say, is how as you queue through that white poly tunnel, it feels like a logic that is emerging from the institution's past, rather than something imposed on it in the present. In this regime of securitisation and surveillance they take everyday objects – I mean, potentially literally every ordinary object in your bag or your pockets, from a pair of tweezers to a cigarette lighter, a Sharpie or a screwdriver – and try to imagine how each everyday item could represent some kind of latent weapon, a tacit threat. In this strange forge, everything is wrought as a potential weapon. Like a sculpture is weaponised when it is stolen and displayed. It's the theory of nonhuman agency all over again. Just don't tell me a monument or a museum or a ballpoint pen 'has agency' in some generic, timeless, depoliticised sense. People have, or do not have, agency. Don't diminish that. There is inequality, but it's due to dispossession and capital, not that mystical entity 'material agency'. It's important because as this vision of material culture resurfaces in the museum, so does a cultural technology dedicated to classifying one group of human beings as different from, inferior to, or more violent than another. And here, one nineteenth-century institution maps onto another and the museum grounds become a policed border. As the border is to the nation state, so the museum is to empire.

In reality, there's another improvised weapon that stands out from documentation of the Morant Bay Race Massacre. Reports placed before Parliament described the rebels as being armed with 'cutlasses, sticks, and spikes', but in addition to their rifles and smooth-bores and nine-pounders and gallows rope, the British forces also carried whips, the ends of which had been tightly wrapped with steel piano wire and knotted to make a cat-o-nine-tails that cut as deeply as possible into the skin.[182] 'Some of these were produced before us, and it was painful to think that any man should have used such an instrument for the torturing of his fellow creatures,' the official Royal Commission report stated. The image of one component of the musical instrument put to work for extra-judicial torture is more than just what Fox calls the combination of tool and weapon, or ploughshares turned into swords – it is an object lesson for how culture itself, in conceptual and tangible forms, can be transformed into a weapon to mutate, to 'improve' through degradation. Steel wire is more than just a metaphor for Fox's account of the adaptation of form. There must have been so much violence that wasn't recorded in the thousands of pages of the Royal Commission report, you say. And as Trouillot observed, claims to innocence can often adopt the shape of silence.[183]

Think back to the atmosphere of the revolutionary spring of 1848. In the early 1850s, one of the first items Fox obtained for his comparative and chronological collections of weaponry was a Moravian percussion rifle used in the Hungarian Revolution of 1848. Today, it's accessioned alongside the Morant Bay revolver in Oxford's Pitt Rivers. In the weeks after the publication of *The Communist Manifesto* on 21 February came the outbreak of the Hungarian Revolution on 15 March 1848, and many other popular uprisings across Europe. In London in the April of that year, in response to the planned Chartist demonstration for universal male suffrage on Kennington Common, organised by a sixty-year-old Black British trade unionist named William Cuffay, the Grenadier Guards received orders to form a large body of troops in central London under the command of the Duke of Wellington, and were placed on alert to make a show of strength. Fox was three years into his army service, and that spring his battalion stationed at St George's Barracks, Knightsbridge. Five hundred soldiers of the Second Battalion stayed overnight at Millbank Prison on Sunday 9 April, part of an overall force of perhaps 6,000 troops. The troops in turn were part of an overall deployment of more than 200,000 police, including perhaps 70,000 or by one estimate 150,000 special constables who were hurriedly sworn in.[184] They arrived at Somerset

House for a day of military counter-demonstration and intimidation.[185] Tens of thousands of Chartists gathered at Russell Square, Finsbury Square, Clerkenwell Green and Whitechapel and marched across the river to gather on the common. Many public buildings had been fortified and guarded.[186] Twenty artillery guns were placed on Waterloo and Blackfriars bridges. The government took possession of the telegraphic systems throughout the country, in an effort to prevent the transmission of news catalysing riots in other cities.[187] The police closed the bridges, and in the heavy rain the crowds dispersed. Somewhere in the cityscape there was Fox, manning a gun on a bridge, perhaps, watching the Thames running east into the night. Or maybe in Bloomsbury where, as the sun rose over Bloomsbury on Monday 10 April 1848, the museum curators were arming themselves, to mount a defence to an attack that might, or might not, have been coming.

There had been alarm at the possibility that a Chartist meeting in Russell Square might march on the British Museum. 'A lawless and infuriated mob' might try to steal or destroy the priceless treasures held there: a crowd of 'infatuated men' who 'so madly dreamed of revolution, and perhaps, of confiscation'. This was how the events were recounted in the memoirs of the museum's assistant librarian Robert Cowtan in 1872.[188] 'It's easy enough after the event to smile and say the threatened something was imaginary,' he wrote, 'but it was seriously felt that a multitude ... was not to be trusted.' Rumours circulated among the keepers that threats had been uttered to burn the institution to the ground. There was agitation from the Irish, it was said, from the Fenians, the 'dissatisfied Sons of Erin'. Two magistrates paid a visit and formally swore in every member of the museum staff, from keepers and librarians to workmen, as special constables, their names called one after another. A garrison of 250 men was mustered, supported by two army officers, fifty-seven soldiers of various ranks and twenty Chelsea pensioners. They were armed with hundreds of pikes, cutlasses and other arms, as well as fifty muskets sent by the Board of Ordnance, along with ammunition. The younger men on the museum staff showed, it was reported, 'a good deal of excitement at the bare thought of not only wielding a truncheon, but possibly being called on to use a cutlass, shoulder a musket, or handle a pike'. Recruitment practices of the time meant that many of the museum porters were retired soldiers.[189] The Royal Engineers barricaded the grounds and the building. Sir Robert Inglis, a trustee of the British Museum and the Tory MP for Oxford University, gave the order to the troops to immediately open fire on the mob upon the first stone being thrown.[190] The museum was becoming an improvised weapon in an imaginary culture war; it was an improvisation that stuck.

The Chartist petition, demanding universal suffrage and other electoral reforms, was submitted to Parliament. As the day wore on, among the armed curators 'protestations of devotion to the museum' and 'a willingness to lay down their lives in its defence' gave way to apprehension and fear, and then finally to relief. The attack on the British Museum never came. In a strange foreshadowing of the Volunteer movement – which from 1859 began to turn British citizens into soldiers at a mass scale to defend the nation against invasion, trained up in drill halls the architecture of which was not so different from a Victorian museum – the museum staff were armed and ready for violence, in a self-imposed siege and a panicked funk.[191] Cowtan kept the constable's staff issued to him that day as a memento, and felt, he wrote, 'as proud of it as any Field Marshal', having warded off, he continued with no hint of irony, the forces of 'anarchy and plunder as things that every Englishman abhors and abominates'.[192] With the pikes and cutlasses and guns in the hands of the curator, the museum was becoming a part of the military infrastructure of the nation in a new way. Necessary fictions, that was the idea: culture as war by other means.

As Fox performed his military duties in the subsequent weeks, the atmosphere among the military was saturated with this febrile energy. That summer, 1848, a series of mock siege operations took place on the practice ground in front of St Mary's Barracks at Chatham, performed in the presence of the Court of Directors of the East India Company.[193] The 21-year-old Lieutenant Fox was among the organisers of this performance of an imaginary attack on a fake redoubt, of London under attack. The timing was no coincidence: elsewhere in London that August William Cuffay was arrested for organising further Chartist protests; he was later charged with 'conspiring to levy war' on the Queen, and sentenced to penal transportation to Tasmania.[194] Watched by a crowd of thousands of spectators, the soldiers constructed a pontoon bridge across St Mary's Creek, and demonstrated escalading, mining and countermining, attacks on stockades and defences of outposts, defence-building and loud explosions.

There were rumours that another war in Europe was coming, a war with the Russians; and fears of rebellions in the colonies in the wake of the vision of freedom that undergirded emancipation. Fears among the aristocracy of revolution following the events of 1848 across Europe, and fears about rebellion in Ireland and India and the Caribbean colonies. An arms race was starting, one in which Fox would be a key figure. More than just guns and bullets was involved: this was about human bodies, and about culture. About fear of the mob, about control. About how to divide the people, because every violent empire needs its foot soldiers.

Spool forward again to the 1860s. There were continued attempts to prosecute the governor, who was now returned from Morant Bay and hiding out in rural Devon. What was at stake was coming to be seen as a question of discrimination between citizens 'at home' and those in the colonies. Within days of the Morant Bay massacre, a leader column in *The Times* claimed that this was about 'the question of the negro's rights':

> While American preachers and orators are proclaiming not only the safety but the necessity of admitting the liberated negro of the South to a full participation in all the privileges of the Constitution, the long-liberated negroes of our own West Indies are doing their best, or their worst, to prove their own unfitness for the privileges which they have long enjoyed.[195]

The Jamaica Committee's final, unsuccessful attempt to prosecute the former governor came in June 1868. The Old Bailey grand jury threw out the bill, preventing the case from going to trial.[196] The House of Assembly was replaced by a Crown Colony government, and under the new Tory administration, the Reform Act of 1867 was passed, expanding the franchise to a new section of British male society.[197] What began as 'a crisis in Victorian consciousness' was resolved through a new set of improvisations and adaptations in the history of state violence and racism in Britain.[198] As the historian Catherine Hall has observed, definitions of human freedom and how, when and where martial law, state-sponsored violence and killing could be constitutional were now debated by Victorian society:[199]

> White male radicals ... had been received within the brotherhood of the nation, whilst black Jamaican males had been condemned to a racialized form of subjecthood and white British women, of every social class, had been firmly positioned within their separate sphere. The nation was a family, as was the Empire, but families, as everyone knew, had rules of belonging.[200]

Indeed, as Priya Gopal has more directly set out, the question was one of governance and human categorisation: about 'black agency – and what was to be done with it'.[201] A cultural logic was emerging that would give a new justification for the ultraviolence of later Victorian corporate-colonial militarism: the 'rule of difference' in which 'small wars' on the edges of empire were extra-judicial and justified. In a letter to the *Daily Telegraph*, John Ruskin summarised the mood among those who, like him, had opposed what he called 'the Radical movement' and 'fatuous outcry' against the former governor. While he 'regretted the need that may exist among savages in a distant island for their governor to do his work sharply and suddenly on them', Ruskin described himself as 'a Conservative in the deepest sense – a Re-Former not a De-Former'. 'White emancipation not only ought to precede black emancipation', he wrote, but must do so 'by the law of all fate'.[202]

A new precedent for unlicensed anti-Black killing had been set for Victorian militarist colonialism, not outside the borders of formal empire as in the case of the emerging 'small wars' of informal militarist colonialism, but against free Black civilians in a longstanding British crown colony. It gave a licence for virulent structures of ethnonationalist violence at a new scale – a history of militarism, not so much what Giorgio Agamben called a 'state of exception' but a kind of 'rule of difference' in which culturally defined racial categories came to justify mass killing, something closer to what Achille Mbembe calls 'necropolitics'.[203]

Militarist realism, by which I mean the creation of militarist-colonial conditions under which it could seem impossible to imagine the world otherwise, involved the gradual formation and reinforcement of the borders of the post-emancipation ethnostate across every conceivable form of cultural Whiteness, limits of the imagination patrolled by volunteer reservists, reinforced by museum displays or changes in suffrage. The governor's savage terrorism in Jamaica, the piano wire that left scars on the body, were early shots above the parapet. Attempts to justify slavery and the Confederate cause through natural science adapted and evolved, bleeding into new forms of racism in which we find, front and centre, the beginnings of anthropology as a science of culture, as a discipline, as a subject. A subject that recreated the idea of the subject. ANT, STS, MET and all the rest won't help us here. But there is a modern name for this violent prejudice too, another acronym: NHI. 'No Humans Involved'.

## 20. FUTURE PROGRESSIVE EXONERATIVE

Of course some people kill people, you say to me. And the gun lobby and the gun trade kills people. The human who holds a gun is never just, as in Latour's example, some generic citizen; sometimes it's a soldier, or a colonial officer, or a police officer, or some random entitled fantasist. Gun violence kills and maims at different scales according to 'race', and gender, and economics, and geography. We need only to compare the guns that were not fired in Hyde Park with those that were fired in Morant Bay. We need to attend to the work of those immense emancipation payments. They brought the conditions for supremacism into a new realm: not just a claim to biology, but the new realisms of capital. Wealth and civilisation were being defined as the future dimensions of humanness in this enduring debt that was more than purely monetary. Of course any such project, however loose and implicit, needed ancient places like the University of Oxford. Just don't tell me a museum or a monument is an 'actor–network'. We'll never get to grips with the legacy supremacism or the histories of cultural Whiteness otherwise.

And what if in Latour's category of universal humanity, the tacit partiality of the generic 'human', is itself a weapon? I mean, you continue, a weapon of around the same age, say, as the mid-nineteenth-century revolver that was kept as a relic or memento of anti-Black violence in Jamaica? Or what if this category of the human is a bullet or shell fired by nineteenth-century anthropological museums as a weapon, which ricochets back into theories of material culture a century later? Latour wrote of 'the war forced upon us by the distinction between subject and object'.[204] In doing so he erased the history and legacy of the fight against the confusion of these categories, against dehumanisation, the enduring struggle for abolition and emancipation. As if they were not, from the very beginning, about trying to end a war that had been fought for a quarter of a millennium – through the violence of treating human subjects as objects. The introduction of the figure of the 'nonhuman' into social science through ANT was concerned with distributing 'agency' away from people into the techno-material environments with which they cohabit the earth. But it was always a reintroduction, a colonial redux, a return of the anthropologists' use of ideas of technology and objects, including Fox's. This wasn't just the *fin-de-siècle* social science of the 1980s business schools, just as the Anthropological Society of London was not simply promoting 'racial science'. Just as culture mediated the category of the human in the 1860s, so material culture mediated humanity in the 1990s. In both cases, there was a deferral of responsibility when some people killed other people, from the past exonerative ('people died') to the material exonerative ('bullets killed the people') to the future progressive exonerative ('there are so many guns around that they end up killing people who happen to be standing at the wrong end of the barrel').

I reread George Orwell's 1936 essay 'Shooting an Elephant' today. In a city in Myanmar, an elephant goes on the rampage, destroying houses and killing a man. The narrator is a colonial police officer who sends at once for a five-cartridge Mauser bolt-action rifle and shoots the beast because he is afraid of the large crowd that is gathering around him.[205] For years I thought of it as a straightforward cautionary tale about the psychology and pathology of British imperial violence. The main thing I remembered was the sidestepping of responsibility. The narrator insists that he didn't really want to kill the elephant, but that once the rifle was in his hands he risked looking like a coward or a fool if he didn't use it. Here was I, he says, the White man with his gun, standing in front of the unarmed native crowd, seemingly the leading actor of the piece; but in reality I was only an absurd puppet. There was always for me an unpleasant aftertaste when I read these sections, reminiscent of Rudyard Kipling's rhetoric of the 'white man's burden', an image of the White patriarch as enslaved by empire, which is surely just the logic of the punitive expedition. I mean, the universal logic of the abuser – 'look at what you made me do'. It works through the deflection of the colonial policeman's agency through the other actors in play: the animal, the gun, the expectation of the crowd.[206] It's like that Bruno Latour piece on guns all over again. That distinctive form of denialism.

Today, though, it feels like there is something further in the text, something about time, and endurance, and thus inheritance. Don't read too much into it, you caution me, remember Orwell himself warned against what he called 'the old mistake of wanting to read too much between the lines'.[207] Then again, a reading can always give way to a retelling, just as a tool can be misused or left unused, applied to a function it wasn't designed for but that's inherent in its form. As the first bullet hits the elephant, every line of its body alters, and it seems suddenly ancient, thousands of years old, Orwell writes. With the second, it climbs slowly to its feet. With the third, the agony jolts its whole body, and it falls but does not die. The last two shots are fired towards the animal's heart and blood pours out. It is still alive, but dying very slowly. Out of ammunition, the policeman-narrator sends back for his small .44 calibre Winchester and pours shot after shot into the animal's throat, but they seem to make no impression. He leaves the elephant still alive, and later learns it lived for another half an hour, its tortured gasps as steady as the ticking of a clock. The animal's slow death, how it won't die for ages no matter how many slugs are shot into it, reads like an image not so much of the brutal logic of colonialism but as an extreme ready-made metaphor for how the man with the gun refuses to stop firing and even when death will not come – to the extent that, impossibly, he comes to appear as the victim as well as the perpetrator. That's the category error, right there.

The fact of an undying, undead imperialism within Euro-American societies as well as in former colonies is perhaps clearest, you tell me, in how stories like that of the governor – the massacre and the acquittal – echo and repeat in the criminal justice system. In London as in so many other places there's an ongoing history of the killing of young Black men being met with inaction and injustice, and a long history of community- and family-led campaigns for justice and truth against police brutality, cover-ups and lethal anti-Black violence. In London it's a history that runs deep, from Kelso Cochrane (aged 32) who was stabbed to death in North Kensington on 17 May 1959 to Stephen Lawrence (aged 18) stabbed to death in Eltham on 22 April 1993; from Colin Roach (aged 23) shot dead in police custody at the entrance of a Stoke Newington police station on 12 January 1983 to Mark Duggan (aged 29) who was shot dead by police in Tottenham on 4 August 2011. Untruths in such cases can take the form of silences or the closing of ranks, or corruption and even collusion between racist groups and police officers; or sometimes even of direct lies, as Isaac Julien's film *Who Killed Colin Roach?*, which documented how the initial inquest ruling that Roach had committed suicide was shown to be untrue.

In the wake of the failure of the Metropolitan Police to convict the group of five White murderers who were witnessed killing Stephen Lawrence in an unprovoked racist attack in 1999 the Macpherson Report of the Stephen Lawrence Inquiry criticised the police force's procedures. More than just incompetence in the investigation, there was the potential for collusion and corruption, for 'serious basic errors made by senior and experienced officers which cannot be explained by accident, oversight or overwork' that amounted to what the report called 'institutional racism'. This was by no means new terminology. The term had come to prominence in the US civil rights movement from 1968, and during the 1970s had been used in Black studies to express the idea that racism can exist not just in obvious and visible ways but also inherently or structurally in sectors such as the military, schools or international relations.[208] In Britain, the conclusions of the 1981 Scarman Report into the Brixton riots stated in broad terms that 'institutional racism does not exist in Britain', but elsewhere in the report Lord Scarman wrote that if 'an institutionally racist society' is understood as one in which 'practices may be adopted by public bodies as well as private individuals which are unwittingly discriminatory against black people, then this is an allegation that deserves serious consideration and, where proved, swift remedy'.[209]

In keeping with the politics of the time, in those heady days of the first term of a New Labour government under Tony Blair, Sir William Macpherson's 1999 report was employing a particular kind of social scientific language. It accepted that institutional racism was described as a 'pernicious and persistent' phenomenon, but described this racism as 'subtle and concealed', 'systematic' and yet 'unconscious', 'collective', 'hidden'. Institutional racism, the report argued, was a 'net effect', a set of 'attitudes, values and beliefs', rather than 'the deliberate actions of a small number of bigoted individuals'. It derived from the 'culture' of the police service: 'the canteen culture, the occupational culture' – 'the white experience, the white beliefs, the white values'.[210]

The official use of the term 'institutional racism' seemed to many people, as Stuart Hall wrote at the time, like 'a real advance'. It offered an acceptance, Hall wrote, of the everyday practices of 'institutional habitus'.[211] And as Paul Gilroy has argued, the concept of institutional racism offered an important alternative to the emerging 'agentic, individuating, rights-based approaches to diversity and difference that characterise neoliberal dogma and corporate multiculturalism alike', which lead towards 'the privatisation both of racial grievances and of the mechanisms of their amelioration'.[212] But the question that was not asked by the report was: how were those laws, customs and practices established? It's not like this is ancient history, after all.

In retrospect, the key failure in the Macpherson Report, you explain to me, related to the kind of social science theory that informed it. Having 'trawled' the academic literature, the report added a third adjective to Scarman's acceptance of the existence of 'unwitting or unconscious racism'. That word was 'unintentional'.[213] And when this question of intentionality was combined with the language of 'established laws, customs, and practices which systematically reflect and produce racial inequalities', the sociology of Anthony Giddens (since 2004 Baron Giddens of Southgate), the centre-left theorist who was close to the New Labour project and often described as the architect of the 'Third Way', was perceptible. Giddens' influential theory of 'structuration' had placed analytical emphasis on institutions and how they are reproduced, which he saw as a constant interplay between structures and the individual agency that is both framed by those structures as outcomes and in turn recreates, perpetuates. Just as the Giddensian sociology was interested in ongoing self-maintenance of institutions, so Macpherson's report wrote about 'outcome' and 'process'.[214]

There is the overt racism of individuals, and the bribes and intimidation to keep people quiet and complicit, and then there is the hidden and unintentional or unwitting racism of institutions, the report argued. But what if the analysis is right but the very framing of 'agency' was itself a kind of unintended theoretical stitch-up? Surely there are racisms that were once intentional, and were hidden or made covert intentionally too, so that over generations they would be inculcated into culture, buried in practice, functionally cemented into institutions? Surely there are institutional racisms that are the conscious creation of hidden prejudice, like loaded dice? Such structures would represent the opposite of the so-called 'material agency' of ANT, in that it is about duration not some timeless present. A generation later in the 2020s, you show me, the improvement narratives inherent in reports like those of Scarman or Macpherson must be measured against the fact, highlighted by Aviah Sarah Day and Shanice Octavia McBean in their book *Abolition Revolution*, that:

> These generational cycles of crisis management – where our anger and energy are syphoned into the latest report into, and admission of, police failures – have made the police better able to protect their power by creating the illusion of change . . . Calls for improved policing are a central part of the machine that legitimises police power, the belief that the police simply need to do better.[215]

Day and McBean thus open up another dimension to the question of institutional reproduction. They point to the reminder by the group Abolitionist Futures that the recommendation of the Macpherson Report was that the ministerial priority for police services was 'to increase trust and confidence in policing amongst minority ethnic communities' – rather than to rid the forces of racism.[216]

The history of this trick begins with the Anthropological Society and the Confederate propagandists; and it winds up now in Oxford, in the colleges and the museum displays and the Rhodes statue and even with how we teach archaeology, art, architecture, anthropology. British, French, German and American universities are only one step away from offering a Masters programme in nonhuman studies, which would doubtless be offered in partnership with one legacy colonial museum or another, you write to me, half joking (or perhaps not joking at all). It's possible for institutions to be set up a certain way after all, during their institutionalisation, like digging a foxhole, or loading a trap, to be consciously designed to make the enduring violence seem unconscious. It takes work to undo such structures, which are infrastructures and superstructures at the same time. Just as state-sanctioned violence against unarmed Black civilian bodies came to be seen as part of a structure rather than a legacy. A past with a surprisingly shallow Victorian time-depth, and one that morphed through the criminalisation of soft drug use, the 'sus' laws of the 1970s and 1980s (arbitrary stop-and-search on the basis of 'suspicion'), media-spun moral panic around 'mugging', and patterns of school exclusion.[217]

The police service, like the museum or the monument, is a memory institution, of course, as is the criminal justice system more generally. Not for nothing were those Confederate statues often placed outside the courthouse. And that's not to mention the invisible statues. The Macpherson Report's model of institutional racism has come to be a touchstone for many working in other sectors, and has even at times been employed in heritage management. But there's a clear danger of basing a twenty-first-century model of anti-racism on a 1990s police report. Not least one that is couched in the language of 1970s sociology, strained through a distinctive Blairite legacy.

These questions have been addressed more satisfactorily in California. In the wake of the acquittal of LAPD police officers in the case of the beating of Rodney King, which sparked the Los Angeles riots of 1992, Sylvia Wynter issued what she called 'an open letter to my colleagues' under the title 'No Humans Involved'. The letter focused on the acronym NHI, which the attention given to the case had revealed was a routine, unofficial way for members of LAPD to refer to young Black unemployed men in inner city ghettoes. Wynter describes NHI as part of a long-term process through which the image of 'the human' has been formed and universalised, but on a partial model. As a code, 'Man' has put forward the heteropatriarchal, White, Euro-American, militarist, extractivist, colonialist, bourgeois-capitalist, lone, exclusionary figure, Wynter argued. 'Man' came to stand for all humankind, as if eternally.

In the mid-1800s, Wynter explained, 'Man' became a prototype for a new secular political subject and Western bourgeois ethnoclass that was inscribed into the conception of humanity itself. She called this ideology 'liberal monohumanism'. A category that claimed universality was always already exclusionary, because human life was reduced to an exclusionary category. One group of people 'overrepresented' themselves as if they stood for the human itself.[218] The emerging generalised image of Man was endlessly reproduced and re-enacted to the point where it could hardly even be seen any more, unmarked in the hope of going unremarked. Call it out, you said to me. Anthropology, and its image of 'anthropos', of course was a central tool in this process in which the supremacist vision of a hierarchy of humanness was valorised. Man was presented as a natural category but was in reality a kind of supernatural image, Wynter showed, that could allow new forms of racism to emerge as an effect of this biocentric conception of the human. Wynter is not, of course, you said, suggesting that this vision of Man was invented unconsciously; and here the gaps in the Macpherson Report become even clearer.

What does Sylvia Wynter's account mean for our conception of humanity in the social sciences, and for the future of those parts of academic knowledge that we still call 'the humanities'? The new regimes of monumentality that emerged from these enduring forms of carcerality certainly revolved around the definition of humanity. They ranged from Fox's theory of the unseen hand to the physical reality of the skull-cup in the college archival box. This is a story of the invention of a history of humanity, then, a colonial worldview which began, say, in the 1860s or 1870s, with the creation of alterity or otherness not simply through the White supremacist ideas of biology – the treatment of some people as subhuman or as animals which was opposed through the anti-slavery movement – but through culture, the idea of people without history or at an earlier stage of civilisation.

The project of monohumanism was surely aligned with the formation of anthropology and archaeology as 'subjects' and the creation of the museum as a universal space full of 'objects', acts that made claims of different kinds to universalism. At the level of thought, knowledge and categorisation, this was a transformation and survival of the enduring horrors of objectification developed under slavery, in that it restricted the work of subjectification to certain humans. And then there's the strange re-emergence of what Bruno Latour called his 'universalist anthropology', against which we might try to fold Wynter's analysis of Man back onto the resurgent figure of the 'nonhuman' as it returns to these legacy colonial academic spaces.

If a certain idea of 'race' is a primary legacy of colonialism, not just a ghost to be exorcised but an ideology to be dismantled in both physical and immaterial forms, a weapon to be disarmed, then it is crucial to attend to the violence of the exclusionary history that Wynter underlines. Wynter describes this work as 'counterhumanism', a rewriting and 'mutation' of knowledge, an attempt to 'unspeak' the category of Man; to dislodge him as a secular political subject: deconstructing the 'genre of human' through which the human past and present has come to be imagined.[219]

There's a phrase in Michel-Rolph Trouillot's book *Silencing the Past* – 'to repress the unthinkable' – that feels relevant here. He uses it in a discussion of the Haitian Revolution of 1791–1804, to express the idea current among French (and British) colonisers at the time that enslaved people could never envision their freedom in the way that the French Revolution did. Trouillot asks his reader: 'How does one write a history of the impossible?' It's a question, he argues, of understanding that archival and historical silences are silencings, just as much actions as 'mentions' are. And acts of silencing, he continues, are concerned with who counts as human – about the definition of 'Man (with a capital M)' as he puts it.[220]

Against the marked or unmarked, overt or covert racisms to which the Macpherson Report pointed, it's possible to read Stuart Hall's account of Whiteness which, as he observed in a seminal paper in 1981, has often come to represent 'the unmarked position'.[221] Hall was discussing the presentation of 'race' in the British media such as TV shows in the 1980s, but this gesture of ultranormalisation of an unmarked, unremarked hegemonic norm has a past. Here is the prehistory of the so-called culture war that rattles down from the flying column formations of the Royal Navy's punitive expeditions in the nineteenth century through the column inches of *The Spectator* and the more extremist corners of the op-eds of the *Daily Telegraph* today. Columns of all kinds marshalled as if they were monuments to what Hall called the unmarked position; partial images passing for the sum of reality, just like Wynter's description of 'Man'. Wynter's argument echoes and reorients Fanon's line: 'When I search for man in the technique and style of Europe, I see a succession of negations of man, an avalanche of murders.'[222]

If we are to understand the techniques and tools used by this image of 'militarist realism' to reproduce itself over time, then we need to do more than take the work of anthropology, or archaeology, or the museum or the monument as timeless projects, as Macpherson did with police racism, but try understand how the representation and misrepresentation of 'others' was from the start an intergenerational technology of endurance. The fiction was that a statue, a display, or a body of knowledge would be immortal, icons of how cultural Whiteness would outlive dying 'races' through technological superiority and civilisation. And thus today we encounter their ghosts in the archives and in the streets as statues and in the museums as we embody them as visitors. But a ghost, the anthropologists tell us, is always a kind of impersonation; an innovation that works in unexpected ways with human mortality.[223]

The Macpherson-Giddensian account of institutional racism is missing a sense of causality, of legacy. How then to join the dots? From stolen lives on Caribbean plantations to stolen objects in museums to the history of criminal justice systems and the emergence of mass incarceration after the Second World War: what if, in the *longue durée* of carceral violence, the monumentality of monohumanism were not an aberration? What if the monument and the museum represent some kind of foundation-trench or post-hole or grave-pit cutting through a layered sequence that runs from enslavement before the mid-nineteenth century, to the regimes of carceral capitalism evolving into the realms of policing and jails from the mid-twentieth century? These monuments, as ideas and images, as objects or subjects, would represent an underpinning cut into the treatment of millions of human beings and human bodies as objects, commodities, chattel, property, currency, at an industrialised scale. They try to naturalise an ideology of timeless supremacy through the display of human cultures and human bones under lock and key. And what would this mean for the fields of anthropology and archaeology, which emerged hand in hand with these new regimes of the museum and the monument? As disciplines, they sought to measure and control time and space and the human body just as the regimes of time-management and the vision of the 'overseer' did on the plantation or in the factory or the prison or the school. As academic subjects, they established themselves through the installation and inheritance of a host of solid objects.

To borrow the terminology of Saidiya Hartman, we might approach the museum and the monument and the 'subjects' of archaeology and anthropology as 'scenes of subjection' – not sites of the spectacular direct violence of a hundred ways in which bodies were broken and violated, but secondary, proxy spaces of 'ordinary terror'. Where subjection meets subjectification, and dehumanisation is worked with the bodies and bones of the dead rather than directly with the living, and with cultural cargo brought from the ship's hold to the gallery, where the 'hold' of slavery is still present like the grip of an unseen hand.[224] Does some trace of the memory of the soldiers in Hyde Park in 1866 live on through the statues that still police its pathways? 'What need have we of all these monuments to Peel?' wrote Marx and Engels in 1850, referring to Sir Robert Peel, the Tory home secretary who'd founded the Metropolitan Police Force in 1829: 'Every policeman in Britain and Ireland is a living monument to him.'[225] Those monuments take different forms, it turns out, each another element of an exclusionary vision of one figure of Man: statues, systems, laws, a police box on every corner, a museum in every city, a Confederate monument outside every courthouse in the American South, and in the streets and parks of London not just the soldiers holding fire but also the statues, wrought in bronze and stone, all those generals, monarchs and colonial-capitalists, still on guard after all these years.

This book you're thinking of writing is turning out to be more about White men than I expected, you tell me. Then again, you reply, I guess there's that line from Sara Ahmed: '"white men" is an institution'.[226] You read me a section from Fox's first lecture on 'Primitive Warfare': 'the savage is morally and mentally an unfit instrument for the spread of civilization, except when he is reduced to a state of slavery.' [227] And one from his second 'Primitive Warfare' lecture, where he dismisses the idea of 'suddenly applying to the inferior races of mankind, laws and institutions for which they are about as much fitted as the animals in the Zoological Gardens'.[228] I tell you about a discussion I read between Kobena Mercer and Isaac Julien from 1994 about the image of the black male youth as a 'mugger', and the 'toughness' that Black men have to resort to, to defend against the prior aggression and violence that is inherent in how Black communities are policed by White male police officers. It's a 'cycle between reality and representation', they write, that produces a kind of 'truth' or, more precisely, a struggle over the meaning of Black masculinity under the 'dominant regime of truth'.[229]

We talk about the culturally White counterparts in that cycle, and how they are inherited; different and dangerous kinds of brutalisation through which the image of a toxic, violent, White masculinity is put forward, and then repeatedly brought into reality. I don't want to hear any more about why cultural Whiteness was created, I say to you, I want to understand how cultural Whiteness was built to last, and is made to endure. And then we read more about how these shifting categories of nonhumanity and inhumanity and humanity itself were the focus of the nascent militarist White supremacist ideology of the mid-century British ruling class, whose estates had been swelled by the 'reparations' paid to slave-holding families.

The head of Victoria on the coin removed from the skull-cup. The Cannibal gavel carved in ivory and ebony. The museum curators behind barricades with their loaded guns. The elephant that won't die. The Prussian helmet transposed from the First World War trenches to Nagaland to Oxford to the cover of a theory book. The Lefaucheux revolver taken as a memento from the race massacre and the piano wire knottily twisted into the cat-o-nine-tails. The transformation of capital from slavery compensation into the purchase of the skull. Blink and in all these images stands the figure of Fox, not the man exactly but his figure in thought and practice. And not just the one figure but hundreds of men like him in a manner akin to what the anthropologist Roy Wagner described as 'the figure ground reversal of thought', that blink of the eye which reveals an inverse, like a significantly less abstract version of that famous black-and-white image in Gestalt psychology where the vase transforms into human faces.[230]

Let me offer my own future progressive. Neither exonerative nor denialist, but something closer to the second law of thermodynamics, a simple statement of entropy, of archaeological taphonomy. The heritage management perspective if you like: without preservation, without conservation, without maintenance, *every monument will fall*. Let them fall then, when they are out of step with the times, when they no longer reflect where a society wants to be going. In the space that opens up, imagine it were possible to try to repair the damage, rather than continually reload the weapon. Demand an expansion, a recalibration of the category of the human, you told me. I mean, understand the history of the category. I was scrolling down my notes on this history of violence, in all its forms; this story of remembering and forgetting that was now unfolding on the screen. I stood up, took my keys from the table and walked out of the flat, ran twice round the park, came back and took a shower, got dressed again for writing, made a pot of tea, poured the milk, opened the laptop again, and then closed my eyes for a moment with a thought of you, before turning the page.

# V

# Panic Attack

*fall*, noun. v) (of a person or animal) the action of falling as a consequence of stumbling, losing balance or becoming dizzy or weak

At the college's request, an archaeologist drills a tiny, powdered sample of the bone for carbon-14 dating. An email arrives a few months later; the lab has processed the results.

> We have the 14C results (162 ± 17 BP). Definitely not Neolithic!

The science suggests a date range for the death of this person of 1788, give or take seventeen years either side. So that's 1771 to 1805. At this kind of proximate timescale, there can be no further calibration or accuracy between one decade and another. But what's clear is that this unnamed person died in the late eighteenth or early nineteenth century. We both cried that evening, when we read those words: 'not Neolithic'.

Radiocarbon dating is a scientific procedure that illustrates a wider truth: that any archaeological method will involve drawing a line connecting the past and the present. The principle is quite simple, as every archaeology undergraduate must learn. Carbon-14 is an unstable isotope of carbon, known as radiocarbon because of its radioactivity. Living organisms continually assimilate carbon into the cells of their bodies, including small, naturally occurring traces of radiocarbon which derive from the effect of cosmic rays on nitrogen in the atmosphere. When a plant or animal dies, no more carbon is taken on and the C-14 in the body begins to decay into nitrogen. The rate at which such decay proceeds is described by nuclear physicists as a 'half-life', and for radiocarbon this is around 5,700 years. The moment of death starts the object's radiocarbon 'clock'.[1] In the 1950s, archaeologists realised that they could use these scientific measurements to determine quite accurately the date of organic artefacts dating from any point in the past 50,000 years or so.

By measuring the amount of C-14 against the pace of decay, radiocarbon dating thus produces a date rendered as 'BP', 'before present', and it is here that the line between past and present comes into focus – because 'before present' counts back not from the current year but from 1950. This convention began with the publication of the first radiocarbon dates in December 1949; but it stuck for one overwhelming reason. The year 1950 pre-dates the large-scale testing of nuclear weapons. During the 1950s and 1960s, the large controlled nuclear explosions that punctuated the Cold War increased the amount of carbon-14 in the earth's atmosphere, which was in turn taken into the bodies of all organisms alive at the time, dramatically elevating their levels of radiocarbon. It did so to such a degree that anyone born after 1950 carries a signature of the enormously elevated levels of carbon in their teeth and bone, an anthropogenic sign of nuclear testing, a quantum written into your body as militarist-realist time went off the scale. Through a technique called 'bomb pulse dating', forensic archaeologists have even developed a method of determining the year of birth of unidentified human bones and skulls from more recent years, measured against the peak in global C-14 and its gradual decline. But for human bones dating from before 1950, the analysis of radiocarbon in the dead organic material – the 'necromass' as scientists call it – operates as a chronometer, a form of time-reckoning based on measurements calibrated against the half-life.

In April 2023, the results of the DNA analysis that the college have commissioned come in – nothing can be ascertained about the place of birth or death. But from the physical size, the experts say, it is clearly the skull of a woman. When I shared the scientist's results with you, we tried to process these facts in silence. Then you read me some lines by Audre Lorde from a poem she called 'A Litany for Survival', and they broke the silence between us in fragments, words she wrote for those 'who live at the shoreline', for those 'imprinted with fear', for those 'who were never meant to survive'.[2]

## 21. A KIND OF WARNING

The art writer Adrian Stokes recalled walking in Kensington Gardens and Hyde Park as a child in the first decade of the twentieth century. Their 'cruel railings', he wrote, seemed to contain nothing but 'a burning cold'. There were fierce swans, and an orange cloud in the sky freighting a thunderstorm that when it arrived made it seem like all the coloured balloons sold by an old woman at Stanhope Gate had burst at once. The ominous, decaying smell of the machine house for the fountains and how they drained into the Long Water – 'the inky-dark medium of the Park suicides', as he put it. And then there were the monuments, their solid, 'pseudo-sacred' matter. 'It took many years for me to discover that art was not a kind of warning,' he wrote.[3] After all, these monuments were warnings all right: 'what else was to be made of the sharp, pale, granite obelisk in the Long Walk, the single word "ALMA" inscribed above two steps and a platform, edged by a decorous iron chain?'

Stoke here was misrecalling the Speke Monument, or reimagining it at least. Cut to a sharp spiked point as if it could burst the clouds above it, it was erected in 1866 to mark not the Battle of the Alma, but the journey of John Hanning Speke, Richard Burton's sometime companion and later rival, as the first European to visit Lake Victoria on his expedition to find the source of the Nile. In 1863, Speke published his racist Hamitic hypothesis of the White origins of the Tutsi, in contrast to the Hutu. You were near Kensington Gardens yesterday and agreed to go and check the actual words carved into the base of this monolith; when you send me your photos of the inscription, it reads:

IN MEMORY OF SPEKE
VICTORIA NYANZA AND THE NILE 1864

Speke's fake race-cultural science merges with Stoke's mnemonic licence. Perhaps the art critic was blending the image on purpose with the Guard Memorial, three soldiers – Grenadier, Scots and Coldstream – above the figure of Honour, which bears the name of three battles of the Crimean War on the pedestal: Alma, Inkerman, Sebastopol. This folded chain of remembrance and misremembrance only makes the sheer unreality of this monumental landscape yet more intense, as I imagine it from Oxford here at my desk in the museum again, googling for images to fact-check, reality continually giving way to militarist realism again.

With the Albert Memorial, installed between 1863 and 1875, militarist realism reached for fantasy at a new scale. The giant golden figure of the prince consort, colonel of the Grenadier Guards, is seated, enthroned within an iconography that depicts his vision of progress spread by empire, by the four Christian virtues, and by figures of the eight sciences of astronomy, chemistry, geology, geometry, rhetoric, medicine, philosophy and physiology – the last of which bears on her left arm a newborn child, 'a representation of the development of the highest and most perfect of physiological forms' as Lytton Strachey described it in 1921.[4] Painted black in the First World War as a protection against Zeppelin bombs, the figure of Albert was re-gilded in the 1990s. The Memorial was conceived by Gilbert Scott as a giant ciborium that enshrines an image of the dead prince at the apex of the world, quartered into sculptural groups symbolising Asia, Europe, Africa and America, a monument to his worldview. And to the south, past the Royal College of Art and the Royal Albert Hall, the Albertopolis, centred on the South Kensington Museum – renamed the Victoria and Albert Museum in 1899, less than two years before the Queen's death, tells further stories, the site of Fox's personal exhibition in the 1870s. But let's not get ahead of ourselves.

In March 1850 at the Mansion House in London Albert, in his capacity as president of the Society of Arts and overseer of the committee for the Great Exhibition, delivered a speech that set out his vision for the Crystal Palace. What times we are living through, he declared: 'a period of most wonderful transition, which tends rapidly to accomplish that great end to which, indeed, all history points – *the realisation of the unity of mankind*'. 'Realisation' is quite a word, you pointed out when I shared that line with you. The biocentric, colonial, economic image of Man described so precisely by Sylvia Wynter was starting to shift shape, solidify, the militarist realism presented as if it were destiny. As distances between nations were vanishing through steam power and the telegraph, he continued, 'thought is communicated with the rapidity, and even by the power, of lightning'. The 'moving power of civilisation', the prince said, 'is being extended to all branches of science, industry and art', and so:

> Man is approaching a more complete fulfilment of that great and sacred mission which he has to perform in this world ... to discover the laws by which the Almighty governs His creation and ... to conquer nature to his use; himself a divine instrument.[5]

Now a transformation was taking place under the crystalline structure at Hyde Park, as if the steel and plate glass of the palace were a hothouse forcing the shoots of a new ideology of technological supremacy. The sheer scale of what was on display was refracted through the glass. Across ten miles of stands were 15,000 exhibitors, six million visitors, half a million pounds in ticket sales, patrolled by hundreds of soldiers and policemen. The introduction to *The Crystal Palace and its Contents* claimed it was an achievement which would 'promote the common weal of the whole human community'.[6] I snag on that word, 'weal' – it is simply an archaic form of the word 'wealth', of course, but I read it like it's a wound or a scar. The military operations around the exhibition were immense. With memories of 1848 still fresh, planning for the exhibition, one soldier recalled in his memoirs, 'was not undertaken without the exercise of precaution against crowded assemblies and consequent disturbances, and notwithstanding his advanced age the Duke of Wellington took measures for the preservation of order involving the employment of troops'.[7] Two days before the opening of the exhibition, *The Times* reported, a violent hailstorm struck the park. Miraculously, the glass structure remained unharmed, every single pane left intact.[8] The hailstones sounded like a rain of bullets from volley fire.

The parkland was being ultramilitarised. The prince consort's world picture began with fear – fear, and a desperate urge to control. Fear and violence, that sounds like a more accurate dialectic than structure and agency, you interject. More than 3,000 soldiers were deployed to London for the duration of the exhibition from as far afield as Dover, Nottingham, Brighton and Dublin to the barracks at Woolwich, Tower of London, Hampstead, Highgate and Uxbridge. The Chelsea Pensioners were issued with muskets, bayonets and swords and stationed at Paddington, Kensington and Hammersmith. The metropolitan and city police, meanwhile, were increased in number by over a thousand men to form a force of 6,500 constables and officers, plus superintendents, inspectors, sergeants, and a reserve and detective force.[9] Hyde Park and its environs were saturated by men with guns, soldiers and police, and among them was Captain Fox, then twenty-four years old.

The watershed for these pronouncements of technological improvement came on 1 May 1851, when to the echoing volleys of artillery, the Queen announced from her throne in the Crystal Palace that the Great Exhibition of the Works of Industry of All Nations in Hyde Park was open, and the first visitors were admitted.[10] Joseph Paxton's prefabricated palace of glass and iron enclosed nineteen acres. The idea was for 'a world jubilee of industry', 'a museum manifesting the progress of man in all countries and under all social circumstances, in the myriad arts and pursuits of civilisation'.[11] The products of empire were displayed across four sections according to a scheme devised by the prince consort himself – I Raw Materials, II Machinery and Mechanical Inventions, III Manufactures (Textile Fabrics, Metallic, Vitreous and Ceramic), IV Fine Arts (Sculpture and Plastic Art) – to which further sections from British colonies and other nations were added.[12]

Within these sections there were thirty classes, ranging from mining and quarrying operations to machines of every kind, to agricultural implements, musical instruments, surgical instruments, silk and velvet manufactures, flax and hemp manufactures, 'cutlery and edge', saddlery, clothing, jewellery, and so on. Steam-hammers and gas-burners and Derrick cranes and pistons and girders and a papier-mâché jewel case and ship-ventilators and daguerreotypes and a great hydraulic press, lace gassing machines, a jewelled hawk, a collection of Indian jewels exhibited by the East India Company, the immense Koh-i-Noor diamond from the Royal Collection, the printing press of the *Illustrated London News*, Prince Albert's own 'model houses for the labouring classes' and the great centrepiece, a crystal fountain.[13] There was art as well, of course. Among the many statues displayed at the Great Exhibition were Hiram Powers' nude white marble *Greek Slave*, standing like the *Venus de' Medici* but with both wrists bound and chained to a post, and Bostonian Peter Stephenson's *Wounded Indian*, as well as a 21-foot-high zinc figure of Queen Victoria made by the Franco-Belgian Vieille Montagne Zinc Company.[14] *Punch* magazine asked why so few of what it called 'the treasures of America' were on display: 'Why not have sent some choice specimens of slaves? We have the Greek Captive in dead stone – why not the Virginian slave in living ebony?'[15] What about the weapons technology on display? you ask me. Or was all of this a weapons technology? The prehistory of the culture war.

Fox was among those deployed to guard the exhibition, the bearskin on his head with its white plume or 'hackle'. It was one of a series of Fox's postings where the Grenadier Guards were policing London for high-profile events: from the eighteen-year-old Ensign Fox who'd been on duty the day of the Chartist demonstration to Acting Major Fox who would defend the Hyde Park monuments in 1866, aged thirty-nine. His biographers have pointed out that the fact that he started collecting so soon afterwards is suggestive of the effect it had on his interests, aesthetics and sensibilities, especially the evolutionary and providential dimensions of the prince consort's thinking. But Fox remained primarily a soldier-administrator throughout: quartermaster, adjutant, instructor and military theorist. In fact in 1875, when Fox was elected to a fellowship of the Royal Society, he insisted that his main contributions to science lay not in the museum he had built, or his many anthropological papers and archaeological digs, but in the field of musketry – the intertwined experiments he undertook to replace the army's smooth-bore musket with the new Enfield rifle, and to improve the training of soldiers to use it effectively; experiments that took the human body and transformed it at scale.[16] Central here was a sense of bodily techniques, of the particular changes that take place through drilling, repetition and the passage of time. What he took away from spending time in the vast barracks-like gallery spaces of the Great Exhibition was, perhaps, something akin to the technology of the drill hall – that for the public to bring their bodies to this place at such scale brought about a particular kind of transformation in culture; a process he came to imagine perhaps in a manner not unlike the parlour game where the snail turns into a bird, or John White's drawings of the timber posts hardening into stone. As a line from the fictional Captain Harry Flashman – born in 1822, the bully from *Tom Brown's School Days* who grows up to be a high-ranking

Victorian British Army officer and antihero – goes, 'In the British Army of course, 'taint the weapon that counts, 'tis the man behind it.'[17]

As it was for the drill hall and the butts, so it was for the exhibitionary spaces of Victorian London. As the soldier Fox gripped his weapon and stood stock still, a blurring of the boundaries between bodies, statues, architecture and the idea of improvement or evolution was taking place in the surreality of Hyde Park. Just as memories of Waterloo were beginning to fade, any image of a half-century of European peace was breaking apart. War was coming. A new war; a new kind of war.

## 22. TECHNOVIOLENCE

When Fox joined up, the British Army were still using the kind of smooth-bore muzzle-loaded muskets that they had used at Waterloo, the so-called 'Brown Bess'. But small arms technologies were developing quickly, with more widespread use of rifling – which added machine-cut shallow spiral grooves to the interior wall of the gun barrel, increasing accuracy at long distance – replacing the smooth bore, the percussion cap replacing the flintlock, and new ammunition systems. Foremost among the new ammo was the conical lead bullet invented in Paris by Claude-Étienne Minié in 1847, for which two years later the Minié percussion-lock rifle had been invented to fire the 'Minié balls'. The rifle allowed rapid muzzle-loading, and when fired the soft bullet was deformed in the barrel, achieving a new scale of physical damage when it struck a human body. There were stories that it would run four inches into a pine tree at 1,000 yards, that it could pass through a soldier and his backpack from a distance of three quarters of a mile, and that at point-blank range one shot could run through six ranks of soldiers as smoothly as a depth charge sinks through the ocean water.

In summer 1850, still in his early twenties, Fox was appointed to the newly convened Sub-Committee of Small Arms, formed to consider the respective merits of adopting a different new gun as a general-purpose firearm in the world's first modern arms race. Much of his professional work in the subsequent years was focused on experiments for a new system of rifle training for the British Army, first at the Royal Gun and Powder Factories and Laboratories in Woolwich and the Small Arms Factory at Enfield in London, then at Hythe in Kent, and later in Malta. Fox described his work as 'the science of gunnery' – by which he meant a synchronicity between new technologies of steel and powder on the one hand and of the drilled human body which fired the weapon on the other. Violence, technology, bodies: all the elements were in play for the discipline of anthropology – for what the theorists would later call the study of 'humans and nonhumans' – to start to emerge.

By 1861, some 2,000 rifles per week were being produced from steel, brass and wood at the Enfield factory by a workforce of 1,700. The remit of the subcommittee came to intersect with that of the Exhibition Committee, as they experimented with many new weapons, including those that were displayed at the Great Exhibition in Hyde Park, the latest revolvers, 'needle' guns and carbines.[18] They conducted experiments in the butts at the Royal Arsenal at Woolwich, using not only specialist artillerymen but also rank and file line regiments, because the interest was in an improved system of efficient use that could be drilled into soldiers at scale, rather than purely the superiority of a weapon's firepower or accuracy.[19]

The production of bullets and trained bodies at the government facilities at Enfield, Woolwich and Hythe was stepped up, and guns began to be procured from private Birmingham gunmakers, as the East India Company had done, rather than being manufactured solely at the government's own armoury at Enfield.[20] During one demonstration of the Colt revolver, which was displayed in the American Department of the Great Exhibition, the Queen attended to hear an explanation of its capacities. The pistol could fire six times in rapid succession without the need for reloading. Prince Albert surprised onlookers by picking one of the guns up. He handled the weapon for a minute or so, then cocked, primed, loaded, discharged the six-shooter, and emptied its chamber in the direction of the steel target.[21]

Handled right, the new Enfield rifle could improve the accuracy of extermination from 100 to as much as 900 yards, they said at the time. The gunman required training in how to observe and calculate his distance from the target and so adjust the sights correctly, allowing for wind and anticipated movement. Fox advocated for a formalised system of teaching the soldier to use this new weapon of precision, and submitted plans for such instruction to his superiors.[22] In 1852 he was appointed to instruct the Second Battalion of the Grenadier Guards in musketry and draw up a new code of instruction: aiming, position, judging distance and other preliminary drills. Fox travelled across Europe to research the most effective elements of systems of codes and instruction in use on the continent and incorporated them into his system.[23] There's no record of the exact route taken, or the letters of introduction to visit a foreign army, as Fox travelled by rail and steamer to musketry training facilities at Vincennes in the suburbs of Paris, at Turin in the Piedmont, at the vast Belgian military camp at Beverlo, Leopoldsburg, and at the musketry experimentation and training facilities of the Army of the Two Sicilies in Naples.[24]

Fox's mode of experimentation with weapons also involved collecting, from the outset, and he brought back a haul of state-of-the-art firearms from his European trip. The trip coincided with his travel to Naples to retrieve the body of his older brother, who died on 13 June 1852, from the British mission at Cava de' Tirreni. The city lies next to Pompeii, and Fox's encounter there with an image of the dead frozen by volcanic catastrophe, at a time of personal loss, was surely another domino falling.[25] He had some guns specially made for his regimes of weapons-testing, each with slight improvements. Weapons that survive in the collection in Oxford offer glimpses of this history. There's a smooth-bore percussion-cap muzzle-loading long gun from the factory of gunmakers Ancion & Cie at Liège, bearing the label '51' which presumably records the year of acquisition.[26] Further Belgian guns include a breech-loading rifle with a cleaning rod and bayonet acquired by Fox from the Great Exhibition of 1851.[27] There was a musket with a revolving chamber, a bolt-action breech-loading rifle such as had been invented in Prussia, and rifles with experimental adjustable sights. It is also during this trip that Fox appears to have collected an item which he donated to the museum of the United Service Institution in February 1853 – a stuffed, life-size model of a French soldier in uniform, with 'knapsack, cap, arms, and accoutrements complete; together with a glass case containing a specimen of every article forming the kit of a French soldier'.[28] Even the clothing and equipment of potential enemy combatant bodies was being assembled in this campaign of military collecting.

In September 1850, the *Birmingham Gazette* reported that a case of model muskets and appurtenances had arrived by steamer from Ostend for the inspector of small arms at the Tower for submission to the committee.[29] Another model rifle was sent to Fox by steamer from Calais in December,[30] and Fox undertook experiments with Minié bullets manufactured for him by Henry Wilkinson, whose company supplied the East India Company with firearms through their Pall Mall office.[31]

Three prototypes for the Enfield Pattern 1853 rifle-musket, as an alternative to the Minié, were manufactured specially for Fox in London, including one by Wilkinson from a drawing supplied by Fox, and another at the Royal Small Arms Factory at Enfield.[32] After years of experimentation, testing, instruction and the formalisation of codes, the British Army adopted the .577-calibre Enfield Pattern 1853 rifle-musket as its first service rifle for infantry on the battlefield. The 1852 prototype made for Fox by Wilkinson is fixed on display in the upper gallery of the Pitt Rivers today, the second firearm from the top.[33] I stood in front of it last week. And I wondered whether Fox encountered the 'mitrailleuse', a manually fired fifty-barrel volley gun developed in Belgium when he was there in 1851, a prototype machine gun. Fox's writing and records are strangely silent on machine guns throughout his gunnery career and after. Then again who knows what's kept in archives and what's considered top secret. Fox is guiding this narrative too much, you tell me, even beyond death. Someone told me he was basically a spy his whole career, using archaeology as a cover in Egypt, America, Ireland, Malta, Prussia, Schleswig-Holstein. There may be some truth in that, I concede. Work from the known to the unknown, that's how Fox described how he worked. It's the approach of the intelligence officer, you said to me; and of the propagandist too.

When the new School of Musketry was established on the Kent coast at Hythe, Fox was appointed first instructor.[34] Occupying two Napoleonic-era blocks about a mile inland, since demolished and replaced by what's now a Sainsbury's supermarket, the school used the wide dunes of the foreshore as ranges for both testing and training. As Woolwich was for artillery training, so Hythe was to be for infantry firepower. In February 1853, Fox and his wife moved to Hythe. During the day there was the continual sound, sight and smell of gunshots.[35]

In July 1853, the Board of Ordnance purchased beach land from the Corporation of Hythe for Minié testing and practice.[36] Here, the 26-year-old Captain Fox introduced musketry instructors to his system of gunnery science, and trained detachments from different regiments sent to Hythe for drill instruction in the use of the new rifle, introducing a system of points through which regiments could compete.[37]

Fox's orders were now to revise the code for adoption across the British Army, and in February 1853 the manual *Instruction of Musketry*, setting out a course for the drilling of recruits, was published. It provided detailed instructions on target practice, and even on the equipment needed for the instruction of soldiers in the manufacture of cartridges, cutting white cartridge paper into a trapezium and rolling it up with a bullet and fine sand used in place of gunpowder: bullets, tin measures and funnels, an iron paper-cutter, a large knife, five cylindrical wooden mandrels to roll the cartridge, and a set of tin patterns for shaping the paper. 'When completed the base of the cartridge must be dipped up to the shoulder in grease, consisting of six parts tallow to one of beeswax', the instructions specified.[38]

In May 1859, when the formation of volunteer rifle corps as part of the Volunteer Force, a part-time national citizen army, came into operation, thousands of recruits undertook residential courses at Hythe for three weeks of training under the system Fox had established in 1853. By the end of the first week, the captain of the Scottish Rifle Volunteers wrote in the *Journal of the Society of Arts* in May 1861, 'men with good sight and ordinary intelligence learn to hit an enemy at half a mile' – underlining that good instruction of men at Hythe was as important as good production of weapons at Enfield.[39] Instruction included 'position drill' in the barrack-yard, teaching posture for firing when standing or kneeling and how to hold the body in position, and a 'judging distance drill' conducted on the shingle beach, where men were placed at fifty-yard intervals to teach the soldiers how to recognise distance by how well the face and the body could be discerned. An 'aiming drill' was conducted on bullseye targets in the firing ranges, and 'theoretical drill' was delivered through lectures with explanatory models and diagrams introducing the principles of the explosion of powder and the flight of the bullet. The soldier's body was becoming another perfectible tool, another weapon stockpiled for the conflict to come.

A sense of the tone and content of the course is conveyed in an account by Henry Edwards of the 5th Norfolk Volunteer Rifles, written shortly after training at Hythe in October 1859:

> Our talk was of trajectories, of groove-cylinders, and frustums of cones; of explosive power and projectile power, of breech loaders, long Enfields and short Enfields, of Lancasters, Whitworths and Westley Richards; of the Bouchier bullet, and the Pritchett bullet. No ladies came upon the *tapis*, except Brown Bess (the rejected) and Minié (the admired). Of Sunday's proceedings I have nothing to note except a curious coincidence in the Psalms of the day, which commenced with the words *Blessed be the Lord my strength, who teacheth my hands to war and my fingers to fight*.[40]

Through serving on this subcommittee as an administrator and an instructor, Fox learned from the new technologies of weaponry through commissioning prototypes and intervening in industrial production and from trials and experiments that led to the discarding of an obsolete weapon. But the new technologies of the drilled body also offered the rudiments of a theory that would inform the rest of his working life, from the barracks to the museum, and from the monument to the academy – a theory of the evolution of material culture.

The so-called 'Great Game' between the Russian and British empires, from Turkmenistan to India, was now threatening war in Europe. And it was in this context that Fox now developed an interest in what he saw as a principle of continuity by observing the very slow gradations of progress in military technology.[41] In 1858, his earliest published lecture was titled 'On the Improvement of the Rifle'.[42] More was at stake than improving weapons technology, comparative research to identify the 'fittest' weapon, and outclassed instruments of destruction being superseded; this was about experiments with the body as well as the weapon itself, about new modes of training and drilling.

'You are another subject because you hold the gun,' wrote Bruno Latour in that argument he made about 'humans and nonhumans', a hundred years after Fox's death.[43] And, in a foreshadowing of such theories, with a different jargon but a parallel vision, Fox wrote that the training of the body and the improvement of the weapon had to be understood together. The technical improvement of the rifle went hand in hand with 'improvements' of the soldier's body that could be taught – technique, skill, the knack of handling a weapon or tool. Here were the seeds of a theory of violence, a kind of bellicose, death-drive Victorian body of thought, an arms race in which the (male) body could be weaponised, tooled up and launched overseas *en masse* to fight for that new, emerging entity, the modern imperial ethnostate.

## 23. DRILLED BODIES

On 22 February 1854, the pace of it all changed. The talk of accelerating technology and improving efficiency got real. For the British military this was no longer just talk, but the biggest expedition for half a century. At St George's Barracks, the men were mustered at 3 a.m. Following a review by Lord Hardinge, the Duke of Cambridge and Albert, the prince consort – who was the colonel of the Guards – the band struck up. At 5 a.m. the column of soldiers began to make its way along a crowd-lined route from Trafalgar Square in near-silence. Fox's battalion was leaving London. Their boots echoed as the men marched in step through the dark, wet streets, a line of bodies that ran down the Strand like a twisted piece of wire towards Waterloo Bridge and across the river to the station, advancing like a second river; a river that seemed wider and deeper and faster than the Thames, with a strong undertow that could carry you away or knock you down and trample you underfoot, advancing like an argument overheard, outside on the street below, that wakes you in the night, filled with the anticipation of violence. Across the unlit flow of the Thames, on the bridge the drizzle was illuminated yellow in the lights and a mass of steel, flesh, leather and red jackets coursed like blood through a vein, arriving at Waterloo, heading to the sea by rail, and thence to a new kind of mechanised, industrialised war.

Opened six years earlier, the railway station bore the name of a battle like a monument to four decades of peace in Europe that was about to shatter. Filing down the steps onto the platform, the soldiers started to board the trains, and the band struck up. The crowds waved handkerchiefs, and as the regimental pipes and drums passed by, some even sang along to the tune of the marching song 'The British Grenadiers':

> Some talk of Alexander, and some of Hercules
> Of Hector and Lysander, and such great names as these.
> But of all the world's brave heroes, there's none that can compare,
> With a tow, row, row, row, row, row, to the British Grenadiers.
>
> Those heroes of antiquity ne'er saw a cannon ball,
> Or knew the force of powder to slay their foes withal.
> But our brave boys do know it, and banish all their fears,
> With a tow, row, row, row, row, row, for the British Grenadiers.
>
> Whene'er we are commanded to storm the palisades,
> Our leaders march with fusees,[44] and we with hand grenades.
> We throw them from the glacis,[45] about the enemies' ears,
> With a tow, row, row, row, row, row, for the British Grenadiers.[46]

Navigating the crush of the crowds, sombrely assembled as though to attend to some accident rather than witness a parade, construction workers were arriving to site. They were breaking ground to expand Waterloo further with a private station for the London Necropolis & National Mausoleum Company. In the coming years, it would transport the bodies of both the dead and the mourners south-westward to Brookwood Cemetery in Surrey, bringing the living back into the city after the funeral and interment. This station within a station, a terminus for the dead, would be completed in the autumn. The arches below the vast brick viaduct that snakes southwards across Lambeth and out of the city served as mortuaries, where bodies were stored before transportation. But for now, shortly before sunrise, cheered off by thousands of onlookers, the troops boarded two London and South-Western Railway trains which steamed out of the station towards Southampton, packed full of sardined soldiers' bodies. At Southampton, the Coldstream Guards arrived by train from Chichester, marching through the streets from the station, and later that morning the Grenadier Guards took the same route. The troops boarded the P&O steamers *Ripon* and *Manilla* and the Royal West India Mail Company steamship *Orinoco*. The shore bell rang, the ships pulled away from the quay and 2,000 men embarked for service in the Eastern Campaign. The *Ripon* arrived in Malta twelve days later on 6 March, slowed down by calling at Gibraltar for coal, and the smaller *Manilla* took a further six days to arrive.[47] But Captain Fox had travelled via another route and was already on the island, readying the facilities for gunnery training.

Following his appointment as Superintending Instructor in Rifle Practice for the Expeditionary Force for the War in the East, Fox made the much faster and significantly more comfortable journey with the headquarters staff officers. The new technoviolence demanded new speeds. The first leg of the journey from London Bridge to Folkestone and thence to Boulogne was by express locomotive and steam-packet specially commissioned for dispatches and government couriers in this time of war. The Channel crossing took just two hours, and Fox's party continued by rail on the express train of the Boulogne and Amiens Railway Company. Twelve hours after departing, they were already in Paris.[48] With a group of twenty other staff officers, Fox's onward rail journey from Paris to Marseille the following day brought them to the Mediterranean coast.[49] The headquarters staff took a mail steamer to Malta.[50] French vessels and the British government-commissioned P&O steamers *Vectis* and *Valetta* provided a dispatch service between Marseille, Valletta and Constantinople. The company claimed they were the world's fastest ocean-going steamers, capable of making the voyage from Marseille to Malta in forty hours.[51] Within four days of leaving London, Fox was in the Maltese capital, with blueprints for instructing and drilling the men in the use of the new rifle while they were still on the transports. With the capital resources at hand for war, time and space were starting to warp.

In those days in early March 1854, more and more war vessels were converging on Valletta, the staging post for more than 20,000 British troops forming the Expeditionary Land Force for the invasion of Crimea. They travelled from Southampton, London and Liverpool to Malta and then across the Black Sea, turning the waters into a lake of steel and brass and human bodies. The massive steamer *Himalaya* arrived at one in the morning with the appearance, one Grenadier Guard recorded, of a huge floating phantom as she glided sluggishly into the harbour.[52] The massing of bluejackets and redcoats was, the special correspondent of the *Morning Post* wrote, 'a rock-bound scene of chivalrous and historical association'.[53] The troop numbers were such that the barracks at the island's forts were full. Some regiments slept in hammocks in the dockyard or under canvas on every available slope and ridge across the landscape. Some even made camp in a graveyard.[54]

This period of waiting was a time for training. Under the command of Adjutant-General Fox, Minié rifle practice began on 9 March at Fort Ricasoli at Kalkara, built by the Knights Hospitaller in the late seventeenth century, and at Fort Tigné.[55] The Crusader heritage ran deep into the Maltese landscape. Fox was superintending instructor in rifle practice.[56] Soldiers were trained to shoot at those iron targets invented in Hythe, six feet in height and two feet in diameter and each marked with a bullseye eight inches in diameter. They were both introduced to firing – drilled in shooting while standing, kneeling, lying down, advancing and retreating – and also instructed in how to use the sights to calculate aim at increasing distance. 'At 150 yards take the sight full' and fire straight at the target, Fox instructed, but when firing from increasing distance, increase the elevation of the barrel, to accommodate the effect of gravity.[57]

Competition was encouraged and rewarded as the hits of each man were recorded by markers against each soldier's name. On 21 March, the *Morning Post*'s special correspondent in Malta reported that under Fox's supervision target practice with the Minié rifles ran daily from 9 a.m. to dusk, and that 'the targets brought in daily tell plainly the rapid strides in the use of the rifle'.[58] The new carbine rifles for the Minié balls had been made at Woolwich to the agreed design: three feet six inches in length including stock and barrel with a light percussion lock, three grooves in the bore, and a sliding sight at the breech of the barrel, the wood of the stock left unstained but polished, the colour of elm. Each gunner was supplied with a sword and steel scabbard, which could be attached to the carbine as a bayonet.[59]

This was no actor–network. But you could call it embodiment if you wanted to. It was the beginning of modern industrialised war. An imperial war that, no matter what they might tell you, no matter what the medals and war memorials might claim to the contrary, still isn't over. If we need a language to describe the men and their rifles, then we might say that they were 'embodied' – a term that has at least three intersecting senses that are in play here:

> *embodied*, adjective. 1) of a spirit or soul: to have a body, to be incarnated; 2) of an abstract idea or principle: to be expressed or exhibited in concrete form, to be actualised; 3) of a militia or other company of soldiers: to be brought together and put into training or action against an enemy

After a month of training and experiments, Fox published a report and memorandum on an adaptation that was required for the use of the Enfield rifle in the warmer climate of Malta. As seen in the instructions given to soldiers, the paper-wrapped Minié cartridges, containing the powder and the bullet, were dipped in grease after manufacture. As the balls were designed to fit the muzzle tightly, the grease ensured that it slipped down freely when loading the firelock.[60] But in the Mediterranean heat, the grease was liable to melt and seep away. Fox conducted a series of experiments to test a possible solution. He had the grease melted off sixty rounds of Minié cartridges in front of a fire, scraped and wiped clean 'so that no grease remained except what had soaked into the paper'.[61] Fox instructed the soldiers to wet the degreased cartridges in their mouths before loading, and to fire them off in the practice range. He compared this firing with sixty rounds of the normal greased cartridges from the store. The results were presented in a table, recording the time taken in firing (a little longer for the wetted cartridges), and the number of hits and misses (a slightly better performance for the wetted cartridges). 'The result proved that wetting the bullet is a perfect substitute for grease under the circumstances', Fox's report concluded, and he issued an official memorandum, setting out 'additional rules suggested to be attended to in the use of the Minié musket', which included the updated instruction.[62]

The cartridges were probably often torn open with the teeth anyway, like tearing the paper from the end of a hand-rolled cigarette. Did the factory process that produced those paper bag cartridges at the Royal Laboratory at Woolwich, manufactured at an immense scale and speed 'without seam or crease', influence the development of pre-rolled cigarettes? you ask me, with another filter between your lips.⁶³ Certainly it seemed natural for Fox to instruct the men to place the bullet on the tongue, in a kind of extension of the remembered loading drill for the musket, where the gunman tore the cartridge open with the teeth 'so as to feel the powder in his mouth', an evolution of this idea, in a shifting series of practices and forms.⁶⁴

## 24. ARGO

Imagine that the killer story that Ursula Le Guin described, when she lifted that framing from Herbert Spencer, began not in some putative Palaeolithic cave after the hunt, but with what people call the first historians, Herodotus and Thucydides and Homer before them. If you were looking for a unit of measurement for the timescales of militarist realism then you might choose war, as the museum and the monument and perhaps also archaeology and art extended that historiography: Trojan, Peloponnesian, Persian, each drawing on fragments of the last, retrofitted in the nineteenth century by historians building a tradition, hammered together to form a pedigree, a canon. On 4 September 1854 that mythography was forming in real time, through a genre of extreme military re-enactment with live ammunition and more than 50,000 British, French and Ottoman soldiers, a combined expeditionary force to take on the Russian Empire. There was even collecting from the battlefield, and live arguments about cultural and technological superiority. An armada of more than 600 vessels, the allied transport across the Black Sea to the Crimean peninsula, set sail.⁶⁵ Fox travelled with the British Army from Malta through the Aegean landscapes and seascapes punctuated by monuments of the ancient world, still discernible after millennia: Trajan's Column, the Varna Necropolis, perhaps suggesting Athens could be sighted in the distance, or speculations about the site of ancient Troy as the troops came past the Dardanelles. But it was the names of the British ships that stand out in the contemporary accounts, citations of the classical antiquity redolent in the newspaper reports: Fox sailed on the General Screw Steamship Company's steamer *Golden Fleece*, then there were the troopships HMS *Apollo*, HMS *Agamemnon*, HMS *Ajax*, HMS *Vulcan* and HMS *Cyclops*, steaming alongside HMS

*Britannia*, HMS *Prince Regent*, HMS *Princess Royal* and HMS *Imperieuse*.[66]

History is never history but 'history-for', Lévi-Strauss once wrote, you remind me. He said it's always partial in that it works with incomplete fragments, and also partial in that it is always biased, even or especially when it denies itself to be so – a self-effacement that is itself just another form of partiality.[67] I think again of the pronouns in the book I was thinking of trying to write, the I and you and we and they, and how these words, the grammar textbooks tell us, can variously be: personal, reflexive, intensive, indefinite, demonstrative, interrogative, relative, archaic. There are three intersecting senses of the partial in play here:

> *partial*, adjective. 1) relating to a part as opposed to the whole; 2) prejudiced or biased; hence in a weakened sense sympathetic (opposed to impartial); 3) (astronomy) of an eclipsed object of which only part is covered or darkened

In a body of thinking that reaches back over the past four decades, anthropologists have come to place this idea of partiality – incompleteness woven together with committedness – at the centre of their accounts of what they call 'personhood'. This word denotes the different ways in which we think of humans: this is not quite subjectivity, as the idea of the subject is itself always shifting across different cultures and ages, but something closer to performance.[68] In the work of Marilyn Strathern, for example, Lévi-Strauss' account of partiality develops into what she calls 'partibility', and 'the partible person'. Strathern offers an image of the person beyond the conventional Euro-American idea of the 'individual', which is presented as an indivisible whole and an indissoluble atom of society. Man. Splitting that particular atom, she offers the figure of the 'dividual', which unleashes new potentials for tracing ongoing fusions and fissions in human lives. The broken-up person involves micro-detonations and releases of energy. It's not exactly that the idea of the individual is one of the 'social construction' of personhood or the self-presentation of identities – but rather that persons across all human societies are constantly becoming part of and at the same time splitting off from or distributing artefacts, events and places and other people, ancestors and descendants and all those with whom any given person can be said to be 'in a relation'. Personhood, in other words, involves a constant interplay of scales in which the extended person reaches out and enlarges themself through objects and sites involved in social relations, such as gift and debt, and how the 'dividual' constantly breaks themself into chunks. Like Rilke's poem reflecting on an *Archaic Torso of Apollo* – in which the stone figure can, it seems, 'burst out from all its edges, / like a star'.[69] Or like how Hannah Arendt evoked the despair of British colonisers when faced with the limits of their ultraviolent, hyperexpansionist ambitions:

> 'Expansion is everything,' said Cecil Rhodes, and fell into despair, for every night he saw overhead 'these stars, these vast worlds which we can never reach. I would annex the planets if I could.'[70]

Sounds like Elon Musk, you said. I read that dictionary definition of partiality as an eclipsed object again, of which only part is covered or darkened, and think of the crescent moon in Fox's lecture illustration, the face degraded until nothing remains but the moustache, or the smile, of the imperialist's dream of colonising dead stars and blazing planets, and of Wynter's account of humanity. On the Black Sea in September 1854, the imperialism of East and West gave way to war: a war that was framed in historical, even classical, terms, as if there were continuities with the ancient wars of poetry and literature.

You cut in to tell me about how in his semi-autobiography *Roland Barthes on Roland Barthes* the French semiotician discussed the familiar image of the ship *Argo*, each component of which the mythological Argonauts gradually replace. Eventually, so the story goes, not a single chunk of the original physical material survived, making it both an entirely new ship and also the same ship as ever. The form persisted, but also the name, Barthes observed. The ongoing substitution of materials went hand in hand with a continuity of nomenclature. This 'eminently structural object' was produced by substitution (one part replacing another) and nomination ('the name is in no way linked to the stability of the parts'). No trace of its origin is left; there is no other cause than its name, and no other identity than its form. Barthes makes an analogy between the rebuilt ship and the speech act of the lover who repeats the words 'I love you'. Each time, there is somehow a renewal without changing the words, the recovery of a new state, like the totally different ship with the same form and the same name, like 'a sign that is never signified'.[71]

A second *Argo* is interleaved on my bookshelves, between the covers of the book *The Argonauts* by Maggie Nelson, where those lines that Barthes wrote reappear, rewritten. Nelson writes: 'I thought the passage was romantic. You read it as a possible retraction. In retrospect, I guess it was both.'[72]

As with vessels so with spoken words, the persistence of form holds no control over the content, then, we learn from Barthes and Nelson. I'm telling you this, you told me, because it seems to open up a different dimension to the container story, I mean to containment. It seems quite like that thing you were saying about the instability of museum collections. That would be a different kind of container history. I want to hold onto that idea of a past that isn't just read differently by different people, but that is physically unstable as it's constantly remembered, renewed and reactivated. A past that is changed. I don't mean like a fragmented story you can try to piece together; but rather one where you can retain form and words and still see it transmogrify, like the *Argo*. Because there are forms of memory, and modes of engaging with the past, that are like a speech act that repeats the same words. To understand it demands not that you fit it back together, but that you disassemble it further. Hasten the process so the spreading out of a myth transforms into a past that is simply falling apart.

There are two more Argos in the mix in my head here somewhere here too: that early animated scene in the 1963 movie *Jason and the Argonauts* that terrified a generation of future archaeologists, where the skeleton warriors rise from the earth wielding swords and shields, their bodily gestures and jabs in stop-motion celluloid. And the name of the foundational text for the functionalist anthropology of the early twentieth century: Bronislaw Malinowski's *Argonauts of the Western Pacific*, which has those memorable lines in the opening sections that imagine the anthropologist's body as a kind of moving container for knowledge, through the process of fieldwork: 'Imagine yourself suddenly set down surrounded by all your gear, alone on a tropical beach close to a native village, while the launch or dinghy which has brought you sails away out of sight.'[73] Just as fieldwork – the anthropologist in their tent on the shoreline, the archaeologist in their trench – is an experiment you undertake with your body, so Fox's experiments with the drilled bodies of the troops were going live.

On 28 March 1854, Britain and France had declared war on Russia. With this starting pistol, onward troop movements of more than 10,000 men east out of the Maltese training camps gained pace and momentum. Following their bombardment of the port city of Odessa (today in southern Ukraine) on 22 April, the British navy gained strategic control of the Black Sea. On the same day, the Grenadier Guards embarked from Malta. On leaving for the Black Sea, Fox was promoted from first instructor in the School of Musketry to deputy assistant quartermaster-general to the 2nd Division under the command of Lieutenant-General Sir George de Lacy Evans, attached to headquarters.[74] Evans was a veteran of military service in India, Spain, Portugal, the Netherlands and America. As quartermaster-general, he had led the storming and looting in the Burning of Washington in 1814, and had in 1828 published an influential book about the threat of the Russian Empire.[75]

On 27 April, the British had pitched camp on a plain to the west of the Necropolis of Scutari, then moved on to the Bosphorus and Constantinople, arriving at the coastal city of Varna on 14 June.[76] In mid-August, a party of officers from the Bashi-Bazouk headquarters at Silistria had built a bridge over the Danube to reconnoitre the earthworks of the Ottoman Medjidi Tabia fortress. (It had been briefly taken by Russian forces during the Siege of Silistria in May and June, leaving thousands dead.) *The Times* reported that there were fragments of shell and shot scattered over the site, and holes in the earthwork that showed where the deadly shower had hit, and open spaces of damp, disturbed and trodden mud indicating the spots of hand-to-hand fighting. Fresh graves surrounded the site, and in all directions the landscape was strewn with fragments of mortar shrapnel from the 50,000 shells that the Russians were said to have launched.[77] I try to picture Fox going along on this field trip to witness a new kind of archaeological site formation, in which the battlefields of industrial war transformed living landscapes into ruins scattered with the Victorian spacejunk of military hardware, as theories of war were put into devastating practice.

Musketry training continued in the Black Sea camps over the summer right until the armada launched. Landing at Old Fort on the Crimean peninsula on 14 September 1854, the march south began in an attempt to storm the port city of Sevastopol, thirty-five miles away.[78] The first engagement was at the strategically critical point where the troops had to cross the River Alma. Tens of thousands of Russian troops had taken up a strong defensive position on the Alma Heights, above the river, and had spent three weeks reinforcing its defences to receive the allied armies.

On the afternoon of 20 September 1854, the allied troops crossed the river and stormed the heights.[79] The sheer bloodshed, carnage and loss of life that took place in the next three hours is hard to fathom. The French formed the western, seaward part of the action, while the British were to the east. The British troops advanced down towards the river across fields, gardens, orchards, vineyards, and to the village of Bourliouk. Here, the Russian soldiers had gathered hay and straw which they set alight as the shooting began at 1.30 p.m., producing thick smoke. Like the walls, trees and buildings, the smoke offered cover for Russian riflemen so the British troops couldn't see the guns.[80] Across the river the ground rose precipitously. The Russians had constructed a large earthen battery with gun emplacements, and infantry and field artillery spread out across the landscape from the flat top of the hill onto the uppermost slopes, a force of perhaps 40,000 men and between eighty and a hundred large-calibre artillery guns. Lord Raglan ordered his troops to lie down, waiting for the French forward movement to get underway from the flank, and then at around half past two he gave the order to cross the water and make the ascent.[81] The foot-soldiers fixed their bayonets, moving in successive thin lines towards the Russian entrenchments, earth newly thrown up in cuts and banks on the skyline of a hill showing the artillery positions. There were repeated attacks by Russian skirmishers, the constant deluge of round shot and shells and grapeshot (small round shots in a canvas bag), the blueish whizz-bang light of the rockets illuminating the fog, the dropping of men to the ground and the thud of officers falling from their horses, the distant glimpse of the brass helmets and gun-barrels of Russian riflemen, the repeated sing of the bullets.[82] The allies were victorious, although with immense casualties. The Russians pulled back to Sevastopol. As Friedrich Engels described it, the infantry fire with the English rifle was 'very murderous', decisive even: killing whole files of soldiers at once and cutting deep into the Russian columns.[83]

Blood stained the earth and the stone walls and the sand and leached into the river-water as men on both sides were butchered in this hell of earthworks and steel and gunpowder. This full-frontal charge never made it into the popular imagination in the same way as the Charge of the Light Brigade, which happened just a month later as the troops advanced. But it was nonetheless decried two years later by the French chronicler of the war in the east, César Lecat de Bazancourt, who described it as a heroic error, 'which inscribes glorious names upon the page of history, but inscribes them upon the records of the dead'.[84] On 20 October, a report in the *Coventry Herald* suggested that the first-hand letters written by soldiers from the frontline at the Alma represented a new genre of reportage: 'the penmanship of the men who wield the bayonet, and who work the gun'.[85]

Those contemporary newspaper eyewitness accounts are added to through archival survivals. For example, in a letter to his wife, the major-general who had ordered his troops across the water and up the slopes, under constant fire, wrote that the attack 'gave me no time fortunately to think of anything but the necessity of exertion, moral and physical'. He described the roaring of guns, the singing of bullets, the cannon fire and shells, and the sharp and strangely unheard fatality of the musket-balls. In the deafening rush of shot and shell and the return fire of our artillery there was the silent way in which death did its work, he wrote. 'No sight or sound betrayed the cause', each bullet hitting an individual body not heard in the immense noise, just evidenced by the men who dropped or rolled over or fell out of ranks into the dust.[86]

It's the aftermath of this swift, bloody battle that leaps out from the pages of these contemporary accounts. The descriptions dwell on the longer period after the thunder and fire and flesh ripped apart, on the wounded soldiers languishing in the dust and the corpses piled high; on how as the troops advanced they stumbled over the bloodied great coats of their own dead and wounded, tripped over knapsacks, dead horses, broken firelocks, spent caps, and the fallen themselves.

A first-hand account by a naval medical officer published by *The Times* described the scene on 25 September:

> For the past two days I have been literally in a sea of blood as I have been attending on the wounded Russians on the battle-field of Alma. No description I could give would realise the horrors of war – the dead, the dying, horses, guns, carriages *pêle-mêle* – headless trunks, bodies minus arms or legs, mutilation of every sort and kind. My blood almost freezes at the recollection ... Our surgical bivouacs were readily known by the number of legs and arms strewn around the scene of our labours. Indeed I cannot liken the field of battle for the two days after the fight to anything better than an *abattoir* ... In the redoubts the Russian dead lay literally heaped on each other. Nearly all the balls I extracted were Minié ones.[87]

Another eyewitness account described how the slope in front of the Russian battery was 'red with the bodies of our troops'. The ground 'thick with the slain'; the sight of the dead and dying 'sickening'.[88] And another wrote: 'It was the hottest engagement ever known; my coatee is completely smothered with blood.'[89] And another:

> My ideas are so confused with what has taken place in the last 15 hours of the battle we have just fought and in which we have come off victorious, driving the Russians from a most formidable position, not, however, without great loss ... It was sad to see the poor fellows, Russian and English, lying on the ground, groaning and suffering so much. They lay all one on the other, killed and wounded, horses and men, English and Russians.[90]

After the carnage at the Alma, then, hundreds of red jackets were smeared redder as the soldiers buried the thousands of British dead and Russian dead, improvised funerals in the heavy rain, and attended to thousands more wounded soldiers.[91] The men dug broad collective graves for the officers to be buried in their mud-splattered uniforms, while hundreds of broken, prone dead bodies, their faces latticed with blood and brain tissue, lying in the shit-smeared ditch of the fort in this machinic landscape were buried by throwing the earthen parapet back down upon them.[92]

The special correspondent for *The Times* recorded that 'the hills of

Greenwich Park in fair time are not more densely covered with human beings than were the heights of the Alma with dead and dying', a slowly shifting landscape in which men 'without legs or arms' were trying to crawl down to the waterside.[93] Pillaging the Russian bodies yielded crosses and Qur'ans, portraits of mothers or wives in coat pockets, and money strapped to the body. One account described how a looter picked up nine revolvers and fifty sovereigns, and another more than £150 in gold. Coats, boots and other articles of dress were stripped from the corpses; gold lace ripped from uniforms.[94]

The troops camped close to the battlefield for two nights, sleeping surrounded by the dead and dying.[95] Becoming accustomed to the horror, to the violence, and thus, as one officer wrote, to their own violent feelings, they witnessed the bodies piled up without feeling the sadness and horror which such scenes would naturally call up at any other moment. 'The dead lay there,' he recorded, 'and all the sad and wonderful attitudes and expressions of sudden and violent death!'[96]

And then there is Fox's own brief first-hand testimony, in the letter home in which he wrote: 'A field of Battle is a horrid sight.'[97]

In the coming days, the allied force pushed forward. The digging of trenches and building of batteries began on 7 October. It grew much colder and the night-time shelling intensified. Fox had moved forward with the force, but by 8 October he was on a hospital ship with his batman at his side, and on Sunday 15 October, ten days before the Charge of the Light Brigade, a medical examination found Fox unfit for service.[98] Although his name does not appear on the official lists of the injured, he was invalided home, through the wards of injured bodies, laudanum, calomel and cholera, having served exactly one month in Crimea.[99] The allied forces fought on, and the siege of Sevastopol commenced on 17 October, but by then Fox was back in London. On arrival, Fox headed straight for the Guards Club on Pall Mall. His brother-in-law saw him there and wrote, 'I hardly knew him. He is quite sallow & had a beard – he looks rather seedy.'[100] The following week, of 14 November, the Great Storm of 1854 hit the Black Sea, wrecking the allied camps, sinking many supply ships, and changing the prospects of the conditions of troops over the winter significantly. In the family papers in an envelope marked 'Dr Bright's

Opinion', countersigned by the physician-extraordinary to the Queen, there is a certificate dated 15 November 1854, which stated that:

> We the undersigned having carefully considered the case of Captain Augustus Lane Fox of the Grenadier Guards are of the opinion that he is at present, altogether unfit for active service in the field, in consequence of which, we think it absolutely necessary that he should for some months give up all idea of rejoining the Army in the East.[101]

On 28 September 1854, Raglan's dispatches from Balaklava stated that George de Lacy Evans included Captain Lane Fox in the list of men whose conduct he eulogised, and he duly received his promotion.[102] But what was this unfitness, this dusty seediness in Fox? There's an albumen print in the Royal Collections of Crimean veterans injured at the Alma and Inkerman, taken at Wellington Barracks in March 1855 and titled 'Men of the Grenadier Guards Wounded in the Crimea'. The man on the right-hand side of the image as I look at it, clean shaven except for the mutton-chops, could almost be Fox: something about his pose, his gloved hand, the look in his eye like he's still digging the trenches, ditches and embankments that furrow his mind.[103] Who knows if it's him? Who knows what that man had seen? Who knows what kind of change had taken place in him and men like him, like a name passed down the line?

## 25. WAR OF POSITION

There's a line that Walter Benjamin wrote in 1940, shortly before he fled from Vichy France to Spain and to his death, about the struggle against fascism. He observed how people will express amazement that fascism is 'still' possible, and asks what kind of concept of history would be required to understand that this 'state of exception' is not the rule, writing: 'One reason fascism has a chance is that, in the name of progress, those who oppose it treat it as a historical norm.'[104] Of course the industrialised violence, mass killing and racial atrocities of the German Reich were not aberrations returning from the past, but unique modern phenomena. What parallel concept of history might then enrich our understanding of the British Empire, of the body horror that was not a hangover from some past imagined barbarism but a new brutishness that sought to present its violence as a continuity with a timeless eternal past, and its weapons technologies as part of a history of unremitting progress?

In the context of the Crimean War and its aftermath, one place to start in answering this question is to point to how its sheer modernity lay in its infrastructures: infrastructures which involved time. The new rifles fired by drilled soldiers destroyed enemy bodies with a new rapidity. The speed of the steam packets and railways destroyed time, ferrying soldiers' bodies along with ammunition, explosive shells, great coats and boots, tents and provisions, sandbags, gabions and fascines for shoring trenches and building earthworks, supplied at a vast scale, dramatically shortening the lag between need and use. As the supply lines choreographed people and matériel, telegraph wires now freighted words at a lightning pace: transmitting messages and commands with a fresh, deadly ease. And just as the new technologies of the gunner, the quartermaster and the telegraph-operator brought novel compressions and disruptions in time and space, so infrastructures of visuality, what was and wasn't seen, were being changed too. Through photography.

Photographs began to capture some of the shock that came in the fallout of industrialised warfare. Roger Fenton was the British Army's first war photographer, and his haunting 1855 image of Lord Balgonie has been described by some as the first photograph of shell shock. Like Fox, he was a semi-aristocratic Grenadier Guard serving in Crimea. He died in 1857 – a death attributed to his experience on the battlefield.[105] There was also Fenton's iconic photograph from the later stages of the Siege of Sevastopol in April 1855, exhibited in London under the title *The Valley of the Shadow of Death*. The large-format glass plate camera captured a still life of perhaps a hundred cannonballs lying on the ground in the aftermath of constant bombardment, as if to present a kind of archaeological assemblage from *just now*, sudden traces that attest to a transformation of the near-present into the immediate past. The acceleration of violence and killing brought a new kind of monumentality to the battlefield and to the image simultaneously. Where normally it would take a thousand or two thousand years for the scale of ruin and patina and cultural life to render the landscape layered and textured in this manner, now the mutation of a place into a kind of archaeological site happened in the closing of a camera shutter. No wonder the soldiers were described as having 'haggard faces, dazed and stupefied'.[106]

In periods of rapid change, language sometimes just can't keep pace with reality. The history of describing and diagnosing the bodily aftereffects of industrial warfare, for those who came out alive, runs from shell shock in the First World War to PTSD and chronic fatigue syndrome in war in the Middle East in the late twentieth and early twenty-first centuries. At the time of the Crimean War in the 1850s, trauma had not yet been defined as a medical condition by military psychiatry. In the aftermath, post-combat disorders were generally diagnosed in terms of a decline in physical health, brought on for example by frostbite, cholera or malaria – or even as the professor of medical medicine of the Army Medical School at Netley near Southampton suggested in the *Journal of the Royal United Service Institution* in 1864, due to restricted circulation caused by tight coats and the design of the army-issue knapsack.

The term 'nostalgia' was used by French doctors treating Crimean veterans. This diagnosis had emerged back in the revolutionary and Napoleonic wars, and was also employed during the American Civil War a decade after Crimea. Nostalgia evoked a kind of homesickness, a deep sense of irreversible loss and enduring pain across both time and space; nostalgia among the Ottoman soldiers making the journey across the Black Sea to Crimea in late summer of 1854 was, according to one account, 'a veritable, often fatal disease in connection with fatalism'.[107] The contemporary accounts recall a line that Dorothy L. Sayers gave to a fictional police surgeon in one of her books, describing an instance of recurrent shell shock as 'nervous shock with well-marked delusions ... A hundred years ago they'd have called it diabolic possession.'[108]

The gradual medicalisation of post-conflict conditions – nerve-stricken emotional disturbance, a racing heart, night sweats, and so on – led in the subsequent years to definitions in 1869 of 'neurasthenia', and in 1871 of 'irritable heart'.[109] By the First World War, a host of new terms came into use to describe the nervous conditions found in soldiers returning from the battlefield. The best known of these, 'shell shock', was first coined in *The Lancet* in February 1915, and quickly picked up by the press.[110] But there was also talk of 'soldier's heart', 'effort syndrome', 'psychogenic rheumatism', 'disordered action of the heart' (DAH), 'valvular disease' (VDH), 'wind contrition' and 'war strain'.[111] A standard text on *The Soldier's Heart and Effort Syndrome* published in the final year of the First World War recorded how the symptoms of this spectrum of conditions included breathlessness, fatigue, exhaustion, pain, palpitations, giddiness, headache, sweating and raised blood pressure and heart rate – as second only to physical wounding and injury in a list of reasons for discharge from the army and navy, far higher than eyesight loss, deafness, epilepsy, frostbite or insanity.[112] In later conflicts came 'gas hysteria', 'flying stress', 'war syndromes' (including post-Vietnam syndrome, delayed stress-response syndrome, Desert Storm syndrome, Gulf War syndrome) and 'combat stress reaction'.

As such battlefield conditions were described and redescribed, there were similarities with the accounts of 'railway spine', that parallel response to mechanical horror among people involved in train accidents who reported illness despite emerging physically unscathed, which the neurologists described as 'the sudden, excessive, exhausting discharge of nervous energy in the excitement, the fright, the horror of the moment . . . [a] general weakness more or less marked, more or less enduring'.[113]

The idea of 'Crimean shell shock', as some historians have called it, is reinforced by some of the case histories in the contemporary literature. For example, in November 1855, a letter from an assistant physician at St Mary's Hospital was published in *The Lancet*, describing an instance of what he called 'Crimean fever'. A 29-year-old captain had recently returned from the frontline, where he had been 'much tasked in both mental and physical exertion', but had been unwell for the final six weeks with what the patient described as 'an overflow of bile'.[114] What began as a kind of jaundice gave way to nocturnal attacks of fever, 'with pains in all the limbs, clammy sweats, parched tongue, and determination of blood to the head'. The doctor prescribed treatments of 'blue pills', calomel, various emetics, taraxacum, bitters, a course of Cheltenham waters, quinine, mercurial and castor oil, recording:

> When I first saw him, he was utterly unnerved, and agitated violently by the merest trifles. His face was much flushed; his head was very hot and aching ... His whole condition was that of complete nervous prostration and disorder ... Once a hysterical paroxysm of sobbing and crying occurred, the mind remaining unaffected.[115]

The man developed an agonising neuralgic pain which was relieved only by a liniment of belladonna, chloroform and opium, and on one early August night, he presented with a distressing feeling of faintness, an uneasy sensation in his heart, and a failing pulse, 'as if he were dying and life was ebbing from him gradually'.[116] In treating this nervous condition, diagnosed as a disorder of the liver, the heart and the bowels, 'resort was had continually to opiates', the doctor concluded, 'both by mouth and rectum'.

In Fox's time, any quiver of the stiff upper lip in the face of roaring guns, bullets, grapeshot and shells might be taken as a lack of moral fibre, a failure of stoic patriotism and the manliness of bodily strength and vigour, a form of treachery to the ethnoclass.[117] Unexplained disorders, stress reactions or breakdowns might even for some represent evidence of hereditary weakness or degeneracy, the eugenicist fantasy of an innate savagery that could re-emerge and hold a man back from a new age of techno-violent civilisation. I imagine that such notions might have played on the minds of men like Fox.[118] Horrors remembered long after the physical conflict was over, the shock of the violence recorded in first-hand accounts: of gunshots that can't be heard above the roar of explosions, of the sight of lacerated, dead and dying comrades, of the enemy corpses that might stop feigning death and shoot you as you tried to drag them into a mass grave, the fear of burial in a dugout when a shell lands, and so on.[119] When Freud wrote about war neuroses in 1919, he described them as emerging from conflict between 'the old ego of peace time and the new war-ego of the soldier', as if the old persona was trying to stop the new persona from killing him.[120]

In 1899, a year before he died in old age, Fox was interviewed from his sick bed by a journalist for the *Salisbury Times* and asked to summarise his military service. 'I was an officer in the Guards,' he replied, 'and served in the Crimea ... I was never wounded.'[121] Not physically, that is. We have no direct record of what palpitations, tremors, irritabilities, emotional numbness, hyperactivity, diminution of self-control or self-belief, avoidances of places or people, waking flashbacks, recurring nightmares, delusions, amnesia, insomnia, paranoia, intrusive images, distressing or self-destructive thoughts, enduring fears and anxieties, fantasies of destiny and fatalism, feelings of sadness, shame, guilt, hopelessness, anger, depression and violence Fox may or may not have experienced. We don't know what downers and uppers, pills and potions he was given by the doctors, nor what patterns of self-medication with alcohol or drugs he adopted. Not that I'm suggesting that we feel sympathy for that 26-year-old officer's psychological maiming as the steamer took him back to London to recuperate. Not least if we look at what he did with his post-trauma. Fox took that trauma, the lasting immediacy of the memory of atrocity, and repressed it by weaponising it in different spheres.

For the emerging discipline of archaeology, the experience of accelerated industrialised war had a particular effect, one that foreshadowed the discipline's use to justify the Nazi regime of the twentieth century. There was the sheer rapidity of the transformation of towns and villages into ruins, looted and burned out, of living human bodies into the dead, the extraction of bullets from the flesh and the amputation of limbs fracturing the skeletons of the living, objects strewn across battlefields as if they were ancient sites that held the traces of the actions of the dead even though the living abandoned these places only hours earlier, and the fires were still burning. The fieldwalking or beachcombing of the conflict zone took place across the sands of the almost present or the just-past; bodies searched and robbed for anything of value: coins, weapons, rings sliced from the fingers of fallen soldiers. This instant archaeology offered another dimension to the temporal displacements of the war as present became past, life death, in the psychotropic, nocturnal, phosphoric, magic-lantern landscapes of modern war. Adrenaline ran through the body witnessing the immediacy of the death of comrades together with the potential proximity of one's own death. The psychological effects of constant shelling of the camps spilled over in time from the present into future, ossifying and hardening as soldiers returned from conflict. I try to imagine the traumatised officers, a brutalising and self-brutalised class of men returned from war, walking the London streets, seated in private clubs and the lecture rooms of learned societies: seeing conflict and danger in everything; imagining explosions in the gas-lit noise of the underground railway stations, building theories of violence. Ideas of the enemy, supremacy on the battlefield, were entering civic society.

For Fox there were the additional, aggravating factors that he had spent so much of the previous four years perfecting the Enfield/Minié, and drilling the soldiers' bodies for slaughter, creating cyborg fighters that brought the new British Army general-purpose weapon up against the Russian muskets, and that he then witnessed at close quarters the physical carnage it caused to tens of thousands of bodies, Russian, French, Turkish, British. The advantage of the allied forces, another correspondent wrote in October 1854, lay not just in the technology but in its empowering effect upon the soldier who carried it:

> Here we witnessed the first splendid effect of the Minié rifle, not only as a superior weapon in itself but also as giving confidence to the soldier, causing him to rely upon the efficiency of his fire, and making him, at the same time, anxious to have every shot of his tell. The men, far from raising their muskets hastily, and popping them off into blue air, paused before they fired, singled out the objects at which they proposed to aim, and, taking their aim coolly and deliberately, discharged their pieces. The fire did fearful execution among the Russians.[122]

There's another piece of shrapnel in this fragmented story, which spun into the new century, after Fox's death, across the generations. You pointed it out to me the other week. It concerns how the study and treatment of shell shock developed during the First World War, and how the history of military medical treatment fused with the development of anthropology.

When the future Cambridge psychiatrist-anthropologist W. H. R. Rivers was born in 1864, his racist uncle was at the height of his powers in the role we have already encountered him, as president of the Anthropological Society.[123] Rivers followed the family tradition, but took it in a different direction. After working as a ship's surgeon and training in medicine, in 1898 he joined the Cambridge anthropological expedition to the Torres Straits, a foundational event for the modern discipline in which a group of male ethnologists travelled to Australia and Papua New Guinea. He conducted further fieldwork in Melanesia in 1908.[124] When the Great War came, Rivers served as captain in the Royal Medical Corps at Craiglockhart War Hospital near Edinburgh, treating airmen and soldiers returning from the Western Front for insanity and shell shock. During this time he developed a particular reading of Freud's account of the unconscious. According to Freud, he wrote in *The Lancet* in 1917, 'forgetting – and especially the forgetting of unpleasant experience – is not a passive but an active process', repressed, dissociated or self-censored. Bodily and mental disorders can result from such repression, Rivers argued, after Freud, in a process that falls somewhere between instinct and memory. Based on his experiences with shell shock, after the war Rivers diagnosed a 'universal psycho-neurosis' across post-war Europe, what he called 'a disorder of the national life' of all European people:

> Since this reawakening of the danger-instincts affects nearly every member of the more civilised populations of the world, it is producing a state which may be regarded as a universal psycho-neurosis which explains much that is now happening in human society.[125]

Following fieldwork undertaken in island Melanesia with Arthur Hocart in 1908, Rivers applied similar thinking to the question of what was euphemistically called the 'depopulation' of the region, arguing that there were psychological dimensions to demographic decline, above other factors such as introduced disease or other effects of colonialism. Indeed he seems to have suggested that colonialism could be seen as a disturbance of such force that it too produced 'anxiety-neurosis', a kind of cultural shell shock among Melanesian people, and that this was a cause of the fall in population numbers.[126] The implication was that as among brutalised soldiers in the trenches, so among colonised people, the instinct for self-preservation was damaged. The idea that Melanesian people were 'suffering from a kind of "shell shock" as a result of colonial traumas', in a move from wartime psychotherapy to demography, was a kind of 'conjectural anthropology', Tim Bayliss-Smith has observed, that was in many ways 'a throw-back to nineteenth-century ways of thinking'.[127] But it was also something cast forward from the Victorians: ideas of survival, and salvage, and extinction as something other than colonial slaughter or genocide. I want to take that diagnosis from Rivers of a 'universal psycho-neurosis' in European nations after the First World War and fold it back onto the 1860s, read it as an idea that emerges from the brutalisations of industrialised colonial warfare.

I think of what Fox took away from the Alma. Not in his head or psyche, not the eulogising mention in dispatches, not the medals and also not the promotion he duly received on 12 December to brevet major by purchase.[128] I mean, I want to think about what this arms-race theorist physically carried back with him, in his baggage, as the steamer cut through the waters of the Mediterranean Sea and rounded Spain and France to arrive at Southampton.

When we take the weapons out of their cases to examine them in the museum research facility, the rectangular boxes of blue latex gloves, small, medium, large, are here not so much to protect the objects as to guard our skin against layers of hazardous and poisonous solutions with which the collections have been brushed, doused and embalmed over decades and centuries to prevent decay, to keep things the same. Some time ago I began, idly, to research what biocides and repellents might be generating in the residues, dust and evaporating gases given off by this museum's 300,000 objects, but I got no further than an incomplete handwritten and carcinogenic A to Z before putting the task aside, in horror at the *Breaking Bad*-style shopping list that was emerging: arsenic, borax, camphor, dieldrin, DDT, flowers of sulphur, leaded gasoline, lindane, mercury, naphtha crystals, phenol, strychnine; an armoury of chemical freeze-frames and fumigations that have meant these things are still here, decades on.

On the table, the dark weapon is lying on white polyethylene foam, bathed in fluorescent light. The database record is printed out and stapled to a transcription of the accession book entry for Pitt-Rivers' 1884 founding collection: 'Smooth-bore percussion-cap long gun. Russian infantry. Muzzle-loading, with a ramrod'.[129]

The gun was made in 1849 at the Russian Imperial Arsenal at Tula. The black wooden shoulder stock has a cheek rest. The steel barrel has bands of brass, bright hoops cross-cutting the metal tube and the trigger guard. The stock is varnished and there are Russian maker's stamps. An ancient square paper label glued to the barrel bears the number 403. It curls at the corners. Next to the number is an ink manuscript note in the hand of some unnamed past curator:

> Infantry percussion musket, m-l, s-b., RUSSIAN, 1849, (CRIMEA). P.R. Coll. [s. 1331] XLVI.

And then there is Fox's own record of this object:

> 403. Russian Infantry musket brought by Col. Fox from the Alma 20 Sept 1854.[130]

Some questions not to ask too quickly of an old weapon: the number of times it was loaded and fired. The names of all who held it or pulled the trigger, or all those it killed, or all, themselves now long since dead, who were touched by the loss of those deaths. What fate their fragmented remains have met. On these questions, the musket remains silent. The only possible initial question is: when? And the answer is always the same: now. We must start in the present if we are to consider how it comes to be here, what its presence means, what it could mean that it has outlived its 50,000 contemporaries. In this museum, violence persists in material form, but at the same time events decompose and fragment, so they can be reassembled in new forms. It's hardly CSI, but here there are the conditions for a kind of forensics, insofar as forensics is concerned with the admissible evidence. And for a sort of pathology, inasmuch as we can enquire into the causes and effects of injury. And autopsy, in the sense of the two Ancient Greek roots of that word, to see (*opsis*) for ourselves (*autos*): a metaphorical dissection on a slab of plastic foam. There's a strange smell to those preservation treatments, you say, as I put the gun into its body bag with its handwritten toe-tag; like something that is decomposing, the atmosphere of death enlivened by this light. How are you meant to tell the carrier bag story when what's being contained is violence? Just don't call it an actor–network of humans and nonhumans, I reply. Sometimes, like you said, you have to tell the killer story.

Antonio Gramsci made a distinction between two tactics of conflict, which he called 'wars of manoeuvre' and 'wars of position'.[131] The decontextualising, timeless locatedness of the curatorial milieu managed to create this place. And how can you be reflexive about the situated nature of your knowledge when you're always already being positioned? A war of position, Gramsci showed, brings certain technologies to the fore: the trench, the rifle, the work of the surveyor, and the changes in tempo as war involves longer periods of waiting. Like a gun in a museum. Like garrison colonialism. Occupation rather than just carceral regimes. To write about the monuments of militarist realism you'd need to be able to describe this process, an object contained so as to create its own context. A Martello tower or a tank-trap, but in the form of a statue, or a museum, or a library. Not necessarily on stolen land, like I said before. But territory of every kind would be at stake. This book might try to tell a counter-story about how the lines between soldiering and thought were blurred and scrambled. How the present and the past were mixed up on purpose, the living conflated with the dead, memory jumbled with imagination, inheritance with self-justification, drilled bodies with drilled minds, brutality and civilisation. Tell the story not to try to undo the past, but to change it, to fold its momentum onto itself, and collapse its inertia onto its own lines. Such a book would be not so much an exercise in history, you tell me, as a kind of return.

# VI

# 'Choc en Retour'

*fall*, noun. vi) (military) the surrender of an army or capture of a fortress. See also (military) to 'fall in': to form and move in a line

LOT 211. A Drinking Bowl formed of a Human Cranium with a silver rim. Resting on a stem and carved wood foot, bound with silver. Underneath is inlaid a shilling of Victoria, round the border is a Greek inscription, *Drink ere you take on this dust*. 5.5.0 Dining Room Rushmore Hinton.[1]

The catalogue description is in Fox's own hand, and accompanied by a small, detailed facsimile. Alongside this watercolour illustration there's the Sotheby's lot number, the price paid recorded again, in pounds, shillings and pence, and its location in the manor house. There are forty or fifty other objects listed in the catalogue volumes as kept in the dining room: candlesticks, decanters, a Persian rug, ceramics and glassware from India, Switzerland, Germany and Scandinavia.[2] As a museum curator, it's the catalogues, databases and other lists of objects that are the places where you see how a collection constantly shifts. Not just in meaning, description or interpretation, I mean, but in substance, in reality: a collection is a heterotopia that involves accumulation, the piling-up of things, and yet comes in and out of focus, precarious and transitory as if growing and shrinking at the same time, so that every time you count 300,000 objects you get to a different number.[3] Given the curatorial language of preservation, conservation and posterity, it's easy to mistake collections as among the more stable bodies of material culture in modern Euro-American societies. But the lines between the thing and the metadata are always blurred. The catalogue is a modifier, like an adjective is. That's what those culture warriors, the iconodulic statue-huggers, venerators of a dead past, I mean the self-styled 'anti-woke' brigade who want to stop every last statue from falling and to hold onto every last looted artwork and stolen skull rather than giving things back, returning stuff when asked, case by case, that's what they miss. The thing they claim they are trying to hold onto, it's not stable, it's not fixed. In a very real sense, the past that they are fighting to preserve is not actually there in the first place. What is there is memory. And memory is very different from how such activists imagine history to be. They understand that of course, these people, you explained to me, they know it's all about the present; that's always been part of the lie of the fake 'culture war'.

The stem and wooden foot and shilling with the head of Victoria were still there at this point, in the 1890s when this volume of the catalogue was made. In addition to the rim there's a silver stand held by four rivets (two missing) and a silver disc within the bowl that's held in place by a small crude bolt tightened from below. Neither of the two silver parts bears a hallmark. The stand seems to have been cut from a poor-quality goblet or chalice before being fixed on in this clumsy manner. Together, they represent a makeshift, twentieth-century fix to replace a broken stem and foot, now missing. The vessel is no longer watertight. The container story starts to leak.

We drove there that time to look around, but it's still hard to picture the setting in which the skull-cup was used towards the end of Fox's life at Rushmore, the dining room of the manor house, where the skull-cup was taken after he'd bought it at Sotheby's in 1884. The private estate grounds at Rushmore Park extended across 300 acres of parkland maintained by a militia of thirty gardeners. The archaeologist Hilda Petrie described a visit she made to see Fox in 1898.[4] She wrote that driving in through the gateposts, which were painted in Pied Piper colours, the bright blue and canary yellow of the Rivers family livery, was like entering 'fairyland', with Fox 'the King of the place with all his magic things about him', a big man with a long bushy beard and long white hair.[5] The house was filled with heaps of 'antika and curiosities' and in the billiard room the table's green baize was not used for play but was covered with antiquities and a human skull. Scattered across the house were further skulls, from his Dorset excavations, from New Guinea and Peru, and beyond, on tables and in cabinets – *memento mori* in every corner. 'There was a large party of grandchildren at lunch', she wrote, and I think of the Grandson, eight years old, sitting in the room with the skull-cup.[6]

Last night you read me a ghost story that Ursula Le Guin told in 1980.[7] A man and a woman are sitting in a tent around the campfire. Three days before, they had killed her husband and run away together across the plains. They are sure they have run far enough to get away without being tracked. But then there is a sound outside the tent. 'Are you afraid?' the woman asked, Le Guin tells us. The man goes out to check and in the dark, in the firelight, sees that it's a skull, the skull of the man they killed, rolling against the side of the tent, trying to get in. The skull has grown much bigger as it rolled after them. They run and the skull follows, catches them up. 'That was the end of them.' Then Le Guin writes something strange. This was a Plains Indian story retold, she says, and passed down 'in English by an anthropologist of German antecedents'. Kroeber, you say to me, interrupting yourself. But the skulls he left behind weren't ghosts, they were human beings. So I really don't know what to make of the following line, you say, and then you read me what Le Guin wrote next: 'Take the tale in your teeth, then, and bite till the blood runs, hoping it's not poison; and we will all come to the end together.'[8]

I try to draw a line in my head back from the college archive to the museum of the United Service Institution, one of the places where Fox's collecting began – an organisation that today with royal approval has evolved into RUSI, a defence think tank. In the early 1840s, when Fox visited the place as a boy, they displayed Chinese imperial trophies in the entrance hall. There was a dedicated models room that contained scale models of an Austrian entrenched camp with artillery towers to the design of Prince Maximilian and a gun salvaged from the wreck of Henry VIII's sunken *Mary Rose*; a natural history room displaying minerals and the skeleton of Marengo, the war horse of Napoleon I of France; an upper floor containing 'miscellaneous articles of ethnological interest and a few antique specimens, Greek, Roman and Egyptian'; and an armoury with 'a chronological series of fire-arms', and a series of earlier hand weapons, shields and armour. The glittering points of bayonets and spears of every clime and age were set out below a ceiling ornamented by two stars formed of arrows taken from scores of different battlefields.[9] Back in 1843, aged fifteen, Fox had donated three scale models of fortifications to the museum.[10] Over the next few years, Fox was involved in the development of this collection and its displays. In 1849, aged twenty-two, he donated a scale model of the Alcántara Bridge in Spain, a remarkable survival of a standing Roman bridge across the River Tagus built in 106 CE by order of the Emperor Trajan. And then in 1853, just back from that tour of European drilling regimes, he made that donation of the stuffed model of the French soldier with his kit.[11] Prototypes for a museum of weapons, for the museum as a weapon.

In the coming years, the progressive arrangement of weapons in the United Service Institution Museum – which Fox said 'may very properly be called our ethnographical military department' – was clearly a key influence in his development of a wider theory of material culture.[12] By 1876, the museum displays ran to the full range of weapons, a vast accumulation of the implements of 'savage warfare', from items of war dress made from skin and feathers to the latest improvements in armour plating, from clubs and bows and arrows to the Gatling gun – the development of military technology traced through every stage.[13] Fast-forward to 2015 and RUSI, now the UK's leading defence and security think tank although with no public memory of its lost museum, was the venue for a speech by NATO's deputy commander for Europe, General Sir Adrian Bradshaw. He warned that Russian expansionism in Crimea posed an 'existential threat' to the West; and as he spoke, the strange ability of Fox's collecting to bend time and space somehow re-emerged.[14]

The skull-cup sits here on the desk, next to the empty archival box. We know nothing of this human life, but we are not witnessing a death – we are encountering an unfinished process of dying, the taking of a body to which there is a continual return every time the claret was poured and the skull-cup passed around from one pair of lips to the next. But where could this skull be returned, to whom? you ask me. After all, any knowledge of who this person was in life has been destroyed, as part of the violence in an unfinished death.

It's possible to imagine many kinds of return. One effect of a monument, for example, is surely to draw people to revisit it. So too a grave. In any of the thousands of legacy colonial collections, to return stolen art to its rightful owners, to give another example, is to imagine the recursive possibilities of the museum label to be more than just a one-way ticket. Or to revisit a display over the years and feel how it changes, falls out of step perhaps. Returns may be about reciprocity, or recompense, or obligation, or debt. A return may be a reburial or a renewal, sometimes a repayment, whether quick or slow, where the rate of return may be gauged. Who gains, and who loses? A return is also an act of documentation: to record current opinion, as with the duties of a returning officer, or to document both wealth and liabilities, as with a tax return. Sometimes we may return the gaze of a monument. At other times the return may mean to answer a violent volley or blow with another; to meet enemy fire. And when a gift is made with the expectation of return, the anthropologist Marilyn Strathern once wrote, there is a 'counterflow contained in that same gesture', which means that 'the form that gesture takes is durable'.[15]

When are you going to explain how the skull-cup came to Worcester College in the first place? you ask me. That would need to be in the final sections of the book I was thinking of writing, I tell you, so that it's possible to trace how the pressure mounted between one generation and another like a bow being drawn back, before we see how the counterflow began.

## 26. GRAND TOUR

If the book I've been talking about were ever to get written then it would have to take stock of a particular nexus of history, topography and statistics through a ten- or fifteen-year slice of Fox's life. You could call it his 'grand tour', although he didn't take the trip to Greece and Rome like those aristocrats of two generations before him. Instead, first he made that journey to see new rifles and drilling techniques in Italy, Belgium and France in 1851; and then from the early 1850s to mid-1860s he took a wider tour of duty at the gunnery ranges, barracks, monuments and museums of Malta, America, Ireland, London and the Kent coast.

Are you sure it's not a biography, that book? you asked me. Don't confuse the man with his image, I replied. Or with the small army of patriarchal images that the White male governing ethnoclass he was part of sought to create for posterity, which they imagined might be spectres that haunt Europe and the world to this day. This book would have to be not about Fox, but about the distribution and transformation of his personhood and his memory. A mode of writing that would be a kind of counter-disarticulation. With an embodiment that's a bit like the *Argo*, or a museum, in that there could be the hope that the story, I mean, the meaning, can change, and with it the past. Not a biography then, but perhaps its inverse, a story traced like an archaeologist would encounter the horizons, layers, deposits and cuts, in its raw form, beginning at the surface, working from the known into the unknown without reversing the sequence to tell the story as a progression. Tell it forwards and it would all seem inevitable. Which it's not. I don't know how this ends. Fight magic with magic like you always said; dig up the archaeologist if you're going to trace the necrography. It would run something like this, if you applied it to those ten years of his life:

**London, 7 December 1866.** The monthly meeting of the Royal Archaeological Institute of Great Britain and Ireland – an institution whose full name continues 'for the encouragement and prosecution of researches into the arts and monuments' – is held in the rooms of the Arundel Society on Old Bond Street. Fox exhibits an object at a learned society for the first time. It's a human heart, embalmed in salt. Contained in a heart-shaped lead cist, eight inches by six, with the remnants of a silver coating, it was found in the medieval crypt of Christ Church, a church in the city of Cork. Four years earlier, when the crypt was being cleared out, a workman had put his hand into a niche in the pillar and discovered the heart. The finder told a story about how the relic 'belonged to some distinguished individual, and was being carried to the east'. 'I attach no value whatsoever to this story,' Fox reports. The name of the Armourer is there in the proceedings, too. In fact, he was the last person to speak, as part of the previous item of business, before Fox stood up, opining on the early history of the rifle.[16]

**London, 23 July 1866.** At the Reform Movement demonstration at Hyde Park, Fox holds fire. In the archive, there's an unfinished text in his hand, written around this time. It's an unsent letter addressed to the Anthropological Society of London. The title reads: 'The Irish Government Difficulty Considered as a Question of Race'. From late 1865, Fox had been investigating and reporting on anti-imperial resistance to British evictions. This was the period leading up to the Fenian Rising of 5 March 1867, a key moment in the Irish Republican struggle. In the February of 1866, Fox had acted as the prosecuting officer in a court martial of two non-commissioned officers in Cork accused of membership of the Fenian Brotherhood. In his letter, Fox calls for an 'anthropological view of this question', criticising 'an undue tendency to attribute to political causes questions the solutions to which must be sought in the social, ethnical, and psychological condition of the people to be governed'. He makes his point clearly: 'Fenianism must be regarded as a war of races.'[17]

**Ireland, Autumn 1865.** Fox is posted to Ireland as assistant quartermaster-general, stationed at Cork from September 1862 to December 1865.[18] Twenty years later a lightly fictionalised image of Fox's presence was presented in a historical novel called *The Two Chiefs of Dunboy*. In this story, a character named General Vavasour is tasked with surveying the region's coastal defences and naval batteries, and through the professional work of military survey becomes a keen amateur antiquarian whose chief pride 'was in the discoveries which he believed himself to have made in the history of the ancient Irish'.[19] Like his fictional counterpart, Fox undertook archaeological surveys at a range of prehistoric and medieval sites, from ringforts to towerhouses.[20] Working with the secretary and custodian of the Royal Cork Institution, Fox wrote that these archaeological monuments were 'fossils' of 'man in his most savage state', built by what they called 'the aboriginal inhabitants of Ireland'.[21] A primary influence was William Wilde (the father of Oscar Wilde), and his belief that a process of successive invading 'races' could be seen in the archaeological record, from monuments to material culture to human skulls. Wilde imagined a 'dolichocephalic' (long-skulled) dark-haired Irish native 'race' who had learned the skills of metalwork from their 'globular-headed' and, Wilde claimed, more intelligent, Celtic conquerors.[22] Wilde held that vestiges of these different waves of immigration and invasion survived in the Irish population to the present, and contrasted what he referred to as 'Firbolg' or 'Danaan' groups with later Anglo-Norman invaders.[23] In the context of British colonialism and the beginnings of the Irish Home Rule movement, Fox's reading of the Cork landscape went further. Fox claimed to be able to discern an 'indigenous' or 'aboriginal' population that had been displaced across the British Isles by an invading population in later prehistory, and suggested connections to contemporary processes of domination and resistance throughout the British Empire.[24]

While in Ireland, Fox also collected Irish antiquities of bronze and stone wherever he could get hold of them, including buying from museums, dealers and other antiquarians.[25] What he acquired ranged from prehistoric flintwork to unique items like the ninth-century silver penannular open-ring brooch known as the Galway Brooch (now in the Metropolitan Museum in New York).[26] Sometimes, though, he just took stuff. In 1865, at Rooves More Ringfort he dug into the souterrain chamber (or 'crypt' as he called it) to examine three early medieval Ogham standing stones, which had been reused as capstones for the structure. These are rare examples of stones that bear incised marks in the early Irish ancient Ogham alphabet. Despite what he called 'the superstitious dread' of 'the natives', he completed the excavation, but judged that the structure was now unstable due to the digging.[27] Given this 'impending ruin', and as his plans for returning to London were formed, he 'prevailed upon the landowner' and arranged for the Cork Steam Company to ship these three large stones, all more than six feet and one almost seven and a half feet in length, to London free of charge, and presented the group – 'remarkable monuments to palaeography' as he put it – to the British Museum.[28] Each inscription records the name and kin of the deceased. All three stones are now in the British Museum, with one on display in the Great Court.[29]

**London, September 1862.** Before he departs for his posting to Ireland, Fox makes a handwritten list of his collection at his house in Clapham.[30] It was a remarkable, if far from unique, collection of arms and armour made by a soldier, which a later biographer recalled 'lined the walls of his London house from cellar to attic'.[31] The soft-cover booklet of lined paper bears a title in Fox's manuscript hand:

> *Catalogue of Arms* belonging to Lt Col A. Lane Fox Gren Guards Taken at Park Hill House Clapham 21st August 1862

The catalogue details 515 items that hung from the walls of his house and were displayed in cabinets in bedrooms and hallways. Many are still identifiable in the Oxford collection. The objects are organised under nine rudimentary subdivisions. Clubs. Paddles. Spears. Axes, adzes and staff weapons. Swords, daggers and knives. Shields. Armour. Bows, quivers and arrows. Firearms, bayonets and cartridges.[32]

**Boston, 16 April 1862.** Fox is recorded with his servant on the steamer *Niagara*, departing Boston for Liverpool.[33] The urgency of his initial task – providing gunnery training for the disparate Canadian militias – had passed in a few weeks.[34] But Fox spent three months in North America, journeying into the United States for the first time: to New York City and Washington, DC by rail, and to the frontline of the Civil War in Virginia by horse. He may have visited the nascent museums: the Arsenal building in Central Park that held the first collections of what would become the American Museum of Natural History, and the Neo-Gothic red sandstone castle of the Smithsonian Institution, housed on the Mall, which had opened just seven years earlier.[35]

What's certain is that at the Navy Yard at Brooklyn, he saw the *Roanoke* being converted into an iron-plated ship. In Washington, DC, he met with Frank Vizetelly – American correspondent and 'special artist' for the *Illustrated London News*, who was later commissioned as an honorary captain in the Confederate Army during his reportage – and with him tried unsuccessfully to visit the Union-held Fort Monroe in Hampton, Virginia.[36] There were rumours that the Union's army of the Potomac was going to be landed there, and the fort was also a site for gunnery experiments. Perhaps Fox hoped to see weapons-testing of the heavy Rodman gun for coastal defences in progress, or perhaps he was more interested in seeing a Gatling gun in use, witnessing the new tempo to mass killing. What is recorded is a journey out on horseback to see the ruins of the town of Manassas, burned down by the Union soldiers, and to visit Bull Run (that infamous site of battlefield relic-hunting), where the Union had been defeated on 21 July 1861, the Confederate victory in the first battle of the Civil War.[37] Fox travelled through an American landscape scarred by bombed-out buildings and dynamited bridges and spent ordnance. War was cutting a fresh layer through the landscape, vitrifying ultramodern mass killing and fossilising the immediacy of death.

A decade on from the Alma, he was on another frontline, on stolen land where perhaps he encountered at first hand examples of the Native American mounds that had the previous year been compared by the antiquarian Thomas Bateman with prehistoric British tumuli.[38] He certainly during this trip collected two steel Indian pipe-tomahawks made by the British government for presentation to Native American chiefs, and a prototype bullet-proof vest.[39] His special military service took him to the frontline of a war about slavery and freedom, about 'race' and humanity. And as with the Crimean War, he brought more home than just the objects he collected.

**London, 14 December 1861.** In the royal bedchamber at Windsor Castle, Albert, the prince consort, aged only forty-two, dies of typhoid. In her grief, Victoria is reported to have held séances to communicate with him. For her biographer Lytton Strachey, Albert's death was a turning point in the Queen's life. 'She herself felt that her true life had ceased with her husband's, and that the remainder of her days upon earth was of a twilight nature – an epilogue to a drama that was done,' he wrote.[40] It was 'like losing half of one's body and soul, torn forcibly away', the Queen wrote; but her 'firm resolve' was that 'his wishes, his plans, about everything, his views about *every* thing are to be my law. And no human power will make me swerve from what he decided and wished.'[41]

The last piece of state business that Albert had conducted before his death was on 1 December, from his sick bed at Windsor Castle. It was a memorandum sent in reply to a letter from the prime minister

Lord Palmerston to Victoria.[42] The letter concerned an incident known as the '*Trent* affair'. On 8 November, in international waters off Bermuda, the Unionist frigate USS *San Jacinto* had intercepted the British postal steamer *Trent* as it travelled from Havana to St Thomas, and seized two Confederate propagandists and envoys to Britain and France who were on board, en route to Europe.[43] The prisoners were now being held in Boston.[44] When news of this incident reached London on 26 November, newspaper headlines described an 'American Outrage on the British Flag'. Eight months into the American Civil War, the *Trent* affair was described as a challenge to British neutrality in the conflict, a violation of the rule of law in international waters, and an attack on the security of British postal services.[45] Palmerston's letter said that the Cabinet considered this incident 'a gross outrage and violation of international law'. Albert's reply called for diplomatic efforts for the release of the prisoners, since 'the British Government could not allow its flag to be insulted'. The envoys would be released on 26 December but this had already become a major international incident, leading to a massive deployment of a British expeditionary force.[46] The fear was that a rapid Union victory over the Confederate States could lead to the invasion of Canada. On 2 December the leader column of *The Times* demanded that 'in the interests of peace' the American people should not 'suppose that there was no limit to our concessions and our forbearance'; Britain would have 'no reason to shrink from such a challenge' as war, it said – asking: 'Do the United States wish to engage in a foreign as well as a civil war ... a war between Canada and the Union?'[47]

The *Trent* affair came close to bringing the British state into war in support of the Confederate cause. The day after Albert's memo, Fox was on the Cunard Royal Mail steamer *Canada*,[48] sailing out of the Liverpool Docks. He was part of an advance party of hand-picked officers that travelled incognito to Boston, and then by train to Montréal, to prepare the ground for a potential military operation against the Union.[49] In the weeks after Albert's death, the widowed Queen oversaw the transport of over 18,000 troops to the Canadian border by ship. 'Canada is alive with soldiers,' one newspaper account said in the February.[50] Thousands of men trekked for days in the snow after arrival, as the Saint Lawrence River was frozen.[51] It was the greatest show of force that Britain had ever made in one of its Atlantic colonies.

On 21 December, *The Times* reported the funeral of the prince consort right next to a news item titled 'The Guards for Canada'. No shots were fired, of course, and the hypothetical American invasion of Canada never came to pass. This troop deployment was a memorial to Albert; a monument moving across the ocean towards the brink of war, like 18,000 breathing statues to commemorate him with a vast show of strength, a warning.

**London, 14 June 1858.** Fox gives the first major public lecture of his career. Titled 'On the Improvement of the Rifle' and delivered at the United Service Institution, it outlines the history of the rifle and the experiments he undertook at Woolwich, Enfield, Hythe and Malta between 1851 and 1857.[52] He gives particular attention to the problems of using greased cartridges in the heat of the Maltese sun, noting how the paper of the Enfield cartridge was of a fine texture, which 'when saturated with grease became like wet leather, and was very liable to crease'.[53]

Four years later Fox would begin to develop his private collection in a new direction, beyond simply arms and armour, into other things that could be weaponised; for now, weapons of every variety lined his large house in Clapham from cellar to attic in increasing numbers.[54] He was involved with a special committee that oversaw the United Service Institution Museum's dismantlement and redisplay, and he bought some items from their collection when the storerooms were cleared out.[55] In the same year, the Commissioners of the Great Exhibition to the Government assigned land to the east of Exhibition Road, where the South Kensington Museum was built as a kind of continuation of the 1851 exhibition. But in 1858, the main inspiration and model for Fox's collecting was the publication of Gustav Klemm's *Die Werkzeuge und Waffen: ihre Entstehung und Ausbildung* ['Tools and Weapons: Their Development and Training'].[56]

Klemm's personal collection in his Dresden house was arranged to present his ideas about material culture as a primary source for the cross-cultural study of human civilisation, and later formed part of the founding collection of Leipzig's Grassi Museum. In 1842, he published *Fantasie über ein Museum für die Kulturgeschichte der Menschheit*

['Fantasy of a Museum for the Cultural History of Mankind'], and set out a vision of the 'universal history' of human cultures over time and space through weapons, art and technology. Ninety years later this fantasy vision provided material for Nazi ideologies.[57]

**Malta, 26 July 1857.** Fox is on the P&O mail steamer *Colombo* from Valletta with his two sons, his wife and his mother, leaving Malta for the final time and returning to London.

'The decline and fall of empires are not affairs of greased cartridges,' Benjamin Disraeli told Parliament the following day.[58] These two events were, it turns out, far from unconnected.

In May 1855, after his post-Crimean convalescence, Fox resumed his duties as instructor of rifle practice in Malta.[59] As the prefabricated sections of the new British Army military hospital were arriving in the Dardanelles to treat the injured and broken soldiers' bodies, at the other end of the supply chain of human bodies Fox drilled fresh recruits in musketry in an expanded operation over the next two years. When his first two sons were born on the island, he gave the second the name St George – not just a statement of English ethnonationalism but also a commemoration of the firing ranges that Fox created on the dunes at St George's Bay.[60] He was promoted to lieutenant-colonel in May 1857. But on 24 July, a report severely attacking Fox's training techniques was published by his successor at what was now the Small Arms School Corps at Hythe.[61] There was now a cloud of controversy over his professional conduct. And the reason seems to have been that his system of musketry had been one factor in the insurgency in India – an early domino in a sequence that would lead to the toppling of the East India Company.

As the ship arrived into Southampton on 4 August 1857 with 143 people on board, it was crowded 'with women and children from India'.[62] More than 100 British subjects were en route as refugees, of a sort, on the vessel, in the wake of the Indian Rebellion.[63] A primary reason offered for the rebellion of Sepoy troops which led up to the Lucknow 'mutiny' has been the enforcement of drilling regulations in which the cartridges of the new Enfield rifles had to be placed in the soldier's mouth. Writing on 30 June 1857, Karl Marx picks up the story:

The alleged cause of the dissatisfaction which began to spread four months ago in the Bengal army was the apprehension on the part of the natives lest the Government should interfere with their religion. The serving out of cartridges, the paper of which was said to have been greased with the fat of bullocks and pigs, and the compulsory biting of which was, therefore, considered by the natives as an infringement of their religious prescriptions, gave the signal for local disturbances.[64]

The 'Greased Cartridge Affair' has been alternatively interpreted by historians as a conspiracy to expose the bodies of Hindu and Muslim troops to beef or pig fat against their religious beliefs on the one hand, and as a pretext in which the actual composition of the grease or the technical processes involved in drilling and loading have been deliberately misunderstood on the other.[65] At the time, some claimed that 'the issue of Enfield rifle-cartridges is utterly without foundation'.[66] But the blame had to lie somewhere. And it was Fox who had written the memorandum, back in April 1854 in Malta, that instructed soldiers to wet the cartridges in their mouths. This bodily practice in which soldiers were drilled was now at the centre of a debate about the future of corporate-militarist colonialism in the British Empire. Fox's mood in this period appeared to his father-in-law as 'discontented and querulous'. But the evidence trail is sparse in terms of what the proceedings against him might have been. 'What does the discontented Field Marshal intend to do with himself?' the father-in-law asked. 'In the meantime I should prefer he does not go out shooting every day as I wish to keep some partridges for the use of the house.'[67] Fox undertook only regimental duties until the matter was resolved, which it was, one way or another, in early 1861, over three years after his return to England.[68] His interests moved inwards in those years, to the museum of weapons. The bullet wetted in the mouth slowly hardened into a memory, and then into the metaphors that started to pour out in writing and lectures, like a counterflow or a ricochet.

**London, 1854 or 1857.** There's another photograph taken by Roger Fenton, no certain date but someone has written '1854' in pencil on the verso, and it's been published with the date 'ca. 1857'. By now, Fenton had moved from war photographer to the first official photographer of the British Museum. It shows a man alongside two other people sketching at an easel in the third Graeco-Roman saloon of the museum, surrounded by a mythological series of statuary of demigods, heroes and centaurs. Bearing the post hoc title *Gallery of Antiquities* the image shows the man drawing one of the Townley Marbles, a Roman life-size marble statue of the muse Thalia, a *pedum* stick in her hand, taken from the maritime baths at Ostia in 1776.[69] Are you saying that's Fox, you ask me? I imagine that it is. Maybe it was the early autumn 1857 and he was recently returned from Malta. Or maybe it was 1854 and he was back from Crimea, another shell-shocked soldier photographed by Fenton.[70]

**London, 1860, no date.** Pull forward in time. There's one part of this tour, from Malta and London to North America and Ireland, that seems to cut through the other horizons. So I've held it back to this point, out of sequence. A kind of truncation, one from the year that the University Museum was opened in Oxford. This is about a different kind of weapon though, not a museum but an acronym. Not ANT or NHI, but NRA this time. In the archive, I am looking at a few pages of undated manuscript notes in Fox's barbed-wire hand, a fragment of text for a lecture that he perhaps never gave. It probably dates from early 1860. I take photos, and read part of the text aloud to you later:

> The spirit of liberty pervades all our institutions and enterprises and produces that individuality and independence of character which make the Englishman a marked man amongst the rest of our species. Our canals, our railroads our navigation all those Institutions which in other countries are regulated by Government are with us conducted by private companies. Until very lately the largest of our Colonial possessions was governed by a private company, and now it appears we are making a private company for the defence of our homes.[71]

The identity of the first company referred to is self-evident. After the Indian rebellion, the British Crown assumed direct control of India from the East India Company, establishing the British Raj. The company was eventually entirely dissolved in 1874, and the British

Army absorbed its military units. Fox's greased cartridges were a key element in its downfall. The second privatisation is a reference to the National Rifle Association – not that American outfit with those bumper-stickers (founded 1871) but the British version. On 18 February 1860, a public meeting at the Thatched House Tavern on London's St James' Street formalised its founding, and celebrated the new volunteer movement.[72] *The Times* printed a summary of the introductory remarks by the chairman Lord Elcho, the Conservative MP for Haddingtonshire (East Lothian), a man who later in 1882 would be founder of the right-wing Liberty and Property Defence League. He reflected on the NRA's sole purpose: 'encouraging rifle shooting'.[73] The aim, he said, was to encourage the use of the rifle, in the same manner that the cultivation of wheat was encouraged by the Royal Agricultural Society, namely by prizes and by periodical meetings held in different parts of the country. I think of Fox's later metaphor here, about an advancing European wave moving like the sickle cuts through the wheat, and read on:

> With such a vast colonial empire as England possesses there are numberless circumstances which render it desirable that civilians should have at least an elementary knowledge of drill. When by the outbreak of the Indian Mutiny our countrymen were called on suddenly to transform themselves into soldiers, and to oppose the storm which burst upon them, of what incalculable advantage would they not have found it to have received some previous training?

Lord Elcho called for more physical education and 'field exercise' for schoolboys; to introduce the preliminary drill to public schools so that learning to handle a rifle would be as natural as learning to use a knife and fork. In the subsequent discussion, he quoted Adam Smith in support of the NRA's objectives, since Smith had written that 'the government of any wealthy and prosperous state must carefully manage their national defences' – so as not 'to lose both their wealth and their liberties at the hands of those nations who cultivated arms rather than commerce'.[74]

We read a speech by Queen Victoria from the summer of that same year together:

> I have witnessed with pleasure the manner in which the ancient fondness of the English people for manly and sylvan sports has been converted by your Association to more important ends, and has been made an auxiliary instrument for maintaining the inviolability of our common country.[75]

It was Monday 2 July 1860 and 15,000 people were gathered on Wimbledon Common to watch the shooting. Most came by train from Waterloo Station. At 4 p.m., the 41-year-old Queen Victoria – with Albert, still alive, at her side – opened proceedings at the inaugural field meeting of the National Rifle Association, making the speech that welcomed the formation of the new volunteer force to defend the nation. She proceeded with her entourage to the tent facing the butts. A Whitworth rifle was bolted to a mechanical sliding rest at 400 yards range. Mr Whitworth himself was there; he handed the Queen a royal blue silk lanyard, tied at one end to the trigger, and the Queen discharged the weapon with a curt tug. As the shot struck the bullseye a great cheer rang from the crowds. Roger Fenton took a photograph of the result: *The Queen's Target*, made of plate iron such as that used in the system of the School of Musketry at Hythe, marked with crosshairs within a circle. It has a strangely abstract quality. Look closely and you can see the mark made by the bullet just above the centre. The rifle used is apparently on display today in the National Rifle Museum at the National Shooting Centre at Bisley, just three miles from the Woking Crematorium where Fox's body would be taken by train and burned four decades after that bullet left the barrel.

Through the work of the NRA, the reserve army of volunteer army riflemen across the country grew quickly, instructed on Saturday afternoons by drill-sergeants who licked them into shape armed with Fox's manual, and reviewed in regular weekend mass gatherings of citizen-soldiers on commons and racecourses to conduct sham fights. In its first year of operation, Engels recorded that this citizen army grew to 120,000 men in strength; their green or grey uniforms hung in bedroom wardrobes like hollow statues, each man a monument waiting to be put into service.[76] Now at Wimbledon Common, volunteer corps trained in musters and drills in their local practice-grounds came together. After the Queen had fired the gun, the shooting competition brought together the four best shots from companies of 500 men or more in their different uniforms from different towns and counties. The prizes given out included twenty Whitworth rifles, 'each to the value of twenty guineas, fitted in oak cases complete', and the winner received the silver medal of the association.[77] The teaching of theory and practice was concerned with the production of skilled bodies as if they were improved guns, using their weapons to their maximum deadly effects.

Just as a militia and the British system of volunteer service were said to be 'disembodied' when not assembled for service (so that the French wars were called 'the long embodiment', as the British militia were engaged on a long-term basis), so the army of statuary that would in the coming decades come to patrol and guard the public spaces of British towns and cities might be said to be an embodiment. As a uniformed volunteer and auxiliary service, the NRA became part of that production of the image of Man described by Sylvia Wynter, now being driven into civic society, into provincial British life. A violent masculinity but also a new identity: a White male militia trained and ready for battle with the enemy, and the attendant cultures – the locker-room, the public house, the sports field, and an emerging cult of public art.

In those years between the Greased Cartridge Affair and Fox's vindication and return to military service, the volunteer movement continued to grow. The model of drilling and training the military body that Fox had been so involved in was evolving, and with it his theories of objects and subjects, materials and agency. In the future, this would be about bodies 'at home', not just bodies on the battlefield. Bodies in museums, galleries and lecture rooms, too. I close the handwritten book, pull the white cord back around it from top to bottom, then loop it left to right before tying with a bow. I place it back in the acid-free box, put the box back on the shelf, set the alarm and double-lock the storeroom door. The archive, like any weapon, requires the trained body, instructed in both words and gestures. Unlock the storeroom, open a book, like you're slipping the safety catch to safely discharge a loaded gun.

## 27. SOME GREAT WAR

But where exactly does the archaeology come in? you ask me. Think back again to London, 28 June 1867. Colonel Fox was on his feet at the Royal United Service Institution delivering his first lecture on 'Primitive Warfare', again, setting out the agenda that he would follow through with force, persistence and immense financial resources. Forty years of age, Fox was now one death away from his inheritance of the necronym, and so was assured of his financial future, because the previous March he'd become next in line to the Rivers estate under the terms of the trust created by the will of his great-uncle, the 2nd Baron Rivers. Any doubts about Fox's intentions to implement his agenda were dispelled when, a week after the lecture, on 5 July, the *Daily Telegraph* confirmed the rumours that Fox was taking half-pay from his military service.[78] He would now devote his time to anthropology, collecting – and archaeology.[79]

Fox's agenda had developed through his 'grand tour' through British militarist colonialism – that decade, the whole of his thirties, which he spent in postings from Malta to America to Ireland before returning to the metropole. This tour of duty was a trajectory that was hardly uncommon among the militarist-administrative sons of the governing classes of Fox's generation. Many saw much more direct violence than Fox did; in India, across the continent of Africa, in the colonial wars that the British were starting up across the globe, and of course in the brutality of army, navy, militia and police; in colonial rule like that seen at Morant Bay. You could give that generation a name, you suggest. Call them 38ers if you like. The men who, like Fox, were born into influential families in the years running up to the emancipation of enslaved people in the British colonies in 1838, you continue. Small children in big houses whose families' influence was growing because of the fortunes they received from some chunk or other of those vast payouts of 'reparation' for White planters and absentees, that injection of capital to shore up that governing ethno-class, to concentrate wealth and land within those families, and to start it cascading across generations, changing form as capital does. The thing then about the 38ers is that they responded to the crisis for

White supremacy by expanding the battleground from science to culture. Fox was more than a foot-soldier here; he played a key role in the wider phenomenon that needs to be my focus here: the fabrication of forms of cultural Whiteness. It was a process of mythography – the one that started, as the stories got told, to slip into militarist realism.

Fox's contribution to the wider informal project of militarist realism – the presentation of corporate-militarist imperialism as if it were an eternal state of nature not a contemporary culture – took the form of an argument he made about the prehistory of war and violence.

Fox's lecture made the case that a military focus on progress meant that attention was fixed 'upon the present and future of war', but it was equally important to look 'back in time and across cultures' to understand conflict. 'The science of war,' he argued, 'should be ethnographically and archaeologically, as well as practically, treated.'[80] Fox started to create evidence that the conflict that the nation state and the bloodlines of the White ethnoclass were fighting with a new violence in every corner of the empire could also be seen in the past, in British soil and the British landscape.

One episode through which this part of the story began came a few months earlier. On 20 October 1866, just back from Ireland, Fox recalled years later, he read a small news item in *The Times* that bore the title 'A Subject for Antiquaries'. It described how in excavations at London Wall, in the City of London, during the construction of the Gooch and Cousens wool warehouse, at a depth of thirty feet, workmen had discovered a large deposit of horse, cattle and deer bone. More than twenty cartloads had already been dug out, along with 'spear handles, partially decayed', the report stated.[81] Fox paid a visit to the spot the next day. You're looking at the map. It's a stone's throw from Liverpool Street Station, you say. Walk west towards the Barbican and that roundabout where the Museum of London used to be and it'd be on the south side of the road, somewhere between the Specsavers and the Boots Opticians, if you wanted to go psychogeographing around EC2 that is, I tell you, but there's really not much to see.[82]

Fox returned regularly over the next two weeks to document and collect the archaeological material that was being removed by the labourers. In this part of the City, the Walbrook, a tributary of the

Thames, ran in brick culverts under the city as it still does today, but in the past it had been an open stream. A rich variety of later prehistoric, Romano-British and post-Roman remains survived in the area around the watercourse. These included extensive deposits of human remains, which have continued to be found at Walbrook since the nineteenth century. Some of these are due to the erosion of burial sites cut into the London gravel, but archaeologists have suggested that some are due to a Mithraic cult associated with anti-Roman rebellions in the 2nd century CE. Whatever the actual detail of the formation of these deposits, Fox undertook an early exercise in 'rescue archaeology', recovering ceramics, metalwork and well-preserved leather shoes as well as human skulls from a sequence of peaty deposits, in order to evidence a particular story. He carefully plotted the locations of rows of well-preserved wooden revetments, along with shell and bone in the waterlogged conditions of the alluvial gravel deposits.

On 18 December, he delivered a lecture to the Anthropological Society of London setting out his interpretation. He argued that the earliest finds were the remains of wooden piles and 'kitchen middens' of the pre-Roman British stronghold of Cassivellaunus, the legendary British warrior king who led the resistance to the Roman invasion in 54 BCE. Fox imagined the town to be situated on the marshes and of necessity therefore built on timber piles.[83] He drew analogies with the prehistoric Swiss lake villages around Lake Zurich that had been excavated in the 1850s, with prehistoric 'shell middens', and with Scottish and Irish *crannogs* (later prehistoric artificial islands or structures built in lakes and estuaries). The finds included scores of 2,000-year-old human skulls, and Fox used two of these as lecture props, drawing a crude distinction between two types. 'One of these skulls is a remarkably fine one,' Fox explained, 'the other quite the reverse, very small in the frontal region, large in the parietal and cerebellum, and somewhat pointed and low in the crown.'

He continued: 'Such a skull might very possibly have belonged to a savage', but then again the Roman legion was composed of many nations, so 'skulls of almost any description' might have be found among them. Fox shared his fantasy that the skulls might have been trophy heads taken from enemies – a 'Gaulish practice'. And in the discussion, the opinion was expressed that while the first skull was definitely Roman, the second 'surely accords with the low type of the Irish skull', not Celtic, that is, but rather more dolichocephalic. And so it must surely be evidence of the ancient Britons who constructed this wooden proto-city on the water – the enemies of the Roman invaders.[84] The seeds of the idea of saving the past – which in the twentieth century would evolve into 'rescue archaeology' that sought to salvage evidence of unwritten histories before it was destroyed by construction at new industrial scales – merged somehow with the sublime scale of the deep excavations that were ripping into the London cityscape. Fox visited many more construction sites in the City, obtained prehistoric metalwork dredged up from the River Thames, observed the many deep railway cuttings being dug for new underground and branch rail lines, and recorded finds from brick-earth pits, gravel quarries and West London housing developments.[85] The self-image of the archaeologist was becoming, in Fox's hands, that of the salvage worker, scouring the building sites as if they were war zones.

Strange, you say, there's an echo here with a section in *Austerlitz*, the novel by W. G. Sebald, where there's a description of the skulls dug up from under Broad Street, the demolished railway terminus just next to Liverpool Street Station. The protagonist takes photographs of the skulls, and talks to the archaeologists doing the excavation, and reflects on the past lives of millions of people who moved through these stations, and how the railway lines on the historic maps look (you quote Sebald) 'like muscles and sinews on an anatomical atlas'.[86] The main thing I remember about that book, I reply, is that the family name that the man reclaims from his past, when he fled the Nazis on the *Kindertransport* in the 1930s, is also the name of a battle from 1805, and also a railway station built in Paris in 1840 commemorating Napoleon's defeat of the Austrian forces at that battle. At some points in the narrative it's unclear which Austerlitz is being referred to: the man, the war, the monument, or all three at once.

A near-obsessive recording of context – of the location, depth and stratigraphic location of finds – gradually developed in Fox's methods. The value of relics, viewed as evidence, he argued, was inverse to their monetary value.[87] He started to write onto the objects he excavated, inscribing and transforming ancient artefacts into a distinctive kind of personal text. 'A discovery dates only from the time of the record of it, and not from the time of its being found in the soil,' he argued.[88] And making a record of an excavation, he later claimed, should take about five times as long as the actual digging.[89] One object in Oxford's Pitt Rivers Museum offers a snapshot of this. Stuck to the bottom of a Romano-British potsherd collected from further works at London Wall, a wide paper label with its corners cut to form a kind of elongated octagon has a message to the future handwritten by Fox, this time giving not just the depth and the soil and the date and the location but an arresting use of the first person:

13 to 14 FT in black PEATY EARTH DEC 28 in ROADWAY by me.

It recalls the medalets Fox later placed in his trenches, this obsession with legacy, this 'found-by-me' context-making – a collapse of past, present and future. But there's also an affinity with how looters often wrote their names onto spoils of war. Like with the decipherment of the Rosetta Stone, which dates from the beginning of the second century BCE, where the known language of Ancient Greek was used as an index for the two other parallel texts carved into the broken stele, the Demotic and the formal hieroglyphs. The artefact now sits, as it did in Fox's day, in the British Museum: taken as spoils of war in 1799 by the savants who accompanied Napoleon's expeditionary army, signed over to the British Crown under the terms of the Capitulation of Alexandria two years later. It was taken away, some reports stated, on a gun carriage. Back in London, officials etched new text in a fourth language, English, onto the sides of this ancient stone document, as if awaiting some future cryptographer:

CAPTURED IN EGYPT BY THE BRITISH ARMY IN 1801.

PRESENTED BY KING GEORGE III.

In April and October 1867, during trips to his cousins' estates in Yorkshire, Fox joined an excavations of Bronze Age tumuli.[90] Here, Fox later wrote, building on his experiences in Ireland, he received training in the techniques of archaeological fieldwork from the man who was leading those digs, the canon of Durham Cathedral.[91] Born in County Durham in 1820, seven years Fox's senior, the Canon William Greenwell had begun studying law at Middle Temple in 1839, but soon returned to the north-east, was ordained and worked as a librarian at University College, Durham. Having previously dug sites in Northumberland, the canon was now moving his fieldwork to barrows in Ryedale, North Yorkshire and the Yorkshire Wolds in the East Riding. He was working in the tradition of 'barrow-digging' established by excavators from the early nineteenth century.[92] But now in the 1860s, these excavations had a very different dimension: one informed by the new narratives of cultural identity being developed in the nascent field of anthropology.

In 1865, in a new twist in the fake racial science of the 1850s, a man named John Thurnam had published a paper in the *Memoirs of the Anthropological Society of London* titled 'On Two Principal Forms of Ancient British and Gaulish Skulls'.[93] It was an analysis of the burial mounds of the later Neolithic and early Bronze Age periods in Wiltshire, which are of different forms: 'long barrows' and 'round barrows' respectively. The paper built on his book *Crania Britannica*, a monumental study with a craniologist from the Royal College of Surgeons that examined the human skulls in the museum of a barrow-digger of the previous generation, Thomas Bateman. Thurnam argued that the skulls shed light on the 'aboriginal and other early inhabitants of the British Isles'. The archaeological record had yielded evidence, he claimed, of a taller, blonder and more civilised population of Celts, incomers from Gaul – and the survival of ancient 'autochthonic' people of the 'interior' of England who might be identified with the pre-Roman Dobunni tribe. There was wider evidence, he continued, of 'Teutonic' people of an Anglo-Saxon and Scandinavian source with British or Celtic ancestors, and of the presence in Gaul of another more numerous 'pre-Celtic' people with brown or black hair and eyes of 'North African or Berber origin'. All these conclusions were made using the arithmetical methods of craniometry and phrenology, and they boiled down to a crude distinction between two different racial types in British prehistory: an earlier *dolichoaphic* (long-headed) 'race' – 'ignorant of metals, rude workers in stone' – who were replaced by a 'more civilised' *brachytaphic* (round-headed) 'race'.[94] The kick came with the connection to the monuments. The round form of the later barrows matched up with the roundness of their skulls, Thurnam claimed, as if earthen mounds and cranial bone could be woven together to tell a single story. He offered a simple rule of thumb or aphorism: 'Long barrows, long skulls; round barrows, round or short skulls.'[95]

Thurnam even interpreted the disjointed state of the bones and skulls in Neolithic chambered tombs – understood today to be a distinctive funerary practice in which the disarticulation of the body allowed for ancestral remains to circulate among the living – as evidence of a cannibalism that confirmed the 'savage state' of the earlier groups, who slayed and ate their slaves, captives and wives.[96]

The skulls from the canon's excavations were studied in turn by George Rolleston, Oxford University's first Linacre Professor of Anatomy and Physiology, who became one of Fox's few close friends.[97] The conclusions were in keeping with Thurnam's scheme: a story about an original dark-skinned, dark-haired, dark-eyed, shorter, smaller-headed Stone Age group, and then the arrival of a taller, fair-skinned, blonde, larger-brained invading group who displaced them. Accordingly, the professor wrote that the Yorkshire barrows showed evidence of 'two stocks of people, having characteristic features of the most distinctive kind; the one being brachycephalic, the other dolichocephalic'.[98] The round-headed invaders, it was argued, were probably originally from Denmark or Germany. And the absence of the surviving long-headed people in the later round barrows was probably evidence that they were kept as slaves by the 'ruling race', and so were not buried in the mounds.[99] There was a strange echo of the English Civil War in these descriptions of round heads. And there was even perhaps even an allusion to Anglo-American White kinship: the mythologies of Confederate soldiers that mixed up narratives of the Norman Conquest and the English Civil War in depicting the American Civil War as a war between different White populations, evoking the image of the Yankee as a 'Norman' or 'Anglo-Saxon' round-headed Cavalier fighting 'Celtic' Puritans. [100]

With this initiation into a new kind of 'scientific' archaeology, over the next thirty years Fox pursued fieldwork across the counties of England, at hillforts, coastal defences and castles. Fox led surveys and digs at scores of sites from Kent to Oxfordshire, from Yorkshire

'CHOC EN RETOUR'

to Sussex: campaigns of excavation that set the tone and the standard for the modern discipline of field archaeology. I'm worried this is going to get boring, you interrupt me. Please don't make me listen to a list of where he dug and what he found. Tell me what he imagined he was doing instead.

Fox surveyed every hillfort along the Sussex coastline in order to study the military strategies of the Iron Age Belgae whose methods of warfare were, he wrote, far in advance of the 'aboriginal' populations of ancient Britons.[101] You read down a list of the points on the coastline – Beachy Head, Chichester, Seaford, Newhaven, Ranscombe, Hollingbury, Plumpton Plain, Lancing, Mount Caburn, Wolstonbury, Highdown Hill, Chanctonbury – places where the chalk crumbles from the edges of the nation, the green grass meeting a sudden drop so it's always dizzying if you walk the coastal path.[102] He even extended these coastal surveys to the other side of the English Channel, including fieldwork in Brittany and at the site of Caesar's Camp, Dieppe. He dug at Danes Dyke at Flamborough, in the East Riding of Yorkshire, interpreting it as evidence of the 'formidable military operations' of an invading body of men advancing from the east, entrenching themselves with stockades and ramparts successively as they invaded.[103] He then surveyed the line of the Danevirke, a medieval system of fortifications in Schleswig-Holstein, in order to compare the forms and consider whether the English monuments were Danish in origin.[104] Digging a prehistoric flint mine at Cissbury near Worthing, he interpreted it as a 'Neolithic armoury' – 'a Woolwich of the Stone Age' producing flint arrow-heads and axes for a long-forgotten war. In rural Oxfordshire, he excavated a Romano-British villa and interpreted fragmented remains as evidence of the everyday lives of enslaved people from 1,700 years earlier – evidence perhaps of an enslaved native population.[105] And at Folkestone in Kent he undertook that massive excavation at Castle Hill ('Caesar's Camp'), where he developed his use of 'relic tables'.

These themes continued in the fieldwork he undertook, at a new scale and with new resources, after inheriting the vast estate in Dorset and Wiltshire. At sites along the Wansdyke and Bokerly Dyke, Fox read the prehistoric earthworks as monuments that evidenced a great unwritten prehistoric conflict. In Fox's view, 'these continuous entrenchments, must necessarily have been the work of a people in a higher condition of civilization, to secure their territory against the depredations of an inferior people, in a lower condition of life'.[106] This was a 'missing page in the history of the country, and is on that account of paramount importance', he concluded. Comparing these earthworks with Roman structures like Hadrian's Wall, and the Limes Germanicus and Pfahlgraben (the Roman imperial borderworks between the Rhine and the Danube), he argued that archaeology was now revealing evidence of 'some great war, in which the whole of the south-western portion of the country was arrayed against the rest of Britain'.[107]

And this is the point, I think, the thing you wanted me to explain – what he thought he was doing. The culmination of Fox's vision of archaeology came in 1894 with his very last major excavation at Wor Barrow on Handley Down, a Neolithic long barrow located just four miles east of his Rushmore mansion.[108] The results were presented in one of Fox's four-volume set of lavishly self-published *Excavations on Cranborne Chase*, bound in gilt-panelled blue cloth, the endpages marbled with a psychedelic weft of peacock feathers in sky blue, navy blue, blood crimson, ivory white and bone yellow. Wor Barrow was the largest funerary monument in the region, and Fox had read Richard Colt Hoare's accounts of digging some sections of the mound, but his plans for the site were on another scale entirely.[109] It would come to be hailed by twentieth-century archaeologists as a landmark in modern scientific excavation. In the twenty-first century, we might start instead with the observation that the exercise would push to the limit his logic of the excavation as a siege.[110] In two seasons of fieldwork, Fox oversaw the physical destruction of every cubic inch of this 6,000-year-old funerary monument, and with military precision. In the photographs taken, the site looks like a sustained bombardment has done its worst, explosives falling backwards from the Victorian era into later prehistory, reducing the chalk of the blast site to ash and fallout. The excavators left just three tall chalk baulks which stood like blank white pyramids.[111] He had removed the whole monument, shovel-load by shovel-load; and later had it reconstructed. In Fox's last dig, his method was pushed to its logical conclusion: total destruction.

Perhaps it would be possible to suggest that English antiquarianism began with war – with the English Civil War, specifically. In the seventeenth century, the aftermath of the Civil War catalysed a new generation of antiquarian texts. Whether William Dugdale's *The Antiquities of Warwickshire*, published in 1656, or John Aubrey's *Antiquities of Wiltshire* begun in the same year, and in many subsequent 'county histories', the recording of monuments in the landscape became a prime concern, not least the careful recording of the genealogies etched on parish church walls confirming the lord of the manor and his pedigree, and the sharp lines of the etched images of medieval knights in cold smooth alabaster, a dog curled around their feet. But with Fox, this latent military context became explicit. He followed the motto of his close friend George Rolleston – that anthropology was an 'armed science' that 'possessed the eye to watch and the arm to strike'.[112] The art of excavation, Fox later wrote, is to attack a site.[113] To excavate, he argued, is to 'besiege a place'.[114] The military skill-sets of engineers, sappers and miners were all in play. So too was the expertise in landscape survey and technical mapping that came to be combined so strangely, and yet in a manner fully comprehensible to Fox no doubt, in the nascent Ordnance Survey. At the Board of Ordnance expertise in the flight of projectiles across time and space laid the foundations for mapping the nation.

As Fox trained his diggers, there was more than an echo of the bodily techniques of the drill sergeant, and of course his expertise in fortification shaped this interest in the earthworks of the past. Alongside all this came the administrative skills of the military quartermaster, applied to the finds-processing and the provisioning of the project equipment. Fox's excavation teams dug into the English landscape like soldiers entrenching their position. And running throughout was a sense of conflict and the sensibility of the gravedigger. His experience of the damage and fragmentation of warscapes now led him to imagine the English countryside as if it were the battlefield at the Alma.[115] 'Our knowledge of prehistoric and early people is derived chiefly from their funeral deposits,' Fox wrote in one particularly dark reflection in 1892, 'and for all we know of their mode of life ... they might as well have been born dead.'[116]

In 1890, in a book chapter titled 'Non-Aryan Survivals in Britain', the director of the Folklore Society George Gomme reported how Fox had found archaeological evidence of 'conflict between a short dwarfy people and the Romans'.[117] Fox's use of archaeology was, then, to generate evidence that seemed to support wider cultural narratives of a forgotten civilisational clash between 'aboriginal' and invading people that could be told in England, as it had been in Ireland. Crucially, however, he wanted to suggest that the same war, in long-term perspective, was now being waged by European forces against 'primitive warfare' in every part of the world. In Dorset, these ideas merged with his attitude to rural populations, whom he imagined to include inferior, miscegenated survivals of ancient Britons. In his published archaeological tracts, Fox created a collective amalgam of agricultural labourers that he referred to as 'Hodge', writing: 'He is better off than he has ever been before, is in a lower condition, morally and mentally, than at any previous period.'[118]

In the museum at Salisbury, they still have his craniometers, on which he published a note under the heading 'Measuring the Profiles of Skulls and Living Heads', describing how the rubber-tipped metal rods could be screwed into the ears with sufficient tightness to enable to skull to revolve on a single point (or the device to swing around the head of a living person), taking precise measurements on a brass scale engraved in millimetres between the *meatus auditorius* (inner acoustic canal) and any point on the skull and the lower jaw.[119] But Fox's racial science was about cultural supremacy, which he expressed through the idea of cultural inheritance – the form of the monument and a form of the weapon as well as the form of the skull.

What Fox was doing in archaeology he also was trying in anthropology. There was an evolution in his collecting practices here. Think back to the Russian musket in Oxford's Pitt Rivers collections, part of what he brought back from the Alma in 1854. I read you out a list of other artefacts collected by Fox from the Crimean battlefield: five further Russian guns; ten Russian swords and bayonets; a black leather Russian marine *shako* cap with a copper alloy badge; a brass triptych worn by Russian soldiers, and two leather Russian helmets – one an officer's and one of an infantryman – each with a bronze badge at the front depicting the double-headed eagle insignia of Imperial Russia, recorded by Fox as 'Trophies of Russian Arms from the Crimea'.[120] Within a few years, he had added to his collections sixteen further trophies from the Battle of the Alma, acquiring mementoes kept by his comrades: three further smooth-bore muskets, seven Russian infantry sabres, two locks from long guns, a bayonet, and three Russian helmets.[121]

These thirty-five salvaged trophies became more than one soldier's personal mementoes of war. They were the seeds of a militarist theory of culture. Thirty-five monuments in a collection through which the modern disciplines of archaeology and anthropology were forged.

From its beginnings with that shell-shocked return from Crimea in 1854, Fox's collection had gradually evolved into a 'Museum of Savage and Barbarous Weapons' over the next decade.[122] Doubtless that's how he first got to know the Armourer, who was building a similar collection. At first, the objects that Fox amassed were limited to two classes of artefact: weapons, and a few locks and keys. That is clear from the list he made when he left for Ireland in 1862 – a simple 'Catalogue of Arms' as he put it. In doing so, his military role in the 'Guards', whose role was to protect and defend the sovereign, came into some kind of dialogue with the figure of the museum 'keeper' and a very new idea of sovereignty, of the museum as a memory palace. But from 1867, Fox's museum of weapons was becoming something very different. Fox became increasingly interested not just in 'salvaging' sites but 'protecting' them, and he involved himself in early efforts towards heritage preservation, from Ireland in 1866 to the Dorchester Dykes in Oxfordshire in 1870.[123] Whether in the British landscape or in the British Museum, the past needed to be not just saved, but defended.

As early as 1868, Fox explicitly rejected polygenist ideas of multiple origins of human 'races' promoted by the outgoing generation of anthropologists. What he offered in place of these ideas was no modern model of cultural relativism, but a new model of hierarchy and manifest destiny. Instead, as he put it in 1868, his aim was to account for what he claimed were differences in intellect between 'Europeans' and 'savages', while claiming that the prehistoric archaeology of Britain shows that his own nation too was once inhabited by people who 'existed in a condition as low or lower than that of existing savages', with the same tools and weapons.[124]

Between the excavation seasons, from 1867 Fox started to forge a theory of human material culture that was not just about weapons or skulls but also about violence and supremacy in other forms, on other grounds. The war that he saw in the past and present was never just about race; it was always already about culture and inheritance, he argued. What Fox wanted was a cultural theory of extinction. And here the question of human intentionality – questions of agency and nonhumanity in the figure of the 'automaton' – came to the fore.

## 28. AUTOMATIC ACTION

In March 1867 on the firing range of the School of Gunnery at Shoeburyness in Essex, the Select Committee on Ordnance was undertaking initial trials of the Gatling gun for the British Army. Manufactured in Hartford, Connecticut it was a technology which had already been adopted by the United States government. It is 'a formidable weapon', the *Illustrated London News* reported, 'and for trenches or a breach, and for street fighting, it would do execution'.[125] And in June 1867, in the week that Colonel Fox gave his first 'Primitive Warfare' lecture, *The Times* reported on its display at the *Exposition Universelle* in Paris, noting that 'in a descriptive pamphlet the inventor claims for his production no less a future than to revolutionise the art of war'. Clearly the weapon would be most effective when its stream of bullets were used in defending a doorway or an embrasure, the correspondent noted: 'the man who turns the handle is not to do so hurriedly, but should retain his *sang froid* and grind away quietly as if he were working a barrel organ for the edification of nursemaids and children'.[126]

As the automatic weapon came into use, Fox was moving on from this particular arms race to another: one fought with language and ideas rather than bullets and powder; since, as he later put it, 'A word may be said to be a tool for the communication of thought, just as a weapon is an implement of war.'[127]

As Fox began to expand his collecting beyond weapons to both archaeology and ethnology, and to make plans for public displays, his thinking began to deploy a different form of automatism: one that sought to provide the justification for the mass destruction of human life that the machine gun would bring.

Fox's attitude to spiritualism offers one point of entry for understanding his ideas about automatism. From the late 1860s, questions about séances, clairvoyancy, mediums, and the supernatural more generally, were being debated by anthropologists – themes that revolved around the idea of communication between the worlds of the living and the dead, of hearing the human past in the present. Some anthropologists were claiming that psychic forces should be studied scientifically, to establish the laws by which the 'spirit' relates to the mind, the brain and the outer world, and the fate of a disembodied spirit after the death of the body.[128] Others saw the current fad for spiritualism in polite society in London, New York and New England as a prime example of how 'traces of the early mental condition of man' can endure into the present – a survival from 'animism', a vestige of 'the religion of savages' that was based on the outdated belief system that life exists in material objects and the natural world, a belief that was being gradually erased by scientific thinking. For these anthropologists, modern spiritualism was nothing but a modern relic of past barbarism. One of these men, E. B. Tylor, Oxford's first professor of anthropology, the man who oversaw the Pitt Rivers Museum in its early days, made ethnological notes on the séances he attended. His records are filed in the museum archives. They were punctuated by racialised descriptions of the American and English female mediums as 'long-nosed', 'dark-browed' and 'half-bred', each adding to the sense of a desire to use an ethnography of contemporary Victorian society to prove that beliefs in the supernatural were survivals to be found among what he saw as inferior people.[129]

Fox steered his own path through these questions. His position on 'spirit-writing', 'spirit attacks', table-rapping, the materialisations of 'psychic force', was consistently agnostic.[130] In one lecture he joked about spiritualists as having 'lost their heads'.[131] But equally, he saw psychic phenomena as a worthy topic of anthropological study. In a letter to *The Times* in 1876, written in his capacity as president of the Anthropological Institute and chair of their Psychological Committee, he argued that no scientific discussion of social phenomena should be taboo, not least since the rapid spread of spiritualist interest derives from 'unexplained psychical phenomena that are occurring daily in families throughout the country'. 'Our study is man,' he wrote, 'and we must take him as we find him, with all his credulity and imposture.'[132]

On 22 September 1876, *The Spiritualist* magazine reported how, at the annual meeting of the British Association for the Advancement of Science in Glasgow on the Tuesday of the previous week, Fox had described how he had conducted séances himself. He and his children had often done so over the previous four years, *The Spiritualist* stated. Fox said they'd used a *planchette* – a kind of early ouija board, a heart-shaped wooden board on metal casters with a pencil fixed downwards, designed for the production of psychography or 'automatic writing'.[133] According to Fox, when questions were posed 'as if addressing an invisible agent', the report continued, answers had been received: sometimes a simple yes or no, other times a whole sentence, or simple drawings. On one occasion the age of a visitor was correctly given, he claimed, and on another the spirit even wrote its name: 'Minnie'. The possibility that answers could be received from 'the unseen world' meant that there should be no shame in studying spiritualism. Indeed, he concluded, 'important biological results might ensue from the investigation'.[134]

To try to understand this claim by Fox, I want to return to his metaphor of the 'unseen hand' and look at it a little more closely. He employed this term to describe the particular conjuncture that came about when he inherited a landscape full of archaeological monuments, having developed knowledge, skills and experience as an archaeologist. 'It was as if an unseen hand had trained me up,' he wrote.[135] Working through his writing from 1867 onwards, it becomes clear that Fox was developing his thinking about unconscious inheritance, which became a kind of theory of cultural supremacy that locked step with an intellectual environment shaped by Darwin's 1871 publication of *The Descent of Man*, by the development of the eugenics movement, and by the merger (in which Fox played the central role) of the Ethnological and Anthropological Societies, creating a new body known as the Anthropological Institute.[136] The clearest summaries of Fox's new body of theory came in quick succession, on 28 May and 1 July 1875, in the form of two lectures that summarised eight years of theory-building. The first was at the Royal Institution of Great Britain and the second at Bethnal Green Museum in East London, where the collection he had been amassing was going on public display for the first time.

They bore the titles 'The Evolution of Culture' and 'The Principles of Classification', and a close reading of these lectures, and some of the earlier papers he gave, reveals much about the mysticism, cultural exceptionalism and violence that lay at the heart of his vision of anthropology.

Fox argued that the progress of material culture was grounded in what he called 'the automatic action of the brain'.[137] That machine-gun metaphor can't have been accidental, I suggest to you. After all, Fox had drilled bodies for volley-firing long before automatic weapons came in. He understood how training with the rifle could develop into knack and skill, the techniques of the body that are needed to operate a gun effectively, like a prefiguration of the mitrailleuse. Sounds like those military theoretics came back in, a century after Fox's death, you reply, I mean in that Bruno Latour stuff about gun violence. As if the image of 'actor–networks of humans and non-humans' that we serve up to our students were simply a resurrection of this Victorian anthropological figure of Man, denialism reloaded, dehumanisation reconfigured.[138]

Fox's argument began with the emerging field of linguistics, and especially with the work of the Oxford professor Max Müller. In the case of language, Fox argued, the idea of design could not be located at the level of individual creativity, since no individual or nation ever invented a grammar, consciously, so to speak.[139] The same observation must apply, Fox argued, to material culture. A builder, a toolmaker, or someone who makes a weapon cannot be said to have devised 'a scheme of arts', he argued; so too the person who coins a new word has not invented a new language. Rather, any word in any language 'bears the impress of human design as clearly as a weapon or a coin'.[140]

In 1861, Müller had given a lecture called 'The Growth of Language in Contradistinction to the History of Language'. In that lecture, the linguist made a fundamental distinction between words (which grow) and things (which have a history).[141] 'If language be the work of man, in the same sense in which a statue, or a temple, or a poem, or a law are properly called the works of man,' his argument ran, then 'the science of language would have to be classed as an historical science'. Instead, Müller said, language is not 'a work of human art' but emerges through decay and regeneration – and so falls within the sciences, not as a topic of human history.

Fox contested Müller's distinction between words and things, suggesting it makes no sense to stop at language, since the world of objects is produced in an analogous manner. 'Words are the outward signs of ideas in the mind,' he continued, 'and this is also the case with tools or weapons':

> Words are ideas expressed by sounds, whilst tools are ideas expressed by hands; and unless it can be shown that there are distinct processes in the mind for language and for the arts they must be classed together.[142]

Unlike words in prehistoric and nonliterate societies, however, objects endure, and their physicality requires its own science:

> Words take seconds to record, hours and days may be spent in the accurate delineation of form. Words cost nothing, are packed in folios, transmitted by post, and stored on the shelves of every private library. Ten thousand classified words may be carried in the coat pocket without inconvenience, whilst a tenth part of that number of material objects require a museum to contain them.[143]

What would Fox's new para-grammatology of material culture look like? Foremost was a theory of the unconscious, or the 'automatic'. Thinking back to Fox's metaphor of human culture as a game of dominoes, it's important to remember that his argument was not simply that 'the fundamental rule of the game is sequence', but also that it's impossible to 'tell beforehand what will be the ultimate figure produced by the adhesions'.[144] The object of enquiry was difficult to perceive, he stated, in the same manner as it would be impossible to 'stand in the position of molecules of paint upon the surface of a picture [and] catch the artist's design'.[145] Fox's approach therefore was to look backwards, rather than ahead. In his mind, anthropology was entering a new scientific phase, akin, he argued, to the development of chemistry from alchemy, or astronomy from astrology.[146] This sense of the improvised, unpredictable nature of human knowledge and perception had also run through his meticulous, hyper-detailed, obsessive recording of archaeological sherds and their contexts, but now it took on a more explicitly mystical tone:

> There is a force within us by which we are moved in the direction of acquiring knowledge for its own sake and for the sake of truth regardless of any material advantage to be derived from such knowledge. Sooner or later such knowledge is sure to bear practical fruits, even though we may not live to realize them.[147]

Fox's position bore similarities to what the man known as the Bulldog later called his 'Zadig method'. Huxley had been the Hunterian Professor at the Royal College of Surgeons in Lincoln's Inn, when he was researching comparative anatomy at the Royal School of Mines. He named this approach after a fictional ancient Babylonian philosopher in an eighteenth-century novella by Voltaire. The Bulldogian image was one of Zadig as a proto-detective who could read traces, like footprints, to understand the past. He used this image to evoke how archaeology, geology, palaeontology and history might be woven together in order 'to forecast retrospectively' – to predict the past, so to speak.[148]

One particular paper delivered by the Huxley at the meeting of the British Association for the Advancement of Science in Belfast in August 1874 was a direct influence on Fox's two lectures. It was focused on the connections between instinct, reason and consciousness in order to assess whether or not animals should be seen as 'unconscious machines' and 'automata'. He argued that both animals and humans alike should be understood as what he called 'conscious automata'. And yet the balance between consciousness and instinct seemed to be variable, and so too was the nature of instinct. Huxley gave one example from a military context, observing how 'that operation called war is a great series of physiological experiments' from which science could learn.[149] It concerned a French sergeant injured during street fighting in the Battle of Bazeilles during the Franco-Prussian War. Shot in the head by a Bavarian bullet and paralysed down one side of the body, the damaged man alternated between conscious and 'abnormal', unconscious states. In the latter, his actions were mechanical and irrational, with lucid hallucinations that he was back on the frontline and under attack. In the context of Belfast in the first months of Disraeli's new Conservative administration in Westminster, the dog-whistle insinuations as Huxley concluded with a discussion of whether 'the brutes have souls' was clear. None of his audience believed he was just talking about animals. And in the longer version of the talk published in *Fortnightly Review*, the post-emancipation context of other British colonies was clearly what Huxley was referring to when he offered the example of a greyhound who's released from his leash. Since he has been bred to be 'a machine impelled to the chase', he argued, his freedom is constrained by more than just the 'external force' – also by his 'inclination'.[150]

The kick galvanic came now with what Fox did with the Bulldog's account of 'inclination', of breeding, of the 'conscious automata'. In Fox's hands, Huxley's account of 'automata' came to be applied to the idea of unconscious memory. We're born into a world of material culture and the bodily techniques of making and using things. Like language, these are not of individual conscious creation. A 'transfer of the action from the intellectual to the automaton brain' can take place through repetition, so that some actions can break free of the control of the 'conscious intellect' and become 'second nature', Fox said, 'an automaton mind capable of acting intuitively in certain matters without effort of the will or consciousness'.[151] Through the ideas of the Bulldog, Fox was taking Darwin's account of 'unconscious selection', as set out in *On the Origin of Species*, in another direction.[152] Kind of like a diachronic proto-theory of nonhuman agency then, you suggest. It is 'by classifying and arranging in evolutionary order the actual facts of the manifestations of the mind, as seen in the development of the arts, institutions, and languages of mankind,' Fox wrote, 'that we shall arrive at a solution of the question, to what extent the mental Ego has been, to use Professor Huxley's expression, a conscious spectator of what has passed'.[153] Here, the Bulldog was repeating the racist position for which he is most famous today, in a paper written about abolition in the context of the end of the American Civil War 1865 called 'Emancipation: Black and White', where he claimed that 'no rational man, cognisant of the facts, believes that the average negro is the equal, still less the superior, of the average white man'.[154]

Since 'modern savages' were just representatives of antiquity, an understanding of 'the hereditary transmission of faculties' was needed, Fox argued.[155] 'History is but another word for evolution,' he claimed.[156] And gradually his militarist theory of the evolution of culture brought in terminology that is suggestive of some prototype idea of manifest destiny, which took the idea that 'the progress of civilization has been continuous and connected' in new directions.[157] It began with what Fox says about the creation – or more precisely what he described, with no hint of irony, as the 'erection' – of 'man'.[158] Fox argued that anthropology and archaeology revealed evidence of 'one vast design', 'the great scheme', 'a work of all time', in which the 'unconscious contributor', 'the agent employed in a work of continuous progression', is, he continued, 'Man':[159] 'Generation has succeeded generation, and race has succeeded race, each contributing its quota to the fabrication of the edifice, and then giving place to other workmen.'[160]

In this construction process, 'Man is not the designer in the sense of an architect,' Fox wrote, 'but he is the constructor in the sense of a brickmaker or a bricklayer.'[161] This edifice, 'the complex civilisation of our own time', he argued, 'has been built on the foundations that were laid by these aborigines of our species'.[162] Fox wanted to understand that 'design'. 'We have sprung from inferior beings,' he later argued, and 'with the help of Providence, notwithstanding frequent relapses towards the primitive condition of our remote forefathers, we may continue to improve in the long run as we have done hitherto'.[163]

In the background was the old White supremacist idea from the president of the Anthropologicals, expressed back in 1863 in no uncertain terms:

> We see enough to know that laws are secretly working for the development of some nations and the destruction of others; which it is both the province and the duty of the politician to assist in discovering.[164]

Behind this fantasy of secret laws that operated to make the White race replace all other people lay Robert Knox's argument, made back in his 1850 book titled *The Races of Man: A Fragment*, which claimed that: 'Human history cannot be a mere chapter of accidents. The fate of nations cannot always be regulated by chance.'

Knox's point was to contend that 'a Negro or Tasmanian accidentally born in England' may be an Englishman, but to say they might 'become also a Saxon or Scandinavian' would be a 'ludicrous error'. 'With me,' Knox had concluded, 'race, or hereditary descent, is everything. It stamps the man.'[165]

In contrast with Knox's fake 'scientific' racism, Fox was contributing to the new mytho-cultural racism that I am calling militarist realism. The question of hereditary descent persisted in his thought, but transformed, like capital transforms, or like the Cheshire cat dematerialised but endured in its smile, or like a body of soldiers evolves, or a soldier's body is drilled, but will inevitably age and decay. Fox's theory concerned how human thought had spilled out to create a differentiated world of objects – in which some humans have different stuff from other humans – but also how this is built into their heredity in an unexplained manner, related somehow 'to the length of time during which the ancestors of the individual have exercised their mind in those particular ideas'.[166]

When man became a tool-using animal, Fox argued, this difference from other creatures marked 'the dawn of a new dispensation'. It was as if human culture were one great *chaîne opératoire* (operational chain) of increasing complexity, with different people standing at different points along the chain like workers in an ammunition factory, or soldiers facing each other in colonial war with different military technologies as slaughter began to be mass-produced.

Fox summed all this up by offering an analogy with that favourite topic of all colonialist thinkers: the railways. In a lecture at the Whitechapel Foundation School in February 1875, he offered the image of a traveller in an express train, who sees a slow train running alongside. It may appear to be stationary, or even going backwards, he pointed out. But this is simply a matter of relativity. The traveller is in fact 'a constituent portion of the more rapidly moving body', and this position means his vision is blinkered, very different from if he could somehow look at both trains from a distance. Then he would see clearly that it was just a matter of two trains in motion at different speeds. So too, 'in viewing savages from a similar narrow standpoint they may appear to us to be stationary and incapable of progress', he concluded; but in fact they are simply 'advancing at the same rate that we ourselves advanced in prehistoric times, before we had acquired that great impulse of speed which is now urging us so rapidly forward'.[167]

Through the metaphor of the train window, Fox thus expressed his longstanding view that 'the difference observable between existing races is one of divergence, and not of origin' since 'one race has improved, while another has progressed slowly or remained stationary'.[168] In the contemporary world, Fox argued, the separation of 'races' leads to arrested development, in which 'the intellect of the nation fossilises and becomes stationary for an indefinite period, or until destroyed by being brought again in contact with the leading races in an advanced stage of civilization'.[169]

Since warfare is such a cross-cultural instinct among all cultures, it must surely 'have been ordained for special objects', he suggested.[170] In these unavoidable, fated, necessary wars of culture, older groups in a condition of 'stagnation' or 'decay' will be, Fox argued, 'destroyed by their own offspring':

> The law of nature must be vindicated. The savage is morally and mentally an unfit instrument for the spread of civilization, except when, like the higher mammalia, he is reduced to a state of slavery; his occupation is gone, and his place is required for an improved race.[171]

The logic was clear: outside Europe and beyond the frontiers of formal empire there was now a psuedo-scientific licence for extra-judicial killings based not on racial superiority but on that parallel lie of inferiority in civilisation, culture, technology. Two nations or cultures at different stages of civilisation could never be amalgamated, he said.[172]

The mass industrialised slaughters in this new phase of corporate-colonial-militarist ultraviolence across the 'informal' dimensions of empire were presented as if attacks were defensive or necessary retaliations. The 'small wars' launched as punitive expeditions by the British would sometimes claim as justification breaches of a treaty, or small incidents that became pretexts for a disproportionate response, or simply as an act of 'disarmament'. At other times, though, the justification would come in the form of a simpler, wider narrative of culture, criticising 'savagery' or the persistence of traditional slavery, or the sheer 'primitivism' of the people being set up for democide. And the unconscious, destined, somehow inevitable aspect of these exterminations was presented as part of the natural order, an inevitable outcome of technological change. Fox's lectures were a masterclass in the future progressive exonerative. It's the technology, not the men. It's the man-with-the-gun, not the man. These are extinctions not exterminations, these populations are dying out automatically because of contact with 'the leading races'. It's just fate. Machinic providence. Technological destiny. So ran the accelerationist denialism, the militarist realism.

And then on 4 July 1879 at the Battle of Ulundi the technological slaughter, which the militarist realism seemed to prove was an inevitable destiny, reached a tipping point of horror. Fox's son was there, and returned with those objects, as we have seen, and Fox's theories of gun technology were now playing out in a real time in a terrible new phase. Perhaps a thousand tribal warriors, armed with assegai spears and hide shields, were mown down by the two Gatling guns that had been brought on this expedition.[173] It was one of the first deployments of machine guns in live combat by British soldiers, and by far the most deadly yet, bringing a decisive victory against King Cetshwayo kaMpande, and thus defeating the most powerful kingdom in southern Africa in a battle that lasted under an hour.[174] The theories of technological inheritance, of machinic automatism, gave carte blanche to destruction, extinction, extermination. Fox doubtless saw this extermination as vindication of his model of the evolution of culture, and his son's loot as its physical proof, taken from the bodies of Zulu people (and still sitting in the cabinets in Oxford today).

Fox's words landed in the lecture rooms like bullets from a mitrailleuse. The Darwinian metaphor that mapped inheritance onto the geography of empire ran together in Fox's mind with the British landscape as filled with the traces of a great prehistoric war. And the language of destiny and the unconscious served, in his denialist-supremacist worldview, to render human agency conveniently entangled, distributed and decentred.

Reminds me of Macpherson, you say, switching back into the conversation, and of exoneration from personal responsibility for racism because of some bigger, intangible process. Or that man with the gun in the French theory. Fox and his comrades were killing off a discredited theory. Their logic was simple. The old fake 'race science' was almost dead. Long live the new mystical militarist-realist pseudoscience of nonhuman agency. At least that's the vibe, it can sometimes feel, in the seminar rooms these days, you tell me. Long live the neo-animistic, semi-spiritualist, retro-vitalist theories of material agency, they say, you explain, without ever actually saying it out loud like that, as if, you continue, they had invented some new magical-realist theory that doesn't have a history. Long like the anthropological museum, unchanged and unchanging. It's as if a disciplinary theory could be based on a repressed memory of what has been made to endure, or based on an unspoken denial, like the denial of humanity for example. But this theory's past is now catching up with it.

## 29. THE ARROW AND THE BOOMERANG

When there's so little to say about the person at the centre of this history, the person whose body was turned into this skull-cup and used for so many years, one thing we can do is tell the stories that we do know, right? I have a story I can tell you, you say. Okay, I have one too; let me go first. Perhaps it could be an antidote to all those quotes from the Victorian lectures. Then again, it's a story about poison, I mean poison in the way that Ursula Le Guin described it when she retold the story of the murder and the skull that caught up with those two people on the run across the Californian plains.

**Story One.** It was the dog days of summer 2007 and I'd been a few weeks in post as a curator at the Pitt Rivers Museum. Not so much a place as an Edwardian state of mind, or so it seemed to me. In the tea room and the corridors, various anecdotes about the institution's past were recounted to me by my new colleagues, all long since retired. Each had that practised and direct quality of those myths that institutions tell and retell to themselves, with the sense of exaggeration and elaboration for dramatic effect, and the mood of something between a cautionary tale and an initiation rite. One was about a former director who became so possessed by the institution over years of service that after her retirement party in the summer of 1959, she still came in to sit at her desk at five to nine the following morning as usual, and continued to do so for a further sixteen years, right up to her death at the age of eighty-six. Another was about a practical session called 'primitive pyrology' in which while demonstrating how to ignite an ember with a bow drill and a block of wood the world's first professor of anthropology set fire to his enormous grey-white late-Victorian beard.

A third concerned a lecturer whose teaching included an annual practical demonstration of boomerang-throwing for students in the University Parks, adjacent to the museum – until on one occasion his throw was interrupted on its return by a nanny pushing a pram, and it knocked her out. An official ban by statute on the use of boomerangs on university land was swiftly drafted by the proctors and adopted by the university's council, and neat hand-painted signs were erected in the parks to enforce it.

A fourth was about another long-serving curator who had a nervous breakdown which culminated in his taking a box of matches from his trouser pocket and setting light to the waste-paper bin under his desk in a fit of anger at what he saw as yet another directorial diktat. When called on by his director to extinguish the fire immediately, he unzipped his flies and pissed on the flames. Taken off to the Warneford Lunatic Asylum, he was never released. From one institution of restraint, seclusion, straitjackets and locked doors, the storyteller said, looking me in the eye, to another.

These apocryphal, off-colour, trivial, tiresome stories formed part of the strange oral tradition of the institution, and were a mix of fact and fiction, just like the museum itself. Perhaps that was the point of them. There was no boomerang statute or sign, of course. At least not literally. No beard fire. And the museum didn't really drive its curators insane or obsess them so much that they could never leave.

But there was a fifth. The unresolved, mythic quality of which has stayed with me like a ghost story or a horror movie might haunt you. I was told it on three or four different occasions by different people (all now long departed from this institutional ship of Theseus that will outlive us all) as it was passed down from one curatorial generation to the next. It took a slightly different form each time it was told, but the gist of the thing was as follows.

One night in late January 1933, after a good college dinner, when over dessert the men had, as etiquette dictates, definitely not discussed transubstantiation or the political situation in Europe, the curator Henry Balfour had returned to the museum and was working late at a table on the upper gallery. A full moon shone down through the glass roof onto the desk where he sat in his shirt sleeves and tweed waistcoat in the vast dark space in the yellowish glare of a single electric light. Balfour was preparing a display of a set of poisoned arrows, brought back from West Africa twenty years earlier. He was cataloguing them one by one, describing the materials, shaft, flight and tip of each, making sketches and attaching explanatory labels, as he had done for countless objects since he joined the museum in the 1880s. Periodically dipping the nib of his pen in the inkpot, the old man carefully recorded the provenance in the accessions register:

> dd. Lieutenant C. Henry, Worcestershire Regiment, Putney Heath, SW London. Specimens collected by himself from the PHRA-PHRA TRIBE, district of Zovaragu, Northern Territories, Gold Coast, W Africa. Poisoned with crocodile gall and by insertion in decomposing human bodies

Tired and perhaps a little drunk, as Balfour pulled out the seventh arrow from the bamboo quiver he pricked his finger on the sharp iron tip, drawing blood. He pulled a handkerchief from his trouser pocket to staunch the red drops that were now falling onto his shoes, onto the floor of the gallery, dripping through the iron grille in the floor. In front of him, held down by two paperweights, was the letter that had accompanied the donation, written by the lieutenant in August 1912:

> Death from wounds from these arrows occurs within 20–30 minutes and no antidote is known to Europeans, though the natives are said to possess one. The range of the arrows is not more than 50 yards. The natives take cover behind rocks etc. or in trees, and fire at close range. I can warrant the poison on the arrows as several of our men were hit & died in about 20 mins in spite of the fact in one case of the doctor actually being next to the fellow hit & consequently able to cut him at once.

Alone in the museum, in that moment Balfour, as he told the story, thought only of his contribution to science and to posterity. He realised at once that seeking medical assistance for this unknown poison would be fruitless. Instead, he filled his pipe and lit it; unhooked his pocket watch from his waistcoat and placed it on the desk in front of him. A ruled notebook open at a blank page and a sharpened pencil in his hand, he waited to document each symptom as he succumbed to the effects of the poison. At least this way some hint of the true identity of the toxic substance might be yet discerned at his autopsy, evidence that could be duly added to the museum documentation. The pocket watch ticked and as the curator watched its hands turn from ten, to eleven, to one in the morning, he was contemplating the mix of reptile gall and the blood or bile of a human corpse.

At first, nothing happened. And then, nothing kept happening. It is from this nothing – every one of my narrators slowed down here for effect, to underline this point – that Balfour drew his conclusion. It became clear to him. *The passage of time had deprived the poison of its effectiveness.*

What is the lesson of this story which balances on an event in which nothing happens, where the material has no agency? In his final years of teaching, before his death on the eve of the outbreak of another world war in 1939, Balfour always included this anecdote in his annual lecture on the anthropology of technology. The moral of the story, he told the students, I was told, is that 'one must take no chances with poisoned arrows'.[175] (The museum archives do not record whether Lieutenant Henry died fighting for his country in the First World War, as so many of his generation did.) But what stayed with me were two other, very different dimensions to the tale that I want to draw out in this retelling. First, there's the sheer hubris that inhered in how Balfour had started to imagine himself as carrying a burden of potentially being killed by the place he had continually rearranged and constructed over half a century of curatorial duties, a burden that eclipsed the countless deaths through which weapons had been taken as the wave of violence swept across Indigenous societies around the world. And second, there's the notion that the efficacy of the poison of this place, of its regime of assemblage and display, might be decaying over time, as if the museum itself were in a constant process of decomposition, year on year, as a new curator comes to stand in the dead man's shoes of the last.

Through imperialism, the White man 'becomes a sort of hollow', Orwell wrote in his essay. 'He wears a mask and his face grows to fit it.' But in institutions and disciplines, it is never a question of successive living occupants of a stable, enduring structure. What unfolds across the generations is a history of position, that hollow is a position in an ever-changing world, where each new generation can choose to repeat the story faithfully for posterity, or retell it for the present. And as I recall the story of the arrow, those bullets entering the elephant's body and the poison on the tip pricking the curator's finger, its deadliness long dried up, start to blur into the sheer Lovecraftian image of the curator consumed by the violence of the museum. Or a devastating line that J. G. Ballard has somewhere in his book *Crash*: 'The images of these wounds hung in the gallery of his mind like exhibits in the museum of a slaughterhouse.'[176]

Okay, your turn, I say.

Well, mine's a bit more technical, you tell me, but we can pick it up with the boomerang-throwing in the park, and that sign against boomerangs that never existed, a story that was always a kind of oddly violent joke. Against that imaginary boomerang, let me hold up a second. It's a strange kind of theoretical story, and it's a little technical and pedantic at points, but bear with me; it's a story about translation and I think it might be important.

**Story Two.** To begin, imagine we're back in the upper gallery of Oxford's Pitt Rivers, this time in front of the display of boomerangs. The case sits alongside the other weapons, between the knuckledusters and the knives, across the walkway from the bows and arrows. There are over 300 records for boomerangs on the database of the museum you work in, you tell me; I looked it up online the other day. Most are from Australia, but there are others from India, Egypt, Sudan, North America, replicas made in Britain; there's even one example from Chad. Just under forty of these were collected by Fox, the others accessioned into the museum in the years since 1884. And that's not counting all the objects recorded as 'throwing sticks'.

There's a lot of stuff on my bookshelves and in my browser history about something called the 'imperial boomerang', or the 'boomerang theory' of colonialism.[177] Often attributed to the Caribbean writer Aimé Césaire, it's a metaphor that's widely used to express the idea of a constitutive relationship between war in the empire and the metropole – and especially how colonial brutality bounced back to Europe, for example in the form of Nazism. My story is about the process, the line of flight, through which that metaphor has taken form. I want to dig back through the literature, and the translations between arguments and languages, to trace how as the story shifted form, so too did this image of the boomerang, transforming like Henry Balfour's picture of the snail that became a bird, or Fox's horse that grew wings, or like that game we seem to keep coming back to, Russian Scandal or Telephone.

The story begins on 26 May 1868, at the Oval in Lambeth. The cricket ground was laid out in the mid-1840s. The site is a few minutes' walk from where William Cuffay's Chartist meeting took place in 1848, the one that fizzled out in the rain, the day when the soldiers closed the bridges across the river and the British Museum curators imagined they were under attack. Kennington Common was long gone by the 1860s, though, transformed through an act of Parliament into the Victorian park which is still there today. Now the Oval was hosting a very different event from the iconic mass gathering of 1848. A group of thirteen Aboriginal men, most from what was then the Crown Colony of Victoria, were starting a national tour. In the subsequent four months, they played forty-seven two-day matches of cricket at various venues in England, from London to Liverpool. Before and after the game, there were performances of their 'traditional skills'. That afternoon, a crowd of 7,000 paying spectators in south London watched them perform sham fights, spear-throwing and demonstrations of the use of the boomerang. Fox, then living not so far away in Clapham, expanding his museum of weapons, was in the crowd. It was less than two weeks before he delivered the second 'Primitive Warfare' lecture at the Royal United Service Institution, in which he offered an extensive comparative analysis of the geographical distribution of the boomerang, which should, he said, be understood as 'a relic of the original Australoid stock' in India and Egypt. Objects and bodies were increasingly merging in his accounts of technological improvement and cultural supremacy. Four years later in 1872, he explained how he made a facsimile of an ancient Egyptian boomerang from the British Museum, and practised with it on Wormwood Scrubs until 'at last obtaining a return of flight, so that the weapon, after flying seventy paces forward, returned to within seven paces of the position in which I was standing'. To deny the 'affinity' between the Australian and South Asian 'Dravidian' boomerang, he argued, simply because the latter does not return, 'would be the same as denying the affinity of two languages whose grammatical construction was the same because of their differing materially in their vocabularies'.[178] *Harper's Magazine* reported how, at the British Association for the Advancement of Science meeting in Brighton, Fox had underlined his view that the importance of the return flight for the performance of the boomerang as a weapon was exaggerated.[179]

One thing about translation is the time lags that it introduces. Those lags hold something in common with memorialisations – the gaps between a life lived and a statue built. When a translation is published it will be read as if it's contemporary, like a statue or like the rebuilding of the ship *Argo*. Let me give an example, one that begins after the Second World War, and runs from the work of Hannah Arendt to that of Aimé Césaire, Frantz Fanon and Jean-Paul Sartre. The image of the boomerang comes in and out of focus in their different analyses of the relationships between colonial and European history, and through a series of translations from French and English.

The idea of a 'boomerang effect' of colonialism is commonly associated with Aimé Césaire's landmark text *Discours sur le colonialisme*, published in 1950. Look up the English translation and the phrase appears in two famous passages. First Césaire describes how colonialism served 'to decivilize the colonizer, to brutalize him in the true sense of the word, to degrade him, to awaken him to buried instincts, to covetousness, violence, race hatred, and moral relativism':

> A poison has been distilled into the veins of Europe and, slowly but surely, the continent proceeds toward *savagery*. And then one fine day the bourgeoisie is awakened by a terrific boomerang effect: the gestapos are busy, the prisons fill up, the torturers standing around the racks invent, refine, discuss.[180]

'If I have recalled a few details of these hideous butcheries', Césaire's argument continues,

> it is by no means that I take a morose delight in them, but because I think that these heads of men, these collections of ears, those burned houses, these Gothic invasions, this steaming blood, these cities that evaporate at the edge of the sword, are not to be so easily disposed of. They prove that colonization, I repeat, dehumanizes even the most civilized man;

that colonial activity, colonial enterprise, colonial conquest, which is based on contempt for the native and justified by that contempt, inevitably tends to change him who undertakes it; that the colonizer, who in order to ease his conscience gets into the habit of seeing the other man as a beast accustoms himself to treating him like an animal, and tends objectively to transform *himself* into an animal. It is this result, this boomerang effect of colonization, that I wanted to point out.[181]

So read the two key passages in the 1972 English translation. But look back at the French edition and things are less straightforward. In both instances the text that the translator has rendered 'boomerang effect' in English, reads in the original French *'choc en retour'*.[182] It's a phraseology that, as Michael Rothberg has observed, presents a very different image from what was rendered by the English translator as 'boomerang effect'.[183] When Césaire writes of *'un formidable choc en retour'* and *'cette action, ce choc en retour'*, a literal translation would be 'shock in return'.[184] The French word *'choc'* has the primary sense of a sudden meeting of one body with another, a violent shock like the clash of swords, an impact, a blow. The metaphor thus evokes not the rotation, tilt, lift, speed and sweeping return of the boomerang, a curved blade resisting gravitational pull, but a backlash or a recoil, like the recoil of a gun. Such is the influence of the English translation, however, that when the German translation was published in 2021, the translator chose the term *Bumerangeinschlag* ('Boomerang impact') in the first instance, and in the second opted for *'Diese Rückwirkung, dieser Bumerangeffekt'*, i.e. 'this backlash, this boomerang effect'.[185]

Where then does this English phraseology come from? Perhaps it comes from Hannah Arendt's book *The Origins of Totalitarianism*, published in 1951, the year after Césaire's book. Arendt described the Nazi regime as a 'boomerang effect of imperialism', something not experienced by Britain because, unlike in Germany and Austria, they did not seek 'to imperialise the whole nation', and 'drew a sharp line between colonial methods and normal domestic policies'.[186] Or maybe the influence was Jean-Paul Sartre.[187] In 1963, Sartre had written the preface to the English translation of Frantz Fanon's *The Wretched of the Earth*, which had been published in

French in 1961. Addressing the contemporary situation in Algeria and Angola, Sartre described a conjuncture in which 'Europeans are massacred at sight', as 'the moment of the boomerang' [*le moment du boomerang*]. 'It is the third phase of violence; it comes back on us, it strikes us, and we do not realize any more than we did the other times, that it's we who have launched it', Sartre wrote.[188] But Fanon, who had been mentored by Césaire, employed very different language in his book. He used, for example, the metaphor of a bomb, arguing that 'laying claim to and denying the human condition at the same time: the contradiction is explosive. And it does explode, as you know as well as I do'.[189]

So the story of the boomerang is not just one of colonial violence and ideologies of supremacism returning from the colonies to Europe in the form of fascism. It also involves something like what Naomi Klein's book *The Shock Doctrine* called 'ideological blowback'.[190] The recoil of a gun becomes, through the voices of Sartre and Arendt, at risk of displacing those of Césaire and Fanon, as in one of Fox's Victorian parlour games, like the line of flight of a boomerang coming back to centre the European. It's like the metaphor could flip at any point into that old hard-right narrative of the risk of 'reverse colonisation', the replacement by colonial populations coming to Europe, which still fuels anti-immigration politics across the continent, from Dover to Leipzig: a parallel history of colonial-militarist ideas brought back to Europe from the edges of empire, moving in a vector that at some point will intersect with the Césaire–Fanon sense of the self-brutalisation of the coloniser.[191] Connections between colonial war and war in Europe, or between colonial racism and Nazism, might be presented as an analogy, or as a historical continuity like the flight of an arrow or a bullet. Remember what Marx wrote about repetition, you say as if your story is coming to some kind of conclusion:

> Hegel remarks somewhere that all facts and personages of great importance in world history occur, as it were, twice. He forgot to add: the first time as tragedy, the second time as farce. [192]

They were the opening lines to *The Eighteenth Brumaire of Louis Bonaparte*, you remind me, as if they could distract us from the news from America that just came in, the election result, November 2024.

Marx was slightly misquoting Hegel of course, you continue; what he actually wrote ran something closer to: through repetition what felt the first time to be just an accident or a possibility comes to seem like reality or truth.[193] I prefer the earlier line from Marx, I reply, you remember it I'm sure: 'History goes through many phases as it carries an old figure to the grave'.[194] The conversation dried up then, and we went back to looking at our phones, and listening to the podcasts, and trying to make sense of what just happened, and what is about to happen. The next day you emailed me a passage from Felix Guattari's 1989 book *Les trois écologies* – the moment in which in his discussion of Western distinctions between nature and culture he compares the 'mutant and monstrous algae' that can take over a water system with an American social ecology characterised by 'the freedom afforded to men like Donald Trump to proliferate' – and thinking of the White supremacism of the 2020s as another kind of return.[195] The subject line of your email was blank, but underneath the quote you'd added the line: 'Hegel might've called it a dialectic, but this seems to me like the recoil of serial untruths.'

## 30. WHEN THE WORLD SCREAMED

'The General took the opportunity of expressing his regret that no collection had been made as yet to illustrate the development of the art of shipbuilding.'[196] I was reading you a news cutting from *The Times* from 1891, describing Fox's final visit to Oxford to see the museum he had donated and then detached from. He gave an address in the lecture room of the University Museum about the arrangement of the collection. He explained how it all started from his professional interest in the development of the rifle. He then applied the same thinking to stone axes and other weapons, and then to musical instruments, and pottery, and boatbuilding, he continued.[197] Musical instruments as a weapon sounds like Morant Bay, you interrupted. Not sure that's what he meant, but yes, that's clearly something we see here – how culture got weaponised. And then there's the boatbuilding example.

In the subsequent years, several boatbuilding displays were added, most obviously today in the form of *Salama*, a double outrigger canoe from the Swahili coast of Tanzania, suspended from the lower gallery above the entrance to the museum, donated in 1967.[198] I go back and look again at the story of the *Argo*, that ship that is constantly rebuilt to the extent that its materials are totally replaced but its form survives, like a word whispered down the line. It's still the *Argo*, its fabric long decayed and substituted. Then, as I read more, I realise this mythic story was never actually about Jason's *Argo*, the vessel of the Argonauts, with which they retrieved the gold fleece, named after its builder Argus. The story of the rebuilt ship was always the ship of Theseus. Theseus' ship sailed from Crete, as described by Plutarch in his *Life of Theseus*, and was preserved as a kind of monument for centuries, supposedly for 500 years, down to the third century BCE. The story was retold by Thomas Hobbes, and repeated from there. Imagine that a man had kept all the old planks as they were taken out, and had made a ship of them, Hobbes wrote.[199] There's a line of citation that runs right down to Gilles Deleuze: like I said before, he compared the ageing human body to 'Theseus's ship, which the Athenians were constantly repairing'.[200]

But Roland Barthes misidentified the ship when he offered his metaphor of how literature operates like the *Argo*, and that's where I picked it up; repeated by Maggie Nelson in her *Argonauts*. I guess they both knew what they were doing, you tell me, Roland Barthes and Maggie Nelson, that Cartesian adverb *ergo* becoming *Argo*. That's the point, after all. The words change as well as the form. You read Barthes' description back to me, an image of a boat 'whose long history admitted of no creation, nothing but combinations; bracketed with an unchanging function, each piece was nonetheless endlessly renewed, without the whole ever ceasing to be the *Argo*'. I want to learn from what Barthes and Maggie Nelson do here, and offer two transformations of Fox, each with a different name; each representing a continuity but also a disjuncture. First the fictional Professor Challenger, then the very real Grandson at last.

In 1853 Fox honeymooned at Penrhyn Castle in Snowdonia, North Wales, the seat of his maternal uncle, the 1st Baron Penrhyn.[201] It lies 150 miles from the Fox estate in Yorkshire along that railway line that runs west from Leeds and hugs the Irish Sea coastline through Chester, Rhyl and Llandudno to Bangor.[202] The uncle had built this massive fantasy castle during the 1820s and 1830s, and it had views over Snowdonia to the south and the Menai Strait to the north. He inherited it through a series of intermarriages between families with Caribbean plantation and mercantile interests, from Liverpool and Yorkshire, including the Pennants, the Dawkinses and most recently the Lascelles.[203]

The Baron had an immense pit at Penrhyn Quarry, Bethesda, six miles away from the castle. One mile in length, and 1,200 feet in depth, it was the largest slate quarry in the world, where 3,000 quarrymen hammered out the Cambrian deposits of Welsh slate. It generated a profit of £100,000 a year. The slate was hauled onto wagons on the six-mile narrow-gauge railway which took it to Port Penrhyn, and out into the Irish Sea, the fifty miles along the coastline to Liverpool and beyond. It was a landscape of gunpowder explosions and men hanging from ropes, described like a battlefield by one visiting German prince because injuries were so common.[204]

You can visit the railway museum today, opened after Penrhyn Castle was given to the National Trust in 1951 along with 40,000 acres of land. Fox must have seen his uncle's vast excavations at the quarry during his honeymoon, and the vast art collection too, which came to be known as 'the gallery of North Wales'. The uncle had also commissioned a monument by Richard Westmacott in the parish church in 1820, depicting an idealised image of a quarryman with his slate knife, a girl wearing an oak leaf, and cherubs above them chiselling slate, dancing at a harvest festival, and learning to read.[205] The National Trust website describes how:

> Behind the formidable architecture, Victorian grandeur and fine interiors, present-day Penrhyn Castle's foundations were built on a dark history. One of exploitation, Jamaican sugar fortunes and the transatlantic slave trade.[206]

It's not a real castle, of course, but an example of the so-called Norman Revival, built with a combination of capital gained from the labour of enslaved people in the Caribbean and the forced labour of Welsh quarrymen: a sham castle, a Normanesque folly. Stylistically a kind of blank, grim picturesque, filled with specially designed Norman-style furniture. It's one of the most enormous houses in Britain, and the baron opened it for public visits as early as 1856. Today, the prime exhibit is a one-ton slate bed specially built for Queen Victoria and the prince consort when they visited in 1859. The Royal Collections Trust holds a nondescript pencil drawing made by the Queen of the view from the bedroom window.[207]

Penrhyn was a site of ongoing exploitation and workers' resistance. In 1866, the baron sacked eighty workers for failing to vote for his son, Fox's cousin, when he was elected, unopposed, as the Tory MP for Caernarvonshire in 1866. There were ongoing disputes from the 1870s, as the baron resisted unionisation, and when the second baron, Fox's cousin, succeeded in 1886 these intensified. The second baron formed a body called the North Wales Property Association, a 'mutual self-protection' society that fought for landowners' rights, and described industrial relations at the quarry as a matter of nationalism and 'race'.[208] In April 1900, years of aggression from the lords of the manor as workers protested pay and conditions came to a head, when a walk-out led to the mounted police of the county being deployed against workers. The result was the Great Quarry Strike, which lasted three years and was an important influence on the formation of the British Labour Party. In 2016, the artist Lisa Heledd Jones installed a lightbox in the fireplace of the castle's Grand Hall, bearing a local Welsh saying handed down generations of local communities:

MI GEWCH CHI'CH CROGI AM DDWYN DAFAD ODDI AR Y MYNYDD, OND AM DDWYN Y MYNYDD MI GEWCH CHI'CH GWNEUD YN ARGLWYDD.

which translates as:

You will be hanged for stealing a sheep from the mountain, but for stealing the mountain you will be made a lord.[209]

Whenever I try to focus on this family connection, I find the figure of Fox gets blurred with a character from early twentieth-century science fiction. Professor Challenger was first introduced in Arthur Conan Doyle's book *The Lost World* in 1912, and then reappeared in some of Conan Doyle's writing over the next two decades, including several short stories published after the silent Hollywood movie of *The Lost World* was released in 1925. The professor made his final appearance in a short story named 'The Disintegration Machine' in 1929.[210] The parallels between the fictional Professor George Edward Challenger FRS and the real-life General Augustus Henry Lane Fox Pitt-Rivers FRS are legion. The aggressive, domineering, toxic, hypermasculine character of Challenger matches so many of the facts and eyewitness accounts of Fox. In later life, Fox forbade his second son from entering his country estate, and when his wife broke with this estrangement by secretly meeting with him, Fox was there in the hallway to meet her when she returned, took the riding crop from her hand, and slashed her across the face.[211]

Conan Doyle's description of Challenger's writing looking like a barbed-wire fence bears a striking affinity with my experience of reading Fox's letters and notebooks.[212] Then there is the sense of a similar lecturing style. I watch the scene of Professor Challenger's lecture in the MGM silent movie adaptation of *The Lost World*, standing below the Union Flag. After one of Challenger's harangues, Conan Doyle wrote, an audience would feel as if their protective epidermis had been pierced and their nerves laid bare. Challenger was appointed assistant keeper in comparative anthropology at the British Museum in 1893, but resigned after acrimonious correspondence later the same year. He planned to open a private museum with the fortune in diamonds he had brought back from his South American expedition.[213] Fox's anthropological collections came to Oxford after a public disagreement with the authorities of the South Kensington Museum and the British Museum, and the aggression of his machine-gun lecture-theatre style leaps off the page. It's got to the point that when reading any description of the fictional Challenger with his spade-shaped beard, I find myself picturing Fox:

> He is a primitive cave man in a lounge suit. I can see him with a club in one hand and a jagged bit of flint in the other. Some people are born out of their proper century, but he is born out of his millennium. He belongs to the early Neolithic or thereabouts.[214]

The Scots-born Challenger lived at the fictional Enmore Gardens in Enmore Park, Kensington West, and the Yorkshire-born Pitt-Rivers lived at several addresses in Kensington, including Onslow Gardens. Challenger held the fantasy that he might one day occupy for posterity the fourth plinth in Trafalgar Square, while Pitt-Rivers erected two museums and commissioned various busts, portraits and other monuments to himself. Pitt-Rivers inherited a vast fortune that can be traced back to the unfree labour of enslaved people on the sugar plantations of the Caribbean which he used to build museums and undertake excavations, and Challenger too inherited an enormous sum, millions of pounds, from a man who made a fortune in rubber, who gave it with the provision it should be used solely for scientific ends.

When I read one of these short stories in particular I found myself blurring the line between Challenger and Fox. (I have the same with Rhodes and Musk, you chip in.) Actively blurring it, as a kind of method of enquiry. It starts with Challenger purchasing a property at an imaginary place called Hengist Down, on the north edge of the chalk country of Sussex. He wires off an immense tract of the landscape and begins to dig – at first apparently searching for oil.[215] 'Science seeks knowledge. Let the knowledge lead us where it will, we still must seek it!' Challenger cries as he engineers a colossal open-cast pit or tunnel boring eight miles deep into the Sussex chalk, at the cost of millions of pounds.

Layer after layer of chalk, clay, coal and granite is cut into with hydraulic shovels and lifted out, skip after skip drawn up on steel wires from the pit. At the very bottom, in depths of immense airless heat, a vast electric steel drill 100 feet in length is positioned to pierce the deepest layer exposed, a greyish shiny stratum that seems to ripple or throb. An audience of dignitaries including lords, members of Parliament, the chairmen of learned societies from London, Paris and Berlin, and international journalists have arrived by special train from Victoria, brought by a fleet of cars from the rural railway station on the edge of the Downs. If you squint, and train your eye along where I'm pointing, across this black and white landscape of words on the page, do you see the figure of Fox silhouetted in the special reserved enclosure, built with sandbags and a corrugated iron roof, set aside for the party of members of the royal family?[216] At last the true purpose of the dig is revealed: to penetrate the soft inner cuticle of Mother Earth. As the machinic iron dart pierces the surface, there is a howl, a shriek, a scream of which the narrator writes, 'No sound in history has ever equalled the cry of the injured earth.'[217]

An enormous geyser of putrid tar shoots up two thousand feet into the air, and the lift shafts are blown as far as Worthing Pier in one direction and Chichester in the other, and then the earth closes the pit like a wound healing with extreme rapidity. In the aftermath, volcanos erupt around the world, from Iceland to Vesuvius to Mexico, while cameras click, and handkerchiefs are waved and cries of admiration for Challenger are raised:

> The June sun shone upon him as he turned, gravely bowing to each quarter of the compass: Challenger the super-scientist, Challenger the arch-pioneer, Challenger the first man of all men whom Mother Earth had been compelled to recognise.[218]

Half a century after 'When the World Screamed' was serialised in *Liberty* magazine, Challenger underwent an unreal reincarnation that was in total alignment with his chaotic character – a transubstantiation not in the science fiction bookstores, but on the continental philosophy shelves of university humanities and social science libraries. In 1980, the French philosophers Gilles Deleuze and Félix Guattari opened Chapter Three of their labyrinthine book *A Thousand Plateaus: Capitalism and Schizophrenia* by imagining a lecture being given by Challenger on the theme of stratification. It was, they tell us, a lecture written by mixing textbooks on geology and biology. Strata are acts of capture, the French theorists make Challenger say: they are like black holes or occlusions striving to seize whatever comes within their reach. A 'machinic assemblage' exists between geological layers, a physical presence on the surface of the stratification so to speak.[219] Never could make much sense of Deleuze and Guattari, you said when I tried to describe this; but it sounds like Professor Challenger was trying to explain the archaeological concept of cuts and layers, the stratigraphy of vertical and horizontal interfaces.

I typed the words GENERAL AUGUSTUS HENRY LANE FOX PITT-RIVERS into an AI text-to-image generator the other day, you tell me, and if your descriptions of Fox's phantom-like presence didn't already give me nightmares, Deleuzian nightmares about sedimented bodies and folds in the fabric of time, after hearing about you working in a place named after him for a decade and a half, now I have this AI-meets-Francis-Bacon rendering of him as some kind of cyborg museum cabinet to try to unsee, to unname, to exorcise.

The writer Christopher Hitchens' attention was caught by how Conan Doyle's image of the earth as a fragile, living organism foreshadowed James Lovelock's Gaia hypothesis of the 1960s.[220] I'm more interested in what it referenced back to, I tell you. To Fox, perhaps. But surely primarily to the Big Hole in Kimberley, South Africa. At a quarter of a mile in diameter, and half that in depth, this void can be seen from space and may be the deepest hole ever excavated by hand anywhere on earth.[221] From 1888 to 1914, hundreds of thousands of men dug thousands of kilograms of diamonds in open cast for Cecil Rhodes' De Beers Consolidated Mines Limited.[222]

There is a degree of prefiguration of Challenger's electric drill in a gun that Rhodes had specially designed and manufactured for the Diamond Fields Artillery at the height of the Boer War in January 1900. (Fox would be dead a few weeks later.) Known as Long Cecil, it had a firing range of four and a half miles and took thirty-pound shells made by the De Beers Company, some supposedly bearing the message WITH COMPTS CJR.[223] After Rhodes' death two years later, Long Cecil served as the gun carriage for his funeral procession, and it is now the centrepiece of a monument to the Siege of Kimberley. As for the void, it became a bleak heritage tourist attraction which has periodically seen attempts, unsuccessful to date, to have it inscribed as a World Heritage Site. And here in Oxford, his statue remains on the High Street, the north façade of Oriel College, this monument to the origins of the colour line and Apartheid, to the fantasy colonisation of the stars themselves. To how 'cultural racism', if we can give it that name, was never simply a degeneration or decline to an old barbarism, but a self-conscious evolution and advance that brought death and horror for a future based on myth. Like Challenger's cannon packed with gun cotton blasting not Jules Verne-style into the sky, but fired into the earth itself.

So is it possible to make sense of these voids: from the empty opencast pit of the diamond mine to Challenger's fictional excavation on the South Downs, the gaps left by what was extracted from the cultures of the world to make the two Pitt Rivers collections, and the space that is already starting to open up as the Rhodes statue starts, imperceptibly, to fall, to the cavity of the skull-cup, and the de-named human life degraded in death? In archaeological terms, each void is a cut into lives and landscapes. A pit or a ditch may be continually recut, or it may silt up over the years. The extractions are real and lasting, but like a monument the myths they are based on will fade unless they are maintained, remembered and retold. And the history of all myths is, after all, Fox argued in his *Evolution of Culture* lecture, you remind me, 'one of continued degeneration'.[224]

Conan Doyle's Challenger was a figure perhaps partly modelled on Fox – just as Austerlitz's encounters with the dead in the excavations near Liverpool Street were a fiction perhaps part-modelled by W. G. Sebald on Fox's accounts of his prototype rescue archaeology. Let me offer another such figure. A second relic table, then, each line like the recoil of a gun, like Newton's third law about the mutual actions of two bodies, action yielding to reaction. An initial account of the man who would return to Oxford as a student bearing the necronym even before he had technically inherited it: the Grandson. To show the evolution of form from one generation to another, how history repeats itself through human lives in constant transformation, in this case from one ideology of supremacy to the next:

FOX-PITT, George 'Joe' Henry Lane FRAI FRGS

BORN: George Henry Lane Fox 22 May 1890, 4 Grosvenor Gardens, London, son of Alexander Edward Lane Fox-Pitt (later Pitt-Rivers) of Rushmore, Wilts (d. 1927) and Alice Ruth Hermione Thynne, daughter of Lord Henry Thynne.

ARISTOCRAT: owned land in Dorset and Wilts. Owner-director of the Pitt-Rivers Museum in Farnham, Blandford, Dorset.

MARRIED: first 1915 his third cousin (great-great-granddaughter of his great-great-grandfather, the 2nd Marquess of Bath) Hon. Emily Rachel Forster (daughter of Lord Forster, an MP and later governor-general of Australia; a film and television actress with the stage name Mary Hinton), div. 1929; second 1931 his second cousin (granddaughter of his great uncle, Fox's brother-in-law the 4th Baron Stanley) Rosalind Venetia Henley FRS d. of Brig-General Anthony Morton Henley, granddaughter of the 4th Baron Stanley of Alderley, separated 1936; third relationship with Stella Edith Howsen Clive (also known as Stella Lonsdale, Stella Maumen, Stella Warner, Stella Magaloff, occasionally Stella Sidoroff, and later Stella Pitt-Rivers), they never married, but on 23 June 1952 she changed her name to Pitt-Rivers by deed poll.[225]

'CHOC EN RETOUR'

EDUCATION: Ascham House prep school, Bournemouth; Eton College, Worcester College, Oxford (degree not completed).

CAREER: Fellow Commoner of Worcester College, Oxford 1920. BSc awarded February 1926, thesis title 'The Clash of Race and the Clash of Culture' (member of the Junior Common Room 1920–26, then member of the Senior Common Room 1927–66).

Personal private secretary (1920–21) and aide-de-camp (1922–24) to his father-in law Lord Forster, governor-general of Australia.[226] Did work in anthropology in New Guinea and Bismarck Archipelago in 1921.

President, Section F (Ethnology and Anthropology), Australasian Association for the Advancement of Science 1923; chairman, British Population Society 1932; chairman, Wessex Agricultural Defence Association 1933; contested North Dorset constituency as Independent Agriculturalist 1935; arrested for espionage in Karlsbad (Karlovy Vary) 1936; detained under Defence Regulation 18B 27 June 1940 (released January 1942); inaugurated Wessex Musical Festival 1945.

MILITARY RANKS AND SERVICE: Royal Wiltshire Yeomanry 1909; captain in the 5th Dragoon Guards 1910. Served in Johannesburg, South Africa 1911–13; fought in the European War 1914–18 ('severely wounded');[227] Reserve of Officers 1919–36.

CHILDREN: Michael Pitt-Rivers (landowner), Professor Julian Pitt-Rivers (anthropologist), Anthony Pitt-Rivers (landowner and lieutenant of Dorset).

FAMILY: grandson of Augustus Henry Lane Fox Pitt-Rivers FRS; great-nephew of philosopher Bertrand Russell; father-in-law of Sonia Orwell (widow of George Orwell);[228] nephew of John Lubbock MP, Ist Baron Avebury; second cousin of Winston Churchill; second cousin once removed of Diana Mitford (second wife of Oswald Mosley, 6th Baronet and fascist); nephew-in-law of the 4th Marquess of Bath (Lord Lieutenant of Wiltshire and trustee of the British Museum); great-great-grandson-in-law of Sir Francis Baring (founder of Barings Bank).[229]

MEMBERSHIPS: Eugenics Society (life member), Royal Anthropological Institute, Royal Geographical Society, British Council against European Commitments, British Population Society (president), International Union for the Scientific Investigation of Population Problems (founder and honorary general secretary and treasurer), Nordic League, The Link, National Front After Victory.

RECREATIONS: 'historical research', 'refuting politicians', 'cultivating any form of Art', 'detesting Bishops'.[230]

PUBLICATIONS: *Conscience and Fanaticism* (1919), *The World Significance of the Russian Revolution* (1920), *Variations in Sex Ratios as Indices for Racial Decline* (1925), *The Clash of Culture and the Contact of Races* (1927), *Weeds in the Garden of Marriage* (1931), *Czecho-Slovakia, the Naked Truth about the World-War Plot* (Sept 1938), revised edition, *The Czech Conspiracy in the World-War Plot* (Nov 1938); various papers on psychological and eugenic subjects.

CLUBS: Cavalry, Arthur's, Athenaeum, Cercle de l'Union interalliée.

ADDRESS: The Manor House, Hinton St Mary, Dorset and 77 Cadogan Gardens, SW3.

DIED: 17 June 1966, aged seventy-six.

WEALTH AT DEATH: £799,416 in probate; £676,746 net; beneficiaries 'Stella Edith Pitt-Rivers *feme sole* and Richard Trehane, Milk Marketing Board' plus further sums, vast estates and vast art and museum collection held by a trust managed by Stella.[231]

The Grandson, Fox-Pitt, 'was totally antipathetic to his parents', a Great-Grandson recalled in 1977, and so the Grandfather-General, who had died when he was ten years old, 'became for him the idealised father-figure throughout life'. He even intended to author his biography, the Great-Grandson continued, 'as a work of grand-filial piety', but he never did.[232] Let me try to set out some of the facts of the life of the Grandson; a life he lived as if dominated by the idea of preparing that biography of his grandfather that he would never write.

George Henry Lane Fox-Pitt was an anthropologist, a soldier and a fascist. He was 'an aristocrat of decidedly "theoretical" bent', as Patrick Wright has put it.[233] Following his father's death in 1927, this 37-year-old eldest son of the eldest son inherited the necronym, along with the second museum collection, the vast Rivers fortune, and a landed estate so enormous that his biographer Bradley Hart has called it 'a small agricultural empire'.[234] (Fox-Pitt was styling himself George Pitt-Rivers, taking the name of the suicidal lord and the Grandfather-General, long before this, however: indeed, from the moment of his Grandfather's death a couple of weeks before his tenth birthday, as if impatiently trying to jump a generation of inheritance in those accelerationist years as Victorian ideas transformed in the new context of a new century.)[235]

Fox-Pitt's early life paralleled that of his Grandfather in certain respects: overseas service in the military, and a growing interest in anthropology and theories of cultural supremacy. Schooled at Eton, he joined the Royal Wiltshire Yeomanry and then the 1st Royal Dragoons. His first deployment was in Mathura in northern India in 1910. Then in November 1911, he was posted to South Africa – like his uncle, the man who'd fought at Ulundi and brought back the Zulu items now in the Oxford Museum. He was stationed near Johannesburg. And in an intergenerational echo of the Hyde Park railings affair to the Penrhyn slate quarry, in July 1913 Fox-Pitt participated in the violent suppression of the miners' strike, when the Dragoons opened fire and killed and injured dozens of demonstrators outside the Rand Club.[236]

When war came to Europe, he fought briefly at the First Battle of Ypres in November 1914, but received a bullet wound to his left leg, below the knee, from German machine-gun fire and returned from Belgium immediately. Apart from light duties in the trenches towards the end of the war, he spent the rest of the war convalescing and reading. He married a daughter of the Tory MP for Sevenoaks in December 1915, and published his first book, *Conscience and Fanaticism: An Essay on Moral Values*, in 1919 – which he described as concerned with 'two aspects of mind', 'objective' and 'subjective', writing that:

The life history of every new individual, in its initial stages, is a (more or less complete) recapitulation of the life history of the race. The earlier ancestral acquisitions have been transformed into habit and have become secondarily automatic, the less are they liable to variation, and the more inexorable and unfailing will be their transmission.[237]

Where the Grandfather's favourite axiom from Leibniz had been 'nature never acts by leaps', the Grandson offered his own: 'Substance, the ultimate reality, can only be conceived as force'.[238] In January 1920, now twenty-nine years of age, Fox-Pitt went up to Worcester College, Oxford. He read social anthropology and psychology as a fellow commoner for two terms.[239] When his father-in-law, newly created the 1st Baron Forster, took up the position of governor-general of Australia, he left Oxford and joined him as his aide-de-camp. Over the next two decades, Fox-Pitt produced a series of anti-Semitic, hardline eugenicist, anti-Bolshevist writings. *The World Significance of the Russian Revolution* was a racist diatribe that introduced the conspiracy theory of a supposed Jewish-Bolshevik revolutionary conspiracy that had caused the First World War.[240] Appearing at the same time as the fake *Protocols of the Elders of Zion*, it offered a parallel set of racist myths of a Jewish-controlled world government. Fox-Pitt's output was part of the wider phenomenon of aristofascism which, as Adam Sacks has observed, was fusing Russophobia with anti-Semitism in the creation of 'Judeo-Bolshevist' conspiracy theories.[241]

Fox-Pitt's publications while in Australia expanded his eugenic ideas on how the 'inter-breeding of races' was causing 'demographic decline'.[242] The degree of interaction he had with the Pitt Rivers Museum in Oxford is unclear, although in 1924 he deposited seventeen photographs of Papua New Guinea to the collections.[243] What is certain is that his supremacist thinking fed into his most influential book, *The Clash of Culture and the Contact of Races* – and that in 1927, just after its publication, he was elected as a life member of the Senior Common Room of Worcester College, a position he held until his death in 1966.[244] This cultural-eugenicist, 'ethnogenetical' text set out an argument developed from the Grandfather's generation, a vision of the clash of 'race', 'population' and 'culture'. One difference was that, unlike the Grandfather, the word 'heritage' was now front and centre in Fox-Pitt's thinking. For instance, in his 1924 discussion of 'the passing of the Maori race and the decay of Maori culture', he stated that 'the general culture level of a people at a particular time' is conditioned by three aspects of heritage: 'culture-forms' like tradition, art and belief, 'culture accessories' like weapons and tools, and 'culture-potential', the last of which 'must be correlated with racial not national history'. This was the language of eugenics, in which racist theories of 'hereditary genius' developed by men like Francis Galton blended into the anthropological study of culture.[245] With his attachment to the Oxford college sealed, in 1928 he founded the International Union for the Scientific Investigation of Population Problems. In his role as its secretary-general, back in Britain, his attempts to present a White supremacist ideology of miscegenation as the work of conservation, or humanitarian care, was taking on a new European dimension.

Little wonder, then, that a year after a meeting with Fox-Pitt, and just as the life membership of the SCR of Worcester College was being agreed, Benito Mussolini wrote in a letter in April 1927 that in his political philosophy: 'We are putting into practice what Pitt-Rivers and his friends have looked forward to.'[246] And Hitler was present at the ceremony in 1936 when Fox's great-grand-niece married Oswald Mosley, you once pointed out to me.

Perhaps now we can start to revisit what Césaire and Fanon were concerned about, you say. The nature of the inheritance from the atrocities and ideologies of corporate-colonial militarism to the ideologies of fascism, like the recoil of a gun. And how that might help to understand the history of the skull-cup. Structures of cultural supremacism inherited from one generation to another. Shifting forms of monumentality and the scream of the earth against the void. Invented traditions made to seem as timeless as the ship of Theseus, or as the *Argo*. Dispossessions naturalised like the theft of a mountain, or the possession of human body parts. Mass slaughter presented as inevitable and predestined through an automaton theory of extermination. An evolving denialist theoretics of nonhuman techno-agency. An enduring militarist realism. An emergent, eugenicist identity politics of cultural Whiteness mapped onto ideas of preservation, inheritance and heritage. An extremist co-option of the idea of the museum, of the monument, and even of the university. The prehistory of a 'war of position' – a culture war that was now entering a new phase.

# VII
# Culture War

*fall*, noun. vii) the decline or closing part of a day, year, or someone's life. By extension, autumn, the season in which leaves fall from trees

The Latin inscription runs around the silver rim of the skull-cup like a curse:

> Fructus Worcester College D.D. in usum Cam. Com. George Lane-Fox Pitt-Rivers B.Sc. Soc. Com. 1920–1926, postea annos XX privilegiis Cam Com.[1]

At Hinton St Mary on 27 June 1940, the arrest by plain-clothes officers proceeded without incident. Worcester College's senior member Fox-Pitt was being detained under Defence Regulation 18B as a Nazi sympathiser. He was never a formal member of the British Union of Fascists, it seems, but he was close to his cousin's husband, Oswald Mosley, having hosted meetings for him in the mid-1930s.[2] And the evidence mounting up against him indicated more than just a theoretical support for the National Socialist regime. In 1936, he'd been arrested in Czechoslovakia on suspicion of working for Hitler. In the September of the following year he attended the 1937 Nuremberg Rally wearing a gold swastika badge, and took photographs of the Deutsche Arbeitsfront, the labour brigades formed after the destruction of the trade unions, as they carried shovels on their shoulders like rifles, tools borne as weapons.[3] In June 1938, he wrote to Hitler expressing a thankfulness that the *Anschluss* had been achieved without bloodshed, and included a typescript copy of the invited lecture he had recently given at the University of Göttingen, titled *'Der Friede welcher höher ist denn alle Unvernunft'* – 'the peace which surpasses all misunderstanding'.[4] Fox-Pitt had doubtless delivered it with the confidence that will always derive from a sense that there's a certain sheen of sophistication and charm to the stilted constructions of an English public-school German. Published in the same year, his book *The Czech Conspiracy* presented the Nazi case for the cultural heritage of the Germans in Bohemia, and claimed that Czech heritage is German.[5] In a typical talk delivered at the British Council Against European Commitments in 1939, he told the audience that 'we have an England to rebuild', and the 'spirit' of England 'is rising everywhere'.[6] And at a meeting at Hinton St Mary in April 1939 he told his audience that Dorset should not take in refugees from Nazi Germany because they would be 'the scum of Europe', and that anyway the idea that a further world war was necessary 'to make the world safe for democracy' was 'another monumental lie'.[7]

After war broke out on 1 September 1939, Fox-Pitt's estate was requisitioned by the military, but he remained vocal, his biographer Bradley Hart records, in expressing his pro-Nazi sentiments.[8] The chief constable of Dorset claimed that the Grandson would walk around the grounds wearing a swastika armlet, and on visits to London, an MI5 report recorded, he was seen 'leaving Nazi propaganda between the pages of books in the library' of one of his clubs.[9] Then in November and December 1939, he took part in joint meetings held between Mosley and the top brass of the National Socialists, the Nordic League, and the British People's Party. Such meetings had continued into 1940.[10] Now, as he was being driven away by the authorities, a search of the manor house recovered a small assemblage of extremist paraphernalia, including a plaque of the Führer, and four pendants designed for a motor car – the Union Jack, the swastika, the Spanish flag and the Italian flag.[11]

Following his arrest, Fox-Pitt was held at first in Brixton Prison. He wrote to the provost of Worcester College and the anthropologist R. R. Marett (rector of Exeter College) asking for academic sanctuary, and intending to make Worcester his 'headquarters', but MI5 vetoed this, determining that he should be kept out of the city since, the intelligence service believed,

> It is most undesirable that he should be in a position to give vent to his objectionable views in the university, as it appears that he proposes to associate with other members of the Senior Common Room of Worcester College.[12]

Instead Fox-Pitt was transferred to Liverpool Prison, and then to the more informal regime of Winter Court Camp – a special internment camp at Ascot Racecourse with twenty-six huts set up in a barbed-wired compound.[13] Eventually released to a nursing home in January 1942, he recorded for posterity, in his *Who's Who* entry for 1965, that he had been 'held a political prisoner by order of Home Secretary 1940–1942'.[14] Forbidden to return to his Dorset manor house, in November 1943 Fox-Pitt wrote to George Lammie at the War Office, stating his wish 'to retire to my College at Oxford and write a treatise on the decline and fall of the British Empire'.[15] But he was banned from returning to Oxford too until the end of the war (although there is a record that he dined in college in 1942). In the final two years of the war, he directed his energies towards support for A. K. Chesterton's National Front After Victory, the organisation that provided the programme for what became the National Front, and to funding a number of far-right blood-and-soil farming campaigns.

But it's what Fox-Pitt did when he finally returned to this city, and to his college – returned to, say, six hundred yards from where I'm typing this now, eight decades ago, that is where this story goes next. Not where it ends, but where it starts to open out.

I translated the Latin text, and got a colleague to check it:

> For the benefit of Worcester College. Donated for the use of the Senior Common Room [SCR] by George Lane-Fox Pitt-Rivers BSc, Junior Common Room member 1920–1926, SCR privileges during the subsequent twenty years.

Just as the war against fascism was won, the fascist war on culture was entering a new phase. In 1946, on one of his first return visits to the college, Fox-Pitt donated this item to the SCR, with this new inscription on the rim, a new layer to this death-history more than sixty years after it had been bought by the Grandfather-General at Sotheby's with the Pitt-Rivers inheritance. And in doing so, he set in train a tradition of its use at the dining table that ran forward almost seventy years, used with more and less frequency under different provosts and different butlers, until the practice was finally stopped, and the skull-cup was boxed up in the archive.

I go back to those lines: 'For the benefit of the college', and 'for the use of the SCR', the place where the college fellows dine and drink and exchange ideas from one discipline to another. That first word, *fructus*, should make you hesitate about how best to translate it, my colleague tells me, because it encompasses more than the simple word 'benefit' suggests, something like a 'yield'. Under Roman law, *fructus* was a technical term used to describe goods born of other property, like wool shorn from a sheep or grapes harvested from the vine, but also the interest paid on a loan by the debtor. The word denoted one element of a trio of potential property rights that together form absolute ownership: 'dominium' over a thing (*res*). A right to *fructus* was distinguished from a right to use (*usus*), or to disposal or destruction (*abusus*). It signals the ability to draw a profit or surplus from what is possessed. It also evokes the idea of *ususfructus* – that form of ownership that was used to describe some forms of servitude. *Fructus* is also a kind of life interest, which means that the rights should expire on the death of the beneficiary. What then exactly are the usufructuary benefits that it is claimed might flow from this skull-cup drinking cup? What did it generate, as the benefits passed from the Blackshirt anthropologist (died 1966) to the immortal Oxford college (founded 1714)? What should the college do with the skull-cup now? And how would the answer to that question relate to the hundreds of thousands of human skulls and bones that remain in cardboard boxes in museums and collections around the world, some with detailed information of provenance so they could be returned to descendants, others where the violence included the destruction of all information or context, as with the case of the skull-cup?

Back in the late 1890s, I suggest to you, as a boy of eight or nine, perhaps Fox-Pitt was passed the skull-cup around the Grandfather's dining table one evening.

Who knows, you reply, and frankly who cares? I'll tell you what, though, the inscription reminded me of how the local historian W. G. Hoskins described in the 1950s how the idea of the 'palimpsest' could be applied to the English landscape, as if you could read it like a document that has been repeatedly written over: look hard enough at any town, city or countryside, he argued, and you might 'get behind the superficial appearances, to uncover the layers'.[16] As if a city, an object or even a human life could be read like a document that's been written on again and again, so much that a constellation of words has built up that could never be fully erased, and will always leave some trace or another if you can only find the right way to read it.

If you ever wrote that book you were talking about possibly writing then perhaps that'd be the most important part of how to tell the story, you say. I mean, you continue, could we even find some glimmer of hope in that thought, that sense of counter-endurance, of survival? Then again like Sara Ahmed says, there's always the risk that 'Whiteness can be reproduced in the spaces where it is supposedly being questioned'.[17] So I want to trace the wider legacies of Fox's thinking, from museums to monuments to the disciplines of anthropology and archaeology with that risk in mind. Because the question that faces Worcester College now is one that faces hundreds of museums, universities and towns and cities from Berkeley to Berlin, and from New York to Oxford. How to recognise, and to deal with, the unfinished legacies of colonialism: enslavement and its transforming afterlives. Three infrastructures of supremacy are coming into focus: the museum, the monument, the subject. They are becoming seen because they are being revealed by three parallel grassroots movements, led by African, African-Caribbean, African-American, Indigenous and Black European thought: restitution, fallism and decolonisation. The challenge is to see the history that lies behind these urgent and necessary attempts to address legacy colonialism in all its cultural forms; a history of the co-option of culture for the purposes of supremacism, the prehistory of this so-called 'culture war', this unfinished war on culture – this 'militarist realism'.

## 31. THE MUSEUM

Lectures and excavations were all very well, but it was the public display of objects that represented the key element of Fox's propagandistic model of militarist realism. To observe that museums became 'temples of Whiteness', as Sumaya Kassim has written, is to show that museums became places where White men laid claim to truth through lies, and still do, 'consecrate(d) race science', 'consecrate(d) the ideal of the white man', and proclaimed their worldview as ' objective in a way nothing else is'; where they claimed and continued to claim that 'My Word [is] objective and neutral, where all else is superstition and magical thinking'. 'I recognise in these buildings systems at work that are cumulative,' Kassim writes, as they 'venerate the actions that produce whiteness'.[18]

Fox's early involvement with ethnological museums had included honorary membership of the Blackmore Ethnological Museum at Salisbury, his role as a committee member organising exhibits at the Museum of Practical Geology in March–April 1869, and a chronological series of exhibitions themed on the Palaeolithic, on 'Neolithic and Savage Stone Implements', and on objects from the European Bronze Age at the Society of Antiquaries of London at Somerset House during 1871 and 1872.[19] When a new exhibition of musical instruments was installed at the South Kensington Museum in June 1872, he loaned some objects, and in the same month he made loans to displays of 'Ancient and Modern Jewellery and Personal Ornaments' at the East London or Bethnal Green Museum. The new museum was an outpost of the South Kensington Museum (not yet renamed the Victoria and Albert Museum), made from a section of the so-called 'Brompton Boilers', prefabricated cast-iron structures manufactured for the Great Exhibition that had served as display spaces in South Kensington for the previous twenty years, reclad in brick.[20]

Dropped into this poor, working-class and ethnically diverse part of the capital, the museum's public educational remit chimed with Fox's thinking.[21] The American novelist Henry James described the museum as an act through which 'half in charity and half in irony a beautiful art collection has been planted in the midst of this darkness and squalor', as an experimental lever for 'the elevation of the masses'.[22] 'Within an easy walk of upwards of a million of people, mostly of the artisan class', the *Journal of the Society of Arts* reported, the Bethnal Green displays were 'intended to be educational in the widest sense of the word', the complement of the 'great economic museum' of South Kensington.[23] Bethnal Green offered Fox an audience of what he called 'the more intelligent portion of the working classes': the target group in his ambition to create museum exhibits 'in which the visitors may be able to instruct themselves' according to his worldview, taking away that Leibnizian message that in his hands was transformed into a kind of counterinsurgent slogan that change never takes place quickly: 'nature never acts by leaps'.[24]

Fox loaned his ethnological collection for display in the basement at Bethnal Green, and the installation opened to the public on 1 July 1874.[25] The building is still there, reimagined in 1974 as the Victoria and Albert Museum of Childhood, and rebranded in 2023 as Young V&A. There were perhaps two or three thousand objects to begin with, but over the ten-year period of the loan Fox constantly added to the displays. Synergies were emerging between his weapons-technology militarism and his civic educationalism. In April 1873, Fox had returned to active army service for a three-year term, taking command as brigadier of the West Surrey Brigade Depot at Stoughton Barracks.[26] In this new military role he involved himself in the volunteer service in the county, commanding thousands of recruits at the annual field days in June, marching the troops through his garden, conducting mock battles at nearby Merrow Downs, and conducting comparative chest measurements of recruits.[27] On Easter Monday 1874 a volunteer review and sham fight was conducted on Wimbledon Common with 12,000 men, with the defending force commanded by Fox and the attacking by Prince Edward of Saxe-Weimar. 'After some excellent and interesting evolutions, the Surrey Army was beaten all along the line,' the newspapers reported.[28]

You know, I remember telling you when we were walking from Bethnal Green tube station along Cambridge Heath Road to take a look at the building, that word, 'evolution', has kept turning up in the reading I've been doing about drilling soldiers and the development of the volunteer forces, as well as in terms of cultural change. So I looked it up in the dictionary, and was surprised by what I read:

> *evolution*, noun. 1) (military and navy) a manoeuvre executed by troops or ships to adopt a different tactical formation; 2) the process of unrolling, opening out, or revealing; 3) (biology) the transformation of living organisms into different forms by the accumulation of changes over successive generations

Sounds like he saw his theory of cultural evolution as a tactical military formation, an unrolling and revealing, and an image of transformation through accumulation over the generations all at once, you pointed out. The line between the drilling of soldiers and the education of the public was blurring from the outset. In both contexts, Fox's contention that 'history is but another word for evolution' rang clear.[29] Museums could train the masses in 'the arts of life', educate them against revolution just as the NRA and the sham fights on the common by brigades of volunteers could turn ordinary men into soldiers rather than protestors. Indeed, the education that museums can produce 'is eminently progressive and conservative', Fox told an audience years later in Salisbury in 1890. 'Using that term in its general, and not in its political sense,' he added with a wink to the MP for Salisbury, the 6th Baronet sitting on the front row (a future captain in the Imperial Yeomanry, and assistant press censor on the military staff in South Africa at the end of the Boer War).[30] By then Fox's second museum at Farnham had been open for a decade, and he had also expanded his efforts in public education and civic recreation further, laying out a public pleasure grounds at Larmer Tree Gardens, with summerhouses, picnic bowers with signs that read 'No Speeches', and a menagerie where he experimented with cross-breeding reindeer, yaks, peacocks, llamas, sheep, kangaroos, wallabies, emus, zebras and oxen. To this landscape in the 1890s he added transplanted Nepalese pavilions that were originally part of the Great Exhibition, an outdoor theatre, a golf links and a race-track.[31] Fox's personal band, made up of estate staff dressed in a uniform of blue and yellow, would play at a specially built bandstand, and he gave away bread and butter and tea to the visitors, who came in their thousands.[32] Like in Hyde Park, both for the Great Exhibition and for the Railings Affair, Fox had embraced a kind of populism, in which culture could be participated in just like the NRA would drill civilians to shoot a gun, in the years running up to the Volunteer Force and the Imperial Yeomanry being sent out to war in South Africa.

Back in East London in 1874, Fox's collection of arms and armour had transformed into what E. B. Tylor described, on seeing the Bethnal Green displays, as 'a museum of weapons, &c., the classification of which has led Colonel Fox to form his theories'.[33] The 'etcetera' included a range of other things transformed into weapons, in the same way as those bag checks at the British Museum today, or a police stop-and-search for example, can find suspicion of violent or criminal intent in pretty much anything.

The displays were in four parts. First came the human skulls, samples of human hair, and photographs of so-called racial 'types' (although Fox advised the public that the best collection of skulls could be seen at the College of Surgeons, in Lincoln's Inn Fields, and in the collection of the Anthropological Institute at St Martin's Place). From 1864, Fox's collection had begun to include human skulls, and his interest in craniology and aspects of 'race science' – which certainly had begun by February 1861 when he was reading Charles Bray's account of phrenology in his book *The Education of the Feelings* – had gained momentum.[34] A dog whistle here or there to the failed 'race science', and a gesture to the promise of the emerging fields of eugenics and population studies, was a favoured element of his talks as well as his museum displays.

Second, weapons (obviously). Third, 'the material arts of modern savages and barbarous races', a vast range of artefact types:

> Pottery, Glass, Enamels, Architecture, House Furniture, Modes of Navigation, Land Transport, Horse Furniture, Tools, Weapons, Weaving Apparatus and Textiles, Metallurgy, Painting, Writing, Music, Mensuration, Sculpture, Ornamentation, Personal Ornament, Agriculture, Hunting and Fishing Apparatus, Trapping, Machinery, Fortification, Modes of Burial, Modes of Punishment, Monuments, Coins, Religious Emblems, Toys, Heating and Lighting, Food, Clothing, Basket-making, Narcotics, Medicine, Domestication of Animals, and so forth.[35]

Finally came a 'pre-historic series' of archaeological objects. Each part was designed to display what Fox called 'typical' specimens, rather than rare objects, and these were arranged in conjectural 'series' so as to trace a 'succession of ideas' in the human mind, from the 'primitive' to the 'complex'.[36] One model for this was how William Wilde, the antiquary whom Fox had met in the 1860s, had rearranged the collections of the Museum of the Royal Irish Academy: according to materials and 'use' or function rather than geographical region – in order to illustrate, as he put it, 'progress from the simplest and rudest to the most complicate and ornate'.[37] But the main influence was how the late prince consort's vision for the Great Exhibition had been 'ever anxious for the advancement of education, had strongly advocated the comparison of like things with like – that is to say, arrangement by classes and not according to geographical position'.[38]

Fox reproduced the centrepiece display as a diagram in his lecture on the 'Evolution of Culture'. It showed his typological method, and his theory of material culture based on improvements in warfare. At the centre of the diagram was a hypothetical wooden stick, standing for the natural forms from which the first humans developed tools and weapons. Fanning out in every direction like the dial of a clock, or like shrapnel flying from an epicentre, were a series of Melanesian and Aboriginal weapons 'acquired', to use the conventional euphemism, from the frontiers of British colonialism in Australia. Fox had bought these wooden items – boomerangs, throwing sticks, lances, shields, clubs – from dealers and auction houses in London, and he had no evidence of their relative ages or dates. Nonetheless, he arranged them into hypothetical 'series', using the fantasy stick as the imaginary point of origin, the vanishing point for the vision of the anthropologist where cultural history folds into natural history, as if that fantasy unaltered stick at the centre of the drawing could stand for some putative beginning of how all material culture and techniques of the body began in nature and started to transform it (a fantasy that was an ancestor of Kubrick's cinematic image of the bone as the first weapon). Fox's lecture about the relativity of train travel makes a little more sense when you picture it being delivered to the schoolboys at Whitechapel the year before the tube station opened, you point out, as his exhibit was going on show just up the road in Bethnal Green.

Outgrowing the East London basement, Fox's displays were transferred to two large ground-floor rooms at the main South Kensington Museum site, opening to the public on Boxing Day 1878.[39] On receipt of his inheritance in 1880, Fox began making plans for the long-term housing of his collection, which was still just on loan to South Kensington.[40] In a letter to the assistant director dated 14 April 1880, he stated that he intended to 'extend much more rapidly than hitherto the Ethnographical collection now exhibited at South Kensington' – and would need 'double the space'.⁴¹ As he spent more and more on his anthropological collections, so also with his new wealth came a new scale to his fieldwork. The museum's report for 1880 recorded that the collections had now grown to 14,860 objects, occupying 7,200 square feet of gallery space.⁴²

Now Fox, applying his newly acquired necronym to the collection, stated that he intended 'to leave it to the nation, or to some other nation, or to some institution that will carry it on'.⁴³ It would not, however, be given to the British Museum, which he saw as an institution for 'savants', a research collection rather than displays for public education, as had been developed by the South Kensington authorities.⁴⁴ Tylor expressed the hope that Fox's 'Museum of Weapons, which illustrates so many problems in his History of Civilisation, and has been already in its collector's hands so fertile a source of new ideas, may in some shape become a national institution'.⁴⁵ Fox made a formal offer to donate it to South Kensington, with various provisos and stipulations. In addition to the commitment of gallery space and basic maintenance, there was a condition that Fox would have total curatorial control as a 'life interest' until his death; that accessioned objects would be the property of the state six months after their deposition, but Fox could nonetheless have items removed if he decided they were inappropriate; and that the government would pay for not only insurance, labels and guidebooks, but also special police supervision of the collection. While he demanded a doubling of the space dedicated to its display, he also offered to pay to the costs of a curator who would report directly to him as the donor.⁴⁶ There was a need for adequate curatorial 'supervision' of the collections, since 'additions are being made daily, and it must be subject to constant re-arrangement as the things accumulate'.⁴⁷

Fox also proposed a statute of limitation on the future arrangement of his museum. It would be continued if it were accepted by 'men of science' – but there would be 'no object in continuing it', he argued, if it were not. 'Views become so much changed as knowledge accumulates,' he wrote, 'that it would be mischievous to hamper the future with ideas of the present.'⁴⁸ On this point, about the future of his own collection, Fox's guidance is worth reflecting on today, you once pointed out to me.

A specially convened subcommittee of the government's Committee of Council on Education considered the offer, and it recommended the acceptance of the collection by the nation.[49] But on 3 June 1881 the rejection of the offer by the committee on behalf of the Department of Art and Science came, in part due to space, but mainly because it was thought to be more appropriate for the British Museum, and 'a distinct line should be drawn between the collections at South Kensington and those at the British Museum'.[50]

During negotiations, Fox had set out his reasons for not directing the offer to the British Museum, stating that:

> My collection differs from others in this, that the arrangement is psychological rather than geographical, that is to say, objects from different countries appertaining to like arts or phases of the human mind have been classed together.[51]

In this respect Fox imagined his museum as belonging to a new phase of informal colonialism, to a new model of militarist realism, quite distinct from the cartographic approach of an institution like the British Museum; it was far less about place, and far more about ideas; about extraction rather than settlement. 'The British Museum, with its enormous treasures of art, is itself only in a molluscous and invertebrate condition of development,' he later argued; it is no use for public education, because of its sheer scale.

> It produces nothing but confusion in the minds of those who wander through its long galleries with but little knowledge of the periods to which the objects contained in them relate. The necessity of storing all that can be obtained, and all that is presented to them in the way of specimens, precludes the possibility of a scientific or an educational arrangement.[52]

Sounds like not much has changed at the British Museum in a century and a half then, you interrupted me. That's right, but we live in hope, I replied. Fox had threatened that if not accepted by the British nation, he might offer his collection to an institution in the United States.[53] Newspaper reports suggested that it was too 'racial' in character for South Kensington and, despite his reply that 'the object of this museum is not racial: it is a museum of primitive arts',

Fox's offer was turned down.[54] The fine distinction between scientific and cultural racism so important to Fox didn't wash with the Department of Science and Art in the Albertopolis, for whom the objection appears in retrospect to have been essentially aesthetic and geographical. There was a better reception in Oxford, however. Here, Fox now offered his collection to the university, imagining it as a kind of memorial to the death of his friend, co-excavator and fellow Yorkshireman George Rolleston, the university's Linacre Professor of Anatomy and Physiology, who had been a member of the committee that had recommended the collection be acquired for the nation – and had died on 16 June 1881, just after the refusal from South Kensington came through.[55]

The collection was formally accepted in a deed of gift on 20 May 1884 and ten days later the vice-chancellor formally confirmed the university council's agreement to accept the collection.[56] The donation was a key part of the establishment of a new chair in anthropology, a post which was taken up by E. B. Tylor on 10 March 1883. Tylor was also supplied by Fox with a text and diagram setting out his vision of the teaching of the subject on a 'four-field' model – physical anthropology, ethnology, culture and archaeology.[57] I prefer the model of the four As, I told you when we looked at the drawing. The university committed the sum of £10,000 to the construction of the new purpose-built museum building to 'contain' the objects; an extension to the 1860 University Museum, with the inscription PITT RIVERS COLLECTION above the entrance.[58] The deed of gift had various conditions, including a provision that:

> changes in details which may be made after the death of the said Augustus Henry Lane Fox Pitt Rivers shall be such only as shall be necessitated by the advance of knowledge and as shall not affect the general principle originated by the said Augustus Henry Lane Fox Pitt Rivers.[59]

The *University Gazette* reported that the museum would address 'such problems as the effect upon barbarous art of contact with civilised peoples and the survival of rude forms of art among civilised peoples'.[60] In long-term perspective, the university's collections had developed over six centuries, punctuated roughly once every 200 years by new benefactions and institutions: from the opening in 1488 of Duke Humfrey's Library, housing the manuscripts donated by Humphrey of Lancaster, 1st Duke of Gloucester, to the benefaction of Elias Ashmole that formed the basis of the future Ashmolean Museum in 1683; and now in 1884 by the donation of the Pitt Rivers collection. Each of these moments – 1480s, 1680, 1880s – was intimately related to new kinds of knowledge: Renaissance, Empiricist, Evolutionary. What new moment will Oxford University have entered, then, by the 2080s? I asked you. One thing's for certain, you replied, it will be defined by the university collections' past having caught up with them.

There are no precise figures for how much of the collection that Fox donated had been purchased since spring 1880, and therefore bought directly with the necronymic inheritance. But what can be said for certain is that by January 1880, two months before the 6th Baron died, the collection loaned to South Kensington was recorded as comprising 14,860 objects.[61] The South Kensington Museum recorded all the items they received in a document variously known as the 'Day Book', 'Van Book' or 'Green Book'. It includes dozens of pages listing the further additions Fox made, month after month, in the five years that elapsed between his receipt of the inheritance in 1880 and the physical shipping of the collection to Oxford in 1885.[62] And Fox continued to add to the collections.[63] One of Fox's biographers, William Chapman, estimated that he 'presented nearly a thousand new items' between March and May 1881 alone.[64] One key addition in this period was a bulk purchase from collections from the defunct museum of the Anthropological Institute in 1880.[65] When it was finally shipped to Oxford in 1885, the number of objects in the founding collection of Oxford's Pitt Rivers is estimated as between 26,000 and 30,000.[66] Somewhere between a third and a half of the founding collection in Oxford, the so-called 'first collection', was therefore purchased by Fox after he had inherited the Pitt-Rivers fortune. Like the skull-cup, a good proportion of this museum was bought with the proceeds of slavery. Funny that, you tell me, because I looked the 4th Baron up on the UCL database, the one run by the Centre for the Study of the Legacies of British Slavery, and the entry doesn't read like that. We open up the page and look at it together:

The vast majority of this collection was acquired before 1880 when Augustus Henry Lane Fox inherited the Rivers estates from the 6th Baron Rivers, the brother of the 4th Baron (and took the name Pitt-Rivers). From 1880, General Pitt-Rivers acquired a second, separate collection, which was housed in a private museum in Farnham, Dorset, and is now dispersed.[67]

It even questions whether there's any evidence that 'the first collection' (the collection transferred to the Pitt Rivers Museum) was bought with the proceeds either of slavery or of slave compensation. I've tried writing to them a few times, but I never heard back. I'll try again. It just goes to show how tricky it is to get the basic facts into the public domain. Or indeed to correct mistakes or misrepresentations.

You might try, if ever you take the train from London to Oxford, to imagine the logistics and the spectacle when the transfer finally happened in 1885: the sheer weight of the hundreds of packing cases, hampers, chests and trunks in which 30,000 objects – from heavy bronzes to delicate ceramic vessels, human body parts and weapons of every conceivable variety, some wrapped in blankets and some packed in newspaper – were carted from the museum to the railway line, perhaps at South Kensington or perhaps across Hyde Park to Paddington, to be loaded onto train carriages and freighted to Oxford; and then how they were carted again across town, from the station, past Worcester College, the Ashmolean Museum and the Bodleian Library, to arrive at the newly built Pitt Rivers Museum, moving through the streets like military hardware and matériel moving into place for some future war, or like the procession following a hearse – to fill vitrines organised not by culture or date but by type in this new 'typological' museum.

Or you might pay a visit, as you and I did last year, to see the building that housed the other museum he built, which stood incongruously in that obscure corner of the English landscape, and has been divided up and sold off as houses as if a statue were being toppled through the pressure of market forces alone, leaving just a few traces, like the PR and 1884 carved on the outsized stone pillars on the roadside, a monument that nobody particularly wanted to be preserved, or to see disappear.[68] You would never notice it as you drove by on this country road just off the A354, just past Blandford Forum. With his immense inherited wealth, the second collection was of a different scale and character from that in Oxford. Each accession was carefully recorded in a register, with precise scale drawings by the illustrator Waldo Johnson and coloured facsimile illustrations traced from photographs made in a dedicated dark room in the mansion house. By the time of Fox's death, more than 20,000 artefacts had been accessioned, recorded in nine massive bound manuscript volumes.[69]

In his will, Fox left £300 per annum for the maintenance of the museum, and bequeathed it to his son. It passed on the son's death in 1927 to Fox-Pitt, the Grandson. At some point the museum was established as a trust, but Fox-Pitt began to sell off and disperse this collection periodically, to raise money for the political causes he supported, maybe, or just to fund his lifestyle. This sustained act of cultural vandalism, dispersing this unique collection of 'world culture' through the art market, accelerated after the war. As a monument, the collection was fungible. And there was a need, in the aftermath of the defeat of Nazi Germany, for money and energy to be put somewhere other than into a museum, if his political agenda were to continue to advance.

Fox-Pitt began his relationship with a woman named Stella Clive in the 1940s – a Nazi agent, who shared Fox-Pitt's extreme right-wing politics, and went under half a dozen surnames (Clive, Lonsdale, Maumen, Warner, Magaloff, Sidoroff) before settling, not through marriage but through a change by deed poll in June 1952, on the name Stella Pitt-Rivers.[70] This fractal woman, Clive-Lonsdale-Maumen-Warner-Magaloff-Sidoroff-Pitt-Rivers, had been born in 1913 into a Birmingham family of brass founders and travelling salesmen (a few months younger than Enoch Powell, and on the same side of town), and, like Fox-Pitt, she had been imprisoned during the war – at Wandsworth, and then Aylesbury.[71]

Fox-Pitt and his partner Clive/Lonsdale/Maumen/Warner/Magaloff/Sidoroff/Pitt-Rivers started to sell off the collection of 20,000 items at an increasing pace, especially after the transformation of the trust in 1964 into a company named 'Pitt-Rivers Museum Trustees Limited'. Far from safeguarding the collection after Fox-Pitt's death in 1966 the company (dissolved 1977) sold off what was left over the next ten years. Sometime in 1966 or 1967, the museum at Farnham closed its doors to the public for what would be the last time. Eventually, in 1974, the bulk of the much less financially valuable excavated British archaeological collections from Fox's digs was donated to Salisbury and South Wiltshire Museum, and can be seen there on display today.[72]

History does not record which far-right interests or organisations Fox-Pitt and Clive supported with the sale of millions of pounds' worth of collections. Everything of any monetary value was liquidated, piecemeal over the previous three decades, or was in the 1970s and 1980s sold off and dispersed internationally through the art and antiquities market.[73] In the coming years, the items regularly fetched high prices due to their provenance in the second Pitt Rivers collection, most notably with Clive's sale of the collection's remaining Benin Bronzes in 1975.[74] An Ecuadorean shrunken head in a domed glass case fetched £1,210 at Sotheby's in London in December 1979 – although the *Guardian* reported that following protests Clive withdrew eight skulls, including those of Native American ancestors, from the sale.[75]

There was also a vast art collection, which Fox had opened to public view at nearby Tollard Royal in 1891. Organised chronologically to illustrate 'the history of painting from the earliest times' (of course), it ran from Egyptian mummy paintings through Margaritone, Tintoretto, Cranach, Bellini, Holbein, Bruegel, Rubens and Hogarth, and up to a selection of nineteenth-century works. The paintings too were largely hawked, just as what was arguably the single most significant personal collection of anthropological and archaeological objects anywhere on the planet was sold off at Sotheby's, Christie's and through scores of private sales. Items were acquired by the Metropolitan Museum in New York, the Smithsonian Institution in Washington, DC, the Musée de l'Homme in Paris, the Berlin Ethnological Museum, and hundreds of other collections and collectors. Countless millions of pounds, francs, marks and dollars changed hands for Asante gold, Māori jade, a Haida totem pole from Canada, Japanese ivory, Sri Lankan silver, ancient Egyptian amber and onyx, Indian textiles, Melanesian barkcloth, Persian ceramics, Renaissance paintings, British and Irish prehistoric antiquities, and the single most significant collection of Benin Bronzes in the world. The Rivers fortune was shape-shifting here again, from the 'compensation' payments of the 1830s to unknown destinations. The shadowy world of the post-war far-right, most likely, you suggest to me.

Capital was moving and transforming again; as the money came in from the sales so the items were scattered to thousands of museums and private collections around the world, like the burst of Victorian shell from which the shrapnel is still falling. Ransacked through this process sixty years ago now, the form of the building remains though the content is gone. The farmhouse converted into a 'Gypsy School' in the 1850s, then turned into the museum in 1884, is now a series of bad Nineties housing conversions, a small, unexceptional example of the ruined landscape of the property market of the early twenty-first century, a kind of negative monument to wherever the money went next. They don't actually care about culture, these people who pretend they want to save it, you tell me. They didn't stop the sales by the Grandson and Clive. And yet they want to protect every last plaque on the wall to Cecil Rhodes. Meanwhile, the thousands of objects bought with those same slavery profits that were given to Oxford are still here, of course. The forms of these museum collections are shifting, but then again, Fox and his generation were experimenting with new forms of monumentality.

## 32. THE MONUMENT

As is by this point clear, something was happening to ideas of monumentality in the 1880s. But how to join the dots from Fox's role as inspector of Ancient Monuments, his theories of salvage, preservationism and conservatism, the wider colonial-militarist project he wanted to push forward, and the broader phenomenon that I am calling militarist realism? When we were in Dorset last year, walking in different chunks of the estate that he inherited, we found the former site of a life-size bronze cast of Fox's namesake, Caesar Augustus, which used to stand facing the entrance to the museum at Farnham, but was removed after it closed. The statue was commissioned from Alessandro Nelli's foundry on Via Luciano Manara, Rome, modelled on the ancient marble original in the Vatican Museum.[76] We looked for the diminutive figure of *The Hunter of the Early Days*, in the

Pleasure Grounds, but couldn't find it. But two monuments that we did see have stayed with me. The first was a recreation of the Temple of Vesta in Rome, the place that housed the holy flame of the goddess of fire, built by Fox in 1890. In limestone ashlar, with a copper domed roof, on a nine-step *stylobate* circular platform, it cost almost £2,000. We found this bleak monument to the east of Rushmore House and Sandroyd School. It was built to mark the birth of his eldest son's eldest son – the Grandson and heir and future Blackshirt, Fox-Pitt.[77] We looked it up and English Heritage listed it in 1966, just before he died.

The second was a white marble portrait bust, an artwork that was among the first things Fox spent his inheritance on, two decades before his death: a statue of himself. It depicts him a little younger than his fifty-something years; a transubstantiation of flesh to stone. He commissioned this self-image in 1882 from Sir Joseph Edgar Boehm, 1st Baronet, RA, a medallist and sculptor best known today for the 'Jubilee head' of Queen Victoria (the coinage portrait for the gold sovereign issued in 1887 to mark five decades of the monarch's reign), and who was also the sculptor of that equestrian statue of the ancient hunter. We opened the narrow, decaying wooden doors to the Roman temple at Fox's Larmer Tree Gardens, an octagonal limestone building with a domed stone roof, which felt like it was part folly, part mausoleum, and there it was. I met his gaze first, saw the slight smirk on his face, believing he will outlive us all. When you took a photo of my face next to his, we saw that his white head was slightly larger than life. Above the entrance, the stained, moss-pocked stone bore the engraved text AVGVSTVS PITT RIVERS EREXIT MDCCCLXXX. On the floor, there was a design of an eight-pointed star around a labyrinth, and on the ceiling an image of a fiery sun, with Fox's characteristic mix of classicism and mysticism. Fox's hair was pushed back above mutton-chop sideburns and a high collar girded his neck, tied with a pinned cravat. The lapels of his waistcoat were encompassed by a coat, and the coat encompassed in turn by drapery vaguely suggestive of antiquity. The bust and pedestal sat on a small ionic column. A few spots of water damage discoloured the white stone, like foxing on the pages of a Victorian book. The bust seemed vain, rootless and melancholic in this setting of light decay.

The next day, a weekday morning in the second week of January, we set out to find what remains of Wor Barrow. I remember talking about Mary, just over two years after she died, as we walked. I was telling you about what she taught me about the power of the unmarked position, and about the counter-power of the modifier. How one word can transform the next, but how in writing, unlike in speech, despite everything, you can always go back and add a word or two, revisit a paragraph or a place, change a phrase here or there and so put the subversive poetics of the postmodifier to work for something important, something good. That, Mary showed me, I told you, is what writing about the past must always strive to do. Perhaps the postmodifier offers a model for heritage management too, as well as for writing about the past. The postmodifier changes the form of the words on the page, adds and edits meaning in a single gesture to maintain coherence, refuses always to be bound by the imagined intentions of an earlier draft, some earlier version of the author of a text or the maker of an object. The counter-power of the postmodifier is a 'subversive poetics' that applies to things as well as to words, as Mary used to put it, and so offers a very different image from always having to rewrite the interpretation panel. Another possibility of changing the world beyond the strangely restrictive textual multivalency of that idea that every monument can only ever be 'retained and explained'.

We parked at Sixpenny Handley, and followed the public footpath as it weaved through an out-of-season campsite, crossed the road and followed the bridleway to join what the Ordnance Survey map shows as the row of green diamonds that indicates a 'recreational route'. When the obliteration of Wor Barrow was completed, in that iconic example of extreme archaeological destruction, Fox ordered that the monument be recreated with banks of earth, at this prehistoric mortuary site, to form a kind of amphitheatre which he imagined would be used 'for games or other amusements and exhibitions'.[78] We were both unsure we'd be able to find his recreated monument, the supposed site of the beginning of the modern scientific archaeological excavation method. On the map, the footpath that took us there is called 'Hardy Way'. It's part of a vast subcircular route punctuated by waymarkers for more than 200 miles, from the author's birthplace at Higher

Bockhampton to the graveyard of St Michael's parish church in Stinsford. We passed a group of four hikers who were slowly making a full traversal of Thomas Hardy's fictional historic landscape of Wessex. The novelist once described how he had at first imagined Wessex as 'a partly-real, partly-dream country' in his novels, but it had taken on a life of its own beyond the page, in the landscape, becoming a provincial definition used in everyday life, to the extent that 'the dream country has, by degrees, solidified into a utilitarian region which people can go to, take a house in, and write to the papers from'.[79]

As we overtook them we saw how the walking poles of the walkers were piercing the ground, leaving a line of small stabs in the path behind them. It's like they're checking it's real, I said to you. While we're walking to the monument, let me tell you about a short story Hardy wrote, you replied. It's part ghost story, part cautionary tale, and was published in the *Detroit Post* in 1885 under the title 'A Tryst at an Ancient Earthwork'. It concerned the theft of artefacts and human remains from archaeological monuments. The tale recounts an excavation at the site of Maiden Castle, in the dead of night. The hillfort lies thirty miles to the south-west of here. Hardy was Fox's neighbour, by the way. He used to attend his parties. You looked up some lines you remembered on your phone, the scene where the nighthawkers have laid out the bones of a skeleton on the edge of their trench, and read them aloud:

> The rays of the lantern pass over the trench to the tall skeleton stretched upon the grass on the other side ... The beating rain has washed the bones clean and smooth, and the forehead, cheek-bones, and two-and-thirty teeth of the skull glisten in the candle-shine as they lie.[80]

They find a figure of Mercury, and the man leading the excavation appears to pocket the object in the dark. 'I was just wiping my hand,' he tells his friend, and his friend takes him at his word. As they try to rebury the bones, they disintegrate in the rain. Then, seven years later, when the excavator dies, the gilded statuette of Mercury is found among his effects. The friend donates it posthumously to the museum of the fictional Wessex town of Casterbridge.

With a map on our phones, we struck out to our left across the fields just before the route crosses the line of what was once the Roman road of Ackling Dyke, now the busy A354, and eventually found the ruined remains of Wor Barrow at the edge of a field, a scrappy patch of land. Clumps of grass clung to the uneven surface of the monument, which had been reconstructed but has sunk and eroded unevenly since, a testament to more than a century of sustained disinterest quite out of step with the story told in the textbooks about the history of archaeological method and practice. A bit like that story about the excavation, I offered, an object lesson in the vanity of trying to hold onto the past, or rebuild a monument. It's definitely a genre, you replied, the way these men were concerned with transforming fact into fiction, and back again, to try to make their worldview last.

As we walked back to the car, I told you about what Fox called his theory of 'persistent conservatism'.[81] In the years running up to the archaeo-destruction of Wor Barrow, this had evolved into a more explicit political agenda. In 1888, Fox stood unsuccessfully for election as an independent to a seat on the county council, and in the same year he joined two political organisations. One was Lord Elcho's Liberty and Property Defence League, a right-wing lobby group founded in 1882 to represent the interests of landowners against socialism, trade unionism and the growing calls for the reform of land taxation inspired by the writing of the American economist Henry George (and clearly an influence on the 2nd Baron Penrhyn's North Wales Property Association, formed in 1886). The other was the Primrose League, a membership organisation established to promote conservative values, whose motto was *Imperium et Libertas* ('Empire and Freedom'). The idea developed out of Primrose Day: an annual memorial for the late Tory prime minister Benjamin Disraeli, established in 1882 by a man named Sir George Birdwood, in which the tradition was to wear the yellow flower in the buttonhole.[82]

(I looked Birdwood up, you tell me. Another mediocre Victorian informal coloniser. An economic botanist, formerly the sheriff of Bombay, then professor-curator of the Grant Medical College in the same city, he returned from empire and became a civil servant in the India Office in London, and the editor of the letter books of the East India Company. And I don't know if you realised but in 1894 it was this same man who chaired Henry Balfour's lecture at the Society of Arts, the one about the evolution of form in art.)

It was getting dark, and as we got closer to where we'd parked at Sixpenny Handley I told you about an address that Fox delivered to a Primrose League meeting right here, in the schoolroom in this village on his estate in Dorset, in 1888. It gives a sense of Fox's politics. I reread the exact words later:

> One word about the much-abused class of Landowners to which I belong. You are told by some people to look at the inequality which exists. Inequality is a law of nature and without it no progress could take place . . . In the old days when conservatism meant the conservation of class privileges, I was not a conservative; now that conservatism means the conservation of our liberties and the maintenance of the Empire, I am as staunch a conservative as any Tory.[83]

In another speech, delivered at Dorchester School of Art in February 1884, Fox claimed that the aim of the democratic socialist is to diminish society, break it up into its 'primitive elements' and to abolish 'all the accumulated wealth, knowledge, and experience which have been bequeathed to us by our forefathers'.[84] Fox borrowed from Herbert Spencer's rhetoric about socialism being a movement that would turn the clock back on civilisation, returning to modes of collective living that prevailed in the past and survived in the 'uncivilised' regions of the present, leading to what he called 'a gradual deterioration of the race'.[85] That's further context for that line from his lecture in Salisbury in 1890, the one about how education in museums should be 'eminently progressive and conservative', I offered.[86]

The wealth generated by this Dorset–Wiltshire farmland and the rents of his tenants would have been, the archaeologist Jacquetta Hawkes once estimated, 'one good Victorian sovereign for every one of those acres' – a figure borne out by the fact that in 1883 the annual gross income of the estate was £35,396.[87] Twenty-seven thousand acres is more than forty square miles. If we ran across Fox's vast estate north to south, it would be a double marathon. We'd start on the chalklands at the edges of Cranborne Chase and look north-east to Salisbury Plain, where in the last few years of Fox's life, they were building among the Neolithic long barrows and Bronze Age round barrows, building a new landscape of training camps for military practice manoeuvres for the Boer War. The camps that would expand again before the First World War, and expand even more before the war against fascism. Like outdoor munitions factories producing drilled soldiers' bodies, like Fox's fantasy of a landscape of war coming real. At the other end of that double marathon we'd reach the coastline, where decaying concrete pillboxes stud the beaches in an irregular line from Weymouth to Swanage, their loopholes still staring out across the waters of the English Channel. A line of anti-fascist monuments, you described them as, washed by the waves, slowly falling into the sea, small reminders of the sacrifice made to fight an ideology that had its origins in the nineteenth century, and hardened into a reality that seemed impossible to do anything other than appease, but eventually was broken. Now there's an alternative model of monumentality, you said when we stood on the beach in front of one of them.

But from the 1860s and 1870s, the way in which regimes of monumentality were shifting involved their recalibration by empire, by patriarchal militarism, by the beginnings of White supremacy, to that image of 'Man' and how to make him seem eternal and sovereign. There's a line in Engels where he claims that the idea of an army, as an organised body of armed men maintained for war, began in states that enslaved people.[88] That seems to be one part of the context for this change, the image of the soldier coming to the fore in a post-emancipation civil society hand-in-hand with the museum and the monument, a society improvising and experimenting with new cultural forms of White supremacy, the militarist realism of the '38ers', the original culture warriors.

Militarist realism moved through the phalanx of statues that runs from Buckingham Palace to Kensington Gardens, past the Serpentine with its iron railings, through the provincial vanity of Fox's 1884 bust and the copper-topped, reconstructed Roman temple built for the fascist Grandson, to the figure of Cecil Rhodes on the High Street in Oxford, the same look on his face after all these years, standing one storey above the figures of the monarchy on the front of Oriel College. Strange, you say to me, how often in anthropologists' accounts of 'first contact' situations the appearance of settlers, or soldiers, or miners was classified by Indigenous people as a return of the ancestors, their skin white, as if the life had drained out of them.

And then you look at Fox's sideburns and cravat, or the face, suit and shoes of Rhodes, the whites of their eyes, hammered out from marble and Portland stone.[89] They presented themselves as bleached white, blank and enduring, as if they could keep returning as ancestors forever. That reversal of perspective, in which it was the Europeans who were thought to be from the past, rather than the view of Fox and men like him that 'primitive' people represented the predecessors of modern humans, feels relevant here. These statues aren't ghosts. It's not a question of haunting. That mystical-Gothic framing was theirs, not yours or mine. Such monuments are best seen as impersonations devised to distribute a man's personhood; a metaphor designed to endure over time; a supremacist fantasy built to outlive us all. It reminds me of something else Engels wrote, about the technology of fortification in nineteenth-century Europe. He observed how it always included the *blindage* – those elements of defence made of wooden boards or sheet metal that prevented the enemy from seeing what is going on.[90]

When we were in Hyde Park the other week, coming down from Bond Street tube station and cutting around the eastern edge along Park Lane, I took you to stand with me in front of the Wellington Monument. It was quite early in the morning, and in the hazy light to the south that barracks tower-block was looking down on us. The baroque fantasy towers of Knightsbridge ran along a hallucinatory skyline to the left: Harvey Nichols and the Mandarin Orient Hotel. This giant, lithe, bronze Achilles, three times as tall as a mortal man and standing on a plinth that doubles that elevation, making the whole thing thirty-six feet in height, dates from 1822. It depicts Arthur Wellesley, 1st Duke of Wellington, the same man as was depicted in that equestrian figure that used to stand on the Wellington Arch, 700 yards to the south. If you'd looked up that night when the railings here were torn down and Fox and his men didn't fire a shot, you'd have seen both fantasy figures of the Duke of Wellington looking down on you, like you were seeing double. The mega-statue depicts a likeness of the duke's face mounted on the heroic body of the Trojan Achilles, modelled on the ancient marble 'horse tamer' figures on the Monte Cavallo Fountain on Rome's Quirinal Hill. The vast plinth is made of Dartmoor granite. Achilles-Wellington raises a round shield with his left arm, his right hand gripping a sword, and his hypermuscular torso nude apart from a cloak draped over his shoulder. His body armour, removed, is at his side. Its scale inspired by the colossal statues of Rome's Capitoline Hill, it was claimed at the time that this superhero fantasy was the largest classical bronze statue cast anywhere in the world for 1,600 years.[91]

In November 1852, after the Duke of Wellington had died, aged eighty-three, his body had lain in state in the Great Hall, Chelsea Hospital. The hall was hung with black cloth and velvet illuminated by colossal candelabra and an enormous chandelier, the coffin covered by a crimson velvet and surrounded by a mass of banners, batons, spears, laurel wreaths, silver lace, gold fabric, flags, pennons and plumes, and when it was opened to the public on Saturday 13 November, from 9 a.m. to 4 p.m., Captain Fox was among the officers recorded as on duty to sit around the coffin in this surreal space, an official mourner and a guard, another initiation, aged twenty-five, after the Great Exhibition of the previous year, to the idea of a public exhibit.[92]

The monument and the arch both commemorated the British victories in the Peninsular War and the latter stages of the Napoleonic Wars as if they were a recapture of the victories of antiquity. Achilles-Wellington weighed thirty-three tons, and was cast from French cannon and ordnance captured at Salamanca, Vittoria, Toulouse and Waterloo and melted down at a foundry in Pimlico. Perhaps this explains its weapon-like aura. The career of its sculptor, Richard Westmacott, reads like an index to the earliest phases of that shift in the regimes of the monumental. On his return from training in Rome in 1797, he married a Jamaican-born woman named Dorothy Wilkinson, and began to specialise in transforming the spoils of war into sculpture.[93] He also advised the committee that oversaw the British government's purchase of the Parthenon Marbles, and he designed the Neoclassical tympanum called *The Progress of Civilisation* that stands on the pediment above the entrance to the British Museum.[94] He made monuments for Caribbean planters, merchants and military heroes, including the 1809 statue of slave trader Robert Milligan at London's West India Docks (removed in June 2020[95]), and the 1813 statue of Horatio Nelson that in November 2020 was taken down from the National Heroes Square in Bridgetown, Barbados and placed in the storerooms of the Barbados Museum and Historical Society.[96] He made that church sculpture of the quarryman and the cherubs for

Fox's uncle too, if you remember. If someone were to write the history of militarist realism as an artistic movement, they might begin it with Richard Westmacott. Inevitably, there's a blue plaque to Westmacott; it adorns the front of the house where he lived and worked at 14 South Audley Street, Mayfair, just a five-minute walk from here.

Gazing up in the early morning sunlight at this transformation of guns looted from the battlefield into an outsized lone giant figure of the male warrior body, it was as if the artist had impossibly recalled from the future that image of the technologised body familiar to us from the *Terminator* movie franchise about a cyborg killing machine who travels across time. At the end of the first film, the Terminator, played by the bodybuilder-turned-actor Arnold Schwarzenegger, future Republican governor of California, returning from the year 2029 to 1984 to make an execution, takes successive hits from bullets and is burned alive, but still rises from the flames, its eyes blown out to expose video cameras, and clothes, hair, skin, flesh and blood scorched away until the hyperalloy endoskeleton of the T-800 robot is revealed as it keeps staggering forward, whirring, scanning, shooting. Its famous catchphrase was: *I'll be back*. Achilles-Wellington seemed like a premonition from 1822, from the age of abolition and emancipation to the age of fascism, one that pushes the male body so far beyond its limits, with machine guns and plane propellors and caterpillar tank-tracks as prosthetics, that it would culminate in what Hitler claimed in July 1937 in his speech for the opening of the Great German Art Exhibition at Munich's Haus der Kunst: 'Today's new era is working on a new human type.'[97]

In 1961, in his book *Les damnés de la terre* [*The Wretched of the Earth*], Frantz Fanon described colonialism itself as 'a world of statues':

> A compartmentalised, Manicheistic, immobile world, a world of statues: the statue of the general who made the conquest, the statue of the engineer who built the bridge. A world that is sure of itself, crushing spines flayed by whips with its stones. Behold the colonial world.[98]

'Every statue,' Fanon wrote, 'all these conquistadors perched on colonial soil never cease to signify one and the same thing: "We are here by the force of our bayonets."'⁹⁹ The monument was a key instrument in how, as he put it, 'the colonial regime owes its legitimacy to force and at no time tries to hide this aspect of things'. That world of statues described by Fanon – they built it here, too. Sometimes violence or the deployment of images of violence isn't unconscious, or even repressed; the false consciousness is just placed in plain sight, then passed along the generations as if it had always been a part of tradition. We were once so worried about that idea of false consciousness, and not repeating the mistakes of an earlier hardline Marxism, you wrote to me in an email; perhaps we ignored what lies in front of our face. Once the wheels are rolling, such juggernauts are quite tricky to stop. They have momentum, these monuments, like a locomotive, or a tank, or a bulldozer.

We walked back down to the Wellington Arch, to take another look. Standing beneath it and turning back, a chill ran down our spines as we saw the massive, outsized statue of a field gun, a Howitzer, carved, improbably, in Portland stone, pointing south – Charles Sargeant Jagger's Royal Artillery Memorial. They installed it in 1925 apparently, I said. If it's possible to say there's a masterpiece of militarist realism, then this is surely it. You don't install a monument like this, you tell me: you erect it.

On each of the four sides of the cruciform base on which this magnified weapon sits is the dark bronze figure of a soldier, hyperrealist and yet oversized – a driver with his cape spread out with arms outstretched like a winged phantom, facing the constant stream of traffic and Apsley House beyond; an officer in his great coat facing St James' Park and Buckingham Palace; an ammunition-carrier facing the Wellington Arch; and then, on the side that faces towards the memorial landscape of Hyde Park, a dead soldier with his tin hat placed on his chest. It commemorates the deaths of '49,076 of all ranks of the Royal Regiment of Artillery who gave their lives for King and Country between 1914 and 1919', the text reads, and then, chiselled letter by letter in a line that encircles the monument, is a limestone geography of the places that they bombed:

FRANCE, FLANDERS, DARDANELLES, MACEDONIA, ARABIA, RUSSIA, PALESTINE, CENTRAL ASIA, MESOPOTAMIA

Circling around to go back into the park in search of coffee, we passed another bronze nude male figure, this time the Machine Gun Corps Memorial, his slim, contrapposto pose bizarrely styled alongside the massive sword in his hand, and the chilling rendering of two life-size Maxim machine guns in bronze to either side, cloaked in metal wreaths the size of car tyres. These figures of generals, soldiers and colonists that began to emerge in cityscapes across Victorian and Edwardian England seemed to combine the genre of the funerary monument with a new secular image of Man, as if, like one of Emily Dickinson's dead narrators, they could not be dead: 'It was not Death for I stood up / And all the Dead lie down'.

Ten minutes later, we are back on the bench by the Serpentine, and I'm describing the blue cloth officer's vest laid out on the table in the research facility of the Pitt Rivers Museum like a human torso, its collar upturned, its eight gilt buttons shining in the white electric light. No ordinary item of military uniform, it weighs five pounds, is lined with two cast light steel plates, one front, one rear, has adjustable metal straps on the shoulders, and is stamped with the words: 'PATENT APPLIED FOR'.

The buttons bear the motto 'CONNECT. SIG. REIP' – the seal of the State of Connecticut, around the arms of the state, three vines in fruit. A display label from when it was exhibited at Bethnal Green in the 1870s reads:

MADE IN NEW YORK AND USED FOR A SHORT TIME BY SOME OF THE AMERICAN OFFICERS DURING THE LAST WAR.

Another label reads:

SMITH'S PATENT, MADE BY G. & D. COOK & CO., NEW HAVEN, CONN.

And the catalogue entry includes the text: 'An attempt to revive the use of armour.'[100]

Fox collected this newly invented prototype flak jacket during his posting to the United States and Canada in 1862. Looking like a standard piece of officer's uniform, the Smith's patent bullet-proof vest offered protection against pistol and musket balls, rifle bullets, shrapnel or the thrust of a sword or bayonet, the manufacturers claimed, and when worn 'it is entirely concealed, keeps the wearer erect, and adds grace and dignity to his form'.[101] In March 1862, one advertisement for the vest claimed that it would 'double the value and power of the soldier'.[102] Another step along the way to the improvement of the military body through training and technology. It would be another eighty years before the British military issued its first flak jackets, for Royal Air Force bomber pilots in the Second World War. In the museum catalogue, body armour – from ancient Greek helmets to the medieval chain mail and to this American vest – is classed as weaponry.

Perhaps that's how the statue of Rhodes will be classed too, you suggest, when he's finally taken down and donated to the Pitt Rivers Museum and put, let's hope, not on display but wrapped in acid-free tissue in a cardboard box in some remote, forgotten storeroom. Each time I cross Hyde Park these days, you continue, it becomes another triangulation of how the worldviews of men like Fox, I mean that ethnoclass-generation of 38ers, are cut into the sedimented layers of our public spaces and civic culture; an impromptu walking tour of militarist realism.

We were walking back from a talk at the Royal College of Art the other day, round the Albert Memorial to cross Hyde Park, and there in Kensington Gardens, that landscape of Adrian Stokes' childhood fears, looming down Lancaster Walk, was the second bronze casting of George Frederic Watts' *Physical Energy*, surveying the western horizon with all its intense proto-fascist masculinist fantasy. It's Rhodes again, I said to you, this copy made of his monument in South Africa. People will try to tell you it's not him. He's not in his business suit but reimagined as a naked cowboy. One way to draw a line back from Watts' statue to Fox's collection of the Civil War flak jacket to show in his museum would be through German cultural historian Klaus Theweleit, who wrote of the psycho-socio-visual effects of the coming together of man and machine in the modern history of industrial militarism and prosthetic masculinity. To do so would be to try to connect the monumental regimes of Hyde Park and Kensington Gardens and the military body in the recent history of 'Man'.

In his 1977 book *Male Fantasies*, Theweleit was discussing the armoured soldier's body of the First World War trenches and the Freikorps, drawing on Ernst Jünger's glorified Nazi eulogy to German 'men of steel' in his first-hand account of trench warfare *In Stahlgewittern* [In Storms of Steel]. Jünger described battle as an 'inner experience', in which 'military technology is but matter from which the soul blindly creates its own imagery'.[103] Armouring, Theweleit argued, took place not just through the donning of protective clothing but through the learned skills and physique born of the routines of the parade, the drill and the military training camp, through the personal experience of killing, and through the mythic armour of the idea of the nation.[104] Above all, it was by putting on a uniform that the soldier gave up some part of their personhood to become part of a military force of millions of men. Jünger's fascist, dehumanising vision was of the drilled body of every foot soldier clenching his teeth inside his steel helmet, being reborn through the fantasy of becoming one of countless integral moving parts of a single vast death machine. Hurtling towards oblivion, this fantasy involved displacing the mass of flesh, skin, hair, bones, intestines and feelings that formerly constituted the living mortal male, as if industrialised warfare and the supply lines from the munitions factory to the frontline could transform not just the mechanical production of the tools of destruction, but the mechanical production of humanity itself. The armoured body of the medieval knight, which Patrick Wright has described as 'a living tank', transformed.[105] The form of 'Man' was being reproduced, a bullet-proof image, its materials replaced like the hull and the yardarm of the ship of Theseus. Or perhaps, just like the name-change from Wellesley to Wellington to Achilles, as the *Argo*, you chip in. To the extent that the nude bronze Rhodes has no need for armour, as if impermeability has sunk into his skin as if touched by Midas.

For Fox, perhaps the mythic armour of this proto-fascist, patriotic metallisation of the body also had something to do with his conception of cultural heredity. Perhaps the 'inner experience' born of the armour-plated death-machinery of modern warfare had, like those curatorial barricades erected in Bloomsbury in 1848, something to do with the technology of the museum. There was a foreshadowing of what Hal Foster has called 'the (proto)fascist obsession with the body as armour', and what Nicholas Mirzoeff has described as a psychophysical blurring of technological, machinic prosthesis with idealised superman images of masculine corporeality and Classical antiquity, from the monumental male sculptures of Nazi artist Arno Breker to the Nazi architect Albert Speer. Speer also had a theory of ruin, you tell me. He called it his *Ruinenwerttheorie* ('theory of ruin value'). In planning for the 1936 Berlin Olympics, he suggested an approach to monumentality that put an aesthetics of ruin at the heart of building a long-lasting legacy for the Third Reich, like the heritage of the Roman Empire. Sounds like Fox rebuilding the Roman temple for his future fascist Grandson, you say, that urge for some semblance of endurance, or eternal life, or ruin value. Sounds like Cecil Rhodes' fantasies about overcoming death.

Fox lived just to the south of here in 1878, at Onslow Gardens, while he was installing his collections in the South Kensington Museum.[106] The Albertopolis, the mnemonic landscape named for the dead prince consort, was taking form; the South Kensington Museum renamed the Victoria and Albert Museum in 1899, the cluster of museums and universities growing, from Imperial College to the Royal Geographical Society, and the intense unreality of the Albert Memorial rising between the avenues and trees from the London gravels. You could've stood there on the afternoon of Wednesday 4 May 1898 and watched the crowds filing into the Royal Albert Hall when prime minister Lord Salisbury, speaking in his capacity as grand master of the Primrose League, addressed 12,000 League members in a famous speech where he issued 'a prophecy and a warning' about the coming wars. 'You may roughly divide the nations of the world into two classes, the living and the dying,' he stated, in a line that chimed with the curator's lecture from four years earlier. The living, he continued, have railways, with which they 'can remove their armies to any given point convenient for the bloody arbitrament of war', while the dying 'are mainly communities which are not Christian'. 'Weak states are becoming weaker, and strong states stronger. What must be the inevitable result?' he asked, rhetorically. Even the strongest have no control over this. Peace is unlikely, until the coming war is won.[107]

When the prime minister mentioned the name of Cecil Rhodes, the *Western Gazette* reported, there was 'an instant storm of cheering'.[108]

When I read about that speech, given a year before the outbreak of the Boer War, I thought of another, also delivered in the Royal Albert Hall, I told you. It was given thirty-six years later, on the evening of 22 April 1934. A British Union of Fascists rally. The windows of the barrel-like building pulsed with light like a regiment of magic lanterns projected one next to the other. A ring of policemen surrounded the venue, and 'strong-arm' Blackshirts marshalled the crowd of more than 10,000 people to hear Fox-Pitt's comrade Oswald, his grandfather's great-grand-nephew, defending what he was now calling 'British fascism'. Mosley responded, the newspapers reported, to the charge that fascism is a foreign import, by observing that all brands of politics had come from outside: liberalism is French, socialism is the idea of the foreigner Karl Marx, and nobody knows where conservatism comes from, he concluded, to cheers, with a carefully practised line, because it's 'prehistoric'.[109] Later that year, Mosley was speaking in Dorset, at the invitation of Fox-Pitt. He spoke in Oxford regularly, too, with the support of William Morris, who ran the city's car factory (in Cowley, just head out of town and past the statue with the gun). That came to an end with the Battle of Carfax, like I told you, a few months before the Battle of Cable Street.

'The dead can only live with the exact intensity and quality of life imparted to them by the living.' Joseph Conrad gave that line to Kyrilo Sidorovich Razumov, a student in St Petersburg, in his 1911 novel *Under Western Eyes*.[110] And with that thought, written down at the height of the monumental regimes of militarist realism at the end of the first decade of the twentieth century, I want to appropriate the preferred verbal formulation of the militarist realists, the future passive exonerative, and try for once to put it to some good. It's possible of course to insist that all the monuments must fall, and to do so convincingly. But the formulation I have adopted here replaces the 'must' with a 'will'. The archaeological observation is simple. It's like what I was calling White taphonomy before. A monument, or a whole regime of monumentality, is only going to survive if it is maintained. For a statue not to fall, you have to keep it standing. The entropy is there already. The question is about what a society chooses to conserve and value. I can't think of any other walk of life, from healthcare to the criminal justice system, where there's the idea that if something is outdated, or causing damage, or racist, then nothing can ever be done to fix it. What is it about art, culture, education, heritage, statues in the town squares and civic museums and universities that makes this a problem? Perhaps it's a basic misunderstanding about what these fields are. As if they are fixed and static entities, rather than things that a society chooses, does, creates.

It's possible for a community, or a nation, or a new generation to choose to stop conserving what it doesn't wish to keep. It happens all the time, in every society on earth, in every culture in human history and prehistory. Monuments are relocated, replaced, removed, or just allowed to fall. What's weird is the idea that nothing would ever change, that an ideology of the late nineteenth century would live on forever through tradition or public art. The question isn't why would people want to remove a monument that celebrates hatred or racism or violence. The question is why would anyone make the false claim that no monument should ever fall? What exactly are they trying to defend? Perhaps that's now getting a little clearer. Just as restitution and fallism have revealed the histories of the museum and the monument, so decolonisation teaches us about the histories of knowledge, universities, and the idea of 'the subject'.

## 33. THE SUBJECT

I found a pressed flower in the archive today. It was folded between two pages of one of Fox's handwritten notebooks from his time in Malta in the 1850s, but it's definitely from later, plucked from the stalk of a common cowslip, *Primula veris*. Alongside the familiar deep yellow flower are two other blooms, one red and one orange, colours that are cross-pollinated from other primulas. The notebook bears the title 'SURVIVALS No. 1'. Maybe the flower is a sign of hope and luck, an artefact of contagious magic, an apotropaic amulet, a votive offering, I think for a moment. Then again maybe it's some kind of index of the Primrose League, a message from Fox or from Fox-Pitt to the future, a foreshadowing, an image of miscegenation or the struggle for survival, a tool for divination or volt sorcery or a bullet shot into the future in order to try to change it. A curse placed on every future curator.

What even is archaeology in your definition, then, you asked me, if it can study not just prehistory or the ancient Romans and Greeks, the ancient Maya and Egyptians, but the medieval, the post-medieval, the modern, the contemporary periods, flowers in the archive and statues in the streets? It seems, you carried on, no longer to be defined by what it studies, by its object of enquiry. So do you now call it a discipline (a word that always sounds like it's about power and punishment)? A lens (a word that always sounds contemplative somehow, like you're just gazing at the world rather than trying to change it)? A practice? Each metaphor brings its own baggage.

I don't really see it as a discipline or a method or a theory, I replied. I want to see it as *a subject*. Like anthropology, like art, like architecture, archaeology is an experiment we perform with our bodies. The four As, those subjects across which I work, were subjects born of empire, but subjects that can be flipped, like the blink of the eye in a figure ground reversal, like the modifier applied to a noun. Think of how third wave feminism transformed the subjects of the humanities and social sciences, and our idea of 'the subject' too. There's a parallel process now taking place with these legacy colonial disciplines. It's still about 'bodies that matter', but also 'subjects that endure'. I mean, how subjects are made to endure. About reconstituting and expanding the conception of humanity, where everybody counts as human. And by flipping the subjects, so that another four As might come to the fore: anti-racism, anti-colonialism, anti-militarism, and the unfinished work of abolition.[111]

When I was a student, there was still a sign hanging in the Pitt Rivers in Oxford that bore the heading 'ARRANGEMENT AND OBJECT OF THIS COLLECTION' and included the line:

> To aid in the solution of the problem whether MAN has arisen from a condition resembling the brutes, or fallen from a high state of perfection.[112]

How many of these framings survive even once the notice is removed? These academic subjects, the four As, have been used for purposes of subjectification, and for subjection, in efforts to contain 'the subject' – personhood, discipline, topic, power. Each has been involved in justifications for territorial dispossessions and for other kinds of dispossession, whether directly by taking ancestors' bodies and ancestral knowledge or building on stolen land, or more indirectly by erasing land rights and traditional sovereignty or promoting ideas of supremacy. As the legacy-supremacist money that came from land-grabs, killings, enslavements and profits of empire is passed down across a generation or two, the connections can come to seem tangential or indirect; it's even more the case when it comes to the legacy-supremacist ideas. Stolen art in the ethnological museum, stolen pasts in the archaeological collections, stolen knowledge in the anthropology library, stolen dead bodies in the anatomical and natural history collections. Attitudes, gestures, framings, assumptions, discipline. How we think about subjects and objects. About humanity itself.

'The barbarian is, first and foremost, the man who believes in barbarism', as Claude Lévi-Strauss said in his essay 'Race and History', written for UNESCO in 1952 as the discipline of anthropology sought to transform itself after the victory against fascism.[113] You'd have to redraft Umberto Eco's list of the traits of what he called 'Ur-Fascism' if you wanted to make all the connections between the Blackshirt Grandson, the ultra-iconography of Rhodes, and the proto-fascism in Fox's cultural supremacism, but it would be possible. Let me try to sketch out that Venn diagram, you said. The creation of a new man. A firmly held and yet self-contradictory belief in the certainty of some future Golden Age and the destiny of an unending struggle. An interest in the collective unconscious and crowd behaviour, and in the slowness of change and thus conservatism, and yet also in irrationalism, automaton behaviour, myth and manifest destiny. A love of railways, of course, and bureaucracy, and theatre and exhibition. An interest in both fine and so-called 'degenerate' art, how both can be used to argue the same supremacist point. The family and public education. An interest in men of action rather than eggheads. Extreme militarism and a fetish for guns. An interest in inheritance and posterity, in tradition and preparing the ground for what is to come. Blood and soil. A semi-mystical ethnonationalism. The list goes on. A kind of medievalism, colonial-aristocratism, or insurgent neo-feudalism, whether in the case of Rhodes' middle-class background or the '38er' new money wealth of Fox and his heirs. Above all, culture. Traditions of culture.

The 'cult of tradition' combined with a virulent White supremacism. European people as the custodians of culture. A fear of how culture might die off. A desire for permanent war couched within the fantasy of ultramilitarisation as the end to all wars. A politics based on the cult of tradition and the fear of difference. A passion for symbols, from the skull on the medalets to the motto that would surely fit it well – *Long Live Death!*[114] If I had to come up with a caption for this particular Venn diagram, then 'militarist realism' would probably do it, you conceded.

It would be possible then to draw another, parallel line from the extremism of the Grandfather following his experience of industrialised imperial war in Crimea and the influence that the brutalisation of war is known to have had on veterans who became fascist thinkers in Germany in the interwar period. If you plotted that line it would run straight through Cecil Rhodes and the Second Matabele War, and Fox-Pitt and his gammy leg from the trenches. The idea of evolution itself evolved, embraced the militarised sense of the word, was set to march for a new vision of heredity, destiny and eugenics, as if cultural Whiteness represented an inherited title to the whole world, from the English landscape to every last 'primitive' culture. As the historian of settler colonialism Patrick Wolfe once put it:

> Evolutionary theory evinced a preoccupation with descent that betrayed a usurper's desire to formulate a pedigree that might measure up to the ancestral legitimacy sustaining the landed order that the bourgeoisie had so rudely displaced.[115]

Katherine McKittrick and Sylvia Wynter have written about what they call the 'biocentricity' in these arguments. They show how there was an attempt to naturalise inequality through the new image of 'Man' as if that were the only possible definition of life and humanity.[116] The definition of the subject was the prime way in which the ideologies of White supremacy, racism and colonialism have been made to last, from the human subject to the academic subject – especially the four As, which have played their role in subjectifications and subjections that are not over. So the processes of abolition and emancipation in the wake of enslavement are not over, as we learn from the abolitionists today – from the carceral industrial state to the warehousing of the bodies of the dead in museums. Today that unfinished work of abolition and emancipation is starting to address what Saidiya Hartman calls a 'process of subjection as one of being held captive by a past not yet past' – the creation of anomalous subjects 'no longer enslaved but not yet free'.[117] How then to reframe or redefine subjects and make a change without undertaking what Eve Tuck and K. Wayne Yang have called 'settler moves to innocence'?

Stuart Hall once wrote that 'when a conjuncture unrolls, there is no "going back". History shifts gears. The terrain changes. You are in a new moment.'[118] Without a doubt, that is what is going on here, as the skull-cup comes into view. It's an intellectual moment, an expansion of historical awareness of the enduring nature of empire, a shift in public consciousness. Through the work of restitution, fallism and decolonisation, the regime of monumentality that I am describing as militarist realism is being made visible, from the new monuments in the London streets to the ancient monuments of the English countryside. New subjects were written deep into the landscape of the nation, and into the heart of the establishment: the academic subjects, ideologies of subjection, and the subjectification of the 'heritage' visitor in these mnemonic spaces of knowledge and patrimony. Each of these subject lines operated through codes of cultural Whiteness: objects, monuments, the landscape itself, and the human body passing through space and time.

The process of change in Oxford is ongoing. In 2019 St Peter's College, Oxford received a donation from a trust named in memory of the grandson of Oswald Mosley, and the plan was to name a building funded by this donation after the grandson – but in 2021 it was decided to find an alternative name.[119] And in 2023, the Bodleian Libraries' Sackler Library, along with the Ashmolean Museum's Sackler Rome Gallery, Sackler Keeper of Antiquities and Sackler Gallery of Life after Death in Ancient Egypt, were all un-named, and so too was the university's Sackler-Clarendon Associate Professorship of Sedimentary Geology. And in 2024 the Rhodes Professorship of Race Relations, created in 1953, was renamed the 'Professorship of African Studies' – just as the Rhodes Professorship of Imperial History at King's College London had been un-named in 2022.[120] Makes sense, you say to me, nobody wants to visit a museum gallery or work in a university library named after a drug dealer. But after the removal of the nineteenth-century images of the slave traders Colston in Bristol and Milligan in London, what I still don't get is why would anyone want to prevent a democratic decision to remove a legacy statue of a White supremacist in Oxford? I mean, if the university can rename the professorship then the college could change the statue.

In 2024, the mayor of London announced that a new public sculpture called 'The Wake' has been commissioned for West India Quay, outside London Museum Docklands, where Westmacott's statue of the slave trader was removed in 2020. That seems to me to be a crucial moment, when one form of monumentality is replaced by another, and a community claim the right to choose whom they remember, and how. I mean, you continued, it's great to see the anti-racist initiatives at Oriel College including scholarships for Black students, just as the Rhodes Trust has over the years opened its scholarship programmes to Black men, and to women, and has more recently expanded its African scholarship programme. But that's work other colleges and institutions are doing anyway. And it's hardly a new story in any case. Stuart Hall studied English literature at Merton College, Oxford on a Rhodes scholarship from Jamaica from 1951 to 1954. And Alain Locke became the first African American Rhodes scholar, going up to Hertford College in 1907 to read philosophy. It's never going to be a substitute for getting rid of the statue, as if public art and public culture didn't matter when it comes to anti-racism. And remember the many forms of monumentality at stake here, how many different forms militarist realism, the memory culture of cultural Whiteness, could take. Grenfell Tower, for example, is a monument to failures in civic policy and social policy, inequality and racism, and it's also named for Field-Marshal Lord Grenfell, the man who returned to the battlefield at Ulundi, dug up the skull of the Xhosa chief Sandile, and kept it as a memento on the mantelpiece of his manor house. These structures, names, framings, losses, inequalities, forms of violence are inherited across the generations. That's how the infrastructures of militarist realism work.

There is still a lot of inertia. At Cambridge, the George Pitt-Rivers Laboratory for Archaeological Science, and an associated professorship of archaeological science, established to commemorate Fox-Pitt as recently as 1989, both still bear the name of the fascist eugenicist Fox-Pitt at the time of writing, commemorations to his racist anthropology. And at St Peter's College, Oxford, the current vice-master is still called the 'Alexander Mosley Fellow', despite a piece in *The Spectator* of all places, claiming that the college 'should not accept money that is tainted by fascism'.[121] Here the right-wing press have again tried to change the framing of the community views in Oxford: it's not about taking supposedly 'tainted' money – there are sound professional ethics committees to review donations already in place. The question is about memory culture – people in Oxford don't want a memorial to the name Mosley, just as they didn't want the Blackshirt thugs at Carfax in 1936.

In the Albertopolis, meanwhile, at Imperial College London in October 2021, a specially commissioned report examined the institution's imperial legacies, including its origin as the Royal School of Mines. That institution was founded for the purpose of 'Science Applied to the Arts', and was where Thomas Huxley, the Bulldog-ethnologist whose thinking influenced Fox's account of automata, his prototype for modern theories of 'nonhuman agency', had been a professor until his retirement in 1885. Strange to think of how actor–network theory emerged from the Paris École des Mines, of all places, a century later, you remarked when I mentioned it. The report recommended that a building that bears Huxley's name should be renamed, and a bust of him removed from display, so as not to commemorate a man who espoused 'a racial hierarchy of intelligence' that 'fed the dangerous and false ideology of eugenics', a legacy which 'falls far short of Imperial's modern values'.[122] These proposals were not followed, however, as others defended the Bulldog's character, on the grounds that he had been against the polygenesis theories of the Anthropologicals, and as president of the Ethnological Society of London he had far more interest in themes like culture and intelligence. Yet again, a failure to understand the nature of the cultural forms of racism that came with militarist realism, and a mixing-up of the named building and the sculpture with the man, were in evidence. Like the story of the poisoned arrowhead, stories about decolonisation can often seem to end with nothing happening. Then again, there's always William Craft's optimistic question about who has painted the picture, and whether that depicts the ways things will actually play out over time.

There's also a lot of hope in these times. It's just important to hold onto the principle that a society can set its own memory culture, its chosen forms of monumentality, and that these can change once in a while. Don't call it presentism, and don't call it a paradigm shift, this transformative period for decolonisation, restitution and fallism: it's just the past catching up with legacy institutions, inherited disciplines, and second-hand forms of public memory, and like the second hand catching up with the minute hand, it will keep on happening.

In the case of Rhodes, Albert Speer's Nazi theory of ruin value is in operation in a rather different way from how he envisioned it, so that the statue they refuse to let fall, without saying why, having voted to remove it, is not just already falling, its ruination underway, the Dickinsonian process of collapse again, but it is also transforming in meaning, becoming a message of refusing to bring the institution into step with its time. Some say they won't remove the statue because of financial risk, of no donor ever giving again. But there are different models of benefaction, just as there are different models of monumentality, and anyway some donors would happily give money for statues to be removed or replaced. In reality there's a far bigger risk, and that is reputational. Who'd want to give money to an institution that can't deal with legacy racism or brutal dehumanisation at the heart of its culture? Rhodes will fall in the first half of this century, you assure me. Just look at what we have learned about how long it has taken for other such figures to be removed. Three, four or even five decades is not unusual. They always fall in the end. The Oriel statue will be gone, removed or replaced, in my lifetime or yours, just like the Parthenon Marbles will eventually be returned to Athens.

Just over the road at the library of All Souls College, however, you see the risks most clearly, you tell me. We went there together the other week. It wasn't even ever formally called the Codrington Library, we learn, it was just paid for by him and has a big 1730s statue of that eighteenth-century Caribbean plantation-owner in the middle of it, looking down on you. It's a chronological outlier, almost like a prototype for all these other art-wash colonialist statues, you say. Same kind of date as the memorial to Rustat at Jesus College, Cambridge, I reply. Another man who profited from slavery. The thing is that after the campaigners said this legacy should be addressed, they left the statue but de-named the un-named library, erecting a stone with letters carved into it to explain this. The stone reads:

IN MEMORY OF THOSE WHO WORKED IN SLAVERY ON
THE CODRINGTON PLANTATIONS IN THE WEST INDIES

I mean, they erected yet another monument to Codrington. And where are the names of those enslaved people? Some of whom, we know, were given the surname Codrington. Talk about the ship of Theseus. I look back to those lines from Stuart Hall about facing things as they are now, not as they were ten years ago, what he called 'the contradictory, stony ground of the present conjuncture'.[123] Rhodes Must Fall in Oxford began in 2015, and the world is continuing to change. At Birmingham University they've even put a blue plaque up for Stuart Hall, so it's not like these forms of monumentality can't be rewired. There's no Stuart Hall blue plaque in Oxford yet, you observe.

The funny thing is, all these questions about remembrance, preservation and heritage management have been part of professional practice for years. In the old days, decisions over listing buildings or protecting archaeological sites lay in the hands of two, often rival, bodies of experts in what used to be called English Heritage, and their colleagues in local authority planning departments. The architectural historians foregrounded historical and aesthetic criteria – the significance of a named architect, or their verdict on the beauty or importance of the physical fabric of a building. The archaeologists, meanwhile, were often interested in little more than the academic importance of the buried, subsurface remains of the past. From the late 1990s, however, under the New Labour government, a different set of criteria came in. A watershed came with the English Heritage Oxford conference on 'conservation planning' in 1999. At the heart of this new thinking was a focus on cultural value, and specifically what James Semple Kerr described as 'the cultural values and character of the participants and the way these have shaped the fabric and function of the place'.[124] In 2001, this was followed up by Kate Clark's English Heritage guidance *Informed Conservation*, which defined the practice of heritage management as 'handing on to future generations what we value'.[125] At the heart of which was the understanding that, as Sir Neil Cossons, chair of English Heritage, put it:

> Caring for this historic environment is a dynamic process which involves managing change in order to allow future generations to understand what we value and something of their origins. This does not mean keeping everything from the past but it does involve making careful judgements about value and significance.[126]

As methods for capturing, recording and acting on community values in decision-making about what is kept and what is not were developed, a landmark event took place that informed this work. A conference called 'Whose Heritage? The Impact of Cultural Diversity on Britain's Living Heritage' convened in Manchester in November 1999 by Arts Council England, set this evolution of professional practice in value-led heritage in the context of diversity and 'multicultural' heritage.[127] The keynote delivered by Stuart Hall, which was published in the journal *Third Text*, remains a touchstone for many in the fields of heritage management today, calling for the twin tasks of 'unsettling "The Heritage"' and 're-imagining the post-nation'.[128] Black British perspectives on 'The Heritage', an entity which had previously been treated as a monolithic unchanging entity, meant it had to be 're-imagined' and 're-invented to include us', Hall argued. As Clara Arokiasamy has observed, his intervention thus disrupted 'the cosy and incomplete national story' that had been created in the years since English Heritage was formed in 1983 (a foundation that marked, as seen above, the anniversary of Fox's appointment as the first inspector of Ancient Monuments).[129]

It's remarkable how, during the 2010s, this intellectual, professional, ethical and practical infrastructure of cultural values was gradually sidelined by the enduring concerns of historians, and by the language of the value defined by the 'cultural economics' of 'heritage assets'. One key example of how the clock has been turned back came with DCMS framework document 'Valuing Culture and Heritage Capital: A Framework Towards Informing Decision Making', published in 2021 (published while the current provost of Oriel College was commissioner for cultural recovery and renewal at DCMS). The price of everything, you said to me when that retrograde report came out, and the value of nothing. Worse than that, I said, they talk about something called 'heritage capital' and say it's about getting a return on heritage. I wonder if any of the advisors ever read what Marx said about capital? And how on earth does this relate to the political injunction, from other parts of government at the time, to 'retain and explain'?[130] It's revealing when you look back at the story of Rhodes, where the cultural economics presumably would argue that any monument to a benefactor should always be retained, in case other benefactors might be put off in the future. As if a college could be bought, and bought for perpetuity. Today's culture of philanthropy begins with a genealogy of donations to institutions from those who profited from slavery and wished to memorialise their benefactions, glorifying themselves to art-wash and gift-rinse their legacy as if it could be a kind of moral admonishment. Another justification for the horror. Just like the propaganda of displaying so-called 'primitive' cultures whose extinction was mystically fated. Or inventing subjects with a sideline in cultural supremacism. The potential to change the subject, to shift the subjectivity, to resist the legacy subjugation – these are all urgent elements of decolonisation. And decolonisation can, by attending to these legacies, serve to reveal the histories, parts of which include these infrastructures of cultural Whiteness, subtle and not-so-subtle. Other cultures of giving and remembering must be possible.

They're decolonising everything now, someone said to me the other day, you told me. The curriculum, the museum, every academic discipline you can think of; pronouns even, apparently. Where will it end? they demanded, you said. Good question. If I were to finish that book I was thinking of writing, it would have to address this theme, the relentless whataboutism and wherewillitendism of those desperate to turn the clock back, impossibly, to those old fake certainties of militarist realism as they crumble. So in the time remaining to us here, let's see if we can make any sense of it together.

## 34. SPITTING ON BRITAIN

Half a century ago, in the mid-1970s, Moses Finley, the leading ancient historian of his generation, was sitting in his rooms at Jesus College,

Cambridge, writing an article to which he gave the title 'Colonies: An Attempt at a Typology'.[131] The paper moved back and forth from classical antiquity to post-war decolonisation, comparing the Greek *apoikia* and Roman *colonia* with South Africa, Rhodesia, Algeria, Nigeria and Ireland in the twentieth century. But Finley's typological approach did not accommodate a type of colonialism that was to be found in two corners of his own college. A kind of militarist realism that was built to endure, hidden in plain sight. One that is coming back into view today and one that, just as its power is almost completely exhausted, is quite possibly at its most destructive.

In the dining hall, a bronze cockerel stood on a wooden base. A small brass plaque screwed to the wood was inscribed with a Latin text that celebrated its provenance. The sculpture, it recorded, had been looted by a colonial businessman and banker during the chaotic British attack that sacked and destroyed Benin City in February 1897.[132] In 1905 that man had donated it to the college, where his son was an undergraduate. Then in 1930, the cockerel was put on permanent display in the dining hall, and it became a kind of college mascot (the college coat of arms depicts three cockerels). Many years later in 2016, following a student-led campaign, the college removed this sacred royal sculpture from its tableside display, and subsequently returned it to Nigeria. This represented the first institutional return of a looted Benin Bronze.[133]

In 2021, as this high-profile restitution was in process, a second monument was being discussed by the governing body of Jesus College. This time it was in the college's medieval chapel. A large memorial dominates the west wall of the nave. Almost fourteen feet in height, three and a half tons in weight, and made from eight separate sections of carved white marble, the memorial has been attributed to the artist Grinling Gibbons. It celebrates a benefactor named Tobias Rustat (1608–94), once the keeper of Hampton Court Palace, who in 1671 endowed eight college scholarships with a donation of £2,000. A head and shoulders portrait of the man carved in high relief in a flowing curled wig looks out blankly from within an oval medallion, flanked by two naked *putti* (cherubs) pulling back folds of drapery. Below, a cartouche inscription is bordered by a festoon of flowers and fruit.

Its text celebrates the man's devotion to the Crown as Yeoman of the Robes to the King, and lists many charitable acts; but it is silent on how he made a fortune from the slave trade as a longstanding investor in the Royal African Company, the Company of Royal Adventurers Trading into Africa, and the Gambia Adventurers – companies that shipped tens of thousands of Africans across the Atlantic as enslaved people.[134] While a courtier, Rustat commissioned three statues of monarchs from the studio of Gibbons, two of Charles II and one of James II. Rustat then commissioned the monument to himself in the mid-1680s. He kept it in his house in Chelsea for the final eight years of his life, periodically exhibiting it to guests.[135] When he died he was interred under a floor-slab in a specially prepared tomb in the chapel's choir, and the wall monument was posthumously installed by his executors in the north transept at the cost of £430. Victorian restorations saw the memorial moved to the west wall of the south transept, and then in 1922 it was moved for a second time to its present, most prominent location.[136] The master of Jesus in 1922 at that time was an antiquarian and author of Gothic ghost stories. We look him up and you read one of his stories to me, a tale called 'The Everlasting Club', published in 1919.

The story concerns a fictitious, secretive, profligate Hellfire dining club founded in the 1730s by a nobleman and courtier named Dermot, a thinly veiled reference to Rustat. The club rules state that its seven members, who are all fellows of the college, must meet for dinner once a year on All Souls' Day, unless four of them meet in the previous month and vote to cancel the annual feast. Breaking the rules will lead to 'mulcting': a word that is not defined, although the president is described as a man with an 'exceptional degree of cruelty and wickedness'. The rules also state that membership does not lapse at death. Over the years, the members die off one by one. Each October the surviving 'corporeal' members meet up so they can cancel the dinner – fearful that otherwise the 'incorporeal' members, which now include Dermot, would attend as riotous, orgiastic spirits. Eventually only one member is alive, so he is unable to meet in with others. In the small hours of 2 November, a 'hideous uproar' is heard from his rooms, and the following morning the don is found dead. Seven chairs stand drawn around a table, the rooms are in chaos as if a wild party had taken place, and Bellasis' lifeless head is 'bent over his folded arms, as though he would shield his eyes from some horrible sight'. The staircase and rooms were shut up thereafter, and remain empty to this day.[137] So what is the moral of this cautionary ghost story about the violent undead of an Oxbridge college? you ask me. Sounds like the same genre as the poison arrow story, I replied; the mistaken, hubristic, inward-looking story that a certain class of Oxbridge don like to tell themselves, that the college privileges they enjoy and the invented traditions they participate in will somehow make them vulnerable.

Across town, the university authorities erected another monument to this man in 1890, 200 years after his death, as part of a Gothic Revival restoration. It should be a familiar pattern by this point on the story. Rustat donated not only to the college, but he is also recorded as the first benefactor to the university library in 1667. His was one of a series of statues of benefactors erected during work on the western gate-tower of the Old Schools. It overlooks what was then the main library and is today the university's administrative building. But you don't learn that from the monument, which just gives the name:

RUSTAT

There was a debate about removing him a couple of years ago, but, like the 1909 statue of Cecil Rhodes here in Oxford, it's still there. He's perched so far back in his alcove that he doesn't even cast a shadow. They left him up but stuck steel spikes on his wig, his gloves, and around his boots, to keep the pigeons from shitting on his face, hands and feet. Looks like they stuck him with pins for witchcraft, you said to me the other day. Is it an act of protection, or some kind of curse? Maybe it's both at once.

I could relate the tedious story of the non-removal of the statue celebrating a slave trader by the university and the non-relocation of the memorial despite the guidance of the college's Slavery Working Party, and the democratic decision of the governing body of Jesus College which voted to move the monument again, this time to another more appropriate, secular space in the college. In this way it could be better appreciated as an artwork and as 'an educational vehicle for discussion on the legacy and history of enslavement', the paperwork stated.[138] A lavish annual feast at Jesus College named for him was also un-named.[139] The desire was simply no longer to celebrate someone so intimately involved in the history of the transatlantic slave trade. As a Grade I listed ecclesiastical building the plans were referred to the Consistory Court of the Diocese of Ely. And a campaign was mounted by a small but powerful activist group mustered to stop the relocation. There were accusations that the college wished to 'cancel' Rustat, to erase history.[140] I remember you telling me at the time that this cultural filibustering felt like it had something in common with the backlash that Trump's neo-fascist supporters had unleashed when they'd stormed the Capitol building in the January after that strangest of years, 2020. On both sides of the Atlantic, a desperate attempt to cling to power was in the air: to 'never concede', to overturn the outcome of a vote, to 'stop the steal', to cry fraud and rigging and fake news. Even somehow to defend the nation, to save something under attack by going on the assault. We watch back the footage of Trump at the Save America Rally on 6 January on YouTube. His small black leather gloves grip the lectern as the Stars and Stripes flies. 'And don't worry,' Trump tells his supporters:

> We will not take the name off the Washington Monument. We will not cancel culture. You know they wanted to get rid of the Jefferson Memorial? Either take it down or just put somebody else in there. I don't think that's going to happen. It damn well better not. They'll knock out Lincoln too, by the way. They've been taking his statue down. But then we signed a little law. You hurt our monuments, you hurt our heroes, you go to jail for ten years. And everything stopped. You notice that? It stopped, it all stopped.

I told you about how one of the emeritus culture warriors trying to revive the old militarist realism gave the Roger Scruton Memorial public lecture in Oxford's Sheldonian Theatre in October 2022. 'The colonial front in the culture war is culturally crucial,' he told the small assembled audience in the vast auditorium. 'What's at stake', the lecture continued, 'is the self-confidence of the British and their identity as a people committed to support and promote a liberal international order.' The rhetoric echoed up the tiers of ancient empty benches as the speaker, a lay clergyman, decried a 'fraudulent ... Corbynite' approach to history that is based on a false equation: BRITAIN = EMPIRE = EVIL. 'Cultural revolutionary decolonisation', he concluded, is an American import from the 'extreme-left Black Lives Matter movement'. It promotes 'imaginary guilt'. To attack 'the British faith' is to threaten 'the liberal international order', he claimed. It amounts to 'a desire to spit on Britain'.[141]

He'll probably get a knighthood for that, you joked, then pointed me to a description of the declining power of the Church in the nineteenth century, the lines with which Karl Marx opened his description of the mass protests in Hyde Park against the Sunday Trading Bill in June 1855:

> It is a long-established truth that a power that has outlived its times, a power that remains nominally in control of every instrument of violence even after its reason for existing has long since rotted away from beneath its feet – clinging on even as fights about the inheritance are breaking out among the heirs before even the notice of death has been printed or the will has been opened – will summon all its strength before the final death throes, and will switch from the defensive to the offensive – making an attack rather than stepping aside.[142]

At first glance, the bureaucratic process of listed building consent was an improbable weapon in a culture war. But red tape was becoming one item of the armoury employed to try to generate a kind of moral panic about British history, encouraged by some government ministers in the last years of a tired administration. Following the revitalisation of longstanding anti-racist movements in the summer of 2020, in which cultural heritage had proved one public space for addressing enduring inequalities, on 22 September 2020, the then culture secretary Oliver Dowden posted an open letter online addressed to the twenty-one 'arm's-length bodies' funded by his department, which included a range of national museums and galleries, the Royal Parks, the British Film Institute, the National Archives, and the Churches Conservation Trust. 'History is ridden with moral complexity,' he wrote. 'Statues and other historical objects were created by generations with different perspectives and understandings of right and wrong.' Further down the first page of the letter, eleven words were underlined, stating that the government '<u>does not support the removal of statues or other similar objects</u>'.¹⁴³

Later that autumn, the self-styled 'Common Sense Group' (CSG) of Conservative MPs launched their attack on heritage bodies including the National Maritime Museum and the National Trust, criticising what it called 'multiple perspectives on history'. In a letter to the *Daily Telegraph*, they argued that 'institutional custodians of history and heritage, tasked with safeguarding and celebrating British values' should not be coloured by cultural Marxist dogma, 'colloquially known as the "woke agenda"'.¹⁴⁴ Then in January 2021, that month of the Capitol attack, the UK's then communities secretary, Robert Jenrick, joined the fray. He took the phrase 'Retain and Explain' – a term previously informally used as a shorthand for one option in cases of managing so-called 'contested' heritage, like using interpretation boards to recontextualise a monument, for example – and elevated it first to the status of a slogan, and then a general policy. A new legal framework was announced, in which any changes to historic plaques, memorials or monuments – even those without 'listed' status – would now require planning permission. 'We cannot – and should not – now try to edit or censor our past,' Mr Jenrick told reporters. 'We believe in explaining and retaining heritage, not tearing it down.' Mr Dowden added:

> I strongly believe that we should learn from our past – in order to retain and explain our rich history. The decisions we make now will shape the environment inherited by our children and grandchildren. It is our duty to preserve our culture and heritage for future generations.¹⁴⁵

Do you know, I asked you, how many applications for listed building consent, to make a change to a listed building, were granted in England and Wales last year? Twenty-six thousand. And also 273 full demolitions of listed buildings were approved.¹⁴⁶ In these cases, Rhodes and Rustat, the processes have the full democratic support of the colleges' governing body. It was just such wilful nonsense. The civil servants around the ministers knew that, and the ministers did too. But that wasn't going to stop the culture warriors. After all, the Ministry of Culture was known informally in Whitehall as the Ministry of Fun. In May 2021, the CSG published a manifesto that claimed the Black Lives Matter movement was 'an inherently far-left movement', an 'extreme cultural and political group fuelled by ignorance and an arrogant determination to erase the past and dictate the future'. 'Britain is under attack,' they wrote. Heritage is being attacked by the 'new orthodoxy' of, yes you guessed it, 'woke ideology'.[147] 'Have the courage to stand up and fight it,' the manifesto exhorted its readers.

In the same month, an organisation called the Restore Trust (no 'the', they try to insist, someone tells me, it's meant to be just 'Restore Trust')[148] was set up as an explicitly entryist project, aiming to gain control of the National Trust by placing its own network on the trustee board of the heritage charity. Its tactics included challenging the National Trust on its position on a range of issues, central among which was historical research into the history of their houses and collections in relation to transatlantic slave trade and LGBTQ+ history. Supporters included the right-wing politician Nigel Farage, who said he hoped the Restore Trust 'knocks a bit of common sense' into the National Trust.[149] And soon afterwards the self-styled 'anti-woke' campaign group History Reclaimed was formed, a blogging collective of emeritus Oxbridge dons and fellow travellers, again with no transparency on its funding. Both the Restore Trust and the History Reclaimed are often cited as prime examples of 'astroturf' (i.e. fake grassroots) projects. Didn't I read somewhere that both these culture-war outfits are funded by Tufton Street? you ask me. Who knows, I reply. But amazing that these groups say they will 'restore trust' but won't say where their funding comes from. There are significant overlaps in memberships. When I was thinking about writing a book on this subject, one thing that was holding me back was the grim sense of those old men desperately combing through the footnotes to find grist for their bad-faith interventions, restating the old colonial position, tone-policing, or simply making direct untruthful attacks. That's how they roll, these emeritus activists, you tell me. The attempt is to intimidate or create a chilling effect for scholarship. Desperate stuff.

Kris Manjapra, author of *Black Ghost of Empire*, has described what happened next as a prime example of 'ghostlining' – a strategy that 'disavows the ongoing effects of slavery, colonialism and racism', and then 'plays the benefactor and the victim at the same time'.[150] Hit-jobs were fired off on every live topic in the so-called 'contested history' field, from Jesus College and Cambridge University to Oriel and Oxford, and from restitution to fallism to decolonisation in all its forms. For example, in November 2021 one retired Cambridge professor of Mediterranean history named Robert Tombs resorted to publishing an open letter to Sonita Alleyne, who had recently been appointed as the first female and the first Black head of Jesus College, Cambridge. The professor's demand that the master of the college should write a text for the History Reclaimed blogspot, justifying the return of the bronze cockerel, had been ineffective.[151] Hang on, you interrupt me, you're telling me that he's trying to stop stolen artefacts being returned and he's literally called 'Rob Tombs'?

The edgelord keyboard warriors at the History Reclaimed HQ marshalled further dad's army culture-warriors. First out of the blocks was a retired director of listing at Historic England and a former council member of the Church Monuments Society, whose doctoral research in art history at Cambridge three decades earlier had focused on 'seventeenth-century funerary monuments of a macabre nature'. He wrote a report that claimed that 'the college's proposals will cause substantial harm to the chapel', arguing that 'monuments must have a voice too'. He said what now? you asked.[152] Then his colleague, an expert on the archaeology of animal bones and chief scientist at English Heritage, who is, I read somewhere, a great-great-great-great-great-great-great-great-nephew of Rustat's, went a step further. In a letter to *The Times*, this man criticised the college for 'wasting money on sad gestures', and the *Daily Mail* reported that he saw 'the removal of the monument as a sort of desecration of his ancestor's grave'.[153] Technical cliometric arguments about the precise sources of Rustat's wealth up to 1671, when he made his donation to the college, or up to 1686, when the monument was made, were produced, and there was an attack on what the emeritus activists described as 'the false narrative that Rustat had amassed much of his wealth from the slave trade'.[154] These were combined with emotional calls for action, such as the idea that 'Rustat is being condemned for acts that were neither criminal nor exceptional in his own time'.[155] A solicitor hired for the group claimed there was 'an unfortunate desire on the part of the College to get rid of an elderly and unpopular relative, albeit one who had been hugely generous towards the College in the past'. 'The dead', he said, discussing the slave trader, 'cannot fight back.'[156]

Persuaded by these arguments at a hearing in March 2022, the deputy chancellor of the Ely diocese rejected the college's proposal.[157] 'Why is it so much agony to remove a memorial to slavery?' the Archbishop of Canterbury reflected.[158] The First Biannual Report of the Archbishops' Commission for Racial Justice also strongly criticised the decision, as did an open letter from 160 clergy published in the *Church Times*.[159] In a reflection on what he called 'the discipleship of Christian memory', the dean of Jesus College chapel warned against 'attending to the past in such a way that its weight stifles the grace that sets us free for a different future'.[160] What should have been a simple decision turned into a convoluted consistory court process, Sonita Alleyne reflected, so that 'Rustat's memorial was given more weight than the 150,000 African people he helped traffic into slavery'.[161]

The governing body's democratic decision to move the memorial from one location of the college to another remains unresolved. The only clear reason given by the diocese for the decision to prevent the change, apart from various opinions expressed about Rustat's ethics, was that the proposals would be to move the monument to 'a physical space to which its monumentality is ill suited' – an aesthetic argument rather than a historical, ethical or practical one.[162] The aesthetics of militarist realism. A monumentality designed never to be changed.

But what type of colonialism is this stoppage, on Moses Finley's terms? The tactics are simple: take an opposite position on every progressive development, let the op-eds claim the middle ground, and allow social media and institutional risk aversion to do the rest. The lie here is that you are not taking a side if you oppose the removal of a statue, or the return of an object to its rightful owner, or a change in the curriculum or in a tradition. In fact it's the classic logic of the punitive expedition, and indeed of a Muskian politics – attack democratic change by pretending it is itself an attack that must be resisted. The aim is to seek to exhaust, embarrass or intimidate institutions with concerns over reputational risk. It is a rearguard action: reactive, opportunistic, vexatious, punitive, disproportionate, bullying, bad faith anti-anti-racism. The effect is to preserve whatever last vestiges of exclusionary infrastructures of cultural supremacy survive from the nineteenth or early twentieth century. And the overall objective is simply to create a chilling effect that ensures that decolonisation in all its forms will never advance in the realms of art, culture and heritage – realms that have been so important for parts of the extreme right for a century and a half. The slogans are familiar distortions of the framing: we can't apologise for the past. Why should we feel guilty for the actions of our ancestors? History is complicated. Woke institutional leadership is destroying our heritage. And so on. Without fail the memorial is confused with the man. Small case-by-case decisions are blown up into a new moral panic, trying to scare institutional leadership into inaction through fear of negative press. There's a word for it in German, as you might imagine. *Vorauseilender Gehorsam.* Look it up. It means something like 'anticipatory obedience'.

Institutional leaders and boards of trustees can find themselves compromised, exposed – accused of aligning with those who are 'spitting on Britain', or making the mistake of commissioning reports from historians to go down rabbit-holes and cul-de-sacs to assess the ethics of the past, only to find out that the answer is that it's complicated. And yet these right-wing culture warriors understand precisely what is at stake. It's about the present, not the past. It's about what a society or community values. The accusation against experts in heritage, curation or teaching is 'identity politics', whereas in reality their culture war has the prehistory that has been traced in this story: from the founding of the Pitt Rivers in 1884, to the erection of Rhodes in 1911, to the skull-cup donation to Worcester College in 1946. The Muskian astroturfers hope to be able to reuse the playbook of the Primrose League. They rely for their success on the risk-averse nature of institutional leaderships who give into their pressure, and on the willingness of historians to wade in on questions that are, it turns out, about memory, heritage, memorialisation and cultural value in the present, rather than about the rights and wrongs of the past.

The tradition of this culture war, the original identity politics of a White patriarchal supremacism, begins with the history of war, violence, killing and dispossession justified on the grounds of culture. The continuity or inheritance takes the form of a kind of information war, a knowledge war, a propaganda war. A war about the idea of common humanity and its alternatives, about equality and freedom. It's as if the American Civil War were not just not over, but is now a transatlantic phenomenon: a war that gets mixed up with the memorials to mass sacrifice of the Boer War and the two World Wars. And even, in the final analysis, perhaps a fake war, I mean like the ones fought on a fake premise, culminating in a sequence that runs something like – 1980s: War on Drugs; 2000s: War on Terror; 2020s: War on Woke. Each another fold in the history of violence and ideologies of cultural supremacy from the opium wars to colonial 'small wars' to the long history of the war on culture. The arguments run deep, not least in historical anthropology, where some have for many years tried to shut down conversations about memory and memorialisation by suggesting that any 'image of colonialism as nineteenth-century racist oppression' will always be too simplistic, going so far as to suggest that 'left-liberal' accounts of a violent and cultural-supremacist Victorian colonial culture have served to 'stereotype' the past in the same way as colonialism defined itself against a stereotyped image of other cultures.[163]

Such arguments extend to the heart of the history-writing establishment too. 'Context is all, and contexts change, and the context has certainly changed in Rhodes's case,' wrote Sir David Cannadine in his introduction to a 2018 book titled *Dethroning Historical Reputations: Universities, Museums and the Commemoration of Benefactors*, based on a conference held at the Institute of Historical Research in London. What a title, I said when you lent it to me – since when was remembrance and heritage management about 'dethroning reputations'? Cannadine's short text asked whether undergraduates' 'preference for vegetarian meals' these days might mean that at some future date universities would be ill advised to accept donations 'from individuals who like their filet mignon or their beef wellington'.[164] Try applying these obfuscatory arguments to repositioning one legacy colonial statue or another, or how best to honour the sacrifice of those who fought fascism, or the college decision to stop using the skull-cup at dessert. To give one example, in January 2024 there was an attempted hit-job on the Pitt Rivers Museum in Oxford, penned by one of those emeritus professors. An op-ed for the *Daily Telegraph* warned university leaders: 'Go woke, go broke', making the claim that the museum was 'being "decolonised" in legal breach of the deed of gift under which the university acquired the collection'.[165] The museum is a 'time capsule', the article claimed, which is 'designed to illustrate the views of the age of empire' because the deed of gift stated, supposedly, that 'the principles governing the organisation and display of the objects had to be adhered to'. The trick here was that the deed does actually makes explicit provision for change. The selective quoting missed out the important line: 'changes in details which may be made after the death of the said Augustus Henry Lane Fox Pitt Rivers shall be such only as shall be necessitated by the advance of knowledge'.[166] A total non-story thus gains traction, corrections in the next day's paper will never get picked up by ChatGPT, and so the world of op-eds continues laying down the groundwork.

Ever felt you've been lied to? By the fantasy that certain parts of the past can't ever be changed, for instance, that a museum must be preserved in amber, that a statue or memorial once erected can never be moved or removed, or that a reading list can't be changed, or a tradition can't ever be changed. Or by the line of argument described so clearly by Frantz Fanon in 1956:

> First comes the assertion of the existence of human groups that have no culture; then the existence of a hierarchy of cultures; and finally the notion of cultural relativity.[167]

It's the process seen again and again in this story: the move from militarist realism (the presentation of cultural supremacy as the only possible state of affairs) to the repetition of myths so that they harden, come to seem solid and certain, through whispers, innuendo and sometimes downright misrepresentation. They know it's about the present, these culture warriors. And yet they use history as their weapon of choice, pick it up like a brickbat. Against this increasingly desperate, but sometimes dangerous, phase of hard-right fightback, the *choc en retour* of colonial-militarist realism, there is ongoing innovation in countermemory, countermonumentality, new forms of remembrance and monumentalism addressing the unfinished work of abolition, emancipation, anti-racism and anti-colonialism, addressing the legacies of enslavement and of proto-fascism, through reparation, restitution, repair, dignity and remembrance. Hold on, I reminded you as we were saying goodbye, to Stuart Hall's deeply humanistic conception of community and heritage, which was, in the words of Ien Ang, concerned not with 'who we are' or 'where we came from' but 'what we might become'.[168] No building will stand for ever. Any society chooses its heritage by deciding what it wishes to retain. This is about legitimacy, transparency and consent. You can't keep everything. Everybody knows it's about choices in the present. Every monument will fall.

## 35. FLATLINE

Incendiary bombs had hit the target earlier in the air raid. But it was the high explosive missile that fell at five to one in the morning on 11 May 1941, exploding on impact, that did the damage. Two people were slightly injured, *The Times* reported, but the loss to the museum collections was catastrophic. The staff had taken precautionary measures, packing the collections deemed most valuable in the basements and sub-basements. A portrait of the founder had been taken out of town, and his statue bricked in for protection; both survived unscathed. More than half the museum pieces were destroyed, the correspondent noted, you told me, including skeletons of kangaroos brought by Captain Cook from Australia, and 'the oldest mummy in the world' from Egypt. The lecture room was decimated, as was 'that grim, but scientifically invaluable collection', one newspaper reported – the army medical war collection, which was made up of plaster casts of every type of wound to the human body.[169] Fire spread to the odontological collection – an assortment of skulls, jaws and teeth – and much of the collection of comparative anatomy was lost.

It must've been a strange sight for the neighbours in Lincoln's Inn Fields, London's largest public square, watching the staff start the clean-up at number 35, the galleries of the Hunterian Museum of the Royal College of Surgeons, the next morning. The building is just round the corner from where the Armourer had practised law, and a stone's throw from Zimbabwe House, where the Epstein statues had been vandalised four years earlier. Some of the human skulls and skeletons, the ones that came through British colonialism collected on battlefields, from morgues, or simply dug up from their graves, the bodies of people whose fate after death was to be turned into a museum specimen, were now dehumanised and desecrated for a second time, blown further into pieces by a new form of supremacist ideology and war. It was another evolution of the violence of militarist realism, this time into something like what Mark Fisher called 'the gothic flatline', which he defined as 'a plane where it is no longer possible to differentiate the animate from the inanimate', where agency has become detached from humanity and life.[170] How then to let the militarist realism flatline, and yet rebuild institutions, communities, knowledge and memory, breaking with legacy supremacism, finding peace despite the ongoing war on culture?

The Hunterian collection in Lincoln's Fields comes back into this story, this necrography, in 1972, three decades later, in an unexpected way. The curator of the Pitt Rivers Museum in Oxford, recently arrived back in Britain after working in museums in Nigeria, wanted to capitalise on the name above the door. With the fascist Grandson dead, and the second Pitt-Rivers Museum shut, there was a once-in-a-generation opportunity to get the descendants to make an endowment, or at least increase name recognition for Fox's necronym, and use it to leverage other funding. The dispersal of the second collection had seen the Pitt Rivers discussed quite often in the national press. The curator had a plan to totally rebuild the museum on a new site, an idea that never materialised because of lack of funds.[171] The curator had failed for some reason in an attempt to republish the four monumental volumes of Fox's *Excavations of Cranborne Chase* in a facsimile edition through Oxford's Clarendon Press, as a way of promoting the museum to new audiences.[172] He was also keen to see a biography written, making it clear that Fox was the discipline's founding father.

Fox-Pitt had always talked about writing a biography of his idolised grandfather, and he had kept a tight grip on the papers and archives that the family had inherited. He'd been dead since 1966, however, and by the late sixties the archaeologist Jacquetta Hawkes was telling people that she was going to write the man's life, co-author it indeed, with Mortimer Wheeler. Born in the same year as Fox-Pitt, 1890, a late Victorian who lived through the next century, Wheeler was a former army major, former director-general of archaeology in

India, emeritus professor from UCL, an archaeologist who had been named British Television Personality of the Year in 1955, known for his wax moustache and Victorian style, an image that inherited much from Fox's mix of militarism, excavation and administration. Hawkes was also a skilled and experienced writer and BBC broadcaster who saw Fox as a hero figure. In 1968, she had made a programme for Radio 4 where she encouraged listeners to imagine this man as 'tall, strong and very handsome – in fact an ideal specimen of the English aristocracy'.[173] The book that would have tried to rehabilitate and celebrate Fox was never written, and other biographers filled the gap. But Hawkes' plans did produce a paper-trail which I worked through in her archive at Bradford University.

I picked up the story from an article that Hawkes wrote about Fox for the *Sunday Times* in June 1969. She said that Fox had left his head to science, at his own express request. The body that went by train from Tisbury for cremation at Woking may have already had its head removed, in other words. The head, Hawkes said, had been deposited in the collections of the Royal College of Surgeons. In her archive it becomes clear that Hawkes believed she had discovered the current location of the skull. At first she thought it had been incinerated when that Nazi bomb hit.[174] But some of the skulls were salvaged and taken to the sub-department of anthropology in the natural history department of the British Museum, which is today part of the Natural History Museum. After Fox-Pitt's death, the Pitt Rivers curator, Hawkes and two of Fox's great-grandsons entered into a correspondence about the head, and the question was addressed to the Natural History Museum.

Typescript replies were received from Rosemary Powers, whose title was 'experimental officer', British Museum (Natural History). On 30 April 1968 she communicated the news of a possible identification. There was no record of the skull in the Royal College of Surgeons archives. But there was an unidentified skull received by the museum from the college in the transfers in 1951. The index card was lost but the number would have fallen straight after the skull of Professor Francis Jeffrey Bell (1855–1924), a comparative anatomist who worked at King's College, London. Perhaps the head sat around in the manor house and was donated by the Grandson when he inherited in 1927, you say. Anything seems possible at this point, I reply. The evidence was thin. The Pitt Rivers curator wrote to one of the great-grandsons enquiring as to whether the family had any record of Fox's hat size, since this would assist in the identification. Hawkes' archive holds a handwritten note from her, slightly desperate perhaps, which reads: 'I believe there may be a death-mask.' In her letter, Rosemary Powers described the skull which she had provisionally identified as that of Fox:

> Only the rear of the skull survives, all the face and frontal are missing and charred patches on both parietals suggest that this was due to the blitz damage. As the edges seemed to be shattered rather than burned through, I hunted through my collection of 'lost' bits from the R.C.S. collection, which are boxed according to their preservation, but the only 'recent' and charred bits were all juvenile, known to be part of a sequence showing dental development. The skull is obviously male, with big mastoids and big attachments for the nuchal muscles, and well-marked temporal lines extending back as far as the lamboid suture. (In other words, he was a muscular man.) The sutures around the lambda are rather below the level of the surrounding bone, so he may have been aware of a slight depression at the crown of the head like an inverted Y. There is a slight suggestion of inflammatory reaction on the occipital ridges inside the skull. That is all I can say. So he was a war casualty after all, whether this be him or not.[175]

December 2022. In a Teams meeting with the keepers at the Natural History Museum, we examine the skull virtually. It may or may not be Fox. The bone is charred. The cheekbones have been blown off by the fascist bomb. I enquire about a radiocarbon date, or further physical or scientific examination, but there would be an ethical review to go through, and it would be unlikely to be granted for such a poorly provenanced item. And what would such an application to examine the skull further really achieve? Is it Fox? Do you believe it to be Fox? you ask. I believe him to be dead, I reply. His skull entering the collection, only to have the back of it blown off four decades later by a Nazi missile while his Grandson was incarcerated as a fascist? Whether true or not, let me say that *it appears to be true*, which is to say it's a kind of hypermetaphorical reality, a *choc en retour*, as if the fate of the proto-fascist general of the Grenadier Guards who believed mass extermination through cultural supremacy was the manifest destiny of his ethnoclass was always going to be not that of the soldier hoist by the petard of his fascist descendants – but of one who like Hamlet 'will delve one yard below the mines / and blow them at the moon'.[176]

'Territories and ideas have to be explored politically through construction and reconstruction,' Isaac Julien once argued, 'then thrown away, if we are to change the master narratives and conventions.'[177] Try to hold up the uncertain history of Fox's body like a lens, or a map, then. Chart its unknown, pathetic story and look again at the museum that bears his necronym, at the university's vain and stubborn memorial to corporate militarism and apartheid, and at the redacted life of the unnamed person whose skull is still there wrapped in acid free paper in that box on the shelf of the college archives. The unfinished story that I have tried to tell here begs the question not just about what late Victorian men did with the intergenerational wealth that came from transatlantic slavery, or how they revived the old East India Company model of corporate militarist colonialism and applied it with a new violence, a violence that they called vigour and physical energy, to the continent of Africa and to the world. No, it requires us to take stock of the cultural worldview that they tried to construct, and how we should inherit it. To understand the incomprehensible, collective abuse of the skull-cup as something other than an aberration. To try to open institutional and disciplinary eyes, to open my own eyes and ears and worldview, to the countless humans whose fate has been for their bodies still to be held as specimens in legacy colonial museums. Whiteness, Sara Ahmed has written, as 'a way of viewing the world can put racism behind closed doors'.[178]

There are some glimmers of hope, and not just in the instances where communities have removed monuments or changed names. In London's Docklands, outside the museum where the statue of a slave trader stood, the London Assembly will be installing a sculpture by Khaleb Brooks, called 'The Wake'; inspired by the form of a cowrie shell and engraved with new poems by Yrsa Daley-Ward, it will be a memorial to the lives of enslaved people, intending 'not just to remember individual stories ... but also counteract the history of forgetting embedded in colonialism'.[179] And in Dorset when some Egyptian human skulls from Fox's second collection came up at auction in 2024, for example, they were withdrawn after the auctioneer realised the public reaction.[180] Who knows, perhaps they'll ban the sale of human remains before too long, you said to me at the time – remarkable that it's still legal to sell body parts. And as for this story, there has to be the hope that this person, whoever they were, de-named and dehumanised in death, then abused in the body horror of this artificial afterlife, might now find some dignity.

And they're decolonising the museums, the newspapers report. But what does that mean exactly for the fate of the ancestral remains in their care? That every ancestor will now be returned to their communities where that is possible? Open the cabinets and the vast storage facilities, even if just metaphorically, and try to discern the human lives, perhaps a hundred thousand people who lived in the nineteenth century whose bodies or body parts are today, so long after death, in collections in the United Kingdom alone, perhaps twice that number we just don't know, because these legacy colonial institutions, museums and universities, the departments of anthropology or the schools of dentistry or the institutes of medicine, often haven't published basic inventories or databases or estimates. It's perhaps a million people or more if you add in the global landscape of museums, from California and New York to Paris, Germany, Sydney and Cape Town, who knows, each box containing somebody's ancestor. There has been no audit. Surely that's the first lesson of the story told here. There's a need for more certainty, for at least some sense of the numbers. Remarkable how some people try to say it's not okay for a community or institution to remove a figurative statue or to rename a building when it decides to, you always pointed out to me, when alongside tens of millions of cultural objects there are these enduring silent posthumous informal incarcerations where they've thrown away the key, unburied and uncremated – skulls, bones, hair, skin, teeth.

And what should be done in those many cases, as with the story told here, where there is no documentation of provenance or culture for the human remains in the box on the archival shelf, sometimes not even a country or continent of origin recorded, so there is no community to which a return could be made? That was how this violence worked of course, as this book has traced, the de-naming, the dehumanisation, the deterritorialisation. But if there can be respect and dignity for unknown soldiers after war then the same must surely be possible for unknown people whose bodies still lie in museums, gathered there through the forces of militarist realism. Doing nothing is after all an action in its own right, one that in this case might continue the violence. Part of the answer may be to recognise this historical movement, what I have been calling militarist realism, which is revealed by the three intertwined movements that have struggled for more than half a century to undo it — restitution in the museums, fallism in public art and memory culture, and decolonisation in the universities. In each case, the ways in which White supremacism flipped from science to the arts, from nature to culture, begin to come into view. The gothic flatline of the so-called culture war, which as this book has traced, meant that from the 1860s the lies of racist 'science' came to be applied to the fields of the arts, culture and heritage, and thus transformed in the process, like those parlour games again, the drawings that seem to evolve as the paper is passed around the table. In every city, society, museum or university these lines of inheritance are now running closer than ever to the surface from one generation to another: from the past to you, like it ran from Fox to Fox-Pitt, from colonialism to fascism. From Rhodes' desire to annex the planets to Elon Musk's 'dark, gothic MAGA'.

The hope must surely lie in holding onto the right that any society or community has to define its own memory culture, rather than always having to hold onto the memories, ideologies, misrepresentations of a hundred years ago or more, the tired propaganda of its ancestors. Holding onto the fact that without the work of maintenance every monument will fall, and what flows from that fact: that communities have the right to choose to keep what they value and face up to what is hurtful, hateful or destructive. Because it's surely possible, when it comes to culture, heritage and tradition, art, archaeology, anthropology and architecture, to care for people more than you do for things, by refusing to hold onto every last thing that's inherited from the past, by not mistaking the statue for the man, or mistaking the human skull in the collection for an object of material culture. It's impossible to hold onto everything. It could even be that to try to do so might be a form of enduring violence. Receive and care for what's good from the past then, but be open to refusing ideas and practices that are toxic or hurtful. Reimagine ideas of tradition, benefaction and heritage, dismantle structures that have no place in our times, find new ways of inheriting and remembrance. Try to find dignity for the ancestors.

Palo Alto, California, mid-November 2024. The election results came in a week ago now, along with the final line edits for this book. We talked about both things over dinner last night in Santa Cruz, and they are now forever intertwined in my head. Before I give my talk at Stanford's Archaeology Center this evening I'm taken outside to see the empty pedestal where a white stone statue of Louis Agassiz stood for decades, until they took it down in October 2020.[181] It was erected in the 1890s, more than two decades after his death. It's a genre that I have come to understand better, this militarist realism. But once you've seen the gap on the main façade of the Stanford campus buildings as you walk up the Oval, you can't miss it. It's a monument in its own right, this gap; an answer to structures of silencing and redaction, a new layer of remembrance and reflection, one surely more enduring than stone or bronze. It's not about history but about memory, you always reminded me. These stories aren't finished. We still don't know how this ends.[182]

So come to Oxford next week, next year, or next decade. I'll buy you a coffee on Little Clarendon Street, or lunch from the sandwich place on Holywell Street, or a drink in the Lamb and Flag, and we can walk to High Street and look up at the pedestal, visit the museum displays, walk in the gardens of Worcester College. We can take stock of the parallel movements of fallism, restitution and decolonisation, and what they continue to reveal, how they continue to address the enduring legacies of militarist realism across the generations; how the old cultural war of position is failing on every one of its chosen fronts, from monuments to museums to universities. And ask each other what more we can do to work towards new forms of remembrance and reconciliation, towards peace, transparency and dignity holding onto this book's two mottos: *Stay with the Fragments*. And, *Sometimes the gap is the monument*.

# Acknowledgements

Acknowledgements should record obligations and express gratitude. In this case the obligations begin with the dead. The writing of this book was bracketed by a sequence of personal bereavement. In August 2020, as I was starting to outline the structure, my father died; and then as I was completing the first draft in May 2022 my mother's death followed. In June 2024, as I was finishing the manuscript, my sister died too, still in her late forties. The practicalities of care and the human fallout of loss were normalised for a period, and then grief was what was left over. Outlive the household you grew up in and a host of shared memories become yours alone, as if an event horizon has closed in upon you. Covid, cancer and addiction: causes can be clear but insufficient facts as you try to make sense of death; of three deaths as it turned out.

There was a fourth. A couple of weeks after my father's funeral my dear colleague and longstanding co-editor Mary Beaudry died too, aged sixty-nine. This book is dedicated to Mary, who always told me you can piece broken sherds together to give shape to human lives without trying to cross-mend every last chunk of a smashed vessel, return it to its former state, make it whole again. Archaeology, she understood, is never about reconstruction, or even the discovery of the past. Fragments of human lives can say more than might be expected, shattered messages not erased but modified and multiplied through the fact of their fractured survival. That goes for the living as well as the dead. Archaeology is the science of human endurance. Hence one of the two mottos that came to guide this book: *Stay with the fragments.*

Strange how that torn strip of time folded into the arc of writing the book, but there you have it.

## ACKNOWLEDGEMENTS

My own experience of loss could hardly be further from the unfinished history of unfinished deaths that I was reckoning with on the page: a story of who gets named and who de-named, whose image an institution posthumously celebrates in monuments and whose body it posthumously abuses. A speculative history of a collective mourning that has not even yet begun because the story has been untold. But in living through grief while trying to write this silenced history, I was learning something about memory, remembrance and our obligations to the ancestors.

People recommended books about bereavement. It was hit-and-miss. Those four years were not a time of magical thinking. It was nothing like the sensation of being afraid.[1] Grief arrived, as it happened, neither like the 'cruel education' of the kind described so beautifully by Chimamanda Ngozi Adichie ('ungentle mourning ... full of anger'), nor like Max Porter's terrifying crow-like thing with feathers ('fourth-dimensional, abstract, faintly familiar ... the fabric of selfhood, and beautifully chaotic').[2] There was no Psalm 30:11, no I Corinthians 15:55. But when I reread Helen Macdonald's sparkling memoir *H is for Hawk* I rediscovered her metaphor of excavation. ('The archaeology of grief is not ordered. It is more like earth under a spade, turning up things you had forgotten.')[3] And I revisited the analogy Walter Benjamin once drew between excavating and remembering. ('Memory is not an instrument for scouting the past, but the medium.') In the library and on the screen my reading traced the sharp contours of the gaps hammered into the archive and the sudden breaks of slope of the voids punched through my life. ('A good archaeological report,' Benjamin concluded, 'records not just the strata in which the finds were made, but also those that had to be dug through to get there.')[4] The folded corners of book pages, light 4H pencil underlinings, constellations of asterisks as marginalia, and quotations copied in blue ink into lined notebooks became a bricolage of reading for writing while grieving. I found grief comprehensible as a mode of archaeology, a medium of fragments: I came to understand grief as a form of memory.

In the bricolage was a line from Roland Barthes' *Mourning Diary* suggesting one might not suppress grief but change its form instead. ('Make it pass from a static state (stasis, engorgement, recurrences,

## ACKNOWLEDGEMENTS

repetitions of the identical thing) to a fluid state'.)[5] An image from Aimé Césaire's poem 'Maison-Mousson' which found its way into the book ('my very worn face on a coin suddenly rediscovered in your excavations').[6] And a fragment from Fred D'Aguiar's poem sequence *For the Unnamed* ('Dead you ask us living / nothing.').[7] Melt it down. Dig it up. Read its silence. Apply such grief-thinking to that other form of memory with which this book is concerned, someone suggested: monumentality. Think through how forms of grieving coincide with forms of monumentalism. Hence the second motto of the book: *Sometimes the gap is the monument.*

Now to the thanks. Conversations and correspondence with colleagues and friends were the weft of the writing, to the extent that the book came to adopt a vocative form (addressing a second person), at some points even becoming invocatory (addressing the dead as well as the living, like a spell or a prayer might do). Two men who taught me archaeology died twenty years ago, both too young, in their fifties. Chris Currie was my first boss and trained me as an excavator for the first three years of my working life at sites, mostly historic gardens, from Birmingham to Worcestershire to Hampshire. Chris instilled a commitment to local, community and public archaeology, and brought a kind of scholarly irreverence and punk DIY sensibility to the politest corners of English landscapes and art history, forever joking with utmost seriousness about British archaeology's twin lines of inheritance: the bourgeois neo-romanticism of hippie counterculture, and the plummy neo-Victorianism of young fogey antiquarianism. Andrew Sherratt, assistant keeper at Oxford's Ashmolean Museum for over thirty years, was one of my undergraduate tutors. Andrew showed me how monumentality took different forms in the human past, and memorably described the Pitt Rivers as a monument to a fallacy: a hegemonic cultural relativism that drew its apparent solidity from 'the metaphor of descent' combined with 'the new, hard imagery of race'.[8] A third teacher, the late poet R. F. Langley who taught me English Literature and Art History at Bishop Vesey's Grammar School in Birmingham, set me onto the connections between archaeology, art, architecture and anthropology. Good teaching stays with you a lifetime, and some lines that Roger read with us in class have returned while writing this book, from T. S. Eliot ('In succession / Houses rise

## ACKNOWLEDGEMENTS

and fall') to Shakespeare ('Not marble nor the gilded monuments / Of princes shall outlive this powerful rhyme'), to Charles Olson ('What does not change / is the will to change'). I am grateful to these three men for their lasting inspiration as my teachers, which shaped this book in such varied ways.

At the Pitt Rivers Museum, thanks are due to Chris Morton, Philip Grover and Mark Dickinson, and to the teams who worked on the 'Characterising the World Archaeology Collections' and 'Excavating Pitt-Rivers' projects in 2009–2014 (funded by Arts Council England and the John Fell OUP Fund), which laid the foundations for this book – Beth Asbury, Carlotta Gardner, Matt Nicholas, Alice Stevenson and Judy White. Thanks are also due to those emeritus colleagues whose 'Rethinking Pitt-Rivers' project undertook crucial collections-based documentation (Jeremy Coote, Chris Gosden and Alison Petch). More than three quarters of a century passed after Pitt-Rivers' death without a biography being written. Then in the space of just fourteen years (1977 to 1991) three came along.[9] Thirty-four years after the most recent of those studies, a reassessment of 'the General' is overdue. In this respect this book is indebted to the primary work of his three biographers – the late Michael Thompson, William Chapman and Mark Bowden – and to the work of Bradley Hart on the fascist grandson.

I am, like all who live or work in Oxford, indebted to those involved in the Rhodes Must Fall in Oxford campaign which has, in its different forms over the past decade, revealed so much about the central role of imperialism in the history of Oxford University. Without the questions raised by that grassroots campaign this book would not have been written. Special thanks are also due to the governing body of Worcester College, Oxford, who in 2019 invited me to look into the provenance, history and ethical questions around the skull-cup on their behalf. The college's ethical commitment to understand and openly to address the difficult questions of its history and what to do next has been an inspiration.

Various aspects of the research presented here were given in the 2021 Strathern Lecture at the University of Cambridge, the 2022 Bernie Grant Memorial Lecture, the 2022 Goethe Lecture at the Goethe Institute, London, and during a Distinguished Lectureship at Stanford University in 2024, as well as in talks at the University of Connecticut,

## ACKNOWLEDGEMENTS

the British School at Rome, Iziko South African Museum in Cape Town, Adelaide University, University of California, Santa Cruz, and at Pushkin House, SOAS, the Royal Academy and the Victoria and Albert Museum in London. I am grateful to all those who came along to hear earlier versions of the arguments in this book, as they took shape, and for the many dialogues from which I have learned so much.

Thanks are due to colleagues, friends, collaborators and students who helped form this book in so many different ways, too many to name here, but including Pio Abad, Sandeep Bakshi, Richard Bradley, Victor Ehikhamanor, Kodzo Gavua, Albert Gouaffo, Sharon Grant, Monica Hanna, Rebekah Hodgkinson, Bryan Knight, Ania Kortaba, Rebekka Ladewig, Philipp Lepenies, Siddhartha Lokanandi, Stuart Mcclean, Diarmaid MacCulloch, Lesley McFadyen, Denis Maksimov, Peter Mandler, Lennon Mhishi, Mary-Ann Middelkoop, Jeremy Millar, Janet Miller, El Hadji Malick Ndiaye, Josh Pollard, Ciraj Rassool, Anthony Richter, Sydney Rose, Mike Rowlands, Bénédicte Savoy, Carole Souter, Jonas Tinius, Kate Tunstall, Hrag Vartanian and Onyekachi Wambu. Thanks also to all I dug alongside over the years who shaped my thinking about archaeology, too many to mention but especially Tim Allen, Adrian Chadwick, Nigel Jeffries, Sadie Watson and Helen Wickstead. Special thanks are due to Isaac Julien and Mark Nash, and to my agent Charlie Brotherstone. At Penguin Random House thanks are due to my two editors – Helen Conford for her vision for the book and Shan Vahidy for her courage, wit and integrity – and to the whole team including Lindsay Davies, Laurie Ip Fung Chun, Vanessa Phan and Isabelle Ralphs. Nick Mirzoeff has played a central role in shaping this book, and I am grateful to him for his comradeship, friendship and commitment.

Thanks are also due to staff at Bodleian Libraries, the British Library, the National Archives, Salisbury and South Wiltshire Museum, University of Bradford Special Collections and the National Army Museum for their assistance with archival- and collections-based research. Thanks also to Nick Lane Fox for his generosity and hospitality in hosting my visit to Bramham in May 2022, and to the Pitt-Rivers family for their archival donations and interactions with the museum project researchers.

Oxford, 31 December 2024

# Notes

## PROLOGUE: LEGACY MONUMENTALITY

1 Trouillot, 1995: 51. cf. Hicks and Stevenson, 2013.
2 Gould, 1981.
3 Gibson, 1984: 289. cf. Hicks, 2021a.
4 Du Bois, 1931: 279.
5 Savage, 2018: 131, 162; Savage, 1994: 130; cf. Mirzoeff, 2023: 89.
6 Winberry, 1983: 108–10.
7 To this day, the UDC issues crosses of military service to 'veterans who are lineal blood descendants of Confederate military personnel', from World War II and Korea to Vietnam to 'the continued Global War on Terror', as well as their 'Pioneer in Space Award'; see https://hqudc.org/medals/.
8 Du Bois, 1928: 97; 1935: 715–6. Du Bois refers to a monument in North Carolina that bears this text, although he does not specify which of the scores of such monuments in the state this might be.
9 Anon, 1910.
10 The governor was William Walton Kitchin (1866–1924). See Daughters of the Confederacy, 1909; Tyson, 2004: 97.
11 'For increased pensions', *Goldsboro Semi-Weekly Argus* 24(97) (6 November 1909), p. 3.
12 William Walton Kitchin had been among the ringleaders alongside his elder brother, Claude Kitchin; see Rutter, 2019.
13 'What will you be?', *Wilmington Messenger* (8 November 1898), p. 1; 'Attention white men', *Wilmington Messenger* (9 November 1898), p. 8.
14 The number of deaths in the Wilmington Race Massacre is disputed, see Tyson and Cecelski, 1998: 5; cf. Prather, 1984; Umfleet, 2020; Gustafson, 2021.

## NOTES TO PROLOGUE

15 Letter from Senator W. Lee Person to the editor, *The Caucasian* 45 (6 October 1898), p. 1. Quoted by Crow and Durden, 1977: 127; see discussion by Rutter, 2019: 160.
16 Cox, 2003: 93, 120; cf. Cox, 2017.
17 Douglass, 1870.
18 'Neo-Nazi James Fields gets 2nd life sentence for Charlottesville attack', *National Public Radio* (15 July 2019).
19 Mirzoeff, 2017; cf. Mirzoeff, 2023.
20 All Monuments Must Fall went from a blog post and social media (Mirzoeff, 2017, 2021) to a collaboratively written syllabus (All Monuments Must Fall, 2017, 2020); cf. Preciado, 2020; Younge, 2021.
21 Davis, 2003.
22 Gaddis, 2022: 486–7.
23 'Blackshirts at Oxford', *Sunday Times* (3 November 1935), p. 26.
24 'Oxford Fascists University Association', *The Times* (2 May 1933), p. 11. 'Mosley dining club aimed to subvert armed forces', *The Times* (10 November 1983), p. 4.
25 'Fight at Blackshirt meeting', *The Times* (26 May 1936), p. 18. An eyewitness recollection of the Battle of Carfax by Elizabeth Longford was recorded in 'The Wit, the Poet and the Haughty Fascist', *The Sunday Telegraph* (10 August 1986), p. 13. The previous February Oxford City Council had cancelled a contract for the Oxford University Fascist Association to hold Mosley's talk in the Town Hall; the Association's president, R. J. M. Gould-Adams (or Goold-Adams) of New College, whose book *South Africa: To-day and To-morrow* was published in the same year, issued legal proceedings against the city council. 'News in brief,' *The Times* (21 February 1936), p. 11; 'Writ against Oxford Corporation', *The Times* (26 February 1936), p. 14; 'Britain and the Commonwealth', *The Spark* (6 December 1963), pp. 2–3. See also Renton, 1996.
26 The porch of the University Church, with its distinctive Solomonic columns, was designed by the architect Nicholas Stone in the 1630s.
27 Stead, 1902: 102. The seven sculptural figures were by Henry Alfred Pegram; see Impey, 2011: 100.
28 Brock and Curthoys, 2000: xv; Rotberg, 1988: 89–90.
29 'Oriel new buildings', *The Times* (29 September 1911), p. 5.
30 Verschoyle, 1900 [1883]: 159, 369, 379; Beinart, 2022: 583.
31 'The real meaning of Rhodes Must Fall', *Guardian* (16 March 2016).
32 'The Rhodes Colossus', *Punch* (10 December 1892), p. 2.

33 In Stephen Greenblatt's terms, 'self-fashioning' is an activity associated with the middle class, with submission to colonial or military administration, and with an urge to attack and destroy something 'alien, strange, or hostile' (Greenblatt, 1980: 9).
34 Marks and Trapido, 2013.
35 Rotberg, 1988: 649, 663; Stead, 1902: 68.
36 Millin, 1933: 398.
37 Horace's *Odes* Book 3, Ode XXX, lines 1–8 (My translation). Postscript to will of 8 September 1893, Wills and related papers of Cecil John Rhodes Bodleian Libraries Archives MSS.Afr.t.1; see discussion by Rotberg, 1988: 665–6.
38 Williams, 1921: 1.
39 Muringaniza, 2002. The 1907 statue at Kimberley was by the sculptor William Hamo Thornycroft RA.
40 The building in question was known as Cecil Rhodes House on Goldington Street, Camden. Chief Inspector Cecil Rolph Hewitt (1901–1994) was named after Rhodes, see 'The Old Bill', *The Listener* (10 October 1974), p. 29. A proposal was made in 2021 to rename *Homo rhodesiensis* (Roksandic et al., 2021).
41 Maylam, 2005: 126.
42 Decision Summary (reference 1469337), Historic England, 11 February 2020, www.heritagegateway.org.uk/Gateway/Results_Single.aspx?uid=1469337&resourceID=7
43 In 2021, the college report listed 'a bronze bust by S. March 1901, a miniature by M. H. Carlisle, an oil painting by P. T. Cole; and drawings by M. Menpes' (Souter et al., 2021: 36–7).
44 William Nicholson 'Cecil John Rhodes' (lithograph, 1899), Government Art Collection accession number 14662, https://artcollection.dcms.gov.uk/artwork/14662/; '"Three Brexiteers" chase buccaneering spirit of empire in choice of art', *Observer* (1 July 2017).
45 'New Rhodesia House', *The Times* (24 April 1935), p. 7. The name 'Rhodesia House' had previously been used to refer to the headquarters of the British South Africa Company in London Wall. 'Future of Southern Rhodesia', *The Times* (11 July 1935), p. 8; 'New statues for Agar House?' *Daily Telegraph* (11 July 1935), p. 16.
46 Correspondence held in the file 'Rhodes Statue', Records of the Royal Fine Art Commission BP/2/13, National Archives.
47 The high commissioner was Stephen Martin Lanigan O'Keeffe (1878–1948). '18 heroic Epstein nudes are for sale', *New York Herald* (22 April 1935), p. 3.

NOTES TO PROLOGUE

48 'Can you change your own building?', *Daily Mirror* (12 May 1935), p. 6.
49 'No reprieve for Epstein statues', *Daily Telegraph* (21 July 1937), p. 12; 'Epstein statues to go', *Daily Mail* (21 July 1937), p. 16.
50 'Epstein statues must go', *Evening Telegraph and Post* (20 July 1937), p. 4; '"Off with their heads!"', *Daily Mail* (18 August 1937), p. 3; 'Epstein statues on Agar House', *The Times* (22 July 1935), p. 17; 'Vandalism, says Epstein of his lifted statues', *New York Herald* (3 May 1935), p. 3; 'Epstein may seek injunction', *Daily Telegraph* (24 June 1937), p. 19.
51 'Royal Academy: Brilliant gathering at the "Private View"', *The People* (1 May 1904), p. 9; 'London's new statue: "Physical Energy"', *Daily Telegraph & Courier* (30 Sept 1907), p. 6; 'Lusaka cheers the Queen Mother', *The Times* (23 May 1960), p. 9.
52 The interpretation of the horse as representing Africa was underlined by the *Sunday Telegraph*'s caption to an image of the statue in 1966, which read 'Salisbury's Black Beauty'; see 'Gift horse', *Sunday Telegraph* (15 May 1966), p. 3.
53 Clodfelter, 2017: 212.
54 The provost was Charles Lancelot Shadwell (1840–1919). 'Oriel new buildings', *The Times* (29 September 1911), p. 5.
55 Colonel Christopher Codrington (1668–1710).
56 'Nineteenth-Century Benefactors of the College and the Legacies of Enslavement' (All Souls College, Oxford), www.asc.ox.ac.uk/sites/default/files/2024-01/Nineteenth%20Century%20Benefactors%20of%20the%20College%20and%20the%20Legacies%20of%20Enslavement%20-%20Lizzie%20Dawson.pdf
57 Stead, 1902: 21–2; Rhodes Trust, 1929.
58 Rhodes House, designed by Herbert Baker, built 1926–29.
59 Meades, 2013: 159–160.
60 Hilton, 2017: 88n4; Symonds, 1986: 172; see Bent, 1895; Fontein, 2016; Chirikure, 2020; cf. Symonds, 2000.
61 Arendt, 1951: 215.
62 Reproduced in Stead, 1902: 58–9.
63 Rhodes described how Ruskin's lecture discussed the 'privileges and opportunities of the young men in the Empire' (Baker, 1934: 10–11, quoting James McDonald, who was describing a conversation between Rhodes, George Wyndham and Lady Eliza Grey in what was then Rhodesia).
64 Ruskin, 1905 [1870]: 42.
65 Rhodes was only sixteen years old at the time of Ruskin's lecture, delivered on taking up his first tenure of the Slade Professorship, on

8 February 1870. It is not impossible that he visited Oxford from his home in Hertfordshire to hear the lecture in the Sheldonian Theatre, a few short months before he left for his first trip to Africa, departing for Durban in the June of that year. More probable perhaps was that he encountered Ruskin's arguments on the page, as the text was published in 1870, and so in wide circulation by the time he matriculated three years later in October 1873 (Foster, 1888: 1189). Almost fifteen years later, on 18 October 1884, a month before the Berlin Conference convened with the purpose of dividing up the continent of Africa between the European nation states, Ruskin opened another Slade lecture, this time on 'The Pleasures of England', by repeating the line about 'northern blood' from the 1870 text, describing it as 'the most pregnant and essential of all his teaching'. Ruskin, 1905 [1884]: 422–3.

66 'The proposed Pan-Britannic or Pan-Anglian Contest and Festival' (letter from J. Astley Cooper), *The Times* (30 October 1891), p. 3. The following year the proposal gained the support of the president of the Oxford University Boat Club: 'The president of the OUBC and the proposed English-speaking Olympic Games', *Sporting Times* (9 April 1892), p. 6.
67 Rotberg, 1988: 666.
68 Maguire, 1897: 9.
69 Mosley, 1932: 8, 154. 'Greater Britain' was term coined by Charles Wentworth Dilke in his travelogue *Greater Britain: A Record of Travel in English-Speaking Countries During 1866–7* (Dilke, 1869), and expanded by Cambridge's Regius Professor of Modern History J. R. Seeley in a series of lectures given in 1883 to describe what he called 'an extension of the English nationality' (Seeley, 1883). It was the name of the periodical that published in 1891 what most biographers of Rhodes understand to be the blueprint for his scholarship scheme (Rotberg, 1988: 664), and then later also the title of Mosley's book of 1932.
70 See for example Quigley, 1981.
71 Rotberg, 1988: 663, 666; Williams, 2000: 717.
72 Rotberg, 1988: 666.
73 Stead, 1902: 36–43, 52.
74 'Rhodes Scholarships', *Daily Telegraph* (9 March 1914), p. 14; Stead, 1902: 44–5.
75 McDonald, 1927: 204–5, 355; Rotberg, 1988: 650–1.
76 'Mr Rhodes wished no memorial statues', *Edinburgh Evening News* (1 May 1902), p. 2; 'A Cecil Rhodes memorial refused', *Shields Daily Gazette* (24 December 1904), p. 5.

77 'Our London correspondence', *Manchester Guardian* (31 March 1902), p. 5; 'The late Mr Rhodes', *Edinburgh Evening News* (31 March 1902), p, 4; 'National memorial to Mr Rhodes', *The Times* (2 July 1902), p. 12.
78 'Memorial plaque to Cecil Rhodes', *The Times* (4 December 1953), p. 10. Development of the Oxford monuments was doubtless aided by Lord Curzon, the chancellor of Oxford University, former viceroy of India, a man who shaped ideas of preservation and memorialisation from the restoration of the Taj Mahal to the National Trust. For Curzon's comments on the Rhodes Memorial in Cape Town see Hilton, 2017: 106.
79 Plomer, 1933: 27, 172.
80 Churchill, 1908: 379.
81 It was moved to the grounds of the National Archives in Salisbury (a city itself renamed Harare in 1982). 'Unwanted statue finds a home', *The Times* (23 December 1964), p. 10; 'Zambia "deports" Rhodes statue', *Daily Mirror* (24 December 1964), p. 20; 'Gift horse', *Sunday Telegraph* (15 May 1966), p. 3. See discussion by Schmahmann, 2022.
82 'Exorcising the ghost', *Daily Telegraph* (1 August 1980), p. 12; 'Another Rhodes statue to go', *Daily Telegraph* (8 August 1980), p. 4; 'Rhodes statue removed in Bulawayo', *Daily Telegraph* (16 August 1980), p. 4.
83 'Cecil Rhodes statue in Cape Town has head removed', *BBC News*, 15 July 2020.
84 Din-Kariuki, 2020. cf. Chigudu, 2021.
85 Rhodes Must Fall Oxford, 2016 [2015]: 3–4.
86 Mockler-Ferryman, 1903; Gildea, 1911: 170. Photograph from 1907, Henry Taut Collection, Historic England Archive, HWT01./01; C50/00504.
87 National Inventory of War Memorials number 31934.
88 'Cecil Rhodes and Oriel College, Oxford', *Times Literary Supplement* (20 December 2015).
89 'Free speech trumps censorship – be it Cecil Rhodes or Adolf Hitler', *Daily Telegraph* (23 December 2015).
90 'Oxford University risks "damaging its standing" if it pulls down Cecil Rhodes statue, warns Tony Abbott', *Independent* (23 December 2015).
91 'Oxford will not rewrite history, says chancellor', *Daily Telegraph* (13 January 2016), pp. 1–2.
92 Reproduced in Amory, 1980: 49.
93 Hicks, 2020a, 2021a.
94 'Oxford v-c: "hiding your history is not the route to enlightenment"', *Times Higher Education* (11 June 2020).

95 'Bishop's Stortford; Rhodes Birthplace Trust to be renamed', BBC News (11 June 2020). In August 2020, the Rhodes Arts Complex was also renamed South Mill Arts.
96 'Oriel College backs removal of Cecil Rhodes statue', *Guardian* (17 June 2020).
97 In February 2020, Historic England had confirmed that the memorial plaque on King Edward Street did not meet the criteria to be protected under Listed Buildings legislation. The Historic England decision stated that it 'lacks the richness of detail and modelling to mark it out as of national interest for its artistic quality'. 'Decision Summary: Memorial plaque dedicated to Cecil Rhodes, 1906', by Onslow Whiting (11 February 2020).
98 'Name change', *The Times* (16 August 1991), p. 5; Renaming Cecil Rhodes House, www.camden.gov.uk/renaming-crh
99 'GLC launch anti-race space game', *Daily Telegraph* (18 January 1984), p. 6.
100 Oriel College, 2021, 'Contextualisation of the Rhodes Legacy'. Archived at https://web.archive.org/web/20211011111102/https://www.oriel.ox.ac.uk/contextualisation-rhodes-legacy. In July 2022 the culture minister, Nadine Dorries, overruled the Historic England decision and had the King Edward Street plaque 'emergency listed'.
101 Oriel College presented a bullet-pointed list of other actions it would take: 'Establish a task force to oversee implementation of the Report's recommendations; Commission a virtual exhibition to contextualise Rhodes's legacy; Contextualise Rhodes's legacy and memorials; Create the office of Tutor for Equality, Diversity and Inclusion (EDI); Develop a strategic plan for improving educational EDI; Fundraise for scholarships for students from Southern Africa; Arrange an annual lecture on a topic related to the Rhodes legacy, race, or colonialism; Institute an annual student prize for work on a topic related to Rhodes legacy, race, or colonialism; Provide additional training for all staff in race awareness; Introduce further outreach initiatives targeted at BME student recruitment'.
102 Michael Gove held the position of minister for housing, communities and local government until he was replaced by Labour Deputy Prime Minister Angela Rayner after the general election on 5 July 2024.
103 Hansard Vol. 255, column 1033 (12 August 1880).
104 Hicks and Mirzoeff, 2020.
105 Younge, 2021.
106 Dickinson, 1960 [1865].

107 The formulation of the idea of the Four As is originally Tim Ingold's (Ingold, 2013).
108 Mitchell, 2021: 105.
109 Bradley, 2023: 14.
110 Service, 1962: 161–3; see Bradley, 2001: 73–4.
111 Childe, 1950: 12; see discussions by Sherratt, 1990a and Bradley, 2023: 44–5.
112 Bradley, 2000.
113 See discussion by Trigger, 1990.
114 McFadyen, 2007; 2018.
115 Smithson, 1995 [1972]; 1966: 27; 1996 [1967]: 342, 345n66; Hicks, 2019a: 188; cf. Hicks, 2016a, 2019b.
116 See discussion in Hicks, 2021b; cf. Hicks 2021c.
117 Cf. Hicks 2021d.
118 Cf. Hicks 2023a, 2023b.
119 Gilroy, 2002; Mitscherlich and Mitscherlich, 1975 [1967].
120 Hall was employing loose translation from the opening sections of Antonio Gramsci's 1951 text *Passato e presente* [*Past and Present*], the famous passage titled 'Del sognare ad occhi aperti e del fantasticare' ['On daydreams and fantasies'], which ends with the phrase 'Pessimismo dell'intelligenza, ottimismo della volontà' ['Pessimism of the intelligence, optimism of the will']. The line in question runs: 'Occorre invece violentemente attirare l'attenzione nel presentecosì com'è, se si vuole trasformarlo' ['Instead, you must violently direct attention to the present as it is, if you wish to transform it'] (Gramsci 1951: 6, my translation).
121 Hall et al., 1987: 151.
122 McGranahan, 2017: 243.
123 Wynter, 1994a: 70.
124 Advice given, in a different form, by Michael Taussig (Taussig, 2017).

## I. THE RULE OF NAMES

1 Wells, 1901: 117.
2 Frost, 1947: 7.
3 'Un livre est un grand cimetière où sur la plupart des tombes on ne peut plus lire les noms effacés' (Proust, 1927: 59).
4 Cf. Wright (1952: 1–4).
5 McClintock, 1992; Dirlik, 1994: 343. On the other hand, Stuart Hall (Hall, 1996: 246) made the case in favour of the term, arguing, rather

unconvincingly, that the Gulf War of 1991 was 'a classic postcolonial event'. Hall's gradual swapping-out of his earlier Marxism for a kind of Derridean discourse analysis 'reaches a peak in this essay, the effects of which are interestingly debatable', as Gregor McLennan puts it (McLennan, 2021: 8).

6  See Jameson, 1991: xii.
7  Lambert et al., 2021.
8  Coates, 2015: 71.
9  Marx, 1887 [1867]: 167, 163.
10 Koram, 2022: 19.
11 Julien, 2017: 335, 341; cf. Lyde, 2019: 191.
12 Goody, 1976.
13 Lambert et al., 2021, 5–6.
14 Ahmed, 2004; 2006; 2021: 80.
15 Gould, 1981; 1983: 59.
16 Wynter, 1994a: 43.
17 'Cependant, il arrive parfois qu'au cours de ce procès, l'intégrité de la formule primitive s'altère. Alors cette formule dégénère ou progresse, comme on voudra, en deçà ou au delà du stade où les caractères distinctifs du mythe restent encore reconnaissables et où celui-ci conserve ce que, dans le langage des musiciens, on appellerait sa "carrure".' ['But it sometimes happens that in the course of this process, the integrity of the original formula is altered. This formula then degenerates or progresses, as you will, below or beyond the point where the distinctive features of the myth are still recognisable and where it retains what, in the language of musicians, we would call its "build" or "lilt".'] (Lévi-Strauss, 1971: 694, my translation; cf. Lévi-Strauss, 1974; see discussion by McKeon, 1981: 144–5.)
18 Serres, 2015 [1987]: 6.
19 Thomas Baker was killed on 21 July 1867, and the punitive expedition took place in August 1868. 'The murder of the Rev Mr Baker at Fiji', *The Standard* (10 November 1868), p. 6; 'Fiji', *Sydney Mail* (19 September 1868), p. 11.
20 Turner, 1884. A database of some of the collections made on the *Challenger* expedition is published at www.hmschallenger.net/.
21 Howse, 2009.
22 Ballard, 1985 [1974]: 5.
23 Wagner, 1981: xi.
24 O'Hanlon, 2007: xvii.

## NOTES TO SECTION I

25. David Binning Monro was the provost of Oriel College at the time. D. B. Monro to A. Pitt-Rivers, 1 March 1886 (Pitt-Rivers Papers, Salisbury and South Wiltshire Museum L220). Rhodes received his DCL in 1892, but only attended the ceremony to receive it in 1899.
26. Professor Edward Burnett Tylor (1832–1917), Henry Balfour (1863–1939).
27. Balfour, 1894: 455.
28. Layers 102 and 202 (Bedford, 2005).
29. 'Houses wrecked in London', *Daily Telegraph* (17 November 1928), p. 13.
30. 'Vergangenes historisch artikulieren heißt nicht, es erkennen "wie es denn eigentlich gewesen ist". Es heißt, sich einer Erinnerung bemächtigen, wie sie im Augenblick einer Gefahr aufblitzt' (Benjamin 1991 [1940]: 695.
31. Pitt Rivers Museum accession numbers 1884.24.84 and 1884.24.165 and also a quiver 1884.17.14, taken by Colonel Charles Napier North of the 60th Rifles. North (1817–1889) established and superintended the manufacture of Enfield rifle cartridges during the Indian rebellion (Hart, 1861: 329; Hart, 1866: 332), and published his journal account of the Indian rebellion in 1858 (North, 1858).
32. Pitt Rivers Museum accession number 1886.1.115.
33. Pitt Rivers Museum accession number 1891.13.1 (taken by Edward Samuel Hamersley).
34. Pitt Rivers Museum accession number 1917.53.256.
35. Pitt Rivers Museum accession number 1884.19.168.
36. Pitt Rivers Museum accession numbers 1908.26.1, 1908.27.1, 1915.15.8, 1917.25.29-32, 1921.15.3, 1930.67.4-7, 1966.1.15.
37. The trope of the human skull as inkstand has gone through various realities and myths (Harrison, 2008: 290). See Moorehead, 1971: 335; Harrison, 2012: 72-4; cf. 'Skulls for inkstands', *Edinburgh Evening News* (18 August 1883), p. 3.
38. Pitt Rivers Museum accession number 1905.81.5.
39. Pitt Rivers Museum accession numbers 1907.72.41-45, 1907.72.51-54.
40. Pitt Rivers Museum accession number 2010.4.1.
41. Pitt Rivers Museum accession number 1966.11.16.
42. Pitt Rivers Museum accession numbers 1990.60.7 and 1997.46.1.
43. See Balfour, 1901 on strangling cords; Balfour, 1925 on thorn-lined traps.
44. Fox's son William Augustus Lane Fox-Pitt (9 January 1858–17 March 1945) spent a career in the British Army, including active service in Sudan in 1885 and in Kitchener's campaign of 1899; Pitt Rivers Museum accession number 1884.74.31.

## NOTES TO SECTION I

45  Pitt Rivers Museum accession number 1886.1.371.
46  Pitt Rivers Museum accession number 1884.44.9.
47  Pitt Rivers Museum accession number 1906.80.1.
48  Pitt Rivers Museum accession number 1918.9.27.
49  Sweet, 2001; Shuttleworth, 1998; Ho, 2012.
50  Tylor, 1881: 224.
51  Trouillot, 1995: 142.
52  Elkins, 2015: 852. On the changing meaning of classification in the colonial museum see Richards, 1993.
53  Burke, 1824 [1757]: 122.
54  Penelope Lively in the 1989 Channel 4 Rear Window film *The Pitt Rivers Museum ... is Shut*, 05.18 minutes in, https://vimeo.com/112940758; Fenton, 1984: 39.
55  Wang, 2018. On the prison-industrial complex see Gilmore, 2021, 2022.
56  'Il faudrait d'abord étudier comment la colonisation travaille à déciviliser le colonisateur, à l'abrutir au sens propre du mot, à le dégrader, à le réveiller aux instincts enfouis, à la convoitise, à la violence, à la haine raciale, au relativisme moral' (Césaire, 1955 [1950]: 77; my translation).
57  Corsín Jiménez and Nahum-Claudel, 2019: 386.
58  Corsín Jiménez (2021: 123) also quotes a discussion by American anthropologist Otis Mason, where he described Native American hunting traditions as 'an invention for the purpose of inducing animals to commit incarceration, self arrest, or suicide' (Mason 1900).
59  De Genova, 2015; 2016: 49.
60  Fisher, 2009: 5.
61  Ursula Le Guin, 'Speech in Acceptance of the National Book Foundation Medal for Distinguished Contribution to American Letters' (19 November 2014), www.ursulakleguin.com/nbf-medal.
62  Orwell, 1949: 28.
63  Marx, 2010a [1857]: 463.
64  Fisher, 2009: 10.
65  Fisher (2009: 4) offers this as a definition of capitalism.
66  Compare this parafabulation with Michael Taussig's rather different account of what he called 'the colonial work of fabulation', in relation to the 'reciprocating fabulations' of 'magical realism' (Taussig, 1987: 94).
67  'There is no art among a shepherd people if it remains at peace. There is no art among an agricultural people if it remains at peace' (Ruskin, 1873 [1865]: 99–100, 102).
68  Malthus, 1803.

69 Darwin, 1859; Spencer, 1864: 444–5.
70 Huxley, 1894 [1893]: 82.
71 Fox, 1869a: 526–7.
72 Fox, 1875a: 304.
73 John Evans (1823–1908); Evans, 1872: 2–3.
74 '... a time arrived when bronze, in its turn, gave way to iron or steel, as being a superior metal for all cutting purposes; and which, as such, has remained in use up to the present day' (Evans, ibid.).
75 'Wenn ich Kultur höre ... entsichere ich meinen Browning' (Johst, 1933, Act I, scene i).
76 Zwicker, 2006: 95–6; Fuhrmeister 2001: 100.
77 Steward et al., 1961: 1044.
78 The brownstone was later converted into the Philip A. Rollins Mansion.
79 Kroeber, 1970: 11; Steward, et al., 1961: 1040. As Franz Boas, the German anthropologist who came to New York's Columbia University in 1896, later reflected, the aesthetic of German Romanticism and the ideals of the 1848 revolution, in the wake of which so many of the so-called '48ers' had emigrated to New York, was still 'a living force' in the German community in the city (Boas, 1938: 201).
80 Kroeber, 1970: 47; cf. Ryan Jobson's account of what he called the 'Boasian fix' (Jobson, 2020).
81 Kroeber's PhD was supervised by Franz Boas at Columbia.
82 James Clifford (2013: 107) takes up one side of this argument when he writes: 'Today one sometimes hears comments to the effect that Ishi was "captured" by the anthropologists, held "prisoner" in the museum. In literal terms this is unfair: Ishi was generously treated, had a job, spending money, and freedom of movement. The comments may, however, express a sense that the refugee was a prisoner of drastically limited options, a narrowed freedom created by colonial violence, with an inability to imagine alternatives.'
83 Clifford, 2013: 91.
84 'Horrible massacre of Indians', *Bradford Review* (17 March 1860), p. 7.
85 Hitchcock and Flowerday, 2020; for a first-hand account of the Three Knolls Massacre see Anderson, 1909: 71–81.
86 Clifford, 2013: 106.
87 See discussion by Starn, 2004. 'Ishi's' cremated remains were placed in a Pueblo jar in the Columbarium at Olivet Gardens of Cypress Lawn Memorial Park in Colma, San Francisco; his brain is buried in Redding Rancheria reservation.

88 'Ishi's Kin to Give Him Proper Burial', *SFGATE* (10 August 2000).
89 O'Dell, 2010.
90 University of California, 2020.
91 Le Guin, 1966; Kroeber, 1961. See also Stone and Gene-Rowe, 2021.
92 Yahi is a dialect of the Yana language. Kroeber, 1961: 126–8.
93 See discussion by Stone et al., 2021: 85ff.
94 Kroeber, 1959: 402.
95 Le Guin, 1996: 27.
96 Nelson, 2015: 1.
97 See Tehrani, 2015; Peters, 2015; Okuleye, 2015; Coleman, 2014.
98 My translation. 'Parfois au contraire on se souvient très bien du nom, mais sans savoir si quelque chose de l'être qui le porta survit dans ces pages' (Proust, 1927: 59).
99 Rothberg, 2019: 2.
100 Sharpe, 2023: notes 23, 25, 85 and 236.
101 Riley, 2019: 1.
102 'On a invoqué toutes sortes de croyances pour expliquer la prohibition si fréquente du nom des morts' [All sorts of beliefs have been put forward to explain the widespread prohibition on the names of the dead] (Lévi-Strauss, 1962: 261; my translation).

## II. THE FOLD

1 Benjamin, 1963 [1928]: 197.
2 Kroeber, 1970: 261.
3 The 1887 reforms had led to the opening of new Militär-Unterrealschulen [military academies], one of which was St Pölten. Rilke's father was an army officer, a period of his childhood that he later described as *'eine Fibel des Entsetzens'* ['a primer in horror'] (Kim, 1973: 30; see Rilke, 1927 [1902]).
4 Rilke, 1919.
5 The exact lines from Edison are: 'the gathering up and retaining of sounds hitherto fugitive, and their reproduction at will' and 'The captivity of all manner of sound-waves heretofore designated as "fugitive," and their permanent retention' (Edison, 1878: 527, 530).
6 The full epigram of Julianus (Book VII, number 32) translates as: 'Often I sung this and I will cry it from the tomb / Drink ere ye put on this garment of the dust' (Paton, 1917: 23; cf. Edwards, 1825: 269 (DLXXVIII)).
7 Barry, 1783; see J. D. Bennett, 2008.

8  Barry, 1793: 50. In the background is a naval pillar, added later in 1801 as a painted monument to Nelson's victory on the Nile, and holding the caduceus, the herald's wand that depicts two intertwined serpents.
9  Saunders, 1843: 365.
10 The previous Charing Cross Station is now Embankment Station.
11 Balfour, 1894: 455; my transposition.
12 Fox, 1876a: 471; see Fox et al., 1874; cf. British Association for the Advancement of Science, 1841.
13 Klemm, 1845–51.
14 'General Pitt-Rivers', *The Athenaeum* 3785 (12 May 1900), pp. 594–5.
15 'Acting upon the principle of reasoning from the known to the unknown I have commenced this catalogue' (Fox, 1877a: xiii); 'Passing now from the known to the unknown, we come to the study of prehistoric times, prepared to find that every fresh discovery helps us to trace backwards the arts of mankind in unbroken continuity towards their source' (Fox, 1868a: 403).
16 Fox, 1875b: 501–2.
17 Pitt Rivers papers M39, Salisbury and South Wiltshire Museum.
18 For a contemporary account of the game see for instance Mackay, 1867. The anthropologist Mary Douglas (1980: 24–5) describes Norbert Wiener similarly transposing Russian Scandal to images in Cambridge in the 1920s (although, in a slip that illustrates her point, she calls him Weiner) to show 'some of the perceptual processes that lead to a steady reproduction or to conventionalisation'.
19 Fox makes the same point about 'historical and non-historical' sciences. See Fox, 1875b: 499–500.
20 Pitt-Rivers, 2014 [1890].
21 The card in the archive records that nine participants took part in the parlour game. Their initials are recorded and indicate the experiment was conducted among eight various Lane-Foxes, Pitt-Riverses and Fox-Pitts, plus one non-family member, a 23-year-old named W. S. Tomkins who had recently joined Fox's staff as his professional archaeological draughtsman, painter and surveyor. Fox's teenage son Douglas went first, and is recorded as 'has drawn for ten years', and his wife Alice, recorded as 'AMPR, aged 55, learned to draw when young', is eighth on the list (Archives of the Natural History Museum, University of Oxford).
22 Fox, 1875b: 515; the coinage example was taken from Evans' paper 'On the Coinage of the Ancient Britons, and Natural Selection', read at the Royal Institution two weeks before Fox's own paper was (Evans, 1875).

## NOTES TO SECTION II

23 John Coleridge Patteson, who had been bishop of Melanesia from 1861, was killed in September 1871 on the island of Nukapu. There is a marble memorial to him in Merton College, Oxford. Fox's transposition of 'Patterson' for Patteson might be counted as another unintentional example of the phenomenon of copying that he was describing.
24 Fox, 1873a: 169–70.
25 Fox, 1868a: 436.
26 Balfour, 1893: 26–8. Balfour's training in animal morphology, and his lifelong interest in ornithology, is a significant part of the context here. The John White image is in the British Museum collections (accession number 1906.0509.1.7).
27 Pitt Rivers accession numbers 1884.71.24-25, 1884.74.31-32, 1884.75.31, 1884.76.4, 1884.82.46-50, 1884.82.62, 1884.82.64-65, 1884.82.73-75, 1884.84.24-27. See also 1884.5.53, 1884.5.55, 1884.140.635.
28 Grenfell, 1925: 65–6. See discussion by Harrison, 2008: 292–5, 299 and Harrison, 2012: 75–7.
29 Van Eynde, 2018: 296, 313–14.
30 Harrison, 2008: 287–8; i.e. Xhosa chief Sandile kaNgqika (c.1820–1878).
31 Harrison, ibid.
32 Lévi-Strauss, 1987 [1950]: 59.
33 Hall, 2021 [1997].
34 Gilroy, 2021: 1–2.
35 Valencia, 2018.
36 Bohrer, 2020.
37 Trouillot, 1991.
38 Carroll, 1865: 93.
39 Pitt-Rivers, 1889: 833.
40 Gould, 1981.
41 Fox, 1868b: xlix.
42 Pitt-Rivers, 1894, 1898; cf. Beddoe, 1881: 375; A. C. Haddon to A. H. L. F. Pitt-Rivers 7 June 1899, Pitt-Rivers Papers, Salisbury and South Wiltshire Museum.
43 Fox, 1875b: 504.
44 Pitt-Rivers, 1897: 336–8.
45 Rowse, 2017.
46 Hacking, 1990: 2.
47 Scott, 1998: 15, 77. See discussion by Rowse, 2017.
48 Scott, 1998: 24.
49 'Un masque n'est pas d'abord ce qu'il représente mais ce qu'il transforme, c'est-à-dire choisit de *ne pas* représenter' (Lévi-Strauss, 1975: 117).

50 Weber 1930: 181; see discussion of the various translations of Weber's *The Protestant Ethic and the Spirit of Capitalism* by Schögler 2025, 182.
51 Needham, 1979: 19.
52 Benjamin, 1991 [1940]: 697.
53 Honorary Doctor of Civil Law from Oxford University 1886; Fellow of the Royal Society 1876; Justice of the Peace. See Gray, 1905: xxxiv; 'Anniversary meeting', *Proceedings of the Royal Society* 25: 92; Chapman, 1981.
54 'War Office', *London Gazette* (19 September 1818), p. 1659; 'Yorkshire Hussar Yeomanry', *London Gazette* (22 November 1823), p. 1949.
55 Hart, 1866: 62.
56 'War Office', *London Gazette* (16 May 1845), p. 1472.
57 Thompson, 1977: 122; Gray, 1905: x; 'War Office', *London Gazette* (2 August 1850), p. 2132.
58 *London Gazette* (12 December 1854), p. 4052.
59 'War Office, Pall Mall', *London Gazette* (19 May 1857), p. 466; Bowden, 1991: 18.
60 'War Office, Pall Mall', *London Gazette* (26 February 1867), p. 1025; 'War Office, Pall Mall', *London Gazette* (28 February 1873), p. 1307.
61 *London Gazette* (2 October 1877), p. 5461.
62 *London Gazette* (14 November 1882), p. 5037.
63 'War Office, Pall Mall', *London Gazette* (11 April 1893), p. 2168.
64 George Hamilton-Gordon, the 4th Earl of Aberdeen (1784–1860), was a Peelite politician and prime minister from 1852 to 1855, during the Crimean War. His second wife was Harriet Douglas (1792–1833, m. 1815), who was the younger sister of Fox's mother Caroline. It was also her second marriage.
65 Fox's sister-in-law (Henrietta) Blanche Stanley (1830–1921), Countess of Airlie, was the grandmother of Clementine Hozier (1885–1977), who was Winston Churchill's wife from 1908 to his death in 1965. Fox died eight years before they married.
66 Hart, 1890: 230; 'Lady Grove's objection', *Daily Mirror* (11 February 1905), p. 4.
67 'Death of General Pitt Rivers', *Boston Spa News* (11 May 1900), p. 7.
68 On the biographical detail see also Foster, 1888: 1203; Haddon, 1900; Tylor, 1901; Gray, 1905; Penniman, 1946; Thompson, 1976; Chapman, 1981; Bradley, 1983; Bowden, 1991; Bowden, 2004.
69 'General Pitt-Rivers', *The Athenaeum* 3785 (12 May 1900), pp. 594–5.
70 Lorde, 1983 [1979]: 100–1.
71 White, 2019.

72  Gilmore, 2021: 70.
73  Fox, 1875a: 308.
74  Deleuze, 1988, 1991.
75  Tylor, 1871: 2. For Fox's use of the Leibniz term see for example, 'The law that Nature makes no jumps, can be taught by the history of mechanical contrivances, in such way as at least to make men cautious how they listen to scatter-brained revolutionary suggestions' (Pitt-Rivers, 1891: 116). His earliest use of the phrase appears to be from 1875, when in a lecture to the Whitechapel Foundation School he wrote: 'The Great Law of Nature *Natura non facit saltum* (Nature makes no jumps) is as applicable to the works of human art as to the succession of species and varieties of the animal and vegetable kingdom.' (Fox, 1875c; see Bowden, 1991: 74).
76  Deleuze, 1988: 148 (my translation).
77  'Death of Lieut.-General Pitt-Rivers', *Western Gazette* (11 May 1900), p. 7.
78  'The last 24 hours', *Bristol Mercury* (5 May 1900), p. 5.
79  The person who was the first quasi-legally person cremated at Woking was an artist named Jeannette Pickersgill.
80  Zaehnsdorf, 1880: 92.
81  Zaehnsdorf, ibid.
82  'Death of Mr Alfred Maltby', *Oxford Chronicle and Reading Gazette* (22 May 1914), p. 12.
83  'Funeral of Lieut.-General Pitt-Rivers', *Western Gazette* (18 May 1900), p. 7.
84  Hartman, 2008: 12. cf. Hartman, 2019.
85  Hartman, 2021: 127.
86  Trouillot, 1995: 26.
87  Hartman, 2008: 11.
88  Hartman, 2021: 129–30. See Beaudry, 2004; Hicks, 2004: 102.
89  Hartman, 2008: 12.
90  NourbeSe Philip, 2008: 201–2.
91  Hartman, 2022a: 759.
92  Beaudry borrows the use of the term 'unmarked' from Joseph Greenberg's *Language Universals* (1966) where he described 'the ambiguous nature of the unmarked term' – drawing in part from a classic study by Alfred Kroeber of 'classificatory systems of relationship' (Greenberg, 1966: 86; Kroeber, 1909; see Beaudry, 1980: 10).
93  Foucault, 2003 [1976]: 240.
94  Bergson, 1932: 111–15. See discussion by McClean, 2017: 38–9.

95 Haraway, 2016: 119–123, 213n4, n8.
96 Tsing, 2015: vii.
97 Deleuze, 1995 [1990]: 174.
98 My translation; the original reads: 'Le monument n'est pas ici ce qui commémore un passé, c'est un bloc de sensations présentes qui ne doivent qu'à elles-mêmes leur propre conservation, et donnent à l'événement le composé qui le célèbre. L'acte du monument n'est pas la mémoire, mais la fabulation'(Deleuze and Guattari, 1991: 158). See discussion by Wiame, 2018: 530–1.
99 Nietzsche, 1997 [1874]: 71.
100 McLean, 2017: 160.
101 Reilly, 2022: 59. See Perry and Challis, 2013, 277; cf. Challis, 2013.
102 Bertrand Russell was Baroness Henrietta Stanley's grandson, and had been brought up by her after his parents both died in 1874–5 one after another, when he was three years old, a fact that makes this testimony all the stronger. (Russell and Russell, 1937: 18; see discussion by Petch, 2012). Fox's mother-in-law was Henrietta Maria Stanley, Lady Stanley (née Dillon-Lee).
103 Le Guin is here following an argument made by Elizabeth Fisher (1980). Le Guin, 1988 [1986]: 166.
104 Le Guin, ibid: 167.
105 Le Guin, ibid: 169.
106 Papers of the Pitt-Rivers family. The text presented here is edited; for the full transcription see Petch, 2013.
107 Theweleit, 1987 [1978]: 233.
108 *Hamlet*, Act III, Scene ii.
109 Browne, 1658: i.
110 Taussig, 1984: 87.
111 Sir John Evans. See Evans, 1872.
112 Pitt-Rivers, 1887a: xviii.
113 Barrett et al., 1983.
114 Carroll, 1865: 123, 132.
115 'Accident on the Brighton Railway', *Illustrated London News* (9 January 1847), p. 23; 'Miraculous escape of the London and Brighton train', *Bell's Weekly Messenger* (8 January 1847), p 3. William Frederick Pitt-Rivers (1845–59, son of the 4th Lord Rivers) had been born at 13 Lewis Crescent, Kemptown, Brighton on 27 Nov 1845.
116 Erichsen, 1867.
117 Erichsen, 1867: 73–6; Gasquoine, 2020: 242.
118 Dercum, 1889: 654.

NOTES TO SECTION II AND SECTION III

119 Dercum, ibid. See discussion by Jones and Wessely, 2001: 1–16.
120 Dickinson, 1959; Rosevear et al., 2019; Robson, 1842: 927.
121 Thompson, 1977: 12.
122 Fox's uncle was George Lane Fox MP (1793–1848).
123 See Leach and Pevsner, 2009: 206.
124 The portrait of the horse may have been by George Hayter. See 'Destruction of Bramham Mansion', *The Times* (1 August 1828), p. 2.
125 'Destructive fire at Bramham-Park near Tadcaster', *Leeds Intelligencer* (31 July 1828), p. 3.
126 'Report – Hope Hall Bramham, Nr Leeds' (29 December 2008), https://web.archive.org/web/20200224074244/https://www.28dayslater.co.uk/threads/hope-hall-bramham-nr-leeds-29-12-08.35860/
127 I owe sincere thanks to Nick Lane Fox for hosting my visit in May 2022. On the house and gardens, see Leach and Pevsner, 2009: 211.
128 A framed survey by Fox held in the collections of Bramham Park, West Yorkshire.
129 Pitt Rivers Museum accession number 1884.140.331; cf. Sidney Hartland, 1893.
130 Ettlinger, 1943: 247–8; cf. Sidney Hartland, 1893.
131 Ballard 1985 [1974]: 5.

## III. THE UNSEEN HAND

1 Hartman, 2022b: xxix–xxx.
2 Hertz, 1960 [1907–1909]: 77, 82; Evans-Pritchard, 1940: 19–20.
3 Second day, Lot number 211, '*Catalogue of the important collection of arms and armour, formed by the late W. J. Bernhard Smith, Esq., consisting of European armour, helmets, swords, daggers, guns and pistols, maces and other furniture of war, offensive and defensive; Asiatic arms and armour of every description, from Persia, Turkey, India, &c. and a small selection of savage arms from Africa, South America, &c. which will be sold by auction at Messrs Sotheby, Wilkinson & Hodge Auctioneers of Literary Property and Works Illustrative of the Fine Arts at their house no. 13 Wellington Street, the Strand, W.C. on Tuesday the 13th day of May 1884, and the following day, at one o'clock precisely*' (Lugt Number 44022, auctioneer's sale catalogue at British Library).
4 British Museum accession numbers As1884,0411.5, As1884,0411.12.a, Af1884,0411.2, Af1884,0411.3.a, Af1884,0411.1.a.

## NOTES TO SECTION III

5   William John Bernhard Smith (1 May 1818–27 February 1881) of 3 Eaton Place, Belgrave Square; see 'Miscellaneous', *Notes and Queries* 6(3) (26 March 1881), p. 259.

6   Commander John Bernhard Smith, RN (1784–11 January 1844) also lived at 3 Eaton Place, Belgrave Square. 'Died', *The Times* (13 January 1844), p. 7. It's likely that he was buried at St George's Burial Ground on Bayswater Road, which was converted into allotments in the First World War and is now the site of a 1970s housing development. John Bernhard Smith's official Royal Navy biography records that 'We first find this officer serving as midshipman of the *Hercule* 74, being the flag of Rear-Admiral J. R. Dacres, on the Jamaica station; where, April 8th, 1805, being then in command of that ship's tender, the *Gracieuse*, mounting twelve guns, he captured a large Spanish schooner, full of passengers, from San Domingo bound to Puerto Rico; and, two days subsequently, drove on shore and destroyed, after a smart action, in which a brother-midshipman and two of his crew were wounded, a French national vessel of five guns, four swivels, and 96 men. He was made a lieutenant on the 8th Sept. 1808; and promoted to his present rank, Dec. 1st 1812' (Marshall, 1833: 90–1).

7   'British Channel Harbours Railway', *Morning Herald* (18 May 1836), p. 4.

8   'Notice', *London Gazette* (6 March 1829), p. 429; 'Obituary', *Gentleman's Magazine* (21 February 1844), p. 216.

9   William John Bernhard Smith's mother was Charlotte Jane Robertson (11 March 1790–16 April 1872), recorded along with her place of birth as a 'British subject' in the 1871 census, buried in Brompton Cemetery.

10  John Bernhard Smith (3 October 1739–28 August 1791), buried in Greenwich. One of the executors of the will is listed as 'General Sir Thomas Trigg[e] of 12th regiment of foot'. They possibly served in Gibraltar together. Trigge was commander-in-chief of the Windward and Leeward Islands, 1799–1802. One further potential clue to the skull-cup's history is that the 12th Regiment of Foot (Suffolk Regiment) served in the New Zealand Wars of the 1860s and Australia in the mid-1850s.

11  'GOETHE, Ottilie von (1796–1872). Collection of 51 autograph letters, mainly signed ('Ottilie von Goethe, Ottilie, Ihre alte Freundin Ottilie'), addressed to Samuel Naylor, Weimar, later Frankfurt, Leipzig and Vienna, 16/17 October 1830 to 23 April 1848', www.christies.com/en/lot/lot-3113442.

12  The entry for cannabis, for example, quotes Swinburne's *Hespera* – 'As a heart that it's anguish divine in / The green bud cloven' (Bernhard Smith, 1923: 8). William Arthur Hans Bernhard Smith (5 August

1867–24 January 1927) was thirteen years old when his father died, and seventeen years old when the skull-cup was sold at Sotheby's. See 'Obituaries: Dr Bernhard-Smith', *The Times* (31 January 1927), p. 15.
13 Patterson, 1982; cf. Bauman, 1992.
14 Hartman, 2008: 12.
15 Williams' 1938 doctoral thesis was published in 2014 (Williams, 2014 [1938]).
16 Williams, 1944; cf. Lester, 2022.
17 Reckford, 1968: 125.
18 Williams, 1944.
19 Nelson, 2009: 4.
20 'Some useful addresses', *Observer* (2 January 1983), p. 31.
21 Wright, 1985: 3.
22 See the description by Joseph Roach in *Cities of the Dead*, of elements of the past that exist 'not only as artifacts, such as cemeteries and commemorative landmarks, but as behaviours' (Roach, 1996: xi).
23 John Lubbock, Baron Avebury (1834–1913) and Lord John Russell, 1st Earl Russell (1792–1878).
24 'The Security Service: Personal (PF Series) Files. Right-Wing Extremists', p. 39 (99a, Extract from Home Office Files 862171/62 and 840766/8), National Archives KV 2/1364.
25 In 1885, the Wellington Statue was moved to Aldershot. 'Moving the Wellington Statue', *Illustrated London News* 82 (5 May 1883), p. 434.
26 https://historicengland.org.uk/research/results/reports/.
27 Thompson, 1960; National Archives Ancient Monuments Notebooks, WORK 39.
28 Saunders, 1981.
29 A marked shift in language had taken place: from salvaging to protecting. Even when it came to foreign antiquities, Fox wrote in 1882, 'the time has passed when antiquities should be regarded as trophies of war'. He wanted to see them as preserved, rather than looted. In a letter to *The Times* on 3 August 1882, sent while staying in the spa resort of Karlsbad, he said that the new connections of steam and railway lines meant that humanity – 'and British humanity in particular' – now travelled in such numbers that 'it is no longer necessary to hoard up valuable specimens of foreign antiquities in European museums': 'the time has passed', he wrote in a memorable phrase, 'when antiquities should be regarded as trophies of war'. The atmosphere of Egypt preserves antiquities like no other climate, he argued, 'and the time may come when subscriptions will be raised to take back obelisks and put them up again in their

proper places' away from the 'weathering and withering in smoke and damp' of European towns. Letter to the editor: 'Scientific exploration in Egypt (from Augustus Pitt-Rivers)', *The Times* (10 August 1882), p. 10. When the architectural commission was awarded for the Oxford Pitt Rivers Museum it was given to the man who'd been the first inspector of National Monuments for colonial Ireland – Sir Thomas Newenham Deane, who with Benjamin Woodward had also been one of the two architects for the 1860 University Museum. Rockley, 2008: 22.

30  The felicitous phrase 'doggedly bloodless' in this context was coined by Jonathan Meades.
31  Galton, 1869.
32  Pitt-Rivers, 1884a; Fox, 1875a: 297; cf. Beliso-De Jesús and Pierre, 2019.
33  Briggs, 2015: 118; Barthes, 2013 [2003].
34  'Death of Lord Rivers', *Sunday Times* (30 January 1831), p. 3.
35  'Death of Lord Rivers', *Cambridge Chronicle and Journal* (4 February 1831), p. 4
36  'Births, deaths, marriages and obituaries', *Jackson's Oxford Journal* (29 January 1831), p. 3.
37  'Melancholy death of Lord Rivers', *Standard* (27 January 1831), p. 2. Lord Rivers was buried on 5 February 1831 in Iwerne Steepleton, Dorset.
38  George Pitt, 2nd Baron Rivers (1751–1828) was the only son of George Pitt, the 1st Baron Rivers.
39  'Inquest on the body of the Right Hon. Horace Pitt, Lord Rivers', *Standard* (28 January 1831), p. 4.
40  'Miscellanea', *Sheffield Independent* (5 February 1831), p. 1 ; 'News', *Reading Mercury* (31 January 1831), p. 2.
41  'Lord Rivers' (letter to the editor), *The Age* (6 February 1831), p. 6; 'Lord Rivers', *The Cabinet Annual Register and Historical, Political, Biographical and Miscellaneous Chronicle for the Year 1831* (Vol. 1), London: H. Washbourne, pp. 412–13.
42  'Domestic miscellany', *Preston Chronicle* (5 February 1831), p. 2.
43  *Bury and Norwich Post* (2 February 1831), p. 4.
44  'Lord Rivers', *The Spectator* (5 February 1831), p. 129.
45  'Foreign', *Fayetteville Observer* (17 March 1831), p. 3.
46  'Police', *Sunday Times* (1 May 1831), p. 4.
47  'The Gleaner', *Ipswich Journal* (25 February 1837), p. 3; 'Lord Rivers' (letter to the editor), *The Age* (6 February 1831), p. 6. Two days later, a letter to the editor of the *Morning Post* from the club suggested that the loss was only £560. 'The late Lord Rivers' (letter to the editor), *Morning Post* (8 February 1831), p. 3.

## NOTES TO SECTION III

48 'Graham's Club', *Sunday Times* (26 February 1837), p. 2.
49 *Bell's Life in London and Sporting Chronicle* (6 February 1831), p. 2
50 'The Serpentine River', *Morning Chronicle* (23 May 1831), p. 3.
51 'Kensington Palace Queen Victoria statue sceptre taken by man with hammer', *The Mirror* (21 October 2019).
52 Durkheim, 1952 [1897]: 212–14.
53 Draper, 2010: 270.
54 Manjapra, 2019; Beckles, 2013.
55 Manjapra, 2019: 180.
56 Olusoga, 2018.
57 Sharpe 2016: 3.
58 'Lord Rivers', *Gentleman's Magazine* 101(1) (1831): 268–9. Frances Rigby (b. 1776), the third Baron's widow, lived at Rushmore until her death on 6 September 1860. Frances' maternal grandfather was Sir Thomas Rumbold, the governor of Madras. In 1835 and 1836, the 4th Baron Rivers was listed as holding Jamaican estates inherited from the 3rd Baron.
59 Peter Beckford of Stepleton (1740–1811). See also Hunter, 2018.
60 Garwood, 2003: 145–7.
61 The 2nd Earl of Harewood received £26,307 in compensation for the freeing of 1,277 enslaved people on the estates of Belle, Fortescues, Thicket and Mount St George in Barbados and Nightingale Grove and Williamsfield in Jamaica. 'Henry Lascelles', www.ucl.ac.uk/lbs/person/view/6180.
62 Born in Barbados into a family of the British plantocracy in 1740, in 1795 Edward Lascelles, 1st Earl of Harewood (1740–1820) inherited the sugar fortune of his childless cousin Edwin Lascelles, 1st Baron Harewood. Edwin had inherited from Caribbean estate-owner Henry Lascelles, who had taken his own life in 1753, and had rebuilt the family seat at Harewood. See Smith, 2006: 87; Finch, 2015: 197; Beckles, 2013: 125.
63 Floud, 2019.
64 The wife of Charles Henry Dillon-Lee, the 14th Viscount Dillon (1810–65) was Lydia Sophia Story, daughter of Lydia Baring (1786–1854), who in turn was the youngest daughter of Sir Francis Baring MP, 1st Baronet (1740–1810). See *UCL Legacies of Slavery Database*, www.ucl.ac.uk/lbs/person/view/25097. Today the house is home to the Ditchley Foundation, an organisation that describes itself as focused on 'renewing the US–UK relationship, of which Ditchley is the spiritual home', 'Ditchley Foundation: Our Purpose', www.ditchley.com/our-purpose.

65 Fox's maternal uncle Colonel Edward Gordon Douglas (1800–86) was married to Juliana Isabella Mary Dawkins-Pennant (1808–42), whose father was George Hay Dawkins-Pennant. Colonel Edward Gordon Douglas took the name Pennant in 1841, after his father's death the previous year, and was created Baron Penrhyn of Llandygái in 1866. After the death of his first wife, he married Maria Louisa FitzRoy (1818–1912), daughter of Henry Fitzroy, 5th Earl of Grafton (Lindsay, 2023, cf. Lindsay, 2004).

66 www.goldsboroughhall.com; https://vimeo.com/514216412.

67 The 6th Baron Rivers had married Eleanor Sutor in 1845, but they were separated in 1846, and there were no children.

68 'Obituary of eminent persons: Lord Rivers', *Illustrated London News* (6 April 1867), p. 22; 'Died', *John Bull* (23 March 1867), p. 16; 'Summary of this morning's news', *Pall Mall Gazette* (18 March 1867), p. 7.

69 'Rushmore', *Western Gazette* (22 March 1867), p. 8.

70 Biographers of Fox have suggested William died of tuberculosis like his father – but a letter from Dr John Roskilly (*c.* 1789–1864) in Naples in the Pitt Rivers Papers at Salisbury and South Wiltshire Museum advises that it was malaria (J. Roskilly to Fox, 10 June 1852). 'Died', *John Bull* (26 June 1852), p. 16. See Foster, 1891: 488; Thompson, 1977: 12–13.

71 'Torquay', *Morning Post* (16 February 1832), p. 3. 'William Augustus Lane Fox (1795–1832)', Taylor, 1865: 285 (note). When he was eighteen years old, Fox's grandfather James Fox-Lane had inherited the Bingley estate, an enormous portfolio of land and property in Yorkshire and Ireland. When James died in Florence in 1821 his estate at Bramham Park and a vast fortune and portfolio of estates in Yorkshire and Ireland passed to the eldest son, George Lane Fox – Fox's paternal uncle, the sporting squire and Tory MP who was responsible for that fire that gutted the manor house at Bramham. But the further sum of £300,000 from the Bingley estate was divided in a settlement between James' widow and the four younger children, Sackville Walter, Thomas Henry, Marcia Bridget and William Augustus (Fox's father). Separately, his widow Marcia received the £120,000 declared at probate, and when she died in London in the summer of the following year the inheritance to her five children included property with an annual return of £10,000 per year. Ward, 1970: 64. 'Fox Lane, James of Bramham Park, Yorks', History of Parliament, www.historyofparliamentonline.org/volume/1790-1820/member/fox-lane-james-1756-1821

72 The *Gentleman's Magazine* explained the threefold nature of this wealth: 'The present Lord Rivers, when he becomes of age, which will be shortly,

comes into the Pitt property, upwards of £40,000 a year, and the Beckford property (in the West Indies), a very considerable one; the Rigby estates, coming through his Lordship's mother, he does not yet touch.' 'Lord Rivers', *Gentleman's Magazine* 101(1) (March 1831): 268–9.
73. 'Friday night's gazette', *Hampshire Chronicle* (8 December 1828), p. 4.
74. James Fox-Lane (1756–1821) and his wife Marcia Lucy Pitt (1756–1822) were Fox's paternal grandparents. John Douglas (1756–1818) and Frances Lascelles (1762–1817) were his maternal grandparents (cf. Smith, 2006: 117–24). John Douglas was the son of James Douglas FRS, 14th Earl of Morton and president of the Royal Society, by his second marriage. James Douglas had sold off his Orkney and Shetland estates to Sir Lawrence Dundas, 1st Earl of Zetland, for £63,000 in 1766.
75. Fox's paternal grandfather James Fox-Lane had inherited the estate of his paternal uncle George Fox-Lane, 1st Baron Bingley, in 1773 (which included Bramham Park). He married Marcia Lucy Pitt in 1779. When Fox's great-uncle, the 2nd Baron Rivers, died in 1828, a provision in his will stated that the Rivers and the Bingley estates 'shall never rest in or belong to the same person', so long as there was male issue of at least two sons of his sister Marcia, Fox's grandmother (d. 1822). Since the majority of the Bingley fortune had gone down the line of her eldest son, George Lane Fox (d. 1848), the Pitt-Rivers estate passed to the second son, Fox's father William (d. 1832). 'Will of George, 2nd Lord Rivers', Dorset History Centre D-PIT/F/28–33. See discussion by Chapman, 1981: 295; Gray, 1905: x.
76. The barony of Rivers became extinct. 'Whitehall, 25 May 1880', *London Gazette* (4 June 1880), pp. 3326–7; 'Memoranda', *London Gazette* (22 June 1880), p. 3591.
77. Smith, 2006: 311–16.
78. Conversation quoted by Butler, 2002: 15. See discussion by Sharpe, 2016.
79. Higginson, 1937: 282.
80. Fox was the second son of his father William Fox, who was the second son of Marcia Fox.
81. Bowden, 1991: 36; Chapman, 1981: 295.
82. 'General Pitt-Rivers', *The Athenaeum* 3785 (12 May 1900), pp. 594–5. The idea of the inheritance being a total surprise is repeated by Gray (1905), who is perhaps also the author of the *Athenaeum* article.
83. Thompson, 1977.
84. Chapman, 1981: 295.
85. Bowden, 1991: 36.
86. Pitt-Rivers, 1887a: xi–xiii; see discussion by Bowden, 1991: 103.

NOTES TO SECTION III

87  The British envoy to whom Fox's elder brother was assistant was Sir William Temple (1788–1856), who left a major collection to the British Museum on his death. Fox had first proposed to Alice Stanley in 1849, but her wealthy and influential family had had concerns about his prospects. The death of his elder brother changed his circumstances. Her parents gave their consent and Alice and Fox were married on 3 February 1853. 'The Spectator marriages', *The Spectator* 1285 (12 February 1853), p. 159.
88  The eldest three sons of the 4th Baron Rivers and his wife Susan Georgiana Leveson-Gower were: George Horace Pitt (20 March 1834–20 December 1850), Granville Beckford Pitt (26 July 1838–20 August 1855) and William Frederick Pitt (21 October 1845–8 July 1859).
89  'I saw the eldest son carried out by a servant & put into a little carriage – he cannot walk at all & is not likely to live; they say the younger one is better than his brother, but I expect not much'. Edward John Stanley to Henrietta Maria Stanley, 2 November 1858, reproduced in Mitford, 1939: 191–2.
90  Fox's father William had retired from the army eleven years previously, and had been staying at Torquay to take the water and the air and recuperate. He was probably suffering from tuberculosis, but when he died on 11 February the newspapers described his illness as 'an abscess of the liver'. 'Torquay', *Morning Post* (16 February 1832), p. 3.
91  Sheppard, 1960.
92  Bruneau, 2020.
93  Pitt Rivers Papers, Pitt Rivers Museum Archives.
94  Among a hundred possible examples, see most recently Stourton, 2022: 82
95  Bowden and Green, 2017. William Chapman (1981: 11) similarly describes Fox as 'a recognized founding father of modern archaeology'. See discussions by C. Evans, 2005: 966; Dyson, 1994: 159.
96  Fox, 1878a: 1097; Spencer, 1873: 25, 32–4.
97  Spencer, 1885, 1896: 233.
98  Spencer, 1873: 34–5.
99  Fox, 1878a: 1098.
100 'Thoughts on hunting', *Monthly Review* 65 (September 1781), pp. 211–20.
101 Taylor, 1865: 390, note; see also Scarth Dixon, 1898: 44.
102 A plaster model of this diminutive equestrian sculpture by Joseph Boehm, which was exhibited at the Royal Academy in 1868, is in the collections of the Victoria and Albert Museum (accession number 1806–1892).

103 Fox 1876b: 359. On one of Pitt Rivers' shoots on Cranborne Chase, Fox reportedly found a flint arrowhead, stopped the shoot and made his guests search for stone tools (Bowden, 1991: 43). See also Rocher, 2020.
104 'Removal of railings Hyde Park 1940' (National Archives WORK 16/1710) shows what was removed and what wasn't. Thank you to Katrina Navickas for pointing this out on Twitter, before we all left the platform because of the algorithmically enhanced fascist reply-guys and Muskian bot-droogs.
105 See the discussion by Awcock, 2019.
106 'The Hyde Park disturbances', *Manchester Guardian* (25 July 1866), p. 3.
107 Fox gave up the role in Cork and returned to London from Ireland in December 1865, although he was back in Cork in February 1866 to prosecute the court-martials (Chapman, 1981: 186; Hamilton, 1874: 332, 423). Fox was living with his family from 1866 to 1873 at 10 Upper Phillimore Gardens, in West Kensington/Holland Park. The 1871 census shows Fox aged forty-three, Head of House at 10 Upper Phillimore Gardens, occupation: Colonel unattached. Wife (age forty-two) and eight children aged four to fifteen, a Mancunian governess named Lavinia Sutcliffe, housekeeper, cook, ladies' maid, parlour maid, house maid, and a nursing maid.
108 'The Hyde Park disturbances', *Manchester Guardian* (25 July 1866), p. 3.
109 'Metropolitan news', *Illustrated London News* (28 July 1866), p. 7.
110 'The disturbances in Hyde Park', *Manchester Guardian* (26 July 1866), p. 3; 'The Hyde Park disturbances', *Manchester Guardian* (25 July 1866), p. 3; 'News of the week', *The Spectator* (28 July 1866), p. 1.
111 'The storming of Hyde Park', *Bradford Observer* (26 July 1866), p. 4.
112 Marx, 2010b [1866]: 299; cf. Jones, 1985 (part of a series of pamphlets on Hyde Park published by the National Museum of Labour History in the 1980s).
113 Dover Wilson, 1932: xxvi.
114 Arnold, 1867: 48, 52.
115 Arnold, 1869: 37.
116 Kroeber and Kluckhohn, 1952: 151.
117 Hall, 1980: 6. Hall made this point about both Matthew Arnold's *Culture and Anarchy* and also F. R. Leavis' book *Mass Civilization and Minority Culture* (Leavis, 1933).
118 Arnold, 1869: 52–3.
119 Darwin, 1859: 382.
120 Fox, 1867a: 620.
121 Fox, 1867a: 615.
122 Fox, 1867a: 620ff.

123 Fox, 1867a: 619.
124 Fox, 1867a: 618; see discussion by Gallagher, 1980: 162.
125 NourbeSe Philip, 2008: 196.

## IV. NO HUMANS INVOLVED

1 Pitt-Rivers, 1895: 19.
2 Hodge, 1990: 202–3, 207–8.
3 'Miscellaneous', *Notes and Queries* 6(3) (12 March 1881), p. 220; 'Obituary', *The Times* (12 March 1881), p. 12.
4 Anon, 1879.
5 *Archaeological Journal* 13 (1856): 269. See also *Archaeological Journal* 13 (1856): 96, 188, 280; *Archaeological Journal* 14 (1857): 280–1.
6 Royal College of Physicians of London, 1860: 68 (item 296).
7 Tarlow, 2024.
8 Harrison, 2008: 294.
9 Draper, 2010: 125 (plate 8). The Sotheby's sale was 'Important Silver, Gold Boxes & Objects Of Vertu' (18 December 2007; lot 153). www.sothebys.com/en/auctions/ecatalogue/2007/important-silver-gold-boxes-objects-of-vertu-l07661/lot.153.html
10 My translation. The original reads: 'ma face de monnaie très usée brusquement redécouverte dans tes fouilles' (Césaire 2017 [1960]).
11 Bernhard Smith's address is given as 3 Eaton Place in Belgravia in letters to *The Times* of 10 December 1874 and 28 May 1879.
12 Balfour, 1897a.
13 Pitt Rivers Museum accession number 1896.11.1; Balfour, 1897a: 340–1.
14 Pitt Rivers Museum accession number 1884.140.984; see Busk, 1870a: 79n.
15 Pitt Rivers Museum accession numbers 1887.33.25, 1900.55.292 (South Australia); 1887.1.279.1, 1887.1.589 (China), 1890.34.2, 1927.10.40 (Tibet), and 1896.11.1 (India). See Balfour, 1897a.
16 Pitt Rivers Museum accession number 1887.1.279; see Busk, 1870a; Busk, 1870b; 'Drinking-cup in the Chinese Court formed of a human skull', *Illustrated London News* (1 November 1862), p. 18; 'The International Exhibition', *Daily News* (2 August 1862), p. 5; 'The Earl of Elgin's collection of works of art', *Manchester Times* (21 May 1864), p. 5. There is a potential link to the supposed 'Confucius' skull in the Pitt Rivers collection and Bernhard Smith, in that Hans Busk, the cousin of George Busk who wrote the 1870 paper on that object, was executor for Bernhard Smith's will in 1881. 'Wills and bequests', *Illustrated*

*London News* (9 July 1881), p. 20. Captain Hans Busk (1815–1882) also played a key role in the development of the Volunteers movement, and was the author of the standard text *The Rifle: And How to Use It* (Busk, 1858). On the 'Confucius' skull see Pearce, 2014.

17  The donor, Gibbes Rigaud (1820–1885), was a major in the 2nd Battalion, 60th Rifles. Pitt Rivers Museum accession number 1887.1.589.
18  'These cups out of which the priests of Buddha drink confusion to their enemies (this one was half full of samshoo, and probably a toast had shortly before been given to the "fat-faced barbarian, the Earl of Elgin and Kincardine"), are made as far as I could learn either out of the skulls of rebels of the highest order, or those of priests of such holy character as to obtain after death the title of "Living Saints". Whether this be the skull of a saint or a sinner, I must ask Dr Rolleston to determine, to whose care I suppose it may go' (quoted by Balfour, 1897a: 354).
19  Ballard, 1985 [1974]: 5.
20  Balfour, 1897b, 1897c.
21  Ruskin, 1905 [1870]: 84.
22  Browne, 1658: 17.
23  Harrison, 2008: 295.
24  Harrison, 2008: 290.
25  'The report of the Joint Committee on the Conduct of the War is described in outrages on our dead', *Boston Daily Advertiser* (1 May 1862), p. 1. Harrison, 2012: 95–6, 173.
26  The Governor-General in question was Sir Reginald Wingate (1861–1953), a former director of military intelligence for the British Army who replaced Kitchener in Sudan when he was transferred to South Africa in 1899. The *Schutztruppe* captain and plantation owner was Tom von Prince (1866–1914). Harrison, 2008: 291.
27  Hodge, 1990: 205.
28  Meier, 2017.
29  'The Golgotheans, or Charnel Club', *Morning Post* (7 November 1816), p. 2.
30  Lovell, 1966: 64–6; 'Place of ghosts', *Daily Telegraph* (21 February 1930), p. 13; 'From The Times of 1823', *The Times* (5 September 1923), p. 13.
31  Meier, 2017; 'Lord Byron's drinking cup', *Augusta Chronicle* (12 July 1828), p. 1; 'Some skull stories', *Newcastle Courant* (5 April 1890), p. 2; 'Letters and journals of Lord Byron; with notices of his life', *The Athenaeum* 117 (23 January 1830), pp. 34–6.
32  The purchaser was Captain (later Colonel) Thomas Wildman (1787–1859). Allen, 1874: 26; Moore, 1844: 87, note 3.

## NOTES TO SECTION IV

33 'Walks round Nottingham, no. VIII: Newstead Abbey', *Nottingham and Newark Mercury* (14 July 1827), p. 1. This account includes a sketch of the Byron skull-cup.
34 *Leicester Guardian* (7 July 1860), p. 3. Others account the Byron skull-cup as having been found beneath the floorboards in August 1900, and it was sold, it appears, at Puttick and Simpson auctioneers in November 1921 before the most recent sale.
35 The Wildmans had been involved in managing the financial affairs and Caribbean estates of William Beckford of Fonthill (1760–1844) from Beckford's childhood. Wildman's father Thomas Wildman MP was a lawyer, a partner in a solicitors at Lincoln's Inn, and from 1770 attorney, guardian and a member of the council appointed to manage the immense fortune inherited of Beckford, then just nine years old. His uncle, James Wildman (1747–1816), was overseer on the Jamaican estate for Beckford's absentee ownership. See the article 'Thomas Wildman' on the Twickenham Museum website, www.twickenham-museum.org.uk/detail.php?aid=268&ctid=1&cid=16.
36 Thomas Newenham Deane and Benjamin Woodward built the Tudor-Gothic quadrangle of Queen's College Cork as well as the Pitt Rivers Museum in Oxford. Cf. Eastlake, 1872: 703–4; White, 1962: 24; Prout, 1989.
37 Ruskin, 1905 [1870]: 41–2.
38 Eyre, 1845, Vol. 2: 311, 345 (Plate IV), 511.
39 Massola, 1961.
40 Heuman, 2008.
41 Hume, 1866. See discussion by Hall, 1996.
42 See Boa, 2002. The governor was Edward John Eyre (1815–1901).
43 See discussion by J. Evans, 2005: 133–4.
44 Wilmot, 2006: 227–8.
45 Hall, 1989.
46 *Report of the Jamaica Royal Commission 1866, Part I*, London: Eyre & Spottiswoode, pp. 11, 132.
47 Hume, 1867: 192–5. The baron was one of the first to be singled out and beaten to death by the protestors on 11 October.
48 Heuman (1994: 6–7) describes twenty-two members of Number 1 Company and eight members of Number 2 Company.
49 F. L. McClintock to Vice Admiral Sir James Hope, 8 November 1865, *Papers Relating to the Disturbances in Jamaica, Part I*, London: Harrison & Sons (1866), pp. 247–8.

50 Mill, 1873: 296. Paul Bogle himself underlined that the rebellion was not against the Queen, but was instead an ongoing struggle to assert the freedom gained through emancipation (Heuman, 1994: xvii; Hobsbawm, 1965: 119–20).
51 'Insurrection in Jamaica', *The Times* (3 November 1865), p. 10.
52 'The outbreak in Jamaica', *The Times* (13 November 1865), p. 9; 'The West India and Pacific Mails', *The Times* (17 November 1865), p. 6. See also Anon, 1866a.
53 Heuman, 1994; Fulweiler, 2000: 122. The role of the Maroons led by Colonel Alexander Gordon Fyfe has been discussed by Bilby, 2012 and Sheller, 2011. *Report of the Jamaica Royal Commission 1866, Part I*, p. 41; *Army and Navy Gazette* (16 December 1865).
54 Underhill, 1895: 50.
55 'Despatch from Governor Eyre, 20 October 1865', *Supplement to the London Gazette* (18 November 1865), pp. 5495–5502.
56 Hall, 2021 [1975]: 178.
57 The court martial court consisted of Lieutenant H. C. A. Brand RN (chair), Lieutenant A. J. Errington, RN and Ensign Kelly (4th West India Regiment). See *Report of the Jamaica Royal Commission 1866, Part I*.
58 Heuman, 1994; *Report of the Jamaica Royal Commission 1866, Part II: Minutes of Evidence and Appendix*, London: Eyre & Spottiswoode, pp. 1135–43.
59 F. L. McClintock to Vice Admiral Sir James Hope, 8 November 1865, *Papers Relating to the Disturbances in Jamaica, Part I*, London: Harrison & Sons, pp. 247–8; Heuman, 1994: 139.
60 *The Times* reported a bounty of $2,000 on the head of Paul Bogle. 'The outbreak in Jamaica', *The Times* (13 November 1865), p. 9.
61 Col T. Francis Hobbs to Major General O'Connor, 9 November 1865, *Copy of Extracts of Correspondence Between the Horse Guards and General O'Connor on the Conduct of Military Officers During the Recent Deplorable Occurrences in Jamaica*, 1867, London: House of Commons, pp. 22–3.
62 Semmel, 1962: 5.
63 'Art V: Report of the Jamaica Royal Commission', *British Quarterly Review* 44: 452–4 (p. 461).
64 Fox's uncle was Lord John Russell.
65 See discussion by Hall, 1992.
66 The governor was Edward John Eyre (1815–1901), formerly an explorer and sheep-drover in Australia and Lieutenant-Governor of

New Munster Province in New Zealand. Semmel, 1969: 120–6; Fulweiler, 2000: 125.

67 Cardwell to Eyre, January 1866, *Jamaica Disturbances: Papers Laid Before the Royal Commission of Inquiry by Governor Eyre, June 1866*.

68 E.g. 'Letter to the Editor from Reverend J. Radcliffe', *The Times* (18 November 1865), p. 6.

69 'The rebellion of Negroes comes very home to the national soul', *The Times* (18 November 1865), p. 8.

70 Hume, 1866: 7–8, 12.

71 Belich, 1986.

72 Major O'Connor to the Military Secretary, 24 October 1865. Reproduced in *Copy of Extracts of Correspondence Between the Horse Guards and General O'Connor on the Conduct of Military Officers During the Recent Deplorable Occurrences in Jamaica*, 1867, London: House of Commons, p. 8.

73 John Tyndall's comments are recorded in *Report of a Meeting of the Eyre Defence Committee held at Willis's Rooms*, reproduced as Appendix C of Hume, 1867. See Hume, 1867: 281, 283, and discussion by Semmel, 1962: 12–13.

74 Said, 1993: 130.

75 'Front Matter', *Transactions of the Anthropological Society of London* 1: xxiv–xxv.

76 The *Société d'anthropologie de Paris* was established in 1859 by pathologist-collector Paul Broca.

77 Stocking, 1987: 247.

78 Gantz, 1939: 183; Hunt, 1866: 20; see discussion by Flandreau, 2016: 19; 'The Anthropological Society', *The Times* (7 March 1863), p. 1.

79 Burton, 1865.

80 Keith, 1917: 20.

81 Chapman, 1981: 174; 'Front Matter Source', *Transactions of the Anthropological Society of London* 1: xxv.

82 Keith, 1917: 20; Clarke, 1868. Cf. Wallen, 2013. Fox to Tylor, 6 June 1879, Box 13 Tylor Papers, Pitt Rivers Museum Archives.

83 Wise, 1920: 98. Keith, 1917: 20–21; cf. Keith, 1919, 1924, 1927.

84 Stocking, 1987: 252.

85 Bertolini's was at 32 St Martin's Street, Leicester Square. See the account by Sir Edward Brabrook summarised by Rooksby, 1997: 115–17.

86 Wise, 1920: 96–9.

## NOTES TO SECTION IV

87 Farwell, 1962: 220–1; Gosse, 1921: 63; Royal Anthropological Institute Papers A60 (Fagg Papers): 1–5, Dining Club. See discussion at 'Dining Club. Sherry Club. Garden Party. Strawberry Teas (A60).
88 Swinburne, 2004 [1865]; see Wise, 1920: 96–9. Note that in 1874 Fox's niece Clementina Gertrude Helen Ogilvy (1854–1932) married Algernon Bertram Freeman-Mitford (1st Baron Redesdale), the cousin of the poet Algernon Charles Swinburne (1837–1909). The issue of that marriage included the future father of the Mitford sisters (David Bertram Ogilvy Freeman-Mitford, 2nd Baron Redesdale).
89 Cf. Sigel, 2002; Lutz, 2011.
90 See discussion by Malchow, 1996: 42.
91 On 31 May 1863, Burton reportedly wrote from Dahomey to Richard Monckton Milnes, 1st Baron Houghton that 'Poor Hankey must still wait for his peau de femme' (Lovell, 1998: 420). See Kabbani, 1986: 56; Bull, 2017: 237; Heilmann and Llewellyn, 2010: 140.
92 Chapman, 1989: 32–3; Flandreau, 2016: 54.
93 Gillian Tett (2021) claims that Fox was a member of the Cannibal Club, although the footnote leads only to Flandreau (2016: 49), who does not make this statement, so this seems to be incorrect.
94 Tylor, 1863.
95 Bischoff, 1863.
96 Anon, 1863a.
97 Guppy, 1864.
98 Anon, 1863b.
99 Lee, 1864.
100 Bouverie Pusey, 1864.
101 Beddoe, 1863.
102 Burton, 1864.
103 Dally and Beavan, 1864.
104 Anon, 1864.
105 'Anthropotomy' (review of 'Anatomy: Descriptive and Surgical'), *Anthropological Review* 2(6): 202–9.
106 Reddie, 1864.
107 Wyman, 1865.
108 Anon, 1865.
109 Anon, 1866b.
110 Jackson, 1867.
111 Anon, 1868.
112 Pike, 1868.

113 Walker, 1866.
114 Gibb, 1866.
115 Davis, 1868.
116 Beddoe, 1866.
117 Beddoe, 1870.
118 Barnard Davis, 1869.
119 Hunt, 1869.
120 Lee, 1864: xcv, xcviii.
121 Eyre, 1845, vol. 1: x.
122 Hume, 1866: 7–8, 14.
123 Evans, 2002: 196.
124 Hunt, 1866; Knox, 1850.
125 But see the commentary by Flandreau, 2016: 41ff.
126 The president of the Anthropological Society of London referred to here was the speech therapist James Hunt (1833–69). The protagonist for the Confederacy was a man named Hotze. Born in Zurich, Henry Hotze (1833–87) moved to Mobile, Alabama in 1849, becoming the editor of the *Mobile Register*. In the 1860s he was arguably the most significant propagandist for the Confederate States in Europe. See Bonner, 2005: 290; Burnett, 2008; S. Bennett, 2008; Oates, 1965.
127 Gobineau, 1856 [1853].
128 Henry Hotze to Judah P. Benjamin, Confederate Secretary of State (27 August 1863), *Official Records of the Union and Confederate Navies in the War of the Rebellion* 2(3), p. 878.
129 See Jameson, 1930.
130 Hunt, 1863a: 3, 6.
131 Hunt, 1863b.
132 Craft, 1864.
133 William Craft's comments at the British Association for the Advancement of Science in 1863 are reproduced in Ripley, 1985: 540–1. 'A long discussion arose after your President's paper', reported the editorial of the *Journal of the Anthropological Society of London*, 'during which, although much feeling was expressed, no scientific fact was elicited' (Carter Blake, 1864: iv).
134 Hunt, 1863a: xvi; see Huxley, 1863.
135 *Anti-Abolition Tracts* was published by a White Supremacist named John H. Van Evrie (1814–96). Hunt, 1864; published in the same year New York by Van Evrie, Horton & Co under the title *The Negro's Place in Nature: A Paper Read Before the London Anthropological Society by Dr James Hunt F.R.S. President of the Association*

136 Flandreau, 2016: 60n17.
137 Pim, 1866: 3–7; Napier, 1868: lix.
138 Pim, 1866: 50.
139 Stocking, 1987: 251.
140 Waitz 1863 [1859].
141 Hotze to Gobineau, 11 July 1856, reproduced in Burnett, 2008: 186–91.
142 Waitz, 1863 [1859]: 13.
143 Waitz, 1863 [1859]: 351. Waitz refers here specifically to the work of Samuel Morton in Philadelphia and Agassiz at Harvard.
144 Waitz, 1863 [1859]: 384–5.
145 Farrar, 1867: 119–20.
146 Bastian, 1881: 64.
147 Hotze, 1863; Bonner, 2005: 301.
148 Pitt Rivers Museum accession number 1966.11.16. This may be a reference to John H. Haughton, who was chief agricultural officer in the Crop Agronomy Division of the Department of Agriculture in Jamaica in the 1950s (Morton and Russell 1954: 262).
149 James Philip Mills (1890–1960); Pitt Rivers Museum accession number 1928.69.200.
150 Saunders, 2003: 183.
151 Herle, 1990: 60; Jacobs et al., 1990: 184.
152 Co-curated by anthropologists Anita Herle and Alan Macfarlane. Email from Bruno Latour to Dan Hicks, 18 May 2018. See Coote et al., 2000: 33, figure 30.
153 Latour, 1993: 69; cf. contributions to Hicks and Beaudry, 2010.
154 Latour, ibid.
155 Fukuyama, 1992.
156 See discussion by Hicks, 2010.
157 Marett, 1909: 76.
158 Hutton, 1921: 128.
159 Malinowski describes how sorcery 'becomes, when looked at from a great distance, and from an alien tribe, a non-human agency, endowed with such super-normal powers as changing of shape, invisibility, and a direct, infallible method of inflicting death' (Malinowski, 1922: 59).
160 Latour, 1999: 178.
161 Latour, 1999: 178–80.
162 Latour, 1999: 271.
163 Latour, 1999: 176; Heidegger, 1977.
164 Or the study of 'cultural techniques' in the work of Leroi-Gourhan.

165 Latour, 1999: 189.
166 Latour, 1999: 109.
167 Latour, 1999: 146–7, 308.
168 Latour, 1999: 199, 201, 289.
169 Latour, 1999: 198.
170 Latour, 1999: 209–11.
171 Latour, 1999: 211.
172 Latour, 1999: 214.
173 Latour, 1999: 15, 22–3, 192.
174 Latour, 1999: 277.
175 Shapin, 1998: 7. See Latour, 1990: 53, 76; cf. discussion by Kochan, 2015.
176 Latour, 1999: 299.
177 'There is only one nonmodern humanity – and in this sense, yes, I believe in a universalist anthropology' (Latour, 1999: 277).
178 Sharpe, 2010: 3.
179 1 Samuel 13:19–22 (King James Bible); Fox, 1868a: 400, 407.
180 In evidence given to the Royal Commission, James Cresser reported that he saw cutlasses being sharpened on a grindstone on 12 October. *Report of the Jamaica Royal Commission 1866, Part I*, p. 137.
181 My emphasis. Fox, 1868a: 407; for reporting of the Paul Bogle quotation see 'The insurrection in Jamaica', *Morning Post* (17 November 1865), p. 6; 'The Negro insurrection', *Daily Telegraph* (17 November 1865), p. 3.
182 *Report of the Jamaica Royal Commission 1866, Part II*, pp. 25–6, 77, 169, 252; *Report of the Jamaica Royal Commission 1866, Part I*, pp. 11–13.
183 Trouillot, 1991: 17.
184 Self, 1938: Appendix VIII, pp. 298–9; 'Kennington Common meeting', *Leeds Times* (15 April 1848), p. 6.
185 Higginson, 1916: 37–9.
186 'Kennington Common meeting', *Leeds Times* (15 April 1848), p. 6.
187 Ibid.
188 Cowtan, 1872: 147–54.
189 See Mansfield, 2016: 147.
190 Miller, 1974: 167–9.
191 Osborne, 2006.
192 Cowtan, 1872: 145–57.
193 'Grand siege operations at Chatham', *Illustrated London News* (19 August 1848), p. 112.

194 Gossman, 1983.
195 'The telegraphic news from Jamaica', *The Times* (4 November 1865), p. 9.
196 John Stuart Mill (1873: 298) wrote that it was clear that 'to bring English functionaries to the bar of a criminal court for abuses of power committed against negroes and mulattoes was not a popular proceeding with the English middle classes'.
197 The legal historian Rande Kostal has observed that 'now it had been established by a court of high authority that colonial legislatures had sovereign jurisdiction to pass laws which might legitimate even the worst excesses of martial law, and shield its worst offenders. It was also beyond dispute that a colonial legislature could prevent the victims from seeking recourse to justice in the mother country. British citizenship, in other words, was now officially divisible' (Kostal, 2008: 450).
198 Fulweiler, 2000: 119. After the failure of the 1866 Reform Bill, in the run-up to the Hyde Park Railings Affair which resulted from it, the Liberal government collapsed and on 25 June 1866 the Liberal prime minister – who had only come to office on 29 October of the previous year just as the facts of Morant Bay were coming to be understood – stepped down. As it happened this resignation was a family matter for Fox, as Prime Minister Lord Russell was his uncle – more precisely, on 8 November 1864 the sister of Fox's wife Alice, Katherine (Kate) Stanley (1842–74), married John Russell, Viscount Amberley (1842–76) – the first son of Lord Russell by his second marriage. At the time of the marriage Lord Russell was foreign secretary under Palmerston, and had been prime minister between 1846 and 1852, as well as variously secretary of state for war and the colonies, secretary of state for the colonies, and lord president of the council; he would be prime minister for the second time between October 1865 and June 1866. The children from the marriage (Fox's nephews and nieces) included the philosopher Bertrand Russell, who was raised by his grandparents (i.e. as if he were Fox's brother-in-law rather than his nephew) after the early death of his parents in the mid-1870s.
199 Hall, 2002: 421; cf. Hall, 1996, 2001.
200 Hall, 1994: 29.
201 Gopal, 2019: 111.
202 'The Jamaica insurrection' (letter to the editor), *Daily Telegraph* (20 December 1865), p. 5. Reproduced in Ruskin, 1905 [1865].
203 Agamben, 2005; Mbembe, 2019; Hicks, 2020b: 127; Wagner, 2018: 224; see discussion by Chatterjee, 1994.

204 Latour, 1999: 308.
205 Orwell's description of a German rifle with crosshairs seems best to fit the Gewehr 98 Mauser, which was the German service rifle from 1898 to 1935.
206 Cf. Guha, 1997: 492.
207 Orwell, 1968 [1930]: 20.
208 On the discussion of institutional racism at the 11th annual meeting of the African Studies Association in Los Angeles in October 1968 see Matthews et al., 1969: 25. See also Cohen et al., 1969; Baratz and Baratz, 1970; Murray, 1971; Carmichael and Hamilton, 1972; Massey et al., 1975.
209 Scarman, 1986: 28, 209.
210 Macpherson, 1999: 47, 52.
211 Hall, 1999a: 194–5.
212 Gilroy, 2012: 381.
213 Macpherson, 1999: 43.
214 Macpherson, 1999: 48.
215 Day and McBean, 2022: 56–7.
216 Macpherson, 1999: 375; Abolitionist Futures, 2021.
217 See for example Hall et al., 1978.
218 Wynter, 2003: 260.
219 Wynter, 1994b: 11; cf. Jackson, 2020; McKittrick and Wynter, 2015: 9.
220 Trouillot, 1995: 73–6.
221 Hall, 2021 [1981]: 107.
222 'Quand je cherche l'homme dans la technique et dans le style européens, je vois une succession de négations de l'homme, une avalanche de meurtres' (Fanon, 1961: 312; my translation).
223 See discussion by Wagner, 1972: 9
224 Hartman, 1997; Hartman, 2022a, 2002b.
225 Marx and Engels, 2010 [1850]: 512. They were adapting lines from 'The Peel Monument', *Red Republican* No. 9 (17 August 1850), p. 69., which had asked of the 'blue-coated bludgeoners': 'What need of any other monument, while these perambulating Peelers grace (?) the streets of the metropolis?'
226 'White men' (Feministkilljoys website, 4 Nov 2014), https://feministkilljoys.com/2014/11/04/white-men/.
227 Fox, 1867a: 619.
228 Fox, 1868a: 438.
229 Mercer and Julien, 1994: 137–8.
230 Wagner, 1986: 140.

## V. PANIC ATTACK

1. Libby, 1961; Rafter and Fergusson, 1957; Buchholz and Spalding, 2010.
2. Lorde, 1978.
3. Stokes, 1972 [1947]: 289–98.
4. Strachey, 1921: 325.
5. Albert, Prince Consort, 1862 [1850]: 110–12
6. Royal Commission for the Exhibition, 1851: 16.
7. Higginson, 1916: 53–4.
8. 'The Great Exhibition', *The Times* (30 April 1851), p. 5.
9. 'Military preparations for the Great Exhibition', *The Times* (30 April 1851), p. 5.
10. 'The Great Exhibition', *Morning Chronicle* (2 May 1851), p. 2.
11. Ibid.
12. Royal Commission for the Exhibition, 1851: 2.
13. Royal Commission for the Exhibition, 1852; Royal Commission for the Exhibition, 1851: 299.
14. Royal Commission for the Exhibition, 1851: 1.
15. 'America in Crystal', *Punch* 20 (24 May 1851), p. 209. See discussion by Flint, 2007: 172.
16. Fox to Tylor 9 January 1875, 'I mention this as you ... think as I do that my Anthropological contributions to Science alone do not afford my very weighty claim to recognition. Even tho you were kind enough to suggest to me to become a candidate for the Society. My School of Musketry work however was the result of many years hard work including experiments in connection with the small arms commission at Woolwich & Hythe and the translation of some of the official codes of foreign countries' (British Library Manuscript Collections Add 50254 f.84). See discussion by Evans, 2020: note 77.
17. *Royal Flash* (1975 movie, 20th Century Fox), 26:45 minutes in.
18. 'Experiments With Fire-Arms', *The Times* (11 September 1851), p. 7. The committee was chaired by Field Marshal Hardinge, who became a strong supporter of the young officer Fox. Hardinge had served in the Grenadier Guards from 1814 to 1827, and was a veteran of the Peninsular War, and had served as an MP in Durham and in Cornwall, as secretary at war and chief secretary for Ireland, and was governor-general of India under the East India Company from 1844 to 1848, before being created Viscount Hardinge of Lahore in 1846. After his return to London in 1848 he went on in 1852 to become master-general of ordnance and commander-in-chief of the forces during the Crimean War.

## NOTES TO SECTION V

19 'Naval and military', *John Bull* (27 July 1850), p. 7.
20 'Committee on Small Arms', *Birmingham Gazette* (22 May 1854), p. 1.
21 'Recollections of the Great Exhibition', *Raleigh Register* (21 January 1852), p. 2.
22 Fox, 1858: 454.
23 Army: Musketry Instruction (Question from Sir Charles Russell), Hansard Vol. 183, column 818 (11 May 1866); Hamilton, 1874: 153.
24 Fox, 1858: 468 (note); cf. Higginson, 1916: 45–7.
25 A powder-flask used by the Piedmontese Bersaglieri collected during this trip survives in the museum collections. Pitt Rivers Museum accession number 1884.28.16.
26 Pitt Rivers Museum accession number 1884.27.52.
27 Pitt Rivers Museum accession number 1884.27.72. Recorded in Fox's Catalogue of Arms of 1862 as '414. Breechloading Zundnadel le Mille brevété à Liege & bayonet'.
28 'United Service Institution', *Morning Post* (7 March 1853), p. 6.
29 'London', *Aris's Birmingham Gazette* (9 September 1850), p. 1.
30 'Model Firearms', *Sunday Times* (8 December 1850), p. 5.
31 Fox, 1858: 469.
32 Fox, 1858: 455; Pitt Rivers Museum accession numbers 1884.27.57, 1884.27.58 and 1884.27.66; cf. Fox, 1861a. See also Pitt Rivers Museum accession number 1884.27.65.
33 Pitt Rivers Museum accession number 1884.27.57.
34 Under Colonel Hay (Charles Crauford Hay, sometimes referred to as Charles Crawford Hay, later General Office Commanding-in-Chief, Cape of Good Hope.). See Hamilton, 1874: 153–4. See also Fosbery, 1869.
35 Their first child was still-born in their rooms in those blocks the following November.
36 'Military Intelligence: The Minié Rifle', *Colburn's United Service Magazine and Naval and Military Journal* 1853 (Part 2, July), p. 455.
37 Fox, 1873b.
38 Fox, 1854a: 27–9.
39 MacGregor, 1861: 474.
40 Edwards, 1860: 4.
41 Rolleston, 1874: 143.
42 Fox, 1858; cf. Fox, 1861b. There is also the possible existence of an undated paper by Fox titled 'Description of a Stadia for Judging Distance Practice, Proposed by Major Lane Fox, Grenadier Guards, Chief-Inspector of Musketry at Malta, Assisted by Captain Lutyens, 20th Regiment; Also a Statement of the Reasons Necessitating an Alteration in the Present

## NOTES TO SECTION V

Method of Ascertaining Distances'. It is referred to in the posthumous bibliography by Gray (1905: xxxvii), but research for this book has not identified an extant copy, nor details of how it was published, if it was, or in which archive it might survive. If it does exist, it would presumably have been written while he was serving in Hythe or Malta in 1853–57.

43 Latour, 1999: 179.
44 'fusees' here refers to a light musket or firelock.
45 'glacis' here refers to a break of slope.
46 James Lambourne, 'Travels of the 1st Bn Grenadier Guards by Sea and Land from England to Montreal, British North America Embarked from England the 19th of December 1861 and Disembarked the 7th February 1862 Written by a Soldier of the above Regiment', bound manuscript notebook, Templer Study Centre, National Army Museum (Accession Number 1970-10-8).
47 'Further arrival of our troops at Malta', *The Standard* (9 March 1854), p. 3; 'The Expeditionary Army at Malta', *Morning Post* (20 March 1854), p. 5.
48 'Paris, Brussels, Cologne, Bordeaux, Marseilles by the South-Eastern Railway', *The Times* (27 February 1854), p. 1; 'Preparations for war', *Morning Post* (23 February 1854), p. 5.
49 'Preparations for war', *Bristol Mercury* (25 February 1854), p. 4.
50 'Preparations for war', *John Bull* (6 March 1854), p. 142; 'Preparations for war', *Morning Post* (23 February 1854), pp. 5–6. On the journey time to Malta via Marseille see 'Preparations for war', *Sheffield Independent* (18 February 1854), p. 6.
51 'The preparations for war', *The Times* (20 February 1854), p. 9; 'Preparations for war', *Manchester Examiner and Times* (22 February 1854), p. 7; Preparations for war', *Bristol Mercury* (25 February 1854), p. 4.
52 Higginson, 1916: 94–5; 'The impending war', *Bath Chronicle* (23 March 1854), p. 1.
53 'The Expeditionary Army at Malta', *Morning Post* (20 March 1854), p. 5.
54 Higginson, 1916: 95–6.
55 W. J. Codrington to M. A. Codrington, 9 March 1854, Correspondence and Crimea War Papers of Sir W. J. Codrington (1804–88), Templer Study Centre, National Army Museum (reference 1968-07-375-1), p. 19; 'The Expeditionary Army for Turkey', *Morning Post* (14 April 1854), p. 5; 'The Expeditionary Army at Malta', *Morning Post* (20 March 1854), p. 5. Fox was staying at Dunsford's Hotel, Strada Froni. 'The Expeditionary Army at Malta', *Morning Post* (29 March 1854), p. 5.
56 'The preparations for war', *Morning Post* (23 February 1854), p. 5.

## NOTES TO SECTION V

57  Fox, 1854b.
58  'The Expeditionary Army at Malta', *Morning Post* (29 March 1854), p. 5.
59  'Royal Artillery', *Morning Post* (29 March 1854), p. 6.
60  A process in which the cartridge was torn open at one end, the powder poured down the barrel, the ball, still in the paper, placed into the bore, the loose cartridge paper that had contained the powder torn from the top, and the bullet rammed home, down onto the powder, before the hammer was half-cocked and the spent cap removed.
61  'Expeditionary Army in the East, from our Special Correspondent, Malta 11 April', *Morning Post* (19 April 1854), p. 5; Fox, 1854b.
62  Memorandum signed A. Lane Fox, First Instructor, School of Musketry, *Morning Post* (19 April 1854), p. 5; *Morning Chronicle* (19 April 1854), p. 3.
63  'The Enfield rifle', *Daily Telegraph* (23 April 1859), p. 5.
64  Harding, 1997: 257; see discussion by LeClair, 2015: 100–101.
65  'The Crimea expedition', *Illustrated London News* (23 September 1854), p. 19; 'From our Special Correspondent, Varna Bay Sept 4', *Morning Post* (21 September 1854), p. 6; 'Progress of the war: landing of the Allied troops in the Crimea', *The Examiner* (23 September 1854), p. 604.
66  A rigged scale model of HMS *Agamemnon* was donated to the Oxford Pitt Rivers Museum in 1940 (accession number 1940.2.1 B).
67  Lévi-Strauss, 1952: 157–8; the French distinction is between '*partial*' and '*partiel*'.
68  Strathern, 2005a: 39; Strathern was in dialogue with the classic statement about 'partial truths' in the *Writing Culture* project (Clifford, 1986).
69  'brächte ... aus allen seinen Rändern / aus wie ein Stern' (Rilke, 1955 [1908]).
70  Arendt, 1951.
71  Barthes, 1977 [1975]: 46, 114.
72  Nelson, 2015: 5–6.
73  Malinowski, 1922: 4.
74  Thompson, 1977: 122; W. J. Codrington to M. A. Codrington, 20 April 1854. Correspondence and Crimea War Papers of Sir W. J. Codrington (1804–88), Templer Study Centre, National Army Museum (reference 1968-07-375-1), p. 66; Hamilton, 1874: 166, 181; 'The war in the East', *Morning Post* (20 May 1854), p. 5; de Lacy Evans to General Yorke, 3 April 1855 (Pitt Rivers Papers, Salisbury and South Wiltshire Museum, A1a).
75  Evans, 1828.

76 Higginson, 1916: 111.
77 'The War in the East', *The Times* (15 September 1854), p. 5.
78 Calthorpe, 1856: 143.
79 Clifford, 1956: 50.
80 Calthorpe, 1856: 168; 'Letter from the Crimea', *Yorkshire Gazette* (14 October 1854), p. 7.
81 Adye, 1860: 42.
82 Mitra, 1921: 32.
83 Engels, 2010a [1857]: 18.
84 De Bazancourt, 1856: 261; cf. 'De Bazancourt's "Crimean Expedition"', *Spectator Supplement* (5 July 1856), p. 728.
85 'Editorial: soldiers' letters from the seat of war', *Coventry Herald* (20 October 1854), p. 2.
86 W. J. Codrington to M. A. Codrington, 9 March 1854, Correspondence and Crimea War Papers of Sir W. J. Codrington (1804–88), Templer Study Centre, National Army Museum (reference 1968-07-375-1).
87 'Letter from a medical officer', *Yorkshire Gazette* (14 October 1854), p. 7.
88 Colebrooke, 1856: 18–19.
89 'Another Warwick man on the Alma', *Coventry Herald* (20 October 1854), p. 2.
90 Clifford, 1956: 49–50.
91 Adye, 1860: 63.
92 Tyrrell, 1858: 255.
93 'The Crimea', *The Times* (11 October 1854), p. 7.
94 'Incidents of the Battle of Alma', *Coventry Herald* (20 October 1854), p. 2.
95 'From a private in the Black Watch', *Coventry Herald* (20 October 1854), p. 2.
96 W. J. Codrington to M. A. Codrington, 27 September 1854. Correspondence and Crimea War Papers of Sir W. J. Codrington (1804–88), Templer Study Centre, National Army Museum (reference 1968-07-375-1), p. 444.
97 A. H. L. Fox to A. M. L. Fox (undated, probably around 25 September 1854) 'Our men behaved manfully and their gallantry is only equalled by their humanity after the battle. I was surprised having heard of men committing all sorts of horrors, to see them just after the excitement of Battle talking so moderately and attentively to the wounded Russians, who did not understand it – many of the wounded men raised themselves up and shot our men in the backs after they had passed them ... A field of Battle is a horrid sight. I found one spot where every

man in the ranks must have been killed, 3 files, apparently by the same ball, lying side by side in the order they stood in the ranks.' Fox, 1977 [1854]: 135.

98  A report in the *Cork Examiner* dated 25 October that 'Captain Lane Fox has been brought down to Scutari wounded in the leg' must refer to Charles Lane Fox, rather than to Augustus who was already on his way home by that date. 'Foreign intelligence: the war in Crimea', *Cork Examiner* (10 November 1854), p. 3.

99  A. M. L. Fox to A. H. L. Fox, October 1854. Pitt-Rivers family archive at Hinton St Mary, number 33. See Thompson, 1976: 122, 144.

100  Johnny Stanley to Henrietta Maria Stanley, 9 November 1854, reproduced in Mitford, 1939: 93.

101  Signed by Prescott Hewitt and Richard Bright; Pitt-Rivers family archive at Hinton St Mary, number 36. See Thompson, 1976: 145. Dr Richard Bright (1789–1858) had been physician-extraordinary to Queen Victoria since 1837 (Berry, 2004).

102  'War Department', *London Gazette* (10 October 1854), p. 3059; 'War Department', *Edinburgh Gazette* (15 December 1854), p. 1187.

103  Royal Collection Trust RCIN 2800741, www.rct.uk/collection/2800741/men-of-the-grenadier-guards-wounded-in-the-crimea

104  See discussion by Benjamin 1991 [1940]: 697.

105  Pare, 2004: 224.

106  See Cooke, 1999: 17: 34; on the wider connections between archaeology and photography see also the contributions to Hicks and McFadyen, 2019; cf. Hodgkinson, 2021.

107  Slade, 1867: 275. See Dodman, 2018: 178–9; McCann, 1941; Rosen, 1975; Jones and Wessely, 1999.

108  Sayers, 1928: 425. See Lott, 2013: 103.

109  E.g. Maclean, 1864; Da Costa, 1871: 18. See Wooley, 2002; Jones, 2006: 533–4; Bourke, 2009: 69–71.

110  Myers, 1915; 'Hypnotism for shell-shock', *Daily Mail* (10 April 1915), p. 3.

111  Anon, 1917; 'Soldier's heart', *Daily Mail* (20 September 1917), p. 3.

112  Lewis, 1918.

113  Dercum, 1889: 654; see discussion by Jones and Wessely, 2001: 103.

114  Cooke, 1999. Cf. Jones and Wessely, 2006; Jones, 2006.

115  Handfield Jones, 1855: 461.

116  Handfield Jones, ibid.

117  See the discussion by Fletcher, 2014: 41ff.

118  Jones and Wessely, 2001: 91–2.

NOTES TO SECTION V AND SECTION VI

119 Lott, 2013: 116; cf. Elliot Smith and Pear, 1917: 2.
120 Freud, 1921 [1919].
121 'The history of Larmer Tree: interview with Lieut-General Pitt-Rivers', *Salisbury Times* (18 August 1899), p. 9.
122 'The Minié rifle', *Elgin Courant and Morayshire Advertiser* (27 October 1854), p. 4.
123 James Hunt (1833–69) was the uncle of William Halse Rivers Rivers (1864–1922).
124 Haddon, 1935.
125 Rivers, 1922: 256.
126 Bayliss-Smith, 2014: 203; Rivers, ibid.
127 Bayliss-Smith, 2014: 194, 210
128 Dolby, 1866: 35; *London Gazette* (2 March 1858), p. 1258; Hart, 1883: 535; 'War Department', *London Gazette* (10 October 1854), p. 3059; 'War Department', *Edinburgh Gazette* (15 December 1854), p. 1187.
129 Pitt Rivers Museum accession number 1884.27.47.
130 'Catalogue of Arms belonging to Lt Col A. Lane Fox. Gren Guards taken at Park Hill House Clapham 21st August 1862', Pitt-Rivers Papers, Pitt Rivers Museum.
131 For Gramsci's account of the 'war of position' see Gramsci, 2007 [1930–1931]: 109, 117, 162–64, 169, 267.

## VI. 'CHOC EN RETOUR'

1 Add.9455vol2_p29 /4, Pitt Rivers Catalogue (CUL) Vol. 2, p. 29; cf. Thompson and Renfrew, 1999.
2 Petch, 2010.
3 Foucault's fourth principle of heterotopias notes how the 'heterochrony' of the cemetery, in which there is a break with the conventional regimes of time-reckoning, is part of how museums and libraries have come to be structured as heterotopias, in a quite different manner to how these institutions functioned in the seventeenth century, in that now 'time never stops building up and topping its own summit', as time is constantly accumulated (Foucault (1984 [1967]: 26)).
4 'The history of Larmer Tree: interview with Lieut-General Pitt-Rivers', *Salisbury Times* (18 August 1899), p. 9.
5 Hilda Petrie to Amy Urlin, 17 September 1898. Drower, 1994: 627.
6 'General Pitt-Rivers', *Salisbury Times* (19 April 1890), p. 3; 'General Pitt-Rivers' Sunday band', *Western Gazette* (18 May 1900), p. 7.

7 Le Guin, 1980.
8 Le Guin, 1980: 199.
9 'The United Service Institution', *Illustrated London News* 97 (9 March 1844), p. 149. Marengo was captured at the Battle of Waterloo, brought back alive to London and sold to Captain John Julius William Angerstein, a horse breeder, captain in the Grenadier Guards and the son of John Julius Angerstein (a banker with business interests connected to Caribbean slavery, whose collection formed the basis of the National Gallery). In 2016 the horse's skeleton was put on permanent display at the National Army Museum in London. The horse's front hooves were turned into a silver snuff box and a silver inkwell, the latter of which is on display three miles away from the skeleton in Chelsea, at the Household Cavalry Museum in Whitehall.
10 The following March, the institution's annual report noted that it had received 28,000 visitors over the previous twelve months, and that the council 'strongly recommended the expediency of forming a collection of arms of all nations, offensive and defensive, including those of antiquity, as well as those of modern invention, and procuring models of military works, and of naval and military machines used in warfare in past and present times'. 'United Service Institution', *John Bull* (4 March 1844), p. 144.
11 'United Service Institution', *John Bull* (2 March 1850), p. 144; 'United Service Institution', *Morning Post* (7 March 1853), 6; Leetham and Sargeaunt, 1908: 181 (accession number 2673).
12 Fox, 1867a: 612.
13 Thornbury, 1876: 335.
14 'Russian expansionism may pose existential threat, says Nato general', *Guardian* (20 February 2015).
15 Strathern, 1999: 15; cf. Strathern, 2005b.
16 Pitt Rivers Museum accession number 1884.57.18. Fox, 1867b. The following week, at the Society of Antiquaries in London, Fox also exhibited two of a collection of eleven ivory peg-top-shaped objects found at Castletown Bearhaven, Bantry Bay (Fox, 1866). Just before Fox's talk, a collection of early guns from the Museum of Artillery at Woolwich was displayed by the brigadier-general responsible for that collection, John Henry Lefroy. The weapons from Woolwich were partly from the collection at the Tower of London, and also included one firearm from the Royal Collection at Windsor. See *Archaeological Journal* 24 (1867), pp. 70–1.
17 Unfinished and undated letter, probably dated 1866. Pitt Rivers Papers, Salisbury and South Wiltshire Museum, A8c. See Thompson, 1976: 4–5;

Thompson, 1977: 123; Chapman, 1981: 247. As Karl Marx put it in a letter in 1865, 'The Irish affair and the Jamaica butcheries were all that was needed after the American war to complete the unmasking of English hypocrisy!'(Marx, 2010c [1865]: 199). The officers were Drum Major James Butler and Sergeant Thomas Darragh of the 1st Battalion of the 2nd Queen's Royal Regiment of Foot. After his conviction for mutiny in April 1866, Darragh was sentenced to death, a punishment commuted to transportation to penal servitude in Western Australia, where in the same month Butler was found guilty of 'complicity with the Fenian conspiracy' and sentenced to penal servitude, but this was remitted due to lack of evidence and he was reduced to the rank of private. 'Ireland', *The Times* (9 April 1866), p. 9; 'Sentence on Drum-Major Butler', *Cork Examiner* (23 April 1866), p. 2. See Pitt-Rivers Papers SSWM A8a.

18 When Fox returned to London from Cork in December 1865, he took up the position of junior acting major of the 2nd Battalion of the Grenadier Guards, stationed at Buckingham Palace. While in Ireland Fox lived with his wife and their growing family at 7 Montenotte Road, Cork. His daughter Agnes and son Douglas were born at Montenotte Road on 25 July 1863 and 17 December 1864 respectively. See Pitt Rivers Papers, Salisbury and South Wiltshire Museum, B388; Bowden, 1991: 20–1; Thompson, 1977: 123; Schneller, 2009.

19 Froude, 1889: 308, 329–30, 335. See discussion by Burrow, 1978.

20 On arriving in Ireland, Fox joined the local archaeological and historical societies: the Royal Cork Institution, its subcommittee the 'Cuvierian Society of Cork' and the Kilkenny Archaeological Society. Richard Caulfield and Fox made measured surveys and undertook excavations at sites including the fifteenth-century towerhouse Kilcrea Castle to the west of Cork, the nearby coastal site of Ovens Caves, Carrigane, 'oratory' sites with early medieval *ogham* inscriptions on the Blasket Islands off the Dingle peninsula, and the prehistoric *rath* or fort at Lisnaran in County Louth. See Rockley, 2008: 149–152; Chapman, 1981: 95; Bowden, 1991: 60–4; Twohig, 1987: 35, 43; Caulfield, 1865; 'Cork Cuverian Society', *The Constitution* (6 May 1864); 'Cork Cuverian Society', *The Constitution* (10 May 1864); 'Antiquarian discoveries', *London Gazette* (14 July 1865), p. 2.

21 'We can consider the antiquary a geologist applying his method to reconstruct the first ages of mankind previous to all recollection, and to work out what may be called "pre-historic history"' (Caulfield, 1865: 710). 'Remains of the Aboriginal inhabitants of Ireland', *Gentleman's*

## NOTES TO SECTION VI

*Magazine* (June 1865), pp. 707–10; 'Cork Cuverian Society', *The Constitution* (6 May 1864); 'Arms No. 7', Templer Study Centre, National Army Museum (reference 1968-07-343).

22  Wilde, 1849: 40, 229, 238.

23  In 1874, when the British Association for the Advancement of Science met in Belfast, Wilde summarised his thoughts on 'The Early Races of Mankind in Ireland', where he described how he imagined a sequence of different characteristics – dark-skinned, 'swarthy' or fair-skinned, blonde, red or raven-haired, shorter or taller, round-headed or long-headed, and so on – matched onto a series of names he offered for successive groups, 'Lapps', 'Celts', 'Firbolgs', 'Dannans' and 'Tuatha-de-Dannans', 'Milesians', Danes and Vikings, and of course the arrival of the English and the Scots. Wilde sought to connect these groups to types of technology, monument or material culture: hunter-gathering, pastoralism, metal-working, building tumuli or building forts, and so on (Wilde, 1874).

24  As early as the 1820s, the Cork antiquarian William Hackett had sought to interpret burnt mounds as evidence of 'a similarity of habits' between Fenians and Native Americans as 'hunting people' (Rockley, 2008: 107–8).

25  Fox was put forward for fellowship of the Society of Antiquaries of London in October 1863 on the grounds of his 'attachment to the study of Antiquities especially ancient arms and armour', and was admitted to the fellowship on 2 June 1864. See Chapman, 1981: 113; Twohig, 1987: 40; Rockley, 2008: 64, 73–6.

26  Fox, 1868d, 1868e, 1869b, 1869c, 1871. Metropolitan Museum of Art accession number 1981.413; Pitt Rivers accession numbers 1884.117.28 and 1884.119.1.

27  Fox, 1867c: 125. See also Fox, 1870a, 1870b; House of Commons, 1867: 23.

28  'Science', *The Athenaeum* 2010 (5 May 1866), p. 601.

29  British Museum accession number 1866,0511.3. The other two *ogham* stones are in the British Museum stores (British Museum accession numbers 1866,0511.1 and 1866,0511.2); see Fox, 1867c; Pitt Rivers Papers, Salisbury and South Wiltshire Museum, P 2, 4, 6, 7 and 8.

30  'The Army', *Irish Times and Daily Advertiser* (18 August 1862), p. 2. It is likely that in December 1861 Fox had stopped over in Queenstown/Cork en route to Canada, as outlined above.

31  Tylor, 1901: 269.

## NOTES TO SECTION VI

32  Unknown to scholars until its donation by the great-grandson Anthony to Oxford's Pitt Rivers Museum in 2012. See http://web.prm.ox.ac.uk/rpr/index.php/article-index/12-articles/750-1862/index.html.
33  Fox and his servant are recorded alongside Major Grey (with wife, four children and two servants) and Colonel Edward Newdigate among others, arriving in Liverpool on 30 April. 'Passengers of *Niagara*', *Boston Daily Advertiser* (17 April 1862); 'America: arrival of the *Niagara*', *Liverpool Daily Post* (29 April 1862), p. 5.
34  Chapman, 1981: 107.
35  Evans 2013; for the Wimburn diary entries see https://sites.google.com/site/laurieletters/6-johns-diary-1861-1862/1862-04.
36  Hoole 1957: 14. Passes for a group of military observers and journalists including Russell of *The Times* were issued to accompany General George McClennan's advance into Virginia – but the denial of passes by Secretary Edwin Stanton was described by Vizetelly in *Illustrated London News*, 26 April 1862 (letter issued 11 April) XL: 409. Cf. Vizetelly, 1890: 91–2.
37  A site today commemorated by the Manassas National Battlefield Park which receives 900,000 visitors per year.
38  Bateman, 1861: xliii.
39  Pitt Rivers accession numbers 1884.21.4 and 1884.101.75.
40  Strachey, 1921: 297.
41  Victoria to Leopold I of Belgium, 24 December 1861; Victoria to Earl Canning, 10 January 1862. Reproduced in Benson and Esher, 1907: 605–6, 608.
42  When he took it to Victoria for her to sign he reportedly said that he could hardly lift his pen. Palmerston to Victoria, 30 November 1861; Victoria to Earl Russell, 1 December 1861. Reproduced in Benson and Esher, 1907: 595–8.
43  Mason and Slidell had travelled to Nassau in the Bahamas on 11 October on the privateer *Gordon*, and had boarded the *Trent* there; see Ferris, 1977.
44  Charles Wilkes, the captain of the USS *San Jacinto*, had been a committee member for the American exhibits at the Great Exhibition of 1851; see Cunliffe, 1951: 117.
45  'The American outrage', *Nottingham and Midland Counties Daily Express* (2 December 1861), p. 3.
46  After an apology by William H. Seward; see Biddulph, 1940: 112.
47  'Leader column', *The Times* (2 December 1861), p. 6. See also 'Leader column', *The Times* (30 November 1861), p. 8.
48  Hamilton, 1874: 321.

49 'Brevet', *London Gazette* (13 December 1861), p. 5374. At the end of the following week, the press was reporting Fox's promotion to lieutenant-colonel as one of a group of officers to be employed 'upon a particular service' in Canada: along with Col A. Law, Col C. F. Fordyce, H. R. Browne, H. H. Crealock, T. Ross, E. Newdigate, A. Naylor; see Evans, 2013. He probably stopped off for some time in Cobh, County Cork (then known as Queenstown) before arriving in Boston on the *Canada* on Saturday 11 January 1862. On arrival he was accompanied by Colonel Edward Newdigate and Charles Francis Fordyce (both veterans of the Crimea) and by his servant. 'Passengers', *Boston Daily Advertiser* (11 January 1862), p. 1. While en route with him across the Atlantic, Fox's younger comrade Assistant Quartermaster-General Garnet Wolseley wrote that 'My own private opinion is that we are on the verge of the greatest war which has taken place in our days', Wolseley to Biddulph, 10 December 1861, reproduced in Biddulph, 1940: 112–14.

50 'Overland from Halifax to Montreal', *Sheffield Independent* (31 January 1862), p. 1.

51 More than 11,000 soldiers were deployed directly by ship, while almost 7,000 men began a ten-day trek on foot and by sleigh in the snow after they had crossed the Atlantic – travelling the 300 miles across New Brunswick from St John to Rivière du Loup because the Saint Lawrence River was frozen, proceeding by rail to Quebec and Montréal.

52 Fox, 1858; cf. Fox, 1861b.

53 Fox, 1858: 474.

54 When returning from Malta in 1857, Fox and his family lodged with his parents-in-law at 40 Dover Street. Here, Alice's mother would regularly hold her influential political *réunions*, hosting Benjamin Disraeli, Thackeray, the Austrian ambassador, Queen Victoria's aunt the Duchess of Cambridge, and members of the Danish royal family among a galaxy of aristocrats, bankers, writers and politicians. Anthony Trollope was a regular attendee and fictionalised some of his experiences in his novels (Strachey, 1918; Bartnum, 1975; Thompson, 1977: 27, 123; Bowden, 1991: 18). Staying also at Fox's mother's house at 1 Chesham Street, Belgravia, by 1858 the family had moved into Park Hill House in Clapham where they lived until 1862. The 1861 census for Belgravia does not survive, but on 28 August 1859, 5 November 1860 and 11 January 1862, the dates of the birth of their next three children, Fox and Alice were living at Park Hill House in Clapham. See 'Births', *Caledonian Mercury* (1 September 1859), p. 3; 'Births', *Morning Post* (7 November 1860), p. 8; 'Births', *The Times* (13 January 1862), p. 1. The 1861 census shows

his mother Caroline Lane Fox (aged 64) lodging with Martha Anderson (aged 46) at 17 Belgrave Place in Brighton along with Elizabeth Gore and Emily Gore (aged 59 and 43, described as visitors), and domestic staff.

55 Many items were disposed of and a policy that rearranged the displays was based on the principle that 'every department should have a distinct object in view . . . and that each should be practical and methodological in arrangement'. See United Service Institution, 1858: 291–2. See also the Sotheby's sale on 24 July 1861, 'Ethnological and Miscellaneous Portion of the Museum of the Royal United Service Institution', documented by the Rethinking Pitt-Rivers project, https://web.prm.ox.ac.uk/rpr/index.php/article-index/12-articles/833-sothebys-sale-of-rusi-items-to-lane-fox-24-july-1861.html.

56 Klemm, 1858.

57 Miller, 2013: 263.

58 Speech by Disraeli, Motion for Papers, Commons Chamber, India: State of Affairs. Hansard Vol. 147, columns 474–5 (27 July 1857).

59 Fox arrived back in Malta on the *Vectis* with Captain Birnie on 30 April 1855. 'Naval and military intelligence', *The Times* (8 May 1855), p. 11; cf. Thompson, 1977: 26, 122; Chapman, 1981: 59. His return to Malta came with a letter of support from George de Lacy Evans that stated that Fox was 'an extremely zealous, hard-working and meticulous young officer': copy of a letter of support for Fox's adopting the role of an assistant on the General Staff rather than a deputy assistant from Sir de Lacy Evans to Major-General Charles Yorke (military secretary), 3 April 1855, Pitt-Rivers Papers, Salisbury and South Wiltshire Museum, A1a. Fox's eldest children, sons Alexander and St George, were born in Malta in November 1855 and September 1856.

60 Chapman, 1981: 57.

61 James Lindsay (commanding officer of the Grenadier Guards) to James Scarlett (adjutant-general), February 1861 (copy in Pitt Rivers Papers, Salisbury and South Wiltshire Museum, A1c); *Third Annual Report of the School of Musketry, for 1856–57* (October 1857), p. 15.

62 'India and China mails', *The Globe* (4 August 1857), p. 2; Edward John Stanley to Henrietta Maria Stanley, 5 August 1857; reproduced in Mitford, 1939: 152.

63 'The Mediterranean', *The Times* (5 August 1857), p. 5; 'East India and China mails', *The Standard* (5 August 1857), p. 5.

64 Marx, 2010d [1857]: 298; written on 30 June 1857 this text was first published in the *New-York Daily Tribune* (No. 5065) on 15 July 1857 as a leading article.

## NOTES TO SECTION VI

65 See David, 2006; Wagner, 2010: 24, 219; LeClair, 2015.
66 North, 1858: 94, 231–3.
67 Edward Stanley to Henrietta Maria Stanley, 10 August 1860, reproduced in Mitford, 1939: 152; Edward Stanley to Henrietta Maria Stanley, 2 September 1860, reproduced in Mitford, 1939: 154; cf. Bowden, 1991: 18.
68 Bowden, 1991: 19–20; Chapman, 1981: 105–6.
69 Statue of the muse Thalia, British Museum accession number 1805,0703.33. Baldwin et al., 2004: 145 (Plate 41); Victoria and Albert Museum accession number RPS.102-2019.
70 In 1883, Oxford University's *Gazette* recorded that he had begun this collection twenty-seven years earlier, i.e. 1856. 'The Pitt-Rivers Collection', *Oxford University Gazette* XII (444) (6 February 1883), pp. 295–6.
71 Undated (?1859) fragment; a draft lecture on rifle shooting (Pitt Rivers Museum Pitt-Rivers papers, Box 3/4/3), p. 2.
72 'The National Rifle Association', *The Times* (27 March 1860), p. 4.
73 Also known as the Thatched Cottage Tavern. See 'National Rifle Association', *The Times* (23 December 1859), p. 5. The man in the chair was the 10th Earl of Wemyss, known as Lord Elcho.
74 'Volunteer drill in public schools', *The Times* (20 February 1860), p. 12. For the important context of the 1860 Royal Commission on the Defence of Britain, and the investment in coastal defences that formed part of the context for Fox's surveys of coastal hillforts, see Royal Commission on the Defence of the United Kingdom 1860.
75 'The Great Rifle Shooting Contest', *Birmingham Daily Post* (3 July 1860), p. 4.
76 Engels, 2010b [1860]: 409.
77 'National Rifle Association', *Western Daily Press* (2 July 1860), p. 3.
78 'Army promotions and appointments', *Daily Telegraph* (8 July 1867), p. 3.
79 On 22 January 1867, Fox was promoted to the rank of lieutenant-colonel by purchase. 'Brevet', *London Gazette* 23223 (26 February 1867), p. 1025; see Chapman, 1981: 252; Thompson, 1977: 123; Gray, 1905: x; 'Army promotions and appointments', *Daily Telegraph* (8 July 1867), p. 3.
80 Fox, 1867a: 612.
81 'A subject for antiquaries', *The Times* (20 October 1866), p. 7; Thompson, 1977: 46; Bowden, 1991: 64; Chapman, 1981: 249.
82 But see Overend et al., 2020.
83 'Roman remains in Finsbury', *London Reader* 8 (2 February 1867), p. 316; Fox, 1867d, 1867e.

84 Fox, 1867d: lxxxii.
85 Fox, 1872; Pitt-Rivers, 1887a: xiii. Some of this salvage archaeology was carried out by Fox through the Exploration Committee of the Anthropological Institute.
86 Sebald, 2001: 182–8; cf. Wood, 2001: xxvi.
87 Pitt-Rivers, 1892: ix.
88 Pitt-Rivers, 1897: 339.
89 Pitt-Rivers, 1897: 336, 338.
90 A press cutting about Greenwell's earlier excavations, from *The Times* (20 June 1865), Pitt-Rivers Papers, Salisbury and South Wiltshire Museum P12 indicates that the general was perhaps aware of the canon's activities two years earlier (Thompson, 1977: 47).
91 'My very first lessons as an excavator were derived from Canon Greenwell, during his well-known and valuable exploration in the Yorkshire Wolds, in the course of which I obtained a large amount of useful experience that has been a constant source of enjoyment and interest to me ever since' (Pitt-Rivers, 1887a: xix).
92 Central among whom were Richard Colt Hoare and William Cunningham who 'opened' 379 barrows on Salisbury Plain (mainly on the estate land that Fox inherited in 1880). Colt Hoare published the results in his five-volume *The Ancient History of Wiltshire* (1810–21). Later there was Thomas Bateman's *Ten Years' Diggings* (Bateman, 1861).
93 Thurnam, 1865.
94 Pitt-Rivers, 1892: ix; Kinnes and Longworth, 1985.
95 'Dolichotaphic barrows, dolichocephalic crania; Brachytaphic barrows, brachycephalic crania', Thurnam, 1865: 158.
96 Greenwell, 1877: 544.
97 Greenwell, 1877.
98 Greenwell, 1877: 126–7.
99 Greenwell, 1877: 129.
100 Bonner, 2002.
101 Pitt-Rivers, 1892: 8.
102 Bowden, 1991: 67, Fox, 1868c, 1869d, 1869e.
103 Greenwell, 1877: 122, 631n; Thompson, 1977: 57; Bowden, 1991: 87–9; Pitt-Rivers, 1882.
104 Pitt-Rivers, 1892: xi.
105 Thompson, 1977: 123, Chapman, 1981: 284; Bowden, 1991: 71.
106 Pitt-Rivers, 1892: 8.
107 Pitt-Rivers, 1892: xii.

108 Technically Fox's last excavation was at Iwerne between September and December, 1897 (unpublished in his lifetime).
109 Colt Hoare, 1812: 242.
110 Pitt-Rivers, 1887a: xiii.
111 Chapman, 1981: 359.
112 In reference to the death of James Graham Goodenough from a poisoned arrow in the Santa Cruz Islands in August 1875 (Rolleston, 1875: 146).
113 Pitt-Rivers, 1892: 22.
114 Pitt-Rivers, 1887a: xiii; see Evans, 2020.
115 Fox, 1867d: lxxix–x.
116 Pitt-Rivers, 1892: xii.
117 Gomme, 1890: 103.
118 Pitt-Rivers, 1892: 306.
119 Pitt-Rivers, 1897.
120 Pitt Rivers Museum accession numbers 1884.27.48-51; 1884.28.41; 1884.24.70-76; 1884.24.81-82; 1884.28.40-41; 1884.32.17; 1884.58.120-121. The helmets are Pitt Rivers Museum accession numbers 1884.32.18 and 1884.32.19; a third Russian infantry helmet (1884.91.125) was destroyed by the museum in 1981.
121 These were all certainly acquired by Fox by 21 August 1862, and some were probably taken from the battlefield in 1854. Smooth-bore long guns/muskets: Pitt Rivers Museum accession numbers 1884.27.47-49, 1884.28.41; locks: Pitt Rivers Museum accession numbers 1884.27.50-51; bayonet: Pitt Rivers Museum accession number 1884.28.40; sabres: Pitt Rivers Museum accession numbers 1884.24.70-76; helmets: Pitt Rivers Museum accession numbers 1884.32.17-19.
122 Pitt-Rivers, 2014 [1890]: 138; Pitt-Rivers, 1891: 118.
123 In 1866, Fox observed how many of the ancient earthwork monuments in Munster that had been mapped in the first edition of the Ordnance Survey of Ireland had been destroyed in the previous generation – a loss which he attributed not to British colonial evictions but to the decline of 'curious myths and superstitions' that had kept these sites unchanged for centuries. Fox, 1867c: 138. In 1868, he joined a committee set up by the International Congress of Prehistoric Archaeology at Norwich to consider the protection of megalithic sites. Thompson, 1977: 59; Chapman, 1981: 296. The following year, he supported the campaign against the destruction of the Tol-Maen in Cornwall, and in 1870 he joined a campaign to restrict the agricultural cultivation of the archaeological site of Dorchester Dykes in Oxfordshire, where the ramparts of an Iron Age *oppidum* (hill-fort) were being ploughed out and levelled (Fox, 1870b).

124 Fox, 1868a: 437.
125 'The Gatling battery gun', *Illustrated London News* (23 March 1867), p. 32.
126 'The Paris Exhibition', *The Times* (22 June 1867), p. 6.
127 Fox, 1875b: 499.
128 Wallace, 1874.
129 Tylor, 1866: 83; Tylor, 1867: 87. The professor in question, Edward Burnett Tylor even gave a lecture, of which only the title survives, on the theme of 'Spiritualistic Philosophy of the Lower Races of Mankind'. See Freire-Marreco, 1907: 378; Stocking, 1971a: 90. Tylor collected 'spirit-photographs', including one that survives in the Pitt Rivers Museum, bought for one shilling at the Burn's Spiritual Institution at 15 Southampton Row in London's Bloomsbury, which claimed to show 'W. John Jones (in the Flesh) and Granddaughter (in the Spirit)'. Cf. Tylor, 1869; Stocking, 1871a; Schüttpelz, 2010.
130 Sometime in 1871 or 1872, Fox and his wife Alice, whose father had died in 1869, had attended a séance together at the house of Lady Harry Vane (Wilhelmina Powlett, Duchess of Cleveland). Tylor's account described how with the lights extinguished a spirit-light was conjured with phosphorus matches, leading Alice to consider the whole business a trick. Tylor Papers, PRM Archive Collections; Stocking, 1971a.
131 Fox, 1875b: 515.
132 'A spirit medium' (letter from Fox to the editor), *The Times* (22 September 1876), p. 10.
133 'Topics of the week: spiritualism at Glasgow', *The Graphic* (16 September 1876), p. 267.
134 'Colonel Lane Fox on psychological phenomena', *The Spiritualist* 9(8) (22 September 1876), pp. 88–9; 'The "Spiritualists" at logger-heads', *The Magnet Agricultural, Commercial and Family Gazette* (18 September 1876), p. 7. Cf. Doyle, 1926.
135 Pitt-Rivers, 1887a: xi–xiii; see discussion by Bowden, 1991: 103.
136 Stocking, 1971b; Darwin, 1871.
137 Fox 1875a: 296.
138 Don't talk of *Homo faber*, Latour tells us, but of *Homo fabricatus* – 'daughters and sons of their products and their works' (Latour, 2013: 230).
139 Fox, 1875b: 499.
140 Fox, ibid.
141 Müller, 1861.
142 Fox, 1875b: 500.
143 Fox, 1875a: 303.

144 Fox, 1875a: 308.
145 Fox, 1873a: 158.
146 Fox, ibid.
147 Fox, 1875b: 497.
148 Ginzburg, 1990: 117; Severi, 2017: 42; Voltaire, 1794.
149 Huxley, 1874a: 364–5.
150 Huxley, 1874b: 576.
151 Fox, 1875a: 296–7.
152 Darwin, 1859: 34ff.
153 Fox, 1875b: 504.
154 Huxley, 1865: 561.
155 Stocking, 1987: 200; Fox, 1875a: 298; Fox, 1875b: 499.
156 Fox, 1875b: 499.
157 Fox, 1868a: 402.
158 Fox, ibid.
159 Fox, ibid.
160 Fox, 1868a: 401–2.
161 Fox, 1875a: 296–7; Fox, 1875b: 500.
162 Fox, 1868a: 401.
163 Pitt-Rivers, 1887a: 22.
164 Hunt, 1863b.
165 Knox, 1850: 6.
166 Fox, 1875a: 297.
167 Fox, 1875c.
168 Fox, 1868a: 437.
169 Fox, 1867a: 615.
170 Fox, 1867a: 622.
171 Fox, 1867a: 615, 619.
172 Fox, 1875a: 308.
173 'The Zulu War', *The Times* (24 July 1879), p. 5. One of the British casualties of the 1879 war was Sackville FitzRoy Henry Lane-Fox of the Natal Native Contingent, the son of Fox's cousin Sackville Lane-Fox, the 12th Baron Conyers. In correspondence home he fantasised about how 'The Zulus ... will be shot down by the thousand, but after the first fight the fun will be over and the nasty work of hunting them in the bush will begin, as they will get such a lesson that they will not show their faces in the open' (Wade, 2011: 10).
174 Faulkner, 2021: 125.
175 Blackwood, 1970: 11. See Pitt Rivers Museum accession numbers 1912.35.1–13.

176  Ballard, 1973: 8.
177  See for example Koram, 2022; Woodman, 2020.
178  Fox, 1873a: 161.
179  Anon, 1873.
180  Césaire, 1972 [1950]: 35–6
181  Césaire, 1972 [1950]: 41.
182  This is the 1972 English translation by Joan Pinkham (Césaire 1972 [1950]: 36, 41); the French text reads: 'Et alors, un beau jour, la bourgeoisie est réveillée par un formidable choc en retour'; and 'C'est cette action, ce choc en retour de la colonisation qu'il importait de signaler.' (Césaire 1955 [1950]: 6, 11).
183  Rothberg, 2009: 36.
184  See discussion by Rothberg, 2009: 70.
185  The German translation reads: 'Und dann, eines schönen Tages, wird die Bourgeoisie durch einen gewaltigen Bumerangeinschlag aus dem Schlaf gerissen ... ', and 'Diese Rückwirkung, dieser Bumerangeffekt ist es, auf den aufmerksam zu machen wichtig ist ... ' by Herbert Becker (Césaire 2021 [1950]: 33, 43).
186  Arendt, 1951: 155, 503.
187  Another potential source of inspiration is the use of the metaphor of the boomerang by Ralph Ellison in the prologue to his 1952 novel *Invisible Man*, where he wrote: 'that ... is how the world moves: not like an arrow, but a boomerang (Beware of those who speak of the spiral of history; they are preparing a boomerang. Keep a steel helmet handy.)' (Ellison, 1952: 4).
188  Sartre, 1963; Fanon, 1961: 28.
189  'Réclamer et renier, tout à la fois, la condition humaine: la contradiction est explosive. Aussi bien explose-t-elle, vous le savez comme moi' (Fanon, 1961: 27–8; my translation).
190  Klein, 2007.
191  See discussion by Woodman, 2000.
192  Marx, 2010e [1852]: 103.
193  The actual line is 'Durch die Wiederholung wird das, was im Anfang nur als zufällig und möglich erschien, zu einem Wirklichen und Bestätigten', i.e. 'Through repetition what seemed at first to be simply accidental and possible becomes a reality and a truth' (Hegel 1848 [1837]: 381, my translation).
194  Marx, 2010f [1844]: 179; note that that the original German reads: 'Die Geschichte ist gründlich und macht viele Phasen durch, wenn sie eine alte Gestalt zu Grabe trägt', so the word rendered in English as 'figure' or 'form' is in the German 'Gestalt' (Marx 1956 [1844]: 382).

195 'Une autre espèce d'algue relevant, cette fois, de l'écologie sociale consiste en cette liberté de proliferation qui est laissée à des hommes comme Donald Trump' ['Another relevant species of alga, in this case in the field of social ecology, is seen in the freedom that is afforded to men like Donald Trump to proliferate'] (Guattari, 1989: 34, my translation).
196 'University intelligence', *The Times* (2 May 1891), p. 13.
197 See discussion by Petch, 2007.
198 Pitt Rivers accession number 2004.2.1.1.
199 Cf. Smart, 1973.
200 Deleuze, 1988: 148.
201 The brothers of Fox's mother Caroline included George Sholto Douglas, the 17th Earl of Morton (1789–1858) and Edward Gordon Douglas-Pennant, the 1st Baron Penrhyn (1800–1886). Both were Conservative politicians. Cf. Lindsay, 2004.
202 'Marriage in high life', *Morning Post* (4 February 1853), p. 5.
203 Penrhyn had been the estate of the Pennants, a family of Jamaican planters and Liverpool merchants into whom the Lascelles family had married through Caroline's grandmother. In the previous generation Penrhyn had passed from Richard Pennant MP (1737–1808), who owned more than 8,000 acres of plantations in Jamaica and more than 600 enslaved people, to cousins of the Pennants, the Dawkinses, another West Indian planter family, who took the name Pennant (Huxtable et al., 2020: 108–9). Then in 1840, Edward Gordon Douglas (Fox's maternal uncle) married Juliana Dawkins-Pennant, heiress to Penrhyn Castle and daughter of Jamaican planter George Hay Dawkins-Pennant. After his father-in-law died in 1840, Edward took the name Pennant through royal licence, and then in 1866 he was raised to the peerage as Baron Penrhyn, of Llandegai. In 1858 on the death of his brother, Edward Douglas-Pennant also became the 18th Earl of Morton.
204 Penny, 2006.
205 Lindsay, 2023; Haslam et al., 2009: 397.
206 'Penrhyn Castle and the Transatlantic Slave Trade', www.nationaltrust.org.uk/penrhyn-castle/features/penrhyn-castle-and-the-transatlantic-slave-trade.
207 'From Bedroom Window at Penrhyn Castle', dated 17 October 1859. Pencil on paper. Royal Collections Trust RCIN 980033.cw.
208 Lindsay, 2004.
209 'National Trust Penrhyn Castle', http://storyworksuk.com/National-Trust-Penrhyn-Castle.

210 Doyle, 1912; for the full novels and short stories see Doyle, 1969. Cf. Holterhoff, 2021.
211 Bowden, 1991: 7.
212 Doyle, 1929: 4.
213 Doyle, 1912: 309.
214 Doyle, 1929: 5.
215 Doyle, ibid.
216 Doyle, 1929: 22.
217 Doyle, ibid.
218 Doyle, ibid.
219 Deleuze and Guattari, 1987 [1980]: 40.
220 Hitchens, 2000: 3.
221 When it came to the end of its operations in 1969, the Jagersfontein mine (acquired by De Beers in 1930), which lies 130 km away from the Big Hole, was marginally larger. 'Big Hole loses claim to fame', *News 24* (20 May 2005), www.news24.com/News24/Big-Hole-loses-claim-to-fame-20050519.
222 Cecil Rhodes was the founder and a life governor of De Beers Consolidated Mines Limited from 1888.
223 Peddle, 1977.
224 Fox, 1875b: 520.
225 'Stella Edith Pitt-Rivers', *London Gazette* (22 July 1952), p. 3965. The deed poll change was enrolled in the Supreme Court of Judicature on 18 July 1952.
226 'Lord Forster's staff', *Daily Telegraph* (14 August 1920), p. 8.
227 'Severely injured' is the claim made by George Pitt Rivers in his entry for *Who's Who for 1965* (Pitt-Rivers, 1965).
228 Michael Pitt-Rivers (1917–99), George Pitt-Rivers' eldest son by his first marriage, married Sonia Brownell (1918–80), the second wife and widow of George Orwell in 1958; they divorced in 1965. In 1954 Michael had been famously put on trial for 'buggery'. He spent most of his life with his partner William Gronow-Davis.
229 Following her divorce from Bryan Guinness in 1932, on 6 October 1936 Fox's great-grand-niece Diana Freeman-Mitford (the granddaughter of his sister-in-law Henrietta Stanley and Lord Ogilvy, the 10th Earl of Airlie) became the second wife of Oswald Mosley in a ceremony conducted in the drawing room of Joseph Goebbels, with Adolf Hitler as a guest of honour.
230 From the entries for George Pitt Rivers in *Who's Who for 1944*, London: Adam & Charles Black, p. 2194, and *Who's Who for 1945*, London: Adam & Charles Black, p. 2431.

231 'Anthropologist leaves £676,000', *Reading Evening Post* (14 July 1966), p. 9; *Calendar of All Grants of Probate and Letters of Administration Made in the Probate Registers of the High Court of Justice in England for 1966*, London: HMSO, p. 231.
232 Pitt-Rivers, 1977a, 1977b.
233 Wright, 2021: 249. He was also 'a notoriously bad speaker', Patrick Wright continues, 'given to overheated rhetoric and rabble-rousing', with the ever-present feeling that the speech might 'suddenly collapse into a foaming harangue about the need to "Keep the Jews out of Dorset"' (Wright, 2021: 255–6).
234 Hart, 2015: 2.
235 George appears with the surname Fox-Pitt on the 1891 census, aged ten months, in the family house at 50 Ellison Road in Streatham, London. But by the 1901 census he is recorded as a boarder at Ascham House prep school, 18 Gervis Road, East Cliff, Bournemouth as George Pitt Rivers, aged ten. He appears as George Henry Lane Fox Pitt Rivers (no hyphen) on the record of his marriage in 1915, and published his first book in 1919 under the name George Pitt Rivers.
236 Hart, 2015: 20.
237 Pitt-Rivers, 1919: 76.
238 Pitt-Rivers, 1919: 18.
239 Fox-Pitt took tutorials in psychology from a eugenicist named William McDougall; see Hart, 2015: 32.
240 George Pitt-Rivers to the Eugenics Education Society, 29 April 1920 (George Pitt-Rivers Papers, Churchill Archives Centre, Cambridge 21/2); see Hart, 2015: 75.
241 Sacks, 2020.
242 See discussion by MacKellar and Hart, 2014: 654; Hart, 2015.
243 Presumably these are the items that Bradley Hart describes as being the subject of an acrimonious and unsuccessful attempt by George Pitt-Rivers to have them returned to him (Hart, 2015: 173). Pitt Rivers accession numbers 1998.276.105.1-17.
244 Pitt-Rivers, 1927.
245 Galton, 1869.
246 Letter from Mussolini to Luigi Villari, quoted in 'War: Defence Regulation 18B Detainees: Pitt-Rivers, George Henry Lane Fox, one-time member of The Link and the Fascist January Club', National Archives HO 45/25725: Home Office: Registered Papers, p. 222.

## VII. CULTURE WAR

1. D.D. stands for 'dono dedit'.
2. See discussion by Wright, 2021: 251ff. Fox-Pitt wrote to Mosley in 1935 to encourage him to renew his membership of his association. 'War: Defence Regulation 18B Detainees: Pitt-Rivers, George Henry Lane Fox, one-time member of The Link and the Fascist January Club', National Archives HO 45/25725: Home Office: Registered Papers, p. 223.
3. 'Recommendation for a restriction or detention order by the Secretary of State under the Defence Regulations or Aliens Order: Pitt-Rivers, George H. Lane Fox' (ref PF.45540/SL), 17 June 1940, p. 3. National Archives KV 2/834: The Security Service: Personal (PF Series) Files. Right-Wing Extremists, p. 165. Hart, 2015: 127 (Figure 6.1).
4. Hart, 2015: 130; George Pitt-Rivers to Adolf Hitler, 22 June 1938, George Pitt-Rivers papers, Churchill College, Cambridge, GPR 17/4.
5. Pitt-Rivers, 1924: 58; cf. Pitt-Rivers, 1927: 3–4; Pitt-Rivers, 1932: 108; Pitt-Rivers, 1938: 61.
6. Aspinal, 2022: 111, quoting 'Minutes of Proceedings at a meeting organised by the British Council Against European Commitments, 16 September 1938', Lymington papers, Hampshire Record Office, 15M84/F255/28.
7. *Western Gazette* (7 April 1939), p. 7.
8. Hart, 2015: 144.
9. Hart, 2015: 5–6. George Pitt-Rivers to Adolf Hitler, 22 June 1938, George Pitt-Rivers papers, Churchill College, Cambridge, GPR 17/4.
10. National Archives KV 2/834: The Security Service: Personal (PF Series) Files. Right-Wing Extremists, p. 103.
11. A close friend, a Nazi sympathiser and former director of naval intelligence and president of the Royal Naval College Greenwich, was staying at his manor house at the time, Admiral Barry Domvile (Hart 2015: 1)
12. 'MI5 objections to release from detention', 27 January 1941; letter from John P. L. Redfern to the Home Office, 29 January 1941, National Archives KV 2/831. Memoirs, File A–D, 1914–1946. George Pitt-Rivers Archive, Churchill College, Cambridge. See discussion by Hart, 2015: 159.
13. Hart, 2015: 149–50; Thomas, 2003: 19.
14. Pitt-Rivers, 1965.

## NOTES TO SECTION VII

15. Hart, 2015: 5, 165. George Pitt-Rivers to Director of Quartering, 17 November 1943, George Pitt-Rivers Papers, Churchill College, Cambridge, GPR 17/1.
16. Hoskins, 1955: 211.
17. Ahmed, 2021: 158.
18. Kassim, 2023: 136, 128.
19. 'Opening of the Blackmore Museum at Salisbury', *Salisbury and Winchester Journal* (7 September 1867), p. 6; Chapman, 1981: 342, 356; 'Exhibition of stone implements', *The Times* (22 November 1871), p. 5.
20. South Kensington Museum, 1873: 28, 31, 71, 86, 93.
21. 'The Bethnal Green Museum', *The Times* (22 June 1872), p. 5.
22. James, 1873: 69.
23. 'East London Museum', *Journal of the Society of Arts* 16: 581; 'Discussion (contribution by the Chair): Proceedings of the Society 26 April 1872', *Journal of the Society of Arts* 20: 484.
24. Pitt Rivers, 1891: 115.
25. Chapman, 1981: 153, 156, 373.
26. 'Brigade depots', *London Gazette* (28 February 1873), p. 1307.
27. 'Brigade field day', *South London Journal* (23 June 1877), p. 7; Fox, 1876c, 1877b.
28. 'Easter Monday Volunteer review', *York Herald* (11 April 1874), p. 15.
29. Fox, 1875b: 499.
30. Sir Edward Hulse, 6th Baronet (1859–1903); Pitt-Rivers, 2014 [1890]: 137.
31. Bowden, 1991: 149–52; 'General Pitt-Rivers', *Salisbury Times* (19 April 1890), p. 3; 'General Pitt-Rivers' Sunday band', *Western Gazette* (18 May 1900), p. 7; 'An experiment in recreation', *The Spectator* (15 September 1894), pp. 11–13.
32. Pitt-Rivers, 1892: 13, 306.
33. Tylor, 1874: 460.
34. Fox, 1877a: 1. Kate Stanley to Edward Lyulph Stanley, 14 February 1861, reproduced in Russell and Russell, 1937: 119–20; see Chapman, 1981: 160.
35. The third and fourth parts of the catalogue were never published.
36. 'The Principles of Classification', read at the Bethnal Green Museum, 1 July 1874. Anon, 1880.
37. Wilde, 1874: 118; Chapman, 1981: 127–8.
38. Cundall, 1890: 507.

39 When the collection opened in South Kensington it comprised 12,662 objects (Science and Art Department, 1880: 541, 552), on display, in Rooms L and K in the West Galleries belonging to the Commissioners of the Exhibition of 1851 at Queen's Gate, on the western side of the Horticultural Gardens. This gallery space had been previously occupied by Frederick Crace's loan collection of maps and prints of Old London (Burton, 1999: 124; Chapman, 1981: 417). A display of 'economic entomology' replaced Fox's displays at Bethnal Green (Science and Art Department, 1879: 558, 565). The Annual Report of the Science and Art Department for 1878 recorded that 'the ethnological collection lent by General Lane Fox to the Bethnal Green Museum for nearly five years has been moved to the Western Galleries, Queen's Gate. So many additions were made to the collection that it became too large for the space that could be given to it, and it was therefore moved to South Kensington. It is a most instructive and interesting collection, and can be well seen in the room now allocated to it' (Science and Art Department, 1879: 558).

40 An earlier idea, from 1877, to offer the collection as a civic display in Guildford had not gone ahead, in the absence of a county museum for Surrey. At a meeting on 14 March 1877 of the Surrey Archaeological Society, held 'in the School of Art Room at the Public Hall, Croydon', Granville Leveson-Gower (brother-in-law of the 4th Baron Rivers), who was chairing the meeting, reflected on the society's lack of a museum: 'A Society like theirs ought to possess a museum, and it was astonishing, if they once created a centre of that kind, how readily they would accumulate a number of interesting objects. Colonel Lane Fox had a large collection, which he offered to Guildford, but the people there did not exert themselves to obtain them, and they had gone to Bethnal-green; but if they had had a County Museum, Colonel Lane Fox would have given them the collection, which he was afraid they had now lost for ever' (Surrey Archaeological Society, 1880: xxxiii).

41 Pitt Rivers Papers, Salisbury and South Wiltshire Museum, B402-460; Chapman, 1981: 296–7.

42 Science and Art Department 1880: 552.

43 Fox to Richard A. Thompson (assistant director, South Kensington Museum), 14 April 1880, in House of Commons, 1881: 1–2.

44 Fox, 1878b; cf. Pitt-Rivers, 2014 [1890]: 138.

45 Tylor, 1881.

46 Chapman, 1984.

47 Fox to Richard A. Thompson (assistant director, South Kensington Museum), 14 April 1880, in House of Commons, 1881: 1–2.
48 Fox to Augustus Wollaston Franks, 1 July 1880; see Chapman, 1984: 194–5.
49 Chaired by Fox's future son-in-law John Lubbock, the membership comprised George Rolleston (Oxford University), Major-General Sir John Donnelly (Science and Art Department), Thomas Huxley (the Bulldog, Royal School of Mines), Sir Philip Cunliffe-Owen (South Kensington Museum), Sir Edward Poynter (Royal Academy) and Sir Augustus Wollaston Franks (British Museum). Report of the Committee appointed by the Lords of the Committee of Council on Education on the offer made by General Pitt Rivers with regard to his collection (House of Commons, 1881: 2–4).
50 'My Lords feel strongly the inexpediency of national museums competing against each other, and wish that, as far as possible, a distinct line should be drawn between the collections at South Kensington and those at the British Museum. Each should be made as perfect as possible, but should occupy different grounds': F. R. Sandford to Pitt-Rivers, 3 June 1881 (House of Commons, 1881: 4–5).
51 Fox to Richard A. Thompson (assistant director, South Kensington Museum), 14 April 1880, in House of Commons, 1881: 1–2.
52 Pitt-Rivers, 1889: 827.
53 'If you could give me the space I require with a life interest in the management of it I should be very glad but you cannot, and South Kensington can. If I cannot get more space at South Kensington to enable me to develop my museum on the plan I had developed hitherto the course I shall take will be this. I shall build a museum in or close to London about the size of the room I have at present. Keep the bulk of the collection in trays and drawers and exhibit only a few things in cases but I shall not have space available to continue the series and I shall make the museum valuable in other ways. I shall become a collector of ethnographic gems and when I die, I shall have received no encouragement to leave anything to the nation. If the nation will not accept my offer now on account of a rivalry between two departments I shall take good care it never gets anything from me. Science is cosmopolitan and I had rather leave everything to the United States': Fox to Augustus Wollaston Franks, 27 June 1880; see Chapman, 1984: 192–3.
54 *The Standard* (3 August 1881), p. 2; *Stamford Mercury* (5 August 1881), p. 3.

55 George Rolleston (1829–81). Fox had worked with Rolleston since the Canon Greenwell excavations in 1867. Fox attended the funeral in Oxford on 20 June. 'To him we are indebted for the only scientific description which exists of crania of the Stone Age in this country,' Fox wrote in his obituary for Rolleston: 'he will be remembered for his earnest love of truth' (Pitt-Rivers, 1882).

56 A Decree of the Convocation of the University on 7 March 1883 formally decided to accept the collection, and on 20 May 1884, the University Seal was added to the Deed of Gift and Declaration of Trust. The terms assigned to the Chancellor, Masters and Scholars of the University and their successors all those the several specimens, objects, articles and things forming the Anthropological Collection of the said Augustus Henry Lane Fox Pitt Rivers now or lately deposited and on exhibition at the department of Science and Art at South Kensington ... except that part of the Collection styled 'Collection of Agricultural Implements' and 'Peasant Collection and other Carvings'. 'VI: Affixing of Seal', *Oxford University Gazette* XIV (489) (13 May 1885), pp. 449–50.

57 Hicks, 2013; cf. Hicks, 2010.

58 Ten thousand pounds is the sum claimed by Pitt-Rivers to have been granted by the university in his September 1888 address to the British Association for the Advancement of Science at Bath (Pitt-Rivers, 1889: 826).

59 Deed of gift gifting the founding collection of the Pitt Rivers Museum to the University of Oxford. This is a transcription of Pitt-Rivers' deed of gift, a copy of which is held in the Pitt Rivers Museum's manuscript collections (Pitt Rivers Museum papers, Box 2: 20).

60 'The Pitt-Rivers Collection', *Oxford University Gazette* XII (444) (6 February 1883), pp. 295–6. The author was probably Henry Moseley, who had the previous month been requested by a Delegation of Council 'to give some explanation to Members of the University as to the value and importance of the Collection'. See 'The Pitt-Rivers Collection', *Oxford University Gazette* (5 December 1882), p. 181. Newspapers reported at the time that the only condition attached to Pitt-Rivers' offer was that a suitable building should be provided for the collection but there was also some commitment to the principles of display, specifically that 'The general mode of arrangement at present adopted in the said Collection shall be maintained, and no changes shall be made in details during the lifetime of the said Augustus Henry Lane Fox Pitt Rivers without his consent, and any changes in details which may be made after the death of the said Augustus Henry Lane Fox Pitt Rivers

shall be such only as shall be necessitated by the advance of knowledge and as shall not affect the general principle originated by the said Augustus Henry Lane Fox Pitt Rivers.' 'A rare collection of antiquities', *Kilkenny Moderator* (14 February 1883), p. 4.

61 The Annual Report of the Science and Art Department for 1879 recorded that Fox's loan comprised 14,860 objects occupying 7,200 square feet, an increase of 2,198 objects on the previous year (Science and Art Department 1880: 541, 552). Cf. Science and Art Department, 1874, 1877.

62 The original is held in the Victoria and Albert Museum archives. There are copies in the archives of the Pitt Rivers Museum ('Green Book') and in Salisbury and South Wiltshire Museum, Pitt-Rivers papers (P116).

63 The Annual Report of the Science and Art Department for 1880 stated that, 'As already mentioned considerable additional space has been assigned to the Anthropological Collection lent by General Lane Fox (now Pitt-Rivers). In the last report it was stated that this collection contained 14,860 objects. By additions made during 1880 it now contained 15,224 objects. It is at present in process of rearrangement' (Science and Art Department 1881: 504).

64 Chapman, 1984: 197.

65 In 1880, the RUSI Council decided to enlarge its library, and to maintain the collection of skulls and skeletons, but to 'give up the attempt to establish [an] ethnographical museum'. The Council of RUSI accepted two offers of purchases: one of £14 for their Burmese gong, and 'one of £40 from Major General Pitt Rivers for the other objects, with a view of their being ultimately deposited at South Kensington'; Report of the Council, *Journal of the Anthropological Institute* 10: 439.

66 The Annual Report of the Science and Art Department for 1883 recorded that 'The Pitt-Rivers Anthropological Collection remains on view in the western galleries. Several of the cases have been re-arranged and many labels added, but no other changes of importance have been made' (Science and Art Department 1884: 524). The following year, the Annual Report of the Science and Art Department for 1884 recorded that 'the Pitt-Rivers collection, which has been presented by the owner to the University of Oxford, has not yet been removed, and remains on display' (Science and Art Department 1885: 248).

67 'George Pitt-Rivers, 4th Baron Rivers', Centre for the Study of the Legacies of British Slavery, https://web.archive.org/web/20230131145950/https://www.ucl.ac.uk/lbs/person/view/23192.

68 'General Pitt-Rivers', *Salisbury Times* (19 April 1890), p. 3.

69  Thompson and Renfrew, 1999.
70  Fox-Pitt's two marriages, to Rachel Forster and then to his second cousin Rosalind Venetia Henley, were dissolved one after another in the 1930s. (Rosalind Venetia Henley's great-aunt Alice was the wife of Fox, and so George Pitt-Rivers' grandmother; see Hart, 2015: 70–1). Although they never married, Stella Lonsdale (also known other the other surnames listed in this chapter) changed her name by deed poll to Stella Pitt-Rivers. Stella Clive (as she was born) had been engaged to Nicholas Sidoroff, and married in Monte Carlo in 1936 in a ceremony that was later declared invalid (Tremain, 2021: 27). In 1939, she married John Christopher Mainwaring Lonsdale, who had been one of the perpetrators of the violent so-called Mayfair Playboy Affair of 1937. Clive changed her name by deed poll in 1952 (Tremain, 2021: 305). When the relationship with George cooled, Stella remarried in 1963, taking the surname of her new husband Raoul R. F. Maumen, and relocating to a vineyard in Provence named 'Stelladoux' – soon after which Maumen was found dead in the bath. Tremain (ibid.) reviews the evidence suggesting that Stella may have been responsible for Maumen's death. Matthew Sweet has written of Stella that: 'There's a strong chance that she killed her last husband by injecting him with floor polish. Certainly getting too close to her could be hazardous' (Sweet, 2011).
71  Stella Clive (born 9 January 1913) grew up at 42 Lyndon Road, Olton; John Enoch Powell, meanwhile (born 16 June 1912), was born on Flaxley Lane, Stechford, four miles to the north, and grew up at 52 Woodlands Park Road, Bournville, seven miles to the west. Clive was educated at the King's High School for Girls, Warwick and Powell at King Edward's Edgbaston, although in the research for this book I have not come across any evidence that they ever met.
72  Saunders, 2014. The Pitt-Rivers papers were also deposited at the Salisbury and South Wiltshire Museum, with further archival material later being donated by the family to the universities of Oxford and Cambridge.
73  See for example the account of a sale of antiquities by Stella in: 'Envoy's papers sold for £33,000', *Financial Times* (25 July 1978), p. 6.
74  'Talking about salerooms', *Country Life* 158(4082) (25 September 1975), pp. 746–7.
75  'Shrunken head sold despite protests', *The Guardian* (27 November 1979), p. 3. The publicly deposited Pitt-Rivers papers do not record which far-right organisations may have been endowed with these vast proceeds in the 1950s, 60s and 70s.

76 The statue is now to be found on the lawn of Salisbury and South Wiltshire Museum.
77 Gray, 1905: xxxiv; Thompson, 1977: 76.
78 Wor Barrow and two bowl barrows on Handley Down (1020066), National Heritage List for England, Historic England, https://historicengland.org.uk/listing/the-list/list-entry/1020066.
79 Hardy made this observation in the preface to the 1912 edition of *Far from the Madding Crowd* (Hardy, 1912: vii).
80 Hardy, 1913 [1885]: 185–6.
81 Fox, 1875a: 300.
82 In May 1888, Fox became ruling councillor of the Handley Habilitaton of the Primrose League. 'The Primrose League', *Morning Post* (9 May 1888), p. 2. On the Liberty and Property Defence League, see Bristow, 1975.
83 Bowden, 1991: 40–2; Salisbury and South Wiltshire Museum, Pitt Rivers Papers, M37a; 3. 'Handley: Primrose League gathering', *Dorset County Chronicle* (17 May 1888).
84 Pitt-Rivers, 1884b.
85 Spencer, 1896: 565–71.
86 Pitt-Rivers, 2014 [1890]: 137.
87 Bateman, 1883: 381; cf. Bateman, 1876: 164; 'General Pitt-Rivers: version for the BBC' (Bradford University Special Collections, Jacquetta Hawkes Papers Folder 4/18), p. 2.
88 Engels, 2010c [1860]: 85.
89 Axelson, 1970. See discussions by Strathern, 1992; Wynter, 1995: 37.
90 Engels, 2010d [1860]: 137.
91 'Fine Arts: Achilles', *The European Magazine and London Review* 82 (July–December 1822), pp. 161–3. See de Smaele, 2016.
92 'Public funeral of the late Field Marshal Arthur, Duke of Wellington, K.G.', *London Gazette* (6 December 1852), pp. 3551–3.
93 In 1798 Westmacott married Dorothy Margaret Wilkinson (1777–1834), daughter of Dr William Wilkinson (born in South Cowton, North Yorkshire in 1754) whose connections to Caribbean society and inherited wealth require further research.
94 Bryant, 2016.
95 Gray and Thom, 2022.
96 Dresser, 2007; 'Barbados removes Nelson statue in break with colonial past', *Reuters* (17 November 2020).
97 In his 'Rede zur Eröffnung der Großen Deutschen Kunstausstellung', Hitler stated that 'Die heutige neue Zeit arbeitet an einem neuen Menschentyp' (Schuster, 1987: 250).

98 'Monde compartimenté, manichéiste, immobile, monde de statues: la statue du général qui a fait la conquête, la statue de l'ingénieur qui a construit le pont. Monde sûr de lui, écrasant de ses pierres les échines écorchées par le fouet. Voilà le monde colonial.' (Fanon, 1961: 53; my translation).

99 'Chaque statue ... tous ces conquistadors juchés sur le sol colonial n'arrêtent pas de signifier une seule et même chose: "Nous sommes ici par la force des baïonnettes."' (Fanon, 1961: 81; my translation).

100 Pitt Rivers accession number 1884.31.12; see Ffoulkes, 1912: 201.

101 Advertising circular from Merwin and Bray, circa 1862, sold by Swann Auction galleries Americana sale, 26 September 2019 (lot 41), https://catalogue.swanngalleries.com/Lots/auction-lot/(CIVIL-WAR)-Smiths-Patent-(Applied-for)-Bullet-Proof-Vest-fo?saleno=2517&lotNo=41&refNo=759987.

102 'The soldier's bullet proof vest', *Frank Leslie's Illustrated Newspaper* (15 March 1862), p. 15.

103 Jünger, 1922, 1925.

104 Tester, 1998: 26.

105 Wright, 2000: 24.

106 30 Launceston Place, known until 1883 as Sussex Place. (For the discussion by Hal Foster see Foster, 1991).

107 'London', *Daily Telegraph* (5 May 1898), p. 8.

108 'Lord Salisbury on coming wars', *Western Gazette* (6 May 1898), p. 8.

109 '10,000 hear Mosley defend British fascism at rally', *New York Herald* (23 April 1934), p. 1.

110 Conrad, 1911: 304.

111 Cf. Wagner, 1972: 9.

112 'Public notice explaining the Arrangement of the collection that was formerly on display' (see Petch, 2007: 107, figure 8).

113 Lévi-Strauss, 1952: 12.

114 Eco, 1995.

115 Wolfe, 1999: 48.

116 McKittrick, 2021: 3.

117 Hartman, 1997: 206.

118 Quoted by Julien, 2017: 343; Hall, 1987: 16 cf. Tuck and Yang, 2012.

119 Castle Hill House Project (St Peter's College, Oxford), www.spc.ox.ac.uk/alumni/support-st-peters/castle-hill-house-project.

120 'The University of Oxford's relationship with the Sackler family – statement' (Bodleian Libraries), www.bodleian.ox.ac.uk/about/media/university-oxford-relationship-sackler-family-statement. 'Rhodes professorship of

race relations renamed', *The Oxford Student*, (12 January 2024); 'Cecil Rhodes professorship dropped by King's College London after row over slavery links', *Independent* (10 January 2022).

121 'Oxford should not accept money that is tainted by fascism', *The Spectator* (27 November 2021).
122 Imperial College London, 2021: 11. The report also considered Imperial's commemorations of the Beit brothers and Julius Wernher, men who made their fortunes alongside Rhodes.
123 Hall et al., 1987: 151.
124 Semple Kerr, 1999: 19; cf. Clark, 2001a.
125 Clark, 2001b: 12.
126 Cossons, 2001: 7.
127 Arts Council England, 1999; see discussion by Ashley and Stone, 2023.
128 Hall, 1999b.
129 Arokiasamy, 2023: 39.
130 Sagger, Philips and Haque, 2021. Since 2018 the Provost of Oriel College has been Neil Mendoza, who has also since May 2020 been the UK government's Commissioner for Cultural Recovery and Renewal.
131 Finley, 1976.
132 George William Neville (1852–1929), chief agent at Lagos of the African Steamship Company from 1880 to 1899, and later director of the Bank of British West Africa.
133 Hicks, 2020b: 240, 248.
134 Edwards, 2024; cf. Renfrew and Robbins, 1990.
135 The suggestion is made by Jane Renfrew and Michael Robbins in their article on the monument (Renfrew and Robbins, 1990: 419).
136 The sequence of locations described here follows that given by Renfrew and Robbins, 1990: 423n31. In his judgement on the memorial, David Hodge (2022: 9) claimed that 'it is thought that the memorial was originally installed the memorial's current location', but offers no evidence to back up this assertion.
137 Arthur Gray (1852–1940) was master of Jesus College, Cambridge from 1912 to 1940. This short story was published in 1919 (Gray, 1919).
138 Crockford, 2021: 7.
139 'Ties that bind', *The Economist* 434 (8 February 2020), p. 24.
140 Hodge, 2022: 61.
141 Scruton Lectures, 2022 – 'Deconstructing Decolonisation' (26 October 2022), www.youtube.com/watch?v=rOc5KOfa_OE. See also Biggar and Stokes, 2021; cf. Hicks and Mallet, 2019.
142 Marx, 1961 [1855]: 322, my translation.

143 Letter from culture secretary on HM Government position on contested heritage (22 September 2020), www.gov.uk/government/publications/letter-from-culture-secretary-on-hm-government-position-on-contested-heritage.
144 'Britain's heroes' (letter to the editor), *Daily Telegraph* (9 November 2020).
145 'New legal protection for England's heritage' (17 January 2021), www.gov.uk/government/news/new-legal-protection-for-england-s-heritage.
146 These are the figures for 2022–23. See https://historicengland.org.uk/research/heritage-counts/indicator-data/planning/.
147 https://web.archive.org/web/20220108150936/https:/www.thecommonsensegroup.com/wp-content/uploads/2021/05/Common-Sense.pdf.
148 The Restore Trust was founded by Cornelia van der Poll, an affiliated lecturer in Ancient Greek at Oxford's now-defunct St Benet's Hall, a 'permanent private hall' affiliated to Oxford University that closed in 2022.
149 York, 2023.
150 Manjapra, 2022a, 2023b.
151 'An open letter to the master of Jesus College, Cambridge' (History Reclaimed website), https://historyreclaimed.co.uk/an-open-letter-to-the-master-of-jesus-college-cambridge/.
152 Hodge, 2022: 58; 'Roger Bowdler', Paul Mellon Centre website, www.paul-mellon-centre.ac.uk/learning/lecturers/roger-bowdler.
153 See Sebastian Payne's letter to the editor in *The Times* (25 February 2021); see also 'A double first in double standards', *Daily Mail* (28 January 2022).
154 Hodge, 2022: 7. The substantive argument of the opponents, that the claim about profits from slavery didn't match the timeline, was demolished in a subsequent detailed analysis by economic historian Michael Edwards. Edwards showed that that Rustat's involvement in slave-trading companies represented 'just over 17 per cent of his estate when he died and more than 30 per cent of the value of his known lifetime giving', and also that 'the £430 4s 1d costs paid by his executors for erecting his memorial in Jesus Chapel' may have derived from this source (Edwards, 2024: 77, 82).
155 Hodge, 2022: 80.
156 Hodge, 2022: 56.
157 The Worshipful David Hodge QC, see https://lawandreligionuk.com/wp-content/uploads/2022/03/Re-the-Rustat-Memorial-Jesus-College-Cambridge-Summary.pdf.

## NOTES TO SECTION VII

158 'Church court rejects Cambridge college bid to move slave trader memorial', *Guardian* (23 March 2022); see also 'I still think Rustat memorial should go, says Archbishop Welby', *Church Times* (13 April 2022), www.churchtimes.co.uk/articles/2022/14-april/news/uk/i-still-think-rustat-memorial-should-go-says-archbishop-welby; 'Contested heritage and racial justice: statement by the Archbishop' (Archbishop of Canterbury website, 12 April 2022), www.archbishopofcanterbury.org/about/anglican-communion-fund/news/contested-heritage-and-racial-justice-statement-archbishop.
159 'Letters to the editor', *Church Times* (1 April 2022).
160 Crockford, 2022.
161 'The Church of England promised to tackle racial injustice. Why is it defending a slave trader's memory?', *Guardian* (14 April 2022).
162 Hodge, 2022. The college chose not to appeal due to the high costs of the legal process, and the complex and expensive procedures have been called into question by some ecclesiastical legal scholars (Sutton, 2023; Taylor, 2023).
163 Thomas, 1994: 2, 10, 12, 170.
164 Cannadine, 2018: 12.
165 'Universities are in for a painful lesson: go woke, go broke', *Daily Telegraph* (29 January 2024).
166 Deed of Gift and Declaration of Trust on behalf of the University in respect of the Anthropological Collection offered to the University by Major-General Augustus Henry Lane Fox Pitt Rivers, F. R. S., and accepted by the University in Convocation on Wednesday 7 March 1883. (Pitt Rivers Museum papers, Box 2: 20).
167 'Est affirmée d'abord l'existence de groupes humains sans culture; puis de cultures hiérarchisées; enfin la notion de relativité culturelle' (Fanon 2001 [1956]: 43).
168 Ang, 2000: 1.
169 'Loss by College of Surgeons', *The Times* (21 May 1941), p. 2; 'Mummy suffers in Blitz', *Aberdeen Journal* (21 May 1941), p. 3; 'City's oldest house bombed', *Daily Telegraph* (21 May 1941), p. 5; 'London's oldest house destroyed', *Evening Telegraph* (20 May 1941), p. 8.
170 Fisher, 2018 [1999]: 2.
171 Hicks, 2016b.
172 Bernard Fagg to Jacquetta Hawkes, 7 November 1972 (Bradford University Special Collections, Jacquetta Hawkes Papers, Archive Folder 4/18).
173 Jacquetta Hawkes, nd. Typescript lecture on General Pitt-Rivers (Bradford University Special Collections, Jacquetta Hawkes Papers, Folder

4/18), p. 2. Hawkes' archive is held the Special Collections of the University of Bradford's J. B. Priestley Library, and includes correspondence about Pitt-Rivers dating from between 1968 and 1983 (3/16), a typescript text, list of slides and series of 35mm slides from a lecture on 'The General' from 1968 (4/18), and a 1973 letter from Tommy Fox-Pitt expressing hopes of a biography of the General (Fox-Pitt to Hawkes, 21 March 1973: 15/4/19/16).

174 'A new drum for the General', *Sunday Times* (22 June 1969), pp. 50–57.
175 Powers notes that the skull's accession number is 4.5849 (or possibly 4.5819).
176 *Hamlet*, Act III, Scene iv.
177 Isaac Julien quoted by Mercer, 1994: 16.
178 Ahmed, 2021.
179 'The Wake by Khaleb Brooks', Mayor of London London Assembly, https://www.london.gov.uk/programmes-strategies/arts-and-culture/diversity-public-realm/memorial-victims-transatlantic-slavery/wake-khaleb-brooks.
180 'Dorset auction house withdraws Egyptian human skulls from sale', *Guardian* (1 May 2024).
181 'Stanford will rename campus spaces named for David Starr Jordan and relocate statue depicting Louis Agassiz', *Stanford Report* (7 October, 2022), https://news.stanford.edu/stories/2020/10/jordan-agassiz.
182 Long before 2020 the statue first fell in the San Francisco Earthquake of 1906, and was re-erected; there's even a photograph from the aftermath showing the figure plunged upside-down shoulder-deep into the concrete. 'Quake 06 Centennial Walking Tour: Memorial Arch and Agassiz Statue' (Stanford University, 2006), http://quake06.stanford.edu/centennial/tour/stop3.html.

## ACKNOWLEDGEMENTS

1 Didion, 2005; Lewis 1961: 3.
2 Adichie, 2021: 6; Porter 2015: 4, 104.
3 Macdonald, 2014: 199.
4 Benjamin, W., 1991 [1932]: 400, 401, my translation.
5 Barthes, 2009: 141, my translation.
6 Césaire, 2017 [1960].
7 D'Aguiar, 2023: 13.
8 Sherratt, 1990b: 6.
9 Thompson, 1977; Chapman, 1981; Bowden, 1991.

# Bibliography

Abolitionist Futures, 2021, 'Policing by Consent', https://abolitionistfutures.com/latest-news/policing-by-consent

Adichie, C. N., 2021, *Notes on Grief*, London: 4th Estate

Adye, J., 1860, *A Review of the Crimean War to the Winter of 1854–5*, London: Hurst & Blackett

Agamben, G., 2005, *State of Exception* (trans. Kevin Attell), Chicago: University of Chicago Press

Ahmed, S., 2004, 'Declarations of Whiteness: The Non-performativity of Anti-racism', *Borderlands*, https://research.gold.ac.uk/id/eprint/13911/

Ahmed, S., 2006, The Non-performativity of Antiracism', *Meridians* 7(1): 104–126

Ahmed, S., 2021, *Complaint!*, Durham, NC: Duke University Press

Albert, Prince Consort, 1862 [1850], Speech given at the Banquet Given by the Right Hon. the Lord Mayor, Thomas Farncombe, to Her Majesty's Ministers, Foreign Ambassadors, Royal Commissioners of the Exhibition of 1851, and the Mayors of One Hundred and Eighty Towns, at the Mansion House, March 21st, 1850, in *The Principal Speeches and Addresses of His Royal Highness the Prince Consort*, London: John Murray, pp. 109–14

All Monuments Must Fall, 2017, All Monuments Must Fall Syllabus (September 2017), https://allmonumentsmustfall.com/

All Monuments Must Fall, 2020, All Monuments Must Fall Syllabus (revised edition), https://monumentsmustfall.wordpress.com/

Allen, R., 1874, *A Souvenir of Newstead Abbey, Formerly the Home of Lord Byron*, Nottingham: Richard Allen & Son

Amory, M., 1980, *The Letters of Evelyn Waugh*, New Haven, CT: Ticknor & Fields

Anderson, R. A., 1909, *Fighting the Mill Creeks: Being a Personal Account of Campaigns Against Indians of the Northern Sierras*, Chico, CA: Chico Record Press

Ang, I., 2000, 'Identity Blues', in P. Gilroy, L. Grossberg and A. McRobbie (eds), *Without Guarantees: In Honour of Stuart Hall*, London: Verso, pp. 1–13

Anon, 1863a, 'The Influence of Race on Art', *Anthropological Review* 1(2): 216–27

Anon, 1863b, 'Pictet on the Aryan Race', *Anthropological Review* 1(2): 232–46.

Anon, 1864, 'Miscegenation', *Anthropological Review* 2(5): 116–21

Anon, 1865, 'Race in History', *Anthropological Review* 3(11): 233–48

Anon, 1866a, 'List of stores sent on board HMS *Urgent*', in Anon (ed.), *Papers Relating to the Disturbances in Jamaica, Part I*, London: Harrison & Sons, p. 89

Anon, 1866b, 'Race in Religion' (review of *A General View of Positivism*), *Anthropological Review* 4(15): 289–320

Anon, 1868, 'Knox on the Celtic Race', *Anthropological Review* 6(21): 175–91

Anon, 1873, 'People using the boomerang', *Harper's New Monthly Magazine* 46(274): 617

Anon, 1879, 'Museum' (Appendix to Proceedings of the Forty-Eighth Anniversary Meeting), *Journal of the United Service Institution* 22: xxv–xxvi

Anon, 1880, 'General Pitt Rivers (Lane Fox) Anthropological Collection', *Nature* 22: 490

Anon, 1910, 'Monument at Oxford, NC.', *Confederate Veteran* 18(3) (March 1910): 109

Anon, 1917, 'The "Soldier's Heart" and the "Effort Syndrome"', *British Medical Journal* 1 (2936): 459–60

Arendt, H., 1951, *The Origins of Totalitarianism*, London: Secker & Warburg

Arokiasamy, C., 2023, 'Race Equality in the Cultural Heritage Sector: Perceptions of Progress over the Last Twenty Years and Actions for the Next Decade', in S. L. T. Ashley and D. Stone (eds), *Whose Heritage? Challenging Race and Identity in Stuart Hall's Post-nation Britain*, London: Routledge, pp. 39–53

Arnold, M., 1867, 'Culture and its Enemies', *Cornhill Magazine* 16: 36–53

Arnold, M., 1869, *Culture and Anarchy*, London: John Murray

Arts Council England, 1999, *Whose Heritage? The Impact of Cultural Diversity on Britain's Living Heritage, National Conference, Manchester, 1–3 November 1999*, London: Arts Council England

Ashley, S. L. T. and D. Stone, 2023, 'Introduction: on Stuart Hall and the imagining of heritage', in S. L. T. Ashley and D. Stone (eds), *Whose*

*Heritage? Challenging Race and Identity in Stuart Hall's Post-nation Britain*, London: Routledge, pp. 1–10

Aspinal, K., 2022, 'Viscount Lymington: The Journey of a Fascist "Fellow Traveller"', unpublished Masters thesis, Canterbury Christ Church University

Awcock, H., 2019, 'The Geographies of Protest and Public Space in Mid-Nineteenth-Century London: The Hyde Park Railings Affair', *Historical Geography* 47: 194–217

Axelson, S., 1970, *Culture Confrontation in the Lower Congo: From the Old Congo Kingdom to the Congo Independent State with Special Reference to the Swedish Missionaries in the 1880s and 1890s*, Uppsala: Gummesson (Studia Missionalia Upsaliensia XIV)

Baker, H., 1934, *Cecil Rhodes by his Architect*, Oxford: Oxford University Press

Balfour, H., 1893, *The Evolution of Decorative Art*, New York: Macmillan & Co

Balfour, H., 1894, 'Evolution in Decorative Art', *Journal of the Society of Arts*, 42(2162): 455–71

Balfour H., 1897a, 'Life History of an Aghori Fakir; with Exhibition of the Human Skull Used by Him as a Drinking Vessel, and Notes on the Similar Use of Skulls by Other Races', *Royal Anthropological Institute of Great Britain and Ireland* 26: 340–57

Balfour, H., 1897b, 'The Pitt-Rivers Museum', in J. Paton (ed.), *Museums Association: Report of Proceedings with the Papers Read at the Eighth Annual General Meeting Held in Oxford July 6 to 9 1897*, London: Dulau & Co, pp. 51–4

Balfour, H., 1897c, 'Comments on the Arrangement of Ethnological Collections', in J. Paton (ed.), *Museums Association: Report of Proceedings with the Papers Read at the Eighth Annual General Meeting Held in Oxford July 6 to 9 1897*, London: Dulau & Co, pp. 61–2

Balfour, H., 1901, 'Strangling-Cords from the Murray River, Victoria, Australia', *Man* 1: 117–18

Balfour, H., 1925, 'Thorn-Lined Traps and Their Distribution', *Man* 25: 33–7

Ballard, J. G., 1973, *Crash*, London: Jonathan Cape

Ballard, J. G., 1985 [1974], 'Preface to the French Edition', in *Crash*, London: Vintage, pp. 1–6

Baratz, S. S. and J. C. Baratz, 1970, 'Early Childhood Intervention: The Social Science Base of Institutional Racism', *Harvard Educational Review* 40(1): 29–50

Barnard Davis, J., 1869, 'On the Weight of the Brain in the Negro', *Anthropological Review* 7(25): 190–92.

Barrett, J., R. Bradley, M. Bowden and B. Mead, 1983, 'South Lodge after Pitt Rivers', *Antiquity* 57: 193–204

Barry, J., 1783, *An Account of a Series of Pictures, in the Great Room of the Society of Arts, Manufactures, and Commerce, at the Adelphi*, London: William Adlard

Barry, J., 1793, *A Letter to the Right Honourable the President, Vice-Presidents, and the Rest of the Noblemen and Gentlemen, of the Society for the Encouragement of Arts, Manufactures, and Commerce, John-Street, Adelphi*, London: Thomas Davison

Barthes, R., 1977 [1975], *Roland Barthes by Roland Barthes* (trans. R. Howard), Berkeley: University of California Press

Barthes, R., 2009, *Journal de Deuil, 26 Octobre 1977–15 Septembre 1979* (ed. N. Léger), Paris: Éditions du Seuil

Barthes, R., 2013 [2003], *The Preparation of the Novel: Lecture Courses and Seminars at the Collège de France (1978–1979 and 1979–1980)* (trans. K. Briggs), New York: Columbia University Press

Bartnum, B. A., 1975, 'A Victorian Political Hostess: The Engagement Book of Lady Stanley of Alderley', *Princeton University Library Chronicle* 36(2): 133–46

Bastian, A., 1881, *Die Vorgeschichte der Ethnologie: Deutschlands Denkfreunden gewidmet für eine Mussestunde*, Berlin: Dümmler

Bateman, J., 1876, *The Acre-ocracy of England: A List of All Owners of Three Thousand Acres and Upwards with their Possessions and Incomes, Arranged under their Various Counties, Also their Colleges and Clubs Culled from the Modern Domesday Book*, London: Basil Montagu Pickering

Bateman, J., 1883, *The Great Landowners of Great Britain and Ireland* (4th edition), London: Harrison

Bateman, T., 1861, *Ten Years' Diggings in Celtic and Saxon Grave Hills in the Counties of Derby, Stafford, and York, from 1848 to 1858 with Notices of some Former Discoveries Hitherto Unpublished and Remarks on the Crania and Pottery from the Mounds*, London: George Allen & Sons

Bauman, Z., 1992, *Mortality, Immortality and Other Life Strategies*, Stanford, CA: Stanford University Press

Bayliss-Smith, T., 2014, 'Colonialism as Shell Shock W. H. R. Rivers's Explanations for Depopulation in Melanesia', in E. Hviding and C. Berg (eds), *The Ethnographic Experiment: A. M. Hocart and W. H. R. Rivers in Island Melanesia*, Oxford: Berghahn, pp. 179–213

Beaudry, M. C., 1980, '"Or What Else You Please to Call it": Folk Semantic Domains in Early Virginian Probate Inventories', unpublished Ph.D. thesis, Brown University

Beaudry, M. C., 2004, 'Doing the Housework: New Approaches to the Archaeology of Households', in K. S. Barile and J. C. Brandon (eds), *Household Chores and Household Choices: Theorizing the Domestic Sphere in Historical Archaeology*, Tuscaloosa: University of Alabama Press, pp. 254–62

Beckles, H., 2013, *Britain's Black Debt: Reparations for Caribbean Slavery and Native Genocide*, Mona, Jamaica: University of the West Indies Press

Beddoe, J., 1863, 'On the Supposed Increasing Prevalence of Dark Hair in England', *Anthropological Review* 1(2): 310–12

Beddoe, J., 1866, 'On the Headforms of the West of England', *Memoirs of the Anthropological Society of London* 2 (1866): 348–57

Beddoe, J., 1870, 'On the Headform of the Danes', *Memoirs of the Anthropological Society of London* 3 (1867–1869): 378–83

Beddoe, J., 1881, 'Anthropological Colour Phenomena in Belgium and Elsewhere', *Journal of the Anthropological Institute of Great Britain and Ireland* 10: 374–80

Bedford, W., 2005, 'Land Adjacent to Pitt Rivers Museum, Oxford', Oxford: Oxford Archaeology, https://library.oxfordarchaeology.com/482

Beinart, W., 2022, 'Cecil Rhodes: Racial Segregation in the Cape Colony and Violence in Zimbabwe', *Journal of Southern African Studies* 48(3): 581–603

Belich, J., 1986, *The New Zealand Wars and the Victorian Interpretation of Racial Conflict*, Auckland: Auckland University Press

Beliso-De Jesús, A. M. and J. Pierre, 2019, 'Introduction: Anthropology of White Supremacy', *American Anthropologist* 122(1): 65–75

Benjamin, W. B. S., 1963 [1928], *Ursprung des deutschen Trauerspiels*, Frankfurt am Main: Suhrkamp

Benjamin, W. B. S., 1991 [1932], 'Ausgraben und Erinnern', in T. Rexroth (ed.) *Walter Benjamin Gesammelte Schriften Volume 4*, Frankfurt am Main: Suhrkamp, pp. 400–1

Benjamin, W. B. S., 1991 [1940], 'Über den Begriff der Geschichte', in R. Tiedemann and H. Schweppenhäuser (eds), *Walter Benjamin Gesammelte Schriften Vol. 1(1)*, Frankfurt am Main: Suhrkamp, pp. 693–704.

Bennett, J. D., 2008, *The London Confederates: The Officials, Clergy, Businessmen and Journalists who Backed the American South During the Civil War*, Jefferson, NC: McFarland & Co

Bennett, S. (ed.), 2008, *Cultivating the Human Faculties: James Barry (1741–1806) and the Society of Arts*, Bethlehem, PA: Lehigh University Press

Benson, A. C. and R. B. B. Esher (eds), 1907, *The Letters of Queen Victoria: A Selection from Her Majesty's Correspondence Between the Years 1837 and 1861 (Vol. III: 1854–1861)*, London: John Murray

Bent, J. T., 1895, *The Ruined Cities of Mashonaland*, London: Longmans & Co

Bergson, H., 1932, *Les deux sources de la morale et de la religion*, Paris: Librairie Félix Alcan

Bernhard Smith, W. A. H., 1923, *Poisonous Plants of All Countries* (revised edition), London: Baillière, Tindall & Cox

Berry, D., 2004, 'Bright, Richard (1789–1858), physician', *Oxford Dictionary of National Biography*, Oxford: Oxford University Press, https://doi.org/10.1093/ref:odnb/3423

Biddulph, H., 1940, 'Canada and the American Civil War: More Wolseley Letters', *Journal of the Society for Army Historical Research* 19(74): 112–17

Biggar, N. and D. Stokes, 2021, 'How "Progressive" Anti-imperialism Threatens the United Kingdom', London: Council on Geostrategy Policy Paper, www.geostrategy.org.uk/research/how-progressive-anti-imperialism-threatens-the-united-kingdom/

Bilby, K., 2012, 'Image and Imagination: Re-visioning the Maroons in the Morant Bay Rebellion', *History and Memory* 24(2): 41–72

Bischoff, T., 1863, 'Extracts from a Lecture Delivered at Munich, 1858, on the Difference Between Man and Brutes', *Anthropological Review* 1(1): 54–60

Blackwood, B., 1970, *The Origin and Development of the Pitt Rivers Museum*, Oxford: Pitt Rivers Museum (Occasional Papers on Technology 11)

Boa, S., 2002, '"Setting the Law in Defiance": Urban Protests and Lieutenant-Governor Edward John Eyre in Post-Emancipation St Vincent, 1838–1861', *Caribbean Studies* 30(2): 130–69

Boas, F. U., 1938, 'An Anthropologist's Credo', *The Nation* 147: 201–204

Bohrer, A. J., 2020, 'Toward a Decolonial Feminist Anticapitalism: Maria Lugones, Sylvia Wynter, and Sayak Valencia', *Hypatia* 35(3): 524–41

Bonner, R. E., 2002, 'Roundheaded Cavaliers?: The Context and Limits of a Confederate Racial Project', *Civil War History* 48(1): 34–5

Bonner, R. E., 2005, 'Slavery, Confederate Diplomacy, and the Racialist Mission of Henry Hotze', *Civil War History* 51(3): 288–316

Bourke, J., 2009, *An Intimate History of Killing*, New York: Basic Books

Bouverie Pusey, S. E. B., 1864, 'The Negro in Relation to Civilised Society (with discussion)', *Journal of the Anthropological Society of London* 2: cclxxiv–ccxc

Bowden, M., 1991, *Pitt-Rivers: The Life and Archaeological Work of Lieutenant-General Augustus Henry Lane Fox Pitt Rivers, DCL, FRS, FSA*, Cambridge: Cambridge University Press

Bowden, M., 2004, 'Rivers, Augustus Henry Lane Fox Pitt-', *Oxford Dictionary of National Biography*, Oxford: Oxford University Press, https://doi.org/10.1093/ref:odnb/22341

Bowden, M. and A. G. Green, 2017, *General Pitt-Rivers: Founding Father of Modern Archaeology*, Salisbury: Salisbury and South Wiltshire Museum

Bradley, R., 1983, 'Archaeology, Evolution and the Public Good: The Intellectual Development of General Pitt Rivers', *Archaeological Journal* 140: 1–9

Bradley, R., 2000, *An Archaeology of Natural Places,* London: Routledge

Bradley, R., 2001, 'The Birth of Architecture', *Proceedings of the British Academy* 110: 69–92

Bradley, R., 2023, *Monumental Times: Pasts, Presents, and Futures in the Prehistoric Construction Projects of Northern and Western Europe*, Oxford: Oxbow

Briggs, K., 2015, 'Practising with Roland Barthes', *L'esprit créateur* 55(4): 118–30

Bristow, E., 1975, 'The Liberty and Property Defence League and Individualism', *Historical Journal* 18(4): 761–89

British Association for the Advancement of Science, 1841, *Queries Respecting the Human Race, to be Addressed to Travellers and Others*, London: R. & J. E. Taylor

Brock, M. G. and M. C. Curthoys, 2000, 'Preface', in M. G. Brock and M. C. Curthoys (eds), *The History of the University of Oxford Vol. VII: Nineteenth-century Oxford, Part 2*, Oxford: Clarendon Press

Browne, T., 1658, *Hydriotaphia, Urn Burial, or, a Discourse of the Sepulchrall Urnes Lately Found in Norfolk*, London: Henry Brome

Bruneau, O., 2020, 'The Teaching of Mathematics at the Royal Military Academy: Evolution in Continuity', *Philosophia Scientiæ* 24(1): 137–58

Bryant, M., 2016, 'The Progress of Civilisation: The Pedimental Sculpture of the British Museum by Richard Westmacott', *Sculpture Journal* 25(3): 315–32

Buchholz, B. A. and K. L. Spalding, 2010, 'Year of Birth Determination Using Radiocarbon Dating of Dental Enamel', *Surface and Interface Analysis* 42(5): 398–401

Bull, S., 2017, 'Reading, Writing, and Publishing an Obscene Canon: The Archival Logic of the Secret Museum, c. 1860–c. 1900', *Book History* 20: 226–57

Burke, E., 1824 [1757], *Philosophical Enquiry into the Origin of our Ideas of the Sublime and Beautiful*, London: A. Robertson & Co

Burnett, L., 2008, *Henry Hotze, Confederate Propagandist: Selected on Revolution, Recognition, and Race*, Tuscaloosa: University of Alabama Press

Burrow, J. W., 1978, 'Digging the Darwinian Way', *Times Literary Supplement* 3955 (13 January 1978), p. 11

Burton, A., 1999, *Visions and Accident*, London: V&A Publishing

Burton, R. F., 1864, 'Notes on Scalping', *Anthropological Review* 1(4): 49–52

Burton, R. F., 1865, 'Notes on Certain Matters Connected with the Dahoman', *Memoirs of the Anthropological Society of London* 1 (1863–1864): 308–21

Busk, H., 1858, *The Rifle: and How to Use It: Comprising a Description of That Valuable Weapon in All Its Varieties and An Account of Its Origin*, London: G. Routledge & Co

Busk, G., 1870a, 'Description of and Remarks upon an Ancient Calvaria from China, Which Has Been Supposed to be That of Confucius', *Journal of the Ethnological Society of London* 2(1): 73–83

Busk, G., 1870b, 'Supplementary Remarks to a Note on an Ancient Chinese Calva', *Journal of the Ethnological Society of London* 2(2): 156–7

Butler, J., 2002, 'Is Kinship Always Already Heterosexual?', *Differences: A Journal of Feminist Cultural Studies* 13(1): 14–44

Calthorpe, S. J. G., 1856, *Letters from Head-quarters; or, The Realities of the War in the Crimea*, London: John Murray

Cannadine, D., 2018, 'Introduction', in J. Pellew and L. Goldman (eds), *Dethroning Historical Reputations: Universities, Museums and the Commemoration of Benefactors*, London: Institute of Historical Research, pp. 1–14

Carmichael, S. and C. Hamilton, 1972, 'Institutional Racism and the Colonial Status of Blacks', in R. C. Edwards, M. Reich and T. E. Weisskopf (eds), *The Capitalist System: A Radical Analysis of American Society*, Englewood Cliffs, NJ: Prentice-Hall, pp. 290–305

Carroll, L., 1865, *Alice's Adventures in Wonderland*, London: Macmillan & Co

Carter Blake, C., 1864, 'Report on the Anthropological Papers Read at the Newcastle Meeting of the British Association for the Advancement of Science in August and September 1863', *Journal of the Anthropological Society of London* 2: i–vi

Caulfield, R., 1865, 'Remains of the Aboriginal Inhabitants of Ireland', *Gentleman's Magazine* 18: 707–10

Césaire, A., 1955 [1950], *Discours sur le colonialisme*, Paris: Présence africaine

Césaire, A., 1972 [1950], *Discourse on Colonialism* (trans. J. Pinkham), New York: Monthly Review Press

Césaire, A., 2017 [1960], 'Maison-Mousson', in *The Complete Poetry of Aimé Césaire: Bilingual Edition* (trans. A. J. Arnold and C. Eshleman), Middletown, CT: Wesleyan University Press, p. 74

Césaire, A., 2021 [1950], *Über den Kolonialismus* (trans. H. Becker), Berlin: Alexander Verlag

Challis, D., 2013, *The Archaeology of Race: The Eugenic Ideas of Francis Galton and Flinders Petrie*, London: Bloomsbury

Chapman, W. R., 1981, 'Ethnology in the Museum: AHLF Pitt Rivers (1827–1900) and the Institutional Foundations of British Anthropology', unpublished D.Phil thesis, University of Oxford

Chapman, W. R., 1984, 'Pitt Rivers and his Collection, 1874–1883: The Chronicle of a Gift Horse', in B. A. L. Cranstone and S. Seidenberg (eds), *The General's Gift: A Celebration of the Pitt Rivers Museum Centenary 1884-1984*, Oxford: *Journal of the Anthropological Society of Oxford* (JASO) Occasional Paper, pp. 181–203

Chapman, W. R., 1989, 'The Organisational Context in the History of Archaeology: Pitt Rivers and Other British Archaeologists in the 1860s', *Antiquaries Journal* 69: 23–42

Chatterjee, P., 1994, *The Nation and its Fragments: Colonial and Postcolonial Histories*, Princeton, NJ: Princeton University Press

Chigudu, S., 2021, 'Colonialism had never really ended: my life in the shadow of Cecil Rhodes', *Guardian* (14 January 2021)

Childe, V. G., 1950, 'The Urban Revolution', *Town Planning Review* 21(1): 3–17

Chirikure, S., 2020, *Great Zimbabwe: Reclaiming a 'Confiscated' Past*, London: Routledge

Churchill, J. J., 1908, *Reminiscences of Lady Randolph Churchill*, New York: Century

Clark, K., 2001a, 'Preserving What Matters: Value-led Planning for Cultural Heritage Sites', *Conservation: The Getty Conservation Institute Newsletter* 16(3): 5–12

Clark, K., 2001b, *Informed Conservation: Understanding Historic Buildings and their Landscapes for Conservation*, London: English Heritage

Clarke, H., 1868, 'Anthropological Society of London', *The Athenaeum* 2142 (21 November 1868), pp. 681–2

Clifford, H., 1956, *Henry Clifford VC, His Letters and Sketches from the Crimea*, London: Michael Joseph

Clifford, J., 1986, 'Introduction: Partial Truths', in J. Clifford and G. Marcus (eds), *Writing Culture*, Berkeley: University of California Press, pp. 1–26

Clifford, J., 2013, *Returns: Becoming Indigenous in the Twenty-first Century*, Cambridge, MA: Harvard University Press

Clodfelter, M., 2017, *Warfare and Armed Conflicts: A Statistical Encyclopedia of Casualty and other Figures, 1492–2015*, Jefferson, NC: McFarland & Co

Coates, T.-N., 2015, *Between the World and Me*, New York: Spiegel & Grau

Cohen, A., B. Huckaby and K. Simmons, 1969, 'An Exploratory Study in Institutional Racism', unpublished co-authored thesis, Master of Social Work, Wayne State University

Colebrooke, T. E., 1856, *Journal of Two Visits to the Crimea: in the Autumns of 1854 & 1855: with Remarks on the Campaign*, London: T. & W. Boone

Coleman, N. A. T., 2014, 'Philosophy is dead White – and dead wrong', *Times Higher Education*, https://www.timeshighereducation.com/comment/opinion/philosophy-is-deadwhite-and-dead-wrong/2012122.article

Colt-Hoare, R., 1810–1821, *The Ancient History of Wiltshire*, London: Lackington, Hughes, Harding, Mavor, & Lepard

Conrad, J., 1911, *Under Western Eyes*, London: J. M. Dent & Sons

Cooke, B., 1999, 'Crimean Shell-shock', *War Correspondent: Journal of the Crimean War Research Society* 17: 34

Coote, J., C. Morton and J. Nicholson, 2000, *Transformations: The Art of Recycling*, Oxford: Pitt Rivers Museum

Corsín Jiménez, A., 2021, 'Anthropological Entrapments: Ethnographic Analysis Before and After Relations and Comparisons', *Social Analysis* 65(3): 110–30

Corsín Jiménez, A. and C. Nahum-Claudel, 2019, 'The Anthropology of Traps: Concrete Technologies and Theoretical Interfaces', *Journal of Material Culture* 24(4): 383–400

Cossons, N., 2001, 'Preface', in K. Clark, *Informed Conservation: Understanding Historic Buildings and their Landscapes for Conservation*, London: English Heritage, p. 7

Cowtan, R., 1872, *Memories of the British Museum*, London: R. Bentley & Son

Cox, K. L., 2003, *Dixie's Daughters: The United Daughters of the Confederacy and the Preservation of Confederate Culture*, Gainesville: University Press of Florida

Cox, K. L., 2017, 'The Confederacy's "Living Monuments"', *New York Times* (6 October 2017)

Craft, W., 1864, 'On a Visit to Dahomey', in Anon (ed.) *Report of the Thirty-third Meeting of the British Association for the Advancement of Science, Held at Newcastle-upon-Tyne in August and September 1863 (Notes and Abstracts)*, London: John Murray, p. 135

Crockford, J., 2021, 'Rustat Memorial: Faculty Application', www.jesus.cam.ac.uk/sites/default/files/inline/files/Introduction%20to%20Faculty%20Application.pdf

Crockford, J., 2022, 'Contested Memorials and the Discipleship of Christian Memory', *International Journal for the Study of the Christian Church* 22(2): 97–110

Crow, J. J. and R. F. Durden, 1977, *Maverick Republican in the Old North State: A Political Biography of Daniel L. Russell*, Baton Rouge: Louisiana State University Press

Cundall, F., 1890, 'Fifty Years of Government Aid in Science and Art Education', *Journal of the Society of Arts* 38: 499–508

Cunliffe, M., 1951, 'America at the Great Exhibition of 1851', *American Quarterly* 3(2): 115–26

D'Aguiar, F., 2023, *For the Unnamed*, Manchester: Carcanet

Da Costa, J. M., 1871, 'On Irritable Heart: A Clinical Study of a Form of Functional Cardiac Disorder and its Consequences', *American Journal of the Medical Sciences* 61: 17–52

Dally, E. and H. J. C. Beavan, 1864, 'An Inquiry into Consanguineous Marriages and Pure Races', *Anthropological Review* 1(4): 65–108

Darwin, C. R., 1859, *On the Origin of Species by Means of Natural Selection, or the Preservation of Favoured Races in the Struggle for Life*, London: John Murray

Darwin, C. R., 1871, *The Descent of Man and Selection in Relation to Sex* (two volumes), London: John Murray

Daughters of the Confederacy, 1909, untitled pamphlet comprising 'Corner stone of Confederate monument laid Monday May 10th 1909, with impressive ceremony' by F. M. Pinnox; Confederate Monument Dedication by E. L. Conn; Address of Hon. A. W. Graham; Address of Acceptance by D. G. Brummitt, Oxford, NC: Orphanage Press (United Daughters of the Confederacy, Granville Grays Chapter; on file at University of North Carolina at Chapel Hill, Wilson Library)

David, S., 2006, 'Greased Cartridges and the Great Mutiny of 1857: A Pretext or the Final Straw?', in K. Roy (ed.), *War and Society in Colonial India, 1807–1945*, New Delhi: Oxford University Press, pp. 82–113

Davis, A.Y., 2003, *Are Prisons Obsolete?*, New York: Seven Stories Press

Davis, J. B., 1868, 'The Brain of a Negro of Guinea', *Anthropological Review* 6(22): 279–85

Davis, J. B. & J. Thurnam, 1865, *Crania Britannica: Delineations and Descriptions of the Skulls of the Aboriginal and Early Inhabitants of the British Islands*, London: Taylor & Francis

Day, A. S. and S. O. McBean, 2022, *Abolition Revolution*, London: Pluto Press

De Bazancourt, C. L., 1856, *The Crimean Expedition, to the Capture of Sebastopol: Chronicles of the War in the East Vol. 1*, London: Sampson Low, Son & Co

De Genova, N., 2015, 'The Border Spectacle of Migrant "Victimisation"', *Open Democracy*, www.opendemocracy.net/en/beyond-trafficking-and-slavery/border-spectacle-of-migrant-victimisation/

De Genova, N. P., 2016, 'The "Crisis" of the European Border Regime: Towards a Marxist Theory of Borders', *International Socialism* 150: 31–54

De Smaele, H., 2016, 'Achilles or Adonis: controversies surrounding the male body as national symbol in Georgian England', *Gender & History* 28(1): 77–101

Deleuze, G., 1988, *Le pli: Leibniz et le Baroque*, Paris: Les Éditions de Minuit

Deleuze, G., 1991, *The Fold* (trans. J. Strauss), Yale French Studies 80: 227–47

Deleuze, G., 1995 [1990], 'Control and Becoming', in *Negotiations 1972–1990* (trans. M. Joughin), New York: Columbia University Press, pp. 169–76

Deleuze, G. and F. Guattari, 1987 [1980], *A Thousand Plateaus: Capitalism and Schizophrenia* (trans. B. Massumi), Minneapolis: University of Minnesota Press

Deleuze, G. and F. Guattari, 1991, *Qu'est-ce que, la philosophie?*, Paris: Les Éditions de Minuit

Dercum, F. X., 1889, 'Railway Shock and its Treatment', *Therapeutic Gazette* 13(10): 649–60

Derrida, J., 1994, *Specters of Marx: The State of the Debt, the Work of Mourning and the New International* (trans. P. Kamuf), London: Routledge

Dickinson, E. E., 1960 [1865], 'Crumbling is not an instant's Act' [997], in *The Complete Poems of Emily Dickinson*, Boston: Little, Brown & Co, p. 463

Dickinson, G. C., 1959, 'Stage-Coach Services in the West Riding of Yorkshire between 1830 and 1840', *Journal of Transport History* 4(1): 1–12

Didion, J., 2005, *The Year of Magical Thinking*, London: 4th Estate

Dilke, C. W., 1869, *Greater Britain: A Record of Travel in English-Speaking Countries During 1866–7*, London: Macmillan & Co

Din-Kariuki, N., 2020, 'After Rhodes Falls', *London Review of Books*, www.lrb.co.uk/blog/2020/june/after-rhodes-falls

Dirlik, A., 1994, 'The Postcolonial Aura: Third World Criticism in the Age of Global Capitalism', *Critical Inquiry* 20: 328–56

Dodman, T., 2018, *What Nostalgia Was: War, Empire and the Time of a Deadly Emotion*, Chicago: University of Chicago Press

Dolby, I. E. A., 1866, *The Journal of the Household Brigade for the Year 1866*, London: William Clowes & Sons

Douglas, M., 1980, *Evans-Pritchard*, London: Fontana Books

Douglass, F., 1870, 'Monuments of Folly', *New National Era* 1(47): 3

Dover Wilson, J., 1932, 'Editor's Introduction', in M. Arnold, *Culture and Anarchy*, Cambridge: Cambridge University Press, pp. vii–xl

Doyle, A. C., 1912, *The Lost World*, London: J. W. Parker & Son

Doyle, A. C., 1926, *The History of Spiritualism Vol. 1*, London: Cassell & Co

Doyle, A. C., 1929, 'When the World Screamed', in *The Maracot Deep and Other Stories*, London: John Murray, pp. 3–28

Doyle, A. C., 1969, *The Professor Challenger Stories*, London: John Murray

Draper, N., 2010, *The Price of Emancipation: Slave-Ownership, Compensation and British Society at the End of Slavery*, Cambridge: Cambridge University Press

Dresser, M., 2007, 'Set in Stone? Statues and Slavery in London', *History Workshop Journal* 64(1): 162–99

Drower, M. S., 1994, 'A Visit to General Pitt-Rivers', *Antiquity* 68: 627–30

Du Bois, W. E. B., 1928, 'Postscript', *The Crisis* 35(3): 96–8

Du Bois, W. E. B., 1931, 'Postscript', *The Crisis* 38(8): 278–9

Du Bois, W. E. B., 1935, *Black Reconstruction: An Essay Toward a History of the Part which Black Folk Played in the Attempt to Reconstruct Democracy in America, 1860–1880*, New York: Harcourt, Brace & Co

Durkheim, D. É., 1952 [1897]. *Suicide: A Study in Sociology* (trans. J. A. Spaulding and G. Simpson), London: Free Press

Dyson, S. L., 1994, 'Archaeological Lives', *American Journal of Archaeology* 98: 159–61

Eastlake, C. L., 1872, *A History of the Gothic Revival*, Cambridge: Cambridge University Press

Eco, U., 1995, 'Ur-fascism', *New York Review of Books* 42(11): 12–15

Edison, T. A., 1878, 'The Phonograph and its Future', *North American Review* 126(262): 527–36

Edwards, H., 1860, *A Volunteer's Narrative of the Hythe Course of Instruction in Musketry with Numerous Extracts from Lectures, Addresses and Instructions*, London: Thew & Son

Edwards, J., 1825, *Epigrammata e purioribus graecae anthologiae fontibus hausit*, London: George B. Whittaker

Edwards, M., 2024, 'Slavery and Charity: Tobias Rustat and the African Companies, 1662–94', *Historical Research* 97: 63–82

Elkins, C. M., 2015, 'Looking Beyond Mau Mau: Archiving Violence in the Era of Decolonization', *American Historical Review* 120(3): 852–68

Ellison, R., 1952, *Invisible Man*, New York: Random House

Engels, F. 2010a [1857], 'Alma', in *Marx and Engels: Collected Works Vol. 18, 1857–1862*, London: Lawrence & Wishart, pp. 14–18.

Engels, F., 2010b [1860], 'A Review of the English Volunteer Riflemen', in *Marx and Engels: Collected Works Vol. 18, 1857–1862*, London: Lawrence & Wishart, pp. 409–16

Engels, F., 2010c [1860], 'Army', in *Marx and Engels: Collected Works Vol. 18, 1857–1862*, London: Lawrence & Wishart, pp. 85–126

Engels, F., 2010d [1860], 'Blindage', in *Marx and Engels: Collected Works Vol. 18, 1857–1862*, London: Lawrence & Wishart, p. 137

Erichsen, J. E., 1867, *On Railway and Other Injuries of the Nervous System*, Philadelphia: Henry C. Lea

Ettlinger, E., 1943, 'Documents of British Superstition in Oxford', *Folklore* 54(1): 227–49

Evans, C., 2005, 'Engineering the Past: Pitt Rivers, Nemo and "The Needle"', *Antiquity* 80: 960–69

Evans, C., 2013, 'Pitt-Rivers in Canada (and America): The Filmer Album and Notman Studio Lane Fox Portraits, and the John Wimburn Laurie Diary Entries', http://web.prm.ox.ac.uk/rpr/index.php/articles-index/12-articles/883-pitt-rivers-in-canada/

Evans, C., 2020, 'Soldiering Archaeology: Pitt Rivers and Collecting "Primitive Warfare"', in H. Lidchi and S. Allan (eds), *Dividing the Spoils: Perspectives on Military Collections and the British Empire,* Manchester: Manchester University Press, pp. 85–105

Evans, G. de L., 1828, *On the Designs of Russia*, London: John Murray

Evans, J., 1872, *The Ancient Stone Implements, Weapons and Ornaments of Great Britain*, London: Longman, Green, Reader & Dyer

Evans, J., 1875, 'On the Coinage of the Ancient Britons, and Natural Selection', *Proceedings of the Royal Institution of Great Britain* 7: 476–87

Evans, J., 2002, 'Re-reading Edward Eyre Race, Resistance and Repression in Australia and the Caribbean', *Australian Historical Studies* 33: 175–98

Evans, J., 2005, *Edward Eyre: Race and Colonial Governance*, Otago: University of Otago Press

Evans-Pritchard, E. E., 1940, *The Nuer: A Description of the Modes of Livelihood and Political Institutions of a Nilotic People*, Oxford: Oxford University Press

Eyre, E. J., 1845, *Journals of Expeditions of Discovery into Central Australia, and Overland from Adelaide to King George's Sound, in the Years 1840–1; Sent by the Colonists of South Australia, with the Sanction and Support of the Government: Including an Account of the Manners and Customs of the Aborigines and the State of their Relations with Europeans* (two volumes), London: T. & W. Boone

Fanon, F. O., 1952. *Peau noire, masques blancs*, Paris: Éditions du Seuil

Fanon, F. O., 1961, *Les damnés de la terre*, Paris: La Découverte

Fanon, F. O., 2001 [1956], 'Racisme et culture', in *Pour la révolution africaine*, Paris: La Découverte, pp. 37–51

Farrar, F. W., 1867, 'Aptitudes of Races', *Journal of the Anthropological Society of London* 5: 115–26

Farwell, B., 1962, *Burton: A Biography*, New York: Holt, Rinehart & Winston

Faulkner, N., 2021, *Empire and Jihad: The Anglo-Arab Wars of 1870–1920*, New Haven, CT: Yale University Press

Fenton, J., 1984, 'The Pitt Rivers Museum', *Newsletter of the Museum Ethnographers Group* 16: 37–40

Ferris, N., 1977, *The Trent Affair: A Diplomatic Crisis*, Knoxville: University of Tennessee Press

Ffoulkes, C., 1912, *European Arms and Armour in the University of Oxford*, Oxford: Clarendon Press

Finch, J., 2015, 'Atlantic Landscapes: Connecting Place and People in the Modern World', *Journal of African Diaspora Archaeology and Heritage* 4(3): 195–213

Finley, M. I., 1976, 'Colonies: An Attempt at a Typology', *Transactions of the Royal Historical Society* 26: 167–88

Fisher, E., 1980, *Women's Creation: Sexual Evolution and the Shaping of Society*, New York: McGraw-Hill

Fisher, M., 2009, *Capitalist Realism: Is There No Alternative?*, London: Zero Books

Fisher, M., 2018 [1999], *Flatline Constructs: Gothic Materialism and Cybernetic Theory-Fiction*, New York: exmiliary collective

Flandreau, M., 2016, *Anthropologists in the Stock Exchange: A Financial History of Victorian Science*, Chicago: Chicago University Press

Fletcher, A., 2014, 'Patriotism, the Great War and the Decline of Victorian Manliness', *History* 99(1): 40–72

Flint, K., 2007, 'Exhibiting America the Native American and the Crystal Palace', in J. Buzzard, J. W. Childers and E. Gillooly (eds), *Victorian Prism: Refractions on the Crystal Palace*, Charlottesville: University of Virginia Press, pp. 171–85

Floud, R., 2019, *An Economic History of the English Garden*, London: Allen Lane

Fontein, J., 2016, *The Silence of Great Zimbabwe: Contested Landscapes and the Power of Heritage*, London: Routledge

Fosbery, G. V., 1869, 'On Mitrailleurs, and their Place in the Wars of the Future', *Journal of the Royal United Service Institution* 13: 539–63

Foster, H., 1991, 'Armor Fou', *October* 56: 64–97

Foster, J., 1888, *Alumni Oxonienses, the Members of the University 1715–1886: Their Parentage, Birthplace, and Year of Birth, with a Record of their Degrees, being the Matriculation Register of the University Alphabetically Arranged, Revised and Annotated Vol. III–IV*, Oxford: Parker & Co

Foster, J., 1891, *Alumni Oxonienses, the Members of the University 1715–1886: Their Parentage, Birthplace, and Year of Birth, with a Record of their Degrees, Being the Matriculation Register of the University Alphabetically Arranged, Revised and Annotated (Vol. II, Later Series)*, Oxford: Parker & Co

Foucault, M., 1986 [1984], 'Of Other Spaces' (trans. J. Miskowiec), *Diacritics* 16(1): 22–7

Foucault, M., 2003 [1976], *Abnormal: Lectures at the Collège de France 1974–1975* (trans. G. Burchell), London: Verso

Fox, A. H. L., 1854a, *Treatise on Instruction of Musketry*, Hythe: Hythe School of Musketry

Fox, A. H. L., 1854b, 'Report and Memorandum on the Use of the Minié Musket', *Morning Post* (18 April 1854), p. 5

Fox, A. H. L., 1858, 'The Improvement of the Rifle as a Weapon for General Use', *Journal of the United Service Institution* 2: 453–88

Fox, A. H. L., 1861a, 'Musketry: Letter to the Editor', *Morning Post* (1 July 1861), p. 2

Fox, A. H. L., 1861b, 'On a Model Illustrating the Parabolic Theory of Projection for Ranges in Vacuo', *Journal of the United Service Institution* 5: 497–501

Fox, A. H. L., 1866, 'On an Ivory Peg-top Shaped Object from Ireland', *Proceedings of the Society of Antiquaries of London* 3: 395–6

Fox, A. H. L., 1867a, 'Primitive Warfare I', *Journal of the Royal United Service Institution* 11: 612–43

Fox, A. H. L., 1867b, 'Account of a Human Heart in a Case Found in Christ's Church, Cork', *Archaeological Journal* 24: 71–2

Fox, A. H. L., 1867c, 'Roovesmore Fort, and Stones Inscribed with Oghams, in the Parish of Aglish, County Cork', *Archaeological Journal* 24: 123–39

Fox, A. H. L., 1867d, 'A Description of Certain Piles Found Near London Wall and Southwark, Possibly the Remains of Pile Buildings', *Journal of the Anthropological Society of London* 5: lxxi–lxxxiii

Fox, A. H. L., 1867e, 'Objects Found at Great Depth in the Vicinity of the Old London Wall', *Archaeological Journal* 24: 61–4

Fox, A. H. L., 1868a, 'Primitive Warfare II', *Journal of the Royal United Service Institution* 12: 399–439

Fox, A. H. L., 1868b, 'Comments on the Rose Collection of Stone Implements (17 December 1867)', *Journal of the Anthropological Society* 6: xliv–xlix

Fox, A. H. L., 1868c, 'Memoir on the Hill Forts of Sussex', *Proceedings of the Society of Antiquaries of London* 4: 71

Fox, A. H. L., 1868d, 'On a Ring Brooch from Lough Neagh, Ireland', *Proceedings of the Society of Antiquaries of London* 4: 61–2

## BIBLIOGRAPHY

Fox, A. H. L., 1868e, 'On a Silver Penannular Brooch Known as the Galway Brooch', *Proceedings of the Society of Antiquaries of London* 4: 141–3

Fox, A. H. L., 1869a, 'Primitive Warfare III', *Journal of the Royal United Service Institution* 13: 509–39

Fox, A. H. L., 1869b, 'Note on a Gold Lunette, Found Near Middleton, County Cork, and a Bronze Spear with a Gold Ferrule, from Lough Gur, County Limerick', *Proceedings of the Society of Antiquaries of London* 4: 195–6

Fox, A. H. L., 1869c, 'On a Bronze Spear with a Gold Ferrule and a Shaft of Bog Oak, from Lough Gur, County Limerick', *Journal of the Ethnological Society of London* 1: 36–8

Fox, A. H. L., 1869d, 'An Examination into the Character and Probable Origin of the Hill Forts of Sussex', *Archaeologia* 42: 27–52

Fox, A. H. L., 1869e, 'Further Remarks on the Hill Forts of Sussex: Being an Account of the Excavations in the Forts of Cissbury and Highdown', *Archaeologia* 42: 53–76

Fox, A. H. L., 1870a, 'On a Supposed Ogham Inscription from Rus-Glass, County Cork', *Journal of the Ethnological Society of London*, 2: 400–402

Fox, A. H. L., 1870b, 'On the Threatened Destruction of the British Earthworks near Dorchester, Oxfordshire', *Journal of the Ethnological Society of London* 2(4): 412–16

Fox, A. H. L., 1871, 'On a Wooden Instrument from Skull, near Skibbereen', *Proceedings of the Society of Antiquaries of London* 5: 222–3

Fox, A. H. L., 1872, 'On the Discovery of Palaeolithic Implements, in Connection with *Elephas Primigenius* in the Gravels of the Thames Valley at Acton', *Quarterly Journal of the Geological Society of London* 28: 449–66

Fox, A. H. L., 1873a, 'Address to the Department of Anthropology of the British Association at Brighton', in Anon (ed.) *Report of the 42nd Meeting of the British Association for the Advancement of Science, Held at Brighton in August 1872*, London: John Murray, pp. 157–74

Fox, A. H. L., 1873b, 'Correspondence: The English System of Musketry and the Hythe School' (letter dated 15 October 1873), *Volunteer Service Gazette* (18 October 1873), p. 803

Fox, A. H. L., J. Beddoe, A. W. Franks, F. Galton, E. W. Brabrook, J. Lubbock, W. Elliot, C. R. Markham and E. B. Tylor (eds), 1874, *Notes and Queries on Anthropology, for the Use of Travellers and Residents in Uncivilised Lands*, London: Edward Stanford

Fox, A. H. L., 1875a, 'On the Principles of Classification Adopted in the Arrangement of his Anthropological Collection, Now Exhibited in the Bethnal Green Museum', *Journal of the Anthropological Institute* 4: 293–308

Fox, A. H. L., 1875b, 'On the Evolution of Culture (Weekly Evening Meeting, Friday May 28, 1875)', in Anon (ed.), *Notices of the Proceedings at the Meetings of Members of the Royal Institution of Great Britain with Abstracts of the Discourses Delivered at Evening Meetings Vol. 7 (1873–1875)*, London: William Clowes & Sons, pp. 496–520

Fox, A. H. L., 1875c, Unpublished lecture delivered at the Whitechapel Foundation School, 2 February 1875, Pitt Rivers Papers, Salisbury and South Wiltshire Museum, P42, transcribed at https://web.prm.ox.ac.uk/rpr/index.php/article-index/12-articles/631-whitchapel-1875/index.html

Fox, A. H. L., 1876a, 'President's Address', *Journal of the Anthropological Institute of Great Britain and Ireland* 5: 465–88

Fox, A. H. L., 1876b, 'Excavations in Cissbury Camp, Sussex, Being a Report of the Exploration Committee of the Anthropological Institute for the Year 1875', *Journal of the Anthropological Institute* 5: 357–89

Fox, A. H. L., 1876c, 'Note on the Chest Measurements of Recruits', *Journal of the Anthropological Institute* 5: 101–6

Fox, A. H. L., 1877a, *Catalogue of the Anthropological Collection Lent by Colonel Lane Fox for Exhibition in the Bethnal Green Branch of the South Kensington Museum, June 1874, with Illustrations, Parts I and II*, London: Eyre & Spottiswoode

Fox, A. H. L., 1877b, 'Report on Measurements of the Whole of the Officers and Men of the 2nd Royal Surrey Militia, According to the General Instructions Drawn Up by the Anthropological Committee of the British Association', *Journal of the Anthropological Institute* 6: 443–57

Fox, A. H. L., 1878a, 'General Fox on Genius and Evolution' (letter to the editor), *The Spectator* 51 (2618) (31 August 1878): 1097–8

Fox, A. H. L., 1878b, 'The Arrangement of Museums', *Nature* 17(442) (18 April 1878): 484–5

Fox, A. H. L., 1977 [1854], 'Description of the Battle of Alma', in M. W. Thompson, *General Pitt-Rivers: Evolution and Archaeology in the Nineteenth Century*, Bradford-on-Avon: Moonraker Press, pp. 134–5

Freire-Marreco, B., 1907, 'A Bibliography of Edward Burnett Tylor from 1861 to 1907', in N. W. Thomas (ed.), *Anthropological Essays Presented to Edward Burnett Tylor in Honour of his 75th Birthday*, Oxford: Clarendon Press, pp. 375–409

Freud, S., 1921 [1919], 'Introduction', in S. Ferenczi, K. Abraham, E. Simmel and E. Jones, *Psycho-analysis and the War Neuroses*, London: International Psycho-Analytical Press, pp. 1–4

Friedman, J., 1997, review of Sahlins' *How 'Natives' Think: About Captain Cook, for Example*, *American Ethnologist* 24(1): 261–2

Frost, R., 1947, 'Directive', in *Steeple Bush*, New York: Henry Holt, pp. 7–9

Froude, J. A., 1889, *The Two Chiefs of Dunboy, or an Irish Romance of the Last Century*, New York: Charles Scribner's Sons

Fuhrmeister, C., 2001, *Beton Klinker Granit: Material macht Politik. Eine Materialikonographie*, Berlin: Bauwesen Verlag

Fukuyama, F., 1992, *The End of History and the Last Man*, New York: Free Press

Fulweiler, H. W., 2000, 'The Strange Case of Governor Eyre: Race and the "Victorian Frame of Mind"', *Clio* 29(2): 119–42

Gaddis, E., 2022, 'Place and Materiality', in L. A. De Cunzo and C. Dann Roeber (eds), *The Cambridge Handbook of Material Culture Studies*, Cambridge: Cambridge University Press, pp. 471–92

Gallagher, T. F., 1980, 'The Second Reform Movement, 1848–1867', *Albion* 12(2): 147–63

Galton, F., 1869, *Hereditary Genius: An Inquiry into its Laws and Consequences*, London: Macmillan & Co

Galton, F., 1892, *Hereditary Genius: An Inquiry into its Laws and Consequences* (second edition), London: Macmillan & Co

Gantz, K. N., 1939, 'The Beginnings of Darwinian Ethics, 1859–1871', *Studies in English* 19: 180–209

Garwood, I., 2003, *Mistley in the Days of the Rigbys*, Thorndon: Lucas Books

Gasquoine, P. G., 2020, 'Railway Spine: The Advent of Compensation for Concussive Symptoms', *Journal of the History of the Neurosciences* 29(2): 234–45

Gibb, G. D., 1866, 'Comments on the Essential Differences Observable Between the Larynx of the Negro and That of the White Man', *Memoirs of the Anthropological Society of London* 2 (1866–1866): 1–13

Gibson, W., 1984, *Neuromancer*, New York: Ace

Gildea, J., 1911, *For Remembrance and in Honour of Those Who Lost Their Lives in the South African War 1899–1902*, London: Eyre & Spottiswoode

Gilmore, R. W., 2021, *Abolition Geography: Essays Towards Liberation*, London: Verso

Gilmore, R. W., 2022, 'The Prison-Industrial Complex Goes Beyond Cops and Jails. It's All Around Us' (interview with Alberto Toscano and Brenna Bhandar), *Jacobin Magazine* (8 February 2022)

Gilroy, P., 2002, *Postcolonial Melancholia*, New York: Columbia University Press

Gilroy, P., 2012, '"My Britain Is Fuck All": Zombie Multiculturalism and the Race Politics of Citizenship', *Identities* 19(4): 380–97

Gilroy, P., 2021, 'Introduction: Race is the Prism', in P. Gilroy and R. W. Gilmore (eds), *Stuart Hall: Selected Writings on Race and Difference*, Durham, NC: Duke University Press, pp. 1–9

Ginzburg, C., 1990, *Myths, Emblems, Clues*, London: Radius

Gobineau, A. de, 1856 [1853], *The Moral and Intellectual Diversity of Races* (ed. and trans. H. Hotz), Philadelphia, PA: J. B. Lippincott & Co

Gomme, G. L., 1890, *The Village Community, with Special Reference to the Origin and Form of its Survivals in Britain*, London: Walter Scott

Goody, J., 1976, *Production and Reproduction: A Comparative Study of the Domestic Domain*, Cambridge: Cambridge University Press

Gopal, P., 2019, *Insurgent Empire: Anticolonial Resistance and British Dissent*, London: Verso

Gosse, E., 1921, *Books on the Table*, London: William Heinemann

Gossman, N. J., 1983, 'William Cuffay: London's Black Chartist', *Phylon* 44(1): 56–65

Gould, S. J., 1981, *The Mismeasure of Man*, New York: W. W. Norton & Co

Gramsci, A., 1951, *Passato e presente*, Turin: Einaudi

Gramsci, A., 2007 [1930–31], 'Notebook 7', in *Prison Notebooks Vol. III* (ed. and trans. J. A. Buttigieg), New York: Columbia University Press, pp. 151–228

Gray, A., 1919, 'The Everlasting Club', in *Tedious Brief Tales of Granta and Gramarye*, Cambridge: W. Heffer & Sons, pp. 1–8

Gray, H. St G. (ed.), 1905, *Excavations in Cranborne Chase Vol. V*, Taunton: privately published

Greenberg, J., 1966, *Language Universals, with Special Reference to Feature Hierarchies*, The Hague: Mouton

Greenblatt, S., 1980, *Renaissance Self-Fashioning: From More to Shakespeare*, Chicago: University of Chicago Press

Greenwell, W., 1877, *British Barrows: A Record of the Examination of Sepulchrall Mounds in Various Parts of England, Together with Descriptions of Figures of Skulls, General Remarks on Prehistoric Crania and an Appendix by George Rolleston*, Oxford: Clarendon Press

Grenfell, F. W., 1925, *Memoirs of Field-Marshal Lord Grenfell*, London: Hodder & Stoughton

Guattari, F., 1989, *Les trois écologies*, Paris: Éditions Galilée

Guha, R., 1997, 'Not at Home in Empire', *Critical Inquiry* 23(3): 482–93

Guppy, H. F. J., 1864, 'Notes on the Capabilities of the Negro for Civilisation', *Journal of the Anthropological Society of London* 2: ccix–ccxvi

Gustafson, K., 2021, 'Death of Democracy, North Carolina', in K. Roberts Forde and S. Bedingfield (eds), *Journalism and Jim Crow: White Supremacy and the Black Struggle for a New America*, Urbana: University of Illinois Press, pp. 171–200

Hacking, I., 1990, *The Taming of Chance*, Cambridge: Cambridge University Press

Haddon, A. C., 1900, 'Pitt-Rivers', *Nature* 42: 59–60

Haddon, A. C. (ed.), 1935, *Reports of the Cambridge Anthropological Expedition to Torres Straits (1901–1935) Vol. 1: General Ethnography*, Cambridge: Cambridge University Press

Hall, C., 1989, 'The Economy of Intellectual Prestige: Thomas Carlyle, John Stuart Mill, and the Case of Governor Eyre', *Cultural Critique* 12: 167–96

Hall, C., 1992, *White, Male, and Middle Class: Explorations in Feminism and History*, London: Polity Press

Hall, C., 1994, 'Rethinking Imperial Histories: The Reform Act of 1867', *New Left Review* 208: 3–29

Hall, C., 1996, 'Imperial Man: Edward Eyre in Australasia and the West Indies, 1833–66', in B. Schwarz (ed.), *The Expansion of England: Race, Ethnicity and Cultural History*, London: Routledge, pp. 129–68

Hall, C., 2001, 'Men and Their Histories: Civilizing Subjects', *History Workshop Journal*, Vol. 52(1): 49–66

Hall, C., 2002, *Civilizing Subjects: Metropole and Colony in the English Imagination 1830–1867*, Cambridge: Polity

Hall, S., 1980, 'Cultural Studies and the Centre: Some Problematics and Problems', in S. Hall, D. Hobson, A. Lowe and P. Willis (eds), *Culture, Media, Language: Working Papers in Cultural Studies, 1972–79*, London: Unwin Hyman, pp. 2–35

Hall, S., 1987, 'Gramsci and Us', *Marxism Today* (June 1987): 16–21

Hall, S., 1996, 'When Was "the Postcolonial"? Thinking at the Limit', in I. Chambers and L. Curti (eds), *The Postcolonial Question: Common Skies, Divided Horizons*, London: Routledge, pp. 242–60

Hall, S., 1999a, 'From Scarman to Stephen Lawrence', *History Workshop Journal* 48: 187–97

Hall, S., 1999b, 'Un-settling "the Heritage", Re-imagining the Post-nation. Whose Heritage?', *Third Text*, 13(49): 3–13

Hall, S., 2021 [1975], '"Africa" is Alive and Well in the Diaspora: Cultures of Resistance: Slavery, Religious Revival and Political Cultism in Jamaica', in P. Gilroy and R. W. Gilmore (eds), *Stuart Hall: Selected Writings on Race and Difference*, Durham, NC: Duke University Press, pp. 161–94

Hall, S., 2021 [1981], 'The Whites of Their Eyes: Racist Ideologies and the Media', in P. Gilroy and R. W. Gilmore (eds), *Stuart Hall: Selected Writings on Race and Difference*, Durham, NC: Duke University Press, pp. 97–120

Hall, S., 2021 [1997], 'Race, the Floating Signifier: What More Is There to Say About "Race"?', in P. Gilroy and R. W. Gilmore (eds), *Stuart Hall: Selected Writings on Race and Difference*, Durham, NC: Duke University Press, pp. 359–73

Hall, S., C. Critcher, T. Jefferson, J. Clarke and B. Roberts, 1978, *Policing the Crisis: Mugging, the State, and Law and Order*, London: Macmillan

Hall, S., R. Samuel and C. Taylor, 1987, 'Then and Now: A Re-evaluation of the New Left (interview)', in Oxford University Socialist Group (ed.), *Out of Apathy: Voices of the New Left Thirty Years On*, London: Verso, pp. 143–70

Hamilton, F. W., 1874, *The Origin and History of the First of Grenadier Guards Vol. III*, London: John Murray

Handfield Jones, C., 1855, 'Record of a Case of Crimean Fever', *The Lancet* 2: 461–2

Haraway, D., 2016, *Staying with the Trouble: Making Kin in the Chthulucene*, Durham, NC: Duke University Press

Harding, D. F., 1997, *Smallarms of the East India Company, 1600–1856 Vol. III: Ammunition and Performance*, London: Foresight Books

Hardy, T., 1912, 'Preface', in *Far from the Madding Crowd*, London: Macmillan & Co, pp. vii–ix

Hardy, T., 1913 [1885], *A Changed Man, and Other Tales*, London: Macmillan & Co

Harrison, S. J., 2008, 'Skulls and Scientific Collecting in the Victorian Military: Keeping the Enemy Dead in British Frontier Warfare', *Comparative Studies in Society and History* 50(1): 285–303

Harrison, S. J., 2012, *Dark Trophies: Hunting and the Enemy Body in Modern War*, Oxford and New York: Berghahn

Hart, B., 2015, *George Pitt-Rivers and the Nazis*, London: Bloomsbury

Hart, H. G., 1861, *The New Annual Army List and Militia List for 1861*, London: John Murray

Hart, H. G., 1866, *The New Annual Army List and Militia List for 1866*, London: John Murray

Hart, H. G., 1883, *The New Annual Army List, Militia List, Yeomanry Cavalry List and Indian Civil Service List for 1883*, London: John Murray

Hart, H. G., 1890, *The New Annual Army List, Militia List, Yeomanry Cavalry List and Indian Civil Service List for 1890*, London: John Murray

Hartman, S., 1997, *Scenes of Subjection: Terror, Slavery and Self-making in Nineteenth-century America*, Oxford: Oxford University Press

Hartman, S., 2008, 'Venus in Two Acts', *Small Axe*, 26: 1–14

Hartman, S., 2019, *Wayward Lives, Beautiful Experiments: Intimate Histories of Social Upheaval*, London: W. W. Norton & Co

Hartman, S., 2021, 'Intimate History, Radical Narrative', *Journal of African American History* 106(1): 127–35

Hartman, S., 2022a, 'The Time of Slavery', *South Atlantic Quarterly* 101(4): 757–77

Hartman, S., 2022b, 'Preface: The Hold of Slavery', in *Scenes of Subjection: Terror, Slavery and Self-making in Nineteenth-century America* (revised and updated edition), New York: W. W. Norton & Co

Haslam, R., J. Orbach and A. Voelcker, 2009, *The Buildings of Wales: Gwynedd*, New Haven, CT: Yale University Press (Pevsner Architectural Guides: Buildings of Wales)

Hegel, G. W. F., 1848 [1837], *Vorlesungen über die Philosophie der Geschichte*, Berlin: Duncker & Humblot

Heidegger, M., 1977, *The Question Concerning Technology and Other Essays* (trans. W. Lovitt), New York: Harper & Row

Heilmann, A. and M. Llewellyn, 2010, *Neo-Victorianism: The Victorians in the Twenty-first Century, 1999–2009*, London: Palgrave Macmillan

Herle, A., 1990, 'Medium and Message in an Anthropological Exhibit: Curating "The Nagas"', *Visual Anthropology Review*, 6 (2): 55–61

Hertz, R., 1960 [1907–1909], *Death and the Right Hand* (trans. R. Needham and C. Needham), Glencoe, IL: Free Press

Heuman, G., 1994, *The Killing Time: The Morant Bay Rebellion in Jamaica*, Knoxville, TN: University of Tennessee Press

Heuman, G., 2008, 'Eyre, Edward John', *Oxford Dictionary of National Biography*, Oxford: Oxford University Press, https://doi.org/10.1093/ref:odnb/33060

Hicks, D., 2004, 'Historical Archaeology and the British', *Cambridge Archaeological Journal*, 14(1): 101–6

Hicks, D., 2010, 'The Material-Cultural Turn: Event and Effect', in D. Hicks and M. C. Beaudry (eds), *The Oxford Handbook to Material Culture Studies*, Oxford: Oxford University Press, pp. 27–99

Hicks, D., 2013, 'Four-field Anthropology: Charter Myths and Time Warps from St. Louis to Oxford,' *Current Anthropology* 54(6): 753–763

Hicks, D., 2016a, 'The Temporality of the Landscape Revisited' and 'Meshwork Fatigue' (with responses by Tim Ingold, Matt Edgeworth and Laurent Olivier), *Norwegian Archaeological Review* 49(1): 5–39

Hicks, D., 2016b, 'Pitt-Rivers, 2065', *Museum i-D* 19: 31–7

Hicks, D. 2019a, 'Event Density', in A. Boyd, J. Meades and D. Hicks, *Isle of Rust: A Portrait of Harris and Lewis*, Edinburgh: Luath Press, pp. 185–90

Hicks, D., 2019b, 'Memory and the Photological Landscape', in S. De Nardi, H. Orange, S. High and E. Koskinen-Koivisto (eds), *The Routledge Handbook of Memory and Place*, New York: Routledge, pp. 254–60

Hicks, D., 2020a, 'Why Colston Had to Fall', *Art Review* (9 June 2020), https://artreview.com/why-colston-had-to-fall/

Hicks, D., 2020b, *The Brutish Museums: The Benin Bronzes, Colonial Violence and Cultural Restitution*, London: Pluto Press

Hicks, D., 2021a, 'Necrography: Death-writing in the Colonial Museum', *Journal of British Art Studies* 19

Hicks, D., 2021b, 'Glorious Memory', in H. Carr and S. Lipscombe (eds), *What Is History Now?*, London: Weidenfeld & Nicolson., pp. 147–67

Hicks, D., 2021c, 'Let's Keep Colston Falling', *Art Review*, https://artreview.com/lets-keep-colston-falling/

Hicks, D., 2021d, Preface to the paperback edition, in *The Brutish Museums: The Benin Bronzes, Colonial Violence and Cultural Restitution*, London: Pluto Press, pp. xviii–xxii.

Hicks, D., 2023a, 'Are Museums Obsolete?' *Architectural Review*, https://www.architectural-review.com/essays/are-museums-obsolete

Hicks, D., 2023b, 'Declining Whiteness', in O. Wambu (ed.), *Empire Windrush: Reflections on 75 Years & More of the Black British Experience*, London: Hachette

Hicks, D. and M. C. Beaudry (eds), 2010, *The Oxford Handbook of Material Culture Studies*, Oxford: Oxford University Press

Hicks, D. and L. McFadyen (eds), 2019, *Archaeology and Photography: Time, Objectivity and Archive*, London: Bloomsbury

Hicks, D. and S. Mallet, 2019, *Lande: The Calais 'Jungle' and Beyond*, Bristol: Bristol University Press

Hicks, D. and N. Mirzoeff, 2020, 'Fallism and Restitution: Removing Racist Statues and Returning Looted Art Objects', *New African Magazine* (17 August 2020) https://newafricanmagazine.com/23931/

Hicks, D. and A. Stevenson (eds), 2013, *World Archaeology at the Pitt Rivers Museum: A Characterization*, Oxford: Archaeopress

Higginson, A. H., 1937, *Peter Beckford, Esquire, Sportsman, Traveller, Man of Letters: A Biography*, London: Collins

Higginson, G. W. A., 1916, *Seventy-One Years of a Guardsman's Life*, London: Smith, Elder & Co

Hilton, J., 2017, 'Cecil John Rhodes, the Classics and Imperialism', in G. Parker (ed.), *South Africa, Greece, Rome: Classical Confrontations*, Cambridge: Cambridge University Press, pp. 88–115

Hitchcock, R. K. and C. Flowerday, 2020, 'Ishi and the California Indian Genocide as Developmental Mass Violence', *Humboldt Journal of Social Relations* 42: 69–85

Hitchens, C., 2000, 'Officer Material', *Times Literary Supplement* 5092 (3 November 2000): 3–4

Ho, E., 2012, *Neo-Victorianism and the Memory of Empire*, London: Continuum

Hobsbawm, E., 1965, *Primitive Rebels: Studies in Archaic Forms of Social Movements in the 19th and 20th Centuries*, New York: W. W. Norton

Hodge, D., 2022, *Judgement of the Worshipful David Hodge QC*, Ely: Consistory Court of Ely, https://lawandreligionuk.com/wp-content/uploads/2022/03/Re-the-Rustat-Memorial-Jesus-College-Cambridge2022-ECC-Ely-2.pdf

Hodge, M., 1990, 'Challenges of the Struggle for Sovereignty: Changing the World Versus Writing Stories', in S. R. Cudjoe (ed.), *Caribbean Women Writers: Essays from the First International Conference*, Wellesley, MA: Calaloux Publications, pp. 202–9

Hodgkinson, R., 2021, 'Overexposed: Looking Around Photographic Texts and Images in the Archive', *Archaeological Review from Cambridge* 36(2): 31–44

Holterhoff, K., 2021, '"An Absurd Parody of the Professor": Illustrating Professor Challenger in *The Lost World*', in N. Clausson (ed.), *Re-Examining Arthur Conan Doyle*, Newcastle-upon-Tyne: Cambridge Scholars Press, pp. 116–40

Hoole, W. S., 1957, *Vizetelly Covers the Confederacy*, Tuscaloosa, AL: Confederate Publishing Company

Hoskins, W. G., 1955, *The Making of the English Landscape*, London: Hodder & Stoughton

Hotze, H., 1863, 'The Natural History of Man', *The Index: a Weekly Journal of Politics, Literature and News Devoted to the Exposition of the Mutual Interests, Political and Commercial of Great Britain and the Confederate States of America* 3(65): 204–5

House of Commons, 1867, 'Account of Income and Expenditure of British Museum, 1866–67', *House of Commons Sessional Papers* XXXIX.233: Paper 249, London: House of Commons

House of Commons, 1881, Pitt Rivers Collection, copies of letter from General Pitt Rivers, in which he offers to present his collection to the nation; of the report of the committee appointed by the government to consider the offer; and, of letter from the government declining to accept the collection,

*House of Commons Sessional Papers* LXXIII.519: Paper 322, London: House of Commons

Howse, C., 2009, 'Pitt Rivers Museum: canoes, monkey skulls and a witch in a bottle', *Daily Telegraph* (2 May 2009)

Hume, H., 1866, 'Edward John Eyre, Governor of Jamaica, with an Account of his Early Life', *British Army and Navy Review* 19(4): 1–15

Hume, H., 1867, *The Life of Edward John Eyre*, London: Richard Bentley

Hunt, J., 1863a, *Introductory Address on the Study of Anthropology Delivered Before the Anthropological Society of London February 24th 1863*, London: Trübner & Co

Hunt, J., 1863b, 'Geography and Ethnology', in Anon (ed.) *Report of the Thirty-Third Meeting of the British Association for the Advancement of Science, Held at Newcastle-upon-Tyne in August and September 1863 (Notes and Abstracts)*, London: John Murray, p. 140

Hunt, J., 1864, 'On the Negro's Place in Nature', *Journal of the Anthropological Society of London* 2: xv–xxiii

Hunt, J., 1866, *Anniversary Address Delivered Before the Anthropological Society of London, 3 January 1866*, London: Trübner & Co

Hunt, S. B., 1869, 'The Negro as a Soldier', *Anthropological Review* 7(24): 40–54

Hunter, D., 2018, 'The Beckfords in England and Italy: A Case Study in the Musical Uses of the Profits of Slavery', *Early Music* 46(2): 285–98

Hutton, J. H., 1921, *The Sema Nagas*, London: Macmillan & Co

Huxley, T. H., 1863, *Man's Place in Nature*, London: Williams & Norgate

Huxley, T. H., 1865, 'Emancipation—Black and White', *The Reader: A Review of Literature, Science and Art*, 5(125): 561–2

Huxley, T. H., 1874a, 'On the Hypothesis that Animals are Automata, and its History', *Nature* 10: 362–6

Huxley, T. H., 1874b, 'Hypothesis that Animals are Automata', *Fortnightly Review* 16 (95): 555–80

Huxley, T. H., 1894 [1893], 'Evolution and Ethics' (the Romanes Lecture), in *Evolution and Ethics and Other Essays*, London: Macmillan & Co, pp. 46–116

Huxtable, S.-A., C. Fowler, C. Kefalas and E. Slocombe, 2020, 'Interim Report on the Connections Between Colonialism and Properties Now in the Care of the National Trust, Including Links with Historic Slavery'

Imperial College London, 2021, *Community Report from the History Group, October 2021*, Imperial College London, www.imperial.ac.uk/media/imperial-college/administration-and-support-services/equality/public/history-group/History-Group-Report---October-2021.pdf

Impey, E., 2011, 'The Rhodes Building at Oriel, 1904–2011: Dynamite or Designate?', *Oxoniensia* 76: 95–105
Ingold, T., 2013, *Making: Anthropology, Archaeology, Art and Architecture*, London: Routledge
Jackson, J. W., 1867, 'On the Value of Phrenology in Anthropological Investigations', *Anthropological Review* 5(16): 71–8
Jackson, Z. I., 2020, *Becoming Human: Matter and Meaning in an Antiblack World*, New York: New York University Press
Jacobs, J., A. Macfarlane, S. Harrison and A. Herle, 1990, *The Nagas – Hill Peoples of Northeast India: Society, Culture and the Colonial Encounter*, London: Thames & Hudson
James, H., 1873, 'The Bethnal Green Museum', *Atlantic Monthly* 31: 69–75
Jameson, F., 1991, *Postmodernism, or, the Cultural Logic of Late Capitalism*, Durham, NC: Duke University Press
Jameson, J. F., 1930, 'The London Expenditures of the Confederate Secret Service', *American Historical Review* 35(4): 811–24
Jobson, R. C., 2020, 'The Case for Letting Anthropology Burn: Sociocultural Anthropology in 2019', *American Anthropologist* 122(2): 259–71
Johst, H., 1933, *Schlageter: Schauspiel*, Munich: A. Langen and G. Müller
Jones, E., 2006, 'Historical Approaches to Post-combat Disorders', *Philosophical Transactions of the Royal Society* 361: 533–42
Jones, E. and S. Wessely, 1999, 'Case of Chronic Fatigue Syndrome After Crimean War and Indian Mutiny', *British Medical Journal* 319: 1645–7
Jones, E. and S. Wessely, 2001, 'The Origins of British Military Psychiatry Before the First World War', *War and Society* 19(2): 91–108
Jones, E. and S. Wessely, 2006, *Shell Shock to PTSD: Military Psychiatry from 1900 to the Gulf War*, Hove: Psychology Press
Jones, L., 1985, *Marx, Lenin and Hyde Park*, London: New Socialist
Julien, I., 2017, 'From *Ten Thousand Waves* to Lina Bo Bardi, via *Kapital*', in N. M. Alter and T. Corrigan (eds), *Essays on the Essay Film*, New York: Columbia University Press, pp. 335–44
Jünger, E., 1922, *In Stahlgewittern: aus dem Tagebuch eines Stosstruppführers*, Berlin: E. S. Mittler and Son
Jünger, E., 1925, 'Der Krieg als inneres Erlebnis', *Die Standarte: Beiträge zur geistigen Vertiefung des Frontgedankens* (11 October 1925): 2
Kabbani, R., 1986, *Europe's Myths of the Orient*, London: Macmillan
Kassim, S., 2023, 'Museums are Temples of Whiteness', in T. Flores, F. San Martín and C. Villaseñor Black (eds), *The Routledge Companion to Decolonizing Art History*, London: Routledge, pp. 128–38

Keith, A., 1917, 'Presidential Address: How Can the Institute Best Serve the Needs of Anthropology?', *Journal of the Royal Anthropological Institute of Great Britain and Ireland* 47: 12–30

Keith, A., 1919, *Nationality and Race from an Anthropologist's Point of View being the Robert Boyle Lecture Delivered Before the Oxford University Junior Scientific Club on November 17, 1919*, Oxford: Oxford University Press

Keith, A., 1924, 'The pre-Saxon Briton of Roman days', *Illustrated London News* (31 May 1924): 1018, 1032

Keith, A., 1927, 'What Should Museums Do for Us?', *Handbook of the Lister Centenary Exhibition at the Wellcome Historical Medical Museum*, London: Wellcome Foundation, pp. 200–8

Kim, B.-O., 1973, *Rilkes Militärschulerlebnis und das Problem des verlorenen Sohnes*, Bonn: Bouvier Verlag

Kinnes, I. A. and I. H. Longworth, 1985, *Catalogue of the Excavated Prehistoric and Romano-British Material in the Greenwell Collection*, London: British Museum Publications

Klein, N., 2007, *The Shock Doctrine: Rise of Disaster Capitalism*, London: Allen Lane

Klemm, G. F., 1845–51, *Allgemeine Kulturgeschichte der Menschheit* (ten volumes), Leipzig: B. G. Teubner

Klemm, G. F., 1858, *Die Werkzeuge und Waffen: ihre Entstehung und Ausbildung*, Sondershausen: G. Neuse

Knox, R., 1850, *The Races of Man: A Fragment*, Philadelphia, PA: Lea & Blanchard

Kochan, J., 2015, 'Objective Styles in Northern Field Science', *Studies in History and Philosophy of Science* 52: 1–12

Koram, K., 2022, *Uncommon Wealth: Britain and the Aftermath of Empire*, London: John Murray

Kostal, R. W., 2008, *A Jurisprudence of Power: Victorian Empire and the Rule of Law*, Oxford: Oxford University Press

Kroeber, A. L., 1909, 'Classificatory Systems of Relationship', *Journal of the Royal Anthropological Society* 37: 77–84

Kroeber, A. L., 1959, 'The History of the Personality of Anthropology', *American Anthropologist* 61(3): 398–404

Kroeber, A. L. and C. Kluckhohn, 1952, *Culture: A Critical Review of Concepts and Definitions*, Cambridge, MA: Peabody Museum Press

Kroeber, T., 1961, *Ishi in Two Worlds: A Biography of the Last Wild Indian in North America*, Berkeley: University of California Press

Kroeber, T., 1970, *Alfred Kroeber: A Personal Configuration*, Berkeley: University of California Press

Lambert, M. C., E. J. Sobo and V. L. Lambert, 2021, 'Rethinking Land Acknowledgments', *Anthropology News* 62(6)

Latour, B., 1990, 'The Force and Reason of Experiment', in H. E. Le Grand (ed.), *Experimental Inquiries*, Dordrecht: Kluwer, pp. 49–80

Latour, B., 1993, *We Have Never Been Modern* (trans. C. Porter), Brighton: Harvester Wheatsheaf

Latour, B., 1999, *Pandora's Hope: Essays on the Reality of Science Studies*, Cambridge, MA: Harvard University Press

Latour, B., 2013, *An Enquiry into Modes of Existence* (trans. C. Porter), Cambridge, MA: Harvard University Press

Le Guin, U. K., 1966, 'The Rule of Names', *Fantastic Stories of Imagination* 38(8) (April 1964)

Le Guin, U. K., 1980, 'It Was a Dark and Stormy Night; or, Why Are We Huddling About the Campfire?', *Critical Inquiry* 7(1): 191–9

Le Guin, U. K., 1988 [1986], 'The Carrier Bag Theory of Fiction', in *Dancing at the Edge of the World: Thoughts on Words, Women, Places*, New York: Grove Press, pp. 165–70

Le Guin, U. K., 1996, 'Which Side Am I On, Anyway?', *Frontiers* 17(3): 27–8

Leach, P. and N. Pevsner, 2009, *Yorkshire West Riding: Leeds, Bradford and the North (The Buildings of England)*, New Haven, CT: Yale University Press

Leavis, F. R., 1933, *Mass Civilisation and Minority Culture*, Cambridge: Minority Press

LeClair, D., 2015, 'The "Greased Cartridge Affair": Re-examining the Pattern 1853 Enfield Cartridge and its Role in the Indian Mutiny of 1857', *International Ammunition Association Journal* 504: 98–109

Lee, R., 1864, 'The Extinction of Races', *Journal of the Anthropological Society of London* 2: xcv–xcix

Leetham, A. and B. E. Sargeaunt, 1908, *Official Catalogue of the Royal United Service Museum, Whitehall SW*, London: Royal United Service Institution

Lester, A., 2022, 'The Realpolitik of Emancipation in the British Empire, 1833–38', in J. Damousi, T. Burnard and A. Lester (eds), *Humanitarianism, Empire and Transnationalism 1760–1995: Selective Humanity in the Anglophone World*, Manchester: Manchester University Press, pp. 119–44

Lévi-Strauss, C., 1952, *Racism and Culture*, Paris: UNESCO

Lévi-Strauss, C., 1962, *La pensée sauvage*, Paris: Plon

Lévi-Strauss, C., 1971, 'Comment ils meurent', *Esprit* 4: 694–706

Lévi-Strauss, C., 1974, 'How Myths Die' (trans. F. C. T. Moore), *New Literary History* 5(2): 269–81

Lévi-Strauss, C., 1975, *La voie des masques (Tome II: les sentiers de la création)*, Geneva: Albert Skira

Lévi-Strauss, C., 1987 [1950], *Introduction to the Work of Marcel Mauss* (trans. F. Baker), London: Routledge & Kegan Paul

Lewis, C. S., 1961, *A Grief Observed*, London: Faber & Faber

Lewis, T., 1918, *The Soldier's Heart and the Effort Syndrome*, London: Shaw

Libby, W. F., 1961, 'Radiocarbon Dating', *Science* 133(3453): 621–9

Lindsay, J., 2004, 'Pennant, George Sholto Gordon Douglas-, second Baron Penrhyn', *Oxford Dictionary of National Biography*, Oxford: Oxford University Press, https://doi.org/10.1093/ref:odnb/32878

Lindsay, J., 2023, 'Pennant, Richard, Baron Penrhyn', *Oxford Dictionary of National Biography*, Oxford: Oxford University Press, https://doi.org/10.1093/ref:odnb/21859

Lorde, A., 1978, 'A Litany for Survival', in *The Black Unicorn*, New York: W. W. Norton & Company, p. 31

Lorde, A., 1983 [1979], 'The Master's Tools Will Never Dismantle the Master's House', in C. Moraga and G. Anzaldua (eds), *This Bridge Called My Back: Writings by Radical Women of Color*, New York: Kitchen Table Press, pp. 94–101

Lott, M., 2013, 'Dorothy L. Sayers, the Great War, and Shell Shock', *Interdisciplinary Literary Studies* 15(1): 103–26

Lovell, E. J. (ed.), 1966, *Medwin's Conversations of Lord Byron*, Princeton, NJ: Princeton University Press

Lovell, M. S., 1998, *A Rage to Live: A Biography of Richard and Isabel Burton*, London: W. W. Norton & Co

Lutz, D., 2011, *Pleasure Bound: Victorian Sex Rebels and the New Eroticism*, New York: W. W. Norton & Co

Lyde, M., 2019, 'Interview with Isaac Julien and Mark Nash', *Framework: The Journal of Cinema and Media* 60(2): 189–200

McCann, W. H., 1941, 'Nostalgia: A Review of the Literature', *Psychological Bulletin* 38: 165–82

McClintock, A., 1992, 'The Angel of Progress: Pitfalls of the Term "Postcolonialism"', *Social Text* 31/32: 84–98

Macdonald, H., 2014, *H is for Hawk*, London: Vintage

McDonald, J. G., 1927, *Rhodes: A Life*, London: Philip Allan & Co

McFadyen, L., 2007, 'Neolithic Architecture and Participation: Practices of Making at Long Barrow Sites in Southern Britain', in J. Last (ed.), *Beyond the Grave: New Perspectives on Barrows*, Oxford: Oxbow Books, pp. 22–29

McFadyen, L., 2018, 'Constructing Monuments, Perceiving Monumentality and the Economics of Building', in A. Brysbaert, V. Klinkenberg, A. Gutiérrez Garcia-M. and I. Vikatou (eds), *Constructing Monuments, Perceiving Monumentality and the Economics of Building: Theoretical and Methodological Approaches to the Built Environment*, Leiden: Sidestone Press, pp. 87–102

McGranahan, C., 2017, 'An Anthropology of Lying: Trump and the Political Sociality of Moral Outrage', *American Ethnologist* 44(2): 243–8

McLean, S., 2017, *Fictionalizing Anthropology: Encounters and Fabulations at the Edges of the Human*, Minneapolis: University of Minnesota Press

MacGregor, J., 1861, 'On the Hythe School of Musketry Instruction in Rifle Shooting', *Journal of the Society of Arts* 9: 473–4

Mackay, C., 1867, 'Russian Scandal', *London Review* 14 (346) (16 February 1867): 199–201

MacKellar, L., and B. W. Hart, 2014, 'Captain George Henry Lane-Fox Pitt-Rivers and the Prehistory of the IUSSP', *Population and Development Review* 40(4): 653–75

McKeon, M., 1981, 'The "Marxism" of Claude Lévi-Strauss', *Dialectical Anthropology* 6(2): 123–50

McKittrick, K., 2021, *Dear Science and Other Stories*, Durham, NC: Duke University Press

McKittrick, K. and S. Wynter 2015, 'Unparalleled Catastrophe for Our Species?: Or, to Give Humanness a Different Future: Conversations', in K. McKittrick (ed.) *Sylvia Wynter: On Being Human as Praxis*, Durham, NC: Duke University Press, pp. 9–89

Maclean, W. C., 1864, 'The Influence of the Present Knapsack and Accoutrements on the Health of the Infantry Soldier', *Journal of the Royal United Service Institution* 8: 105–15

McLennan, G., 2021, 'Editor's Introduction', in G. McLennan (ed.), *Stuart Hall: Selected Writings on Marxism*, Durham, NC: Duke University Press, pp. 1–16

Macpherson, W., 1999, *The Stephen Lawrence Inquiry*, London: Home Office, https://assets.publishing.service.gov.uk/media/5a7c2af540f0b645b a3c7202/4262.pdf

Maguire, J. R., 1897, *Cecil Rhodes: A Biography and Appreciation*, London: Macmillan

Malchow, H. L., 1996, *Gothic Images of Race in Nineteenth-century England*, Stanford, CA: Stanford University Press

Malinowski, B., 1922, *Argonauts of the Western Pacific: Robert Mond Expedition to New Guinea, 1914–1918*, London: George Routledge & Sons

Malthus, T. R., 1803, *An Essay on the Principle of Population: or, a View of its Past and Present Effects on Human Happiness* (new edition), London: Johnson

Manjapra, K., 2019, 'The Scandal of the British Slavery Abolition Act', *Social and Economic Studies* 68(3/4): 165–84

Manjapra, K., 2022a, 'Beware the "ghostliners": people who mask Britain's slavery shame and mute calls for justice', *Guardian* (27 August 2022)

Manjapra, K., 2022b, *Black Ghost of Empire: The Long Death of Slavery and the Failure of Emancipation*, London: Allen Lane

Mansfield, N., 2016, *Soldiers as Workers: Class, Employment, Conflict and the Nineteenth-century Military*, Liverpool: Liverpool University Press (Studies in Labour History 6)

Marett, R. R., 1909, *The Threshold of Religion*, London: Methuen

Marks, S. and S. Trapido, 2013, 'Rhodes, Cecil John', *Oxford Dictionary of National Biography*, Oxford: Oxford University Press, https://doi.org/10.1093/ref:odnb/35731

Marshall, J., 1833, *Royal Navy Biography: or, Memoirs of the Services of all the Flag-officers, Superannuated Rear-admirals, Retired Captains, Post-captains and Commanders Vol. IV Part 1*, London: Orme, Brown, Green & Longman

Marx, K., 1887 [1867], *Capital: A Critique of Political Economy Volume 1: The Process and Production of Capital* (trans. S. Moore and E. B. Aveling), London: Swan Sonnenschein

Marx, K., 1956 [1844], 'Zur Kritik der Hegelschen Rechtsphilosophie', in *Karl Marx Friedrich Engels Werke Vol. 1*, Berlin: Dietz Verlag, pp. 378–91.

Marx, K., 1961 [1855], 'Kirchliche Agitation (Hyde Park)', in *Karl Marx Friedrich Engels Werke Vol. 11*, Berlin: Dietz Verlag, pp. 322–7

Marx, K., 2010a [1857], 'Circuit and Turnover of Capital' (Economic Manuscripts of 1857–58), in *Marx and Engels: Collected Works Vol. 28*, London: Lawrence & Wishart, pp. 439–72

Marx, K., 2010b [1866], Letter to Engels, 27 July 1866, in *Marx and Engels: Collected Works Vol. 42, Letters 1864–1868*, London: Lawrence & Wishart, pp. 299–301

Marx, K., 2010c [1865], Letter to Engels, 20 November 1865, in *Marx and Engels: Collected Works Vol. 42, Letters 1864–1868*, London: Lawrence & Wishart, pp. 198–9

Marx, K., 2010d [1857], 'The Revolt in the Indian Army', in *Marx and Engels: Collected Works Vol. 15, 1856–1858*, London: Lawrence & Wishart, pp. 297–300

Marx, K., 2010e [1852], 'The Eighteenth Brumaire of Louis Bonaparte', in *Marx and Engels: Collected Works Vol. 11, 1851–1853*, London: Lawrence & Wishart, pp. 99–197

Marx, K., 2010f [1844], 'Contribution to the Critique of Hegel's Philosophy of Law', in *Marx and Engels: Collected Works Vol. 3, Karl Marx March 1843–August 1844*, London: Lawrence & Wishart, pp. 175–87

Marx, K. and F. Engels, 2010 [1850], 'Review', in *Marx and Engels: Collected Works Vol. 10, 1849–1851*, London: Lawrence & Wishart, pp. 490–532

Mason, O., 1900, 'Traps of the Amerinds: A Study in Psychology and Invention', *American Anthropologist* 2(4): 657–75

Massey, G. C., M. V. Scott and S. M. Dornbusch, 1975, 'Racism Without Racists: Institutional Racism in Urban Schools', *Black Scholar* 7(3): 10–19

Massola, A., 1961, 'A Victorian Skull-cup Drinking Bowl', *Mankind: Official Journal of the Anthropological Societies of Australia* 5(10): 415–19

Matthews, D. G., G. Gappert, M. Snyder and F. A. Kornegay, 1969, 'Washington Task Force Black Paper on Institutional Racism', *Africa Today* 16(5/6): 25–31

Maylam, P., 2005, *The Cult of Rhodes: Remembering an Imperialist in Africa*, Cape Town: David Philip

Mbembe, A., 2019, *Necropolitics*, Durham, NC: Duke University Press

Meades, J., 2013, *Museum Without Walls*, London: Unbound

Meier, A., 2017, 'Skull-cup Associated with Lord Byron Heads to Auction', *Hyperallergic* (17 Oct 2017)

Mercer, K., 1994, 'Introduction: Black Britain and the Cultural Politics of Diaspora', in K. Mercer (ed.), *Welcome to the Jungle*, London: Routledge, pp. 1–31

Mercer, K. and I. Julien, 1994, 'Black Masculinity and the Sexual Politics of Race: True Confessions', in K. Mercer (ed.), *Welcome to the Jungle*, London: Routledge, pp. 131–70

Mill, J. S., 1873, *Autobiography*, London: Longmans, Green, Reader & Dyer

Miller, E., 1974, *That Noble Cabinet: A History of the British Museum*, Athens: Ohio University Press

Miller, P. N., 2013, 'The Missing Link: "Antiquarianism", "Material Culture", and "Cultural Science" in the Work of G. F. Klemm', in P. N. Miller (ed.), *Cultural Histories of the Material World*, Ann Arbor: University of Michigan Press, pp. 263–82

Millin, S., 1933, *Cecil Rhodes*, New York: Harper & Brothers

Mirzoeff, N., 2017, 'All the Monuments Must Fall #Charlottesville' (14 August 2017), www.nicholasmirzoeff.com/bio/all-the-monuments-must-fall-charlottesville/

Mirzoeff, N., 2021, 'All the Monuments Must Fall #Charlottesville', *The Funambulist* (31 August 2021)

Mirzoeff, N., 2023, *White Sight: Visual Politics and Practices of Whiteness*, Cambridge, MA: MIT Press

Mitchell, P., 2021, *Imperial Nostalgia: How the British Conquered Themselves*, Manchester: Manchester University Press

Mitford, N. (ed.), 1939, *The Stanleys of Alderley: Their Letters Between the Years 1851–1865*, London: Chapman & Hall

Mitra, S. M., 1921, *The Life and Letters of Sir John Hall*, London: Longmans, Green & Co

Mitscherlich, A. and M. Mitscherlich, 1975 [1967], *The Inability to Mourn: Principles of Collective Behavior*, New York: Grove Press

Mockler-Ferryman, A. F., 1903, 'The South African War Memorial', *Oxfordshire Light Infantry Regimental Chronicle: An Annual Record of the First and Second Battalions Formerly the 43rd and 52nd Light Infantry* 12: 60–8

Moore, T., 1844, *The Life of Lord Byron*, London: John Murray

Moorehead, A., 1971, *The White Nile*, London: Hamish Hamilton

Morton, J. F. and O. S. Russell, 1954, 'The Cape Gooseberry and the Mexican Husk Tomato', *Proceedings of the Florida State Horticultural Society* 67: 261–6

Mosley, O. E., 1932, *The Greater Britain*, London: British Union of Fascists

Müller, M., 1861, 'Lecture II. The Growth of Language in Contradistinction to the History of Language', in *Lectures on the Science of Language: Delivered at the Royal Institution of Great Britain in April, May, and June 1861*, Longman, Green, Longman, and Roberts, pp. 28–76

Murinyaniza, S. J., 2002, 'Heritage That Hurts: The Case of the Grave of Cecil John Rhodes in the Matopos National Park, Zimbabwe', in C. Fforde, J. Hubert and P. Turnbull (eds), *The Dead and their Possessions: Repatriation in Principle, Policy and Practice*, London: Routledge (One World Archaeology 43), pp. 317–25

Murray, P. T., 1971, 'Blacks and the Draft: A History of Institutional Racism', *Journal of Black Studies* 2(1): 57–76

Myers, C. S., 1915, 'A Contribution to the Study of Shell Shock: Being an Account of Three Cases of Loss of Memory, Vision, Smell, and Taste, Admitted into the Duchess of Westminster's War Hospital, Le Touquet', *The Lancet* 185 (4772): 316–20

Napier, C. O. G., 1868, 'Notes on Mulattoes and Negroes', *Journal of the Anthropological Society of London* 6: lvii–lx

Needham, R., 1979, *Symbolic Classification*, Santa Monica, CA: Goodyear (Goodyear Perspectives in Anthropology)

Nelson, M., 2009, *Bluets*, Seattle, WA: Wave Books

Nelson, M., 2015, *The Argonauts*, Minneapolis, MN: Graywolf Press

Nietzsche, F., 1997 [1874], *Untimely Meditations* (trans. R. J. Hollingdale, ed. D. Breazedale), Cambridge: Cambridge University Press

North, C. N., 1858, *Journal of an English Officer in India*, London: Hurst & Blackett

NourbeSe Philip, M., 2008, *Zong!*, Toronto: Mercury Press

Oates, S. B., 1965, 'Henry Hotze: Confederate Agent Abroad', *Historian* 27(2): 131–54

O'Dell, C., 2010, Cylinder recordings of Ishi, 1911–1914, www.loc.gov/static/programs/national-recording-preservation-board/documents/Ishi.pdf

O'Hanlon, M., 2007, 'Foreword', in C. Gosden, F. Larson and A. Petch (eds), *Knowing Things: Exploring the Collections of the Pitt Rivers Museum 1884–1945*, Oxford: Oxford University Press, pp. xvii–xviii

Okuleye, Y., 2015, 'Why Isn't My Professor Black?', www.dtmh.ucl.ac.uk/isnt-professor-black-reflections/

Olusoga, D., 2018, 'The Treasury's tweet shows slavery is still misunderstood', *Guardian* (12 February 2018)

Orwell, G., 1949, *Nineteen Eighty-Four*, London: Secker & Warburg

Orwell, G., 1968 [1930], *Review of Herman Melville* by Lewis Mumford, in S. Orwell and I. Angus (eds), *The Collected Essays, Journalism and Letters of George Orwell Vol. 1: An Age Like This, 1920–1940*, London: Secker & Warburg, pp. 19–21

Osborne, M., 2006, *Always Ready, The Drill Halls of Britain's Volunteer Forces*, Leigh-on-Sea: Partizan Press

Overend, D., J. Lorimer and D. Schreve, 2020, 'The Bones Beneath the Streets: Drifting Through London's Quaternary', *Cultural Geographies* 27(3): 453–75

Pare, R., 2004, 'Roger Fenton: The Artist's Eye', in G. Baldwin, M. Daniel and S. Greenough, *All the Mighty World: The Photographs of Roger Fenton, 1852–1860*, New Haven, CT: Yale University Press, pp. 221–30

Paton, W. R., 1917, *The Greek Anthology, Vol. II*, London: William Heinemann

Patterson, O., 1982, *Slavery and Social Death: A Comparative Study*, Cambridge, MA: Harvard University Press

Pearce, N., 2014, 'From Relic to Relic: A Brief History of the Skull of Confucius', *Journal of the History of Collections* 26(2): 207–22

Peddle, D. E., 1977, 'Long Cecil: the Gun Made in Kimberley During the Siege', *Military History Journal* 4(1)

Penny, N., 2006, 'In Pursuit of an Heiress', *London Review of Books* 38(12)

Perry, S. and D. Challis, 2013, 'Flinders Petrie and the Curation of Heads', *Interdisciplinary Science Reviews* 38, 275–89

Petch, A., 2007, 'Notes on the Opening of the Pitt Rivers Museum', *Journal of Museum Ethnography* 19: 101–12

Petch, A., 2010, 'Rushmore Room by Room' (Rethinking Pitt-Rivers website), https://web.prm.ox.ac.uk/rpr/index.php/article-index/12-articles/240-rushmore-room-by-room.html

Petch, A., 2012, 'Death-related Artefacts in Pitt-Rivers' Collections' (Rethinking Pitt-Rivers website), http://web.prm.ox.ac.uk/rpr/index.php/article-index/12-articles/275-death-a-pitt-rivers/index.html

Petch, A., 2013, 'Brief Account of Such Events of my Life' (Rethinking Pitt-Rivers website), https://web.prm.ox.ac.uk/rpr/index.php/articles-index/12-articles/882-brief-account-of-such-events-of-my-life.html

Peters, M. A., 2015, 'Why Is My Curriculum White?', *Educational Philosophy and Theory* 47(7): 641–6

Pike, L. O., 1868, 'What is a Teuton?', *Anthropological Review* 6(22): 246–57

Pim, B., 1866, *The Negro and Jamaica*, London: Trübner & Co

Pitt-Rivers, A. H. L. F., 1882, 'Anniversary Address to the Anthropological Institute of Great Britain and Ireland', *Journal of the Anthropological Institute of Great Britain and Ireland*, 11: 487–509

Pitt-Rivers, A. H. L. F., 1884a, *Opening of the Dorset County Museum: Inaugural Address*, Dorchester: J. Foster

Pitt-Rivers, A. H. L. F., 1884b, 'Address Delivered at the Annual Meeting of the Dorchester School of Art on 31 January 1884', *Dorset County Express and Agricultural Gazette* (5 February 1884), p. 4

Pitt-Rivers, A. H. L. F., 1887a, *Excavations in Cranborne Chase Near Rushmore on the Borders of Dorset and Wilts Vol. 1*, Rushmore: privately printed

Pitt-Rivers, A. H. L. F., 1887b, 'Inaugural Address at the Annual Meeting of the Archaeological Institution Held at Salisbury', *Archaeological Journal* 44: 261–77

Pitt-Rivers, A. H. L. F., 1889, 'Section H, Anthropology; President's Address', in Anon (ed.), *Report of the 58th Meeting of the British Association for the Advancement of Science, Held at Bath in September 1888*, pp. 825–35

Pitt-Rivers, A. H. L. F., 1891, 'Typological Museums, as Exemplified by the Pitt Rivers Museum at Oxford, and his Provincial Museum at Farnham, Dorset', *Journal of the Society of Arts* 40: 115–22

Pitt-Rivers, A. H. L. F., 1892, 'Excavations in Bokerley Dyke and Wansdyke Dorset and Wilts 1888–91', *Excavations on Cranborne Chase Vol. III*, Rushmore, privately printed

Pitt-Rivers, A. H. L. F., 1894, 'On a New Craniometer' (no abstract given), *Report of the Sixty-fourth Meeting of the British Academy for the Advancement of Science Held at Oxford in August 1894*, London: John Murray, p. 784

Pitt-Rivers, A. H. L. F., 1895, *Catalogue of Pictures and Objects of Art Exhibited at the Larmer Grounds 1895*, London: Harrison & Sons

Pitt-Rivers, A. H. L. F., 1897, 'Presidential Address to the Dorchester Meeting of the Archaeological Institute', *Archaeological Journal* 44: 311–39

Pitt-Rivers, A. H. L. F., 1898, 'Craniometer for Measuring the Profiles of Skulls and Living Heads', *Excavations in Cranborne Chase Vol. IV*, Rushmore: privately printed, pp. 118–27

Pitt-Rivers, A. H. L. F., 2014 [1890], 'On the Uses and Arrangement of Arts Museums: Illustrated by Series from the Pitt-Rivers Museums at Oxford and Farnham, Dorset', *Museum History Journal* 7(2): 135–54

Pitt-Rivers, G. H. L. F., 1919, *Conscience and Fanaticism: An Essay on Moral Values*, London: William Heinemann

Pitt-Rivers, G. H. L. F., 1924, 'A Visit to a Maori Village: Being some Observations on the Passing of the Maori Race and the Decay of Maori Culture', *Journal of the Polynesian Society* 33(1): 48–65

Pitt-Rivers, G. H. L. F., 1927, *The Clash of Culture and the Contact of Races: An Anthropological and Psychological Study of the Laws of Racial Adaptability, with Special Reference to the Depopulation of the Pacific and the Government of Subject Races*, London: George Routledge & Sons

Pitt-Rivers, G. H. L. F. (ed.), 1932, *Problems of Population*, London: George Allen & Unwin

Pitt-Rivers, G. H. L. F., 1938, *The Czech Conspiracy: A Phase in the World War Plot*, London: Boswell Publishing Co

Pitt-Rivers, G. H. L. F., 1965, 'Pitt-Rivers, George', *Who's Who*, London: Adam & Charles Black, p. 2431

Pitt-Rivers, M., 1977, 'Cultural General', *Books and Bookmen* 22(9): 23–5

Plomer, W., 1933, *Cecil Rhodes*, Edinburgh: Peter Davies

Porter, M., 2015, *Grief is the Thing with Feathers*, London: Faber & Faber

Prather, H. L., 1984, *We Have Taken a City: Wilmington Racial Massacre and Coup of 1898*, Rutherford, NJ: Fairleigh Dickinson University Press

Preciado, P., 2020, 'When Statues Fall' (trans. M. Faguet), *Artforum* (December 2020)

Proust, M., 1927, *Le Temps retrouvé (À la recherche du temps perdu VIII)*, Paris: Gallimard

Prout, D., 1989, '"The Oxford Society for Promoting the Study of Gothic Architecture" and "The Oxford Architectural Society", 1839–1860', *Oxoniensia* 54: 379–91

Quigley, C., 1981, *The Anglo-American Establishment: from Rhodes to Clivedon*, New York: Books in Focus

Rafter, T. A. and G. J. Fergusson, 1957, '"Atom Bomb Effect" – Recent Increase of Carbon-14 Content of the Atmosphere and Biosphere', *Science* 126 (3273): 557–8

Reckford, M., 1968, 'The Jamaica Slave Rebellion of 1831', *Past and Present* 40: 108–25

Reddie, J., 1864, 'Slavery', *Anthropological Review* 2(7): 280–93

Reilly, M. C., 2022, 'Archaeologies of Whiteness', *Archaeological Dialogues* 29: 51–66

Renfrew, J. M. and M. Robbins, 1990, 'Tobias Rustat and his Monument in Jesus College Chapel, Cambridge', *Antiquaries Journal* 70(2): 416–23

Renton, D., 1996, *Red Shirts and Black: Fascists and Anti-fascists in Oxford in the 1930s*, Oxford: Ruskin College Library

Rhodes Must Fall Oxford, 2016 [2015], 'Rhodes Must Fall in Oxford founding statement', in *Rhodes Must Fall: The Struggle to Decolonise the Racist Heart of Empire*, London: Zed, pp. 3–5

Rhodes Trust, 1929, *Will and Codicils of the Rt Hon Cecil John Rhodes*, Oxford: Rhodes Trust

Richards, T., 1993, *The Imperial Archive: Knowledge and the Fantasy of Empire*, London: Verso

Riley, D., 2019, *Time Lived, Without its Flow*, London: Picador

Rilke, R. M., 1919, 'Ur-Geräusch', *Das Inselschiff* 1(1): 14–20

Rilke, R. M., 1927 [1902], 'Die Turnstunde', *Gesammelte Werke (Volume 4)*, Leipzig: Insel, pp. 211–20

Rilke, R. M., 1955 [1908], 'Archaïscher Torso Apollos', in *Sämtliche Werke Vol. 1*, Frankfurt am Main: Insel Verlag, p. 557

Ripley, C. P. (ed.), 1985, *The Black Abolitionist Papers Vol. 1: The British Isles, 1830–1865*, Chapel Hill: University of North Carolina Press

Rivers, W. H. R., 1922, 'Appendix VII: Psychology and War', in *Instinct and the Unconscious: A Contribution to a Biological Theory of the Psychoneuroses*, Cambridge: Cambridge University Press, pp. 248–59

Roach, J., 1996, *Cities of the Dead: Circum-Atlantic Performance*, New York: Columbia University Press

Robson, W., 1842, *Robson's London Directory, Street Key, Classification of Trades and Royal Court Guide and Peerage (23rd Edition)*, London: Robson & Co

## BIBLIOGRAPHY

Rocher, P., 2020, *Gazer, mutiler, soumettre: politique de l'arme non-létale*, Paris: La Fabrique

Rockley, J., 2008, *Antiquarians and Archaeology in Nineteenth-Century Cork*, Oxford: Archaeopress (British Archaeological Reports 454)

Roksandic, M., P. Radović, X.-J. Wu and C. J. Bae, 2021, 'Resolving the "Muddle in the Middle": The Case for Homo bodoensis sp. Nov', *Evolutionary Anthropology* 31(1): 20–29

Rolleston, G., 1875, 'Address to the Department of Anthropology', in Anon (ed.), *Report of the Forty-Fifth Meeting of the British Association for the Advancement of Science, Held at Bristol in August 1875*, London: John Murray, pp. 142–56

Rooksby, R., 1997, *A. C. Swinburne: A Poet's Life*, Aldershot: Scolar Press

Rosen, G., 1975, 'Nostalgia: A "Forgotten" Psychological Disorder', *Psychological Medicine* 5: 346–51

Rosevear, A., D. Bogart and L. Shaw-Taylor, 2019, 'The Spatial Patterns of Coaching in England and Wales from 1681 to 1836: A Geographic Information Systems Approach', *Journal of Transport History* 40(3): 418–44

Rotberg, R. I., 1988, *The Founder: Cecil Rhodes and the Pursuit of Power*, Oxford: Oxford University Press

Rothberg, M., 2009, *Multi-directional Memory: Remembering the Holocaust in the Age of Decolonization*, Stanford, CA: Stanford University Press

Rothberg, M., 2019, *The Implicated Subject: Beyond Victims and Perpetrators*, Stanford, CA: Stanford University Press

Rowse, T., 2017, 'The Statistical Table as Colonial Knowledge', *Itinerario* 41(1): 51–73

Royal College of Physicians of London, 1860, *Catalogue of the Contents of the Museum of the Royal College of Surgeons of England, Part 1: Plants and Invertebrate Animals in the Dried State*, London: Taylor & Francis

Royal Commission for the Exhibition, 1851, *The Crystal Palace and its Contents: An Illustrated Cyclopedia of the Great Exhibition of the Industry of All Nations*, London: W. M. Clark

Royal Commission for the Exhibition, 1852, *Reports by the Juries on the Subjects in the Thirty Classes into which the Exhibition was Divided*, London: William Clowes & Sons

Royal Commission on the Defence of the United Kingdom, 1860, *Report of the Commissioners Appointed to Consider the Defence of the United Kingdom, Together with Minutes of Evidence and Appendix*, London: Eyre & Spottiswoode for HMSO

Ruskin, J., 1873 [1865], 'War', in *The Crown of Wild Olive: Four Lectures on Industry and War*, London: Smith, Elder & Co, pp. 98–145

Ruskin, J., 1905 [1865], 'A Letter to the *Daily Telegraph*, 20 December 1865', in E. T. Cook and A. Wedderburn (eds), *The Works of John Ruskin Vol. 18*, London: George Allen, pp. 550-1

Ruskin, J., 1905 [1870], 'Lectures on Art', in E. T. Cook and A. Wedderburn (eds), *The Works of John Ruskin Vol. 20: Lectures on Art and Aratra Pentelici*, Cambridge: Cambridge University Press, pp. 17-179

Ruskin, J., 1905 [1884], 'The Pleasures of England, Lecture 1', in E. T. Cook and A. Wedderburn (eds), *The Works of John Ruskin Vol. 33*, Cambridge: Cambridge University Press, pp. 441-520

Russell, B. and P. Russell (eds), 1937, *The Amberley Papers: The Letters and Diaries of Lord and Lady Amberley Vol. 1*, London: Hogarth Press

Rutter, E. R., 2019, 'Troubled Inheritance: Confronting Old Hierarchies in the New South', *Southern Cultures* 25(3): 156-62

Sacks, A. J., 2020, 'The Fascist Sympathies of Britain's Aristocracy', *Tribune Magazine* (25 October 2020)

Sagger, H., J. Philips and M. Haque, 2021, *Valuing Culture and Heritage Capital: A Framework towards Informing Decision Making*, London: DCMS

Said, E., 1993, *Culture and Imperialism*, New York: Knopf

Sartre, J.-P., 1963, 'Preface', in F. Fanon, *The Wretched of the Earth* (trans. C. Farrington), New York: Grove Press, pp. 7-31

Saunders, J., 1843, 'CXXIII The Society of Arts. &c. in the Adelphi', in C. Knight (ed.), *London Vol. 5*, London: Charles Knight & Co, pp. 353-68

Saunders, N. J., 2003, *Trench Art: Materialities and Memories of War*, Oxford: Berg

Saunders, P., 1981, 'General Pitt-Rivers and Kit's Coty House', *Antiquity* 55(213): 51-3

Saunders, P., 2014, '"The Choicest, Best-arranged Museums I Have Ever Seen": The Pitt-Rivers Museum, Farnham, Dorset, 1880s-1970s', *Museum History Journal*, 7(2): 205-23

Savage, K., 1994, 'The Politics of Memory: Black Emancipation and the Civil War Monument', in J. R. Gillis (ed.), *Commemorations: The Politics of National Identity*, Princeton, NJ: Princeton University Press, pp. 127-49

Savage, K., 2018, *Standing Soldiers, Kneeling Slaves: Race, War, and Monument in Nineteenth-Century America* (revised edition), Princeton, NJ: Princeton University Press

Sayers, D. L., 1928, *The Unpleasantness at the Bellona Club*, Boston: G. K. Hall

Scarman, L. G., 1986, *The Scarman Report*, London: Penguin

Scarth Dixon, W., 1898, *A History of the Bramham Moor Hunt*, Leeds: Richard Jackson

Schmahmann, B., 2022, 'Whatever Happened to Cecil? Monuments Commemorating Rhodes Before and After #RhodesMustFall', in E. Costandius and G. de Villiers (eds), *Visual Redress in Africa from Indigenous and New Materialist Perspectives*, London: Routledge, pp. 95–108

Schneller, B., 2009, 'Grove, (Agnes) Geraldine [née (Agnes) Geraldine Lane Fox; afterwards (Agnes) Geraldine Fox-Pitt], Lady Grove', *Oxford Dictionary of National Biography*, Oxford: Oxford University Press, https://doi.org/10.1093/ref:odnb/55591

Schögler, 2025, 'Translation in Sociological Research', in S. Tyulenev and W. Luo (eds), *The Routledge Handbook of Translation and Sociology*, London: Routledge, pp. 181–95

Schuster, P.-K., 1987, *Nationalsozialismus und 'entartete Kunst': Die 'Kunststadt' München 1937*, Munich: Prestel Verlag

Schüttpelz, E., 2010, 'Animism Meets Spiritualism: Edward Tylor's "Spirit Attack", London 1872', in A. Franke (ed.), *Animism Vol. 1*, Berlin: Sternberg Press, pp. 154–69

Science and Art Department, 1874, *Twenty-first Report of the Science and Art Department of the Committee of Council on Education*, London: George E. Eyre & William Spottiswoode

Science and Art Department, 1877, *Twenty-fourth Report of the Science and Art Department of the Committee of Council on Education (for 1876)*, London: George E. Eyre & William Spottiswoode

Science and Art Department, 1879, *Twenty-sixth Report of the Science and Art Department of the Committee of Council on Education (for 1878)*, London: Eyre & Spottiswoode

Science and Art Department, 1880, *Twenty-seventh Report of the Science and Art Department of the Committee of Council on Education (for 1879)*, London: Eyre & Spottiswoode

Science and Art Department, 1881, *Twenty-eighth Report of the Science and Art Department of the Committee of Council on Education (for 1880)*, London: Eyre & Spottiswoode

Science and Art Department, 1884, *Thirtieth Report of the Science and Art Department of the Committee of Council on Education (for 1883)*, London: Eyre & Spottiswoode

Science and Art Department, 1885, *Thirty-first Report of the Science and Art Department of the Committee of Council on Education (for 1884)*, London: Eyre & Spottiswoode

Scott, J., 1998, *Seeing Like a State: How Certain Schemes to Improve the Human Condition Have Failed*, New Haven, CT: Yale University Press

Sebald, W. G., 2001, *Austerlitz* (trans. A. Bell), London: Penguin

Seeley, J. R., 1883, *The Expansion of England: Two Courses of Lectures*, London: Macmillan & Co

Self, G. M., 1938, 'The Chartist Incident on Kennington Common, April 10th 1848, Critically Examined, More Particularly in the Light of the Home Office Papers at the Public Records Office, London', unpublished Masters thesis, McGill University

Semmel, B., 1962, 'The Issue of "Race" in the British Reaction to the Morant Bay Uprising of 1865', *Caribbean Studies* 2(3): 3–15

Semmel, B., 1969, *Democracy Versus Empire: The Jamaica Riots of 1865 and the Governor Eyre Controversy*, Garden City, NY: Anchor Books

Semple Kerr, J., 1999, 'Opening Address: The Conservation Plan', in K. Clark (ed.), *Conservation Plans in Action: Proceedings of the Oxford Conference*, London: English Heritage, pp. 9–20

Serres, M., 2015 [1987], *Statues: The Second Book of Foundations* (trans. R. Burks), London: Bloomsbury

Service, E. R., 1962, *Primitive Social Organization: An Evolutionary Perspective*, New York: Random House

Severi, C., 2017, *The Chimera Principle: An Anthropology of Memory and Imagination*, London: HAU Books

Shapin, S., 1998, 'Placing the View from Nowhere: Historical and Sociological Problems in the Location of Science', *Transactions of the Institute of British Geographers* 23: 5–12

Sharpe, C., 2010, *Monstrous Intimacies: Making Post-slavery Subjects*, Durham, NC: Duke University Press

Sharpe, C., 2016, *In the Wake: On Blackness and Being*, Durham, NC: Duke University Press

Sharpe, C., 2023, *Ordinary Notes*, New York: Farrar, Straus & Giroux

Sheller, M., 2011, 'Hidden Textures of Race and Historical Memory: The Rediscovery of Photographs Relating to Jamaica's Morant Bay Rebellion of 1865', *Princeton University Library Chronicle* 72(2): 533–67

Sheppard, F. H. W., 1960, 'St James's Square: No 3', in F. H. W. Sheppard (ed.), *Survey of London: Vol. 29 and 30, St James Westminster, Part 1*, London: London County Council, pp. 83–8

Sherratt, A. G., 1990a, 'The Genesis of Megaliths: Monumentality, Ethnicity and Social Complexity in Neolithic North-West Europe', *World Archaeology* 22(2): 147–67

Sherratt, A. G., 1990b, 'Gordon Childe: Paradigms and Patterns in Prehistory', *Australian Archaeology* 30: 3–13

Shuttleworth, S., 1998, 'Natural History: The Retro-Victorian Novel', in E. S. Shaffer (ed.), *The Third Culture: Literature and Science*, Berlin: Walter de Gruyter, pp. 253–68

Sidney Hartland, E., 1893, 'Pin-Wells and Rag-Bushes', *Folklore* 4(4): 451–70
Sigel, L., 2002, *Governing Pleasures: Pornography and Social Change in England, 1815–1914*, New Brunswick, NJ: Rutgers University Press
Slade, A., 1867, *Turkey and the Crimean War: A Narrative of Historical Events*, London: Smith, Elder & Co
Smart, B., 1973, 'The Ship of Theseus, the Parthenon and Disassembled Objects', *Analysis* 34(1): 24–27
Smith, S. D., 2006, *Slavery, Family and Gentry Capitalism in the British Atlantic: The World of the Lascelles, 1648–1834*, Cambridge: Cambridge University Press
Smithson, R., 1966, 'Entropy and the New Monuments', *Art Forum* 5(10): 26–31
Smithson, R., 1995 [1972], 'Hotel Palenque', *Parkett* 43: unpaginated insert
Smithson, R. 1996 [1967], 'The Artist as Site-seer: or, a Dintorphic Essay', in J. Flam (ed.), *Robert Smithson: The Collected Writings*, Berkeley: University of California Press, pp. 340–45
Souter, C., P. Ainsworth, G. Austin, S. Aziz, Z. Badawi, W. Beinart, L. Van Broekhoven, M. Casely-Hayford and M. Codrington-Rogers, 2021, *Report of a Commission of Inquiry Established by Oriel College, Oxford into Issues Associated with Memorials to Cecil Rhodes*, Oxford: Oriel College, www.oriel.ox.ac.uk/wp-content/uploads/2023/06/oriel_rhodes_commission_full_report-CC.pdf
South Kensington Museum, 1873, *Catalogue of the Loan Exhibition of Ancient and Modern Jewellery and Personal Ornaments*, London: John Strangeways
Spencer, H., 1864, *The Principles of Biology Vol. 1*, London: Williams & Norgate
Spencer, H., 1873, *The Study of Sociology*, London: Henry S. Green & Co
Spencer, H., 1885, *The Principles of Sociology Vol. 1* (third edition), London: D. Appleton & Co
Spencer, H., 1896, *The Principles of Sociology Vol. 3*, London: Williams & Norgate
Starn, O., 2004, *Ishi's Brain: In Search of America's Last 'Wild' Indian*, New York: W. W. Norton & Co
Stead, W. T. (ed.), 1902, *The Last Will and Testament of Cecil John Rhodes, with Elucidatory Notes*, London: Review of Reviews
Steward, J. H., A. J. Gibson and J. H. Rowe, 1961, 'Alfred Louis Kroeber, 1876–1960', *American Anthropologist* 63(5): 1038–87
Stocking, G. W., 1971a, 'Animism in Theory and Practice: E. B. Tylor's Unpublished *Notes on "Spiritualism"*', *Man* 6(1): 88–104
Stocking, G. W., 1971b, 'What's in a Name? The Origins of the Royal Anthropological Institute (1837–71)', *Man* 6(3): 369–90

Stocking, G. W., 1987, *Victorian Anthropology*, New York: Free Press

Stokes, A., 1972, 'Childhood', in R. Wollheim (ed.), *The Image in Form: Selected Writings of Adrian Stokes*, New York: Harper & Row, pp. 289–310

Stone, K., E. Lee and F. Gene-Rowe, 2021, 'The Language of the Dusk: Anthropocentrism, Time and Decoloniality in the Work of Ursula K. Le Guin', in *The Legacies of Ursula K. Le Guin: Science, Fiction, Ethics*, Cham: Palgrave Macmillan (Palgrave Studies in Science and Popular Culture), pp. 83–105

Stourton, J., 2022, *Heritage: A History of How We Conserve Our Past*, London: Head of Zeus

Strachey, L., 1918, *Eminent Victorians*, London: Chatto & Windus

Strachey, L., 1921, *Queen Victoria*, New York: Harcourt, Brace & Co

Strathern, M., 1992, 'The Decomposition of an Event', *Cultural Anthropology* 7(2): 244–54

Strathern, M., 1999, *Property, Substance and Effect: Anthropological Essays on Persons and Things*, London: Athlone Press.

Strathern, M., 2005a, *Partial Connections* (updated edition), Walnut Creek, CA: Altamira Press

Strathern, M., 2005b, *Kinship, Law and the Unexpected: Relatives are Always a Surprise*, Cambridge: Cambridge University Press

Surrey Archaeological Society, 1880, 'Report of Proceedings at Croydon, in March 1877', *Surrey Archaeological Collections* 7: xxxiii–xxxix

Sutton, T., 2023, 'Contested Heritage and the Consistory Courts', *Ecclesiastical Law Journal* 25: 171–91

Sweet, M., 2001, *Inventing the Victorians*, London: Faber & Faber

Sweet, M., 2011, *The West End Front: The Wartime Secrets of London's Grand Hotels*, London: Faber & Faber

Swinburne., A. C., 2004 [1865], 'The Cannibal Catechism', in J. McGann and C. L. Sligh (eds), *Major Poems and Selected Prose*, New Haven, CT: Yale University Press, pp. 423–5

Symonds, R., 1986, *Oxford and Empire: The Last Lost Cause?*, London: Macmillan

Symonds, R., 2000, 'Oxford and the Empire', in M. G. Brock and M. C. Curthoys (eds), *The History of the University of Oxford Vol. VII: Nineteenth-century Oxford, Part 2*, Oxford: Clarendon Press, pp. 689–716

Tarlow, S., 2024, 'The Names of the Dead: Identity, Privacy and the Ethics of Anonymity in Exhibiting the Dead Body', *Public Archaeology* 2(1): 1–20

Taussig, M., 1984, 'History as Sorcery', *Representations* 7: 87–109

Taussig, M., 1987, *Shamanism, Colonialism, and the Wild Man: A Study in Terror and Healing*, Chicago: University of Chicago Press

Taussig, M., 2017, 'Trump Studies', *Cultural Anthropology* (18 January 2017), https://culanth.org/fieldsights/trump-studies

Taylor, A., 2023, 'The Case of the Rustat Memorial – Does Duffield Pose All the Right Questions?', *Ecclesiastical Law Journal* 25: 38–51

Taylor, R. V., 1865, *The Biographia Leodiensis; or, Biographical Sketches of the Worthies of Leeds and Neighbourhood, from the Norman Conquest to the Present Time*, Leeds: John Hamer

Tehrani, N., 2015, 'Why Is My Curriculum White?', https://theoccupiedtimes.org/?p=14056

Tester, K., 1998, 'Aura, Armour and the Body', *Body and Society* 4(1): 17–34

Tett, G., 2021, *Anthro-vision: A New Way to See in Business and Life*, New York: Simon & Schuster

Theweleit, K., 1987 [1978], *Male Fantasies* (trans. E. Carter and C. Turner), Minneapolis: University of Minnesota Press

Thomas, N., 1994, *Colonialism's Culture: Anthropology, Travel and Government*, Princeton, NJ: Princeton University Press

Thomas, R., 1993, *The Imperial Archive: Knowledge and the Fantasy of Empire*, London: Verso

Thomas, R. J. C., 2003, *Prisoner of War Camps (1939–1948)*, London: English Heritage (Twentieth-Century Military Recording Project)

Thompson, M. W., 1960, 'The First Inspector of Ancient Monuments in the Field', *Journal of the British Archaeological Association* 23: 103–24

Thompson, M. W., 1976, *A Catalogue of the Papers of Lieutenant-General AHLF Pitt-Rivers in the Salisbury and South Wiltshire Museum*, London: Royal Commission on Historical Manuscripts

Thompson, M. W., 1977, *General Pitt-Rivers: Evolution and Archaeology in the Nineteenth Century*, Bradford-on-Avon: Moonraker Press

Thompson, M. W. and C. Renfrew, 1999, 'The Catalogues of the Pitt-Rivers Museum, Farnham, Dorset', *Antiquity* 73(280): 377–92

Thornbury, W., 1876, *Old and New London: A Narrative of its History, its People and its Places Vol. III*, London: Cassell, Petter & Galpin

Thurnam, J., 1865, 'On Two Principal Forms of Ancient British and Gaulish Skulls', *Memoirs of the Anthropological Society of London* I: 120–68, 534–41

Tremain, D., 2021, *Agent Provocateur for Hitler or Churchill? The Mysterious Life of Stella Lonsdale*, Barnsley: Pen & Sword

Trigger, B., 1990, 'Monumental Architecture: A Thermodynamic Explanation of Symbolic Behaviour', *World Archaeology* 22: 119–32

Trouillot, M.-R., 1991, 'Anthropology and the Savage Slot: The Poetics and Politics of Otherness', in R. G. Fox (ed.), *Recapturing Anthropology: Working in the Present*, Santa Fe, NM: School for Advanced Research, pp. 17–44

Trouillot, M.-R., 1995, *Silencing the Past: Power and the Production of History*, Boston, MA: Beacon

Tsing, A., 2015, *The Mushroom at the End of the World*, Princeton, NJ: Princeton University Press

Tuck, E. and K. W. Yang, 2012, 'Decolonization is not a metaphor', *Decolonization: Indigeneity, Education and Society* 1(1): 1–40

Turner, W., 1884, *Report on the Human Crania and Other Bones of the Skeletons Collected During the Voyage of H.M.S. Challenger in the Years 1873–1876*, London: Longmans & Co

Twohig, E., 1987, 'Pitt-Rivers in Munster 1862–65/6', *Journal of the Cork Historical and Archaeological Society* 92: 34–46

Tylor, E. B., 1863, 'Wild Men and Beast-Children', *Anthropological Review* 1(1): 21–32

Tylor, E. B., 1866, 'The Religion of Savages', *Fortnightly Review* 6: 71–86

Tylor, E. B., 1867, 'On Traces of the Early Mental Condition of Man', *Proceedings of the Royal Institution* 5: 83–93

Tylor, E. B., 1869, 'On the Survival of Savage Thought in Modern Civilisation', *Proceedings of the Royal Institution* 5: 522–35

Tylor, E. B., 1871, *Primitive Culture: Researches into the Development of Mythology, Philosophy, Religion, Art and Custom*, London: John Murray

Tylor, E. B., 1874, 'Review of Catalogue of the Anthropological Collections Lent by Colonel Lane Fox for Exhibition in the Bethnal Green Branch of the South Kensington Museum', *The Academy* 6 (129): 460

Tylor, E. B., 1881, 'President's Address', *Journal of the Anthropological Institute of Great Britain and Ireland* 10: 440–58

Tylor, E. B., 1901, 'Pitt-Rivers, Augustus Henry Lane Fox', *Dictionary of National Biography (Supplement Vol. 3)*, London: Smith, Elder & Co, pp. 268–70

Tyrrell, H., 1858, *The History of the War with Russia: Giving Full Details of the Operations of the Allied Armies Vol. 1*, London: London Printing & Publishing Co

Tyson, T. B., 2004, *Blood Done Sign My Name: A True Story*, New York: Three Rivers Press

Tyson, T. B. and D. S. Cecelski, 1998, 'Introduction', in D. S. Cecelski and T. B. Tyson (eds), *Democracy Betrayed: The Wilmington Race Riot of 1898 and its Legacy*, Chapel Hill: University of North Carolina Press, pp. 3–13

Umfleet, L. S., 2020, *A Day of Blood: The 1898 Wilmington Race Riot* (revised edition), Chapel Hill: University of North Carolina Press

Underhill, E. B., 1895, *The Tragedy of Morant Bay: A Narrative of the Disturbances in the Island of Jamaica in 1865*, London, Alexander & Shepheard

United Service Institution, 1858, 'Proceedings at the Twenty-seventh Annual Meeting', *Journal of the United Service Institution* 4(1): 283–94

University of California, 2020, *Proposal to Remove the Name from Kroeber Hall* (University of California Berkeley Building Name Review Committee, 30 October 2020), https://web.archive.org/web/20210204082625/http://chancellor.berkeley.edu/sites/default/files/bnrc_kroeber_recommendation.pdf

Usener, H., 2010, *Kleine Schriften (Volume 4)*, Frankfurt am Main: Suhrkamp, pp. 400–1

Valencia, S., 2018, *Gore Capitalism* (trans. J. Pluecker), South Pasadena, CA: Semiotext(e)

Van Eynde, J., 2018, 'Bodies of the Weak: The Circulation of the Indigenous Dead in the British World, 1780–1880', unpublished Ph.D. dissertation, University of Michigan

Verschoyle, J. (under the pseudonym Vindex), 1900 [1883], *Cecil Rhodes: His Political Life and Speeches, 1881–1900*, London, Chapman

Vizetelly, H., 1890, *Glances Back Through Seventy Years: Autobiographical and Other Reminiscences Vol. 2*, London: Kegan Paul, Trench, Trübner & Co

Voltaire, 1794, *Zadig, or the Book of Fate: An Oriental History*

Wade, S., 2011, *Empire and Espionage: Spies in the Zulu War*, Barnsley: Pen & Sword

Wagner, K. A., 2010, *The Great Fear of 1857: Rumours, Conspiracies and the Making of the Indian Uprising*, London: Peter Lang

Wagner, K. A., 2018, 'Savage Warfare: Violence and the Rule of Colonial Difference in Early British Counterinsurgency', *History Workshop Journal* 85: 217–237

Wagner, R., 1972, *Habu: The Innovation of Meaning in Daribi Religion*, Chicago: University of Chicago Press

Wagner, R., 1981, *The Invention of Culture* (revised and expanded edition), Chicago: University of Chicago Press

Wagner, R., 1986, *Symbols That Stand for Themselves*, Chicago: University of Chicago Press

Waitz, T., 1863 [1859], *Introduction to Anthropology* (ed. J. F. Collingwood), London: Longman, Green, Longman & Roberts (Publications of the Anthropological Society of London 1)

Walker, R. B. N., 1866, 'On the Alleged Sterility of the Union of Women of Savage Races with Native Males, After Having Had Children by a White Man, with a Few Remarks on the Mpongwe Tribe of Negroes', *Memoirs of the Anthropological Society of London* 2 (1866–1866): 283–7

Wallace, A. R., 1874, *Miracles and Modern Spiritualism: Three Essays*, London: James Burns

Wallen, J., 2013, 'The Cannibal Club and the Origins of 19th Century Racism and Pornography', *The Victorian*, 1, 1–13

Wang, J., 2018, *Carceral Capitalism*, South Pasadena, CA: Semiotext(e)

Ward, J. T., 1970, 'The Saving of a Yorkshire Estate: George Lane Fox and Bramham Park', *Yorkshire Archaeological Journal* 42: 63–71

Weber, M. C. E., 1930, *The Protestant Ethic and the Spirit of Capitalism* (trans. T. Parsons), London: G. Allen & Unwin

Wells, H. G., 1901, *The First Men in the Moon*, London: Collins

White, J. F., 1962, *The Cambridge Movement: The Ecclesiologists and the Gothic Revival*, Cambridge: Cambridge University Press

White, M., 2019, 'The Master's Tools: The Wisdom of Audre Lorde', www.activistgraduateschool.org/on-the-masters-tools

Wiame, A., 2018, 'Gilles Deleuze and Donna Haraway on Fabulating the Earth', *Deleuze and Guattari Studies* 12(4): 525–40

Wilde, W. R., 1849, *The Beauties of the Boyne, and its Tributary the Blackwater*, Dublin: James McGlashan

Wilde, W. R., 1874, 'Upon the Early Races of Mankind in Ireland, their Remains and Present Representatives', in Anon (ed.), *Report of the Forty-Fourth Meeting of the British Association for the Advancement of Science*, London: John Murray, pp. 116–28

Williams, E. E., 1944, *Capitalism and Slavery*, Chapel Hill: University of North Carolina Press

Williams, E. E., 2014 [1938], *The Economic Aspect of the Abolition of the West Indian Slave Trade and Slavery*, London: Rowman & Littlefield

Williams, E. T., 2000, 'The Rhodes Scholarships', in M. G. Brock and M. C. Curthoys (eds), *The History of the University of Oxford Vol. VII: Nineteenth-century Oxford Part 2*, Oxford: Oxford University Press, pp. 717–26

Winberry, J. J., 1983, '"Lest We Forget": The Confederate Monument and the Southern Townscape', *Southeastern Geographer* 23(2): 107–21

Wise, T. J., 1920, *A Bibliography of the Writings in Prose and Verse of Algernon Charles Swinburne Vol. II*, London: privately printed

Wolfe, P., 1999, *Settler Colonialism and the Transformation of Anthropology: The Politics and Poetics of an Ethnographic Event*, London: Cassell

Wood, J., 2001, 'Introduction', in W. G. Sebald, *Austerlitz* (trans. A. Bell), London: Penguin, pp. 1–9

Woodman, C., 2020, 'The Imperial Boomerang: How Colonial Methods of Repression Migrate Back to the Metropolis', www.versobooks.com/blogs/4383-the-imperial-boomerang-how-colonial-methods-of-repression-migrate-back-to-the-metropolis

Wooley, C. F., 2002, *The Irritable Heart of Soldiers and the Origins of Anglo-American Cardiology: The US Civil War (1861) to World War I (1918)*, Aldershot: Ashgate

Wright, M., 1952, *British Colonial Constitutions 1947*, Oxford: Clarendon Press

Wright, P., 1985, *On Living in an Old Country*, London: Verso

Wright, P., 2000, *Tank: The Progress of a Monstrous War Machine*, London: Faber & Faber

Wright, P., 2021, *The Village that Died for England: Tyneham and the Legend of Churchill's Pledge* (revised edition), London: Repeater

Wyman, J., 1865, 'Observations on the Skeleton of a Hottentot', *Anthropological Review* 3(11): 330–5

Wynter, S., 1995, '1492: A New World View' in V. L. Hyatt and R. Nettleford (eds), *Race, Discourse, and the Origin of the Americas: A New World View*, Washington, D.C.: Smithsonian Institution Press, pp. 5–57

Wynter, S., 1994a, 'No Humans Involved: An Open Letter to my Colleagues', *Forum N.H.I: Knowledge for the 21st Century* 1(1): 42–73

Wynter, S., 1994b, 'A Black Studies Manifesto', *Forum N.H.I: Knowledge for the 21st Century* 1(1): 3–11

Wynter, S., 2003, 'Unsettling the Coloniality of Being/Power/Truth/Freedom: Towards the Human, After Man, its Overrepresentation: An Argument', *CR: The New Centennial Review* 3(3): 257–337

York, P., 2023, 'Who are the Culture Warriors? A Closer Look at the Group Piling Pressure on the National Trust', *Art Newspaper* (10 November 2023)

Younge, G., 2021, 'Why every single statue should come down', *Guardian* (1 June 2021)

Zaehnsdorf, J. W., 1880, *The Art of Bookbinding*, London: George Bell & Sons

Zwicker, S., 2006, *Nationale Märtyrer: Albert Leo Schlageter und Julius Fučík. Heldenkult, Propaganda und Erinnerungskultur*. Paderborn: Ferdinand Schöningh

# Index

*2001: A Space Odyssey* (1968 movie), 126, 359
38ers, the, 304–5, 373, 385
48ers, 432n79

Abbott, Tony, 23, 31, 426n90
abolitionism, 8, 33, 75, 148, 236, 242, 376, 386–7; *Abolition Geography* (Gilmore), 115; *Abolition Revolution* (Day and McBean), 240; Abolition of the Slave Trade Act 1807, 35, 145, 148, 149, 167, 171; Abolitionist Futures, 240; anti-abolitionism, 171, 213–15, 322; *Anti-Abolition Tracts* (Van Evrie), 214, 454n135; 'museum abolitionism', 75; unfinished nature of, 384, 386, 405. *See also* emancipation; Craft, Ellen and William; racial justice; police; racism; slavery
Aborigines' Protection Society, 215
actor–network theory (ANT), 221–4, 227, 235–6, 240, 264, 284, 300, 319, 389; as 'symmetrical anthropology', 224–5. *See also* Latour, Bruno; nonhumans, ideas of
Adsumvola (Zulu woman), 100–1, 103, 108, 133

Agassiz, Louis, 3, 455n143; statue of at Stanford University, 413, 493n181–2
Ahmed, Sara, 52–3, 245, 354, 410
Algeria, 25, 335, 394
All Monuments Must Fall (activist collective), 8, 422n20
American Civil War, 3–8, 26, 28, 195, 201, 206–7, 212–19, 277, 294–8, 310, 379–80, 404; comparisons with English Civil War, 310. *See also* Confederate States of America; Trent Affair; wars
American Museum of Natural History, 83, 294
Anatomy Act of 1832, 191
Anglo-Zulu Wars, 101, 111; Battle of Ulundi, 69, 101, 326, 347, 388
animism, ideas of, 223, 317, 326
Anthropological Institute of Great Britain and Ireland (later Royal Anthropological Institute), 346, 358; dispersal of the museum of, 66, 363; creation through merger of the Ethnological and Anthropological Societies of London, 318; Exploration Committee of, 473n85;

Fox as President of, 109, 112, 317; Psychological Committee of, 317
Anthropological Society of London, 112, 207–18, 236, 240–1, 281, 292, 306, 452n75, 452n78, 452n81, 454n126; Confederate funding of through Henry Hotze ('the Protagonist'), 213, 215–16, 218, 454n126; *Journal of the Anthropological Society of London*, 454n133; 'logo' of the society, 209–10; *Memoirs of the Anthropological Society of London*, 309; merger with the Ethnological Society of London, 318; role of Edward Eyre ('the Governor'), 212; role of James Hunt, 207, 212–14, 454n126, 454n135. *See also* Cannibal Club
anthropology, 3, 27–9, 40–2, 46, 52–60, 62, 65, 71, 75–6, 80–113, 121–7, 131, 143, 149–50, 156, 175, 187, 194–5, 207–27, 235–6, 240–6, 254, 256, 267–70, 281–2, 292, 304, 309, 314–20, 323, 327–8, 330, 340, 349, 354, 359–60, 366, 373, 384–5, 404, 408, 411–12,

545

anthropology – *cont.*
417, 431n58, 432n79, 432n82, 434n18, 454n126, 455n152; 'American school of anthropology' (Waitz), 216; *Anthropologie Générale* (Topinard), 105; *Anthropologie der Naturvölker* (Waitz), 215–7, 220, 455n143; *Anthropology* (Tylor), 71; anthropology of lying (McGranahan), 33; as an 'armed science' (Rolleston), 313; Cambridge anthropological expedition to the Torres Straits, 282; 'conjectural anthropology', 282–3; 'ethnographic immersion', 127, 269–70; 'four-field' model of (Fox), 362; Fox-Pitt's anthropology, 345–8, 353, 389; museums of anthropology, 84, 89, 222, 385; relationship with archaeology, 96, 103, 108; Tylor as first Professsor of Anthropology, 65, 362; 'universalist anthropology' (Latour), 456n177; visual anthropology, 54. *See also* four As, the

anti-racism. *See* racial justice

anti-semitism, 14, 348. *See also* racism

anti-vaccination campaigns, 111

Antigua, 167, 201

anxiety 25, 135, 176, 193, 280; as a response to colonialism (Rivers), 282

apartheid, 10, 21, 27, 86, 343, 410

archaeology, 36, 65, 73, 75, 81, 87–8, 99, 104, 107, 113, 116, 118, 123, 127, 133, 155–8, 165, 168, 172–8, 194, 220, 244–5, 248–9, 254, 266, 280, 291–4, 304–16, 318, 320–1, 323, 342–4, 354, 358, 362, 366, 369–72, 382, 384, 388–9, 391, 401, 407, 415–8, 434n21, 446n95, 467n20, 473n85, 474n123; *Archaeological Journal*, 190–1; and espionage, 258; and photography, 276, 299–300, 464n106; and war, 305, 311, 313, 326; as a 'subject', 40, 46, 76, 79–80, 96, 242, 381; as the study of duration, 27, 48, 130, 247; contemporary archaeology, 276–7, 382; excavation of Great Zimbabwe, 17; feminist archaeology, 122; museums of archaeology, 63, 69, 89, 222, 385; re-excavation of South Lodge (Wiltshire), 132; relationships with anthropology, 96, 103, 108, 187, 412; 'rescue archaeology', 306–7, 344, 473n85. *See also* four As, the

Arendt, Hannah, 333, 335; comments on Cecil Rhodes, 18, 268

*Argo* (mythological ship), 291, 333, 337, 349, 380; Argo

Navis (constellation), 102; *Argonauts of the Western Pacific* (Malinowski), 223, 269; *Jason and the Argonauts* (1963 movie), 269; named after Argus 337; Orpheus, 95; *The Argonauts* (Nelson), 86, 269, 337; transposition with the Ship of Theseus in Barthes, 268–9, 337. *See also* myths; Ship of Theseus (paradox)

armour, 16, 68, 129, 186, 190, 222, 289, 294, 297, 357, 375, 379–80, 439n3, 468n25; bullet-proof vests, 378; and *Male Fantasies* (Theweleit), 380–1. *See also* Bernhard Smith, William John ('the Armourer')

Arnold, Matthew: blue plaque to, 151; *Culture and Anarchy*, 184, 206–7, 447n117; 'Culture and its Enemies' (lecture), 183–5; Professorship of Poetry at Oxford University, 183; support for the Eyre Defence and Aid Fund, 205

Arokiasamy, Clara, 392

art history, 4, 33, 79, 89, 224, 401, 417. *See also* four As, the

Australia, 95, 193, 199–201, 331–2, 440n10; Aboriginal Australian people, 67, 69, 100, 199, 211, 332, 359; ancestral skulls from, 193, 205, 207; Australasian Association for the Advancement of

# INDEX

Science, 345; Cambridge anthropological expedition to the Torres Straits, 282; Captain Cook collections from, 405; Cullin-la-ringo massacre (Queensland), 69–70; Edward Eyre in, 201, 205–7, 212, 451–2n66; George Fox-Pitt in, 344, 348; Fox's diagram of Australian Aboriginal weapons, 359; Murray River (South Australia), 199, 201; penal servitude to, 467n17; prime minister of, 23

automatism, 316–22, 385; and extinction, 326, 349; 'automatic writing' (Spiritualism), 318; Hypothesis that Animals are Automata (Huxley), 322; perspectives of Fox on, 319–22, 389; Fox-Pitt's theories of, 347–8. *See also* extinction, ideas of

Balfour, Henry, 64, 72, 95–6, 99–100, 430n26, 430n43, 435n26, 'story of the arrow', 327–31
Ballard, J. G., 140, 194, 331
banking, 105, 148, 171, 180, 394, 466n9, 470n54; Barings Bank, 168, 345; Bank of British West Africa, 490n132
Barbados, 203, 375, 443n61, 443n62, 448n96; Windward and Leeward Islands Station (Royal Navy), 146
barbarism, ideas of, 3, 35, 60, 71–2, 79, 95, 97, 100, 102, 149, 178, 180, 184–7, 194–5, 204, 209, 212, 215, 227, 234–5, 245–6, 276, 279, 289, 292, 306, 310, 315, 317, 322–7, 333, 340, 343, 355, 358, 361–2, 372, 374, 386, 393, 449n18; and 'cannibalism', 71, 179, 194–5, 310, 429n19; definition by Lévi-Strauss (1952), 385; 'Primitive Warfare' (Fox), 79–81, 185, 188, 209, 225, 227, 245–6, 304, 315–16, 332; 'savage slot' (Trouillot), 103. *See also* civilisation, ideas of
Baring, Francis, 1st Baronet (Fox-Pitt's first wife's great-great-grandfather), 168, 345, 443n64
Barons Penrhyn. *See* Douglas-Pennant (surname)
Barthes, Roland, 156–7, 177, 268–9; on the *Argo*, 268–9, 337; *Mourning Diary*, 416; *Mythologies*, 157; *Roland Barthes on Roland Barthes*, 268
Bastian, Adolf, 217
Bateman, Thomas, 295, 309, 473n92
Beaudry, Mary Carolyn, 36n, 123–4, 369, 415, 437n92
Beckford (surname), 16, 171, 198; Peter Beckford (Fox's great-uncle, wife of Louise Pitt, father of the 3rd Lord Rivers), 167, 180, 198; *Thoughts on Hunting*, 180; Caribbean plantations of, 167; William Thomas Beckford (William Beckford of Fonthill) 16, 171, 198, 450n35; potentially Fox's biological great-uncle, 198; *Vathek* (gothic novel), 198. *See also* Pitt-Rivers, George, 4th Baron Rivers (George Beckford); Pitt-Rivers, Horace, 3rd Baron Rivers (Horace Beckford)
Beckles, Hilary, 164
Belgium, 177, 219, 257–8, 290, 347, 460n27, 469n41
Benin, Kingdom of, 50, 69, 366, 394. *See also* Nigeria
Benjamin, Walter, 67, 91–2, 108, 275, 416
Bergson, Henri, 124–5, 225
Bernhard Smith, John (Royal Navy commander) (father of the Armourer), 145–6, 148, 440n6
Bernhard Smith, William Arthur Hans (son of the Armourer), 146–7, 440n12
Bernhard Smith, William John ('the Armourer'), 145–6; 153, 190–2, 291–2, 315, 406, 439n3, 448n11, 448n16; studying at Oriel College, Oxford, 145
Bethnal Green Museum, 63, 110, 318, 355–9, 378, 483n39–40; 'Principles of Classification, The'

547

Bethnal Green
  Museum – *cont.*
  lecture (Fox), 115,
  319. *See also* Fox's
  'first collection'; South
  Kensington Museum;
  Victoria and Albert
  Museum
Bible, the: Isaiah 2:4, 228;
  I Corinthians 15:55,
  416; 1 Samuel 13:19–21,
  227–8; Psalm 30, 416;
  Psalm 144, 260
Birdwood, George
  Christopher
  Molesworth, 96, 371
Birmingham, 95, 256, 365,
  39, 417, 487n71
Black Lives Matter (civil
  rights movement), 7,
  23–4, 33, 398, 400. *See
  also* fallism
Blue Lives Matter (right-
  wing slogan), 196
blue plaques 150, 151,
  155, 376, 391
Board of Ordnance,
  231, 259, 313; Select
  Committee on
  Ordnance, 316
Boas, Franz, 432n79–80
Boehm, Joseph Edgar, 163,
  368, 446n102
Bogle, Paul, 201–2, 204,
  228, 451n50, 451n60,
  456n181
bookbinding, 117–20
boomerang effect, idea of,
  331–5; in Ralph Ellison,
  477n187. *See also choc
  en retour*
boomerangs, 42, 66, 328,
  331–5, 359
border regimes, 35, 77,
  154–5, 188–9, 229, 234,
  312; 'border spectacle'
  (De Genova), 77. *See
  also* police

Boston (USA), 36n, 89,
  253, 294–6
Bradley, Richard, 29, 132
Bray, Charles, 358
Breker, Arno, 381
Briggs, Kate, 157
Bright, John, 25
Bright, Richard, 274–5,
  464n101
Brighton, 133–4, 198, 252,
  333, 470–1n54
Bristol, 24–5, 148, 388.
  *See also* Colston,
  Edward (statue of)
British Army, 41, 68,
  80, 89, 153, 185, 193,
  229–30, 255, 258–9,
  266, 281, 298, 300–1,
  316, 430n44, 449n26;
  regiments of: 1st
  West India Regiment,
  203; 2nd West India
  Regiment, 197, 203;
  12th Regiment of Foot
  (Suffolk), 146, 440n10;
  17th Regiment of Foot
  (Leicestershire), 153,
  181; 19th Lancers
  (British Indian Army),
  193; 5th Dragoon
  Guards, 345; 60th
  Rifles, 430n31, 449n17;
  91st Highlanders, 60,
  111; Buffs (Royal East
  Kent Regiment), 203;
  Grenadier Guards,
  41, 109–110, 128,
  138, 182, 230, 250–1,
  254, 257, 262–3, 270,
  275–6, 294, 410,
  459n18, 460n42, 466n9,
  471n61; Household
  Cavalry Mounted
  Regiment, 181;
  Imperial Yeomanry,
  9–10, 357; Natal Native
  Contingent, 476n173;
  Oxfordshire Light

Infantry, 22; Royal
  Artillery, 203, 253;
  Royal Horse Guards
  Blue, 169; Royal
  Wiltshire Yeomanry,
  345, 347; Scottish Rifle
  Volunteers, 259; South
  Lancashire Regiment
  (Prince of Wales
  Volunteers), 111; West
  Surrey Brigade Depot,
  111, 356; Yorkshire
  Hussar Yeomanry
  Cavalry, 109. *See also*
  police; Royal Navy
British Association for the
  Advancement of Science
  (BAAS), 104–5, 112,
  213, 318, 321, 333
'British Grenadiers, The'
  (marching song), 261–2
British Medical
  Association, 13
British Museum, 100,
  143, 176, 229, 332, 345,
  435n26; as part of a
  'heritage route' (Norman
  Foster), 229; as 'the
  deck of some Predator
  spacecraft' (Fisher), 78;
  barricading of (1848),
  231–2, 332; differences
  from the South
  Kensington Museum
  (Fox), 360–1, 484n49;
  'Gallery of Antiquities'
  photograph (Fenton),
  299–300, 472n69; Karl
  Marx's favourite seat in,
  50; Ogham stones looted
  by Fox in, 293, 468n29;
  'Progress of Civilisation'
  (tympanum), 375;
  security measures in,
  229, 358; Professor
  Challenger in, 340;
  purchases from
  Bernhard Smith's

# INDEX

collection, 145; Rosemary Powers (Experimental Officer for Natural History), 408–9; Rosetta Stone in, 308; separation from the Natural History Museum, 408

Broca, Paul, 104–5; founding of Société d'anthropologie de Paris, 452n76. *See also* craniometry

Bronze Age, 69, 131, 194, 308–9, 355, 372

Brooks, Khaleb, 410

Brown, Michael, 7

Browne, Thomas, 130, 195

Buckingham Palace, 151, 153, 159, 176, 182, 373, 377, 467n18

Buddhism, 193

Bulawayo, 12–3, 21

Bulgaria, 266, 270

Burke, Edmund, 73–4, 78

Burton, Richard, 207–10, 250, 453n91

Byron George Gordon, 6th Baron Byron (Lord Byron), 197–9

California, 458n208; Los Angeles 241; Stanford University, 413, 418; Three Knolls Massacre (1866), 84; University of California Berkeley, 82–5

Cambridge University, 23, 222, 296, 401. *See also* Jesus College, Cambridge; universities;

Canada, 12, 19, 40, 70, 165, 296, 366, 378, 470n49, 470n51; potential United States invasion of, 294–7. *See also* Trent Affair

cancellation (right-wing slogan), 31, 397

Cannibal Club, 207–10, 453n93; ceremonial mace of, 208. *See also* Anthropological Society of London; clubs

capitalism, 48, 50, 114, 241–2, 245; *Capitalism and Slavery* (Williams), 147–8, 171; *Capitalist Realism* (Fisher), 77; 'capitalism and schizophrenia' (Deleuze and Guattari), 342; *Carceral Capitalism* (Wang), 75, 244; disaster capitalism, 47; feudal capitalism, 162, 171; 'gentlemanly capitalism', 47; *Gore Capitalism* (Valencia), 102; racial capitalism, 47, 165–6; 'snuff capitalism', 103. *See also* Engels, Friedrich; Marx, Karl

carcerality, 8, 47, 75–6, 78, 82, 127, 149, 242, 244, 285, 386–7. *See also* Wang, Jackie

Carlyle, Thomas, 178, 205

Carrington, Frederick, 101

Carroll, Lewis, 103, 132, 324

Cassivellaunus (legendary king), 306

Césaire, Aimé, 75, 192, 331, 349, 417; *Discours sur le colonialisme*, 333–5. *See also choc en retour*

Cetshwayo kaMpande (Zulu king), 326

Challenger (name): Challenger Expedition (1872–1876), 60, 429n20; *Challenger* (space shuttle), 59–60; Dodge Challenger (car), 7; HMS Challenger, punitive expedition of, 60; Professor Challenger (George Edward Challenger, fictional anthropologist), 131, 337, 339–44

Chartism, 230–2, 254, 332; Chartist movement, 182, 230–2, 254, 332, 457n198; Reform Bill of 1866, defeat of, 182, 187, 457n198; Second Reform Act 1867, 183, 233, 292. *See also* Cuffay, William; Hyde Park Railings Affair

Chaudhuri, Amit, 11

Cheshire cat (Carroll's *Alice's Adventures in Wonderland*), 103, 132, 324

Childe, Vere Gordon, 29

*choc en retour* (Césaire), 333–5, 405, 409, 477n182. *See also* boomerang effect

Churchill, Lady Randolph (Jeanette Spencer-Churchill) (Fox's niece), 20

Churchill, Winston (Fox's great-nephew), 111, 138, 345, 436n65

*Cities of the Dead* (Roach), 441n22

civilisation, ideas of, 18–21, 28, 35, 45, 60, 79, 84, 97, 102–3, 149, 156, 184–7, 207, 210, 212–17, 227, 235, 242, 244, 252–3, 279, 285, 297, 309, 314, 323, 325, 360, 362; and socialism, 372; 'de-civilisation' (Césaire), 333; *Progress of Civilisation, The* (British Museum tympanum), civilisation, ideas of – *cont.* 375. *See also* barbarism, ideas of

Clark, Kate, 391–2

classification, ideas of, 33, 53, 73, 89–90, 102, 106–8, 115, 131, 141, 320, 357, 373, 431n52, 437n92; and 'classified' information, 73; 'The Principles of Classification' (Fox), 319; 'vernacular classification', 123–4; resisting classification, 124. *See also* militarist realism; types, ideas of

Clifford, James, 84, 432n82, 462n68

Clive, Stella Edith Howsen (aka Lonsdale, Magaloff, Maumen, Pitt-Rivers, Sidoroff and Warner), 344, 346, 365, 479n225, 487n70–1, 487n73; 'Stelladoux' (property in Provence, France), 487n70

clubs: Army and Navy Club, 176; Arthur's, 346; Athenaeum, 112, 346; Bulawayo Club, 13; Bullingdon Club, 10; Cavalry Club, 346; Cercle de l'Union interalliée, 346; Charnel Club ('the Golgothans'), 197; Constitutional Club, 13; East India Club, 176, 'the Everlasting Club' (short story), 395–6; Graham's, 162; Guards Club, 274; Hellfire Club (fictional club), 395, Oswald Mosley's British Union of Fascists dining club, 9; Vincent's, 10; Kimberley Club, 13; North Foreland Golf Club, 13; Rand Club, 347. *See also* Cannibal Club

Coates, Ta-Nehisi, 50

Cochrane, Kelso, 238

Codrington, Christopher, 16, 390–1

colonialism, 2–5, 15–26, 31–5, 44–9, 52–3, 65–71, 74–7, 81, 86–7, 96, 101–2, 106, 114, 123, 148–9, 176, 180, 185–91, 194, 199–206, 209, 212, 214, 217–19, 226–7, 234–45, 251, 282–5, 290, 293, 299–304, 324–5, 333–5, 349, 354, 359, 367, 384–6, 390, 394, 397, 400–6, 410–12, 423n33; as a 'world of statues' (Fanon), 376–7; metaphors of *choc en retour* and 'boomerang effect', 331–6, 405, 409; typological approach to (Finley), 393–4, 402. *See also* capitalism; decolonisation; extractivism; missionaries; postcolonialism, ideas of; Rhodes, Cecil; settler colonialism; slavery; wars

Colston, Edward (statue of), 24, 388

Confederate States of America, 26, 195–6, 201, 218, 235, 240, 294–6, 310; 'Lost Cause', 6–7; monuments to, 5, 15, 24, 241, 245; United Daughters of the Confederacy (UDC), 5, 421n7. *See also* Hotze, Henry; Trent Affair; Vizetelly, Frank; White supremacism

Confucius, 193

conjuncture, concept of, 27, 33, 37, 44, 318, 335, 387, 391

Conrad, Joseph, 151

conservatism: Fox's theory of, 115–16, 357, 367, 371–2; 'in the deepest sense' (Ruskin), 234; as 'prehistoric' (Mosley), 382

Conservative Party (UK), 111, 182, 187, 301, 321–2, 371–2, 478n201; 'Common Sense Group', 399; Benjamin Disraeli, 182, 298, 321, 371, 470n54; Nadine Dorries, 427n100; Oliver Dowden, 398–9; Michael Gove, 24–5, 427n102; Henry Forster (Fox-Pitt's father-in-law), 344–5, 348; Henry Hardinge, 261, 459n18; Edward Hulse, 357, 482n30; Robert Inglis, 232; Robert Jenrick, 24–5, 399; George Lane-Fox (Fox's uncle), 136–7, 439n122, 444n71, 445n75; Lord Elcho, 301, 371, 472n73; Chris Patten, 23; Margaret Thatcher, 13, 150, 226

Cook, James, 64, 95, 406

Cornwall, 58, 155, 459n18, 474n123

Corsín Jiménez, Alberto, 76

Countess of Airlie. *See* Stanley, Henrietta Blanche

Craft, Ellen and William Ellen, 213–14, 454n133; William Craft's story of

550

# INDEX

the lion and the man, 214, 389–90

craniometry, 3, 104–5, 309, *Crania Britannica* (Davis and Thurnam), 309; craniometers, 314; 'dolichocephalic' and 'brachycephalic' skulls, ideas of, 105, 293, 306–7, 310, 473n95. *See also* Broca, Paul; Fox, Augustus; eugenics

cremation, 29, 84, 116–17, 120, 125–6, 130, 132, 302, 432n87, 437n79; of Fox's body, 116, 126, 131, 408

Crimean War (1853–56), 15, 28, 41, 80, 102, 110, 152–3, 250, 261–85, 289, 295, 298, 300, 314–15, 386, 436n64, 459n18, 463–4n97; 464n98, 470n49. *See also* Russia; wars

critical fabulation (Hartman), 122–5, 147. *See also* fabulation; Hartman, Saidiya

*CSI: Crime Scene Investigation* (TV series), 284

Cuba, 5, 177

Cuffay, William, 230–2, 332; transportation to Tasmania, 232

cultural supremacism, 21, 26, 29, 35, 68, 71, 73, 75, 175, 179, 188, 215–20, 242, 305, 322, 325, 348–9, 354, 393

cultural techniques, 225, 244, 254, 290, 298, 308–9, 313, 319, 322, 359, 455n164

culture, ideas of, 8, 19, 21, 27–33, 46–50, 53, 55, 61, 70–1, 75, 79, 85–8, 93, 127–8, 143, 149, 155, 175–80, 187, 190, 217, 230, 233, 236, 254, 305, 362, 383–6, 399, 403; anthropology as 'the science of culture', 115–16, 224, 235, 362; 'culture areas', 83; 'cultural dupes', 27–8; *Clash of Culture and the Contact of Races, The* (Fox-Pitt), 346, 348; *Culture: A Critical Review of Concepts and Definitions* (Kroeber and Kluckhohn), 184; *Culture and Anarchy* (Arnold), 181–8, 206–7; *Culture and Imperialism* (Said), 206; 'Culture and its Enemies' (Arnold), 183; *Culture and Society* (Williams), 184; institutional culture ('canteen culture'), 239–40, 303, 393; *Kulturvölker* ('culture people'), idea of, 215; *The Progress of Human Culture* (Royal Society of Arts), 95–6; nature–culture distinctions, 336, 412; 'Racisme et culture' (Fanon), 405; 'When I hear the word culture, I slide the safety-catch off my Browning.' (Johst, *Schlageter*), 82; 'world culture' (in museums), 32, 72, 74, 87, 89, 244, 297–8, 365. *See also* Fox, Augustus (*Evolution of Culture*); material culture; memory culture

culture war, idea of, 4, 15, 26, 31, 48, 52–3, 67, 82, 188, 220, 232, 243, 254, 287, 349, 352, 373, 397–413; relationships with 'militarist realism', 315–16, 325, 336, 348–9. *See also* militarist realism

*Daily Telegraph*, 61, 243–4, 304, 399, 404–5; letter from John Ruskin, 234

Daley-Ward, Yrsa, 410

*Darkest Hour* (2017 movie), 138

Darwin, Charles, 80, 105, 185, 208, 213, 318, 322, 326; support for the Jamaica Committee, 205

Davis, Angela Y., 8

Dawkins-Pennant (surname): George Hay Dawkins-Pennant (Fox's great-uncle), 443n65, 478n203; Juliana Isabella Mary Dawkins-Pennant, (Fox's aunt), 443n65, 478n203

Day, Aviah Sarah, 240

decolonisation, 20, 48, 50, 354, 383, 387, 389–90, 393–4, 398, 401–3, 405, 411–13. *See also* colonialism; postcolonialism, ideas of: degeneration, ideas of: Munich Degenerate Art exhibition (1937), 14; Nazi ideology of degenerate art, 376, 385; of art (Fox), 81; of myths (Fox and Lévi-Strauss), 56, 343–4; 'realistic degeneration' (Fox), 99. *See also* myths

dehumanisation, 44, 77, 79, 87, 93–4, 102, 121, 131, 142, 190, 192, 199, 205, 219, 236, 245, 319,

# INDEX

dehumanisation – *cont.*
380, 390, 411–2. *See also* humanity; NHI
Deleuze, Gilles, 115–16, 125, 337, 342
denialism, 53, 237, 319, 326
dereliction tourism, 138
Dickens, Charles, 173; support for the Eyre Defence and Aid Fund, 205
Dickinson, Emily, 36, 390; 'Crumbling is not an instant's Act', 26; dead narrators, 378
Dilke, Charles Wentworth, 425n69
Dillon-Lee, Charles Henry, 14th Viscount Dillon (Fox's uncle by marriage), 443n64
Din-Kariuki, Natalya, 21
Dirlik, Arif, 48, 428n5
Disraeli, Benjamin, 182, 298, 321, 371, 470n54, 471n58
DNA analysis, 249
dominoes, 115–16, 257, 298, 320
Dorset: A354 (road), 364, 371; Ackling Dyke, 371; Blandford Forum, 364; Dorchester, 100–1, 106, 112, 372; Higher Bockhampton, 369–70; Rushmore and Hinton St Mary, 112, 120–1, 174, 196–7, 286–7, 312, 344, 346, 350–1, 368, 443n58; Iwerne Steepleton, 442n37, 474n108; Maiden Castle hillfort, 370; Sandroyd School, 368; Sherborne, 196–7; Sixpenny Handley, 369, 372; Stinsford, 370, Wansdyke, 311; Wor Barrow, 312, 369, 371. *See also* Wessex (imaginary landscape); Wiltshire

Douglas (surname): Caroline Douglas, (Fox's mother), 109, 128–9, 138, 167–71, 174, 298, 436n64, 470–1n54, 478n201, 478n203; George Sholto Douglas, 17th Earl of Morton (Fox's uncle), 111, 478n201; Harriet Douglas (Fox's aunt), 436n65; James Douglas, 14th Earl of Morton (Fox's great-grandfather, President of the Royal Society), 445n74; John Douglas (Fox's maternal grandfather, husband of Frances Lascelles), 167, 445n74

Douglas-Pennant (surname): Edward Gordon Douglas-Pennant, 1st Baron Penrhyn, 18th Earl of Morton (Fox's uncle), 337–39, 375–6, 443n65, 478n201; 478n203; George Sholto Gordon Douglas-Pennant, 2nd Baron Penrhyn (Fox's cousin), 339, 371

Douglas, Mary, 434n18
Douglass, Frederick, 7
Doyle, Arthur Conan, 131, 339–42, 344
drilling (military), 20, 41, 62, 232, 254–66, 270, 276, 281, 285, 289–90, 298–303, 313, 319, 324, 356–7, 373, 380. *See also* Greased Cartridge Affair

Druids, 10, 117, 119
Du Bois, W. E. B., 4–5, 421n8
Dugdale, William, 313
Duggan, Mark, 238
Duke of Wellington. *See* Wellesley, Arthur (1st Duke of Wellington)
Duke of Westminster. *See* Grosvenor, Hugh Richard Arthur Grosvenor (2nd Duke of Westminster)
Dundas, Lawrence, 1st Earl of Zetland, 445n74
Durham (UK), 139, 309, 359n18
Durkheim, Émile, 163, 165

East India Company, 146, 167–8, 193, 207, 232, 253, 256, 258, 298–300, 371, 410, 459n18. *See also* India
Eco, Umberto, 385
Edison, Thomas, 93, 433n5
*Education of the Feelings, The* (Bray), 358
Edwards, Michael, 491n154
Egypt, 94, 101, 165, 177, 214, 258, 288, 308, 331–2, 366, 384, 387, 406, 411; Fox's letter to *The Times* on looting (1882), 441n29
Elizabeth, Queen Mother, 14
Elkins, Caroline, 73
emancipation, 8, 35, 145, 148–9, 164, 166, 171–3, 188, 201, 205–7, 213–14, 233–4, 236, 304, 322, 373; as unfinished, 386–7, 405, 451n50; 'compensation' payments from, 164–5, 168, 192,

552

# INDEX

198, 200, 235, 246, 364, 366–7; *Emancipation: Black and White* (Huxley), 322; Emancipation Proclamation (Lincoln), 213; 'white emancipation' (Ruskin), 234. *See also* 38ers, the; abolitionism; Legacies of British Slavery, Centre for the Study of the; slavery; Williams, Eric

Engels, Friedrich, 245, 302, 458n225; *Communist Manifesto*, 230; on the battle of Alma, 272; on blindage in defences, 374; on slavery as the origins of armies, 373. *See also* Marx, Karl

English Heritage, 153–5, 368, 391–3, 401; 'A Monumental Act' (2013 exhibition), 154; *Informed Conservation*, 391–2. *See also* heritage management; Historic England

Epstein, Jacob, 13–14, 406

Ethnological Society of London, 112, 193, 207–8, 212, 389; and Edward Eyre, 207; merger with the Anthropological Society of London, 318; origins in the Aborigines' Protection Society, 215

Ettlinger, Ellen (folklorist), 140

eugenics, 3, 84, 104–5; 155–6, 179–80, 279, 318, 348–9, 358, 386, 388–9, 480n239; Eugenics Education Society, 480n240; Eugenics Society, 346. *See also* Fox-Pitt, George; Galton, Francis; racial 'science'

Evans-Pritchard, E. E., 143

Evans, George de Lacy, 270, 275, 462n74, 471n59

Evans, John, 98–99, 432n74, 434n22, 438n111; design of Fox's 'logo' 131–2

excarnation, 199

excavation, 26, 40, 57, 65, 69–70, 88, 96, 104–5, 108, 111–12, 125, 132–3, 157, 168, 172, 174–5, 191–2, 200, 210, 228, 288, 293, 305–13, 315–16, 338, 341, 343–4, 354, 362, 365–6, 369–71, 406–8; archaeological excavation as 'to besiege a place' (Fox), 313; as a metaphor for grief, 416; as an unrepeatable experiment, 130; as speculative, 123; excavation at Pitt Rivers Museum, Oxford, 69–70; for diamond mining, 50, 343; for mass graves, 273; of the Mahdi's body (Kitchener), 68; of the skull of Xhosa chief Sandile kaNgqika by Lord Grenfell, 101, 388; Walter Benjamin's account of excavation, 416

extinction, ideas of, 57, 83, 142, 149, 186–7, 210–12, 215–18, 283, 316, 326, 393; 'Angel of Death' (Bastian), 217; 'unseen hand' (Fox), 174–5, 179–80, 188, 242, 318; 'Wheat Before the Sickle' (Fox), 187, 301; discussion by Hotze, 215–16; discussion by Waitz, 216; extinction of the Rivers barony with Fox's inheritance, 169, 175. *See also* future progressive exonerative

extractivism, 47, 64, 78, 85–6, 241–2

Eyre Defence and Aid Fund, 205, 452n73. *See also* Jamaica Committee

Eyre, Edward John ('the Governor'), 199–207, 212, 233–5, 237–8, 451–2n66. *See also* Eyre Defence and Aid Fund; Jamaica Committee; Morant Bay Race Massacre

fabulation: in Michel Foucault, 124; in Henri Bergson, 124–5; in Donna Haraway, 124–5, 128; in Anna Tsing, 125; 'fabulous memory' (Guattari), 125; 'fabulatory comparativism' (McLean), 125, 'the colonial work of fabulation' (Taussig), 431n66; critical fabulation (Hartman), 122–4, 128

fallism, 25, 354, 383, 387, 390, 401, 412–13. *See also* Black Lives Matter; Rhodes Must Fall

Fanon, Frantz, 244, 333–5, 349; colonialism as a 'world of statues', 376–7; 'Racisme et culture' (essay), 405

553

# INDEX

Farage, Nigel, 400
fascism, 7–9, 19, 42, 45, 49, 102, 111, 151,176, 181, 216, 275–6, 335, 345–9, 372–3, 376, 380, 386, 389, 397, 409–12; 'aristofascism', 348; Battle of Cable Street, 382; Battle of Carfax, 9, 382, 422n25; British Union of Fascists, 8–9, 350, 382; defeat of in 1945, 32, 352, 385; National Front After Victory, 352; Oxford University Fascist Association, 9, 422n25; proto-fascism, 37, 379–81, 385; 'Ur-fascism' (Eco), 385. *See also* Fox-Pitt, George; Hitler, Adolf; Mosley, Oswald; White supremacism

Fenianism, 205, 231, 292, 466–7n17

Fenton, James, 74

Fenton, Roger, 276, 299–300, 302

figure ground reversal (Gestalt psychology), 246, 384

Finley, Moses, 393–4, 402

First World War (Great War), 82, 129, 221, 246, 251, 277–8, 282–3, 330, 347–8, 373, 380, 404, 440n6

Fisher, Mark, 77, 78, 431n65, on the British Museum, 78; *Capitalist Realism*, 'gothic flatline', 407

Fitzroy (surname): Henry Fitzroy, 5th Earl of Grafton (Fox's great-uncle), 443–4n65; Maria Louisa FitzRoy (Fox's aunt), 443–4n65

Flandreau, Marc, 131, 452n78, 453n93, 454n125

Flashman, Harry (fictional character), 131, 254–5; in *Royal Flash* (1975 movie), 459n17

Forster, Henry, 1st Baron Forster (Fox-Pitt's father-in-law), 344–5, 348

Foucault, Michel, 124, 465n3

Four As, the (Archaeology, Anthropology, Art, Architecture); 28, 40, 55, 88, 240–1, 362, 384–6, 412, 417, 428n107

Fox (surname): Marcia Bridget Lane Fox (Fox's aunt), 444n71; Sackville Walter Lane Fox (Fox's uncle), 444n71; Thomas Henry Lane Fox (Fox's uncle), 444n71; William Augustus Lane Fox (Fox's father), 128, 138, 170, 444n71, 445n80; William Edward Lane Fox (Fox's elder brother), 170, 174, 253, 257, 444n70, 445–6n87. *See also* Douglas, Caroline (Fox's mother); Lane Fox (surname)

Fox-Lane, James (Fox's paternal grandfather), 170, 444n71, 445n74–75

Fox-Pitt, George 'Joe' Henry Lane (George Pitt-Rivers) (Fox's grandson), 42, 45, 64, 88, 144, 288, 344–54, 365, 367–8, 382–3, 386, 388–9, 407–8, 412, 480n235, 480n239, 481n2, 487n70; anti-semitism of, 348, 480n233; aide-de-camp in Australia, 345, 348; as soldier in India, South Africa and France, 345, 347, 386, 479n227; attitude to his grandfather 346–7, 407; tutored by eugenicist William McDougall, 480n239; *Conscience and Fanaticism: an Essay on Moral Values* (1919), 347–8; *World Significance of the Russian Revolution, The* (1920), 348; *Clash of Culture and the Contact of Races, The* (1927), 348–9; arrest for espionage (1936), 350; attending Nuremberg Rally (1937); relationship with Adolf Hitler, 350–1, 481n4, 481n9; relationship with Benito Mussolini, 349, 480n246; relationship with Oswald Mosley, 111, 345, 349–51, 382, 481n2; detention under Defence Regulation 18B (1940), 350–52; founding Wessex Musical Festival 1945, 345; donation of the skull cup to Worcester College (1946), 350–3; marriages to Emily Rachel Forster (third cousin) and Rosalind Venetia Henley (second cousin), 344–5, 348, 487n70; relationship with Stella Clive, 344, 346, 365–7, 479n225, 487n70–1, 487n73; role in the dispersal of the Pitt Rivers Museum

# INDEX

(Dorset), 365–7, 487n73; professorship and laboratory named for him in Cambridge, 388–9

Fox, Augustus Henry Lane (Augustus Pitt-Rivers), passim. *See also* Douglas, Caroline (Fox's mother), Fox-Pitt, George (Fox's grandson), and other branches of Fox's family under the surnames: Baring, Beckford, Churchill, Dawkins-Pennant, Dillon-Lee, Douglas, Douglas-Pennant, Fitzroy, Fox, Fox-Lane, Fox-Pitt, Freeman-Mitford, Hamilton-Gordon, Lascelles, Lane Fox, Leveson-Gower, Lubbock, Mitford, Mosley, Ogilvy, Pitt, Pitt-Rivers, Stanley, Swinburne, Thynne

Fox's 'first collection', 294, 363–4; as a 'museum of savage and barbarous weapons', 315; seen as too 'racial', 361; donation rejected by the Committee of Council on Education, 350–62, 484n49; number of objects acquired after the Pitt-Rivers inheritance, 359–60, 363–4, 468n61–63; idea of donating to Surrey Archaeological Society, 483n40. *See also* Bethnal Green Museum; Pitt Rivers Museum (Oxford)

Fox's 'second collection', 121, 347, 365, 407, 411; art collections displayed at Tollard Royal, 366; dispersal of, 293, 365–6. *See also* Pitt Rivers Museum (Dorset)

Fox's other descendants: Agnes Geraldine Fox-Pitt, Lady Grove (Fox's daughter), 111, 467n18; Alexander Edward Lane Fox-Pitt-Rivers (Fox's son, father of Fox-Pitt), 298, 344, 347, 471n59; Douglas Henry Fox-Pitt (Fox's son) 111, 434n21, 467n18; St George William Lane Fox-Pitt, (Fox's son), 111, 298, 471n59; William Augustus Fox-Pitt, (Fox's son), 69, 101, 111, 326, 347, 430n44; Thomas (Tommy) Stanley Lane Fox-Pitt, (Fox's grandson), 492–3n173; Anthony Pitt-Rivers (Fox's great-grandson), 345, 469n32; Julian Pitt-Rivers, Fox's great-grandson), 345, 408–9; Michael Pitt-Rivers (Fox's great-grandson), 78, 346, 408, 479n228

France, 82, 152, 182, 190, 205, 218, 266, 270–2, 275, 288, 290, 296, 303, 321, 375, 377, 382; Cercle de l'Union interalliée, 346; Dieppe, 311; École des Beaux-Arts, 92–3; École des Mines, 224, 389; *Exposition Universelle* (1867), 316; French Empire, 67, 148, 243; French expeditionary army to Egypt (1798–1801); French Revolution, 243; French soldier, stuffed model of, 257, 289; Marseille; Paris, 70, 92, 104, 207, 224, 255, 263, 316; musée de l'Homme, 366; société d'anthropologie de Paris, 112, 207–8, 452n76; 'Stelladoux' (Provence), 487n70; Storming of the Bastille; Vincennes (military facility), 257

Freeman-Mitford, Algernon Bertram, 1st Baron Redesdale (Fox's nephew), 111, 453n88

Freud, Sigmund, 194, 279, 282

Frost, Robert, 44

future progressive exonerative, 217–18, 227, 235–47, 325. *See also* extinction; institutional racism

Galton, Francis, 104–5, 349; *Hereditary Genius*, 156. *See also* eugenics

Garner, Eric, 7

Gaza, 2, 48

Geoghegan, James, 202

Germany, 14, 19, 32, 48, 129, 165, 196, 286, 310, 334, 338, 351, 365, 386, 411; Berlin Olympics (1936), 381; Berlin Wall, fall of (1989), 48, 222; Brandenburg Gate, 153; Dachau concentration camp, 82; Danevirke (Schleswig-Holstein), 258, 311; Dresden, 297; German ambassador to London, 151; German East Africa, 196; German South West

# INDEX

Germany – *cont.*
Africa (Namibia), 68;
German emigration to
America (the '48ers'),
83, 432n79; German
revolutions of 1848–49,
220, 432n79; Grassi
Museum (Leipzig), 297;
Munich Degenerate Art
exhibition (1937), 14;
Munich Great German
Art Exhibition (1937),
376; Marburg, 216;
Nuremberg Rally of
1937, 350; Saxe-Weimar
(Duchy), 356; Weimar,
146, 440n11
Ghana, 145, 186, 329;
Asantehene Osei Bonsu,
195
Gibbons, Grinling, 394
Giddens, Anthony, Baron
Giddens of Southgate,
239–40, 244
Gilmore, Ruth Wilson,
115, 431n431, 437n72
Gilroy, Paul, 32, 102, 239
Glasgow, 148, 318–9
Gobineau, Joseph Arthur
de, 213–16; *Essai sur
L'inégalité des Races
humaines,* 213
Goethe, Johann Wolfgang
von, 146, 150
golf, 13, 357
Goodenough, James
Graham, 474n112
Goody, Jack, 52
Gopal, Priyamvada, 234
Gordon, Charles George
('Gordon of Khartoum'),
206
Gordon, George, 201,
204
Göring, Hermann, 82
gothic (genre), 4, 33, 37,
44–5, 56, 58–9, 61,
66, 71–3, 79, 92, 121,
131, 197–9, 209, 294,
333, 374, 395; Gothic
Revival (architecture),
17, 62, 74, 91, 198,
396, 450n36; *Vathek*
(William Beckford's
Gothic novel), 198;
'gothic flatline' (Fisher),
407, 412; 'gothic dark
MAGA' (Musk), 412.
*See also* horror
Gould, Stephen Jay, 3, 53,
105
Governor, the. *See* Eyre,
Edward John
Gramsci, Antonio, 33,
178, 428n120, 465n131;
on Caesarism, 176; on
wars of manouevre'
and wars of position,
284–5
Greased Cartridge Affair
(1857), 265–6, 297–303
Great Exhibition, 181,
251–7, 297, 355, 357,
359, 375; 'Brompton
Boilers', 355. *See
also* Hyde Park and
Kensington Gardens
great-man history,
113, 130, 178–80;
Bonapartism (Marx),
176; Caesarism
(Gramsci), 176; 'hero-
myths', 46; *On Heroes,
Hero-Worship and
the Heroic in History*
(Carlyle), 178. *See also*
myths; Le Guin, Ursula
K.: 'killer story'
Greater Britain, idea of,
19, 425n69
Greenwell, William
(Canon Greenwell),
308–9, 473n90,
473n91
Grenfell Tower fire, 102,
388
Grenfell, Francis, 1st
Baron Grenfell, 101,
388. *See also* Sandile
kaNgqika
grief, 32, 89–90, 119–20,
123, 158, 295, 415–18
Grosvenor, Hugh Richard
Arthur Grosvenor, 2nd
Duke of Westminster,
151
Guattari, Félix, 125, 336,
342
gunmakers, 256; Ancion
& Cie, 257; Auguste
Francotte & Companie,
219; Charles William
Lancaster, 260; Casimir
Lefaucheux, 68, 218–19,
246, Mauser brothers,
236, 458n205; Hiram
Maxim, 10–11, 378;
Westley Richards, 260;
Joseph Whitworth,
260, 302–3; Henry
Wilkinson 258, 375
*Guns don't kill people*
(NRA slogan), 224
guns: air rifles, 99; Brown
Bess (musket), 255, 260;
Browning light machine
gun, 82, 432n75;
Colt 45 revolver,
68, 256; displays at
Royal United Service
Institution, 80, 190,
471n55; Enfield rifle,
41, 72, 80, 254, 256,
258–9, 265, 281, 297–9,
430n31; Gatling gun,
5, 101, 108, 289, 295,
316, 326; Gewehr 98
Mauser, 458n205;
Mauser bolt-action
rifle, 236; Maxim
machine gun, 10, 378;
muskets, 203–4, 231,
252, 254–5, 257–8,
265–6, 281, 284, 314–15,

# INDEX

367–9, 461n44, 474n121; 'Long Cecil' (gun), 343; revolvers, 68, 218–19, 230, 235, 246, 256, 274; Rodman gun, 295; Uzi 9mm submachine gun, 68; Winchester rifle, 5, 237; Whitworth rifle, 260, 302–3. *See also* gunmakers; Howitzer (artillery weapon)

Hacking, Ian, 106
Hall, Catherine, 233–4
Hall, Stuart, 33, 37, 172, 184, 239, 387, 391–2, 405–6, 428n120; blue plaque to, 391; on the 'post-colonial', 428–9n5; on Whiteness as 'the unmarked position', 102, 243–4, 369; Rhodes Scholarship to Merton College, Oxford, 388
Hamilton-Gordon, George (4th Earl of Aberdeen) (Lord Haddo) (Fox's uncle), 111, 436n64
Hampshire, 112, 117, 146, 166, 417; Aldershot, 153; Bokerly Dyke, 311; Army Medical School, Netley, 277; Southampton, 262–3, 283, 298; Stratfield Saye House, 153. *See also* Wessex (imaginary landscape)
Haraway, Donna, 124, 128
Hardy, Thomas, 370, 488n79; Hardy Way (walking trail), 369–70. *See also* Wessex (imaginary landscape)
Harewood, Earls of. *See* Lascelles (surname)

Harrison, Simon, 101–2, 191, 195, 430n37
Hart, Bradley, 347, 351, 418, 480n243
Hartman, Saidiya, 124, 142, 147–8, 172, 245, 387
Harvey, David, 51
Hawkes, Jacquetta, 372, 407–9 492n172–3
head-hunting, ideas of. *See* barbarism, ideas of
Hegel, Georg Wilhelm Friedrich, 335–6, 477n193
Herero-Nama genocide, 68
heritage management, 3–4, 28–37, 40, 46, 53, 71, 73, 149, 151–6, 229, 241, 247, 315, 368–9, 383, 387, 391–2, 398–413; conservation planning, 391; 'contested heritage', idea of, 24–5, 400–1; Fox-Pitt's use of the term 'heritage', 348–9, 351; 'ruin value' (Nazi ideology), 381; 'heritage capital' (economics), 392–3; LGBTQ+ heritage, 400; 'Whose Heritage?' conference (1999), 392. *See also* English Heritage; Historic England; National Trust
Hertz, Robert, 143, 147
Heuman, Gad, 204, 450n48, 451n50
Heyer, Heather D., 7
Hidatsa people, 76
Hinduism, 193, 212, 299
Historic England, 401, 427n97, 427n100; listed building consent, 24, 31,

398–9, 427n97. *See also* English Heritage
Hitchens, Christopher, 342
Hitler, Adolf, 349–50, 376, 479n229, 488n97
Ho, Elizabeth, 71
Hoare, Richard Colt, 2nd Baronet, 312, 473n92
Hobbes, Thomas, 80, 184; on the Ship of Theseus, 337
Hobsbawm, Eric, 36
Hocart, Arthur, 282
Hodge, Merle, 189–90, 196
Horace (Roman poet), 11–12, 17, 147, 423n37
horror (genre), 71, 209; body horror, 42, 144, 196, 275–6, 411; *Gore Capitalism* (Valencia), 102; 'Horror in the Museum, The' (Lovecraft), 65. *See also* gothic (genre)
horses: escaped cavalry horses in London (2024), 153, 181; Marengo (skeleton of), 288, 466n9; Old Jack (portrait of), 137
Hoskins, W. G., 353–4
Hotze, Henry (Confederate agent) ('the Protagonist'), 213–15, 218, 235, 240, 454n126; publication of *The Index*, 218; translation of Gobineau, 213. *See also* Anthropological Society of London; Hunt, James; Vizetelly, Frank
Howitzer (artillery weapon), 377
humanitarianism, 147–8, 215, 218, 349

557

humanities, the, 3, 32, 60, 62, 114, 207, 221, 223–7, 235–6, 241–2, 246, 295, 327, 342, 384. *See also* subjects, ideas of
humanity, 35, 45, 62, 78–9, 93–4, 149, 192, 201, 206–7, 380, 385–6, 403, 407, 441n29; in Bruno Latour, 456n177; 'liberal monohumanism' (Wynter), 242, 244. *See also* inhumanity; NHI; nonhumans, ideas of
Hunt, James, 207–8, 454n126, 465n123
hunting, 76, 126–7, 197, 302, 358, 431n58, 468n24; fox hunting, 180; 'Hunter of Early Days' (Joseph Boehm statue), 180, 367–8; *Thoughts on Hunting* (Beckford), 180
Huxley, Thomas Henry, 80, 321–2, 389, 484n49
Hyde Park and Kensington Gardens, 14–15, 152, 159–66, 171, 181–3, 206, 245, 250, 255, 292, 357, 364, 373–4, 377, 379; Albert Memorial, 251, 379, 381; Hyde Park Barracks, 153; Hyde Park Corner, 154–8, 182, 184, 187; Machine Gun Corps Memorial, 378; Physical Energy, 14–15, 152, 379; Serpentine (lake), 156, 158–62, 166, 176, 250, 373, 378; Speke Monument, 250; Sunday Trading Bill protests, 398; Wellington Arch, 152–3, 374, 377; Wellington Monument, 374. *See also* Great Exhibition; Hyde Park Railings Affair
Hyde Park Railings Affair (1866), 182–4, 235, 245, 457n198

*Illustrated London News*, 253, 294, 316; Frank Vizetelly (reporter), 294, 469n36
improvement, idea of, 80–1, 95–6, 127, 240, 255, 257, 260–1, 289, 332, 359, 379
'Improvement of the Rifle' (Fox), 260–1, 297. *See also* degeneration, ideas of; drilling
*Inability to Mourn, The* (Mitscherlich and Mitscherlich), 32
India, 42, 64, 145, 193, 206, 253, 270, 300, 304, 331–2, 366, 371, 426n78; Fox-Pitt's deployment to Mathura (Uttar Pradesh), 347; Grant Medical College (Mumbai), 371; Indian Rebellion (1857), 67, 205, 298–301, 430n31; Lucknow, 67, 298; Koh-i-Noor diamond, 253; Naga people, 221–3, 246. *See also* East India Company; Greased Cartridge Affair; rebellions
*Indiana Jones* (movie franchise), 131
inhumanity, 246. *See also* humanity; nonhumans, ideas of
institutional racism, 238–44, 326, 458n208. *See also* future progressive exonerative; racism; police
*Invisible Man* (Ellison), 477n187
Ireland, 80, 110, 168, 175, 182, 205, 206, 208, 233, 245, 258, 291–4, 300, 304–6, 308, 314–15, 358–9, 394, 444n71, 447n107, 459n18, 467n20, 468n24; Christ Church (Triskel Christchurch, Cork), 291; Cuvierian Society of Cork, 112, 467n20; Fenianism, 205, 231, 292, 466–7n17, 467n18, 467n20, 468n24, 470n49; Fox's looting of Ogham stones, 293, 468n29; Galway Brooch, 293; Home Rule movement, 293; Inspectorship of National Monuments (Irish Board of Works), 441–2n29; Kilkenny Archaeological Society, 112, 467n20; Ordnance Survey of Ireland, 474n123; Rooves More Ringfort, 293; Royal Cork Institution, 467n20; Royal Irish Academy, museum of, 112, 358; Royal Society of Antiquaries of Ireland, 112. *See also* Wilde, William
Ishi, Yahi man, known as, 83–5, 128, 432n82
Islam, 70, 212, 299
Italy, 165, 290; British Mission at Naples (Kingdom of the Two Sicilies), 174, 257, 444n70; Ostia, 300; Rome 374–5; Turin, 257

# INDEX

Jagger, Charles Sargeant, 377
Jamaica Committee, 205, 233. *See also* Eyre Defence and Aid Fund
Jamaica, 68, 148, 160, 167–8, 198–214, 219–20, 228, 233–6, 338, 375, 388, 443n58, 443n61, 450n35, 455n148, 478n203; Jamaica Station (Royal Navy), 146, 444n6; Maroons, 203, 451n53. *See also* Morant Bay Race Massacre
James, C. L. R., 148
James, Henry, 355
Jameson, Fredric, 48
*Jane Eyre* (Brontë), 199
Japan, 67
*Jason and the Argonauts* (1963 movie), 269
Jesus College, Cambridge, 390, 393–4, 396–7, 401–2, 490n137. *See also* Cambridge University; Rustat, Tobias
Jones, Lisa Heledd, 339
Julianus the Egyptian, 94
Julien, Isaac, 51, 238, 246, 410; *Who Killed Colin Roach?*, 328
Jünger, Ernst, 380

Karlsbad (Karlovy Vary) (Czech Republic), 345
Kassim, Sumaya, 354–5
Kensington Gardens. *See* Hyde Park and Kensington Gardens
Kent, 13, 104, 110–11, 146, 154, 162, 256, 258, 291, 310–11; Folkestone, 104, 263, 311; Hythe, 110, 256–60, 264, 297–8, 302, 459n16, 460–1n42;

Kit's Coty House (Neolithic monument), 154; St Mary's Naval Barracks (Royal Marine Barracks) Chatham, 232; Royal East Kent Regiment, 203
Khalifa, the (Abdullah ibn-Mohammed al-Khalifa), 196
King, Rodney, 241
Kipling, Rudyard, 12, 237
Kitchener, Horatio Herbert (1st Earl Kitchener), 430n44, 449n26; receipt of Oxford DCL alongside Rhodes, (1899), 66; treatment of the Mahdi's body, 68, 181, 196
Klein, Naomi, 335
Klemm, Gustav, 97, 104–5, 215, 297
Knights Hospitaller, 177, 264
Knox, Robert, 210, 212, 323–4
Koram, Kojo, 50–1
Kroeber, Alfred L., 83–5, 92–3; 184, 288. *See also* Le Guin, Ursula K.
Kroeber, Theodora, 83, 85
Ku Klux Klan, 5, 20. *See also* White supremacism
Kubrick, Stanley, 126, 359

Lady Grove. *See* Fox-Pitt, Agnes Geraldine
Lady Susan. *See* Leveson-Gower, Susan Georgiana
land acknowledgements, 47–9, 52–3
Lane Fox (surname): George Lane Fox, (Fox's uncle), 136–7, 439n122, 444n71, 445n75; Sackville

FitzRoy Henry Lane Fox (Fox's first cousin once removed), 476n173; Nick Lane-Fox, 137–9; 419, 439n127; Sackville George Lane-Fox, 12th Baron Conyers (Fox's cousin), 476n173. *See also* Fox (surname)
Lascelles (surname), 16, 170–1, 338, 478n203; Edward Lascelles (1st Earl of Harewood) (Fox's great-grandfather), 109, 167, 443n62; Frances Lascelles (Fox's maternal grandmother), 445n74; Henry Lascelles (2nd Earl of Harewood) (Fox's great-uncle), 180, 443n61
Latour, Bruno, 221–7, 235–7, 243, 260, 319, 455n152, 475n138. *See also* actor–network theory
Lawrence, Stephen, 238
Le Guin, Ursula K., 77, 82–3, 90, 125–9, 431n61; 'Carrier Bag Theory of Fiction', 126–8, 178–81, 192, 200, 284; *Earthsea Trilogy, The*, 82; influence of Elizabeth Fisher on, 438n103; influence of Herbert Spencer on, 178–9, 266; 'It Was a Dark and Stormy Night', 288, 327; 'killer story', 127–9, 140, 176, 178–80, 192, 200–1, 266, 284; 'The Rule of Names', 82–3, 85; 'Which Side Am I on, Anyway?', 86

559

# INDEX

Legacies of British Slavery, Centre for the Study of the (UCL), 363–4, 443n61, 443n64, 443n67
Leibniz, Gottfried Wilhelm, 115, 348, 356, 437n75
Leicestershire Architectural and Archaeological Society, 197
Leveson-Gower (surname): Granville Leveson-Gower, 2nd Earl Granville (Lord Leveson) (brother-in-law of the 4th Baron Rivers) 483n40; Susan Georgiana Leveson-Gower (Lady Susan, wife of the 4th Baron Rivers), 170, 446n88
Lévi-Strauss, Claude, 56, 61, 76, 90, 102, 107, 267, 385
Liberty and Property Defence League, 301
Lively, Penelope, 74, 431n54
Liverpool, 148, 168, 188, 263, 294, 296, 332, 338, 469n33, 478n203; Liverpool Prison, 352
Locke, Alain, 388. *See also* Rhodes Trust
looting, 6, 35, 49–50, 66–70, 75, 103, 194–5, 200, 206, 280, 287, 308, 326, 376, 394; in the Burning of Washington (1814), 270; of Russian bodies after battle of Alma (1854), 274; of Ogham stones from Cork (by Fox), 293, 467n20; Fox's letter to *The Times* about looting in Egypt, 441n29; fictional looting in Thomas Hardy, 370; of the Beijing Summer Palace, 193
Lord Balgonie (Alexander Leslie-Melville, Viscount Balgonie), 276
Lord Eddisbury. *See* Stanley, Edward, 1st Baron Eddisbury
Lord Elcho (Francis Richard Charteris, 10th Earl of Wemyss), 301, 371, 472n73, 488n82
Lord Lucan (John Bingham, 7th Earl of Lucan), 151
Lord Malvern (Godfrey Martin Huggins, 1st Viscount Malvern of Rhodesia and of Bexley in the County of Kent), 14–15
Lord Palmerston (Henry John Temple, 3rd Viscount Palmerston), 295–6, 457n198, 469n42
Lord Raglan (FitzRoy Somerset, 1st Baron Raglan), 271, 275
Lord Salisbury (Robert Arthur Talbot Gascoyne-Cecil, 3rd Marquess of Salisbury), 38
Lorde, Audre, 114–15, 249
*Lost City of Z, The* (2016 movie), 131
Lovecraft, H. P., 66, 331
Lubbock, John, 1st Baron Avebury (Fox's son-in-law), 111, 151, 345, 441n23, 484n49

McBean, Shanice Octavia, 240
McClintock, Anne, 48
McFadyen, Lesley, 30, 464n106
McGranahan, Carole, 33
McKittrick, Katherine, 386. *See also* Wynter, Sylvia
McLean, Stuart, 125
Macpherson, William Alan of Cluny, 6th of Blairgowrie, 238–44, 326
Mahdi (Muhammad Ahmad, al-Mahdī al-Muntaẓar), treatment of body of, 68, 196. *See also* Kitchener, Horatio
main character syndrome, 108–9
*Male Fantasies* (Theweleit), 380–1
Malinowski, Bronislaw, 223, 269, 455n159
Malta: 80, 110, 165, 256, 258, 263–6, 270, 291, 297–300, 304, 383, 460–1n42, 470n54, 471n59; Kalkara, 264; St George's Bay, 298; Valletta, 263, 298
Malthus, Thomas, 80
Manjapra, Kris, 164, 400
Marett, Robert Ranulph, 223, 351
Marrow, Henry Dortress, 7
martial law, 6, 182, 202–5, 233–4, 457n197
Marx, Karl, 50–1, 178, 225, 335–6, 393, 398, 477n194; *Communist Manifesto, The*, 230; *Eighteenth Brumaire of Louis Bonaparte, The*, 335; favourite seat at the British Museum, 50; on 'Bonapartism', 176; on monuments of Robert Peel, 245, 458n225; on the Greased Cartridge Affair, 298–9; on the Hyde Park

560

# INDEX

Railings Affair, 183; on the Morant Bay Race Massacre, 466–7n17; Marxism, 27, 50, 377, 399, 428–9n5; Oswald Mosley's commentary on, 382. *See also* Engels, Friedrich

material culture, ideas of, 69, 71–3, 79–81, 108, 220, 221, 229, 236, 260, 286–9, 293, 297, 319–24, 349, 359, 412, 468n23; 'material agency', 55, 223, 229, 240, 326–7. *See also* humanity; nonhumans, ideas of

Maxwele, Chumani, 21

Maylam, Paul, 13

Meades, Jonathan, 17

memory culture, 4, 8, 11, 15, 16, 67, 86, 388–90, 412

memory, 1, 4, 7–8, 13, 20, 30–2, 36–7, 40;, 46, 58, 61, 67, 71, 92–4, 107, 130, 132, 149, 176–7, 181, 200, 245, 250, 269, 280, 282, 285, 287, 291, 299, 387, 391, 402–4, 407, 413, 416; and autobiography, 129; and loss, 45, 415–17; as artificial, 107; as choice, 86; collective memory, 43, 73; counter-memory, 140, 405; 'fabulous memory', 125; faulty memory, 25, 135; involuntary memory, 89; memory palace, museum as a, 315; policing as memory, 241; public memory, 32, 289, 390; shared memory, 108; repressed memory, 327; unconscious memory,

322. *See also* fabulation; naming; nostalgia

Mercer, Kobena, 246

militarist realism, 72–81, 87, 125, 149, 165, 190, 194, 220, 223, 234, 251, 266, 285, 305, 324, 326, 349, 354, 361, 367, 373, 376–7, 379, 382, 386–9, 394, 397, 402, 405, 407, 412–13

Mill, John Stuart, 202–3, 457n196; support for the Jamaica Committee, 205

Milligan, Robert (statue of), 375, 388

missionaries, 47, 50, 60, 65–6, 99, 218, 435n23. *See also* colonialism

Mistley, Essex, 167

Mitford sisters (Fox's great-grand-nieces), 111, 453n88; Diana Freeman-Mitford, 78, 151, 345, 479n229. *See also* Mosley, Oswald

Mkwawa, Chief (Mkwavinyika Munyigumba Mwamuyinga), 196

models, 83, 176, 253, 288–9

modifier (grammatical term), 123–4, 287, 369, 384

monumentality, 4, 7–8, 12, 14–16, 20, 25–6, 29–37, 44, 46–7, 55, 74, 89, 129, 140, 158, 242, 244, 276, 349, 367–91, 402, 405, 417

Morris, William, Viscount Nuffield (Oxford motor manufacturer), support for Oswald Mosley, 382

Morton, Samuel, 3, 104–5, 455n143

Mosley, Alexander (Fox's great-great-great-grand-nephew and Oswald Mosley's grandson), 387, 389

Mosley, Oswald (6th Baronet) (Fox's great-grand-nephew), 8–9, 111, 151, 345, 350, 387, 389; marriage to Fox's great-grand-niece Diana Freeman-Mitford, 78, 111, 479n229; collaboration with Fox-Pitt, 350–1, 382, 481n2; dining clubs of, 422n24; addressing Oxford University Fascist Association (1935 and 1936), 8–9; 'Battle of Carfax', 8–9, 382, 422n25; support of William Morris (motor manufacturer) for, 382; *The Greater Britain* (1932), 19, 425n69

Müller, Max, 319–20

mummies, 214, 406; mummy paintings, 366. *See also* shrunken heads

Musk, Elon, 268, 403, 412. *See also* Rhodes, Cecil; Trump, Donald

Mussolini, Benito, 349. *See also* Fox-Pitt, George

myths, 5, 25, 36, 39, 42, 49, 54, 57, 71, 79, 88, 131, 149, 158, 184, 190, 195, 225, 269, 300, 310, 327–8, 337, 343–4; 348, 380, 385, 405; 'degeneration' of (Fox), 99–100; 'how myths die' (Lévi-Strauss), 56–7, 61, 145; 'mythic matter' (Lévi-Strauss), 56; mythography, 266, 305;

# INDEX

myths – *cont.*
  *Mythologies* (Barthes), 157. *See also* Argo (mythological ship); Challenger (name); militarist realism; racial 'science'

naming, 1, 3–4, 15, 39–40, 45, 53, 55, 57–8, 65–8, 97, 134, 171, 192, 200, 284, 380, 390–1; as remembrance, 22, 35, 90, 391, 416; as silencing, 45, 391; necronyms, 42, 63, 88, 90, 109, 347, 364, 407, 433n102; *noms de guerre*, 196; patronyms, 106; 'rule of names' (Le Guin), 82–3, 85; Maggie Nelson on, 86; names of Stella Clive, 344, 365, 487n70; names of the stars, 102; naming 'militarist realism', 33–6, 73, 79; naming 'the 38-ers', 304–5, 373, 385; nominative determinism, 401; of Emancipation Park (Charlottesville), 7; of the *Argo*, 337; of Fox's sons, 298; of Grenfell Tower, 102, 388; of places after Albert Leo Schlageter ('Schlageter cult'), 82; of Space Shuttle *Challenger*, 59; of ships, 366–7; of storms, 42; of the gates of Hyde Park, 162–3; of the George Pitt-Rivers Laboratory and Professorship at Cambridge, 388–9; of the Pitt Rivers Museum (Oxford), 16, 61, 67, 86, 88, 116, 342, 407; of things after Cecil Rhodes, 11–13, 17, 20, 423n40; of things after the Mosley family, 387; of things after Prince Albert, 381; South Kensington Museum renamed Victoria and Albert Museum, 251, 355, 381. *See also* memory; memory culture; un-naming
Napoleon Bonaparte (Napoleon I), 137, 286
National Portrait Gallery, 13, 208
National Rifle Association (UK), 300–3, 357
National Rifle Association (USA), 224
National Rifle Museum, 302
National Trust, 151, 338, 399–400; and Lord Curzon, 436n78
Naturvölker, idea of, 97, 215, 217
necrography, 46, 90, 109, 176, 194
necronyms, 90, 96, 101, 109, 121, 129, 144, 150, 160, 171, 175, 304, 344, 347, 360, 363, 407, 410
necroscapes, 77
Needham, Rodney, 108
Nelson, Maggie, 86, 150, 269, 337
Neo-Victorianism, 71, 417
New York City, 83, 114, 195–6, 293–5, 317, 354, 366, 378, 411, 432n78–9
New Zealand (Aotearoa), 201, 206, 211–12, 349, 440n10; Māori people, 186, 349, 366
Newcastle, 213; Society of Antiquaries of Newcastle-on-Tyne, 112
Newton, Isaac, 27, 51, 58, 179; third law of motion, 344
NHI (No Humans Involved), 200, 235, 241, 300. *See also* Wynter, Sylvia
Nietzsche, Friedrich, 125, 222
Nigeria, 70, 394, 405. *See also* Benin, Kingdom of
non-performativity (Ahmed), 52
nonhumans, ideas of, 220–1, 223, 226, 241, 243, 246, 256, 322, 326, 349, 389; in Fisher's 'gothic flatline', 407, 412; in 1920s anthropology, 223, 455n159; in Bruno Latour, 224–9, 236, 260–1, 284, 319; nonhumanity, 192, 246. *See also* actor–network theory; humanity
Norman Conquest, 293, 310; Caesar's Camp (Norman castle), 104
Norman Revival (architecture), 338
nostalgia, 6, 48, 71, 79; as a medical diagnosis, 277–8. *See also* memory; shell shock
NRA. *See* National Rifle Association (UK); National Rifle Association (USA)

O'Keeffe, Stephen Martin Lanigan (high commissioner), 13–14, 423n47
objectivity, ideas of, 78, 123, 225, 347, 355. *See also* subjects, ideas of
Occupy Wall Street, 114

# INDEX

Odd Fellows, 119
Ogilvy, David Graham Drummond Ogilvy (10th Earl of Airlie) (Fox's brother-in-law), 111, 453n88, 479n229
Okuleye, Yewande, 87
Olusoga, David, 164–5
Olympic Games, 381, 425n66
Ordnance Survey, 139, 313, 369; Ordnance Survey of Ireland, 474n123. *See also* Board of Ordnance; surveying
Oriel College, Oxford, 9–13, 16–17, 22–4, 26, 63, 86, 88, 145, 343, 373, 388–92, 401, 427n101, 430n25; Oriel's Rhodes building and statue, 223, 240, 373–4, 396, 399, 403; King Edward St plaque (1906), 13, 24, 427n97. *See also* Rhodes Must Fall; Oxford University
Orkney, 155; sale of estate by 14th Earl of Morton, 170, 445n74
Orwell, George, 78, 345, 479n228; *Nineteen Eighty-Four*, 77; 'Shooting an Elephant', 236–7, 330, 458n205
Ottoman Empire, 266, 270, 277
Oxford (UK): Cowley Barracks, 22; Little Clarendon Street, 86, 413; Magdalen Bridge, 22–3; Museums Association meeting (1897), 194; Radcliffe Square, 25, 50; Randolph Hotel, 20;

Rhodes House, 17, 103, 147, 388, 424n58; St Michael's Street, 118–19; Slade Park Barracks, 22; South African War Memorial, 22; University Church, 9, 422n26; Warneford Lunatic Asylum, 328
*Oxford Dictionary of National Biography*, 11, 113–14
*Oxford English Dictionary*, 42
Oxford University, passim. Ashmolean Museum, 64, 88, 143–4, 363; Member of Parliament for Oxford University, 232; Oxford University Apollo Chapter (Masonic lodge), 10; Oxford University drag hunt, 10; Oxford University Fascist Association, 9, 422n25. *See also* Pitt Rivers Museum (Oxford); universities
Oxford University, colleges of: All Souls College, 16, 390; Balliol College, 20; Christ Church, 64, 291; Exeter College, 351; Hertford College, 388; Merton College, 388, 435n23; New College, 422n25; St Benet's Hall (defunct Oxford permanent private hall), 491n148; St Peter's College, 387, 389; Trinity College, 64; Wadham College, 17. *See also* Oriel College, Oxford; Worcester College, Oxford

Oxford, North Carolina, 5–8
Oxfordshire: Dorchester Dykes, 315, 474n123; Ditchley Park, 168, 443n64; Edward Brooks Barracks (Abingdon), 22. *See also* Wessex (imaginary landscape)

Patterson, Orlando, 147
Patteson, John Coleridge, 99, 435n23
Pennant, Richard, 1st Baron Penrhyn (first creation) (Fox's great-uncle), 478n204. *See also* Douglas-Pennant, Edward Gordon, 1st Baron Penrhyn (second creation)
Petrie, William Flinders, 125–6, 191; visit to Rushmore with Hilda Petrie (1898), 287, 465n5
Philip, Marlene NourbeSe, 123, 188
Philippines, 5; Bud Dajo (Moro Crater) Massacre, 68
Pitt Rivers Museum (Oxford), 16–17, 61, 64–6, 95, 110, 118, 192–3, 218–19, 308, 317, 327–31, 348, 364, 378–9, 404–5, 418. *See also* Fox's 'first collection'
Pitt-Rivers Museum (Dorset), 64, 110, 344, 357, 364–7, 407. *See also* Fox's 'second collection'
Pitt-Rivers, George, 4th Baron Rivers (George Beckford; Fox's second cousin, son of the 3rd Baron Rivers), 170–1, 174–5, 443n58,

# INDEX

Pitt-Rivers, George – *cont.* 446n88; brother-in-law's role in offer of first collection to Surrey Archaeological Society, 483n40; Jamaican estates of, 171, 363–4, 486n67; marriage to Susan Georgiana Leveson-Gower, 170, 446n88; pro-slavery lobbying, 171; sickness of the children of 173, 446n88
Pitt-Rivers, Henry Peter, 5th Baron Rivers (Fox's second cousin once removed), 169, 174–5
Pitt-Rivers, Horace, 6th Baron Rivers (Fox's second cousin, son of the 3rd Baron Rivers), 109–10, 169, 171, 175, 363–4, 444n67, 445n76
Pitt-Rivers, William Horace 3rd Baron Rivers (Horace Beckford; Fox's first cousin once removed), 152, 160, 163, 170, 173; gambling debts of 161–3, 173, 175. 442n47; marriage to Francis Hale Rigby, 167, 443n58, 444n72; sources of wealth of, 166–7, 444n72; suicide of, 158–163, 171, 443n58
Pitt, George, 1st Baron Rivers (Fox's great-grandfather), 109, 167, 442n38, 445n75
Pitt, George, 2nd Baron Rivers (Fox's great-uncle), 109–10, 137, 152–3, 170, 174, 304, 442n38, will of 174, 304, 445n75

Pitt, Louisa (Fox's great-aunt), 152, 167, 170, 198
Pitt, Marcia Lucy (Fox's paternal grandmother), 167, 170, 445n74–5, 445n80
*Planet of the Apes* (1968 movie), 60
police, 7, 8, 10, 12, 15, 48, 68, 75, 154, 160–1, 182–3, 196, 202–3, 205, 229–31, 235–41, 244, 246, 252–4, 277, 304, 339, 358, 360, 382, 388, 400; monuments to Robert Peel (Marx and Engels), 245. *See also* abolitionism; border regimes; institutional racism; Morant Bay Race Massacre; Hyde Park Railings Affair
polygenism. *See* racial 'science'
pornography, 209
postcolonialism, ideas of, 48, and academic disciplines, 384; 'legacy colonialism', 49–50, 77, 86, 151, 227, 241, 243, 290, 354, 410–11; *Postcolonial Melancholia* (Gilroy), 32. *See also* colonialism; decolonisation
Powell, Enoch, 151, 365, 487n71
Powers, Hiram, 253
Powers, Rosemary, 408–9, 493n175
*Predator* (movie franchise), 78
preservation, ideas of, 'retain and explain' (political slogan), 31, 393, 398–9. *See also* heritage management

primitiveness, ideas of. *See* barbarism ideas of
Primrose League, 111, 371–2, 381, 383, 403, 488n82; 'Primrose Day', 371
Prince Albert of Saxe-Coburg and Gotha, Prince Consort, 163, 251, 253, 256, 261, 295–7, 302. *See also* Victoria, Queen
Princess Mary. *See* Mary, Princess Royal, Countess of Harewood
pronouns, 33, 35, 55, 87, 212, 226, 267, 393
Protagonist, the. *See* Hotze, Henry (Confederate agent)
Proust, Marcel, 45, 88
Punisher, the (Marvel Comics character), 196
punitive expeditions, 60, 186, 206, 222, 228–9, 237, 243, 325, 402, 429n19

race, ideologies of, 8, 179, 227, 234, 244, 246, 292–3, 309, 315, 323–6, 346, 348–9, 358, 468n23, 475n129; 'Aryan race', 208, 210, 213, 313–14; 'English-speaking race' (Rhodes), 20; Nordic League, 346, 351; 'Nordic strain', 213; racial 'types' (Fox) 309, 314, 358. *See also* extinction; racial 'science'; types, ideas of; White supremacism
racial 'science', 3, 89, 104–5, 125–6, 156, 195, 207–8, 213, 215, 217, 236, 315, 324, 362, 389, 412. *See also* myths

564

# INDEX

racial capitalism, 47, 165–6
racial justice, 5, 24–5, 31, 86, 149, 384, 388, 398, 402–5, 410. *See also* abolitionism
racism, 3–7, 21, 33, 35, 53, 66, 75, 86–9, 102, 114–15, 142, 148–9, 164–5, 187, 204–10, 213–14, 217, 233, 235, 238–44, 250, 275, 281, 317, 322, 335, 349, 382–3, 386, 388–90, 400, 410; 'anti-anti-racism', 402–4; anti-semitism, 348; 'cultural racism', 324–5, 343, 362; racist murders, 5–7, 200–6, 237–8. *See also* eugenics; fascism; institutional racism
radiocarbon dating, 248–9, 409
rag trees, 34, 140
Ranger, Terry, 36
Ranke, Leopold von, 31
rebellions: Fenian Rising, 205, 231, 292, 466–7n17; Indian Rebellion, 67, 205, 298–301, 430n31; Kościuszko Uprising, 228; Mau Mau rebellion, 68; Morant Bay Rebellion, 68, 200–7, 212, 218–19; November Uprising, 228 (Poland); Sunday Trading Bill protests, 398. *See also* Hyde Park Railings Affair; revolutions; wars
Reform movement. *See* Chartist movement
restitution, 49–50, 354, 383, 387, 390, 394, 401, 405, 412–13

Restore Trust, the (right-wing astroturf activist group), 400, 491n148
'retain and explain' (political slogan), 31, 393, 398–9. *See also* Conservative Party (UK); fallism
revolutions, 115–16, 222, 231, 357, 398, 437n75; 1848 pan-European revolutions, 215, 230, 233; French Revolution (1789–1799), 243, 277; German revolutions of 1848–49, 220, 432n79; Haitian Revolution (1791–1804), 148, 205, 234; Hungarian Revolution (1848), 228, 230; Russian Revolution (1917), 346, 348. *See also* 48ers; Chartist movement; rebellions; wars
Rhodes House (Oxford), 17, 103, 147, 388, 424n58
Rhodes Must Fall (civil rights movement), 21; Rhodes Must Fall in Oxford, 21, 23, 37, 391, 418. *See also* Black Lives Matter; Fallism
Rhodes Trust, 17–19, 23; Rhodes scholarships, 19–23, 388. *See also* Hall, Stuart; Locke, Alain
Rhodes, Cecil John, 8–26, 31, 37, 64, 74, 87, 101, 103, 268, 343, 367, 379–81, 385–7; and *Physical Energy* (Watts), 379–80, 390, 393, 404, 412, 423n40, 423n44, 42463, 425n69; 'Confession of Faith'

(1879), 18; description by Hannah Arendt, 268; influence of John Ruskin, 18, 424n63, 424–5n65; portraits by Mary Helen Carlisle, Philip Tennyson Cole and Mortimer Menpes at Oriel College, 423n43; vision at Madeira, 19. *See also* Musk, Elon
Rigby, Francis Hale (wife of the 3rd Baron Rivers), 167, 171, 174, 443n58, 444–5n72
Riley, Denise, 90
Rilke, Rainer Maria, 92–3, 128, 145, 198, 222; 'Archaic Torso of Apollo', 296; in Sankt Pölten, 92, 433n3
Rivers, William Halse Rivers (nephew of James Hunt), 281–3
Roach, Colin, 238
Rocher, Paul, 180
Rodin, François Auguste René, 12–13
Rolleston, George, 310, 313, 362, 449n18, 484n49, 485n55
Roman Empire, 10, 394; Ermine Street (Roman Road), 136; Hadrian's Wall, 312; *Limes Germanicus* and *Pfahlgraben*, 312; Trajan (emperor), 266, 289
Rosetta Stone, 308
Rothberg, Michael, 89, 334
Royal Albert Hall, 251, 381–2
Royal Navy, 60, 89, 145–9, 195–6, 202–4, 243, 266–7, 273, 429n20, 440n6, 462n66; Australia Station, 60; Jamaica

# INDEX

Royal Navy – *cont.*
Station, 146, 440n6;
Windward and Leeward
Islands Station, 146,
440n10, 481n11. *See
also* British Army
royal patronage,
institutions with: Cork
Royal Institution,
112; Royal Academy
of Arts, 14–15, 419,
446n102, 484n49; Royal
African Company, 395;
Royal Agricultural
Society, 301; Royal
Archaeological Institute
of Great Britain and
Ireland, 106, 109,
112, 192, 291; Royal
Asiatic Society, 112;
Royal Collections, 13,
253, 275, 339, 466n16,
478n207; Royal College
of Art, 251, 379; Royal
College of Surgeons
(Hunterian Museum),
68, 101, 125–6, 134,
191, 309, 321, 406–8;
Royal Fine Art
Commission, 423n46;
Royal Geographical
Society, 112, 201,
346, 381; Royal Gun
and Powder Factories
and Laboratories
(Woolwich), 255–6;
Royal Horticultural
Society, 112; Royal
Humane Society, 158,
160; Royal Institution
of Great Britain, 97,
112, 318, 434n22;
Royal Mail, 262, 296;
Royal Medical Corps,
282; Royal Military
Academy (Woolwich),
79; Royal Military
Academy (Sandhurst),
110; Royal Naval
College (Greenwich),
481n11; Royal School
of Mines, 321, 389,
484n49; Royal Society
of Arts (Royal Society
for the Encouragement
of Arts, Manufactures
and Commerce), 95–7,
112, 251, 259, 355, 371,
482n23; Royal Society,
60, 112, 254, 436n53,
445n74; Royal United
Service Institution
(RUSI), 79–80, 112,
185, 190, 227, 257,
277, 288–9, 297,
304, 332, 466n9–11,
471n55, 486n65. *See
also* Anthropological
Institute of Great Britain
and Ireland
ruins, 26, 30, 57–61, 78,
86, 92, 137, 154, 172,
198–9, 270, 277, 280,
293, 295, 371; 'ruin
porn', 138; 'ruin value'
(*Ruinenwerttheorie*)
(Speer), 381, 390
Rushmore Park. *See*
Wiltshire
RUSI. *See* royal patronage,
institutions with
Ruskin, John, 18, 61, 195,
199, 234; support for
the Eyre Defence and
Aid Fund, 205, 234;
lecture at the Royal
Military Academy
(1865), 79, 82; influence
on Cecil Rhodes, 18,
424n63, 424–5n65
Russell (surname):
Russell, Bertrand, 3rd
Earl Russell (Fox's
nephew), 111, 126, 345,
438n102, 457n198;
Russell, John, 1st Earl
Russell (Lord John
Russell) (Fox's uncle),
111, 151, 205, 441n23,
451n64; Russell, John,
Viscount Amberley
(Fox's brother-in-law),
457n198
Russia, 177, 284, 314–15,
377; Kronstadt (St
Petersburg), 146;
annexation of Crimean
peninsula (2014), 289;
invasion of Ukraine
(2022), 48; Russian
revolution, 346, 348;
Tula, 283. *See also*
Crimean War; Russian
scandal
Russian scandal (parlour
game), 98, 174, 195,
217, 219, 332, 434n18
Rustat, Tobias, 390–402,
491n154. *See also*
Cambridge University;
Jesus College,
Cambridge

Sackler name, removal of,
387, 489–90n120
Said, Edward, 206
Salisbury and South
Wiltshire Museum,
488n76; *General Pitt-
Rivers: founding father
of modern archaeology*,
177; Pitt Rivers Papers
held at, 98, 116, 314,
366, 419, 430n25,
434n17, 435n42, 444n70,
462n74, 466n17, 467n18,
468n29, 471n59, 471n61,
473n90, 483n41, 486n62,
487n72, 488n82. *See
also* Pitt Rivers Museum
(Dorset); Pitt Rivers
Museum (Oxford);
Wessex (imaginary
landscape); Wiltshire

## INDEX

salvage, ideas of, 34–5, 87, 137, 155, 218, 283, 307, 367, 473n85. *See also* archaeology; extinction; heritage management; looting; preservation
St Vincent, 201
Sandile kaNgqika (Xhosa chief), 101–2, 388
Sartre, Jean-Paul, 333–5
Saussure, Ferdinand de, 97
Savage, Kurt, 4
savagery. *See* barbarism, ideas of; civilisation, ideas of
Save Our Statues (Twitter account), 35
Sayers, Dorothy L., 277
Scarman Report, 238–40
Schlageter, Albert Leo, 82
School of Musketry (Hythe), 256–260, 270, 298–7, 302, 459n16. *See also* Kent; Malta
Scipio Africanus (Roman general), 177
Scott, Gilbert, 251
Scott, James, 106
Scutari (Üsküdar, Turkey), 270, 464n98
Sebald, W. G., 307, 344
Second Boer War, 10, 15, 22–3, 102, 343, 357, 372, 382, 404
*Second Sex, The* (de Beauvoir), 114
Second World War, 14, 22, 32, 49, 139, 163, 181, 222, 244, 307, 333, 365, 379, 404, 408–10, 421n7
*Seeing Like a State* (Scott), 106
self-fashioning (Greenblatt), 11, 423n33
Semple Kerr, James, 391
Service, Elman, 29

settler colonialism, 19, 47–8, 52, 75, 84–7, 102, 199, 201, 211, 268, 373, 386–7; 'settler moves to innocence' (Tuck and Yang), 387. *See also* colonialism
Shakespeare, William, 95, 147, 214; *Hamlet* 130, 410, 438n108, 493n176; *Sonnet 55*, 418
Sharpe, Christina, 172, 227; *In the Wake*, 165; *Ordinary Notes*, 89
shell-shock, 276–83, 300, 315
Ship of Theseus (paradox), 328, 337, 349, 380, 391. *See also Argo* (mythological ship); myths
shrunken heads (*tsantsas*), 70, 366. *See also* mummies
silver, slavery and ships as 'the three Ss' (Sherratt), 191
skull cup, history of, passim; other examples of skull cups, 192–9 449n18
skulls: skull of Chief *Mkwawa (*Mkwavinyika Munyigumba Mwamuyinga), 196; skull of the Khalifa (Abdullah ibn-Mohammed al-Khalifa), 196; skull of *the Mahdi* (Muhammad Ahmad, al-Mahdī al-Muntaẓar), 68, 191, 196. *See also* craniometry
slavery, 5–8, 50, 75–6, 123, 142, 147–9, 160, 164–5, 167, 170–2, 175, 188, 191, 194, 203, 210, 212–14, 227, 235,

242–6, 295, 325, 363–4, 367, 391, 393, 396, 400–402, 410; Engels on slavery as the origins of armies, 373; Slavery Abolition Act of 1833, 149, 164, 200. *See also* abolitionism; capitalism; colonialism; emancipation; Legacies of British Slavery, Centre for the Study of
Smith, Adam, 301
Smithson, Robert, 30
social death (Patterson), 147
socialism, 218, 371–2; Fox's criticisms of as going back in time, 372; Mosley's criticisms of as a 'foreign import', 382. *See also* Marxism
South Africa, 10, 12–14, 60, 87–8, 206, 343 345, 347, 394, 479n221; British South Africa Company, 13, 14, 17, 423n45; Diamond Fields Artillery, 343; Johannesburg, 345, 347, Kimberley, 12–13, 343, 423n39; South African Miners' Strike (1913), 347; Rhodes Memorial (Cape Town); 14–15; University of Cape Town, 21. *See also* Anglo-Zulu Wars; apartheid; Second Boer War; Rhodes, Cecil; Rhodes Must Fall
South Kensington Museum, 63, 110, 251, 297, 340, 355, 359–64, 381, 483n39, 484n49 'Brompton Boilers', 355; perceived differences from the British Museum, 360–2,

South Kensington Museum – *cont.* 484n50; rejection of the offer of Fox's 'first collection', 361–2, 484n5; renamed Victoria and Albert Museum, 251. See also Bethnal Green Museum; Fox's 'first collection'; Victoria and Albert Museum

space exploration, 59–60, 78, 126–7; Elon Musk and, 412; Pioneer plaque, 132; Rhodes' comments on, 268; United Daughters of the Confederacy Pioneer in Space Award, 421n7

Spence, Basil, 181

Spencer, Herbert, 80, 178, 205, 372; influence on Ursula Le Guin, 178–9, 266; support for the Jamaica Committee, 205; 'survival of the fittest', 80

Spiritualism, 316–19, 475n129

Stanley (surname): Alice Margaret Stanley Pitt-Rivers (Fox's wife), 110, 168, 174, 258, 298, 340, 434n21, 445–6n87, 447n107, 457n198, 467n18, 470n54, 475n130, 487n70; Edward Lyulph Stanley, 4th Baron Stanley of Alderley, 4th Baron Sheffield and 3rd Baron Eddisbury (Fox's brother-in-law and Fox-Pitt's great-uncle and (by his second marriage) grandfather-in-law), 344, 482n34; Edward John Stanley, 1st Baron Eddisbury of Winnington in the County Palatine of Chester, 2nd Baron Stanley of Alderley, the Lord Eddisbury (Fox's father-in-law), 110, 175, 299, 472n67; Henrietta Blanche Stanley, Countess of Airlee (Fox's sister-in-law), 436n65; Henrietta Maria Stanley, Baroness Stanley of Alderley, née Dillon-Lee (Fox's mother-in-law), 110, 126, 191, 438n102, 464n100, 479n229; Johnny Stanley 464n100; Katherine (Kate) Stanley, 482n34

Starn, Orin, 85, 432n87

Stokes, Adrian, 250, 379

Strachey, Lytton, 251

Strathern, Marilyn, 267, 290, 418, 462n68

subjects, ideas of, 46, 55, 156, 220, 223–7, 234–6, 244, 267, 303, 383–93; academic subjects, 28, 62, 227, 242, 245; 'British subjects', 205, 207, 298, 440n9; *Implicated Subjects* (Rothberg), 89, 93; 'scenes of subjection' (Hartman), 142, 245; 'subject races', 10, 188; subjectification, 188, 225, 227, 242–3; subjecthood, 234; subjectivity, 1, 27, 62, 78, 98, 123, 267, 347. See also anthropology; humanity; nonhumans, ideas of; objectivity, ideas of

Sudan, 64, 111, 196, 331, 430n44, 449n26; Omdurman, 67–8

suicide, 151, 238, 250, 431n58; of the 3rd Baron Rivers, 158–64, 166–7, 176 ; *Suicide* (Durkheim), 163

Surrey, 111, 356, 483n40; Brookwood Cemetery, 262; Guildford, 110, 483n40; National Shooting Centre, Bisley, 302; Stoughton Barracks, 356; Merrow Downs, 356; Surrey Archaeological Society, 483n40; Woking crematorium, 116–7, 120 126, 149, 302, 408, 437n79

surveying, 43, 81–2, 84, 87, 106, 131–2, 149, 155, 177, 285, 292–3, 313, 434n21, 467n20; ethnographic surveys, 155; Plan of Black Fen (1847), 138, 439n128; survey of the Danevirke, 311; Sussex hillfort survey, 310–11, 472n74. See also Ordnance Survey

survival, ideas of, 96–7, 99, 113, 143, 155, 185–6, 272, 283, 309, 313–4, 317, 354, 362, 383–4, 415; 'survival of the fittest', 80; 'A Litany for Survival' (Lorde), 249

Sussex, 104, 146; Chichester, 262, 341; Cissbury, 311; Hengist Down (fictional Sussex landscape), 341; Mount Caburn hillfort, 104; Worthing, 218, 341; Sussex hillfort survey, 310–11 472n74

Sweet, Matthew, 71, 472n69

# INDEX

Swinburne, Algernon Charles (Fox's first cousin once removed), 209–10, 440n12, 453n88
Switzerland, 92, 286, 454n126; Lake Zurich (Swiss Lake Villages), 306

tacit, forms of the, 7, 13, 26, 28, 31, 33–4, 47, 49, 56, 75, 89, 93, 116, 229, 235,
Tarlow, Sarah, 191
Taussig, Michael, 131, 428n124, 431n66
Tehrani, Neda, 87
telephone (children's game), 54, 174, 332
Tennyson, Alfred Lord, 205
*Terminator* (movie franchise), 376
Thalia (mythological Muse), 300, 472n69
Thurnam, John, 309–10
Thynne (surname): Alice Ruth Hermione Thynne, (Fox's daughter-in-law), 344; Henry Frederick Thynne, (Lord Henry Thynne, Fox-Pitt's uncle by marriage), 344; Thynne, John Alexander 4th Marquess of Bath (Fox-Pitt's uncle by marriage), 345; Thynne, Thomas, 2nd Marquess of Bath (Fox-Pitt's great-great-grandfather and his great-grand-uncle by marriage), 344
*Times, The* (London), 19, 190, 205, 233, 252, 270, 273–4, 296–7, 301, 305, 316, 317, 336, 401, 406, 448n11;

Fox's letter to *The Times* in 1882, 441n29, 491n153; reporting of the American Civil War, 469n36
*Tom Brown's School Days* (Hughes), 254
trade unionism, 8, 230, 350, 371. Great Quarry Strike (1900–1903), 339; South African Miners' Strike (1913), 347
tradition, ideas of, 2, 4, 6, 16, 19, 25, 27–8, 41, 43–4, 46, 53, 56, 73, 113, 140–2, 149, 172, 189, 195, 220, 221–2, 266, 281, 309, 328, 332, 349, 352, 371, 385, 396, 402–5, 412–13; 'cult of tradition' (fascism), 386; *Invention of Tradition* (Hobsbawm and Ranger), 36
translation, 11–12, 56, 90, 107–8, 143, 146, 198, 213, 215, 221, 226, 331–6, 339, 352–3, 428n120, 433n6, 436n50; Kate Briggs on, 157
Trent Affair (1861), 295–7, 469n43. *See also* Confederate States of America
Trouillot, Michel-Rolph, 2–3, 73, 82, 103, 122, 230, 243
Trump, Donald, 336, 397. *See also* Musk, Elon
tuberculosis, 84, 169–70, 174, 444n70, 446n90
Tuck, Eve, 387
Tylor, Edward Burnett, 64, 71, 115, 317, 357, 360, 362, 430n26, 475n129–130

Tyndall, John, 205–6. *See also* Eyre Defence and Aid Fund
types, ideas of, 125, 179, 211, 306–8; 'a new human type' (Hitler), 376; prototypes, 258, 289, 295; 'typological' approach to material culture (Fox), 187, 211, 264, 322–3, 358–9; typological approach to colonialism (Finley), 393–5, 402. *See also* race, ideologies of

Ukraine, 48, 270. *See also* Crimean War
un-naming, 3, 33, 35, 45, 66, 68, 86–7, 89, 188, 192, 396–7, 410–11, 416; *For the Unnamed* (D'Aguiar), 417; of Codrington Library, 390–1; of Kroeber Hall (University of California, Berkeley), 84–5; of Jameson Avenue (Bulawayo), 21; of things named after Cecil Rhodes, 20–1, 24, 387–8, 426n81; of the Rustat feast (Jesus College, Cambridge), 396–7; of spaces named after David Starr Jordan at Stanford University, 493n181; of Lee Park (Charlottesville), 7; of things bearing the Sackler name, 387–8; de-naming and the skull-cup, 39–40, 44, 86, 89, 109, 121–2, 147, 192, 343, 412, 416. *See also* memory; memory culture; naming

569

# INDEX

Union Jack (flag), 168, 340, 351
United Service Institution. *See* royal patronage, institutions with
universities: Birmingham University, 391; Boston University, 36n; Bradford University, 408; Cambridge University, 23, 40, 222, 282, 388, 390–4, 401; Columbia University, 83, 432n79–81; Göttingen University, 351; Harvard University, 3, 222, 455n143; Howard University, 147; Imperial College London, 389, 490n122; King's College London, 387, 408; Stanford University, 413, 418; University College, Durham, 309; University College London (UCL), 87, 363, 408; University of California Berkeley, 82–5; University of Cape Town, 21; University of Pennsylvania, 3; University of Utah, 30. *See also* Cambridge University; Jesus College, Cambridge; Oriel College, Oxford; Oxford University
unmarked position, Whiteness as (Hall), 243–4, 369
unmarked words (Beaudry), 124, 369; *Language Universals* (Greenberg), 437n92
unthinkability (Trouillot), 243

Valencia, Sayak, 102–3
Victoria and Albert Museum (V&A), 63, 251, 340 355–6, 381, 419. *See also* Bethnal Green Museum; South Kensington Museum
Victoria, Queen, 15, 68, 134, 143–4, 163, 189, 196, 246, 253–42, 286–7, 295–6; 301–2, 338–9, 368, 464n101, 469n42. *See also* Prince Albert
Virginia, 7, 294, 469n36
Vizetelly, Frank, 294, 469n36. *See also* Hotze, Henry
volunteer movement (British Army), 111, 232, 235, 259–60, 301–3, 356–7, 448–9n16, 472n74
von Ribbentrop, Joachim, 151

Wagner, Roy, 62, 246
Waitz, Theodor, 215–7, 220, 455n143
Wales, 168, 337–40; North Wales Property Association, 299, 371; Penrhyn, 443–4n65, 478n201, 478n203; Great Quarry Strike, 339, 347
Wang, Jackie, 75
wars, passim. *See also* American Civil War; Anglo-Zulu Wars; Second Boer War; Crimean War; punitive expeditions; rebellions; revolutions; First World War; Second World War; World War Zero
Washington, DC, 84–5, 165, 270, 294, 366, 397;

attack on the Capitol (2021), 397
Washita River Massacre (Texas), 67
Watts, George Frederic, 14–15, 20–1, 152, 379
Waugh, Evelyn, 23
Weber, Max, 107
Wellesley, Arthur, 1st Duke of Wellington, 152, 184 230, 252, 374–5, 380
Wells, H. G., 39, 59
Wernher, Julius, 490n122
Wessex (imaginary landscape), 369–70; Wessex Agricultural Defence Association, 345; Wessex Musical Festival, 370. *See also* Hardy, Thomas; Dorset; Hampshire; Oxfordshire; Wiltshire
Westbrook, Harriet, 161
White supremacism, passim. *See also* Whiteness, cultural
White, Micah, 114
Whiteness, cultural, 3–4, 15, 28, 71, 74, 151, 234–5, 244, 246, 305, 349, 386–8, 393; as identity politics, 28, 46, 151, 349, 403; museums as 'temples of Whiteness' (Kassim), 354–5; as 'the unmarked position' (Hall), 124, 243–4; straight White feminism, 114; 'white emancipation' (Ruskin), 234; 'white man's burden' (Kipling), 237, 330; 'White taphonomy', 53, 382. *See also* White supremacism
Wilde, William, 292–3, 358, 468n23

570

Wildman, James Beckford, 198, 450n35
Wildman, Thomas, 197–8; captain in the 2nd West India Regiment, 197; obtaining Caribbean estates from William Beckford of Fonthill, 450n35; purchase of Newstead Abbey from Byron, 449n32
Williams, Eric, 147–9, 171–2, 441n15
Williams, Raymond, 184
Wilmington, North Carolina, 5–6
Wilson, John Dover, 183
Wiltshire, 40, 64, 110, 120–1, 160, 309, 311, 372, 473n92; *Ancient History of Wiltshire* (Colt Hoare), 473n92; *Antiquities of Wiltshire* (Aubrey), 313; Blackmore Ethnological Museum (Salisbury), 66, 355, 482n19 (lecture at: 357, 372); Lord Lieutenant of Wiltshire, 345; Royal Archaeological Institute meeting at Salisbury (1887), 112; Royal Wiltshire Yeomanry, 345, 347; Tollard Royal, 120–1, 128, 131, 366; Tisbury railway station, 116, 120, 408; Rushmore Park, 112, 120–1, 174, 197, 286–7, 312, 344, 368, 443n58; Salisbury, 120; Salisbury Cathedral, 198; Salisbury Plain, militarisation of, 372; *Salisbury Times*, 280, 465n121, (section VI) 465n4, 465n6, 482n31, 486n68; Wiltshire Archaeological and Natural History Society, 112. *See also* Dorset; Salisbury and South Wiltshire Museum; Wessex (imaginary landscape)
Wingate, Reginald, 1st Baronet ('Wingate of the Sudan'), 196, 449n26
Worcester College, Oxford, passim. *See also* Fox-Pitt, George; Oxford University
World War Zero, idea of, 206. *See also* punitive expeditions
Wright, Patrick, 347, 380, 480n233
*Wuthering Heights* (Brontë), 199
Wuttke, Adolf, 215
Wynter, Sylvia, 34, 53, 241–4, 251, 303, 386

Yang, K. Wayne, 387
Yorkshire: Boston Spa, 139–40; Bradford, 133, 136, 168, 408; Bramham Biggin, 137–8; Bramham cum Oglethorpe, 136; Bramham Park country house, 137–8, 167; Danes Dyke, 311; Doncaster Races, 137; Goldsborough Hall, 167–8; HMP Wealstun, 140; Hope Hall, 109, 137; Leeds, 136–7; Leeds Festival, 137; Ryedale, 309; River Wharfe, 136, 140–1; ROF Thorp Arch, 139; St Helen's Spring, 141; Swaledale, 136; Tadcaster, 136–7, 139; York Minster, 137
Younge, Gary, 25–6

Zambia, 10, 14, 20–1, 25
Zimbabwe, 10, 13, 17, 20–1; 25, 145; Great Zimbabwe (archaeological site), 17; Zimbabwe House (London), 14, 406
*Zong!* (NourbeSe Philip), 123, 188
zoos, 246